Ramesses III

Ramesses III

The Life and Times of Egypt's Last Hero

ERIC H. CLINE

&

DAVID O'CONNOR

Editors

The University of Michigan Press · *Ann Arbor*

Published in the United States of America by
The University of Michigan Press
Manufactured in the United States of America
∞ Printed on acid-free paper

2015   2014   2013   2012   4   3   2   1

A CIP catalog record for this book is available from the British Library.

Library of Congress Cataloging-in-Publication Data

Ramesses III : the life and times of Egypt's last hero / Eric H. Cline
    and David O'Connor, editors.
          p.   cm.
       Includes bibliographical references and index.
       ISBN 978-0-472-11760-4 (cloth : acid-free paper)
          1. Ramses III, King of Egypt.   2. Ramses III, King of Egypt—
    Influences.   3. Pharaohs—Biography.   4. Heroes—Egypt—Biography.
    5. Egypt—History—New Kingdom, ca. 1550–ca. 1070 B.C.   I. Cline, Eric H.
    II. O'Connor, David B.
    DT88.8.R36   2011
    932'.0140920—dc22
    [B]   2011011893

In Memoriam
CATHLEEN KELLER
1945–2008

Preface

Ramesses III (1184–1153 BC) is a king well known, to scholars and to the public more generally, as a pivotal figure in the Eastern Mediterranean world at a time when the foundations of the classical and biblical worlds were being laid. He is associated not only with a brilliant and complex phase of Egyptian civilization but also with the Shasu of the Levant, from whom the Israelites may descend, and with the Sea Peoples, who might in large part have been Mycenaean Greek in origin and whose descendants include the Philistines, the future foes of the Israelites.

The reign of Ramesses III was prosperous and culturally rich, and he successfully resisted external attacks from the Sea Peoples and the Libyans that might otherwise have led to a virtual collapse of the Egyptian state and its civilization. In Egypt, the reign of Ramesses III produced the great temple of Medinet Habu, frequently visited by scholars and tourists; an elaborately decorated royal tomb; and other significant monuments. The art of private tombs continued to flourish, albeit with important changes in emphasis, and a rich variety of literary forms were produced. Our clearest picture of Egyptian administrative practice and social structure, as well as of the economy (documented by, e.g., Papyrus Harris I and the Wilbour Papyrus) is derived from his reign and immediately contiguous ones, while amazingly we also have a long account (in a judicial document) of the events leading to the assassination of Ramesses III and their aftermath.

Yet for many scholars and others, Ramesses III's reign is tainted by ominous shadows, and this seemingly vibrant society appears to have been already shot through by a fatal degeneration of spirit and values. For them, the process that led to the political fragmentation, social stress, and cultural decline of the Third Intermediate Period (Dynasties 21–24: 1069–715 BC) had already begun under Ramesses III. But this evaluation is perhaps unfair and at the least suggests a paradoxical situation, a complex picture of achievement and decay, a time of "sunshine and shadow."

There is no comprehensive treatment in English of Ramesses III, his achievements, and the culture of his times, and there are very few recent books about him in any language. A recent French study by Grandet is a distinguished historical treatment, but in the present book, we wished to bring together a wider range of perspectives and a rich variety of ideas by presenting, in an orderly, logically structured form, a series of related essays on most major aspects of the reign of Ramesses III.

In the following pages, therefore, we begin with a historical survey of Ramesses III and his reign, written by Kenneth Kitchen, one of the leading experts in the field of Ramesside studies. In chapter 2, Emily Teeter of the Oriental Institute presents a fascinating discussion of the change and continuity observable in religion and religious practices in Egypt during the time of Ramesses III. Carolyn Higginbotham, a specialist on governmental issues during the Ramesside period, discusses the administrative structure of Ramesses III's government in chapter 3, while in chapter 4, Christopher J. Eyre of the University of Liverpool contributes a brilliant discussion of society, economy, and administrative process in late Ramesside Egypt.

Chapter 5 is a survey of Ramesses III's foreign contacts. It appears in three parts, with Peter Haider discussing the links with Anatolia and the Aegean, James Weinstein covering the Levant, and Eric Cline and David O'Connor exploring the Sea Peoples in detail. The astute reader will note a number of overlaps between the three sections of this chapter, particularly concerning the Sea Peoples, who form such an integral aspect of Ramesses III's life and reign. Although there are occasional contradictions between the sections, it has been decided to leave these in place, in part to showcase the level of debate that continues among scholars today.

In chapter 6, David O'Connor, of the Institute of Fine Arts at New York University, presents a detailed discussion and analysis of the mortuary temple of Ramesses III at Medinet Habu, while in chapter 7, Bojana Mojsov gives us a look at the major monuments of Ramesses III, including his tomb, the tombs of six princes, and a variety of temples, sculptures, and reliefs. Between these two chapters, virtually all of Ramesses III's construction projects are covered. Unfortunately, an additional chapter covering Ramesside art in general, to be authored by the late Cathleen Keller, never achieved fruition.

In chapter 8, Ogden Goelet, of New York University, presents an intimate and important treatise on literature and the literary environment in Egypt during the age of Ramesses III. Steven Snape, of the University of Liverpool, ends the book in dramatic fashion by discussing both the legacy of Ramesses III and the Libyan ascendancy, in a complex study that places Ramesses' reign within the context of the later Twentieth Dynasty and the period that followed his death.

In closing, we would like to thank all of the contributors as well as the several acquisitions editors at the University of Michigan Press, particularly Ellen Bauerle, for their patience during the long years while this book was in the process of completion. We hope that it has been worth the wait.

ERIC H. CLINE *and* DAVID O'CONNOR

Contents

Abbreviations

AJA	*American Journal of Archaeology*
ASAE	*Annales du Service des Antiquites de l'Egypte*
BAR	*Biblical Archaeology Review*
BASOR	*Bulletin of the American Schools of Oriental Research*
BES	*Bulletin of the Egyptological Seminar*
BIFAO	*Bulletin de l'Institut français d'archéologie orientale*
BM	British Museum
BN	*Biblische Notizen*
BSFÉ	*Bulletin de la Société française d'égyptologie*
CAH³	*Cambridge Ancient History*. 3rd ed. Cambridge University Press, 1970.
CRIPEL	*Cahiers de recherches de l'institut de Papyrologie et d'Egyptologie de Lille: Sociétés Urbaines en Égypte et au Soudan.*
DE	*Discussions in Egyptology*
E/W	Edgerton, W. F., and Wilson, J. A. *Historical Records of Ramses III: The Texts in "Medinet Habu" Volumes I and II Translated with Explanatory Notes.* Studies in Ancient Oriental Civilization 12. Chicago: University of Chicago Press, 1936.
Excavation II	Hölscher, U. *The Excavation of Medinet Habu.* Vol. II, *The Temples of the Eighteenth Dynasty.* Oriental Institute Publications 41. Chicago: University of Chicago Press, 1939.
Excavation III	Hölscher, U. *The Excavation of Medinet Habu.* Vol. III, *The Mortuary Temple of Ramesses III.* Pt. 1. Oriental Institute Publications 54. Chicago: University of Chicago Press, 1941.
Excavation IV	Hölscher, U. *The Excavation of Medinet Habu.* Vol. IV, *The*

	Mortuary Temple of Ramesses III. Pt. 2. Oriental Institute Publications 55. Chicago: University of Chicago Press, 1951.
Excavation V	Hölscher, U. *The Excavation of Medinet Habu.* Vol. V, *Post-Ramesside Remains.* Oriental Institute Publications 66. Chicago: University of Chicago, 1954.
Giornale	Botti, G., and T. E. Peet. *Il Giornale della Necropoli di Tebe.* Turin, Bocca, 1928.
GM	*Göttinger Miszellen*
HO	Černý, J., and A. H. Gardiner. *Hieratic Ostraca I.* Oxford: Griffith Institute, 1957.
IEJ	*Israel Exploration Journal*
JARCE	*Journal of the American Research Center in Egypt*
JEA	*Journal of Egyptian Archaeology*
JNES	*Journal of Near Eastern Studies*
JSOT	*Journal for the Study of the Old Testament*
Khonsu I	Epigraphic Survey. *The Temple of Khonsu.* Vol. I, *Scenes of King Herihor in the Court.* Oriental Institute Publications 100. Chicago: Oriental Institute, 1979.
Khonsu II	Epigraphic Survey. *The Temple of Khonsu.* Vol. II, *Scenes and Inscriptions in the Court and the First Hypostyle Hall.* Oriental Institute Publications 103. Chicago: University of Chicago Press, 1981.
KRI	Kitchen, K. A. *Ramesside Inscriptions, Historical and Biographical.* Vols. I–VIII. Oxford: Blackwell, 1969–90.
KRI II	Kitchen, K. A. *Ramesside Inscriptions, Translated & Annotated Notes and Comments.* Vol. II. Oxford: Blackwell, 1979.
KRI III	Kitchen, K. A. *Ramesside Inscriptions, Historical and Biographical.* Vol. III. Oxford: Blackwell, 1980.
KRI IV	Kitchen, K. A. *Ramesside Inscriptions, Historical and Biographical.* Vol. IV. Oxford: Blackwell, 1982.
KRI V	Kitchen, K. A. *Ramesside Inscriptions, Historical and Biographical.* Vol. V. Oxford: Blackwell, 1983.
KRI VI	Kitchen, K. A. *Ramesside Inscriptions, Historical and Biographical.* Vol. VI. Oxford: Blackwell, 1983.
KRI VII	Kitchen, K. A. *Ramesside Inscriptions, Historical and Biographical.* Vol. VII. Oxford: Blackwell, 1989.
KV	Valley of the Kings
LÄ	Helck, W., Otto, E., and Westendorf, W., eds. *Lexicon der Ägyptologie.* Wiesbaden: Harrassowitz, 1975–92.
LEM	Gardiner, A. H. *Late-Egyptian Miscellanies.* Bibliotheca Aegyptiaca

MIFAO	Memoires publies par les membres de l'Institut francais d'archeologie orientale du Caire
MIO	*Mitteilungen des Institut für Orientforschung*
MMJ	*Metropolitan Museum Journal*
OA	*Oriens Antiquus*
Or	*Orientalia*
P. Harris	Papyrus Harris
PM	Porter, B., and Moss, R. *Topographical Bibliography of Ancient Egyptian Hieroglyphic Texts, Statues, Reliefs, and Paintings.* 7 vols. 1927–1951 (Reprints 1961–). Oxford: Oxford University Press.
QV	Valley of the Queens
RAD	Gardiner, A. H. *Ramesside Administrative Documents.* Oxford: Griffith Institute, 1968.
RAPH	Recherches d'Archeologie, de Philologie et d'Histoire (Paris)
RdÉ	*Revue d'Égyptologie*
RIK I	Epigraphic Survey. *Reliefs and Inscriptions at Karnak.* Vol. I, *Ramses III's Temple within the Great Inclosure of Amon.* Pt. 1. Oriental Institute Publications 25. Chicago: University of Chicago Press, 1936.
RITA I	Kitchen, K. A. *Ramesside Inscriptions, Translated and Annotated: Translation.* Vol. I. Oxford: Blackwell, 1993.
RITA II	Kitchen, K. A. *Ramesside Inscriptions, Translated and Annotated: Translation.* Vol. II. Oxford: Blackwell, 1996.
RITA IV	Kitchen, K. A. *Ramesside Inscriptions, Translated and Annotated: Translation.* Vol. IV. Oxford: Blackwell, 2003.
RITA V	Kitchen, K. A. *Ramesside Inscriptions, Translated and Annotated: Translation.* Vol. V. Oxford: Blackwell, 1993.
RITANC I	Kitchen, K. A. *Ramesside Inscriptions, Translated and Annotated: Notes and Comments.* Vol. I. Oxford: Blackwell, 1993.
RITANC II	Kitchen, K. A. *Ramesside Inscriptions, Translated and Annotated: Notes and Comments.* Vol. II. Oxford: Blackwell, 1999.
SAK	*Studien zur Altägyptischen Kultur*
TT	Theban Tomb
Urk IV	Kurt Sethe and Wolfgang Helck. *Urkunden des ägyptischen Altertums.* Vol. IV, *Urkunden der 18. Dynastie.* Leipzig: J. C. Hinrichs; Berlin: Akademie-Verlag, 1958.
ZÄS	*Zeitschrift für Ägyptische Sprache und Altertumskunde*
ZDPV	*Zeitschrift des Deutschen Palästina-Vereins*

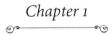

Chapter 1

Ramesses III and the Ramesside Period

KENNETH A. KITCHEN

In the tumultuous and vivid history of New Kingdom Egypt, Ramesses III occupies a unique position and mainly played a role that foreshadowed Egypt's lot in later centuries, when the country was repeatedly on the defensive against external forces rather than imposing its ascendancy on them. The old saying runs, "Some are born to greatness, some achieve greatness, and some have greatness thrust upon them." In some measure, all three clauses apply to Ramesses III. As the son of a man who took over Egypt's throne at a time of crisis, Ramesses III was born to a role for greatness; by his initially vigorous rule and responses to Egypt's needs of the time, he in some measure achieved greatness; and those very pressures in some measure thrust greatness upon him. Later generations have certainly done that. In antiquity, his successors partly took him as a model, while in modern times, an oft-repeated commonplace would make of him "the last great pharaoh of Egypt"—which might be true of the New Kingdom but does scant justice to some outstanding rulers of later epochs. This chapter looks concisely at several facets of this king's reign and career, while leaving ample scope for the fuller treatments that follow.

ORIGINS

As the founder of the Twentieth Dynasty, Setnakht reigned but briefly, not beyond his year 4 at any rate,[1] and so Ramesses III was quite quickly catapulted into the seat of supreme power in Egypt, after his father's success in reaching Egypt's throne. Here, the most remarkable fact is that after some two hundred years of very active Egyptology, we still know absolutely *nothing* explicitly factual about the family and social origins of Setnakht and his son. This is in stark contrast to both the Eighteenth Dynasty, when Ahmose I succeeded his brother in an established Theban local line of kings, and the Nineteenth Dynasty, in which Ramesses I came of a military family from the East Delta and was appointed heir of the realm by his predecessor Haremhab. In our slim surviving sources, Setnakht makes no claim to royal descent; he was exclusively the choice of the gods. And we have no "private" monument of his, from before his accession, to unveil his place in society before he took power.

Therefore, any attempt to "place" him before accession has to be 100 percent speculation and must remain as limited as possible. The meaning of Setnakht's personal name, "Seth is victorious," would speak for an East Delta origin, in the context of his persistent honoring of Re alongside Amun in his standard cartouches. In his prenomen, following Seti II's example, he frequently adopted the double epithet of *Setepenre* and *Meryamun* together, not solely as free variants. In his nomen, he almost universally called himself "Setnakht (ever) beloved of Re and Amun," giving (again) equal prominence to both Re of Heliopolis (where Seth was a hero god) and Amun of Thebes.[2]

As for role and rank, we have only two explicit sources, necessarily in some measure propagandistic: Setnakht's own stela from Elephantine and the appreciation of him in Papyrus Harris I, penned at the accession of his grandson Ramesses IV, just over thirty years later. The stela is an almost-contemporary document, if highly rhetorical. Before its year 2 dateline, in an Egypt "in confusion . . . (that had) lapsed into forgetting God," the gods chose their man "out from millions, dismissing myriads." The new king professedly "banished distress, . . . removed all chiefs (*tpw*) . . . ; . . . flexed his arms to purge Egypt of who(ever) led it astray; . . . (his) opponents (panicked), . . . they fled like flocks(?) of sparrows with a falcon after them." Then, remarkably, "they (= the opponents) abandoned silver and gold [within] Egypt, that they had assigned for these Asiatics, to bring allies quickly for themselves, (as) chiefs (*tpw*) (of) Egypt; . . . troops and chariotry were powerless." The gods had acted in Setnakht's favor. After the year 2 dateline, the text continues as an address to the king: no more opponents exist; divine promise is fulfilled; all is now well. In short, Setnakht did *not* come to the throne by normal and agreed, peaceful succession. There was evidently no clear heir. He arose to claim the throne, while others disputed his claim—simply because no one claimant had a clearly superior status. Setnakht won out in the struggle and presumably did away with his would-be rival(s) and their supporters. The reference to "troops and chariotry" would suggest that he had or won control over armed forces and may have had to defeat at least one rival force. If Setnakht were himself a general and army leader (rather as Haremhab and Ramesses I—Pramessu— had been), then the scenario makes sense, of an East Delta–born generalissimo who struck out for supreme power at Queen Tewosret's decease (or dethronement?) but had to fight for it. His opponents' seeming intention to buy in "Asiatic" help (from the province of Canaan?) might favor an East Delta setting for the conflict.

Papyrus Harris I is consistent with the earlier report. It speaks of the land "abandoned," under unruly local potentates, but adds the brief hegemony of a Syrian termed "Irsu" (Self-made); the gods raised up Setnakht to put things right, slaying the "rebels." It is still appropriate to identify Irsu with the highly ambitious Chancellor Bay, who (with the dowager queen Tewosret) stood behind Siptah's throne, even though his death in fact preceded those of Siptah and Tewosret rather than followed them.[3]

Thus, the Twentieth Dynasty came to power (in effect) by a coup d'état, not by any form of formal handing-on of power. Like the Nineteenth Dynasty, it was comprised of "new men," but unlike their predecessors, they lacked endorsement at a human level. Therefore, the position of both Setnakht and his son (and so soon successor) Ramesses III must have depended all the more on how they could satisfy the aspirations of all Egypt and guard its interests in a now unstable world. If Setnakht were a general and (like his distant predecessors) of a regularly military family, then one might further infer that Ramesses III had in turn begun his career as an aspiring military officer under his father's eye. If so, such military acumen as he possessed was soon to be tried and tested.

ACCESSION: TONE AND STYLE OF PROGRAM

The accession date[4] of Ramesses III (and hence the date of his father's death) was first month of Shomu, day 26. His formal titles echoed great rulers of the past. His Horus name, "Strong Bull, Great in Kingship" (*ꜥ3 nsyt*), was fresh and original[5] and took its distinctive elements from the Horus names of the founders of the Eighteenth and Nineteenth Dynasties no less. Thus, Ahmose I was Horus **ꜥ3**-*khepru*, while Ramesses I was *Wadj-***nsyt***. So, Ramesses III combined the elements in boldface here to form *ꜥ3-nsyt*, linking him with both. In his other titles, he went boldly for an outright association with Ramesses II, as pointed out long since.[6] Thus, in his prenomen, he retained

Ramesses II's basic *Usimare* but substituted *Meryamun* for *Setepenre*. In his nomen, conversely, he substituted a Heliopolitan epithet for the *Meryamun* already in his prenomen—itself reminiscent of the "(God and) Ruler of Heliopolis" epithet used by Ramesses II from his year 42 onward. Moving back to the "Two Goddesses" (Nebty) name, Ramesses III adopted "Mighty of Jubilees like Tatonen," which was taken directly from the second half of Ramesses II's expanded Horus name from his year 34 onward, perhaps in hope of the many jubilees (Sed feasts) that his long-lived predecessor had enjoyed. For a regular Golden Horus name, Ramesses III adapted that of Ramesses II, keeping "Rich in years" (*Wsr-rnpwt*), but replacing "great in victories" by "like Atum." But then he took his cue from Merenptah by adding a second pair of epithets attached to the middle term *ity,* "Sovereign," in fact simply annexing here the whole of Ramesses II's original Nebty name, "Protector of Egypt, curbing the foreign lands." This practice with Golden Horus names (first epithets, "Sovereign," second set of epithets) then stayed in use for the rest of the Twentieth Dynasty, in imitation of Ramesses III.

Thus, through his formal titulary and while retaining his own identity, Ramesses III was in effect announcing, "Another Ramesses II is here."

FOREIGN AFFAIRS: NUBIA

Commonly, it is assumed that this reign saw no conflict in this great southern province of Egyptian rule, by contrast with the other two potential theaters of war, Libya in the northwest and the Levant and Mediterranean in the northeast. Placed on the south half of the rear wall of the king's Medinet Habu temple,[7] the set of three formal scenes portraying warfare in Nubia has been customarily dismissed as having only symbolic force: a pharaoh would be expected to claim supremacy on all three fronts (south, northwest, and northeast), and these anodyne scenes would fulfill that role. In favor of such an assessment, it must be said that there is no individualizing detail in these scenes. The southern foe is uniformly called "Kush," "land of Kush"—which can cover everything south of Aswan!—and there are no occurrences of other specific terms for places or people groups or of any dateline or geographical peculiarity. So, it is little wonder that these scenes are considered as purely symbolic and ideological; and, by original intention, they may well be.

But these very formal scenes are not our total potential evidence; and the political profile of repeated Nubian protest at Egyptian rule is worth bearing in mind. Let us look briefly at this latter factor first. What seems to have happened was a series of intermittent rebellions whenever a new generation that had not tasted Egyptian armed power (as their parents had done) became fed up with Egyptian taxation and exploitation and then (unwisely) tried to throw off the Egyptian yoke by armed rebellion. Inevitably this was sharply crushed, and the whole cycle slowly began again.

This phenomenon embraced both the settled, sedentary groups along the Nile and also the desert-based, more nomadic groups away from the river, but *not* necessarily in conjunction. Thus, during the late Eighteenth Dynasty, a revolt was crushed in Akhenaten's reign (Akuyata; his Buhen stela, year 12),[8] but there was no more trouble until Haremhab's time, between twenty and thirty years later, as indicated by his Silsilah Nubian war scene.[9] The next revolt (Irem) occurred in (probably) year 8 of Seti I,[10] probably twenty to thirty years later still. Then, there was relative peace and quiet, until Irem again revolted under Ramesses II, as commemorated by the scenes at Amarah West that must date after year 21 (1259; -*sw* nomen in use and most likely within years 38–43 [1242–37 BC]; Setau warred in Irem and Akuyata). So, from late in the reign of Seti I, there was peace for between twenty and forty years.[11] Then, peace reigned again for another twenty-five years or so, until the Libyans goaded the people of Wawat into rebelling against Merenptah (year 5, 1209 BC) to distract him from their intentions (unsuccessfully).[12] Finally, until the opening years of Ramesses III, up to twenty-five years or so elapsed before the question of a Nubian revolt arose again (and perhaps twenty-five to thirty years more until [Ramesses IV], for a final such occasion).

So now, secondly, if the Medinet Habu formal reliefs do not directly attest any such event, do we have any other trace? Perhaps we do, as I noted some time ago.[13] The first possible such allusion is a passage in Ramesses III's address to Amun that prefaces his great Festival Calendar on the South Wall of the Medinet Habu temple. Here, the king says, "I have done this by my power, being what my Will has brought about, even my booty from the land of Nubia and the land of Djahy."[14]

Such a passage may imply action in Nubia as well as up north; but just as the calendar proper was substantially copied from that of Ramesses II (Ramesseum), so this speech might also have been taken over, which would then rule it out as evidence for Ramesses III's own activities. The account of the reign in Papyrus Harris I mentions no Nubian campaign by the king; but any local action by the viceroy would not count for royal commemoration—just as Seti I did *not* include his viceroy's success against Irem in his official war reports and temple scenes. (We owe knowledge of the event only to the viceroy's own two stelae.) However, in a second trace (in passing), that papyrus does allude in its prosaic lists[15] to "Syrians and Nubians of the captures of His Majesty, LPH, whom he gave to the Estate of Amen-Re, King of the Gods, to the Estate of (the goddess) Mut, and to the Estate of Khons, . . . : people, 2,607." This kind of incidental mention, with listing of persons, *does* suggest that Nubians had been taken during some action, be it minor or major.

But our third indicator is perhaps the most explicit. This is the rhetorical stela engraved in the "oratory" chapel C, just southwest of Deir el-Medina village.[16] In what is the second of four "geographical" stanzas, we read:

[The Strong Bull] has traversed the countries of the Southland,
—namely the Nubians: the Tiriwaya and Irem.
He makes them cease from [bragging?], (as) they reach the King's
   Domain;
they are turned into shield-bearers and charioteers,
retainers and fan-bearers in the King's retinue, [even of Ramesses] III.

The first stanza celebrates the historical conflict with Libya, naming Libu and Meshwesh; the third celebrates the northern victory over the north ("Khurru"), naming specifically "the Philistines and the Tursha from the midst of the Sea (*yamm*)." The fourth is a general summing-up. As the first and third stanzas are specific for north/east and west and as the second is equally so for the south (with the rare name *Tiriwaya*), the fourth, too, should probably be treated as historical. A viceregal action against some disturbance affecting Irem and Tiriwaya could well fit the bill on all counts—a real event conducted not by the king himself but simply in his name by the viceroy (as did Amenemope for Seti I). What is more, the spelling of *Tiriwaya* used on this stela is unique to that monument and stands in sharp contrast to the merely traditional occurrences of the name in the formal (and oft-recopied) topographical lists.[17] This fact, also, may speak for the authenticity of this unique occurrence; the viceroy had reported back his success, using a spelling that reflected the name as he heard it and thus as was used for the text of this stela, whereon it was certainly *not* just copied from some old list (with radically different traditional orthography).

None of this may count as final proof of a minor campaign successfully waged in the king's name in Upper Nubia by his viceroy (one of the Horis), but the occurrence and special spelling of *Tiriwaya* plus the formal listing of Nubian as well as northern prisoners in a real list of people added to the estates of the Theban trio (Papyrus Harris I) would certainly favor such a view. Dating any such action is not strictly possible; but the onset of a new dynasty and reign may favor a date very early in the reign of Ramesses III (if the Nubians sought to test out a new regime), possibly even before his involvement with Libya and other northerners from year 5 onward.[18]

FOREIGN AFFAIRS: LIBYA

This sphere comes in three phases: the conflict in year 5 (ca. 1180 BC, minimum date); a second conflict six years later, in year 11 (ca. 1174 BC, minimum), bracketing the Sea Peoples' conflict of year 8 (ca. 1177 BC, minimum); and finally Libyan penetration of the Nile Valley south as far as Thebes (via the oases) by year 26 (ca. 1159 BC, minimum). This section briefly considers each phase.

The Year 5 War

For this war, we have three principal sources at Medinet Habu: the reliefs on the rear and north exterior walls of that temple, the allied reliefs spanning the southeast interior angle of the second court, and a rhetorical war report, officially of year 5, directly adjoining these latter scenes (south wall). The undated exterior scenes give more attention to the prebattle preliminaries (four scenes, divine commissioning, etc.) than to the battle and victory (just two scenes). The legends interchangeably use the old-fashioned traditional terms *Temehu* and *Tehenu*, which are of little or no geographical value here, except to identify the foe as west of Egypt. If it were not for two specific features in the third and sixth scenes, this series would have been almost as formal as the adjoining, oft-dismissed Nubian series. However, two specific features preclude such overskepticism. One is that in the third scene, the Tehenu are specifically denominated as "consisting of Libu, Soped and Meshwesh."[19] The other (in sixth scene) is that detailed statistics are given for amputated parts of slain foes.[20] The three group-names mentioned link these scenes with those in the interior southeast angle of the second court that mention Libu and Meshwesh (and have variant statistics) and link both sets of scenes with year 5, the official date[21] of the great text that adjoins the interior scenes and also links Libu, Soped, and Meshwesh (in contrast with the sources for year 11, for a purely Meshwesh war). No detail on the geography of this Egypto-Libyan clash is given, except that the Libyans (1) set themselves up against Egypt (*KRI* V.12.4–5; E/W 7); (2) transgressed Egypt's frontier (*KRI* V.12.6; E/W 8); and, more precisely, (3) were "robbers, damaging Egypt daily" and "treading Egypt which was wasted" (*KRI* V.15.1, 2–3, 8; E/W 13, 14), which implies plundering in the West Delta margins at least.

That ways "untrodden in the past" (*KRI* V.11.4–5; E/W 5) were to be opened to Ramesses III is certainly hyperbole, given the campaigns of Seti I and Merenptah in this quarter. That the "heart of the land of Temehu is overthrown" (*KRI* V.16.9; E/W 12) was simply the consequence of the pharaoh defeating the foe in and on his borders and pursuing them westward, back whence they had come, for some unknown distance. The Libu/Soped/Meshwesh alliance clearly had felt need to expand its territory beyond the rather narrow west-east tongue of land between sea and desert (traditionally, old Temehu/Tehenu terrain) and thus sought to take over pastoral and agricultural areas in the West Delta, a partial cause of the conflict. The coming of a new regime in Egypt may also have seemed a suitable occasion to try their luck.

But the year 5 text brings in another factor. It cites a succession of rulers of the Libu: Didi, Mishken, Mariyu, Wermer, and Tjetmer (line 47; E/W 29–30). Earlier therein (lines 28–31; E/W 25–26), Ramesses III claimed that the Libyans had asked him for a chief, in pretense; he in turn had produced his own protégé, a boy prince (line 30; E/W 25). This begins to look like a double game. First, at Wermer's death, Tjetmer claimed the chiefship but was not unopposed—the others involved sent to Egypt for support for some rival candidate. Second, Ramesses III then seized the seeming opportunity to enthrone a boy puppet chief of his own choice, thus ruling out any local rival candidates. As a result, his puppet was unceremoniously disregarded, the Libyans closed ranks behind Tjetmer, and war was the result. It is not clear by which route the Libyans attacked on this occasion: via the north route eastward, then south along the Western River zone; or (as with Merenptah's opponents) by the south route via Wadi Natrun, emerging opposite the branching of the Nile (itself southwest from Heliopolis). Either way, the king celebrated his victory at an Egyptian fort (north exterior wall, Medinet Habu, last scene; E/W 13), presumably within reach of the West Bank of the Nile at some point, which bore the official name "Usimare Meryamun is Repeller (*khesef*) of the Libyans (*Temehu*)." This place does not recur either in Merenptah's account (with his name) or in the year 11 war of Ramesses III, which may suggest that year 5 was linked to the north route, whereas Merenptah and the year 11 war of Ramesses III were associated with the southern route (cf. the discussion on year 11 just below).

The Year 11 War

After the first clash with Libya, Ramesses III may have had three years respite until the Sea Peoples came down in year 8 (but see below) and, thereafter, three more years before his second clash with Libya in year 11. He had inflicted considerable losses, in killed and captured men, on the Libyan alliance,[22] and he may even have made them into client communities, paying at least nominal tribute. The efforts of the Libu and Soped had failed; it was now the Meshwesh who took over the leadership against Egypt, led by Meshsher, son of their chief, Kaper.

In the great war scenes of this episode, the pharaoh is said to have slaughtered his foes for a distance of eight *iters* between the "town of Ramesses III on the mountain of Up-to" and "the town of Hat-sha," given in opposite order in the two scenes. Which of these two limits is nearest (and furthest) from the Nile? Here, we may profitably turn to the war texts of Merenptah. His invaders had specifically been preceded by Libyans who had gradually penetrated the Nile Valley where (north of Memphis and Letopolis) the river first split into separate streams to span the Delta. Across the river, going northeast, was the Aty Canal, and by it was Heliopolis. Before the year 5 war of Merenptah, Libyan infiltrators and settlers had got that far (*KRI* IV.3.5ff.; cf. 4.10). As pointed out by others,[23] the most direct route to that point from [ancient] Libya was to go southeast along Wadi Natrun and so emerge at precisely that zone. North of Letopolis, near the settlement of Pi-Iru, on Egypt proper's western frontier (*KRI* IV.4.3, 5.14; *RITA* IV.4, 5), Merenptah's forces engaged the Libyans. Close by Pi-Iru was the "guard-post of Merenptah who [encloses] the Libyans" (*KRI* IV.8.3, 22.3; *RITA* IV.7, 19), hence also near the Nile or its valley. And we are there told that the Libyans were slain along the stretch from Pi-Iru/the guard-post of Merenptah out to "the mountain of Up-to," or, more precisely, out to "the settlements of the desert land beginning from Merenptah [*x-y*] as far as [somewhere else]." Those settlements may have been simply minor points at the series of wells along Wadi Natrun.

This information enables us to interpret the backward/forward mentions by Ramesses III in his year 11 scenes. In the first (E/W 61), the span of eight *iters* "from the town of Ramesses III on the mountain of Up-to, to the town of Hat-Sha" mirrors the course of the Libyan advance (west to east) of "the Meshweh who came to Egypt," in the immediately preceding phrase. Conversely, in the other scene (E/W 62) and equally logically, the pharaoh conducted his pursuit and slaughter back from east to west, "beginning from the town Hat-Sha, to the town of Usimare Meryamun which is on the mountain of Up-to," for the same eight *iters*. Hat-Sha must have been somewhere in the same area as Pi-Iru and Merenptah's old guard-post (later known as "Usimare Meryamun is Repeller of the Libyans," from year 5?— E/W 13). Daressy wrongly placed Hat-en-Sha/Hat-Sha in the oasis of Siwa, equally wrongly dividing the full name from the genitive adjective *en* plus *Sha* to make the "name" for Nesha, which he more correctly set in Behera province, south-to-north from Khatatbeh (thirty kilometers northwest from Ausim/Letopolis) toward Lake Mariut.[24] But the town Hat-Sha may have been well south of Khatatbeh, while a region called "Sha" (meaning "sand(y)") might indeed have been merely the desert-edge strip along the west margin of the Lower Egyptian province.

The Up-to "settlement" (more probably a fort or guard-post) was certainly the same place as the Up-to of Merenptah. At 6.5 miles/10.5 kilometers to one *iter*, the eight *iters* here represent about fifty-two miles/eighty-four kilometers in modern terms. From Ausim/ancient Letopolis and area, traveling fifty-two miles westward into Wadi Natrun would well bring us to at least Qaryet Dahr, an intermittent guard-post since the Middle Kingdom as Grandet has pointed out,[25] if not in fact still further west.

Thus, we may gain a better idea of the topographical background of the Libyan invasions under Merenptah and Ramesses III (year 11, if not also year 5).

The Year 28 Incursions down South

By successfully driving back the successive waves of attempted invasion of Egypt by Libyan groups, the pharaohs Seti I, Merenptah, and Ramesses III (plus Ramesses II, with his chain of forts) probably considered that the problem was solved, at least for their own individual reigns. But denial of access to Egypt's rich pastures and grain fields was no solution to the problems of the Libyans. It is very clear that after centuries of nonconflict with neighboring Egypt, the Libyan groups must have been impelled into trying to invade Egyptian territory under the pressure of very real needs. They did *not* do it for fun. Seti I does not deign to tell us why the Libyans "transgressed his boundaries." It is Merenptah who gives us a clear and explicit statement: "They spend all day roaming the land, fighting to fill their stomachs daily; they come to the land of Egypt to seek out (life's) necessities for their mouth[s]" (*KRI* IV.4.14; *RITA* IV.4). Settlement in Egypt's broader pastures was intended: "[. . . .] tents in front of Pi-Barset, making their abode on the edge of the Aty canal" (*KRI* IV.3.5; *RITA* IV.3); "the families of Libya are scattered along the dykes like mice" (*KRI* IV.21.3; *RITA* IV.18). Allowing for incidental rhetoric, these passages make it plain that the Libyans and their allies *needed land* on which to live and from which to feed themselves. Their existing resources in Libya, therefore, were no longer adequate to feed their people (and Sea People immigrants, with Merenptah) satisfactorily; unless they found additional living space and food resource (productive land), they would be in crisis—not yet in famine, but with such a prospect pending.[26] This would be true regardless of what form their social organization took, whether nomadic, seminomadic, or even modestly agricultural.

Therefore, if Egypt was barred, these people had to look elsewhere. Perhaps they would look back toward Cyrenaica, though not if the area was already fully populated. The other overland option was to go south, down through the line of oases that paralleled the Nile Valley out to its west. And this was precisely the solution that some of them adopted, probably from Seti I's time onward. Already a few decades later, in year 44 of Ramesses II, the viceroy Setau of Nubia seized manpower from the "Nubian" oases to build such temples as Wadi es-Sebua—and the men concerned were Libyans, not Nubians. Over a century later, under Ramesses IX–XI, we find Libyans raiding from the oases into the Nile Valley at Thebes, as the Deir el-Medina records show. Ramesses VI earlier had to repulse such Libyans from Thebes, and a similar record of the coming of "the enemy" into Western Thebes is known as early as year 28 of Ramesses III himself. That king built fortified precincts in Upper Egypt for temples at Siut and Abydos, whither desert routes led from the oasis regions. Thus, Egypt was still not clear of its "Libyan problem" long after Ramesses III's vaunted military solutions.[27]

FOREIGN AFFAIRS: THE LEVANT

Here, the most prominent feature is the famed conflict with the Sea Peoples at the (eastern) Nile mouths, dated by the main text to Ramesses III's year 8 (ca. 1177 BC, minimum; 1180 BC, maximum). But it is not the only northern conflict. Papyrus Harris I (76.10–11) records a clear campaign against the Seirites amid the clans of Shosu, looting tents (Semitic word *ohel!*) and livestock. In that narrative, this episode falls between a summary of his defeat of the Danuna, Philistines, Sherden, and so on (76.6–9; the Sea Peoples), which Medinet Habu dates to year 8, and a brief account of defeating the Libyans and Meshwesh (variant Meshwesh and Libyans) in the Western Region (76.10–77.5). If this is the war of year 11 (or even a summary of years 5 and 11), then the Seir episode may have been a direct follow-up of the year 8 battle, in that year or just afterward.

So far, so good. But in the year 5 text at Medinet Habu, scholars have long been troubled by (1) the occurrence of conflict with Amurru early in that text, before Ramesses III's battle with the Libyans, and (2) a further passage near the end, dealing with war involving the Philistines and Tjekkeru (Sicels) at the Nile mouths—seemingly, a clear reference to happenings in year 8. These two items need to be considered separately. And to both, we must add two sets of scenes (interior and exterior of the first court, Medinet Habu) professing to portray warfare in Syria—against Ullaza (not Arzawa!) and Tunip (exterior) and against Amurru (interior).

Here, opinions vary all the way from taking these scenes in some measure seriously to treating them as pure fiction, just recopies of scenes of Ramesses II at the Ramesseum—the more so as the Chicago translators (E/W 95; cf. 94 n. 3b) wrongly identified one "Hittite" fort as Arzawa (deep in Asia Minor!) instead of Ullaza (Phoenician coast). Not even Ramesses II could ever have reached Arzawa; and this spurious identification lent Ramesses III's Syrian reliefs an equally spurious air of unreality that has stimulated widespread skepticism among scholars (myself included) ever since. However, Ullaza (like Tunip) was well within reach of any Egyptian army traversing Phoenicia and outflanking (or threatening) Amurru. So, on the one hand, a more open approach may be indicated. On the other hand, by far the greater part of the vast topographical lists on the facade of the first pylon at Medinet Habu is copied from older lists of the Eighteenth to Nineteenth Dynasties; they are of value not for history but only for the textual tradition and transmission of such lists.

That said, we can return to problems 1 and 2 themselves. Let us first take problem 1: the mention of Amurru as defeated and conquered *before* the Libyan battle of year 5 (lines 13–17). We need to remember the state of Egypt's Levantine dominions from *before* the Sea Peoples' irruption in year 8. Ramesses II had ruled all western Palestine from its deep south up to Galilee and then up the Phoenician coast to Simyra; his stelae and other sources punctuate the route via Accho, Tyre, Byblos, Nahr el-Kalb, Beirut, Adhlun, and so on. Inland, he had cowed Seir (Edom) and Moab, plus Golan (cf. Sheikh Said stela) on to the Biqa Valley (to Kemuat Hermil) and out to Damascus. That same imperium was held by his successors; Merenptah had envoys going up regularly to Tyre (year 3, postal register), and he quickly reaffirmed his hold on Ascalon and Gezer and up to Yenoam (close to Galilee), snuffing out opposition, with knowledge of an Aramean enclave already, further north. Of Amenmesses, we lack record. Seti II is attested in the south (Tell el-Fara S.), Siptah by the odd scarab and so on, and finally even queen regnant Tewosret (as independent pharaoh with full cartouches) by a vessel from Deir Alla in the Jordan Valley.

That same inheritance passed to Setnakht largely intact and so to

Ramesses III, as known records clearly show. When all gathered together, the witnesses to the reign of Ramesses III in western Palestine are a respectable collection. They show his effective control over the main route from Egypt out to Tel Sera/Tell esh-Sharia (Ziklag?), to Lachish and Gezer (on the inland flank from the main south–north coastal plain route), and on to Megiddo and Beth-Shan (with its royal statue) in the transverse Vale of Jezreel, from all of which centers we have traces of his reign. Far south, rock texts at Nahal Roded and Timna (northeast Sinai) also attest this king. Some items—the Egyptian ostraca—bear dates from years 4 to 22 attributable to this reign.[28] Up in Phoenicia, Byblos was presented with a statue of Ramesses III. This is no surprise, because Ramesses III claims to have built anew the great river bark of Amun of coniferous timber,[29] which had to come from Phoenicia and very likely via Byblos. So, there is no reason to believe that, down to year 8, Ramesses III held any less domain than Merenptah—namely, Canaan from Timna and the Negeb up the coastal plain to Jezreel, probably Galilee (and Upe?), and S. Phoenicia certainly to Byblos. After year 8, the ostraca from Lachish (year 10 or 10 + x) and especially Tel Sera (year 22) demonstrate very clearly that his authority remained in Canaan as before, well after the victory of year 8. Egyptian tax collectors and messengers would have to have had freedom of movement through Philistia, even to reach centers such as Tel Sera, Lachish, or Gezer, besides going the main road north. Thus, it is clear that in year 8, Ramesses III did not merely defeat his Sea People opponents on the day of battle but had them also as his vassals in Philistia when they settled down in Gaza, Ashkelon, Ashdod, Gath, and Ekron, as well as up north in Dor and perhaps around Beth-Shan. Like their Canaanite neighbors, they, too, would have been taxed by Egypt, for most or all of his reign.

So, what about Amurru before year 5? Ramesses III very consciously took Ramesses II as his model and, like his exemplar, may have decided to try and restore Amurru to Egyptian control. Back in Merenptah's time, Egypt and Hatti were still allies, and Merenptah even sent grain supplies to the Hittites, probably during the reign of Tudkhalia IV; a sword in his name was found at Ugarit (a Hittite vassal). After Merenptah's reign, we have no further record of any contact between the last two Hittite great kings, Arnuwandas III and Suppiluliuma II, and the Egypt of Seti II, Siptah, or Tewosret. Under Setnakht, the new dynasty may have had no contact at all with the old ally or any sense of obligation toward him. During ca.1200–1180 BC, the last two Hittite emperors were beset with difficulties, culminating in the fall of Hattusas to Gasgeans and Mushku (Phrygians), so finally ending their rule. Their cousins, the kings of Tarhuntassa (north and west of the Taurus) and of Carchemish (in north Syria) would then lack any further central support, were potential rivals as much as allies, and were unlikely to interfere southward in Syria.

Thus, it is probable that Ramesses III judged he might go for Amurru without fear of trouble from the north. Sometime within his years 2–4, he may thus have chosen to lead his army through Canaan to remind his vassals of Egypt's suzerainty, entered Phoenicia, overcome Amurru, and then proceeded north (1) to take Ullaza (and perhaps Simyra, too) and (2) to venture via the Eleutherus gap northeast to attack Tunip—rather like Ramesses II in the latter's year 10. Thereby, he could claim to have equaled the northernmost push by his hero, even if (like that hero) he may have kept Ullaza but not Tunip. Thus, the reliefs concerning Ullaza and Tunip at Medinet Habu would reflect reality, as would the *first* mention of Amurru in the year 5 Libyan War inscription. There is no final proof of this, but of the king's hold on Canaan proper there can be no doubt.

That brings us to the passage in the year 5 text, near the end (lines 51–56), that mentions conflict with Philistines and Tjekkeru (Sicels) in terms that directly mirror the conflict of year 8, three years later than this text (e.g., at the Nile mouths). Nobody is prepared to credit Ramesses III's scribes with the gift of predictive prophecy. The solution to this conundrum most likely lies in two factors: the chronology of the construction of the temple at Medinet Habu and the king's desire to placard his later triumph as promptly as possible.

Freestanding Egyptian temples (new ones) followed a definite order of construction. First, the ground plan was decided and laid out; then, construction began at the rear, with the holy of holies, the sanctuary, and moved steadily forward to the front and facade. Thus, the rear half of the Medinet Habu temple was built first and could be decorated while the front courts were still in course of construction—first the second court, then the first court and front pylon. So, as they occupy the rear wall of the temple and its north wall from the rear to the back of the second pylon, the Nubian reliefs and exterior scenes of the First Libyan War were executed first, once the outer walls of the main temple (from the hypostyle hall to the rear sanctuaries) had been built. But only when the second court had been built could the other set of scenes of the First Libyan War and the year 5 text be engraved within it. In parallel with all this, the Sea Peoples war scenes (year 8) on the north exterior wall could begin to be engraved, once the north wall was complete forward to the second pylon (fronting the second court). So, "year 8" could be inscribed on the north outside, while a "year 5" text was being done on the south inside of the second court.

Building of the temple probably began in year 4, the date of its calendar of offerings. Certainly by year 5, large quantities of stone were being shipped out from the great Silsila sandstone quarries, as graffiti there make clear, with mention of three thousand men and forty-four ships.[30] So, full construction of the rear half of the temple (forward to the second pylon) could hardly have preceded year 8. Thus, the great inscription commemorating the First Libyan War in year 5 kept the date of the event it commemorated but was not finalized and engraved until year 8, when the Sea People reliefs were also being engraved on the exterior north wall. Therefore, in the event, the king had his scribes include a brief paragraph on the year 8 victory (lines 51–56) at the end of the official "year 5" text, just before the concluding praises of the king (lines 57–75).

In turn, the year 8 main inscription was placed on the facade of the second pylon, which would have to await its completion (years 8–9?). The first court and first (front) pylon were built thereafter, such that the scenes and texts of the Second Libyan War (year 11) could be engraved on the exterior of the northern wall between the first and second pylons and within the first court, and on the first pylon, inner face. The two Libyan wars and the Sea Peoples conflict had been the major crises—and military successes—by the king, so these were given priority. But in the first court, both inside and outside on the north wall, his earlier exploit in Phoenicia and to Tunip could be included, to show his former far-flung activity in the Levant, just as his hero Ramesses II had placed Levant and Kadesh war scenes on the north wall of the Ramesseum's first court, inside and out. Minor wars in Transjordan found no place in the memorial temples of either king or even in other temples in Ramesses III's case; so, even in his exclusions, the later king imitated the earlier one.

At this point, it may be useful to clear up some confusions over the "Sea Peoples" and the year 8 episode. First, the term "Sea Peoples," or "Peoples of the Sea," is not a modern invention but in effect was coined by the scribes of Merenptah and echoed by those of Ramesses III. Merenptah speaks of "[Tursha], Sherden, Shekelesh, Aqaywasha, *of the foreign countries of the Sea.*"[31] Ramesses III speaks of "the foreign lands that came from their land in the isles amidst the Sea."[32] The suggestion, occasionally made, that these peoples had been native to Canaan from of old is nonsense, contradicting both the clear statement of these firsthand texts and the evidence of these peoples' material culture once they did settle in southwest Canaan under Ramesses III and onward. Such a suggestion owes everything to the sociological/anthropological idiot dogma that nobody in antiquity ever emigrated anywhere (especially in any quantity), in the teeth of abundant evidence to the contrary at all periods in recorded human history. It owes nothing to the facts of the case.

This is not the only misconception regarding the Sea Peoples' episode in year 8 of this king. Second, and long since, Lesko ingeniously suggested that the years 5 and 8 wars of Ramesses III at Medinet Habu had simply been copied from Merenptah's wars in his now-destroyed memorial temple.[33] However, this is contradicted by the data available, as clearly demonstrated by Yurco.[34] The style and content of the year 5 texts of Merenptah and Ramesses III are different, and the latter's year 8 text is also different from the year 5 text of Merenptah (there is—and was—no year 8 war and text of Merenptah, or we would have heard about it by now). The events and protagonists are different; Merenptah's Libyan/Sea Peoples' war was on the *west* side of the Delta on land, whereas Ramesses III's conflict with the Sea Peoples was wholly on the *east* flank of the Delta and into Canaan/Djahi, (uniquely) on both water and land. The Sea Peoples of Merenptah were *not* wholly identical with those of Ramesses III. Merenptah fought no Philistines, while Ramesses III faced no Aqaywasha, and so on.

Third, in her very dense analysis of the Ramesses III texts, Cifola made the mistake of confusing literary variation in those texts with varying degrees of historical (un)reality.[35] The claims that there was no decisive military encounter in year 8 are based exclusively on a set of astonishing non sequiturs,[36] as well as considerable failure to understand either text or reliefs. The land and water scenes *are*, precisely, scenes of battle, and the main text gives their specific date (year 8). The enemy are not "vague"[37] but are named, more than once: for example, specifically as Philistines, Tjekkeru, Shekelesh, Danuna, Washash (year 8); the scene labels take this for granted. People coming from afar could and did come in large unitary groups, not solely in minor units as falsely claimed;[38] compare the nine to twelve thousand plus in the statistics of both Merenptah and Ramesses III on other occasions. The lack of statistics in the year 8 text and scenes proves nothing; there are no statistics for prisoners after Ramesses II's battle of Kadesh or in his records for years 4, 8, or 10, but nobody (I hope!) is foolish enough to dismiss the reality of his wars on so frivolous and limited a basis. The "different geographical references"[39] boil down to two: *only one each* for the land battle (Djahi) and the waterborne conflict (Nile mouths). In other words, they are unitary in each case. The supposed "absence of the enemy's fight" and "not many" foes[40] is a simple misreading of the scenes. In war scenes, it is customary to show the pharaoh and his forces overwhelming the foe, not the foe making a massive fight back; numbers are irrelevant, as the amount of people shown is simply a factor of the artistic composition and triumphalist intention of the scenes. Superficialities of this kind are of no evidential value whatsoever.

Fourth, to support a spurious and artificial lowering of archaeological dates of levels and pottery in Palestine in the twelfth through the tenth centuries BC, Finkelstein finds himself inventing a *third* wave of Sea People invasion of Canaan at about 1140/35 BC,[41] in order to introduce sub-Mycenaean Monochrome ware there at that particular date (itself based on other false premises). However, 1140/35 BC would correspond to Ramesses VI's time, when there is no trace whatsoever of any such phantom invasion. That king was very militaristic, as his full titulary exhibits, and he did not hesitate to fight off Libyan intruders at Thebes very promptly in his year 1 and to celebrate this with special statuary and a triumphal scene at Karnak;[42] his is a bronze statuette base found at Megiddo, we are often reminded. Such a king would not have hesitated to challenge any real irruption into Philistia or threat to the Delta and would not have failed to let us know, either. The archaeology of Philistia also forbids any such phantom "third wave"; the new Sea People–originated walled settlements at Ashkelon, Ashdod, and so on were not further substantially destroyed until the tenth century. The blunt truth of the matter is that the Philistines, Tjekkeru, and so on came in ca. 1177 BC (with a taste for Monochrome pottery and all), *not later*. Ramesses III carried off some of these people into Egypt from his twin battles in "Djahi" (probably north of the Egyptian base at Gaza) and at the Nile mouths; the rest of such immigrants, still in South Canaan, stayed there. The victorious pharaoh imposed Egyptian overlordship on them as well as on their Canaanite neighbors, levying the customary taxes on both lots (as attested, e.g., for Canaan by ostraca from Lachish and Tel Sera).[43]

Much fuss is sometimes made as to where Ramesses III settled his Sea People captives. In Papyrus Harris I (76.8), we are explicitly told that he "brought (them) as booty to Egypt, settled them in forts, subjected by my name." This could be anywhere in Egypt, not just in the Delta—in fact, deliberately elsewhere, further south. Ramesses II and III both practiced "exile," settling westerners in the east, easterners in the west, northerners in the south, and southerners in the north. In fact, a few decades later, under Ramesses V (ca. 1144 BC), we find Sherden and others settled in Middle Egypt, well away from the Delta or Canaan, in the lists of the great Wilbour Papyrus.

Nearer home than Canaan, in Egyptian eyes, were the copper mines of Timna, at and near which Ramesses III left his mark[44]—rock inscriptions at Nahal Roded and Timna itself, plus a ring stand there. These mines find mention as the land of 'Atika, whither the king sent ships to collect the copper,[45] after the account of digging a great, enclosed desert well at 'Ayna (unlocated) and the expedition to Punt. All three episodes are narrated in Papyrus

Harris I (77.6–78.5) after its summary (76.6–77.6) of his wars with the Sea Peoples (= year 8), Seirites (no known date), and Libyans (= year 11). If the sequence is chronological rather than merely thematic, then the mentioned activities at 'Ayna, Punt, and 'Atika (Timna) might have followed year 12.

HOME AFFAIRS: THE ROYAL BUILDER

Like many pharaohs, Ramesses III saw himself as a builder king, a reputation that he still has today. But that repute merits careful scrutiny. Many who merely go to modern Luxor and see his great memorial temple at Medinet Habu and his quite impressive way-station temple that projects conspicuously into the grand forecourt at Karnak are suitably impressed—the more so, if they recall his major tomb in the Valley of the Kings, visit tombs of his sons in the Valley of the Queens, and are observant enough to notice (or are told of) his large-scale reliefs on the exterior of the rear half of the Luxor temple and his great double stela of year 20 on the walls of the south approach of the Karnak temple. A cursory reading of Papyrus Harris I also confirms (at first sight) his having built grandly for the gods, not only at Thebes.

However, first impressions are not always wholly accurate impressions. Ramesses III (at thirty-one years) reigned just under half the span of his admired predecessor Ramesses II (sixty-six years). So, in theory, one might expect that Ramesses III might in turn have contributed about half as much to Egypt's monumental landscape as his hero did—more if he was specially active, but less if otherwise. In practice, of course, all manner of possible factors could affect the actual outcome and modify any purely theoretical projection. What do we find? Let us proceed from north to south, from Syria to the Sudan, so to speak.

The Levant. Here, Ramesses II left traces of monumental gateways at Byblos up north and at Joppa down south and a swathe of stelae: at Nahr el-Kalb (2), Tyre, Byblos, Adhlun, Beth-Shan, and Sheikh Said and now one of year 56 from near Damascus.[46] For Ramesses III (in monumental terms), we have but one statue each for Byblos and Beth-Shan (plus items of his men there) and report of a temple.[47]

The Delta. (a) Pi-Ramesse. Here, Ramesses II built an entire city (four miles north to south by about two miles west to east); to this, Ramesses III could but add a fresh section, plus a "chapel" (way station?) to the temple of Seth.[48] *(b) Heliopolis.* Ramesses II and his father seemingly added a pylon and large court and a series of obelisks; Ramesses III, a sanctuary, shrine, and chapel (way station?) for Re[49] and a temple for Iusaas.[50] Both kings show up at nearby Tell el-Yahudieh. *(c) Memphis.* Here, Ramesses II and his father built a hall equivalent to that at Karnak (but now lost) and the great West Hall, besides various lesser structures, and established the new Serapeum. Ramesses III was content with a way station in Ptah's forecourt[51] and minor structures and had to fund three Serapeum burials. *(d) The rest of the Delta and so on.* Elsewhere (so far), we find practically no monumental buildings by Ramesses III at all (with none in Papyrus Harris I either). By contrast, we have Ramesses II up at Balamun in the north down to Athribis in the south, via Leontopolis. Out east, he built local centers at Tell er-Retaba (also a trace of Ramesses III!) and Tell el-Maskhuta (as contemporary records prove) and a minor fort at Gebel Hassa en route to Suez. Down the west side, we have seven sites (from El-Gharbaniya to Ashmun) featuring Ramesses II (buildings, or blocks), plus the forts out in northern "Libya." But there is virtually nothing of Ramesses III in this whole region, by finds or in Papyrus Harris I, in striking contrast. In his wars, he names two frontier posts, one probably a remake of Merenptah's by Pi-Iru, the other simply old Up-to renamed (Libyan war scenes).

Mid- to Upper Egypt. Materially, we have (so far) no known temples of Ramesses III between Memphis and Thebes, in strong contrast to Ramesses II. However, Papyrus Harris I does modify this modestly, attributing twin contributions by Ramesses III at five centers in this region: Siut (58.12–59.1), Hermopolis (58.1–6), Abydos (58.7–8), Thinis (57.11–12), and "Ombos" (Nubt; 59.4–5). In each case, Ramesses III contributed a "chapel" at the temple, most likely a way station as elsewhere. Much more significantly, he threw a stout brick enclosure around each temple precinct and twice even tells us why (57.13, 58.6): "(to) restrain the Libyan aliens who had transgressed their bounds from of old." Those Libyans who had taken the road south into the oases were now seeking to penetrate the Nile Valley at a half-dozen points, of which Thebes was but one. With these modest temple structures and badly needed brick enclosures, we may contrast whole main temples of Ramesses II, such as that at Heracleopolis, that at Antinoe, and one to Seth at Matmar, besides his own major temple at Abydos and major works in his father's great temple there.

Thebes. Here, Ramesses III contributed (as before) way stations, of some size, at Karnak for both Amun and Mut, plus the rear half of a new temple to Khons. Perhaps his "temple" at Luxor (so far known only from P. Harris I.5.1–2) was another way station. These were by no means negligible but are still dwarfed by the vast Karnak hypostyle hall of Ramesses II and his father and by Ramesses II's great pylon and forecourt at Luxor. On the West Bank, things are—for once—more equal. Ramesses III made sure that his memorial temple (Medinet Habu) equaled that of Ramesses II in scale; and each had a large tomb in the Valley of the Kings and families' tombs in the Valley of the Queens. Here again, though, Ramesses II scored over everyone else, with his incredible family labyrinth in tomb KV 5.

Upper Egypt (South). No major building work of Ramesses III, going on to Aswan, is yet attested (or listed in P. Harris I). But for Ramesses II, we have good traces of temples at Armant, Edfu ("Ramesside pylon"?), and Elephantine.

Nubia. Here is the greatest contrast of all. Papyrus Harris I (8.13) attributes one temple (so far undiscovered) to Ramesses III in Nubia. But for Ramesses II, we have over a dozen temples from his hand or in which (in two or three cases) he had a major interest; suffice it to list Beit el-Wali, Quban, Gerf Hussein, Wadi es-Sebua, Derr, Abu Simbel (2 temples), Aksha, Amarah West, and Gebel Barkal, with work also at, for example, Aniba and Buhen.

In short, the known and reported major works of Ramesses III are not merely less than those of Ramesses II (to half the latter's output, without benefit of reports) but very substantially so. They consist of refurbishments at Pi-Ramesse and some highly visible moderate-sized works at the three great national centers (Heliopolis, Memphis, and especially Thebes), plus lesser additions elsewhere (in Middle Egypt, with defense walls against Libyan incursions, a threat unheard of in Ramesses II's time).

There are good reasons for the difference. There was (religiously) little point in exhausting national resources in trying to erect still vaster courts, higher pillared halls, and yet more massive pylons in front of the gigantic structures that already prefaced such temples as Karnak, Luxor, Memphis, and Heliopolis, especially if revenues were less than in the balmier days of Ramesses II. Nubian gold revenues were probably in decline; and the current disturbances in the Levant would have limited direct revenues by taxation and would have also inhibited foreign trade (and its profits) in some measure. Centuries passed before anyone tried to prefix still larger structures to the great Nineteenth Dynasty temples, until Shoshenq I set out larger courts before the Karnak temple of Amun and the Memphite temple of Ptah (with a pylon) and, later, Taharqa set up just simple (but tall) central colonnades such as we still see in Shoshenq's forecourt, to be matched still later with Nectanebo's huge pylon, forever left unfinished. So, it would always have been unrealistic to expect Ramesses III in any way to match his old hero or even try to. He achieved a creditable amount for his particular time and circumstances.

A CLOSING ROUNDUP: ADMINISTRATION, TOP PEOPLE, THE ARTS, AND THE END

It would be wrong to expound any further on the remaining major facets of this reign in a mere opening chapter. Instead, I simply remind readers of the presence of such other aspects (besides foreign affairs and monumental buildings) merely as a preface to all that follows in this book.

The Great and the Good (and Not So Good). During the closing years of the Nineteenth Dynasty and the brief crisis of succession from which Setnakht emerged to establish his throne and bequeath it to Ramesses III, it is interesting to note especially the continuity in tenure of the highest administrative offices of state. *In Egypt,* the vizier Hori who had already served Seti II and Siptah continued to officiate under both Setnakht and Ramesses III before (from at least year 16) a new man, To, was vizier,[52] certainly for Upper Egypt originally. After some inner conflict,[53] To was appointed in year 29 as sole vizier over all Egypt,[54] which no doubt doubled his responsibilities. This may well have had an adverse effect at that time, when failures in the regular provisioning of the workmen's village at Deir el-Medina led to strikes in year 29 and the intervention of other notables, such as the high priest of Amun. (It may here be significant that, in due course, Ramesses IV unhesitatingly dumped To in favor of a new man, Neferronpet.) *In Nubia,* a parallel continuity appears with the viceregal regime there. Hori (I) son of Kama was in office from year 6 of Siptah and recurs explicitly so named under both Setnakht and Ramesses III.[55] His son Hori (II) son of Hori (son of Kama; KRI VI.81) lasted into at least the reign of Ramesses IV, after succeeding his own father under Ramesses III. Clearly, the new dynasty found solid and loyal supporters in the Horis, both vizier and viceroys, who had probably kept ordinary state affairs running normally despite the court crisis of change of regime.

By contrast, the top priesthood of the cult of Theban Amun (the most prestigious and best endowed in all Egypt) suffered drastic changes in incumbents all the way from after Merenptah through to Ramesses III and IV. After briefly serving Ramesses II, Roma-roy officiated throughout Merenptah's reign and into that of Amenmesses (represented by erased cartouches in the pontiff's inscriptions at Karnak). In consequence, the ultimately triumphant Seti II felt it politic to dismiss him and appointed his own personal secretary, Mahy ("Mahuhy"), as next high priest of Theban Amun. Under Siptah, all is obscure, although the little-known pair Minmose and another Hori (origins unknown in both cases) may each have briefly served then. What *is* clear is that Setnakht found it politic to appoint an entirely new man, one Bakenkhons (B), son of a lay official, a "Commander (*imy-r*) of recruits (*nfrw*) of the Estate of Amun," and once "general," Amenemope. The father may simply have been a retired military general subsequently placed in charge of the manual work-force of Amun's temple and estates, while his son was made high priest. This looks like a strictly political appointment, openly supplanting the priestly families previously "regnant" in Thebes. Amenemope and Bakenkhons were clearly "king's men," owing their position and allegiance to the new king above all else and, in turn, to Ramesses III.[56] Later, when a new incumbent was needed, the king drew on another family that had close association with the Twentieth Dynasty regime: that of Merybast, chief taxing master (from Hermopolis), dealing with state finances. By year 26, an Usimare-nakht was Amun's high priest, followed in the last year or so of Ramesses III or after the accession of Ramesses IV by one Ramesses-nakht, a son of Merybast. It is pos-sible that both pontiffs were brothers, each a son of Merybast. However that may be, Ramesses-nakht shrewdly formed marital links and on-the-ground alliance with the old priestly families of Thebes, giving his daughter Aatmeret as wife to Amenemope, third prophet of Amun,[57] whose priestly pedigree reached right back to the time of Bakenkhons A and Roma-roy of Ramesses II's day. In that context, the "dynastic principle" of the late Nineteenth Dynasty, evicted by Setnakht, arose again, as Ramesses-nakht officiated along with two sons after him for most of the rest of the Twentieth Dynasty. Like Tutankh-amun, Haremhab, and Merenptah, Ramesses III ordered an inspection of the temples of all Egypt and their affairs, a reforming move carried through in year 15 by one Penpato.[58]

Internal Decline. In the later years of this reign, troubles seem to abound, at least in our available sources. These include (a) intruders (oasis Libyans?) from the desert into Western Thebes in year 28; (b) the vizieral trouble in Athribis about then or after (mentioned just above); (c) the breakdown in workmen's supplies and consequent strikes in year 29; (d) the onset of finan-cial corruption (discerned from about year 28 in one case) that ran on unde-tected (or simply undisturbed?) throughout the reign of Ramesses IV and was only turfed out in year 4 of Ramesses V;[59] and (e) the conspiracy to mur-der the old king himself. The collocation of troubles may indicate that Ramesses III was losing his grip as chief executive in his closing years and also that, at some levels at least, injudicious appointments had been made of individuals lacking in loyalty to the throne (as with the conspirators) or lack-ing the equivalent of financial probity at lower levels.[60] Clearly, factions had developed at court, and the official heir Prince Ramesses (future IV) found himself vulnerable and used the full weight of the pharaonic propaganda machine to shore up his reign thereafter—a sad ending.

Other Spheres. During the Nineteenth Dynasty, alongside merely formal, rather "mass-produced" artwork in statuary and relief carving, extremely fine work was produced on occasion, not lacking in extent (temple of Seti I at Abydos, parts of that of Ramesses II also, and in their tombs), variety (items of jewelry), or experimentation (e.g., the shading of the cheeks of Queen Nefertari in the paintwork of her tomb in the Valley of the Queens). What is more, fine-quality work continued in the royal tombs, as under Merenptah and Siptah. But under Ramesses III, the royal art in Western Thebes changed in some measure and not for the better (at least from a modern point of view). The tombs of his offspring in the Valley of the Queens show this well. The coloring of the carved scenes is blatantly garish, compared with what we find, for example, in earlier tombs like those of Ramesses I and Seti I. And the style of the inscriptions is much cruder, with stumpy signs garishly painted, almost barbaric compared with the fine work in tombs like those of Ramesses I, Seti I, and Ramesses II and even later. In a way, the great rhetorical victory inscriptions of Ramesses III at Medinet Habu show this in verbal form—a level of bombast set to outstrip the shrillest notes of any previous king and full of highly colored, rarer words, both exotic foreign (usually Semitic) and Egyptian, presenting a thoroughly florid style to the reader. Never was such styling exceeded by any later pharaoh. Ramesses III had sought to be another Ramesses II in his own way, in different and more difficult circumstances—and, in turn, to be a model for the future.

IN CONCLUSION: AN OVERALL PERSPECTIVE?

Seti I and Ramesses II had sought to outdo the Eighteenth Dynasty in both war and peace, leading to a period of unparalleled monumental works for the gods (temples great and numerous) and the new city of Pi-Ramesse. Theirs was seemingly a period of not only peace but a fair measure of prosperity, as private monuments (even at fairly modest levels) abound at this epoch. Merenptah was the afterglow; his successors saw the failure of the line but cast no shadow on the great Ramesses II himself, who was now the measure for any later king. In due course, Ramesses III entered into this tricky inheritance, in more dangerous times. Of almost certainly military background, he took his chance to shine on the battlefield against both the Libyans and the Sea Peoples and to impose an outward political ascendancy on both fronts for the rest of his reign. So, in his public war records, he could indeed pose officially as a victorious king in the best tradition. But the suppressed Libyan menace merely moved south, and he had to fortify Upper Egyptian temple precincts against them; Libyan overflows into the Nile Valley were to trouble

Thebes from his time via Ramesses VI to that of Ramesses IX–XI. The Canaanite province stayed in part Egyptian for less than twenty years after his time; and it is probable that Nubia became steadily less profitable.

How did Ramesses III fare posthumously? His son Ramesses IV looked (as did Ramesses III) to Ramesses II for exemplar, as his own Abydos and Karnak texts show. In the mold of an "Usimare Ramesses Meryamun" (and likewise in their fuller titularies when preserved), so probably did Ramesses V, VII, and VIII. However, Ramesses VII, as Usimare Setepenre Meryamun, drew on both Ramesses II and III; Ramesses VI, VII, and XI used the epithets "God, Ruler of Heliopolis" of Ramesses II and re-echoed by Ramesses III; and on offering stands, Ramesses IX chose to commemorate Ramesses II, III, and VII (KRI VI.462)—"ancestor" (II), grandfather (III), and probably uncle (VII). Ramesses III stood too close to his successors (and doubtless to their knowledge of his final decline) to become a figure gilded by a "legendary" haze, transmitting only the glory and not the darker crevices of a reign. So, he did not attain to the same stature either with them or in later times. In modern times, his memorial temple at Medinet Habu (readily accessible, with its impressive war reliefs) has stood him in great stead and has brought him the title "last great king" in some degree—probably for the New Kingdom. But in later days, the shrewd Shoshenq I and still shrewder Psammetichus I (if not also Nectanebo I) would easily rival him as intrinsically strong and clever rulers, in terms of either reuniting Egypt (Shoshenq I temporarily) and/or fending off Egypt's series of later foes (Psammetichus I and Nectanebo I). But let us not begrudge Ramesses III his just place at an important juncture in ancient history when, in turbulence, Bronze Age empires gave way to Iron Age kingdoms and people-groups in new constellations of power.

Notes

1. Accession and death dates of Setnakht: cf., e.g., Altenmüller (1992) 158; Altenmüller (1994a) 25. Year 4 is now attested on a stela from Karnak; see Boraik (2007) 119–26 with pl. 24.

2. Convenient grouping of Setnakht's cartouches: von Beckerath (1984) 244.

3. See Altenmüller (1996) 1–9, basing himself on the (technically) undated P. Greg, of the years 5–7 in an unspecified reign, either Siptah or Ramesses III; cf. KRI V.437, 445. See now Grandet (2000) 339–45 and, for the full publication, Grandet (2003) 59–60, 294, no. 886.

4. References: cf. Beckerath (1997a) 106.

5. It had not been used by Ramesses II, contrary to von Beckerath (1984) 89, 237 as H.13. His example is actually from Ramesses III, as cited in parallel with Ramesses II for the "Blessing of Ptah" text (KRI II.259.13!).

6. See Kitchen (1987) 137 with references.

7. Published in *MH* I, pls. 8–11; texts also in *KRI* V.8–9. Transl.: Edgerton-Wilson (1936) 1–2.

8. Text: Helck (1980) 117–26, following from Smith (1976) 124–29, pls. 29, 75.1–4.

9. References: Porter and Moss (1937) 211(34–36); cf., e.g., Wreszinski (1923) II, pls. 161–62.

10. Amarah West and Sai stelae; cf. *KRI* VII.8–11. Transl. and notes: *RITA* I.85–87; *RITANC* I.81–90.

11. We may here discount the tiny *razzia* by Ramesses II as youthful prince regent against a few villagers in Wawat (*KRI* II.198–99; transl.: *RITA* II.61–62), conducted at most as a training exercise; cf. *RITANC* II.112–13.

12. The Amada stela of Merenptah and its parallels; *KRI* IV.33–37. Transl.: *RITA* IV.1–2; cf. *RITANC* IV.ad loc.

13. Cf. my remarks in Endesfelder et al. (1977) 224–25.

14. Lines 42–43; *KRI* V.117 end. Transl. and notes: *RITA* V and *RITANC* V.ad loc.

15. P. Harris I.10.15; text in Erichsen (1933), 13. Transl.: Grandet (1999) I.236.

16. Text: *KRI* V.90–91 (plus VI.662.6 to fill a lacuna). Transl. and notes: *RITA* V.90–91; *RITANC* V.ad loc.

17. Occurrences: see Zibelius (1972) 175 (under *trwt*) with references to older discussions.

18. It is curious to find Hori II, the viceroy of Nubia, erecting two virtually identical stelae in years 5 and 11 of Ramesses III (*KRI* V.382–83), both honoring the king as Egypt's Nile flood and sustenance. These (by their dates) look like Hori II's way of honoring his king as deliverer from the Libyan attacks in those years and hence provider also. Precisely this role of the king features in the great texts of both year 5 (line 71; E/W 34) and year 11 (line 59; E/W 86). Perhaps such texts were circulated to such as the viceroy, with Hori II taking his cue from them.

19. *KRI* V.12.3–4. Transl.: Edgerton and Wilson (1936) 7.

20. *KRI* V.15.12–14. Transl.: Edgerton and Wilson (1936) 14.

21. For the occurrence of "Sea People" and other references in the text apparently reflecting the events of year 8, see the section "Foreign Affairs: The Levant" below.

22. Cf. O'Connor (1990) 41–45 on possible population figures under Merenptah and Ramesses III; his entire paper is an invaluable contribution to our appreciation of the Libyans at this general period.

23. Notably Grandet (1993) 209–10.

24. See Daressy (1917) 224 (col. 9) and 226 (col. 11), texts, with his pp. 237 (correct) versus 239/240 (wrong; cf. Gardiner [1918] 135).

25. Grandet (1993) 209–10.

26. Dismissal of food shortage and land hunger (with additional population) by O'Connor (1990) 92–93 is clearly contradicted by Merenptah's statements and by the self-evident attempts by the Libyan groups to take over land in Egypt for pasture and so on (Merenptah, Ramesses III); this is *not* modern theory but fact stated by first-hand contemporaries. It is not the firsthand sources but irrelevant anthropological theory that should be ditched.

27. See Kitchen (1985) for this whole topic.

28. All inscriptions are collected in *KRI* V.251–57 and VII.259–60 with references.

29. So in P. Harris I.7.5; Byblos statue, *KRI* V.256.

30. Transcriptions (esp. "C"): *KRI* V.228; cf. 419. Cf. Grandet (1993) 102–4, 365–66 (notes); A. J. Peden (2001) 126–27.

31. Great Karnak text, line 52; *KRI* IV.8.8; *RITA* IV.8. Athribis stela, verso 13; *KRI* IV.22.7; *RITA* IV.20.

32. *KRI* V.33.4; E/W 42.

33. Lesko (1989) 153.

34. Yurco (1997) 502–4.

35. Cifola (1988); Cifola (1991).

36. Cifola (1988) 303; Cifola (1991) 55.

37. Cifola (1988) 303.

38. Ibid.

39. Cifola (1991) 55.

40. Ibid.

41. Finkelstein (1995) 229.

42. Amer (1985) 67–68.

43. For a more factual and refined assessment of the year 8 conflict than the three preceding, flawed approaches, see O'Connor (2000).

44. Texts: *KRI* V.257.

45. P. Harris I.78.1–5.

46. For the last, see Taraqji and Yoyotte (1999a) and (1999b); Kitchen (1999a). For the rest, see, e.g., in Porter and Moss (1951) and *RITANC* II.

47. P. Harris I.9.1–3.

48. P. Harris I.9.2, 60.2–3.

49. P. Harris I.25.12, 26.7, 29.1.

50. P. Harris I.30.1.

51. P. Harris I.45.3, as at Karnak.

52. Kitchen and Ockinga (1992).

53. P. Harris I.59.11, at Athribis.

54. *KRI* V.530.1f.

55. *KRI* V.2 and 381.

56. *KRI* V.397–99.

57. Cf. the convenient chart in Bierbrier (1977) 1245–46 for most of these people.

58. Grandet 1990.

59. Turin Indictment Papyrus; cf., e.g., Peden (1994a) 69–72.

60. Cf. the Turin Indictment Papyrus.

Chapter 2

Change and Continuity in Religion and Religious Practices in Ramesside Egypt

EMILY TEETER

The nature of religion in the Ramesside period and its relationship to religion of the Eighteenth Dynasty is a topic that has been much debated. Most scholars agree that religious beliefs (especially the conception of god) and cult activities were heavily impacted by the Amarna experience and hence that religion is significantly different in the Ramesside period than in the pre-Amarna era. However, there is little agreement as to the forms and depth of that impact. Evaluations contending a dramatic change include the conclusion that "Egypt had lost its security, self-confidence, and tolerance, had become nervous, tense, arbitrary and exacting."[1] According to Van Dijk, "The Amarna episode . . . left deep scars on the collective consciousness. . . . Superficially, the country returned to the traditional religion of the time before Akhenaten, but nothing would ever be the same again."[2] Others have suggested that the culture was not changed so radically, that the Ramesside period continued much in the tradition of the Eighteenth Dynasty, with an overlay of personal piety.[3] Assmann has posited the greatest impact, suggesting that religion of the Ramesside period was radically different, the changes being primarily in the changing role of Maat and the status of the king. According to this reconstruction, Ramesside religion was decadent and devoid of true spirit: "the world has become unintelligible, incalculable and unstable. It no longer inspires comfort and confidence. There is nothing firm and stable within and without but god, the sole fixed point in a turning world."[4] According to this point of view, individuals were no longer comforted by their gods; rather, they were reduced to beings who cringed before the increasingly capricious deities, praying to them for the breath of life. In this reconstruction, the divinity of the pharaoh was eroded to the point that he was merely a figurehead who fought leagues of sinister priests for control of the Two Lands.[5]

The great range of opinions about continuity and discontinuity of religion and religious practices in the Ramesside period is due primarily to the selection of primary sources and how they are employed. The sources for reconstructing the fundamental aspects of Ramesside belief—such as the status of the king, his relationship to his subjects, consciousness of the divine, the nature of the pantheon, the relationship of the people to the gods and how they worshiped them—are everywhere. Virtually every letter, inscription, and relief can be mined for its religious content. Conclusions have, in some cases, been reached employing only certain categories of source material, a methodology that potentially skews the final conclusions. For example, Assmann's important and influential studies of the rise of personal piety are based on hymns, instructions, and prayers,[6] and he acknowledges that he is dealing with a deliberately restricted scope of sources. When, for example, the reliefs and inscriptions of the Ramesside temples are added to that corpus of material, one can reach a rather different conclusion.[7]

So, too, the social and cultural background of modern scholars has colored the discourse. For some of them, Ramesside consciousness of god is akin to Christianity in the search for a transcendent deity resembling the Judeo-Christian supreme being.[8] As Hornung has commented about some of the arguments concerning the nature of god, "The reasoning has become circular—the conclusion that is to be proved is assumed in advance."[9]

In the following comments about the nature of the divine and the relation of the king to his subjects, an attempt has been made to be inclusive, rather than exclusive, in the use of source material. But as will be seen, it is often difficult or impossible to draw clear and concise conclusions, because there was probably not a unanimity of belief but, rather, a complex and often contradictory or complementary system of beliefs and cult activities, not only in the Ramesside period, but throughout Egyptian history.

THE RAMESSIDE CONCEPTION OF GOD

One of the most debated issues in the discussion of Ramesside religion is the nature of the gods and whether the sense of "god" changed in the Late New

Kingdom. It is clear that the process of syncretism—the temporary combination or indwelling of one god within another—continued to be a feature of Ramesside religion.[10] Among the most vivid illustrations is the scene in the Nineteenth Dynasty tomb of Nofertari, where a god with the corkscrew horns of the archaic ram is labeled "This is Re who has come to rest in Osiris; Osiris who has come to rest in Re." One of the most important and often-cited documents of Ramesside theology, the Leiden Hymn to Amun, reflects this temporary indwelling, or syncretistic union, of the many in one:

> Re himself is mingled in his bodily form, and he is the fashioner dwelling in Heliopolis. Wherever is said of Tatenen is referring to him, and Amun, who came forth from chaos—that is God's image above. Another of his forms is the Eight Great Gods; he engendered the primeval gods, brought forth Re, Completed himself as Atum, who began existence.

Another section of the same text reads:

> All the gods are three;
> Amun, Re, and Ptah, who have no equal.
> Hidden (*imn*) is his name as Amun,
> He is Re in people's sight,
> His body is Ptah.[11]

As argued by Horning, one should conclude that this grouping of gods is not a prelude to monotheism but, rather, a strong "counter-current" to it.[12] The phrase "all the *gods* are three" (*3-nw nṯrw nbw*), confirms the essential polytheistic and the syncretistic nature of the pantheon. The contrast of that phrase with the following description of each god in the singular ("He is . . .") refers to the nature of each of the many gods, namely, that they are manifested in all realms of experience—the hidden transcendent form like Amun, the immanent and visible element of nature like the sun (Re), and the corporeal form (Ptah), which was the focus of cult.[13]

Texts from the Ramesside period that refer to syncretistic combinations of gods have been taken as evidence of the emergence of a transcendent god, an omnipresent deity in whom all the gods of the pantheon were expressed.[14] It has been suggested that this deity went beyond the traditional syncretistic forms to become a superdeity who was present in all aspects of nature.[15] According to Assmann, "The relationship between 'god' (in the singular) and 'the gods,' perhaps the most critical of all antinomies, was treated as the opposition between openness and hiddenness, immanence and transcendence."[16] The sense of the multiplicity of forms is indicated by such texts as "Greetings, you sole one who makes himself into millions." He suggests that as a part of this transcendence, "the eulogies of Amun-Re could be transferred to other deities . . . This phenomenon shows that we are not dealing purely with the theology of Amun-Re, but with formulations of a more general concept of the divine that—if the somewhat disrespectful comparison be permitted—could display the images of other deities like a clip-on picture frame."[17] This is reflected in the Leiden Hymn to Amun:

> Lord of Lords, who fashioned himself by himself; Lord of the Goddesses—He is the lord! Those who were dreaming, he shines for them all to brighten their faces in another of his Forms . . .

> The eight great gods were your first incarnation to complete this world, while you were one alone. Your body was hidden among the oldest primordial beings, for you had concealed yourself as Amun from the face of the gods. You fashioned your form as Tatenen, the Land to bring the first gods to birth back in your primeval time. Your comeliness was honored as Kamutef, strong bull of his mother.[18]

A passage addressed to the rising sun in the tomb of Imyseba (reign of Ramesses IX) suggests that the deity could be conceived of as being as transcendent as the cosmos itself:

> Your two eyes are the sun and the moon,
> Your head is the sky,
> Your feet are the netherworld.[19]

This same sentiment is reflected in the Cairo Hymn to Amun (P. Cairo 58032) of the early Third Intermediate Period:

> Mighty in power, sacred in majesty, secret the contours of his bodily form; His right eye and his left eye are the sun and moon . . . With thousand eyes and hearing ears, who guides the millions when he shines; Possessor of life who offers his love, who encompasses the world within his care; who offered forth creation . . .[20]

A similar sentiment is found in another section of the Leiden Hymn: "Light was his incarnation in the Beginning."[21] The same text suggests that the transcendent god becomes unknowable to humankind: "God crafted himself, none know his nature; his perfect features came into being by means of a sacred mystery."[22] A hymn to Amun-Re in the temple of Ramesses III at Karnak describes Amun-Re as one "Whose name has been hidden and his image concealed, none have known his form from the beginning."[23] The Leiden Hymn elaborates:

> But One alone is the hidden God, who hides himself from them all, who conceals himself from gods, whose features cannot be known. He is further above than heaven, deeper down than the world below and no god at all can know his true nature. No picture of him blossoms further in the writings; there is no witness concerning him. He is mysterious to the depths of his majesty—great beyond any perception of him, mighty beyond comprehension . . . "No god can know him by means of it—God is a Spirit, hidden his Name and his Mystery.[24]

These passages seem particularly appropriate for Amun, whose name literally means "the Hidden One."

However, not all Egyptologists agree that a transcendent, unknowable god was a dominant feature of Ramesside religion. Hornung has commented, "But in Egypt one cannot speak of a true transcendence that would raise a deity above space, time, and fate and extend his being into the realms of the absolute and limitless"; "At no time was there a transcendent God in Egypt." He further comments, "The 'anonymous' god of the instruction texts is no exception [to the existence of a transcendent god], even though he is often cited as the chief evidence for transcendent features or 'monotheistic tendencies' in the Egyptian conception of god."[25]

Perhaps one is better advised to look for a multiplicity of experiences of god and gods, rather than to insist that there was only one conception of the divine in the Ramesside period.[26] Indeed, the same texts that are used to support the existence of the transcendent god contain references that suggest that the conception of god was not significantly different than in the Eighteenth Dynasty. For example, the often-cited Leiden Hymn to Amun contains references to the individual differentiation of deities, suggesting that the conception of polytheism existed alongside the sense of a single great god: "Divinest of gods who came into being on his own—all gods came to be after he began with himself." The god is described as one "who conceals himself from gods,"[27] which seems to reflect the relationship of deities to another, but separate, great god. As the Leiden Hymn describes the deity, "God is three of all gods: Amun, Re, Ptah, without any others,"[28] which may be interpreted in two ways. Does the reference to "any others" mean that no god(s) existed other than the three or that the supreme god is made up of only three of the many gods? In any case, the reference to the component gods may be taken as the traditional syncretistic indwelling rather than the formation of an omnipotent transcendent god.

Other sections of the Leiden Hymn suggest that polytheism was still a prominent feature of Ramesside religion: "All that comes forth from his [Amun's] mouth is hidden, so the gods administer for him what is commanded."[29] The Wisdom texts, which are such a prominent part of the documentation for Ramesside religion and thought, also attest to the persistence of traditional polytheism. As stated by Wente, "later Wisdom texts actually mention specific deities even more frequently than earlier Wisdom texts, casting doubt on any supposed trend toward monotheism."[30]

This documentation for polytheism in a conventional pre-Ramesside fashion is suggested by the epithet of Amun (and other gods) "king of the gods."[31] The epistolary formula of the Late Ramesside Letters also reflects a conventional conception of the pantheon that is vastly different from the Leiden Hymn: "In life prosperity and health and in the favor of Amun Re king of the gods. I every day tell Amun Re, Mut, Khonsu, and all the gods of Thebes to cause you to live, to cause you to be prosperous."[32] The Berlin Hymn to the Creator God dating from the reign of Ramesses IX calls on the deity to "protect the *gods* who have come into being in this land."[33] Stelae from Deir el-Medina that call on the deity for a long life and health may be addressed to several gods.[34]

The tombs in the Valley of the Kings also provide evidence for continuity rather than discontinuity of belief in the Ramesside age. The religious texts that appear in the Eighteenth Dynasty or the beginning of the Nineteenth, such as the *Amduat, Book of Gates,* and *Book of Caverns,* continue to be used throughout the Ramesside period with very little modification.[35] For example, the Litany of Re, in which the sun god is called by his seventy-four names, is employed for royal tombs from the time of Thutmose III through Ramesses VI. Extracts of the text appear in the tombs of Ramesses IX and X,[36] suggesting that the underlying conception of Re as expressed in that text did not change throughout the New Kingdom.[37]

The sense that emerges from examining the conceptions of god in the Ramesside period presents innovative ideas of the divine as a more abstract and transcendent being. However, the often-cited hymns that are the primary sources for positing belief in a transcendent god are not numerous, raising the question of how widespread their appeal may have been and how characteristic such a belief was in the practice of religion by Egyptians in the Late New Kingdom. Although one might wonder if such texts were more prevalent than their survival suggests, the inconsistency of the theology of the hymns—the mixing of references to a transcendent god with those that reflect a traditional association of gods—suggests that such a belief was not uniformly held, and it may not have been even widely held. The limited sources for such beliefs and the continuity of old polytheistic-syncretistic beliefs suggest that there were several contemporary conceptions rather than a single unified conception of god.

PERSONAL PIETY IN THE RAMESSIDE ERA

Personal piety is widely considered to be a hallmark of Ramesside religion.[38] Personal piety, a term coined by Erman in 1911,[39] is characterized by an individual's direct contact with the god(s), sense of insecurity, and striving for the blessings of the god as an individual's action and his fate are disassociated,[40] as well as the appearance of penitential hymns, which often take the forms of confession. Personal piety is generally associated with a diminution of the status of the king as the traditional intermediary between the gods and humankind.

The rise of personal piety has been linked to the Amarna age,[41] during which time devotees were cut off from contact with their god(s) by the king, who became the "unique" and sole interpreter of the god's will. The traditional festivals, with their processions of the gods, in the course of which people had contact with their deities, were eliminated in favor of processions of the royal family. Rather than praying to the god(s), the people were forced to rely on the favor of the king and thus strove to be in his good graces. As related in the tomb of Aye, "Oh each one who loves life and desires a good lifetime, worship the king, unique like the Aton, without another who is great except for him."[42] With the near elimination of the other gods (at least at Tell el-Amarna), people no longer relied on their own cognizance of the principles of Maat to guide their behavior, because piety was replaced by loyalty to the king, who was the source of Maat. No longer did they need to live their lives according to Maat, because their fate would be decided by the king. A text in the tomb of Aye relates:

I was one true to the king, the one whom he fostered . . . I was in front of officials and companions of the king, (being) the first of my lord's followers. He has set Maat in my inner being, and my abomination is lying. I live only by worshipping his Ka, and I am fulfilled only by seeing him.

And: . . . worship the king, unique like the Aton, without another who is great except for him, and he will grant you a lifetime in tranquility, (with) food and provisions which are his to give.[43]

According to this reconstruction, people in the post-Amarna period reacted against the king's domination of cult and divine access. They rejected the primacy of the king and strove to be in the praises and presence of the gods, creating a new, intensely personal relationship between human and god. According to Assmann, the resulting personal piety was nothing other than "that new sphere of religious experience beyond cult, cosmos and myth, whose horizon was the human heart and personal history, in which personal destiny could be interpreted directly as the personal will of the deity . . . The only resort was the internal. The gods and goddesses hibernated 'in the hearts' of their adorants as objects of longing, mourning."[44]

Personal piety is documented in many aspects of Ramesside culture. The theophoric names of the form "[god's name] says he/she will live" (e.g., *Djedkhons-iwesankh*) and those that incorporate the divine names *Shed* (the Savior) or *Shai* (fate)[45] became increasingly common in and after the Ramesside period, suggesting a more intimate and immediate relationship with the gods. The scenes of daily life typical of earlier New Kingdom tomb decoration are replaced by densely configured compositions of the deceased before the gods, suggesting that the concern for the realm of the gods had replaced that of daily existence.

Stelae showing an individual praying to a god or gods without reference to the king, which become so popular in the Twenty-first Dynasty,[46] have also been cited as documents of personal piety. The general scheme of development of this composition[47] echoes the changes in religion from the Eighteenth Dynasty through the Ramesside age. In the earlier period (and before), private stelae rarely showed the individual before the god but, rather, portrayed the king adoring the deity. By the early Ramesside period, the stela may be divided into two registers, with the upper showing the king and the god while the lower showed the dedicator of the stela, often with his family. The final development is the removal of the figure of the king, leaving the petitioner directly before the god. This stylistic development parallels the modification of the role of the king from intermediary with the gods to the rejection of the king in that role.

The chapels of Ramesside temples where petitioners could appeal to their god(s)[48] are also cited as documents of personal piety. These structures, many of them called *swt sḏm sprw,* "places of hearing petitions," are located at the outside wall of the temples and were therefore accessible to the general populace. They provided intimate and direct contact with the god. In a similar way, the intercessory statues of the Ramesside and the Third Intermediate periods are cited as documents of personal piety, for they allowed the individual more direct access to the deity.[49] Oracles, which allowed direct access to the deity and become an important part of local jurisprudence and conflict resolution in the Late New Kingdom, are likewise regarded as elements of piety.[50]

Assmann has suggested that the rise of personal piety in the Ramesside age is due primarily to the modification of the conception of Maat, which had previously served as the traditional standard of morality and correct behavior. He suggests that the ideas traditionally inherent in Maat were so closely associated with Akhenaton that with the diminution of the status of the king as the intermediate between the divine and earthly spheres in the post-Amarna period, Maat became a sense of "social solidarity" rather than a personification of moral behavior.[51] As a result, rather than being assured that living one's life according to the precepts of Maat would assure a happy afterlife, one's fate was decided indiscriminately by capricious gods.

The references to one's fate being judged directly by the gods rather than on account of living a moral life based on the principles of Maat are the most compelling evidence for this new "fourth dimension" or "direct causation," as Assmann has called the intense personal relationship with the deity.[52] The most often cited of the texts that document this is *The Instruction of Amenemope:*

Do not lie down in fear of tomorrow:
"Comes day, how will tomorrow be?"
Man ignores how tomorrow will be;
God is ever in his perfection,
Man is ever in his failure. (XIX.11–15)

If a man's tongue is the boat's rudder,
The Lord of All is yet its pilot. (XX.5–6)[53]

The sense that the gods judge the individual and that one loses the ability to direct one's own fate by adherence to Maat is documented by penitential hymns from Deir el-Medina, such as that on the stela of Nebre (Dynasty Nineteen):

> You are Amun, lord of the silent,
> who comes at the call of the poor.
> I called to you when I was in sorrow,
> And you came to save me.
> You gave breath to the one who was imprisoned,
> and saved me when I was in bonds.
> You are Amun-Re, lord of Thebes,
> you save the one in the netherworld.
> You are the one who is gracious to him who calls on him,
> You are the one who comes from afar.[54]

A difficulty in reconstructing the nature of religion in the Ramesside period is that the documents of personal piety are contemporary with other sources that indicate continuity of tradition from the Eighteenth Dynasty through the Ramesside age. Stelae that show an individual directly adoring the god(s) can be cited from the early and middle parts of the Eighteenth Dynasty[55] and are, therefore, not exclusively an expression of post-Amarna personal piety. Oracles also are attested from at least the Middle Kingdom.[56] Although they indeed become more common in the Late Ramesside period, they are not exclusively of that time; hence they reflect a degree of continuity of belief. Intercessory statues, too, are attested prior to the Ramesside period, the most famous being those of Amunhotep son of Hapu.[57] The decoration of private tombs also shows considerable continuity. Scenes of the deceased before the god in Ramesside tombs, which are cited as documents of personal piety, are also attested in the Eighteenth Dynasty.[58] This suggests that such compositions are not exclusively Ramesside and that they do not express a major revision of theology. The chapels where individuals could address the gods, which may also be taken as evidence for a new closeness of human and god, are also not restricted to the Ramesside period. Earlier shrines, such as that of Hatshepsut and Thutmose III on the east side of the Akh-Menu, indicate that this tradition started earlier.[59]

The assertion that people abandoned the conception of living their lives according to the precepts of Maat because their fate was judged by the willful gods is also countered by many documents that indicate that Maat continued to be an important feature of Ramesside theology. In fact, the number of texts that express aspects of personal piety is quite small,[60] and many texts that reflect the continuity of traditions of the Eighteenth Dynasty can be cited. For example, a passage from the great Abydos stela of Ramesses IV relates, "As for the deciding of my fate, according as I am one who is beneficial, (may it [fate] be) a prolonged reign upon earth, the land at peace, . . . strength for my body, brightness for my eye, (and) joy for my heart daily." Here, the fate of the king is based on the goodness of his pious actions, which were enumerated in the previous sections of the stela, rather than on any arbitrary action of the gods. The traditional tone of the text, reflecting the idea that moral behavior results in a good fate, is further emphasized by the scene of the lunette that shows the king presenting Maat to Osiris.[61]

Even *The Instruction of Amenemope,* one of the primary documents of personal piety, does not uniformly express such precepts. The text is in the form of an instruction that was intended to guide the individual in correct behavior, a sentiment that is wholly in keeping with Maat and an individual's responsibility to make correct choices. The individual is exhorted:

Give your ears, hear the sayings,
Give your heart to understand them;
It profits to put them in your heart,
Woe to him who neglects them! (III.10–12)

If you make your life with these in your heart,
You will find it a success. (III.17–18)[62]

Throughout the text, the individual is encouraged to be quiet, meek, and modest—elements of Egyptian behavior reflected in instructions from the earlier period. According to Lichtheim, "In sum, Amenemope teaches the traditional values in the spirit of New Kingdom piety, with unimpaired confidence in the right order (Maat) by which, despite reversals of fortune, the good succeeds and the evil-doing brings failure."[63] This continuity is evident in other types of texts, as summarized by Lichtheim's comparison of Ramesside and earlier texts:

When one compares the texts of these [six Ramesside] officials with those of their 18th dynasty colleagues, one observes a direct continuation of the 18th dynasty trend of piety and an intensification of that trend. The changes in phrasing add up to a significant increase in the intimacy with the gods, as when Huyshery speaks of the Maat whom "he had put in his heart" as the personal goddess rather than the concept of rightness.[64]

References to Maat as an ethical value are not uncommon in the Ramesside era,[65] although the continued reliance on Maat is theoretically incompatible with personal piety.[66] Such references include "May those of the *duat* say to me: 'Come, come in peace, for you have done Maat (*ir.n.k M3ꜥt*) for Thebes' lord, and he will green the west for you'"[67] or, from the stela of Huyshery (reign of Seti I), "I say to you, future people coming after me: I was one worthy, cool . . . who had put Maat in his heart without neglecting her occasion. Since I left the womb she was joined to my heart."[68] The stela of Tjia (reign of Ramesses II) relates, "I am trustworthy, good-natured, intent on doing right (*irt M3ꜥt*), one truly straight (*mty M3ꜥt*), who is not partial."[69] Even the texts on the stelae that call directly on the god(s) may include references to Maat: "my eyes seeing, ears hearing, my mouth filled with truth (*M3ꜥt*) daily."[70] Such references to the continued veneration of Maat in the Ramesside and Third Intermediate periods have led Lichtheim to conclude, "Evidently, knowledge of good and evil was intact, and so was trust in Maat."[71]

However, it is evident that the older tradition rooted in the value of Maat was augmented by new references to fate and what the god knows and desires. Such references reflect a more complex worldview, but not necessarily one that was "unintelligible, incalculable and unstable" or that "no longer inspires comfort and confidence."[72] This mixing of old and new theologies is reflected by a text on the doorjamb of the tomb of Usherhat that relates, "O gods of Abydos, lords of life on earth, . . . I am a true one who acts on your water [i.e., is loyal], I did not consort with an evil man, I did not follow the path of hostility . . . I know what my god abhors."[73] Here, the speaker asserts that he tries to be in the favor of the god by being aware of what the god "abhors," and he avoids the potential wrath of the god by being conscious of good and evil behavior, making deliberate choices between right and wrong. His actions are motivated by the traditional values of Maat, yet one gets the impression that he is aware of potential punishment by the god for incorrect behavior.

The continued veneration of Maat among the same part of the population that was writing penitential hymns is another indication of the complexity of Ramesside beliefs. As Maat took on more epithets that associated her with the necropolis (see below), she was increasingly depicted in private tombs and on funerary stelae.[74] This coexistence of penitential hymns alongside texts that reflect traditional Maat-related theology is seen in *The Tale of Truth and Falsehood*, the earliest copy of which dates from the Nineteenth Dynasty. In that tale, Truth is abused by his wicked brother Falsehood. The son of Truth, setting out to orchestrate a meeting with the ennead, declares, "I will avenge you!" In his plot, he is guided not by the will of the gods but by his own actions and understanding of right and wrong, yet the ultimate judgment and punishment of Falsehood is decreed and inflicted by the ennead. [75] Although the final judgment is made by the gods, the actions of the son of Truth, which stress the strength and victory of right, influence the decision.

The Contendings of Horus and Seth, from the reign of Ramesses IV, reflect this same combination of old and new attitudes. The story details the debate over who was to receive the office of Osiris. The question was put to the gods, and the ennead declared, "Should one not act according to the word of Atum, Lord of the Two Lands?" (8.2–3), a reflection of the sense of god's will over human action. Yet the ability of an individual to determine right from wrong is a recurring theme of the story, as Seth argues that might, rather than virtue, makes right: "I am Seth, greatest of strength among the ennead. For I slay the enemy of Pre every day, standing in the prow of the bark of millions, and no other god can do it. I should receive the office of Osiris!" (4.3–5). The brothers are judged in "the Hall, or Way of Truths" (*wsḫt wꜣ mꜣꜥw*, 2.7; *wꜣt mꜣꜥw*, 14.2), and the ennead declares, "Right will be given to him who is right" (4.13). Even as the god Banebdjede is brought to adjudicate, there is the call "Let us not decide in ignorance," a reference to hasty, unthinking, or capricious action—exactly the qualities that are the antithesis of Maat. The inability or unwillingness of the gods to make a capricious judgment may be reflected in a lament of Horus: "For it is now eighty years that we are in the court and they (the gods) don't know how to judge between us" (13.12–14.1).

The penitential hymns that reflect god's will over humanity's fate are contemporary with texts that reflect individual ability to determine one's fate through making decisions based on wisdom and morality personified by Maat. This suggests that the relationship of humans to god(s) was neither one of complete continuity from the Eighteenth Dynasty nor one uniformly characterized by an individual cringing before the god but perhaps a more complicated combination of the two attitudes. As with the sense of the nature of the divine, although there was a rethinking of theology and relationships, the documentation suggests that was no single, dominate synthesis and that one should not draw sweeping conclusions based on a limited number or selective use of texts.

THE STATUS OF THE KING

The diminution of the status and power of the king is considered to be another aspect of Ramesside religion. Assmann has suggested that "royal prestige had gradually eroded in the course of the 19th and 20th Dynasties" and that this erosion continued through the Twentieth Dynasty, culminating in the theocracy of the priests of Amun in the Twenty-first Dynasty. He further comments, "In the new fourth dimension, the god was recognized as the true, authentic king of the land."[76] As with so many other aspects of Ramesside beliefs, this change is considered to be a reaction to the Amarna age, when the king took the role as sole communicant with the god.[77] This relationship is a constant theme in texts of the time: "You [the god] are in my heart, and there is none who knows you except your son, . . . for you make him aware of your plans and your strength."[78] Texts indicate that during that time, one's fate was decided by virtue of one's loyalty to the king, in essence substituting political loyalty for piety. The Great Hymn to the Aton in the tomb of Ay relates, "I was one true to the king, one whom he fostered . . . I live only by worshiping his *ka*, and I am fulfilled only by seeing him [the king]." In reference to the standard funerary boons, the text records, "It is the king, the Aten's son, who decrees it to you continually."[79]

Because one's fate was decided by the king, living one's life according to the precepts of Maat and even being aware of those precepts became less important. Texts in the tomb of Ay relate: "Lifetime is in your hand and you grant it to whomever you [the king] wish. The land lives only on what you assign. How prosperous is the one who places you in his heart, for then he will achieve old age and good fortune";[80] "May you [the king] grant me a good old age like a favorite of yours."[81] It has been suggested that in reaction to the exclusivity of the king and god relationship, the people of the Ramesside period increasingly bypassed the king, striving to be directly in the praises of the reestablished god(s), thereby eroding the status of the king.[82] The status of the king was further eroded as Maat, traditionally associated with and protected by the king, was replaced by the decrees of the willful gods. No longer did one live life according to the precepts of Maat, for one's fate was decided not with regard to individual action but by loyalty to the god(s).[83]

Scholars have perceived a further erosion of royal power following the long reign of Ramesses II, suggesting that, as a result, Ramesses III's grasp on kingship and rule of the land was increasingly unstable. However, sources that document the erosion of power of the formal office of the king, as opposed to those that attest to the clearly eroding economic situation of the kingdom[84] or the rise of hereditary priesthoods,[85] are scant. The formalized and certainly idealized scenes that decorate the temple walls show virtually no modification from the Eighteenth Dynasty through the end of the Twentieth. In those scenes, the king does not assume humble postures, such as bending or kneeling, any more than he did in the Eighteenth Dynasty.[86]

The Kadesh poem of Ramesses II has been cited as evidence for the erosion of the status of the king in the Ramesside period.[87] In that text, the arrival of the forces and the eventual victory is seen as the result of Amun answering the plea of the king.[88] However, as with the other aspects of Ramesside religion already discussed, the status of the king is often ambiguous. The appeal to Amun in the Kadesh poem (P.) is countered by other sections of the text that stress the cooperation between the king and the god: "Stand firm. Steady your hearts, my army, that you may observe my victory, I being alone, for Amun will be my protector, his hand with me." In other parts of the narrative, the victory is attributed to the initiative of the king, with no reference to the assistance of the god:

> My army came to praise me at seeing what I had done . . . I took on millions of foreign lands, along with Victory-in-Thebes and Mut-is-Content, my great chariot horses! They it is whom I found to support me when I was alone fighting the many foreign countries!

The battle texts at Medinet Habu reflect the traditional Eighteenth Dynasty idea that the king is acknowledged to be appointed and supported by the gods. But there is a continuing sense that the wisdom of the king, rather than direct action of the gods, accounts for the pharaoh's military successes. The king exhorts: "Pay attention to my instructions that you may know my plan for sustaining you"; "pay attention to my instructions, listen to them."[89] In the Sea Peoples' campaign, the king is credited with the victory: "I am powerful and brave and my plans come to pass. That which I have done cannot fail."[90]

The texts contain references to the "fear" and "renown" of the king, not the god. The sovereign is called the "shelter" or "shield" over Egypt,[91] and the safety of Egypt is attributed to him: "Egypt is joyful in the possession of a protector and so the land is [relaxed] . . . their hearts confident for his strong arm is their protection."[92] The plan of the enemies was "turned aside by the wish of the god [i.e., the king]."[93] The text compares the king to Montu and Amun, and the ruler is said to provide the breath of life to the people, "to nourish the Two Lands with his sustenance." Rather than being in a subservient role to the powerful gods, Ramesses III is called the "protector of the Ennead."[94]

In the historical retrospect of Papyrus Harris I (75.1–79.12), Ramesses III claims, "I was with them as the defense and protection of their limbs. I sustained alive the whole land."[95] Although he claims that he was crowned by Amun, the account of his foreign successes are phrased in the first person, emphasizing that his achievements, rather than the god's will, are responsible for his many successes. The relationship between the king and god can be expressed in terms of tenderness, rather than as one of a meek king cringing before the god: "you [Amun-Re] are the great lord to be trusted, the protector whom one can approach."[96]

The continuing sense of the enduring power and wisdom of the king is reflected through the Ramesside period. In a hymn to Amun in the temple of Ramesses III at Karnak, the god is described as one "Whose name has been hidden and his image concealed, none have known his form, from the beginning," yet the king claims later in the text, "I know your nature, and I know your form,"[97] expressing the wisdom and power of the king. A hymn to Ramesses IV attributes the peace and order of the land to the king: "Heaven and earth are in joy (since) you are the Great Lord of Egypt!" The text enumerates elements traditionally associated with *isfet* (dirt, nakedness, hunger, thirst) and attributes their reversal to the power of the king, without any reference to the god.[98] A text in praise of Ramesses VI relates, "Amun has turned himself around (again) to the Black Land."[99] This renewed attention to the care of the land was motivated not by the imperious will of the god but by the king catching fowl (a metaphor for the quelling of chaos). Here the action of the king apparently influenced the god's favor. A hymn to Ramesses VI attributes the rise of the Nile to the power of the king.[100] And in another hymn in honor of Ramesses VII, the king is compared to the gods Re, Khepri, and Baal. He "pulls in those who [go adrift?]," (the aforementioned people) who have "turned their backs on their gods" and who have "forgotten the temples."[101]

Other texts refer to the power of the god affecting the outcome of events. Yet these references are stated as a cooperative effort of king and god, rather than the work of a capricious deity who overrides any plan of the king. Such texts give the impression not of a king whose power was undiminished by the rise of the gods but of a supportive relationship much like that encountered in earlier texts, such as the Poetical Stela of Thutmose III.[102] A passage concerning the Libyan Wars of Ramesses III indicates that the relationship of king and god was obvious even to foreigners, for the Libyans claimed that "gods returned and answered us, to slay us, since we knowingly attacked their district(s). We know the great strength of Egypt and that Re has given her a victorious defender." The king himself acknowledged the assistance of the god: "He [the god] has assigned victory to me (and) his hand is with me so that all who attack my frontier are slain in my grasp."[103] In the historical section of Papyrus Harris I, it is stated that the god "established their son [Sethnakht], who came forth from their limbs to be ruler. He set in order the land of Egypt,"[104] again expressing a cooperative, not a subservient, relationship.

A hymn to Ramesses VII expresses the same sense of cooperation between the king and god:

> Those who have plotted, you act according to their plotting, your force has slain them. Those who say in their hearts, "We shall act by ourselves! Let us divide up the sea!"—in whom is the (self-) assurance of a god—he (Amun) heeds not what they say. . . . Their voices are hoarse from calling out aloud, "How beautiful is your name!" a million times O' Pharaoh, l.p.h., the hand of Amun is in your hand. When you call out to him in the depth of the night, you find him standing behind you. May he act on your behalf.[105]

This text presents the king in a dynamic and powerful light, with the ability to rule the land. According to it, Amun does not rule the land, but he stands ready to assist when summoned.

The text of the campaign of Ramesses IX against the bedouin continues the tradition that the king acts in concert with the god(s), rather then being overshadowed by them. This text clearly indicates that the king's successes were due to "assistance" by the gods, rather than being primarily due to them: "The strong arm of Pharaoh my Lord, l.p.h., has overthrown entirely these enemies . . . It was Amun-re . . . who came with you in order to assist you."[106]

The idea of the god and king working in concert expressed in these texts contrasts with the notion that action and result were disassociated in the Ramesside age.[107] The two Abydos stelae of Ramesses IV clearly indicate that the action of the king influenced the god: "Give [me] the reward for the services that I have done for you," the king says to the god.[108] It is also telling that both these texts have a version of the negative confession, enumerating truisms of morality that are inherent in Maat. In the great Abydos stela of Ramesses IV, the king claims, "Ever since I arose as king upon the throne of Horus I have brought [back] Maat to this land which had been without it, for I know that you [the gods] are troubled when it is lacking throughout Egypt."[109]

Most of the documents that express the power and undiminished status of the king come from contexts that were designed to promote the status of the king—temples,[110] dedicatory inscriptions, and hymns. However, such texts are also found in the nonroyal context during the Ramesside period. A text on a block statue of Tjia, the chief treasurer of the Ramesseum in the reign of Ramesses II, relates that an official's success was still considered to be dependent on the king rather than on the will of the gods:

> With the king's favor did I come from my town,
> having done what his *ka* desired.
> Knowing what the god abhors,
> I did no wrong,
> I gave bread to the hungry,
> water to the thirsty,
> clothes to the naked.[111]

The autobiographic text of Djedkhonsefankh from the reign of Osorkon I indicates that officials in that era continued to feel that their association with the king was the key to success:

> The country's nobles strove to copy me, because my favor with the king was great. I strayed not from his majesty at the palace, He did not exclude me from his falcon-ship ... The god esteemed me for attending to him agreeably, I was advanced in keeping with my worth.[112]

References to the wrath of god in the penitential hymns, which are so characteristic of personal piety, are roughly contemporary to more traditional-flavored texts related to the displeasure of the king, suggesting that the influence of the king was not greatly eroded. The text on the block statue of Nakhtefmut from the reign of Osorkon II contains the phrase "May you [Amun-Re] give me the reward of a good old age, daily seeing Amun as my heart desires, and serving kings while safe from their wrath!"[113]

Passages from texts of the Late New Kingdom and Early Third Intermediate Period already cited give a sense of continuity of the status of kingship, but with an overlay of the god's action working with and on the action of the king. Modifications of the king-god relationship in the Ramesside period can also be documented by the reliefs of Ramesses III at Medinet Habu, particularly by comparing them with the reliefs at the Ramesseum.[114] The reliefs and inscriptions from the temple of Ramesses III were copied so slavishly from the earlier temple of Ramesses II that modern restorers mistakenly inserted blocks originally from the Ramesseum into the walls of the later temple.[115]

Perhaps most telling for a study of continuity and change of ritual and religious practices in the Twentieth Dynasty is the fact, commented on by Nims, that "a large number of the ritual scenes in the latter temple [Medinet Habu] had their origins in the former [Ramesseum]."[116] The scenes of the festival of Min from the Ramesseum were modified only slightly to fit into the available space at Medinet Habu.[117] Scenes that attest to mythology and cult were duplicated, such as the astronomical ceiling in the Royal Mortuary Complex. Even the schedule of the rituals and festivals and the material requirements for those celebrations as recorded in the great calendar at Medinet Habu were largely copied—mistakes and all—from the earlier monument,[118] again suggesting continuity of religion and ritual.

However, a modification of the underlying theology of the relationship of god to king can be documented by a comparison of the offering scenes in the two temples. The iconography of offering scenes shows very little change from the Nineteenth to the Twentieth Dynasties, but the brief inscriptions that narrate those scenes show a significant change, indicating a modification of the underlying theology of the offering ritual.

These short, seemingly stereotypical texts are, in the full form, made up of three phrases: the recitation of the divine recipient of the offering (*di.n.(i) n.k. . . .*, "It is to you that I have given . . .");[119] the king's dedication of the offering to the divine recipient, phrased in the infinitive (e.g., *rdit ḥnḳt n it.f,* "giving beer to his father"); and the phrase *ir.f di ʿnḫ,* "he has made given life," which, into the Nineteenth Dynasty, usually follows the dedication. Individual offering scenes may omit one or more of the phrases, depending on space. These phrases are not linked to a specific offering; indeed, the same general formulas are used for a wide variety of different offerings.

Both the meaning of these phrases and their subsequent modification should be considered in the context of the overall offering scene and their formulas. The divine recipient's speech, preceded by the particle for direct discourse (*ḏd mdw in*) *di.n.(i) n.k. . . .*, "Words spoken by *x*, it is to you that I have given . . ."), is always in the perfect tense, suggesting that it refers to a donation on the part of the god that had already occurred. There is a clear correspondence of the verbal tense to the pose of the deity to whom the text refers, for he or she is always shown statically seated or standing. The dedication of the offering by the king to the god is phrased in the infinitive—an active tense—which clearly was used to correspond to the action of the king, who is shown in the act of making the presentation to the deity. These two sections of the offering formulas show no change from at least the Eighteenth Dynasty into the Late Period.[120]

A comparison of the texts of Ramesses II and III (and his successors) show that the *ir.f di ʿnḫ* phrase was reinterpreted during the Nineteenth and Twentieth Dynasties. This is evident in the modification of to whom the verb *ir* refers, the donor or the divine recipient. This can be easily determined when the donor and recipient are of different genders. For example, in the hypostyle hall at Karnak, when Ramesses II offers to a goddess, the formula appears as *ir.f di ʿnḫ,* "may he [the king] make given life."[121] The same pattern is followed in the Ramesseum.[122] In contrast, at Medinet Habu, when the king offers to a goddess, the phrase is *ir.s di ʿnḫ,* "may she [the deity] make given life [for the king]," indicating that the subject of *ir* is the goddess rather than the king.[123] This pattern is consistently followed for the remainder of the Ramesside and Third Intermediate periods. For example, in the reliefs of Herihor at the Khonsu temple, when the king offers to a goddess, the formula appears as *ir.s di ʿnḫ,*[124] while a scene of Shepenwepet I offering to Amun in the temple of Osiris Hekadjet has the formula *ir.f di ʿnḫ.*[125]

This change can also be discerned in the more numerous scenes where the king offers to a male deity. There, the verb *ir* is reversed to be in the same orientation as the recipient rather than the donor.[126] Another way of indicating that the phrase had been reinterpreted by the reign of Ramesses III was by placing the phrase *ir.f/s di ʿnḫ* in a different area of the overall offering scene. In the Eighteenth and Nineteenth Dynasties, the phrase, when used, was usually directly appended to the dedication phrase,[127] as if they were a continuous idea. However, at Medinet Habu and more commonly at the later Khonsu temple, the phrase is clearly separated from the dedication, being either placed in a separate line or separated from it by an obvious gap.[128]

What does the modification of the *ir.f di ʿnḫ* formula mean for later Ramesside religion? In the earlier version of the *ir.f di ʿnḫ* formula used at the Ramesseum, when the subject of *ir* refers to the donor, the verb *ir* is a circumstantial related to the infinitive of the dedication, to which it is so closely tied in the texts of the Eighteenth and Nineteenth Dynasties. At that time, the phrase meant "[giving *x* to the deity] in so much as he [the king] acts [for the god] who has given life [to the king]."[129] This phrase, in the context of the formula *di.n.(i) n.k,* "It is to you that I have given life and stability," serves as an acknowledgment of the fact that the god has given life to the king, but there is no implicit link between the gift of the king and any future action of the god.

The presence of the revised formula *ir.f di ʿnḫ* at Medinet Habu and on monuments of the later Ramesside period reflects an altered relationship between god and king. Nims proposed that the verb *ir* in the phrase should be a clause of purpose[130] and hence that the formula must be translated "[presenting *x* to *y*] in order that he [the god] may act, he who has given life." Thus, in the reign of Ramesses III, there was a rethinking of the theology and a deliberate expression that the donation of the offering was linked more closely to motivating future action of the god than in previous times. This may be regarded as a manifestation of personal piety elevated to the uppermost level of the state and as an indication of the new approachability of the deity. Just as hymns from the nonroyal context call on the god for assistance, the offering became a new form of dialogue between the king and god, a dialogue composed of the offering, which was then viewed as a means by which the king could obtain the assistance of the god. This reciprocal action of the king and god is yet another manifestation of their cooperative relationship in the Ramesside era.

Not only do the reliefs and inscriptions of Ramesses III document a new dialogue between king and god in the offering rituals, but they also attest to the king's association with specific gods, which, in turn, suggests a newly elevated status of the king rather than a diminution of his status. In the temple of Ramesses III at Karnak, the bark of the king is shown in the expected manner, with the head of the king on the bow and stern and a frieze of cartouches on the shrine. The bark is preceded by the double cartouches of the king. Yet the voice that emanates from the cabin of the bark is that of "Amun-Re of United-with-Eternity," the form of Amun who dwelled at Medinet Habu.[131] As noted by Haeny, "All this clearly indicates that Amun United-with-Eternity and the king were seen as one."[132] This association of king and god is also indicated by the dockets on the wrappings of the king's mummy that include a seated figure of Amun, labeled "Amun-Re United-with-Eternity." This is accompanied by a notation that the daughter of Piankh ordered the wrappings—a pious act that was undertaken "for her lord, Amun, United-with-Eternity, within the Temple."[133] The link between the king and Amun was emphasized by the new interest shown by Ramesses III in the Decade Festival (see further below).

Ramesses III, like his predecessors Seti and Ramesses II and some of his successors, also claimed an association with the goddess Maat through the ritual presentation of the king's name equated with that goddess. This ritual is first depicted in the reign of Seti I.[134] In such scenes,[135] the name, most commonly the prenomen that was compounded at the coronation of the king, is explicitly labeled "Maat," thereby equating the name and hence, by extension, the king's whole being with Maat.[136] This type of ritual scene is attested for Ramesses V, Ramesses VI, and Ramesses XI.[137] This association of the king with the most fundamental principle of correct rule and authority suggests a new vitality, vigor, and confidence of the king in the Ramesside period.

Although it is so often stated that the status of the king eroded rapidly after the reign of Ramesses III, virtually the same documentation of the king's association with Maat and hence his cognizance of proper rule can be cited for his successors in the Twentieth Dynasty. The Abydos stele of Ramesses IV claims that he "brought back Maat to this land which had been without it,"[138] and a hymn to Ramesses VII praises the king as "one who [loves] truth and hates falsehood, and who causes Maat to exist."[139]

The texts from private statues, historical texts, and offering scenes, discussed above, all argue for a largely undiminished status of the king in the reign of Ramesses III. However, the manner in which the king expressed his deification took an entirely different form than that of his patronymic ancestor Ramesses II. The earlier king expressed his divinity during his own lifetime in both Egypt and Nubia.[140] In contrast, Ramesses III was deified in his form of the Osirid king who merged with Amun United-with-Eternity, whose name, according to Nelson, "was still to be invoked for another century or so . . . [as] a deity of the necropolis."[141]

OSIRIANIZATION IN THE RAMESSIDE PERIOD

The architecture, reliefs, and inscriptions at Medinet Habu indicate a growing emphasis on the funerary deities Sokar, Ptah-Sokar-Osiris, and Osiris. Certainly, all of Western Thebes had prior associations with Osiris, and the cult of Ptah-Sokar-Osiris was a feature of the temple of Amunhotep III at Kom el-Hetan.[142] However, comparing the monuments of Seti I and Ramesses II to the mortuary temple of Ramesses III reveals a new emphasis on those funerary deities.

The prominence of the funerary god Ptah-Sokar-Osiris in his form of Sokar is especially notable when comparing the Ramesseum to Medinet Habu. The feast of Sokar is a prominent part of the decoration of the south and east wall of the second court at Medinet Habu,[143] and a shrine was dedicated for the god's bark off the first hypostyle hall.[144] This is in contrast to the lesser attention given to this god at the temple of Seti I at Gourna, whose room IX "perhaps . . . should be attributed to Sokar," and at the Ramesseum, where there was "probably a chapel of Sokar . . . , since the festival of Sokar was celebrated there."[145]

Emphasis on the cult of the god is also reflected in the calendar of Ramesses III, which refers to offerings for Ptah-Sokar-Osiris as well as Amun, the king, and the ennead, indicating that the god was a major focus of the cult. The introduction to the text states:

> I [Ramesses III] made splendid Ptah-Sokar and the *ḥnw*-bark on the *mfḫ* sledge. As for Osiris-Wennefer, whenever he approaches your throne, I have caused him to appear in my house at the introduction of Sokar.[146]

The festival calendar lists ten feasts of Ptah-Sokar on ten consecutive days, and on those days, offerings were made exclusively to Ptah-Sokar: they were not shared by Amun, the king, or other deities, as was usual in other festivals. The quantity and also the variety of offerings for the feasts of Ptah-Sokar were second only to those provided during the feast of Opet.[147] The oldest version of "The Ritual for Bringing Forth Sokar" in the fifth scene of the festival of Sokar appears at Medinet Habu.[148] In the texts of scene 3 of the festival, the king calls the god "in all his names,"[149] referring to the forty-five forms of the god. This may be seen as a counterpart of the litany of Re[150] and hence a reflection of the fusion of celestial and chthonic deities.[151] The king's special veneration of Ptah-Sokar is also indicated by the statement of Ramesses III in the introduction to the calendar that "the king has taken over this cult from the House of Ptah at Memphis.[152]

The Osiris suite at Medinet Habu (rooms 20–27, *MH* VI, pls. 445–81) further documents the new emphasis on the underworld gods. This greatly expanded suite of an "irregular group of rooms" for the mortuary cult of the king was located in a prominent position on the south of the main sanctuary. The reliefs and inscriptions trace the stages of the king's resurrection, culminating in the final scene depicting the king as Osiris inside a portable shrine.[153]

One of the most significant differences that distinguishes the mortuary cult of Ramesses III from those of his predecessors is that the mortuary chapel at Medinet Habu was for the Osirid form of the king himself, not his father, as at the Gourna temple of Seti I, where the focus of the cult was Seti's father, Ramesses I.[154] This change in the focus of the cult to the Osirid king may be another reflection of the king's expression of his divinity and power. As indicated by Pyramid Text Spell 601, which accompanies the relief of the king as Osiris in his shrine (fig. 2.1), the name of the king was to endure like the name of ten other deities.[155]

Nelson has suggested that the identification of the king as Osiris was acknowledged during his lifetime and that this aspect of the king was venerated

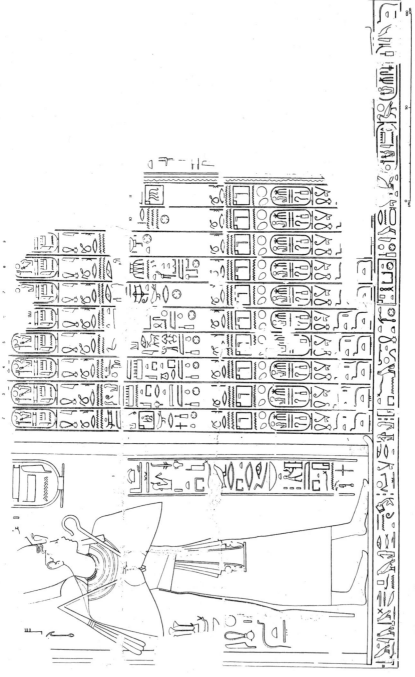

Fig. 2.1. The Osirid king Ramesses III in a shrine, with Pyramid Text Spell 601 that equates the name of the king with deities, from the royal mortuary chapel, room 20, at Medinet Habu. (After *MH* VI, pl. 451. Courtesy of the Oriental Institute of the University of Chicago.)

even before his death. He wrote, "The mystical conception involved in the performance of mortuary services for the Osirid king while the king himself was still alive does not seem to me to be incompatible with other contradictory ideas apparently accepted by the Egyptians."[156] Indeed, the Osirid form of the king seems to have been a potent vehicle for the king's veneration. As suggested by Stadelmann, a statue of the Osirid king, rather than the king himself, may have occupied the palace.[157] It would have been positioned before the window of appearances in the palace, to the south of the temple, where it would witness the processions that entered the court.[158]

The Osirid king was increasingly associated with Amun. The mummy of the king, the most Osirian form that can be imagined, bore a docket identifying him as Amun-Re of United-with-Eternity.[159] As indicated by the reliefs at Medinet Habu, the god resident in the bark of the king was Amun-Re of United-with-Eternity (fig. 2.2).[160] The mortuary aspects of this deity are documented by his identification as a deity of the necropolis who was venerated in Western Thebes for a century after the death of the king.[161] The merging of Amun and Osiris is evident in the precinct of Amun at Karnak, where a series of small chapels to Osiris were built from the Third Intermediate Period onward.[162] Catacombs northeast of the temple of Thutmose III at Karnak and intended for the burial of Osiris statuettes have been dated to the New Kingdom.[163] They were used and expanded into the Ptolemaic period, attesting to the continued fusion of Amun and Osiris.

This Osirianization is also evident with the mortuary associations of Maat, who was traditionally linked with cosmic order, the legitimacy of the king, and the judgment of the deceased. Although she continued to act in her traditional role at the weighing of the heart[164] and in temple offering scenes in the Ramesside period, she was closely associated with the personification of the West (*'Imntt*). By the Nineteenth Dynasty, the Theban necropolis itself was called *st Mꜣꜥt*, "the place of Truth."[165] A text in the Thutmose III temple at Deir el-Bahari from the reign of Ramesses III refers to the Gourna peak that dominates the necropolis as "The Great Peak of the West in this its name of Maat, the daughter of Re who resides in the sacred necropolis."[166] In the tomb of Qen, the "West" is referred to as "the place for those who have done Maat."[167] Ramesside texts include Maat in funerary offering formulas and indicate that she was one of the deities who was capable of granting a good burial.[168] The Four Sons of Horus may hold Maat feathers,[169] and Maat feathers are a common part of the decorative scheme of the Twenty-first Dynasty coffins.[170]

This emphasis on Osiris is reflected in the many references to mortuary

Fig. 2.2. Bark of Amun (top) and bark of Ramesses III in which Amun-Re of United-with-Eternity resides (bottom), from the temple of Ramesses III at Karnak, east side of the court. (After *RIK* I, pl. 21A [lower]. Courtesy of the Oriental Institute of the University of Chicago.)

festivals of Western Thebes in the reliefs and texts at Medinet Habu. The calendar on the south wall of the temple indicates that new endowments were made for the Feast of the Valley.[171] The Decade Festival also gained new prominence under Ramesses III. Although the first specific reference to this feast, during which the god Amenemopet traveled from Luxor to the Small Temple at Medinet Habu, dates to the Twenty-first Dynasty,[172] the fact that Ramesses III enclosed the temple within his precinct suggests a special patronage of the structure and the rituals enacted therein.[173] A Late Ramesside Letter dating to year 10 *wḥm mswt* contains the reference "I say everyday . . . to Amenemopet at each and every decade when he comes to pour water [for] the great living *bas* . . . *nty ḥtp m tꜣ st n ꜣmn ḫnm nḥḥ ḥry-ib tꜣ st pꜣ ḫꜣ sw 10* . . ."[174] This passage has been interpreted several ways in the effort to make the text correspond to the temple. Wente translated the passage "the great living Bas, who rest in the place of Amon, United with Eternity, resident in the place of the appearance of the decade . . ."[175] He interpreted this to indicate that the procession of the Decade Festival visited the Great Temple (*ḥwt-nṯr ꜣmn ḫnm nḥḥ*) to visit the *bas* who were within that structure. Yet he found it difficult to correlate the reference to the *bas* to any chapel there, suggesting that the procession may have visited the Re chapel, a wall of which is decorated with reliefs depicting the *bas* of Re (*MH* VI, pls. 423–24).[176]

Doresse translated the text "grandes *Ba* vivants qui reposent dans la place d'Amon *ḫnm-nḥḥ*, et qui résident dans la place de l'apparition . . . ," assuming that water was poured for the *bas* at Medinet Habu and that their place of appearance was also there. Despite his translation, he suggested that the text referred to two different places. The place where water was poured for the *bas* may have been "dans l'enceinte du temple, probablement dans un reposoir correspondant à celui de Luxor d'ou la statue de dieu embarquait pour Médinet Habu," and the "place d'apparition," he suggests, was also within the enclosure wall but has disappeared because it was made of perishable material.[177]

It is important to note that the adverb *ḥry-ib* in the Ramesside letter is singular and therefore cannot be in reference to the plural *bas*. Rather, it must refer to Amun United-with-Eternity. Hence the passage should be rendered, "the great living *bas*, who rest in the place of Amun United-with-Eternity, who is resident in the place of the appearance of the decade . . ." This rendering of the text indicates that it refers to two separate locations, one where water was poured for the great living *bas* and another where Amon United-with-Eternity appeared on each decade. Rather than *tꜣ st ḫꜣ* being a reference to the Great Temple itself, it may more likely refer to the High Gate, the eastern side of which is carved with a relief of Amun-Re of United-with-Eternity (*MH VIII*, pl. 617B).[178] Its very prominent location in the center of the east side of the tower ensured that it would be among the first sacred images visible to those who approached the temple. In the Twentieth Dynasty, when the Late Ramesside Letter was written, the only access to the Small Temple, which, as attested by later texts, was the resting place of the *bas* of the gods,[179] was through this gate. Thus, according to the letter, the procession entered the precinct through the High Gate, the place where Amun-Re of United-with-Eternity would appear before it, then the procession turned north to enter the Small Temple, where water was offered to the living *bas*. The incorporation of the Small Temple into the temple precinct suggests that the Small Temple was the destination of the procession of the Decade Festival that crossed the Nile from Luxor to Medinet Habu by the reign of Ramesses III and that it was associated in the Twentieth Dynasty with the divine living *bas*, a tradition that is more fully documented only later.

Further evidence that the procession of the Decade Festival was being performed in the reign of Ramesses III is provided by a fragmentary stela of that king, recovered from the first court of the Luxor Temple. The text refers to the construction of a shrine *m 'Ipt swt ḥr imntt gs n it.f 'Imn Rᶜ nty ḥtp.f im.s ḥr-tp hrw 10*, which translates "in Luxor on the right bank for his father Amun-Re, foremost of his *ipt*, in which he rests on the first day of the decade."[180] Although the original location of the shrine is unknown, it has been suggested that it stood "somewhere between the Ramesses II court and the Nile."[181] If so, this suggests that the shrine was intended as a stopping place for a riverine procession, which, according to the text on the stela, was the Decade Festival.

Although the first explicit reference to the association of the Small Temple with the Decade Festival is dated to Pinudjem,[182] the fact that Ramesses III enclosed the Small Temple within the precinct of Medinet Habu, built what may be a Nile-side way station, and placed an image of Amun United-with-Eternity prominently on the High Gate, a structure that the Late Ramesside Letter associated with the Decade Festival procession, strongly suggests not only that the procession from Luxor to the west was being celebrated in his reign but also that the Small Temple was, at that time, associated with the festival.

The role of Medinet Habu in the festivals of rejuvenation represented by the Decade Festival and Feast of the Valley accounts for the orientation of tombs on the axis of the temple's entry. By the Twenty-second Dynasty, tombs were built on both the north and south sides of the processional way to the

Great Temple.[183] By the Twenty-third Dynasty, the south side of the processional way was adopted as the location for the tomb chapels of the God's Wives of Amun, another indication of the sanctity of the route.[184] Just as the great tombs of the Late Period were orientated to the causeway of the temple of Hatshepsut at Deir el-Bahari because of the role that temple played in the Feast of the Valley, the entry to Medinet Habu became another sacred route and a desirable location for tombs.[185]

The association of that area of the temple with Osiris and rejuvenation is also attested by depositions of Osiris figurines at the site. Hölscher excavated a deposit of scores of bronze statuettes of Osiris near the Eastern High Gate,[186] indicating that there was a popular cult in which votives of Osiris were brought to the site.[187] It is impossible to determine whether the statuettes were originally deposited in the hole as a way of symbolically reaching the underground realm of Osiris or if they represent a cachette of material gathered for ritual burial.

SUMMARY

Religion in the Ramesside period shows general continuity of traditions with the earlier New Kingdom, but with some significant modification. The conception of god shows the most continuity, reflecting the traditional sense of polytheism with marked trends for syncretistic merging of deities. References to a transcendent, supreme deity occur in hymns and prayers that are contemporary with texts that reflect traditional polytheism, suggesting a mosaic of belief, rather than a thorough reformulation of theology. As in other periods, the texts suggest a multiplicity of religious experience, without a dominant pattern.

A recurring theme in discussions of Ramesside religion is the impact of the Amarna period. An examination of the continuities of religion through the New Kingdom suggests that the impact of Akhenaton's theology may be overestimated. The roots of personal piety, the rise of which is attributed to the Amarna experience, were already present in the pre-Amarna era. Penitential prayers, confessional shrines, and oracles are attested in the Eighteenth Dynasty. It seems very likely that the Amarna experience accentuated the rise of personal piety, but its roots predate it. One of the greatest impacts of Amarna on Ramesside religion may be the acceptance of the multiplicity of religious experience, as indicated by the contradictory ideas in such texts as the Leiden Hymn to Amun. These inconsistencies, which make an appraisal of Ramesside religion so difficult, may be a reaction to the period in which, at least for the elite at Amarna, deviations from the official dogma were prohibited.

The status of the king also shows continuity from the Eighteenth Dynasty. He is confirmed by the god(s), but as indicated by Ramesside texts, he undertakes his actions based on his own cognizance of right and wrong. The relationship between ruler and the gods is cooperative. The historical texts of Ramesses III stress the power and might of the pharaoh, rather than the role of the god(s), in determining the outcome of battles. The perceived decline in the power of the Ramesside king may indeed be fictive—a convenient way of explaining the tremendous rise of power of the priests of Amun at the end of the Twentieth Dynasty and the following Third Intermediate Period. Indeed, the rise of hereditary officials and priests may be unrelated to the status of the king in the later Ramesside period.

The many reliefs on temples and textual references to Maat suggest that she was still revered and recognized as the standard of right and wrong. The presentation of the Ramesside kings' name equated with Maat is another indication of her continued veneration, and her many funerary epithets suggest an expanded realm of her influence.

One of the most evident changes in religion of the Twentieth Dynasty is growing Osirianization. Not only does Maat take on funerary epithets, but there is an increase in syncretistic unions of Osiris, Amun, and Re. This is most evident in the establishment of chapels and catacombs of Osiris in the precinct of Amun at Karnak and in the decoration of coffins in the following Twenty-first Dynasty. Ramesses III was deified as a form of Osiris in his lifetime, and the texts on his mummy indicate that he was also considered to be a form of Amun.

Notes

1. Wilson (1956) 242.

2. Van Dijk (2000) 287.

3. Lichtheim (1992) 99–101.

4. Assmann (1995) 195. See Assmann (2001) 222 for the comment "But its [the Amarna period's] consequences were so deep and so wide ranging that they cannot be underestimated."

5. Assmann (1989) 81: "The sources of the period . . . draw a picture of the social life in the time of the later New Kingdom which is rather sinister. The temples prosper from the donations of pious kings whereas the people, bereft of the protection and confidence in Maat suffered from violence, distrust and poverty."

6. Assmann (1975); Assmann (1995); Assmann (2001).

7. Teeter (1997).

8. See, e.g., the comments in Hornung (1982a) 190 about Morenz (1964). Morenz ([1973] 98 n. 84) defends his discussion of cult and piety with the comment "This remark should not be misunderstood as a personal profession of faith by the author but as an endeavour to assess properly the historical data about Egyptian religion."

9. Hornung (1982a) 195.

10. Morenz (1973) 137–42; Hornung (1982a) 91–99.

11. Zandee (1947) pl. IV.20–21. See also the translations in Assmann (1975) 318; Assmann (2001) 238; Foster (1995) 76–77. See Posener (1956) 155 for *m Ḥr* as more concretely referring to people's visual perception, in contrast to Foster's "He is Re in his features" and Assmann's (2001) "he is Re in countenance."

12. Hornung (1982a) 98–99.

13. See Assmann (2001) 238–39 for this text illustrating the "three successive stages of the god's becoming the world," constituting preexistence (Amun), the primeval hill (Ptah), and the course of the sun (Re).

14. This was most forcefully suggested by Morenz (1964). See also Hornung (1982a) 188; Assmann (1995) 230–44; Assmann (2001) 237. See Assmann (1989) 75 n. 85 for the comment "Morenz clearly over emphasized this aspect of the Ramessid conception of god."

15. Morenz (1973) 142: "Behind the plurality of gods there was a basic unity."

16. Assmann (2001) 237.

17. Ibid., 192.

18. Foster (1995) 69, 74–75.

19. Assmann (2001) 235. Assmann commented that "the god of Ramesside theology was the cosmos, in that he embodied it."

20. Foster (1995) 66–67.

21. Ibid., 75.

22. Ibid., 72.

23. *KRI* V.222, 2–4; Seele (1935) 234–35. Further on this text, see the discussion of the status of the king below.

24. Foster (1995) 77.

25. Hornung (1982a) 191, 194–95.

26. Cf., e.g., Assmann (2001) 237: "There seem to be only two solutions to this problem [of the reality of individual gods vis-à-vis the transcendent god]; the monotheistic one, which categorically denies the reality of the plurality of deities, and the pantheistic one, which explains the various deities as aspects, names, forms of manifestation—in brief, as immanent refractions of the transcendent unity of the single god."

27. Foster (1995) 76, 77.

28. Ibid., 77.

29. Ibid., 78.

30. Wente (2001) 432.

31. Hornung (1982a) 234–35.

32. Wente (1967) 43.

33. Hornung (1982a) 233; Assmann (1975) 240 n. 65.

34. Lichtheim (1992) 78.

35. See Hornung (1999) as a convenient source for the chronology of the underworld books.

36. Piankoff (1964); Hornung (1999) 136.

37. However, see comments below about the association of Re and Osiris in the Ramesside period and later.

38. E.g., the chapter on the Ramesside period in Breasted's *Development of Religion and Thought in Ancient Egypt* (1912) is entitled "The Age of Personal Piety—Sacerdotalism and Final Decline." This title seems to reflect the American attitude that excessive piety is dangerous and leads to the decay of the state and culture.

39. Erman (1911).

40. See, in particular, Assmann (1984); Morenz (1973) 101–6.

41. Cf. the comment of Assmann (2001) 227: "The old religion emerged from its Babylonian Captivity as a confessional religion. Thereafter, people knew of the absolute reality of the gods, but also that they shed light only on him who put them in his heart and were 'found' only by him who sought them." Brand (2000) 382 described piety as motivated by "fear" and as "traditional religion [that] went underground" under the pressures of Akhenaton's religious program. See also Van Dijk (2000) 287: the Amarna period "left deep scars on the collective consciousness of its [Egypt's] inhabitants." However, see Assmann (1989) 69–71, which traces personal piety to the First Intermediate Period, although it "break[s] through into full dominance only after the collapse of the Amarna religion." See also Van Dikj (2000) 310–13.

42. Sandman (1938) 99.16; Murnane (1995) 118.

43. Sandman (1938) 99.12–14, 99.16–100.1; Murnane (1995) 118.

44. Assmann (2001) 228–29.

45. Brunner (1958) 17–19; Baines (1987) 94–96; Ockinga (2001) 44; Wente (2001) 432.

46. See Munro (1973) for these stelae.

47. See Baines 1995 for how "decorum" predicated how individuals were shown in the company of the god(s). Baines (1991) 138 states that "the general effect of decorum was probably to slow the proliferation of religious materials in public contexts."

48. Nims (1954); Nims (1955); Sadek (1988) 11–84.

49. For comments about such statues, with bibliography, see Baines (1991) 183–84. Although Baines suggests that intermediary statues were restricted to the elite, apparently because of the cost of the statue itself, it is very possible that intermediary statues or objects, such as less formal baked clay figurines, were used as intermediaries by the nonelite. See also Morenz (1973) 102.

50. Assmann (1995) 191; Assmann (2001) 193–94; Kruchten (2001) 609.

51. Assmann (1983) 278, 283–85; Assmann (1984) 696; Assmann (1989) 73§b, 79; Assmann (1995) 194. See Assmann (1989) 67 for the comment "On the cosmic level, the concept of Maat disappears." See Assmann (1989) 74–76 for the idea of indirect causation (traditional Maat theology) verses direct, in which the sense of confidence inspired by Maat is replaced by reliance on the god(s).

52. Assmann (1989) 75–78; Assmann (2001) 231–32.

53. Translation from Lichtheim (1976) 157–58.

54. Assmann (1975) 352; Assmann (2001) 225.

55. From Florence, nos. 2510, 2589, 2548, 2593, 2570; Bosticco (1965) nos. 16, 22, 23,

29, 36, 37, 38, 39, 40). According to Lichtheim (1992) 48, "The appearance of gods is the major innovation in the representational scheme of 18th dynasty private tombs and stelae. Men and women are now depicted worshiping the gods, and in the texts the gods are invoked more directly and more frequently than had hitherto been done."

56. Vernus (1982–83); Baines (1987) 94–97. The oracle of the deified Amunhotep I was also a feature of pre-Amarna Theban cult practices (Sadek [1988] 132). For public oracles in the pre-Amarna period, see Baines (1987) 94–97. One of the clearest indications of the importance of oracles in the pre-Ramesside period is the oracular selection and confirmation of Thutmose III and Horemheb.

57. Morenz (1973) 102.

58. Theban tombs 38, 52, 69, 139, and 161 from the reigns of Thutmose IV and Amunhotep III. See Hartwig (2004) 126–27, 129–30.

59. Porter and Moss (1972) 215–18; Nims (1971) 109–11. Cf. Sadek (1988) 10: "Ordinary people in these periods [Old and Middle Kingdom] already had their personal beliefs and could often practice their rites outside the official priesthood and temple cult."

60. According to Lichtheim (1992) 77, "it can easily be determined that the penitential texts, which aroused so much interest and are so often cited, are very few in number." See Assmann (1975) 349–417 (nos. 147–200) for a compilation of these texts.

61. *KRI* VI.25 l. 4–5; Peden (1994b) 171.

62. Translation from Lichtheim (1976) 149.

63. Lichtheim (1997) 42–43.

64. Lichtheim (1992) 75–76.

65. Ibid., 66–80; Teeter (1997) 84 n. 20.

66. See Assmann (1989) 77 for the comment "The concepts of Maat and of divine intervention seem to be mutually exclusive."

67. Tomb of Paser (reign of Seti I) in Lichtheim (1992) 66.

68. Ibid., 67.

69. Ibid., 75. See other Third Intermediate Period biographies with references to Maat in Lichtheim (1997) 63–64, 66.

70. Lichtheim (1992) 78–79.

71. Lichtheim (1997) 62.

72. Assmann (1995) 195.

73. Lichtheim (1992) 70.

74. Simpson (1995) 87, from the Third Intermediate Period.

75. See Lichtheim (1992) 80 for the interpretation of this tale as a reflection of more, rather than less, continuity with Eighteenth Dynasty traditions.

76. Assmann (2001) 242: "In Dynasty 21, the final step was taken and the god was installed *de jure* as king." See also Assmann (1980) 22; Assmann (1984) 11–14, 232–81; Assmann (1989) 66–68. See Van Dijk (2000) 310 for the comment "It is undeniable that royal prestige had gradually eroded in the course of the 19th and 20th Dynasties"; Baines (1995) 34 for "The New Kingdom crisis of belief that culminated under Akhenaten attacked central elements in the definition of kingship." But Baines also suggests that the result was not so much that kingship was diminished as that the status of the gods in relationship to the king was elevated. See Redford (1995) 174 for comments about "the gradual weakening of the monarchy"; Faulkner (1975) 247 for

the assessment "with the death of Ramesses III the glory departed, and Egypt was never again an imperial power."

77. See also Baines (1995) 34; Van Dijk (2000) 310–11.

78. Murnane (1995) 115.

79. Ibid., 120.

80. Sandman (1938) 97.10–11; Murnane (1995) 117. This text is addressed jointly to the king and the Aton, merging their beings

81. Sandman (1938) 92.9–10; Murnane (1995) 112.

82. Assmann (1989) 78–79.

83. Referred to by Assmann (1989) 75–78 as "the theology of will" or "direct causation."

84. Gardiner (1941–48). See Faulkner (1975) 248 for the comment "The nation was being bled white by so much of its wealth going in one direction." See also Janssen (1975a) 550–58; Černý (1934); Černý (1954); Katary (1989) 216–17.

85. O'Connor (1983) 229–31 stresses the role of the rise of officials, rather than an actual erosion of the status of the office of the king, in the growing instability of the country.

86. Teeter (1987) 85. But see Brand (2000) 383 for the "deferential manner" in which Seti is shown before the gods, and see Brand's note 72 for deference not being universal (in the reliefs of Horemheb).

87. Van Dijk (2000) 313.

88. Gardiner (1960) P94–110. For its interpretation, see Assmann (2001) 231; Assmann (1983–84); Van Dijk (2000) 298.

89. KRI V.39.6, 66.7–8; Peden (1994b) 29, 51.

90. KRI V.42.10; Peden (1994b) 35.

91. KRI V.39.4, 41.14; Peden (1994b) 9, 27.

92. KRI V.26.10–11; Peden (1994b) 21.

93. KRI V.22.15; Peden (1994b) 13.

94. KRI V.21.13; Peden (1994b) 11.

95. P. Harris I.78.12–3 in Grandet (1994) 1.339.

96. KRI V 239.7–8; Peden (1994b) 117.

97. KRI V.222.4, 222.13; RIK I, pls. 22–23; Seele (1935) 234–35, 238.

98. KRI VI.68–69; McDowell (1999) 159.

99. Condon (1978) 20.4.

100. Ibid., 21, 41.

101. Ibid., 20–21.

102. Urk IV.610–19, especially the sentiment that Amun is a "guide" (613.7).

103. KRI V.39.10–11; Peden (1994b) 29.

104. P. Harris I.75.6–7 in Grandet (1994) 1.335.

105. After Condon (1978) 18.

106. KRI VI.520.6–7; Peden (1994b) 75.

107. Assmann (1984). See Morenz (1973) 97 for the comment that "service brought an automatic reward" in regard to cult actions.

108. KRI VI.20.4–5; Peden (1994b) 157.

109. KRI VI.23.6–7; Peden (1994b) 163.

110. Leblanc (1997).

111. Lichtheim (1992) 75.

112. Jansen-Winkeln (1985) 91; Lichtheim (1997) 61–62; Jansen-Winkeln (2007) 96.

113. Jansen-Winkeln (1985) A4; Lichtheim (1997) 64; Jansen-Winkeln (2007) 143.

114. See Nims (1976) for general comments about the similarities between the two temples.

115. See scenes of ritual combat and sports around the window of appearance in *MH* II, pls. 111–12, 114; *Excavation* III.44.

116. Nims (1976) 175; see table on 172.

117. Ibid., 170.

118. Nelson (1934) 26; Nims (1976) 170; el-Sabban (2000).

119. See Teeter (1997) 49–80 for a full discussion of the grammar, uses, and relationship of these formulas with references.

120. Ibid., 59–68.

121. Nelson (1981) pls. 103, 122, 168.

122. Nims (1975); Nims (1976) 173.

123. *MH* V, pls. 294A, 280C (bottom).

124. *Khonsu* II, pls. 158, 164

125. Porter and Moss (1972) 205 (6) I.1; Teeter (1997) 113. The reversion to the pattern where the subject of *ir* is the donor occurs in the reign of Amunirdis and Shepenwepet. See Teeter (1987) 58, 82.

126. *Khonsu* I, pls. 40, 49, 51, 99; *Khonsu* II, pls. 141C, 141D, 157A, 158, 189.

127. There are a few examples of this separation that predate the Twentieth Dynasty; see, e.g., Fischer (1977) fig. 103 (Sobekhotep of Dynasty Thirteen). See also Fischer (1977) 98 (for the chronology of reversals), 106 (on the significance of the reversal). See also Teeter (1997) 58–59.

128. *Khonsu* I, pls. 15, 40, 49, 51, 74, 81, 99, 104; *Khonsu* II, pls. 157A, 164, 189. See also Fischer (1977) 98.

129. See Teeter (1997) 55–56 for the derivation of *ir.f di* from *ir.f n.f di ʿnḫ* and the form *ir n.f m di ʿnḫ* at Beit el Wali (Ricke, Hughes, and Wente [1967] pls. 31B, 32C, 32F). For the grammatical form of *di* in *di ʿnḫ*, as a perfective active participle, see Teeter (1997) 65–69.

130. Nims (1975) 76. See also Teeter (1997) 60.

131. Loc. K. 40, *RIK* I, pl. 21A; Nelson (1942) 134, fig. 2. In that scene, the name of the god is *Ỉmn ḫnmt nḥḥ*, "Amun of United with Eternity." See Nelson (1942) 132–40 for the distinction of *ḫnmt nḥḥ* and *ḫnm nḥḥ*.

132. Haeny (1997) 109. See Nims (1965) 164 for the comment "This Amon [*ḫnm nḥḥ*] was Ramesses himself."

133. Nelson (1942) 135, 152.

134. Teeter (1997) 28.

135. See ibid., 75–76, 85, 92–93, and 107–12 for a listing of such scenes.

136. Ibid., 78; Spieser (2000) 154.

137. Although Ramesses IV presents his name in the same format, it is never equated with Maat through the dedication. See Teeter (1997) 75–76 (with notes about the relevance of this to the perceived legitimacy of Ramesses IV), 91, 109–10. See ibid., 75, 111, pl. 21 for the post-Ramesside scenes of the presentation of the name where the god and king jointly hold, or elevate, the king's cartouches.

138. *KRI* VI.23.6–7; Peden (1994b) 163.

139. Condon (1978) 17.

140. Habachi (1969).

141. Nelson (1942) 154.

142. Brunner (1979a); Ricke (1981) 31–37.

143. *MH* IV, pls. 218–26; Schott (1934) 80–85.

144. Room 4, *MH* IV, pls. 227–28; *Excavation* III.32.

145. Brovarski (1984) col. 1064. For the Gourna temple, see Porter and Moss (1972) 413 (62); for the Ramesseum, Porter and Moss (1972) 432 (1), 438 (18), 441 (26). Sokar's presence is indicated by references to him: Helck (1972) 132 (95), 164 (5), Sokar-Osiris 101 (106), Ptah-Sokar-Osiris 91. See Graindorge (2001) 306 for the more positive statements "At Gurneh, the Hall IX . . . was dedicated to Sokar" and "A group of rooms in the Ramesseum was consecrated to him [Sokar]." Scenes of Ramesses II with the bark of the god on the south wall of the enclosure wall of the temple of Amun at Karnak (Porter and Moss [1972] 128 (468) 23; Heck [1968] 27, pl. 23) and at the temple of Seti at Abydos (Porter and Moss [1937] 26 [236–37]) suggest that he celebrated the festival of Sokar. However, Gaballa and Kitchen ([1969, 30]) have commented that "on the West bank direct evidence of Sokar's participation in the royal cult is meager in the Nineteenth Dynasty" but that judging from the similarities of the calendars at the Ramesseum and Medinet Habu, "one is able to infer from sparse fragments that the Festival of Sokar was celebrated at the Ramesseum. . . ."

146. Nelson and Hölscher (1934) 9; el-Sabban (2000) 61.

147. Nelson and Hölscher (1934) 18–20, 59; el-Sabban (2000) 130–31.

148. Schott (1934) 85; Gaballa and Kitchen (1969) 40–41. This ritual was celebrated into Ptolemaic times.

149. *MH* IV, pls. 221–22.

150. Piankoff (1964); Hornung (1999) 136–47.

151. One of the most famous attestations of this fusion appears in the tomb of Nofertari, where the god Re and Osiris are said to "rest in each other" (Hornung [1982a] 94–96). See also Leahy (1999) 192 for a shrine at Karnak for Osiris and Re. This is already alluded to in Pyramid Text Spell 191–92 ("This Osiris has risen like Re") and in the sixth hour of the *Amduat*, when Re is united with his mummy in the form of Osiris. The axial plan of the Ramesside royal tombs likewise echoes this union, as the rays of the sun penetrate the hallways to illuminate and thereby revive the Osiris who symbolically sleeps in the sarcophagus. For the fusion of Re and Osiris as an expression of the king's own divinity, as the son of Re and the deceased Osirid king, see the scenes of Seti I in the Osiris rooms at Abydos (Calverly and Broome [1938] pl. 35), where the king is shown as the syncretistic form of Amun-Re and Osiris being conducted to the god Horus. See also Luft (2001) 142–44; Brand (2000) 383; Osing (1977) 50–51; Cooney (2000) 41.

152. Schott (1934) 66.

153. Room 20, *MH* VI, pl. 451, fig. 1. For commentary on these scenes, see Murnane (1980) 53–60. On the west wall of room 20, the king wears the crown of Osiris and holds the crook and flail.

154. The contiguous temple at the Ramesseum is destroyed, and it is not known if Seti was venerated there or if it was dedicated to the Osirid form of Ramesses II (*Ex-*

cavation III.74). At Medinet Habu, the cult of Ramesses III's actual father, Sethnakht, is nowhere celebrated or even mentioned. Instead, the king honors his more illustrious forefather Ramesses II in a chapel on the south side of the first hypostyle hall (room 14).

155. For the equation of the name with the individual, see Spieser (2000) 11–13.

156. Nelson (1942) 146.

157. Stadelmann (1996) 228. Perhaps this is what is depicted in room 20 of the Osiris suite (*MH* VI, pl. 451).

158. See below for further comments about mortuary festivals in the Great Temple.

159. Nelson (1942) 135, 152. See Cooney (2000) 41 for the comment "In the New Kingdom, a cult of divine rebirth was celebrated either in the guise of the sun god Re, often associated with Amen as Amen-Re, or in the form of Osiris, but an obvious syncretization between the two had not yet taken place." This conclusion seems at odds with the evidence from the reign of Ramesses III.

160. Nelson (1942) 147–49, 151–52.

161. Ibid., 154.

162. Leclant (1965); Grimal and Larché (2007) 25–31. The earliest of these may be chapel I (Porter and Moss [1972] 203), dated to the Twenty-second Dynasty, although almost none of the decoration remains. Its placement and form, which are echoed by other Osiris chapels in the vicinity, suggest that it had the same function. See Redford (1986) 12 for the identification of the chapel of Osiris Wep-Ished built by Osorkon (Porter and Moss [1972] 203) as a chapel to Isis. The gradual domination of Amun by Osiris is nicely summed up in Kees (1983) 401–10, in the chapter entitled "Der Sieg des Osiris."

163. Leclère (1996); Coulon, Leclère, and Marchand (1995) 205–52.

164. Seeber (1976).

165. Ventura (1986) 38–63; Jankhun (1973).

166. Ventura (1986) 47.

167. *KRI* III 681.1.

168. Teeter (1997) 88.

169. Ibid., 89 n. 56.

170. Niwinski (1987–88).

171. Nelson (1934) 42–43. See Murnane (1980) 27 for the comment that none of the reliefs, even the bark processions on the north wall of the second court at Medinet Habu, can definitively be identified as depicting the Feast of the Valley. He notes an apparent reference to the festival "on the first day of the year" (*m ḥb.f tp(y) rnpt*) on the parapet of the ramp leading from the first court to the second court (*MH* V, pl. 354C) and therefore concludes that "this was *not* the Feast of the Valley—so it seems likelier that the reliefs on the north wall refer to any one of Amon's several visits to the temple throughout the year." However, Wente has suggested (personal communication) that the text is not *ḥb.f tp(y) rnpt*, "his festival on the first of the year" but, rather, *ḥb.f nw tp rnpt*, "his festival of upon the year" or "his annual feast," which would have to be the Feast of the Valley. For the circle in that text being the *nw* jar, see *MH* V, pl. 356A. For *nw* as *n*, see Edgerton and Wilson (1936) 6 n. 22a. For *tpy rnpt*, see

Parker (1950) 61–62. For *tp* as a generalizing term in reference to time (as in *Urk* IV.175.13, *m ḥbw.f ꜥꜣw nw tp rnpt*, "in his great annual feasts"), see Caminos (1972) 220 n. 3 and Graefe (1979) 52–53.

172. Dedication inscription of Pinudjem; Doresse (1979) 40.

173. *Excavation* III.1. There is some difficulty with Hölscher's assertion that the Small Temple was enclosed in the temple precinct only later in the reign of Ramesses III and was not an original part of the plan of the temple complex. According to the excavator (*Excavation* V.26), "the original plan [of Medinet Habu] did not encroach upon the Small Temple," and it was "probably not until the second part of his reign" that the outer wall was built and the Small Temple brought within the walls. However, Hölscher does not state his evidence for a later, separate building phase. On the contrary, the presumed "later" sections of the temple complex appear to be very much a part of an original, unified plan. The walls of the hypostyle hall, like the High Gate are carved in raised relief. The bound prisoners on the gate's windowsills are like those incorporated into the earlier palace of Ramesses III. The basin in front of the palace was apparently not modified (although the quay was; see *Excavation* IV.12–13), suggesting that the basin was dug in a location that took the future High Gate into account. The figure of Ptah that decorates the southern reveal of the Eastern High Gate (*MH* VIII, pl. 607) is referred to on a doorjamb in the first pylon (*MH* IV, pl. 245C) and on a column in the second court (*MH* V, pl. 262B), suggesting that the High Gate and its decoration were part of the original decorative scheme of the complex. See also Nims in *MH* VIII, xi, n. 9. I thank Edward F. Wente for bringing these scenes to my attention.

174. This letter is dated to the Twenty-first Dynasty in Doresse (1979) 41 and Cooney (2000) 35 n. 130.

175. Wente (1967) 78 and comments on 79 (b).

176. *MH* VI, pls. 423–24.

177. Doresse (1979) 41–42.

178. I thank E. F. Wente for bringing this scene to my attention.

179. See Parker, Leclant, and Goyon (1979) 83, 85; Doresse (1973) 121–22; Cooney (2000) 31–33 (for the association of *bas* with the Decade Festival). For the *bas* of the gods, see Žabkar (1968) 5–15; Assmann (1995) 133–34, 142–49.

180. Doresse (1979) 39. See Nims (1965) 131 for the suggestion that this chapel may have been in use during the time of Ramesses II, when it "may have been the first way station for a journey which is first recorded at the beginning of the Twenty-first Dynasty."

181. Schaedel (1936) 25–26; Wente (1967) 79.

182. A dedication of Pinudjem at the Small Temple at Medinet Habu refers to the presentation of offerings on the first day of each decade. See Doresse (1979) 41–42.

183. *Excavation* V.16–17.

184. See Cooney (2000) 47 for the special interest of Taharka in the Decade Festival. This may also account for the Kushite rebuilding of the Small Temple. See *Excavation* II.26–27. Hölscher's conclusions about the Kushite additions have been considerably revised by recent (yet-to-be-published) work of the Epigraphic Survey.

185. Eigner (1984) 99–100, fig. 73. Eigner compares the Assasif and Medinet Habu approaches and suggests that the palace of Ramesses III functioned much like the

chapels of the God's Wives. He notes that the palace and chapels of the God's Wives share the same orientation to the processional way as do the great tombs located to the south of the processional way in the Assasif. See Cooney (2000) 25 for the argument that "the king was a necessary responsible component in the successful cycle of the sun" and hence that one may suggest that the window of appearances allowed the king, whose statue resided in the palace as the Osirid king, to participate in the cycle of rebirth inherent in the Decade Festival. For the statue as the resident of the palace, see Stadelmann (1996) 228.

186. For the so-called Osiris Grave (Medinet Habu 27.34–35 and 27.45 E 4.5/9 8, under the Ptolemaic pavement, at the northwest corner of the High Gate), see *Excavation* II.40; *Excavation* V.30, 33. This deposit consisted of many (the exact number cannot be computed from the excavation records) standing and seated statues of Osiris, *atef* plumes, and circlets from Osiris's crown. The statues range from small figurines to seventy-eight centimeters in height. Other groups of Osiris statues were recovered from Medinet Habu 27.16, the so-called Grave of the Monkeys (tomb 5), a "late" grave between the so-called Wall of Nectanebo and the "Dallage" near the High Gate. The statuettes appear to be from various periods spanning the Third Intermediate Period into the Ptolemaic era. Daressy (1897) 170 reported that he discovered many bronze and stone statuttes, most of which represented Osiris. These were recovered from under the floors of the rooms in the back of the temple of Ramesses III.

187. The statuettes, many of which were accessioned into the collection of the Oriental Institute, are the subject of a forthcoming study. It is hoped that analytic testing of the metal and cores will provide information about the similarities and dissimilarities of the statues, regardless of their style. This group probably constitutes one of the largest groups of excavated bronzes from Egypt.

Chapter 3

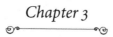

The Administrative Structure
under Ramesses III

CAROLYN R. HIGGINBOTHAM

"L'état c'est moi" (I am the State)—this (in)famous pronouncement by King Louis XIV of France might just as easily have been made by Ramesses III. According to the royal ideology of ancient Egypt, the state was virtually identified with the person of the king. As the living Horus, the son of Re, the king was the sole ruler of the land. All Egypt lived by his command. His authority was absolute and unbounded. His word was law. By his command, the fields were surveyed, sown, and harvested. By his command, the produce of the land was distributed to his grateful subjects. By his command, service was rendered to the gods of Egypt. By his command, the armies marched to war. Everything proceeded according to the dictates of the king.

The reality, of course, was otherwise. Although the king was the final authority in all matters, the specific commands that directed the affairs of Egypt were issued in the king's name by a vast cadre of officials. Viziers, overseers of treasury and granary, stewards and scribes, military commanders and mayors, they formed a complex bureaucracy with intertwining duties and responsibilities. To disentangle the threads of that system is no simple task, because of its distance from us in both time and culture.

THE NATURE OF OUR SOURCES

Sadly, we lack an administrative manual for Ramesses III's government. No document outlining the administrative structure or providing job descriptions of key officials survives from his reign. One document describing the role of the vizier, appropriately known as "The Duties of the Vizier,"[1] is extant, but it dates from the Eighteenth Dynasty. Although there was clearly a great deal of continuity in the governance of Egypt throughout the New Kingdom, some changes in the administrative structure certainly occurred in the centuries between the writing of "The Duties of the Vizier" and the reign of Ramesses III.

A quick comparison can illustrate the dangers of relying too heavily on centuries-old documents. Suppose I were to pull off the shelf the book that my father used to teach American government half a century ago. How accurately would that text describe the structures of the federal government? The basic division of powers has remained constant, but some of the details have changed significantly over the decades. For example, the cabinet has expanded to include departments of energy, education, and homeland security. Therefore "The Duties of the Vizier" can only be used to suggest a general framework of the vizierate and the system within which the vizier operated. It cannot provide a detailed reconstruction of that office or of the overall administrative structure in the Twentieth Dynasty.

We are not entirely without sources, however. A collection of documents dating from the reigns of Ramesses III and his immediate successors, Ramesses IV and V, and attesting to the activities of various officials provides evidence for the administrative structure during this period. The most important of these texts are Papyrus Harris I,[2] the Wilbour Papyrus,[3] the Turin Strike Papyrus,[4] and several documents related to the Harem Conspiracy—especially the Turin Judicial Papyrus,[5] the Rollin Papyrus,[6] and the Lee Papyrus.[7] Also of significance are the reliefs and inscriptions carved on temple walls to commemorate major events, including military victories and religious ceremonies, which provide more detailed information about the army and the temple administration than is available for other sectors of the bureaucracy.

Since these texts focus not on the administrative system per se but, rather, on specific actions taken by specific individuals, they must be used with care. They provide only momentary glimpses into the structures and functions of government. They testify to what a certain official did on a particular day, not to what the normal duties of that official were. The attested actions may not reflect an official's usual role. They may denote special assignments, temporary duties, or the exercise of personal initiative.

At the same time, we must guard against overinterpreting silences in the textual corpus. The texts we have do not mention every governmental office or function. Some aspects of the administrative system escaped mention in the texts because their smooth functioning was taken for granted by the Egyptians. Other aspects are unattested because of the fragmentary nature of our corpus. Our collection of texts comprises only a small portion of the administrative records of ancient Egypt. Furthermore, it is not a representative sample of the ancient archives but only the odd bits and pieces that have survived the accidents of preservation and discovery.

PRINCIPLES OF ADMINISTRATION

As we interpret the available documents, we need to resist the temptation to impose modern principles of public administration on the ancient Egyptian system. The Egyptians organized their governmental departments and divided the responsibilities of governance on the basis of a conceptual framework different from our own. Some distinctions that seem basic to us, like the differentiation between military and civilian personnel, were not fundamental to the Egyptian system. Thus the army was as likely to be dispatched on a stone-quarrying expedition as on a military campaign. There was also no separation of powers into judicial and executive branches.

Nonetheless, the Egyptian government was not simply an ad hoc administrative structure. There were underlying organizational principles. We can identify several distinctions that gave shape to the massive bureaucracy: (1) Egyptian and foreign, (2) civil and religious, and (3) royal and state.

The Egyptians clearly distinguished between Egypt proper and the foreign lands that surrounded them. Not even the entire Nile Valley belonged inside. Although the precise southern boundary fluctuated over the centuries, the upper reaches of the Nile Valley always lay outside of Egypt. Conceptually, regardless of the political or geographic reality, foreign lands remained external to Egypt's self-definition. Individuals from those lands could, nevertheless, be incorporated into Egyptian society without prejudice.

Although there was certainly no separation of church and state, there were separate administrative structures for the civil and religious institutions. The temples were supported by endowments from the king; in the case of the more prominent cults, these endowments added up to large estates that produced great wealth. Since they could be exempted from conscription or taxation, these religious institutions exerted considerable economic power. Their independence was held in check by the royal power to appoint priests and to send inspectors to monitor their affairs.

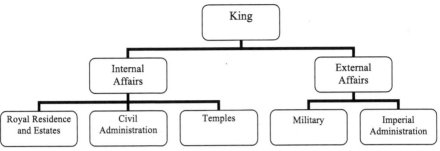

Fig. 3.1. Ancient Egyptian administrative structure

The Egyptian administrative system generally differentiated between "royal" and "state" properties and functions, although the boundaries were not drawn where we would draw them today. Royal properties included the royal residence (despite the governmental functions conducted there) and the estates that supported the royal household and the palace administration. "State" properties belonged to the king as ruler of Egypt and were employed more broadly in the redistributive economy of Egypt.

On the basis of these distinctions, we can posit a bipartite administrative structure. The administration of internal affairs incorporated the royal residence and estates, the civil administration, and the temples. The administration of external affairs included both the military and the imperial administration (see fig. 3.1).

In practice, the boundaries between the branches of government were somewhat porous, with some officials bearing long-term or short-term responsibilities in more than one division. The nature of Egyptian society mediated against rigidly linear models of governance. Cruz-Uribe has noted that the prominence of a handful of dominant families produced overlapping spheres of influence and strategic alliances between various sectors of the government.[8] Prominence, due to position or familial connections, translated into power that was not easily contained in a neatly defined office.[9] Other officials deferred to those with power or access to power even if they were not in a direct supervisory role. Thus the power of the vizier derived as much from his access to the king as from his position at the top of the civil administration. Although organizational schemes like the diagram in figure 3.1 are useful heuristic devices, we must keep in mind that they represent only the formal power structures and not the informal ones.

THE SYSTEM OF ENDOWMENTS

The Egyptian administration was built on an interconnecting network of autonomous and semiautonomous institutions, often referred to as "estates" because they derived their support from a system of endowments. The ancient Egyptian estate was a socioeconomic institution organized to support a particular function or organization. Rather than developing an annual state budget with appropriations designated for each governmental department or activity, the king created distinct estates, each supported by its own endowment (land, animals, personnel, raw materials, workshops, etc.). He executed a legal document (*imyt-pr*) that transferred the assets to the estate and restricted their use to the legitimate functions of the estate. Thus the endowment of a temple could only be used to support the temple, its rituals, and its personnel. Resources were not supposed to be diverted to serve other purposes. The king could choose to protect an estate by exempting it from taxation or conscription. A copy of the *imyt-pr* was deposited in the archives of the vizierate.[10] The execution of an *imyt-pr* ensured that the transfer of property was irrevocable; the property was not merely lent to the institution but was deeded over to it in perpetuity.[11]

In theory, since all the resources of Egypt belonged to the crown, each king had the authority to redistribute those resources as he saw fit. In practice, the king inherited a system of endowed estates that remained largely intact from reign to reign. Kings frequently added to the estates of major temples, replenished estates that had become impoverished, and created estates to support new projects.

These practices are particularly well illustrated in the documents of Ramesses III's reign. Ramesses III gave generously to the temple complexes in Thebes, Heliopolis, and Memphis, enriching their endowments through extensive construction projects and gifts of personnel, cattle, grain, waterfowl, fruits and vegetables, and all sorts of raw materials.[12] He also restored temples and temple endowments in Abydos, Siut, Ombos, and Arthribis.[13]

Every king made certain to endow an estate to support his funerary temple, so that offerings would continue to be made forever—or at least until the endowment was depleted. Ramesses III was no exception. The act of endowment is recorded in the dedicatory inscription, which mentions all three constitutive features of an estate (purpose of the estate, endowment of resources, *imyt-pr* document):

> I placed my temple under Your authority, my Noble Father; I recorded its possessions in documents, which are held tight in Your grasp. I

made a property-deed (*imyt-pr*) for You with regard to all my possessions; they exist forever, enduring in Your name . . . I built farms in
Your name in the Beloved Land (and) in the country of Nubia, as well
as in the country of Asia. I charged them with their produce as a yearly
requirement. All towns whatsoever are brought together with their
inw, in order to send them to Your Ka. (. . .) Your food is brought
inside it (the temple), Your nourishment to its shrine. Your Ba and
Your Birth-stone increase its children(?); they are *wab*-priests and
god's fathers for You, in order to call You to Your meals (and) to adore
Your Ka. Others are at their tasks in every work, in order to provide for
Your fixed portion of daily requirements.[14]

An inscription on the first pylon of the temple details the property included
in the endowment: "gold, silver, all types of linen, incense, *nḥḥ*-oil, and
honey, . . . god's fathers and *wab*-priests doing their duties, serfs, fields, and
herds without limit, good and enduring grain(?) in heaps reaching the sky."[15]
From these inscriptions, we can infer that Ramesses III intended to establish
a largely self-sufficient estate to support his funerary temple.

These inscriptions record the endowment in rather general terms. They
are intended to celebrate the generosity of the king and to remind the
gods (and the priests) that Ramesses III was the source of this largesse.
They are not legal documents. The *imyt-pr* would have contained a drier
and more precise accounting of the endowment and any exemptions bestowed on it.

We do find a reference to exemptions in a dedicatory inscription from
Elephantine in which Ramesses III confirms the legal status of the estate of
the temple of Khnum. The king decrees "[that the inhabitants of this field be
not taken for enforced labor] by an officer of the royal estate or any people
sent on a commission to the field; that their ships be not stopped by any pa-
trol; that their ships be not taken by (lawful) seizure, in order to carry out any
commission of the Pharaoh, by any people sent on a commission [to the
field.]"[16] Although the text is broken, the preserved portion indicates that the
original inscription provided a very detailed listing of the workers from
whom goods could not be requisitioned, including fishermen, fowlers, natron gatherers, salt gatherers, honey collectors, and priests.

Notice of the exemption might be posted at some distance from the estate
proper. A dedicatory inscription of Seti I from a small rock temple in the
Wadi Mia in the Eastern Desert specifies certain exemptions that were attached to the endowment of his cenotaph temple in Abydos:

I speak as follows in assigning my troop of gold-washers to my temple. They are appointed to transport to my House [in Abydos, to furnish gold to] my sanctuary . . . In particular, the troop of gold-washers that I have appointed for the House of *Menmare* shall be exempted and protected. It shall not be approached by anyone in the whole land, by any controller of gold, by any inspector of the desert. As to anyone who shall interfere with any of them so as to put them in another place, all the gods and goddesses of my House shall be his adversaries. For all my things belong to them by testament for ever and ever.[17]

The location of this inscription, far from Abydos, was not accidental. Since the gold-washers were frequently dispatched to the Eastern Desert in the pursuit of gold, they might encounter unscrupulous officials in their travels. The inscription reminded the inhabitants of the Eastern Desert that the gold-washers were protected by a royal exemption and could not be conscripted for other duties.

Some estates, such as the estate of Amun, were quite large and exercised considerable economic and political power. At the other end of the scale were the tiny estates that supported minor shrines or a private individual's mortuary cult. A large estate might comprise several smaller, semiautonomous estates. Large estates would have been virtually self-sufficient, producing most of the goods required for their own support. They could easily have acquired through trade what they could not produce themselves. Smaller estates would have produced sufficient resources only for very specific functions, such as regular offerings on the behalf of a deceased individual.

We are most familiar with the temple estates, but evidence suggests that many other institutions, including the army, were supported by similar endowments. Officials were supported both by the estates of the institutions they served and by their personal estates, which might be enhanced by gifts from the king.

Each estate was managed by a steward (*mr-pr*). He was assisted by a cadre of overseers and scribes. Herders, cultivators, artisans, and other specialists filled out the roster of the estate. The work of the estate was organized by commodity, with overseers supervising the production of a single type of goods, such as cattle or grain. In an agrarian society, overseers of cattle and overseers of fields were ubiquitous. An estate would have employed other overseers as needed, depending on the commodities it produced.

Nonetheless, agricultural production was quite decentralized. Despite the image conjured up by the term *overseer*, the ancient Egyptian estate was not a plantation employing large numbers of slaves and/or wage laborers to work the fields as part of a "unified enterprise."[18] Estates often held numerous small, widely scattered parcels of land that could not have been efficiently managed through a centralized system. Under such conditions, sharecropping and land leases were more effective means of exploiting the agricultural potential of the land.

This system of land management was used by individual landowners as well as by large estates. Most landowners were not themselves cultivators but absentee landlords who delegated the management of their fields to agents (*rwḏw*). The role of the agent was to manage the share contracts under which the peasants labored. Eyre describes the benefits of this system:

> Profitable land management requires constant supervision from somebody with a personal interest in productivity. The farmer works harder if his livelihood depends on his own effort and the size of his residue, and a maximum of local delegation reduces the bureaucratic cost of revenue production.[19]

The owner or his agent oversaw the annual assignment of the fields to the peasants after the inundation and returned at the end of the season to collect a portion of the harvest. In between, the peasant bore personal responsibility for the cultivation of the field, in exchange for his share of the crop.

BIPARTITE ADMINISTRATIVE STRUCTURES

Another fundamental principle of Egyptian administration was the division of responsibilities between two officials or departments.[20] Some forms of this "duality" are well known. Until recently, such divisions have been viewed as specific to their contexts and not generalized into an organizing principle.

The division of Egypt into two administrative regions, Upper and Lower Egypt, was well established by the time of Ramesses III. Most offices associated with the internal affairs of the kingdom were duplicated in the north and the south. Thus there were two viziers, two overseers of the treasury, and two chief stewards. Scholars have tended to explain this practice as a vestige of the earliest history of Egypt, when the first kings unified the two lands of Upper and Lower Egypt into a single kingdom. This pattern was replicated in the Nubian empire, which was divided into two regions, Wawat and Kush.

The workforce was often divided into two crews or teams.[21] The best-documented example comes from Deir el-Medina. The workforce at the royal necropolis was organized into two crews labeled "left side" and "right side." Each had its own foreman, although the entire workforce usually shared a single chief administrative scribe.[22] One might attribute the need for two crews to the layout of the tombs in which the men labored, with one crew for the right side and one for the left. However, there is no evidence that the two crews were deployed in that fashion, and "similar divisions are known elsewhere, among tomb excavators, building workers, temple traders, and men producing dates for the state granaries."[23]

The principle of duality was not consistently employed throughout the administrative system. Some departments and tasks remained largely undivided. The dual administration of the granary during the reign of Tuthmosis III[24] was the exception rather than the rule. By and large, the collection and distribution of grain was centralized in a single granary of Upper and Lower Egypt, with one overseer. Even the division of the vizierate was suspended, for reasons that remain enigmatic, during the later years of Ramesses III, when To was appointed vizier of Upper and Lower Egypt. Furthermore, the staff of an expedition might include single as well as paired officials in various capacities.[25]

INTERNAL AFFAIRS

There were two primary levels of government: local and central. By the Ramesside period, the provincial system had long since been eliminated, so that there was no layer of bureaucracy between the local officials and the central administration. The local officials were directly responsible to the central government. The void left by the disappearance of the nomarchs (as the provincial governors were called) was filled by the mayors of the larger cities, whose sphere of influence extended far out into the countryside.

The Egyptian government was a unitary, rather than a federal or confederate, system. No rights or powers were reserved for local officials. Officials from the central administration always had the right to intervene in local affairs. Most of the time, of course, they paid little attention to what went on in the towns and villages of Egypt. Occasionally, however, they chose to step in and exercise their authority, perhaps because of personal or familial connections. The on-again, off-again nature of these interventions makes it difficult to define lines of authority and responsibility. We are not always certain which duties were regularly, as opposed to sporadically, performed by a particular administrator.

The Vizierate

The most powerful men in Egypt, after the king, were the viziers. Although the office has often been compared to that of prime minister or minister of the interior, there is no precisely equivalent office in modern Western government. Of critical importance to our understanding of the office is its division, throughout most of the Ramesside period, into two offices, one for Upper Egypt and one for Lower Egypt. Thus the vizier was not the singular head of the administrative structure. Rather, the two viziers shared responsibility for the central state administration, especially with regard to the internal affairs of the kingdom.

Our sources provide little information about how the two viziers coordinated their work. In some cases, a simple geographic division of responsibilities was undoubtedly quite effective. Most governmental departments were divided along the same geographic lines as the vizierate, and each department head would have reported to his respective vizier. In other cases, the duties of the viziers must have differed based on their setting, specifically the location of the vizier of Lower Egypt in the royal residence and the proximity of the vizier of Upper Egypt to the royal necropolis.

According to "The Duties of the Vizier," the vizier functioned much like a modern-day chief of staff, controlling access to the king. He provided the king with his daily briefing, serving, therefore, as the primary conduit through which the king received information.[26] The vizier controlled the flow of information in the other direction as well, since he was responsible for transmitting the king's degrees to local officials and to the people of Egypt.

Only the vizier of Lower Egypt could have regularly performed the function of the chief of staff. The other vizier would have been miles away and able to communicate with his sovereign only via messenger, except for those rare occasions when the king traveled south for a religious ceremony or an inspection tour. Although none of our sources describes their relative standing, we can only assume that the northern vizier outranked the southern vizier, in fact if not in principle. Certainly his access to power far exceeded that of his colleague.

The vizier also provided security for the royal residence. During the reign of Ramesses III, this duty would have fallen to the vizier of Lower Egypt. He appointed the head of the security detail (*mr šntw*) who was stationed in the reception hall of the royal residence. He also appointed the military escort that accompanied the king when the king traveled. The vizier did not, however, accompany the king on his journeys. Instead he remained behind to manage the civil administration of Lower Egypt.[27]

The vizier of Upper Egypt often bore responsibility for the construction of the king's tomb. Thus it is not surprising to find the vizier To with the title "overseer of the work of the horizon of eternity and in the house of mourning." The vizier To regularly appears on ostraca and graffiti from Deir el-Medina dated to years 16–29, especially in the company of Amunnakht, whom To appointed necropolis scribe in year 16. Viziers were sometimes tasked to supervise other construction projects, such as the renovation of the temples of Maat at Karnak, which was assigned to To in year 12 (or perhaps year 22—the date is poorly preserved).[28]

Civil administration included both executive and judicial functions. Actions of the civil bureaucracy could always be appealed to the vizierate, which served as a kind of court of final appeals over matters like tax assessment.[29] If a civil servant was derelict in his duty, abused his power, or committed a crime while functioning in an official capacity, the vizierate had judicial authority over the case.

References to this judicial function are ubiquitous, appearing in sample letters, stories, and historical documents. During year 29, when the royal tomb workers went on strike over nonpayment of wages, they demanded that a report of their situation be sent to the king, "our good lord," and to the vizier, "our superior."[30] Their immediate supervisors had not fulfilled their responsibilities, so the aggrieved workers appealed to the king as the titular head of the land and to the vizier as the head of the administrative system. The language of the text clearly expresses their belief that if the king and vizier knew what was going on, they would surely set things right.

The judicial system operated on two levels: local and vizierial. Most cases, whether civil or criminal, would have been heard initially by the local tribunal or kenbet-council (*ḳnbt*). Such cases would only have come to the vizier's "great kenbet-council" on appeal. Cases in which the central government had a compelling interest, such as crimes against state institutions or allegations of corruption, might be tried before the great kenbet-council.

The great kenbet-council was chaired by the vizier and composed of high-ranking bureaucrats, sometimes including priests. The kenbet-council of a city or town was chaired by the mayor and composed of local dignitaries.[31] In the case of the workmen's village of Deir el-Medina, the kenbet-council often included crew foremen, scribes, and other officials, as well as ordinary workmen.[32]

The evidence from the workmen's village of Deir el-Medina suggests that the lines between jurisdictions were not hard and fast. Some cases were heard by "mixed" tribunals, comprising representatives of multiple jurisdictions. Although some rather routine matters were adjudicated by "mixed" kenbet-councils, scribes of the vizier or other "outside agents joined the court particularly when a troublesome case was being heard."[33] Scribes of the vizier were most likely to be included on the tribunal when the case involved theft of state property.[34] A special tribunal might be appointed by the king to deal with especially heinous crimes, such as the attempted assassination of Ramesses III. That tribunal consisted of two overseers of the treasury, a fanbearer, five butlers, a royal herald, two scribes, and a standard-bearer of the garrison.[35]

The ancient Egyptians did not distinguish between civil and criminal law, at least not in terms familiar to modern jurisprudence. The primary categories were (1) cases involving two private individuals and (2) cases involving official misconduct or acts against the state. When both parties were private individuals, the responsibility for investigating and prosecuting the case fell to the complainant; there was no district attorney to bring the case to trial. However, when the case involved a state institution or official, the tribunal had the power to conduct an investigation.

A prime example comes from the late Ramesside period. In the sixteenth year of Ramesses IX, the vizierate received a report indicating that a number of tombs had been robbed. Several high-ranking administrators were dispatched to West Thebes to examine the tombs in question. The vast majority were found to be intact, although thieves had attempted to penetrate some of them. The investigators also interrogated the suspects. The evidence was presented to the great kenbet-council, which declared the accusations false and set the accused free. A record of the proceedings was deposited in the archives-office of the vizierate.[36] The archives-office of the vizierate served as the central depository for administrative and juridical documents. The task of keeping these records fell to the scribes of the vizier, who were, as a result, men of considerable power and standing.

Two men served as vizier of Upper Egypt during the reign of Ramesses III: Hori and To. Little is known of the man (or men) who served as vizier of Lower Egypt prior to year 29. Hori had a long and distinguished career as vizier. The son of a high priest of Memphis of the same name, Hori is first attested as vizier of Lower Egypt in the reign of Seti II, before being transferred to the southern vizierate under Siptah, where he also served as the steward of Siptah's mortuary temple.[37] He survived the transition to the Twentieth Dynasty, continuing in the post of vizier of Upper Egypt under both Setnakht[38] and Ramesses III. He is last attested in year 10 of Ramesses III.[39]

To succeeded Hori as vizier of Upper Egypt sometime around year 12. His career saw both triumph and tumult. On the one hand, he was entrusted with the honor of escorting the gods (i.e., the cult statues) to Ramesses III's jubilee celebration.[40] On the other hand, he was in charge of the work in the royal necropolis at the time of the strikes when the workmen protested the lack of supplies and rations. He must have been a singularly effective vizier, because in year 29, the king made To vizier of both Upper and Lower Egypt, abolishing the dual vizierate.[41]

What happened that led the king to make such a radical change in administrative structure? Helck has suggested that the vizier of Lower Egypt was removed from office for an act of malfeasance: interference in the affairs of the temple of Athribis.[42] Unfortunately the relevant passage in Papyrus Harris I is somewhat cryptic. The king states that he has restored the estate to the control of the priests and agents of the estate and prevented the vizier from interfering with them.[43] One might interpret this passage, as Helck does, to mean that the vizier had unlawfully interfered in the affairs of the temple, perhaps even to the extent of appropriating its resources for his own use. However, the context of this passage is a rather lengthy description of the restoration of the temple, its offerings, and its estate. The account leaves an impression of an impoverished cult lacking the means to support itself. The passage detailing the reorganization of the temple administration need not be read as alluding to criminal activity on the part of the vizier. If the temple's endowment had become depleted, the vizier might have exercised temporary oversight until the king restored the temple to its previous status. According to this latter reading, the prohibition against vizierial interference implies only the restoration of the temple estate's autonomous status, not any impropriety on the part of the vizier. When the estate could not manage its own affairs, the vizier acted as a trustee. That trusteeship was now ended, and authority and responsibility were returned to the temple officials.

Other plausible explanations for To's appointment exist. The consolidation of power might have been a response to growing civil unrest[44] or a means to facilitate preparations for the jubilee.[45] If the vizier of Lower Egypt died in office,[46] either (or both) of these factors might have led to the decision to unify the office of the vizierate temporarily under To. In any event, the unification of the office did not continue after the death of Ramesses III.

The Royal Residence

The royal residence (*pr-nsw*, literally "house of the king") was the center of the Egyptian administrative system. A walled compound within the royal

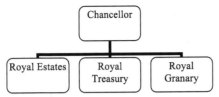

Fig. 3.2. Responsibilities of the chancellor in the Eighteenth Dynasty

city, rather than a "house," the royal residence comprised the private apartments of the king and the various central government departments. From here, the king, through his trusted officials, administered the affairs of state.

The administration of the royal residence is best documented in "The Duties of the Vizier." According to this text, the royal residence was jointly administered during the Eighteenth Dynasty by the vizier (*t3ty*) and the chancellor[47] (*mr ḥtm*), who met daily to coordinate their activities. The vizier bore responsibility for the security of the residence and for oversight of the government departments. The chancellor supervised the daily operations of the residence.[48] Other sources indicate that he also managed the king's private property, including the royal estates, the royal treasury, and the palace granary (see fig. 3.2).[49]

By the Twentieth Dynasty, the office of the chancellor had disappeared, and his functions had been taken over by other officials. The management of the royal estates was assumed by the chief royal steward (*mr pr wr*). The palace granary fell under the authority of the overseer of the granary of Upper and Lower Egypt (*mr šnwt šm3w mḥw*).[50] It is likely that the other functions of the chancellor devolved to the overseer of the treasury (*mr pr ḥd,* literally "overseer of the house of silver").[51] After all, we are concerned here primarily with the collection of valuable commodities and the supervision of the workshops that processed those commodities. The overseer of the treasury already bore those responsibilities for the central administration (see fig. 3.3).

These changes are significant because they weaken the distinction between royal and state properties. Certainly the Egyptians had never insisted on a rigid separation between the royal estates and state lands. There was no ethics committee hovering over the government to guard against the commingling of assets. However, with the demise of the office of the chancellor, the distinction between the king's private possessions and those of the state became significantly blurred. A single hierarchy managed all the valuable commodities belonging to both the palace and the state.

The royal residence was served by a host of servants, although we know little about their precise functions or place within the hierarchy. Among them

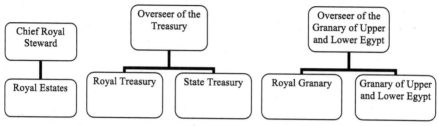

Fig. 3.3. Division of responsibilities in the Twentieth Dynasty

were the royal secretary and the royal herald. The royal secretary was the private secretary of the king. He was the official to whom all royal decrees were dictated. The royal herald was responsible for disseminating the decrees.

Perhaps the most difficult servant to assess is the butler or cupbearer (*wbз*). On the one hand, some sources suggest that the title "butler" could be applied to low-ranking individuals.[52] For example, in Papyrus Anastasi IIIA, "slaves of Kerke and striplings from the priest phyle" are determined to be "fit to be butlers of Pharaoh" and are set to work in the provision house.[53] On the other hand, the monumental inscriptions of Ramesses III often include the royal butlers among the high officials addressed by the king.[54]

Certainly the butler originated as a household servant with primary responsibility for the preparation and serving of food. This function is well attested in the Middle Kingdom and depicted in the Eighteenth Dynasty tomb of Suemnut, "royal butler, clean of hands." Although the tomb painting is badly damaged, the nature of the scene is quite clear. King Amenhotep II sits enthroned in the upper left corner of the scene. Smaller figures of servants, organized in registers, prepare food and drink and present it to his majesty. Suemniwet stands in the lower right corner of the scene, supervising the work of the servants like a good food service manager.[55]

Nevertheless, in the Ramesside period, some of the king's most trusted aides bear the title "butler." These butlers carried out important official duties that had nothing to do with the preparation and serving of food. They led expeditions to Nubia and the Sinai[56] and served as inspectors.[57] Of the twelve magistrates appointed to judge the accused in the Harem Conspiracy, five were butlers: Pabasa, Kendedenna, Maharbaal, Paerswana, and Djehuty-rekh-nafa. Seven of the accused, including the judge Pabasa, were also butlers.[58] As Schulman notes, "At the battle of Kadesh royal butlers clearly [had] a military function, forming at least part of Ramesses II's bodyguard or household troops."[59] The common denominator among these disparate tasks is their sensitive nature. In most of these cases, the butler served as the king's personal emissary. Apparently the butlers were attached to the king's personal service rather than to a particular administrative department.[60] They were available for special assignment at the pleasure of the king.

How did the butler evolve from menial servant to royal confidante? Surely there was no more sensitive position in the royal household than that of butler. The king relied on his butlers to ensure that his food and drink were not only tasty and elegantly served but also free of poison. The Harem Conspiracy provides ample evidence that the king could not trust the members of his own household, including some of his butlers. A good butler, then, had to be a man of unimpeachable integrity who could be trusted with the king's very life.

Given the evidence for royal butlers of both low and high rank, it seems likely that there were a number of grades of butler. Schulman has suggested that the highest ranking butlers bore the title "royal butler, clean of hands," though they might still be referred to by the shorter title "royal butler."[61] We can only speculate about how the office of butler was organized. Since multiple royal butlers seem to have belonged to the king's inner circle at any given time, we cannot identify a position of chief royal butler. We cannot even trace the career of the royal butler to determine whether one typically began at the bottom of the ladder and climbed through the ranks of food service personnel or whether the post of "royal butler, clean of hands" was reserved for trusted individuals of high rank. Perhaps once a butler had proven his trustworthiness and discretion in managing the king's table, he was admitted to the king's inner circle and assigned other equally sensitive duties. Or perhaps the office itself came to symbolize loyalty and integrity and evolved into a designation for trusted aides whose service was unrelated to the kitchen and dining room.

We do know that the role of butler was at least sometimes hereditary: Ptahemwia served as royal butler under Ramesses III;[62] his son Hori filled the same office under Ramesses IV.[63] The royal butler Ramessesemperre is attested in year 7 of Merenptah and again in the reign of Ramesses III. The name is rare enough to suggest that Ramessesemperre either enjoyed a long and successful career culminating in an expedition to the copper mines at Timna or bequeathed his office of royal butler to his son (or grandson).[64]

The Royal Estates

The central administration of the royal estates was handled by the chief royal steward. Both the king and other members of the royal family, especially queens and princesses, possessed individual estates that belonged to the royal residence. Since these estates were scattered throughout Egypt, their day-to-day management was overseen by numerous royal stewards (*mr pr*) under the authority of the chief royal steward.

Helck discusses four individuals who may have served as chief royal steward under Ramesses III: Ptahmose, Pa-ir, Meribastet, and Khaemwast. Of the four, only the identification of Ptahmose is certain. The cartouches of Ramesses III on his statue place him securely in this reign. We know little of his career except that he bore the title of mayor as well as chief royal steward. The others—Pa-ir, Meribastet, and Khaemwast—are all attested in the Wilbour Papyrus, which dates from the reign of Ramesses V. Helck suggests, however, that they appear there as retired officials, who might well have been active in office under Ramesses III.[65]

The most likely of these is Meribastet, who bears the titles "chief royal steward of the lord of the two lands," "chief royal steward of the royal tomb," and "overseer of the god's servants of all the gods of Hermopolis." The family of Meribastet was quite prominent in the Twentieth Dynasty. His son Ramessesnakht was first priest of Amun. His grandson Usermaatrenakht followed him as chief royal steward under Ramesses V, while other grandsons held high positions in the priesthood of Amun. According to Helck, Meribastet rose from the priesthood to the position of chief royal steward. In retirement, he was given the position of overseer of Medinet Habu.[66] Since Meribastet's grandson Usermaatrenakht was "chief royal steward of the lord of the two lands" under Ramesses V, it seems quite plausible that Meribastet himself would have been retired by that time.

It is more difficult to date the careers of the other two. The documents in which they are attested are either undated or from the reign of Ramesses V. Whether they held the office of chief royal steward under Ramesses III cannot be determined with certainty.

The Harem

The royal domain included the harem, or women's quarter. In fact, there were multiple harems scattered across Egypt. The king may not have had a girl in every port, but he had a harem in every major palace, as well as a traveling harem that accompanied him on his journeys. There was a harem at the royal residence in the Delta, another at Thebes (which the king visited frequently, especially for religious ceremonies at the Karnak and Luxor Temples), and a third at the entrance to the Faiyum (where the king retired for rest, relaxation, and hunting).[67]

The documents of the Harem Conspiracy provide the best evidence for the administrative structure of the harem. Although the texts record the trial of the conspirators rather than the daily functioning of the harem, they do preserve the titles of a number of harem officials. They were, in order of rank, the overseer (*mr*) of the harem, the deputy or adjutant (*idnw*) of the harem, the harem scribe (*sš*), and the agent (*rwḏw*) of the harem. Two of the central conspirators were harem officials: the overseer of the traveling harem, known only as the Snake,[68] and one of his scribes. Eight other harem officials—a deputy, a scribe, and six agents—were convicted as accomplices because they failed to report the plot.[69]

The Granary and Treasury

Grain was administered separately from other commodities, which fell under the purview of the treasury. The granary was not subordinate to the treasury but existed as a parallel department of government. The overseer of the granary and the overseer of the treasury shared the same rank within the Egyptian hierarchy.

In contrast to the vizierate and the treasury, the granary remained a single, unified department through most of Egyptian history. Although the grain might be physically stored in many locations, it was centrally administered by the overseer of the granary.

The local threshing floor provided a convenient mechanism for collection of the grain tax. When farmers brought their grain to the threshing floor, the local officials assessed the tax due on each plot under cultivation. These plots would have been previously "registered" in the name of the cultivators when the fields were surveyed at the end of the inundation. The town and village leaders then delivered the grain to the city, where it became the responsibility of the mayor. The role of the mayor in tax collection derived not from a strict hierarchy of local officials but from his authority over the quay where the taxes were collected by the chief taxing master and the granary scribes.[70]

The great fear of the landowner or farmer was to be assessed for land that he was not cultivating. Thus the mayor of Elephantine, Meron, writes to the chief taxing master to appeal an assessment of 100 *khar* of barley for a farm near Kom Ombo. He argues that the liability is not his because that farm was being cultivated by someone else, who had in fact already paid the taxes due.[71] (Unfortunately the outcome of the case remains a mystery, since the response of the chief taxing master has not been preserved.)

The treasury was divided into two administrative units: one for Upper Egypt and one for Lower Egypt. Each was administered by an overseer of the treasury (*mr pr ḥḏ*). Although the name of this institution was literally "the house of silver (and gold)," the treasury was not just a storehouse for precious metals; it was a department of government for the management of a wide range of commodities, including stone, wood, ivory, cloth, leather, oil, wine, honey, salt, natron, incense, and, of course, precious metals. These goods entered the state economy through foreign trade and tribute, domestic taxes, and mining and quarrying expeditions. In addition to the grain taxes assessed on cultivators, each head of household had to pay an annual tax assessed in gold, silver, copper, and fabric.[72]

The treasury included the workshops in which the raw materials were processed and crafted by highly skilled artisans. From the term "department of work," we can infer "that there was a unified control over the workshops of individual temples or of the state."[73] However, we have little evidence for the internal governance of the workshops. Given the variety of skills required, it seems most likely that there would have been separate shops for each craft, each with its own master.

The necropolis workers obtained the tools and the raw materials for their work by requisitioning them from the treasury. Several letters from the Nineteenth and Twentieth Dynasties record the complaints of workmen when these supplies were not forthcoming. One workman went so far as to send the vizier a detailed list of the missing items that ought to have been provided: "yellow ochre, gum, (yellow) orpiment, (red) realgar, red ochre, (dark blue) lapis-lazuli, green frit, fresh grease for lighting, old clothes for wicks."[74]

The Temples

As the Living Horus, the Son of Re, the king was *the* representative of the gods on earth. He mediated between the divine and human realms, restoring and maintaining order (*mꜣꜥt*). In one sense, no one but the king could perform the divine service. In practice, the king appointed priests to play his role in the regular temple rituals. The king could not, of course, be acquainted with each and every priest in all the temples of Egypt. Only the high priests of the major temples would have been selected by the king himself. The others would have been named by their superiors and affirmed by the court through the office of the vizier.

The highest category of priest was the *ḥm nṯr*, literally "god's servant." The traditional and still very common English translation of the title is "prophet." Nevertheless, the *ḥm nṯr* was not a prophet in the usual sense of the English word. He was not primarily an oracular figure, predicting the future or interpreting the divine will. He was a priestly figure, officiating in the cultic rituals and overseeing the affairs of the temple.[75]

The chief priest of a major temple was known as the first god's servant[76] of the temple's primary god (e.g., first god's servant of Amun). Among the other god's servants of that temple, there might be individuals bearing the rank of second, third, or even fourth god's servant. It was not unusual for a man to serve as second god's servant for a number of years before being elevated to the role of first god's servant, much as religious leaders today might ascend through the ranks from priest to bishop to archbishop.

Some temples employed traditional titles for their high priests in place of the more generic "god's servant." These titles often reflected key attributes of the chief god of that temple. Thus the high priest of Ptah at Memphis was known as the "sem" of Ptah.

The ordinary priests were known as "pure ones" (w'bw). These wab-priests were not full-time religious specialists. They were men of some standing in the community who gained prestige and economic benefit from their priestly posts. They supplemented their income from other economic activities with the rations they received from the temple. The wab-priests were organized into units known as *phyles*. Each phyle served in rotation, one month on and three months off. During his month on duty, the wab-priest was subject to strict purity regulations. At the end of his rotation, he returned home and participated in the everyday life of his community.

The priesthood was often a family affair, with several members of the same family in service simultaneously or successively. Although the posts were not strictly hereditary, connections (by blood or marriage) seem to have played a role in the selection of a successor. This pattern is especially clear in the case of the temple of Amun at Karnak. Three interrelated families dominated the priestly ranks at Karnak during the Twentieth Dynasty: the families of Bakenkhons, Ramessesnakht, and Tjanefer (see fig. 3.4). Members of these families also held important civil posts (e.g., mayor of Thebes) and high priesthoods in other cults (e.g., Mont and Mut).[77]

The family of Bakenkhons had a priestly lineage dating back to the reign of Ramesses II, when Bakenkhons himself was the first god's servant of Amun. He was succeeded by a close relative, Roma-roy, either his son or his younger brother. Although the family fell from favor at the change of dynasties, they returned to prominence a generation later, producing two mayors of Thebes, Paser (under Ramesses III) and Amenmose (under Ramesses IV). The sister of Paser and Amenmose, Nefertiry, married Tjanefer, third god's

	Family of Bakenkhons	Family of Tjanefer	Family of Ramessesnakht
Ramesses II	Bakenkhons, high priest (unknown daughter)		
Ramesses III–IV	Paser, mayor of Thebes Amenmose, mayor of Thebes **Nefertiry,** wife of Tjanefer	**Tjanefer,** 3rd god's servant	Usimaarenakht, high priest (brother of Ramessesnakht?) Ramessesnakht,[b] high priest
Ramesses III–X		*Amenemopet,*[a] 3rd god's servant of Amun, high priest of Mut Penpare, 3rd god's servant	*Aatmeret,* wife of Amenemopet Nesiamun, high priest Amenhotep, high priest

[a]Amenemopet began his career under Ramesses III. [b]Ramessesnakht is first attested in year 1 of Ramesses IV.

Fig. 3.4. Priestly families of Thebes (organized by generations)

servant of Amun. Through Nefertiry and Tjanefer, the Bakenkhons family was linked to succeeding generations of high priests.

Sometime before year 26 of Ramesses III, when he is attested on an ostracon from Deir el-Medina,[78] Usimaarenakht was named first god's servant of Amun. Although little is known about him for certain, Usimaarenakht was probably the son of the chief taxing master Meribast and the brother of Ramessesnakht, who succeeded him as first god's servant of Amun. Ramessesnakht seems to have been a man of great political acumen. He solidified his position in Theban society by marrying his daughter into a family that included mayors of Thebes and third and fourth god's servants of Amun. His influence continued after his death: his sons Nesiamun and Amenhotep followed him in the role of high priest.[79] Thus one family provided the chief priest of the temple of Amun at Karnak from the reign of Ramesses III to that of Ramesses X.

The family of Tjanefer served as the link between the Bakenkhons and Ramessesnakht families: Tjanefer married a granddaughter of Bakenkhons; his son Amenemopet married a daughter of Ramessesnakht. The family of Tjanefer was not without its own significance. Tjanefer was himself third god's servant of Amun and came from a line of god's servants that included his father, Amenhotep, and his uncle Harmose. His son Amenemopet not only succeeded him as third god's servant of Amun but also achieved the rank of first god's servant of Mut.[80]

Certainly not every high-ranking priest at Karnak came from a narrow circle of Theban families. At the beginning of the reign of Ramesses III, the first god's servant of Amun was one Bakenkhons, son of a military officer named Amenemopet. Despite his name, he was apparently no relation to the Bakenkhons who was first god's servant during the reign of Ramesses II.[81] The two subsequent first god's servants, Usimaarenakht and Ramessesnakht, were originally from Hermopolis, not Thebes.[82] Family connections certainly aided a career, but they were no guarantee of succession.

One family connection did ensure a high post: royal birth. Two prominent high priesthoods were bestowed on sons of Ramesses III. Prince Khaemwaset was high priest of Ptah at Memphis.[83] Prince Meryatum was high priest of Re-Atum at Heliopolis.[84] These appointments not only provided suitable occupations for ambitious princes but also kept the temples closely linked to the royal throne.

The administration of the temples involved much more than just the priests who performed the daily liturgy and seasonal festivals. The temples were supported by endowments—gifts of land, servants, livestock, and various commodities. Haring explains:

> Temples estates founded during the New Kingdom (1550–1070 BC) included lands—agriculture being the basis of Egyptian economy— animals, workshops and storerooms, ships, and personnel producing and transporting the necessary items. Their revenues served the upkeep of the offering-cult, the temple personnel, and the temple buildings.[85]

In the case of local shrines, these endowments would have been small and could have been managed by a minimal staff. The large temples, however, possessed extensive estates requiring an administrative structure rivaling that of the state. The structure included stewards, scribes, and overseers of every sort of commodity and activity, including cattle, grain, and "works." Individual cultivators and their families farmed many of the temple fields as tenant farmers, turning a share of the produce over to the temple. The grain was collected in temple granaries and redistributed as rations for temple employees.

EXTERNAL AFFAIRS

To the military fell the task of managing Egypt's engagement with the wider world. This engagement was not merely a matter of defense (or offense), although the army was certainly deployed to protect the borders of the Nile Valley and to do battle with Egypt's enemies. Also of paramount importance were diplomacy and economic exploitation. The army could expect to be involved in all of these spheres of external relations.

Military garrisons were stationed, for longer or shorter periods, at outposts across the empire. From these vantage points, they could guard against rebellion, protect key trade routes, and collect tariffs and taxes.

Expeditionary forces were dispatched to "expand the borders of Egypt," to defend the Nile Valley from invaders, to collect tribute from reluctant vassals, to raid distant lands, to inspect the empire, to negotiate with foreign princes and kings, and to mine copper and turquoise. While a show of force was certainly useful in each of these ventures, that does not fully explain the predominance of military personnel in every aspect of external affairs. Here we encounter the fundamental distinction between internal and external, between *t3-mri* ("the beloved land" = the portion of the Nile Valley within the boundaries of Egypt) and *ḫ3swt* ("the hill countries" = all territories outside the boundaries of Egypt, regardless of their topography). Conceptually the military were associated with the *ḫ3swt*, and thus military personnel were in the majority in most foreign expeditions, regardless of their function.

We ought not jump to the conclusion, however, that the imperial administration was fully incorporated within the military chain of command. The evidence indicates that most imperial officials had military experience. Whether they continued to function as military officials or "transferred" to a separate department of government (some sort of department of state or ministry of the empire) is unclear.

The army was also employed in heavy labor at building sites within Egypt, especially for hauling and erecting heavy stone blocks and monuments.[86] The troops no doubt provided a ready source of muscle for such projects. Yet the satirical texts largely focus on the travels of the soldier, not the backbreaking work of construction, as the source of his misery. The reference to general labor by soldiers in the Lansing Papyrus is exceptional: "'Give him who knows how to work!' He is awakened while there is (still) an hour (for sleeping). He is driven like a jackass and he works until the sun sets beneath its darkness of night. He hungers and his belly aches. He is dead while he lives."[87] The text goes on to describe at great length the perils of military expeditions: lack of food and clothing, steep terrain, dysentery, enemy arrows, and so on. Clearly, in the mind of the Egyptian scribe, the role of the infantryman as construction worker was a minor, secondary aspect of his profession.

Interestingly, the specific construction tasks assigned to soldiers are not unrelated to the military's function as an expeditionary force. Army units were often dispatched to quarry and transport stone for buildings and statues. Perhaps the work at the construction site arose as the final step in the fulfillment of the expedition's mission. Having hauled the stone all the way from the distant quarries, the troops were pressed into service to muscle it into place. Their work as heavy laborers, though not always directly connected to an expedition, was, in this sense, a natural extension of their military function.

The Army

Military terminology can be confusing to the uninitiated. Some titles indicate rank (relative position in the hierarchy), whereas others specify the particular post to which someone has been appointed (e.g., commander of Fort X or captain of Ship Y). Still other terms refer to a broad category (e.g., "officer" or "NCO").

The Egyptian army was led by many "military officers" (*mr mšꜥ*),[88] ranging in rank from "standard-bearer" (*ṯ3y sryt*) to "general" (*mr mšꜥ wr*). The "platoon leader" (*ꜥ3 n 50*) is never referred to as a "military officer." From this, we might suppose that he was a junior officer or NCO whose rank placed him outside the "military officer" category.

As the title, literally "great one of fifty," implies, the platoon leader was in charge of a unit of fifty men. This platoon was the basic building block of the Egyptian army.[89] Schulman suggests that platoons may have consisted of five squads of ten men each. He bases this conjecture on references to a "squad leader," literally "great one of ten" (*ꜥ3/ḥry n 10*), on two unpublished objects of late Ramesside date and on analogy to modern military structure.[90]

Companies (*s3*) were composed of several (usually five) platoons and led by a standard-bearer (see fig. 3.5). The term meaning "standard-bearer" referred to rank and was not a functional title. The standard-bearer's title might vary depending on the task to which his company was assigned: for example, commander of the company, commander of the ship's contingent, quartermaster of the army, and so on.[91] Only one standard-bearer is known from the reign of Ramesses III: Panehsy, standard-bearer of the company "Ruler of On."[92] Unfortunately nothing more is known of him or his company.

The standard-bearer was assisted by two other senior officers: an adjutant (*idnw*) and a scribe. Both the adjutant and the scribe were administrative officers: the adjutant coordinated logistical functions, such as the provisioning of the company,[93] while the scribe kept the company's daybook and other records.[94]

The next largest unit in the Egyptian army was the host, or troop (*pḏt*).

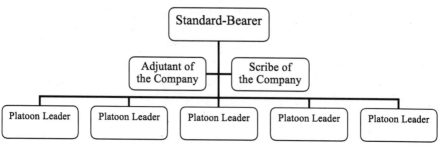

Fig. 3.5. Structure of a company

The host varied greatly in size, from several hundred to several thousand. The minimum size for a host was two companies. The host was led by a "host commander" (ḥry pḏt). He might hold such posts as fort officer, garrison officer, commander of assault officers, or commander of quartermasters of the army.[95] The host commander was undoubtedly assisted by high-ranking military scribes, such as the scribe of the infantry, the scribe of the "elite troops," and the scribe of the assemblage of the army.[96]

The adjutant of the army would have assisted the host commander in the same way that the adjutant of the company assisted the standard-bearer. The Egyptian idnw, translated "adjutant," means "deputy" or "assistant." Since the adjutant of the army ranked just below the host commander, it follows logically that he would have served as his assistant.[97]

The rank of general was bestowed on the commander in chief of the army and, therefore, held by only one individual at a time. Ramesses III followed custom in appointing the crown prince Ramesses commander in chief.[98] This practice ensured the loyalty of the army to the ruling dynasty and provided military training and experience for the future king.

We do not know who commanded the army during the early years of the reign, before Ramesses was designated crown prince. Ramesses had several older brothers, some of whom were named crown prince in turn before their deaths. Yet none of these was placed at the head of the army.

Many princes made a career of military service. Those who did not rise to the post of commander in chief usually served in the chariotry, which was the most prestigious branch of the military. Six sons of Ramesses III held chariotry ranks:

Pre-hir-wenmef   first charioteer[99]
Set-hir-khopshef I   first charioteer[100]

Montu-hir-khopsef	first charioteer[101]
Amen-hir-khopshef I	chief chariot officer[102]
Amen-hir-khopshef II	chief chariot officer[103]
Set-hir-khopshef II	chief chariot officer[104]

The latter three held ranks at the top of the chariot corps.

The organization of the chariotry paralleled that of the rest of the army. Military officers indicated that they were posted to the chariotry by appending "of chariotry" to their titles. Thus we find commanders of a host of chariotry, standard-bearers of chariot warriors, and adjutants of chariotry. Ranks unique to this branch of the military include first charioteer, charioteer, chariot warrior, *tkm*-bearer, and runner. A shield-bearer might hold the rank of either first charioteer or charioteer.[105]

The Egyptians also maintained a modest naval force, which was incorporated into the army. The naval officers bore the same titles as other military officers of comparable rank. From this, we conclude that the navy used a similar command structure.

Military justice was likely administered by a system of military tribunals under the authority of the commander in chief. In the Eighteenth Dynasty, we have references to a "court of the army" and a "judge of the army," who held the rank of host commander.[106] The Nauri Decree of Seti I details the punishments that could be inflicted on a military officer who abused his authority: "one shall invoke against him a statute, namely beating him with two hundred blows and five pierced wounds, as well as exacting the work of the person belonging to the House."[107]

The Imperial Administration

The Egyptian empire consisted of two geographically and administratively distinct regions: Nubia and Syria-Palestine. The exact boundaries of these territories varied over the course of the New Kingdom. In the reign of Ramesses III, Egyptian control in Nubia must have extended at least as far south as Soleb, which was visited, during the course of a tour of inspection, by the crown prince Ramesses.[108] Egyptian control in Syria-Palestine certainly extended no further north than the extreme southern portions of modern-day Lebanon and Syria. Ramesses II signed a treaty with the Hittites ceding control of Kadesh on the Orontes to the Hittites. There is no reason to believe that later kings were successful in expanding the boundaries; in fact, the sphere of effective control was gradually reduced over time.

Although the administrations of the two regions share some superficial similarities, there are marked differences. On the one hand, the top officials of both regions were called "overseers of foreign lands" and usually maintained their primary residences in Egypt proper. On the other hand, the manner in which they were integrated into the larger Egyptian bureaucracy and the structures that they oversaw differ in accordance with their context.

The Administration of Nubia

Nubia was the older and more established part of the empire. Although the New Kingdom marked the pinnacle of Egyptian domination of the region, that dominance began in the Middle Kingdom. The Eighteenth Dynasty kings merely reasserted control over a region that had previously been securely within Egypt's grasp.

This long history of contact and domination shaped the administrative structure of the territory. Egyptian colonial officials predominated, replacing most local political structures. The top official was the "king's son of Kush," commonly known in English as the "viceroy." Both he and the "host commander of Kush" (the chief military officer in Nubia) bore the additional title "overseer of southern (foreign) lands."[109]

Most scholars take it for granted that the viceroy reported directly to the king. S. T. Smith, however, suggests that "the Viceroy was ultimately under the authority of the Vizier."[110] He goes on to propose that the viceroy had close connections to the treasury. In his tomb, Huy, viceroy under Tutankhamen, depicts himself receiving his office from the overseer of the treasury, not directly from the king. In the same scene, the vizier receives the tribute from the foreign lands on behalf of the king.[111] The implication is that the viceroy reported to the overseer of the treasury and, through him, to the vizier.

Tantalizing as it may be, this evidence derives from the late Eighteenth Dynasty. Even if Smith's analysis is correct, there is no comparable evidence from the Twentieth Dynasty. It is equally possible that the case of Huy marks the exception rather than the rule. In fact, if the imperial administration did fall within the responsibilities of the vizierate, we would expect to find some other indications of vizieral involvement in the empire. The complete absence of such evidence suggests that, under normal circumstances, the imperial administration stood apart from the vizierate and reported directly to the king. This interpretation is reflected in figure 3.6.

To a large extent, the internal Egyptian bureaucracy was replicated in Nubia. The territory was divided into two administrative regions—Wawat

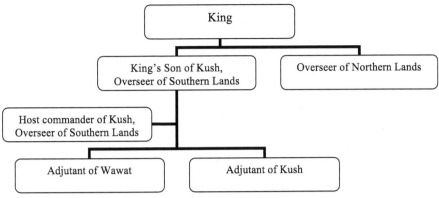

Fig. 3.6. Structure of the imperial administration

(northern Nubia) and Kush (southern Nubia)—paralleling the division of Egypt into Upper and Lower Egypt. The viceroy was assisted by two adjutants (*idnw*), one for each region. The adjutant of Wawat governed from Aniba, and the adjutant of Kush governed from Amara West (see fig. 3.6).[112] In each of these regions, we find the standard administrative personnel, such as overseers of the treasury, overseers of the cattle, mayors, and so on.

There is some evidence to suggest that the southernmost provinces of Upper Egypt were incorporated into the Nubian administration. Smith cites several texts that establish the northern boundary of Nubia at Nekhen (el-Kab).[113] Following Säve-Söderbergh, Smith links this realignment to the "consolidat[ion of] gold mining operations in Egypt and Nubia."[114]

In the earlier part of the New Kingdom, the viceroys were closely associated with Thebes. At least five Eighteenth Dynasty viceroys were buried in Thebes, as were two Ramesside viceroys. Seni, who was viceroy during the reign of Thutmose I, not only chose Thebes as the site of his tomb but also bore two titles that link him closely with that city: mayor of Thebes and overseer of the granary of Amun.[115]

The reign of Siptah marked a sharp break with the past, as a Bubastide family rose to the position of viceroy. Hori son of Kama was appointed viceroy in year 6 of Siptah and survived the change of dynasties, continuing in office well into the Twentieth Dynasty. His son, also named Hori, succeeded him, serving as viceroy under Ramesses III and IV. These viceroys had no known links to Thebes and apparently established their residence in Buhen.[116]

We are able to trace the outline of the first Hori's career. He began his career in the chariotry. Then, in year 3 of Siptah, he was sent to Nubia as a royal envoy (*wpwty nsw*). Since there are no fixed duties associated with the role of royal envoy,[117] we have no way of reconstructing his assignment. Nevertheless, he must have served with distinction, because he was appointed viceroy three years later.

A lintel from Buhen bearing the name of Hori son of Kama and the cartouches of Ramesses III indicates that his career lasted into the reign of Ramesses III. On the lintel, Hori is called the mayor (*ḥȝty ʿ*) of Buhen, as well as viceroy and overseer of southern lands. He also bears the honorific titles "royal scribe" and "fanbearer on the right hand of the king."[118] Undoubtedly Hori administered Nubia from this house in Buhen.

By year 5, however, his son had succeeded him in office, according to a stela from Amara West dated to that year. On a second stela, dated year 11, the younger Hori is paired with the adjutant of Kush, Paser, as both kneel before the king.[119]

We know the names of two host commanders of Kush from the reign of Ramesses III, Bakenseth and "Binemwaset."[120] Although Bakenseth is known only from an undated graffito in the Southern Temple at Buhen, the relative order of the two is assured, since "Binemwaset" is named in the Harem Conspiracy trial at the end of the reign.[121]

Bakenseth must have led a varied and illustrious career spanning the military and the temple bureaucracy. According to his titles, he served as chief steward and chief overseer of cattle of the high priest of Amun-Re. His status markers include royal scribe and fanbearer on the right hand of the king.[122]

We know little about "Binemwaset" prior to the Harem Conspiracy, although we do know his fate: he was condemned to death for his role in the plot. In fact, his real identity has been obscured behind the pseudonym— *Binemwaset*, "Evil-in-Thebes"—that was given to him in the trial documents.[123] Grandet suggests that *Binemwaset* could be a reflex of *Khaemwaset*. About his family, we know only that his sister was one of the women of the harem. She was the one who recruited him for the ill-fated rebellion.[124]

The Administration of Syria-Palestine

The Levant was the younger part of the empire. Strong traditions of local governance continued despite the region's incorporation into the Egyptian orbit. Rather than replacing all those local rulers with Egyptian officials, the Egyptians developed a shared system of administration. The princes of the city-states were allowed to manage their own local affairs, so long as they remained loyal to Egypt and paid whatever taxes or tribute were levied on them.

The loyalty of the princes was assured because their sons were held "hostage" in Egypt; the boys were taken to Egypt to be educated in the royal court. This practice had two benefits for Egypt: the future city-state rulers were fully inculturated in the Egyptian language and customs, and their fathers dared not rebel, for fear of what would happen to their sons.

The Egyptian presence in the Levant was always quite limited. Small garrisons were posted on a permanent basis at only a few sites. One permanent post was located at Beth Shan, at the juncture of the Jezreel and Jordan valleys. It was ideally situated to guard the road north into Syria and to oversee the agricultural production of the rich Esdraelon Plain. Another permanent post was probably located at the end of the coastal road, at Gaza or Deir el-Balah. Garrisons might be temporarily assigned to other locations as the need arose but did not establish permanent bases there. Although Egypt clearly dominated the region, the physical presence of Egyptian officials was intermittent and primarily focused on discreet missions.

The overseer of northern lands was not a resident governor but a circuit official. He made periodic tours of the Levant, to remind the princes of their allegiance to Egypt, to settle disputes among the princes, and to collect their tribute. Confusion over the role of the overseers of northern lands has arisen because of the way in which their title was rendered in Akkadian. They are frequently referred to as governors (*šakin mati* in Akkadian). However, the Akkadian scribes were imprecise in their use of titles, interchanging the titles *šakin mati, rabisu* (commissioner), and *rabû* (great one) when referring to Egyptian officials, regardless of their role or rank.[125] Therefore the Akkadian terminology cannot be used to define the function of the Egyptian official.

Royal messengers (*wpwtyw nsw*) were dispatched to the Levant as needed. These officials varied greatly in rank and function. Some were mere emissaries delivering letters from the royal court, whereas others were true plenipotentiaries "empowered to conduct negotiations on behalf of the pharaoh."[126]

Income from Egypt's foreign possessions was often directed to the estates of the great temples. Documents from the reign of Ramesses III provide a unique glimpse into how this system operated. We know from Papyrus Harris I that the tax revenues of some Levantine cities were assigned to the temple of Amun at Karnak. The papyrus also describes the building in Canaan of a small temple belonging to the estate of Amun. Called the House of Ramesses III in PaCanaan, it housed a cult statue, known as Amun of Ramesses III, before which the people of the region presented their tribute (*inw*).[127] We ought not imagine anything on the order of the great processional temples of Karnak and

Luxor. This "house of religious mysteries" (*ḥwt št3t*) was probably little more than a modest chapel with extensive storehouses to receive the region's grain taxes.[128] From the small bowls bearing hieratic inscriptions found at multiple sites in southern Israel, we might infer that the delivery of the tax was accompanied by a ritual of presentation.[129] Although all of the texts are broken, they clearly record the date on which specific quantities of grain were delivered. At least one inscription uses the term "harvest tax" (*šmw*).[130] Perhaps each local prince presented a symbolic bowlful of grain to the temple priest while his servants unloaded the wagons at the storehouse. The inscribed bowls were not merely records of tax payment but a dedication of the land's produce to Amun.

Ramessesuserkhepesh is one of the few officials of the northern imperial administration known from the reign of Ramesses III. Ramessesuserkhepesh was the ranking official at Beth Shan in northern Israel, one of the few permanent garrison posts in Syria-Palestine. There he built a sturdy Egyptian-style house (house 1500) complete with inscribed doorways bearing his name and titles, as well as those of Ramesses III. From these inscriptions, we know that Ramessesuserkhepesh came from a well-connected family, being the son of Djehutymes, a host commander and overseer of foreign lands. Ramessesuserkhepesh himself bore the titles host commander, royal scribe, and chief steward.[131] Surprisingly, he is never termed "garrison commander," despite his role as the top administrator of a garrison city. His military rank was host commander, but his post in the imperial administration was chief steward. Perhaps the latter title was deemed a more accurate description of the wide-ranging managerial duties to which Ramessesuserkhepesh had to attend as the administrator of a settled post. He must have functioned like the steward of an estate, overseeing agricultural production, artisan's workshops, and building projects, as well as monitoring the security of the region. His reports back to the imperial court would have included both administrative records (production, disbursements, tax collection, personnel matters) and intelligence regarding the local princes, traffic (diplomatic and/or trade), and other potential security concerns.

CONCLUSION

The preceding analysis of the Egyptian administrative structure has revealed a number of key principles governing the organization and function of government under Ramesses III. These principles were informed by the cultural, geographic, and historical context. Thus it is not surprising that they differ substantively from modern Western public administration.

Despite an ideology of absolute royal power, we have seen many examples of how administrative functions were allowed to devolve to local officials. As long as the king could maintain the fiction of absolute authority and control, he was content to allow local systems to function. The king "appointed" sons to the offices they inherited from their fathers. He provided for the support of the institutions of state through gifts of endowment, which allowed those institutions to function largely autonomously. Officials of the central government intervened only sporadically in local affairs—to inspect, to adjudicate a dispute, or otherwise to ensure the interests of the state.

The genius of this system was the limited cost of administration. The Egyptians consistently expended no more effort or resources than necessary to run the government. They maintained order. They collected taxes. They conscripted labor and materials for royal projects. But they did not waste resources maintaining tight centralized control over a far-flung empire. When they "wasted" resources, it was on lavish displays of power like palaces, temples, and tombs, not on micromanagement.

Notes

1. See Boorn (1988).

2. See Erichsen (1933); Grandet (1994).

3. See Gardiner (1948).

4. See *RAD* 45–58.

5. See *KRI* V.350–60.

6. See *KRI* V.360–61.

7. See *KRI* V.361–63.

8. Cruz-Uribe (1994).

9. Such interplay between formal structures and informal personal relationships is typical not only of Egypt and the ancient Near East but of many societies. See Gibson (1987).

10. Grandet (1993) 77–79.

11. Logan (2000) 71.

12. P. Harris I.2–56.

13. P. Harris I.58–60.

14. *KRI* V.117–18; translation after Haring (1997) 46–47.

15. *KRI* V.74; translation after Haring (1997) 49.

16. *KRI* V.343–44; translation after Breasted (1906) §147.

17. *KRI* I.65–70; translation after Lichtheim (1976) 55.

18. Eyre (1994a) 110.

19. Ibid., 126–27.

20. Megally (1975).

21. In the scholarly literature, these crews are often referred to as "gangs," a word that carries negative connotations not appropriate to the ancient Egyptian context.

22. Steinmann (1984) 35–37; Eyre (1987a) 173.

23. Eyre (1987a) 185–86.

24. Megally (1977) 274–78.

25. Steinmann (1984).

26. Neither "The Duties of the Vizier" nor any other text from the period contains any suggestion that other officials regularly participated in these daily briefings. Although they may occasionally have been summoned into the royal presence, their access to the king was quite restricted.

27. For a more detailed discussion of this function of the vizier as described in "The Duties of the Vizier," see Boorn (1988) 312–14.

28. *LÄ* VI.133.

29. P. Bologna 1094.5.8–7.1; LEM 5–6.

30. *RAD* 54.1–3.

31. Lorton (1995) 355.

32. *LÄ* II.538.

33. McDowell (1990) 165.

34. Ibid., 163.

35. *KRI* V.350.11–16.

36. P. Abbott.

37. *LÄ* III.2.

38. *KRI* V.4.14.

39. *LÄ* VI.134.

40. *RAD* 15.5.

41. O. Berlin 10633.

42. Helck (1958) 331.

43. P. Harris I.59.11.

44. *LÄ* VI.133–34.

45. Grandet (1993) 91.

46. Helck (1958) 25.

47. This title is variously translated in the literature. Other common translations include "treasurer," "overseer of the seal," and "overseer of the treasury." The last creates confusion because it is identical to the accepted translation of *mr pr ḥd*.

48. Boorn (1988) 311.

49. Helck (1958) 78–81.

50. Ibid., 81–82.

51. Grandet (1993) 94.

52. Schulman (1976) 123.

53. Caminos (1954) 117.

54. E.g., *KRI* V.33.1: "Spoken by his majesty to the royal princes, the officials, the royal butlers, and the charioteers . . ."

55. Wreszinski (1923) I.295–97.

56. Helck (1958) 272.

57. Ibid., 275.

58. Redford (2002) 11, 23–25.

59. Schulman (1976) 123; see *KRI* II.84 and 133.

60. Grandet (1993) 85.

61. Schulman (1976) 123.

62. *KRI* V.392.

63. *KRI* VI.83–84.

64. Schulman (1976) 124–25.

65. Helck (1958) 381–83.

66. Ibid., 382.

67. Ibid., 262–63.

68. The execration of the conspirators by rechristening them with condemnatory pseudonyms was part of their punishment.

69. *KRI* V.352–59.

70. Eyre (1999a) 44.

71. P. Valençay 1.

72. Helck (1958) 182–83.

73. Eyre (1987a) 195.

74. *KRI* III.44; translation after Kitchen (1982a) 196.

75. During the Ptolemaic period, this title was rendered *prophetes* in Greek. English-speaking scholars adopted the translation "prophet" from the Greek.

76. In scholarly literature, the first god's servant is often referred to as "high priest."

77. The genealogies of these three families are studied extensively in Bierbrier (1975a) 2–18.

78. *KRI* V.505–6.

79. *LÄ* II.1244–46.

80. Seele (1959) 5–9.

81. Ibid., 7.

82. Ramessesnakht's father bore the title "overseer of the god's servants of all the gods of Hermopolis." See Bierbrier (1975a) 11.

83. *KRI* V.368.16.

84. *KRI* V.375.9–10.

85. Haring (1997) 1.

86. Eyre (1987a) 187–88.

87. P. Lansing r. 9.7–8. See Schulman (1964) 108.

88. See Schulman (1964) 41–44 for a discussion of this title.

89. Ibid., 26–27.

90. Ibid., 28.

91. Ibid., 26–30, 85.

92. *KRI* V.394.

93. Schulman (1964) 35.

94. Ibid., 65.

95. Ibid., 30–33, 85.

96. For the relative ranks of the military scribes, see ibid., 82–86.

97. For the relative ranks of the commander of a host and the adjutant of the army, see ibid.

98. *KRI* V.373.6.

99. *KRI* V.368.9.

100. *KRI* V.374.3.

101. *KRI* V.375.7.

102. *KRI* V.369.15.

103. *KRI* V.375.3.

104. *KRI* V.375.5.

105. Schulman (1964) 86.

106. Ibid., 13, 154.

107. After ibid., 111.

108. Grandet (1993) 74.

109. Säve-Söderbergh and Troy (1991) 6–7.

110. Smith (1995) 183.

111. Davies (1926) pl. VI, cited in Smith (1995) 183.

112. Grandet (1993) 26.

113. Smith (1995) 181–83.

114. Ibid., 183.

115. Ibid., 180.

116. *LÄ* III.635.

117. The royal envoy was a plenipotentiary of the king and might be entrusted with any of a variety of missions; see below and Vallogia (1976).

118. *KRI* V.381.

119. *KRI* V.381–82.

120. Grandet (1993) 75.

121. *KRI* V.352.

122. *KRI* V.383.14–15.

123. The execration of the conspirators by rechristening them with condemnatory pseudonyms was part of their punishment.

124. Grandet (1993) 333.

125. Higginbotham (2000) 43.

126. Ibid., 137.

127. P. Harris I.9:3.

128. Higginbotham (2000) 57.

129. Ibid., 63.

130. Tufnell (1958) 133–34.

131. James (1966) 161–73.

Chapter 4

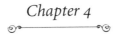

Society, Economy, and Administrative Process in Late Ramesside Egypt

CHRISTOPHER J. EYRE

INTRODUCTION: LEGITIMACY AND RULING FAMILY

The reign of Ramesses III began, if his own statements are to be believed, in social and administrative chaos, resolved when Amon chose him and his father as the founders of a new dynasty:

> He chose whom he found among hundreds of thousands.
> I am established on his throne satisfactorily (*ḥr ḥtpw*).
> Egypt had been dispersed, without a shepherd.
> They were under the plague of the 9 bows.
> I (re)assembled them, and (re)established them by my active arm.
> I am risen like Re as king over Egypt.[1]

Ramesses III then drove out the foreigners who had conspired against Egypt.

The rise of the new dynasty is explained partly as a reunification. The gods appointed first Sethnakhte, their son, as ruler,[2] and then Ramesses as heir apparent: "*rpˁt* in the place of Geb, to be the Great Chief (*ḥri ˁ3*) of the lands of Egypt, in every task (*sḥn*) of the entire land united together."[3] This chaos was not merely the consequence of dynastic competition for the throne and resulting civil war. The Elephantine stela of Sethnakhte describes the underlying situation.[4] The enemy is specifically foreign: when driven out, "they left the silver, gold [and] ... of Egypt, which they had given to those Asiatics (*nn n stt*) to seek for them champions (*nḥtw*) [... the bor]ders of ([... *t3]šw*) of Egypt."[5] The general tenor of the complaint is clear. Papyrus Harris I similarly describes the land in disarray, every man for himself. Local rulers were in control. There was public and divine disorder, and the gods' offerings were not made.[6] More specifically, "the Libu and Meshwesh had been settled (*sndm*) in Egypt, having seized the towns of the western margin (*rwd*) from Memphis (*Ḥwt-k3-Ptḥ*) to Qarbana. They had reached the great river, along all its bank. It was they who had wrecked(? *fḫ*) the towns of Xois during the many years they were in Egypt."[7]

Although the immediate context of these texts is that of military action—the Libyan and Sea Peoples wars of the early years of Ramesses' reign—they seem to reflect a wider background of long-term ecological change and the resulting continuous pressure of immigration on the western margins.[8] The string of forts that Ramesses II had built there seem to have been designed to control wells and pasturage, and so the movement of herds, rather than simply to act as a fortified borderline.[9] The situation described by Papyrus Harris I is not a sudden invasion, but a long-term chronic conflict between immigrant pastoralists and the settled towns and villages of the Western Delta. It is impossible to quantify in detail the socioeconomic effects of these long-term processes. The major military campaigns of years 5, 8, and 11 are presented by Ramesses as responses to specific crises, and as individual incidents in a policy to take and maintain firm central control in the hands of the crown, but they point in reality to significant economic and demographic crises in the parts of the country affected, and to changes in sociopolitical structures—to a general "militarization" of society as a whole—mediated by a local search for security and by a government struggle to maintain sociopolitical order and central authority. Both the stela of Sethnakhte and Papyrus Harris I imply that control of provincial magnates—ethnically diverse—was a major issue for central government.

The real background to the new regime lay in military force, even if no clear territorial or military unit can be identified as the power base of the new dynastic family. The claim to legitimacy of Sethnakhte and Ramesses III as kings lay, however, in their choice by Amon. Ramesses III claims to have been chosen as a child by Amon: he was Amon's choice as founder of the dynasty. Identified with Re, he performed the will of god.[10] Indeed, the wording of the Elephantine stela of Sethnakhte implies oracular approval: "[Then] all the gods and goddesses appeared (*ḫʿi*), that they might give signs biA for the Good God in predicting (*sr*)" that his enemies would be defeated.[11] A stela of Ramesses III from Edfu records a specific oracle: the appearance (*ḫʿi*) of Amon-Re "to predict (*r sr*) the many benefits (*nfr*) of the great kingship of Pharaoh, his son, . . . to the gods, the Lords of Upper and Lower Egypt and to the people of the entire land of Egypt." They are told to "cause to rejoice the people of the districts (*kʿḥ*) which you are in."[12] The concern with provincial attitudes again seems marked. The ideology of these oracles is not new: the motif of specific divine choice—divine birth—and quasi-oracular approval is particularly familiar, for instance, from the reigns of Tuthmosis III and Hatshepsut.[13] There is, however, a change in emphasis, and the motif of the oracle takes a wider significance in the political and administrative process of the Twentieth Dynasty (see below).

Ideologically, the evidence for choice by god—the proof of legitimacy— was seen in events—in the success that Ramesses recounted in the self-justifying address to a public, characteristic of his reliefs and inscriptions at Medinet Habu and elsewhere. Papyrus Harris I itself stands as a self-justification to posterity, in a format that owes at least something to private tomb autobiography in its rationale.[14] The same motif of political self-justification seems explicit in the records of the Harem Conspiracy at the end of the reign.[15]

The key political and ideological themes asserted at the foundation of the new dynasty are repetitive. A stela of Seti I dedicating the chapel he built for his father, Ramesses I, at Abydos[16] is striking in this respect. Chosen by god, Ramesses I (re)created order by his accession to the kingship of Re, although he exercised it so briefly before his death and his translation to his new function as a god in the other world. The inscription stresses the divinity of the person (*ḏt*) of these two kings. Yet as king, Ramesses I "made my family (*ʿbwt*) great in (public) opinion (*ibw*, "hearts")." He educated Seti as his assistant. Abroad, Seti led the army, securing the integrity of the borders, while in Egypt, he "organised [Ramesses'] kingship for him (*ṯs=j n=f nsyt=f*)." At his accession, Seti promoted the cult of his ancestors. He portrayed the mother and brother of Ramesses I in this chapel, and indeed displayed the whole family of Ramesses I to surround him on his monuments: in life, Seti "did not banish his family (*ʿbwt*) from my sight (*ḥr*)" but continued to provide for them at the royal table.

Key themes of the text are the choice by god and the family solidarity within which the continuity and function of kingship are asserted. There is stress on the value of monuments, and on the cult and imitation of kings of the past, but there is also a new emphasis on portrayal of the wider royal family, in processions of princes and princesses. There is also limited but direct reference to the approval of public opinion, and to extension of the fate (*š3y*) of the king through divine favor.

In two stelae from Abydos, Ramesses IV develops the themes of legitimacy and of apology for the regime of the Twentieth Dynasty. The smaller stela is a prayer to Osiris;[17] the larger addresses a wider group of gods, together and individually.[18] Unusually for royal inscriptions, these stelae mobilize the format of a "negative confession,"[19] in which a majority of the clauses relate to ritual conduct and behavior toward the gods. The theme of apology and self-justification is strong, but any possible reference to specific political events is too deeply coded in the text to define in more than general themes.[20] The smaller stela conventionally asserts that Ramesses has created order in his role as son of Osiris.[21] In the larger stela, he specifically asserts: "I am legitimate king (*ink ḥk3 n bs*). I do not usurp (*ḥwrꜥ*). I am in the place of my begetter";[22] "I do not oppose my father. I do not reject my mother";[23] "I do not attack a man on the seat of his father."[24] Toward the end, he calls on the gods for the proper succession: "Appoint my great office to my heirs—look the *bwt* of Your Majesties is *ḥ3kw-ib*."[25] So he called on Osiris in the shorter text: "Appoint my seed kings in the [land for ever]."[26] He ends by calling on Osiris to "double for me the long lifetime and the great kingship of King Usermaatre Setepenre"—Ramesses II—since he has done more for Osiris in four years of rule than Ramesses II did in his sixty-seven.[27] Osiris clearly did not believe him: his reign was cut short, and Osiris left Egypt with kings whose building was on a miserable scale—the definition of an intermediate period.

These texts give a clear focus to kingship as a family business, stressing solidarity in the royal family, in a way that is unlikely to represent simply piety but an important theme in control of the central political machine for both these two dynasties. In both cases this seems also to be followed by political uncertainty in the aftermath of the dominant long-reigned kings Ramesses II and Ramesses III. To judge from the names known for children of Ramesses II, the family was huge, but the role and importance of the family and descendants of Ramesses II in the later Ramesside period is wholly obscure.

Ramesses III clearly mimicked his predecessor in adding the procession of princes to the decoration of his temple at Medinet Habu, but names were not added to this list until after his death, in the reigns of his successors. The evidence for the detailed family relationships at the court of Ramesses III and the order of succession is incomplete, and reexaminations of the problem characteristically have to rely on speculative hypotheses.[28] The procession shows ten named princes: it need not be complete, and it certainly includes princes who died during the reign and were buried in the Valley of the Kings. It is, however, noticeable that those princes who did come to the throne all bear high military titles: Ramesses IV as great overseer of the army; Ramesses VI and VIII both as great overseer of horse. Two other princes, Paraherwene-mef and Montuherkhepeshef, are both great first charioteer of his majesty. Only Ramesses-Meryatum, as great chief of seers, and Ramesses Khaemwase, as *setem*-priest of Ptah, carry priestly titles, implying family control of the temple at Memphis; and both these princes probably died young. The roles of these princes again mimics that of the sons of Ramesses II, but strongly emphasizes the importance to the succession of the control of the army—the militarization of the kingship, the military focus of royal policy, and possibly a political focus on Memphis. The struggle for power at the end of the reign of Ramesses III remains obscure: was it a purely personal rivalry within the royal house, or does it reflect a more complex political and military conflict within the ruling elite? The mere fact that any sort of record survives—of the struggle itself and the trials of the Harem Conspiracy—may imply that it left Ramesses IV politically damaged, despite his apparent ambition for good and effective government.

THE PROCESS OF GOVERNMENT AND THE PROBLEM OF EVIDENCE

The prime duty of kingship is security: external, internal, and cosmic. The royal ideology of the New Kingdom—its presentation of the role of the king—does not draw clear lines between these notions of security, whether in government, in warfare, or in ritual. It does not, therefore, stray often into the practical politics of how the king performed his functions. For Egypt, the rel-atively rich collection of individual events known for the Ramesside period can easily lead to excessive interpretation, appearing to provide a thorough structural and apparently coherent narrative. The problem is one of distin-guishing cause and effect from mere contemporaneity: the contexts in which things happened. Native Egyptian visions of history—call it "ideology"—en-visaged narrative history as cyclical rather than linear-evolutionary. Kings are trying, in their assertions of policy, to repeat the cycle in a better way (and therefore sometimes explicitly in a historically new way) but not to define events as a continuous historical evolution of new cause as the reason for new effect.

In practice, the proof of an effective central regime in Egypt is always the existence of a substantial monumental record, and the absence of such record is an indication of an economically weak regime. But this provides a very limited sort of evidence. The central epistemological problem for Egyptology is whether differences in the preserved data represent real change or merely changes of emphasis, whether they genuinely document variations in social order, and in particular variations in bureaucratic process and the penetration of the central government into local administration. The real issues here are the extent to which a central bureaucracy was ever efficiently in control of Egypt—that is, fully penetrating the provincial government of the country—and the practical interchange between government and people in the functioning of society and economy.[29] Who actually exercised authority, and how? And how did an apparently effective central government in the earlier New Kingdom collapse into a fragmented, effectively independent local and regional government in the reign of Ramesses III and its aftermath? Put another way, how governable was Egypt, both in general and in the Ramesside period specifically? This is the problem of history as process, and not as structure or simple narrative. Also at issue is why people recorded what they did, which poses questions that are largely matters of process.

Discussion here has to focus on Thebes, because the data amenable for the argument is almost entirely Theban. The preserved monumental and inscriptional record is mostly Theban, as is the documentary record: the papyrus archives from Medinet Habu and the documents from Deir el-Medina. Although these make up a very substantial and varied body of texts, they give an uneven and incomplete picture, even of the texts written at that date. As a result, the socioeconomic history for the period is largely one of the local concerns of the West Bank at Thebes, and of the separation of Upper Egypt from central authority. In fact, the importance of Luxor as burial place of high officials of the central state in the Eighteenth Dynasty, and so as source of information for the central regime, is probably a mixture of the religious significance of the site and the Theban origin of many of the leading families.[30] The Theban necropolis of the Twentieth Dynasty belongs to local officials: the highest officers of the central regime, like the ruling family, had different origins. Memphis is the presumed burial site for the court of Ramesses III[31] and his successors, but Memphis is not well documented from the period, since relatively little is known of the Twentieth Dynasty necropolis at Saqqara. Memphis was doubtless already the main royal residence and administrative center, even at that date. The royal residence of the later Ramesside monarchs is assumed to be either Memphis or possibly Per-Ramesses.

DEMOGRAPHY AND ECOLOGY

There is no specific evidence for significant failure of the inundation in the Ramesside period, to provide a cause for the economic failings. Butzer's analysis of historical lake levels in central Africa implies that water flow down the White Nile at least dropped at this date from the extraordinarily high levels of the Middle Kingdom to a more typical long-term norm, but hard data for the New Kingdom proper is very sparse, and dating of this medium-term variation is uncertain.[32] Probably a decline in rainfalls led to gradual decline in Nile heights through the New Kingdom, in ways that were not critical in the long term for Nile-based cultivation in Egypt proper but that were disastrous for pastoral populations in Libya and extremely difficult in Lower Nubia. Occasional graffiti from the Theban West Bank give dates for the peak of the inundation,[33] showing the interest of the tomb workers, but provide no detailed comment about the actual height. In contrast, a Nile height recorded at Medinet Habu in year 7 of Ramesses IX appears to represent a freak high Nile.[34] The royal cities of the Eastern Delta do seem, however, to have been hit by ecological crisis, with movement in the course of the Nile tributary that fed them and their hinterland, leading to a transfer of government function and also presumably of population to Tanis at the end of the period.[35]

The Egyptian record stresses foreign intervention as the cause of disorder,[36] and the context of the mass immigration is evidently long-term ecological pressure in Libya and more widely throughout the Near East. The inscriptions of Merenptah stress starvation and the hunt for food as motivation for Libyan invasion in his reign.[37] In principle, a long-term ecological decline in Libya—presumably a sign of poor rainfall exacerbated by overgrazing—need not be reflected in disastrous inundations in Egypt. A continuous movement into the Nile Valley by pastoralist groups from the Western Desert (consequent on decline in pasture available to them) and their incursions onto grain fields provides sufficient explanation for a collapse in productivity and depopulation in the north of Egypt. Papyrus Harris I implies that Memphis itself was under Libyan pressure (see above), and later it was clearly in a region dominated by districts of immigrant population. It is impossible to assess the level of farming and population stability in the Delta and Memphite regions, but the picture is likely to be one where only a strong local power base could provide any social security against pressure from encroachment by pastoralists, with their strong tribal loyalties and organization. The settled farmer has little defense against even small herds if their owners are both violent and persistent.

This theme of social disorder caused by foreign intervention and resolved by the new regime is a literary and ideological commonplace, but it is also a key policy statement. The wider socioeconomic context is seen in the formal establishment of ethnically distinct immigrant populations in the Delta and at least northern Middle Egypt. In dealing with defeated Sea Peoples, Ramesses "settled (*šnty*) them in strongholds (*nḫtw*), subdued in my name; their young were as numerous as tadpoles. I salaried (*ḥtr*) them all with clothing and grain rations from the Treasuries and Granaries annually."[38] In the same way, in pacifying Libyan ethnic groups, he brought those not killed "as plunder, many, bound like birds, in front of my horses; their women and children in tens of thousands, and their flocks in number like tadpoles. I established (*grg*) their leaders (*ḥꜥwty*) in strongholds (*nḫtw*) in my name; I gave to them great chiefs of bowmen of the tribes, branded and made as slaves stamped with my name, their women and the children likewise, and I presented their flocks to the House of Amon, made for him as herds for ever."[39] The policy is forced settlement and conversion to a sedentary population.

The establishment of immigrant settlements—formally defined as "prisoners," whatever the reality of their immigration—is a recurring theme in Egyptian history from the earliest periods, providing the personnel necessary for internal colonization and agricultural development or for the resettlement of devastated areas. Yet the settlements of Ramesses III are characterized by real focus on a military imperative, seen both in his political address to the populace and in patterns of landholding. The reference to these ethnic settlements as *nḫtw*, "strongholds," rather than "towns" or "villages" emphasizes the military focus:[40] the word *nḫtw* is used, incidentally, in the Sethnakhte stela to refer to foreign "champions" attempting to control Egypt (see above). The security of the country is described in Papyrus Harris I:[41]

I made the entire land flourish with trees and plants(? *ꜣḫꜣḫ*). I caused the populace (*rḫyt*) to live (*ḥmsi*) in their shade. I ensured that the woman of Egypt went about where she wanted, with nobody else molesting her on the road. I caused the army and chariotry to rest (*ḥmsi*) in my time—the Sherden, Qeheq in their towns (*dmi*), lying on their backs, unperturbed, without Nubian conflict, nor Syrian war—their bows and equipment put into storage.

In the reign of Ramesses V, the Wilbour Papyrus indicates that there was a significant military presence in the districts between Heracleopolis and Hermopolis, south of the Fayum. This is seen partly in place-names that imply military settlement[42] and partly in the high proportion of recorded land-holders with military or military-related function: most frequently stable master (*ḥry-iḥ*), soldier (*wˁw*), and Sherden—or their widows.[43] A peculiarly interesting example is seen in a stela from this region[44] that records the royal decree for delimitation of an area of endowment land (*ḥnk*)—both "rental" land (*ȝḥt ḳdby*)[45] and cattle pasturage—for a statue of Ramesses III, associated with the temple of Ramesses-Meryamon-beloved-of-his-army. This land was the possession of a chief of *thrw*-troops[46] of the stronghold (*nḫt*) of Ramesses-Meryamon-beloved-of-his-army, but was under the control of his wife and was hereditary, passing from son to son and heir to heir. A similar picture is found in the Adoption Papyrus of the reign of Ramesses XI, coming from the town of Sepermeru at the northern end of this district.[47] Both protagonists and witnesses here are stable masters and Sherden: landholders, military, and at least partly of foreign origin, they evidently formed a close group and were leading members of local society. These are districts where the floodplain is relatively wide and highly productive, but population levels are extremely sensitive to fluctuations in the security of the water regime, and they are historically areas where repeated cycles of agricultural development through (re)settlement and (re)colonization can be traced into the modern period.[48] While some of the local military settlements evidently go back to the beginning of the Eighteenth Dynasty, the characteristic presence of "stable masters" and the use of the ethnic term *Sherden* as the characteristic term for soldier-colonist imply clearly that such settlement was characteristic of the Ramesside period itself[49] and crucial to security in facing the Libyan and "Sea Peoples" threat. There is a striking emphasis here on the importance of pasturage—specifically land to support chariot horses. It is also significant that there is a strong presence of foreign names among the wine producers of the northern Egyptian countryside:[50] wine production was a characteristic use of development land. Immigrants from either Libya or Syria/Palestine would not naturally be ordinary arable farmers.

The most intriguing reference to this immigration and military settlement appears in a stela of Ramesses III dedicated to Meretseger at Deir el-Medina. Here the reference is to captive Libu and Meshwesh, brought to Egypt: "They were established (*iri*) in strongholds (*nḫtw*) of the victorious (*nḫt*) king, speaking Egyptian (literally "hearers of the speech of people") in following the king. He suppressed their speech, and reversed (?) their tongues."[51] Defeated Nubians are similarly spoken of as integrated into the Egyptian military. By the reign of Ramesses III, it seems clear that the important political power base lay with the military,[52] in which immigrants—both individually and as "tribal" groups—played a major part. But it is equally clear that immigration had significantly changed the demography of rural Egypt as a whole and not just that of a class of military elite.

The monuments of Ramesses III characteristically address a named audience, to whom the king speaks in self-justification as he celebrates his achievements. For instance, his "rhetorical" stela of year 12 from the north wing of the pylon at Medinet Habu addresses[53] the "magistrates, leaders of the army, the chariotry [. . .] land, who are in this land" (*srw ḥȝtyw n mš' nt-ḥtri* [. . .] *tȝ nty m tȝ pn*). Similarly, the "historical" section of Papyrus Harris I is in the format of a royal address, calling on an audience to listen:[54] "magistrates, leaders of the land, army, chariotry, Sherden, ordinary bowmen, all the soldiers(?) of the land of Egypt" (*srw ḥȝtyw nw tȝ mš' nt-ḥtri šrdnw pḏtyw 'šȝ 'nḥ nb nw tȝ n tȝ-mri*). While priests may be included in such address, when the context is that of a specific temple endowment, it is evident that the brokerage of power—the audience to be addressed—lay in the control of military force, both at the beginning and the end of the reign. The success of Sethnakhte is defined in the second year of his reign, in the public address to the king that ends his Elephantine stela: "One said to His Majesty, l.p.h., 'Your heart is joyful, Lord of this land! What god predicted has happened. Your enemies, they are no longer on earth, while there is no force (*pḥty*) of army or chariotry apart from (that of) your father. All temples are open.'"[55]

THE SIZE OF THE ECONOMY AND TEMPLE ENDOWMENTS

Quantification of the economy of Ramesside Egypt as a whole is surprisingly difficult, in light of the extensive documentation and the apparent abundance of detailed figures.[56] The proportion and distribution of immigrant population in Egypt are impossible to quantify in detail.[57] The accounts of the First Libyan War show five heaps of trophies of the dead, with figures ranging from 12,535 to 12,759,[58] and depict four files of presentation, each "1,000 men, 3,000 hands, 3,000 phalli."[59] Perhaps this represents overall totals of roughly 4,000 live and 12,000 dead in the campaign. Figures given for the Second Libyan War add up to 2,175 dead, 2,052 prisoners, and 42,721 captured animals—not huge numbers, with an interesting ratio of approximately ten animals to each Libyan or twenty animals to each captive Libyan. The inscriptions of Ramesses III do not preserve figures for his other campaigns.

Any global assessment of the size of the economy begins in evaluation of the temple economies, particularly in the figures given in Papyrus Harris I for donations made by Ramesses III to the temples as a whole,[60] and in the

Wilbour Papyrus for the revenue incomes administered by the Amon temple in Middle Egypt in the reign of Ramesses V. For Papyrus Harris I, the key question is what the endowments represent: completely new endowment additional to earlier temple holdings, or a process of endowment renewal, mixing old and new. For the Wilbour Papyrus, the key question is the proportion of cultivated land in Middle Egypt that the figures cover. The central nomes of Middle Egypt provide opportunities for expanded productivity in periods of good Niles, but they seem to suffer correspondingly severely when Niles are low,[61] and their weighting in the economy as a whole is correspondingly difficult to assess.

Despite the apparent bureaucratization of economic data and processes, the question also arises of the reliability and idealization of figures. Ostracon Gardiner 86,[62] dating to year 24 of Ramesses II, is a model letter reporting on the income of the Temple of Amon from its endowments in northern Egypt—from the entire Delta and (although the text is broken) probably the northern part of the Nile Valley proper.[63] As such, it provides the basis for some detailed comparisons. The text lists 8,750 cultivators producing two hundred *khar* of grain a man—apparently a standard assessment or expectation of endowment productivity[64]—but it lists much higher numbers of herdsmen (for cattle, sheep/goats, and donkeys) and of men dealing with birds and fish. Although many of the figures are lost, those surviving pose serious questions. Cowherds are each said to be in charge of 500 animals; nearly 4,000 donkey men each control 870 animals, while 22,350 men are each said to be in charge of 34,230 birds. The balance of production between arable farming, on the one side, and herding, fishing, fowling, salt production, and exploitation of reed and papyrus beds, on the other, may be plausible for the north of the country, but the specific figures are questionable. Herds of 500 cattle or 870 donkeys are immense, and nearly 35,000 birds are beyond the ability of a single man to control. While it is possible to envisage the production quotas as in some sense contracted out, with the individual responsible for providing or administering necessary additional labor, the figures are evidently idealized and rounded.

Kitchen compares these figures for gross annual income of grain at 1,752,000 *khar*[65] against the figures given in Papyrus Harris I[66] of 2,981,674 *khar* over thirty-one years—96,183 anually—as donation to the Karnak Temples. When this is added to the gross income of Ramesses new foundations (the temple of Medinet Habu and his other minor Theban temples), quoted at 309,950 *khar* a year from the whole of Egypt,[67] Kitchen estimates the figures to represent an additional endowment of around 10 percent.[68]

That figure makes no allowance, however, for restoration of endowments or possible transfers or lapses of endowment within the overall system with transfers of land and personnel displaced by the wars. A realistic evaluation might be that the actual size of the overall temple endowment did not change greatly in the reign of Ramesses III, even if movements of personnel and the inhabitants of particular plots of land may have changed as the result of new settlements of immigrants following his wars.

Governmental success is defined by the statement that all the temples are open, their storerooms supplied and their cults performed: that is, the economic and ritual funding of the functioning of the temple is (re)assured.[69] While the actual state of the temple endowments at the beginning of Ramesses' reign is impossible to define, it is clear that an explicit focus on the health of the temple economies lay at the center of public policy, although actual building works were not extensive. The balance of endowment seen in Papyrus Harris I, almost all flowing to Medinet Habu, seems to reflect quite accurately the balance of building effort. Immense and impressive, that monument took the majority of the investment and virtually the entire new building effort.

While it is evident that the Karnak endowment remained strong, the specific endowments of other temples and the extent to which their endowment was maintained are not clear from the preserved data. The Turin Strike Papyrus shows other temples functioning on the West Bank of Thebes, although the degree of economic independence of these temples is questionable.[70] Kitchen made the telling observation that the addition of *bandeau* texts to standing monuments was characteristic of the reign of Ramesses IV but is not then attested again until the reign of Ramesses IX.[71] Royal concern for the renewal of endowment seems absent.

GOVERNMENT BY MISSION AND LOCAL POWER STRUCTURES

Typical of the focus on temple economies is an assertion to the gods in a stela from Karnak of year 20: "See, Pharaoh has sent out people (*rmṯ*) to examine (*šn*) the jobs (*sḫ[nw]*) . . . your temples in respect of divine offerings, treasuries, granaries, workshops (*šnꜥw*), poultry yards, all valuable tasks (*zḫn*) which Pharaoh has done for you."[72] This particular stela provides a listing and key summary—on a smaller scale and in less detail than Papyrus Harris I—of the endowment and economic health of the temples.[73] In return, his prayer to Amon requests health, long life, and successful reign, and also asks the god to "cause that the needs of great inundations are satisfied in the [land]."[74] It is characteristic that such texts focus on restoring "temples which had been in decay (*w3s*)"[75] and on reactivating their economic structures, not on new buildings as such.

The policy of grand inventory and reestablishment of temple economies is most explicitly demonstrated in a royal command for a thoroughgoing restoration of order through reestablishment of temple organization, issued in year 5 and followed up in the succeeding years.[76] Incidental evidence is found in the records of inspections made in a number of Upper Egyptian temples in year 15 by the "Chief Archivist (*ḥry s3wty z3*) Penpato of the Treasury of Pharaoh," specifically based on action initiated by the decree of year 5.[77] His task was, explicitly, to inspect (*sip*) the temples between Memphis and Elephantine,[78] but mention is also made of the temples of the Delta,[79] and the prime focus is on the temple treasuries, granaries, and offering provision. This general inventory parallels one initiated in year 2 of Merenptah.[80] In both cases, it is possible to envisage a deliberate policy of reconsolidation in the aftermath and context of genuine economic disorder, but these inventories also represent, at least to a degree, a policy of visible and active government penetration into provincial economic centers. Neither Papyrus Harris I nor the later Ramesside land registers—most notably Papyrus Wilbour and Papyrus Reinhardt—provide, in any real sense, a Domesday Book to inventory the economic state of the country as a whole and so a government tool to control or administer it.[81] The temple sector did, however, provide one context in which royal investment is well attested and in which royal authority, if not constantly present, was formally, ideologically, and visibly asserted during the reign of Ramesses III.

In practice, military endowments must have taken a major part of state expenditure, even allowing for the extent to which "military" settlements of immigrant populations were classified as donations to a temple endowment.[82] The precise way in which temples were integrated in the local and state economies in the Ramesside period remains as obscure as the majority of the rural administration and the taxation regime.[83] What is clear, however, is that temples during the Twentieth Dynasty formed effective socioeconomic units—units of local government or administration parallel to the towns and villages of Egypt, acting as the instruments of resident local political authority. The temples evidently provided a stable reservoir of bureaucratic competence at the local level. There is not, in any simple sense, a clash between temple and state, although one might envisage a rivalry in Thebes in the late Twentieth Dynasty between priesthood, which was genuinely local in origin, and military authority, which was often of nonlocal origin. The issue is rather one of a clash between central and local authority in maintaining a process of stable government at a local level, involving the collection and administration of resources and the relationship between localities and political authority with wider claims and ambitions.

From the early New Kingdom, the text known as "The Duties of the Vizier" describes a situation in which local councils—resident local authorities—act in response to orders sent out by the vizier's office.[84] In reality and at all periods, the central government of Egypt consistently gives the impression of a sort of government by expedition—a relatively small central bureaucracy, acting through visitation to control local officials of, generally speaking, low prestige in the ranking system of the central state.[85] For most of Egypt in the early Twentieth Dynasty, there is little direct evidence. There are the negative comments of Papyrus Harris I (referred to above) that the country was under the control of local rulers.[86] There is also the obscure reference in that papyrus to the action of the king in placing the temple of Athribis under its priests and administrators, removing a vizier "who had entered among them" and taking away "all his people who had been with him."[87] The reference is apparently to the demolition of a localized politico-economic power base.[88] Where extensive and detailed documentation does survive, however, in the Theban area, this picture of resident local administration based on a small group of powerful local families, with which the central administration interfered erratically and on the basis of occasional formal visitation, is highly characteristic of the whole of the Twentieth Dynasty. Despite the fact that Medinet Habu appears to have been the main building project and greatest beneficiary of royal endowment, the king and his court can at best only rarely have visited Luxor,[89] and government bureaucratic presence in the city was local and regional, not national.

DEIR EL-MEDINA AND THE ADMINISTRATION OF THE TOMB

The documentation from Thebes refers firstly to the administration of the royal necropolis, "the Tomb." The basic organization and administrative processes of the Tomb are documented in considerable detail and reasonably well understood.[90] This was a royal project, under the direct personal authority of the vizier, to whom the leaders of the workforce reported. The project existed purely and simply to excavate and decorate the tomb of the king—to quarry out the stone, then carve and paint the tomb walls. The skills required were those of quarrymen, sculptors, and painters. The men employed directly on this work—referred to as "the crew"—were housed, with their immediate dependent families, in their own village of Deir el-Medina, situated a short distance into the desert, outside the cultivable plain but accessible to their work in the Valley of the Kings. Possibly the original model was that of a military/quarrying expedition and work camp,[91] but the basic architecture of the village—with closely packed housing, probably multistoried, on an enclosed site—is evidently fairly typical of both rural villages in the floodplain and small urban communities. The social and administrative processes seen in this community can, with provisos, serve as a wider paradigm for the organization of Egyptian society. Egypt should in no way be envisaged as an open society: people lived in closely knit and focused communities, where family relations, residence, and profession were inextricably linked. This is fairly obvious for the vast majority of the farming population of village Egypt[92] but was characteristic also both within the smaller urban context, where focus on the service and administration of a temple or residence in a military colony places an emphasis on communal identity, and within larger urban contexts, such as Amarna, where focus lay on particular craft or professional functions.

The workmen of the crew were divided into two teams—the "left" and "right" sides—each with their own chief workman. These acted with "the scribe of the Tomb" as a group of three "leaders" with responsibility for the organization and control of the work and the workmen. The leading draftsman/painter was included as a fourth "leader" in the later Twentieth Dynasty. The chief workmen characteristically also had identifiable "deputies." This community functioned as a distinct and coherent social unit: their own "leaders" ran the work and acted as local headmen, providing external representation for the community in dealing with outside authorities and leading the village "council" to provide a self-contained local self-administration for purely internal matters. This can be regarded as typical for Egyptian village society.[93] Egyptian central authority preferred to work through local intermediaries, expecting them to take communal responsibility. The exercise of control from the center is characteristically energetic and traumatic at the moments of visitation but is for the most part loose, delegated, and wholly localized.

The core salaries of the crew were paid directly from the state treasury and granary. A generous grain wage was delivered at the end of each month: four *khar* of emmer and one and a half *khar* of barley per man, with five and a half *khar* of emmer and two *khar* of barley for each of the leaders.[94] With a *khar* measuring just under seventy-seven liters,[95] this represents four to five times the basic subsistence wage for a nuclear family. Edible oils were also supplied regularly. Clothing was issued at more irregular intervals, as were a wider range of more luxury foodstuffs, provided by the central state. A very limited quantity of offering reversions from the local temples formed a normal part of the endowment and deliveries made on a day-to-day basis to the "gatehouse" of Deir el-Medina;[96] these perhaps came in connection with the performance of royal cults in the local chapels, rather than formally as workmen's "wages."

Local produce was supplied by a separate group of men—"the staff" (*smdt*)—specially employed for the purpose, under the supervision of their own scribes, to supply the two sides of the crew. Fish, fresh vegetables, and firewood were delivered to weekly quotas by fishermen, gardeners, and woodcutters. Water carriers brought the necessary drinking water, apparently both to the work and to the village. Coppersmiths dealt with the tools of the workmen. Local potters provided necessary containers. These staff were not resident at Deir el-Medina, and they formed a marginal part of the community or a separate community, although their members visited the necropolis on a daily basis to make deliveries. Other necessary equipment for the work—metal for the tools, leather for baskets, material for lamp wicks, and oils to burn in the lamps—was supplied from the central state resources: responsibility for organizing their receipt and use fell entirely on the local administrators. A small number of local "guardians" controlled the "storehouse" in which equipment and supplies for the work were held, and a separate group of "gatekeepers" supervised the deliveries made to the village and carried some degree of responsibility for the deliveries made by the supply staff. A small group of "police" (*mdꜣy*) acted as watchmen and security guards in the necropolis. All these personnel were marginal to the community and never seem to have lived in the village of Deir el-Medina.

Despite the huge body of texts preserved from the administration of the Tomb in the Ramesside period, it is clear that this record is not fully representative and that the format of documents varied in detail[97] from scribe to scribe and (particularly later in the dynasty) under the pressure of changing security and work pressures. Ostraca diaries and aide-mémoires recording deliveries are typical of the village site of Deir el-Medina, as are records of the control of tools and supplies and the private archives of individual workmen. Ostraca work registers and aide-mémoires for the control and administration of the work, including use of lamp wicks, are typical of the Valley of the Kings. Few papyri survive from the earlier Twentieth Dynasty, but by the reign of Ramesses IX—presumably from about the date that the workmen moved residence from Deir el-Medina to Medinet Habu for security—a single more composite papyrus journal is characteristic of the record, reflecting change in organizational detail. Ostraca become very rare in the record after this date.

The administrative process documented for the early Ramesside period is one in which the local authorities control and record the daily work administration and the day-to-day arrivals of visitors or deliveries at the village. Visitors and deliveries came to the "gatehouse" (*p3 ḥtm*) of the Tomb, at or near the entrance to the village, where they were recorded by the gatekeeper and by two workmen, one from each side, taking turns on a daily watch rota. Wages were shared out here, under the supervision of the scribe and foremen, on days when there was no work: the ninth and tenth days of each ten-day week were typically rest days, as were a large number of festival days. Otherwise, urgent business required the dispatch of a messenger to the Valley of the Kings, where the scribe and foremen supervised the work, documented its progress, and kept the work registers. Written aide-mémoires—either inserted in the diaries or written as separate ostraca—provide more extended notes of events, both regular (e.g., details of grain distributions) and less predictable (e.g., outside visitors). External control lay formally with the vizier, to whom the officials reported. Surviving administrative letters on ostraca are largely anodyne and nonspecific in content—often apparently model letters for scribal training. It is not possible to tell whether full detailed accounts were normally written up and sent as reports to the vizier, but it seems unlikely. The vizier and other officials of the central state bureaucracy or royal household visited when appropriate.[98] Again it is impossible to tell whether they normally inspected the scribe's written accounts and diaries in any detail, but it seems unlikely. The overall picture is that of a highly delegated administration—a central administration that is essentially reactive and at arm's length, issuing commissions and checking on progress during highly fraught personal visits, carried out to check on good order and to hold local authority responsible for appropriate global performance.

The final decade of the reign of Ramesses III and the early years of Ramesses IV are particularly well attested in documents from the village of Deir el-Medina. This was the period of office of the scribe Amonnakhte son of Ipuy. Originally a draftsman/painter, Amonnakhte was the first of six generations who succeeded to the office of scribe, father to son, through into the Twenty-first Dynasty, when the organization of the Tomb disappears from the documents along with the abandonment of the Valley of the Kings.[99] In two graffiti, Amonnakhte records his appointment as "scribe of the Tomb" by the vizier To, on the occasion of a visit To made in year 16.[100] Amonnakhte seems to have felt the personal connection strongly. The vizier To was the key official for the workmen in the second half of the reign, the official of central government who was directly and personally responsible for their work, their discipline, and their payment. At issue here is the motif, whether realistic or not, of a quasi patron-client relationship between the local officials and the vizier—an assertion of personal relationship, loyalty, and access. A similar association is seen with other members of the community. For instance, the foreman Khonsu and the crewman Iierniuetef both depict To on their stelae from the Ptah and Meretseger sanctuary in the Valley of the Queens.[101] However, the association is most explicit in references made by the scribe Amonnakhte:[102] in his graffito recording his appointment and in the frequent addition of the name of To to his other graffiti.[103] He even named a son after To.[104]

In one case, Amonnakhte defines himself as "scribe of the Tomb Amonnakhte, under the charge of the vizier To."[105] This appears at the end of a note from year 25 recording "the deficit of the scribe Amonnakhte of the Tomb"— these were wood deliveries—next to a text dealing with vegetable deliveries. On the other side of the ostracon is the clichéd introduction to a letter from Amonnakhte to the vizier. More pointed, perhaps, is an ostracon with the "report" by Amonnakhte to the crew that on 2 *akhet* 21 of year 29, despite being twenty days into the month, no grain rations had been provided "to us." He then went to the temple of Horemheb and brought back forty-six *khar*, which he shared out on day 23. He concludes with the apparently disconnected note that "the vizier To was appointed vizier To of Upper and Lower Egypt."[106]

Ramesside viziers were not buried at Luxor: the exception is Paser, who appears to have been a man of Theban origin.[107] And despite the fact that there seem generally to have been two viziers at this period, nominally for Upper and Lower Egypt, there is no indication that a vizier was regularly present, much less resident at Luxor.[108] It is recorded as a particular disappointment in the Turin Strike Papyrus that To came to Luxor on 4 *peret* 28 of year 29—to collect the (statues of the) gods to participate in the Sed Festival[109]—but only sent a message by the hand of a chief of Medjay to the local chiefs waiting for him: "Now I haven't come to you for a reason. I haven't not come because there is not something to bring for you. As for your saying 'Do not take away (*nḥm*) our grain rations!' am I, the vizier, appointed to take away! Will I not give that which others like me have done? It happens that there is nothing in the granaries themselves, but I am giving you what I have found." And the scribe Hori of the Tomb said to them, "Half grain ration has been issued to you, and I am to distribute it to you." Hori was probably a scribe responsible for the service "staff" and presumably therefore the portage to the village.

Work on a royal tomb began early in a reign, and unless there were serious disruptions, the basic excavation of a tomb took no more than a few years. Tombs were neither extended indefinitely nor "completed" in advance; they were finished off rapidly following the king's death. By the middle of the reign of Ramesses III there can have been no serious pressure to work in the Valley of the Kings. The workmen were occupied at this period on tombs in the Valley of the Queens—documented by a significant number of ostraca from that site—but the central state seems to have shown little concern in general for their activities. Wage payments were coming in reasonably regularly, if often partially in deficit or delayed. Visits by outside officials were, however, rare at this date: there was simply no significant business.[110] The records then document a series of difficult events for the people of Deir el-Medina, beginning with a visit[111] on 3 *akhet* 18 of year 26 by the vizier To, about "the business [*n3 mdt*] of Penanqet." Interrogations followed on days 19–21, carried out by a commission including a scribe of the place of writings, Amenemope; the overseer of the treasury, Khaiemtore; the high priest Ramessesnakhte; the mayor of Thebes (not named); and two (unnamed) "soldiers of the garrison." On day 23, the vizier failed to arrive in "the Great Field"—the Valley of the Kings—where the crew waited for him, but on day 29, the crew were taken to "the riverbank" for further interrogation, in which the vizier joined on day 30. The implication of these events is that serious accusations of misbehavior had been made within the community, or at least that there was a serious security problem for the necropolis.[112]

A flood of activity in 1 *akhet* of year 28 is probably associated with the new plan laid on day 17 for the tomb of a prince.[113] However, on 2 *peret* 24 of that year, the chief of Medjay warned that "the enemy has descended":[114] the crew ceased work, waiting to see what would happen. Probably this represents a raid from the desert, in view of the endemic problems with Libyan raiders seen later in the dynasty, although other sources of civil disorder cannot be excluded.

In year 28, a sequence of references to chronic problems with grain supply to the village appears in the documents. An ostracon in Turin[115] provides a personal account of ration deficits from 4 *shemu* of year 28 until 2 *akhet* of year 29. It deals only with the emmer ration of 5.5 *khar* and so presumably belonged to one of the "leaders." Only twice in that period is full payment recorded. Generally payments fell about 0.75 *khar* short: the worst payments were in 2 *peret* of year 28, when only 1.5 *khar* was received, and in 1 *shemu* of year 29, when only 3 *khar* came in. The verso of this text continues from 3 *peret* of year 29 to 3 *shemu* of year 30, still with significant deficits: the worst month here was 4 *peret* of year 20, when only 2 *khar* were received. In 3 *shemu*, full rations were again paid. According to a final summary, each leader was in deficit by 22 *khar* over this two-year period, and each of the thirty-seven ordinary workmen was in deficit by 35 *khar*.

A medium-term deficit of less than a *khar* a month may have caused limited hardship for the leaders; for the ordinary workmen, an average loss of 1.5 *khar* from the 4 *khar* of emmer due each month might cause hardship but is not obviously an indication of serious famine. The payments made should have provided sufficient to eat. They are above minimum subsistence level. Even so, a socially disruptive uncertainty and a lower standard of living are marked, while erratic payments and a depletion of reserves will have threatened (and may have caused) periods of real hunger.[116] The low payment in 2 *peret* of year 28 coincides with the notice that "the enemy has descended." The month of 2 *akhet* of year 29 is missing in the Turin ostracon, but this was the date on which the account of the Turin Strike Papyrus begins: its scribe, Amonnakhte, "reported" on day 21 that no rations had been paid. He personally obtained 46 *khar* from the temple of Horemheb, which was issued to the crew on day 23. The share cannot have been more than a *khar* a man, an emergency measure.[117]

As a whole, the Turin Strike Papyrus does not fit readily into a standard format for recording the administrative process at Deir el-Medina.[118] Apparently written in the hand of the scribe Amonnakhte,[119] it is perhaps best understood as a semipersonal collection of reports intended to document his official conduct in the best possible light over this difficult period and to put the actions of other people in a correspondingly poor light.[120] Registers and appointment lists to the local service staff are included—even some records of the issue of grain rations and of vegetables, water, and fish—indicating that all possible efforts had been made to ensure the local supply chain. According to his own account, Amonnakhte consistently discouraged the workmen from direct action,[121] urging them to stay where they belong and not to put themselves in the wrong; his colleagues are sometimes said to advise direct action.[122] The "strike" texts characteristically record workmen acting on their own initiative to pass out of the necropolis area. Sometimes this was at night or at the "weekend," when they would not have been working anyway, but their actions have the general appearance of food riots. In his refusal to obey, one individual is specifically accused of words that appear to be blasphemy against the pharaoh.[123] The workmen demand food, either at one of the West Bank temples or at "the riverbank." Their primary channel was to approach local officials, asking them to address "Pharaoh our Lord" and "the vizier our

Chief, so that they will provide us with subsistence" (*iry=w n=n ꜥ-n-ꜥnḫ*).[124] Their aim was to bring pressure to bear on the local representatives of the chain of state administration.

Amonnakhte obtained some grain from the temple of Horemheb on 2 *akhet* 21–23.[125] In their demonstrations, the crew targeted the West Bank temples: Medinet Habu,[126] the temples of Tuthmosis III[127] and Seti I,[128] and especially the temple of Ramesses II.[129] On one occasion, the local official they found there—the *setem*-priest (?)[130]—went off to Luxor to report to the high priest of Amon and the mayor but refused to give them food from the divine offerings of Ramesses II: his action is glossed as "a great wrong."[131] Admittedly, offering reversions were delivered regularly from the Theban temples to Deir el-Medina, but these were not substantive wages. The crew here seem to be addressing local institutions that they believed had resources to feed them, when the state bureaucracy had failed them. It is noticeable that their complaints, in this and the following years, focus clearly on failures in the local provisions due from their own service staff (*smdt*) as well as their grain rations.[132] Despite the measures taken to employ sufficient people, recorded in the Turin Strike Papyrus, they were not providing the quotas of food required.

The final entry in the Turin Strike Papyrus falls on 1 *shemu* 25, the last day of the regnal year and presumably the natural end of an accounting or reporting period.[133] The difficulties over wage payments did not end, and the crew continued to react in the same way through the middle of the dynasty. At his accession, Ramesses IV significantly increased the size of the workforce at Deir el-Medina, where, to judge from the frequent mention of his name, he was personally well remembered.[134] The beginning of his reign seems to have been marked by an energy and political intention to reform and restore political order. His policy was marked by large building plans, to judge by the initial layout of his mortuary temple, which rivaled that of his father. But the medium-term effect was small. Supply problems continued at Deir el-Medina through his reign, and the number of men employed was cut soon after his death.[135]

The Turin Strike Papyrus also records that on 1 *shemu* 16 of year 29, the workman Penanqet made a complaint to the scribe Amonnakhte and the foreman Khonsu in their official roles as chiefs of the Tomb, making a series of formal accusations against two men and noting specifically the attitude formerly taken by the vizier Hori over similar accusations made against his father, the foreman Paneb.[136] He demanded to see what they would do and threatened to report directly to the pharaoh and the vizier. The accusations include tampering in some way with the tomb of Ramesses II. Paneb and his family do seem to have lost control of the post of foreman as the result of intervention by the vizier, late in the Nineteenth Dynasty; and in view of the investigation involving Penanqet, made by the vizier To in year 26, it would appear that he was bent on creating trouble for his chiefs.

The events of the Turin Strike Papyrus seem to characterize the sociopolitical situation in Luxor during the Twentieth Dynasty. Personal tensions and rivalries in such a close community are no great surprise, but their appearance so clearly in the record may be a symptom of a general lack of self-confidence and a degree of defensiveness in the local hierarchy. The ambiguous personal standing of Amonnakhte may be illustrated by the record of a theft of clothing in year 5 (probably of Ramesses IV).[137] A list of the houses in the village was read out to the oracle of Amenhotep, who identified the house of the scribe Amonnakhte and declared that the stolen clothes were in the possession of his daughter. In answer to Amonnakhte's direct question, the oracle affirmed that she had indeed taken the clothing. A record of this sort cannot be taken simply at face value. The procedure of the oracle, which involved the public observation of the movement of the statue of the god carried on the shoulders of its priests, might, at a crude level, be open to corrupt manipulation. More characteristically, it might be expected to reinforce public prejudice—that is, to provide and give authority to the expected answer. In general, the scribe and foremen at Deir el-Medina do not appear as litigants in the recorded transactions of the local "court," either as plaintiffs or defendants. As local headmen, they acted as core local mediators, without whom the local tribunal could not function. It was both inappropriate and impractical for them to litigate in this context: a complaint against them required the intervention of higher authority. The complaint of Penanqet, like the earlier complaints made by and against Paneb, addressed the vizier and required a focus on accusations of corruption and maladministration ("and he is not fit for this office")[138] and not simply to detail the personal claims and resentments that underlie these texts. The very fact that the oracle was used against the family of Amonnakhte reflects poorly on his local prestige and his personal standing in the community, to say nothing of the oracle's conclusion.

The documentary record from the Theban West Bank gives a very confused picture of political and social conditions through the middle of the Twentieth Dynasty. The leading families at Deir el-Medina retained their positions to the end of the dynasty, particularly the descendants of Amonnakhte in the office of scribe,[139] the family of Qaha as foremen of the left side,[140] and the descendants of Sennedjem on the right side (although there seems to be a break in their control of the office after the Tomb Robbery arrests of years 16 and 17 of Ramesses IX, in which family members were implicated).[141] Magnificent tombs were built at least for Ramesses IV, VI, and IX and even for Ramesses XI, but the numbers of workmen employed fluctuated widely, in a situation where wage payments remained erratic, and the order of succession the family relationships of the kings who employed them remain problematic.[142] It is not clear whether political conflict over the succession included outbreaks of actual violence in the Theban area, but it is clear that respect for the contemporary kings was diminished in a situation of deteriorating public order.

The particular historical importance of the documents from the royal necropolis lies in the way that the local concerns of these workmen reflect in microcosm the events and policies crucial to the government of the state: they provide insights into the role of the temple of Karnak, and both the clashes and the integration of the authority of its priesthood and administrators with those of the resident "state" officials and particularly the local "mayors." Often, indeed, they provide the only evidence in detail. Local crimes and concerns may not always provide an accurate reflection of wider national trends. To a considerable extent, the local picture of a constant and endemic concern about food supply in the Ramesside period, and of a central government that is distant, erratic, and inconsistent in its interventions, may simply reflect the normal political and economic realities of the Egyptian state. In this respect, the evidence may be insufficient to provide a satisfactory explanation of specific cause and effect within the historical narrative. Concern for food supply at Deir el-Medina—even hungry years—does not necessarily point to a developing natural crisis, ecological or agricultural. Evidence for particularly high values for grain are more likely to reflect local and temporary conditions than a general price inflation in the Ramesside period. Similarly, a change in the equivalent values of silver and gold for use in commercial transactions—a depreciation in the exchange valuation of silver—seems to predate the reign of Ramesses III, and its wider economic significance is quite obscure.[143] Individual cases of personal corruption do not necessarily point to a growing institutional and political crisis in government: these may simply document the ordinary concerns of ordinary Egyptians. They do, however, represent the documented picture of Upper Egypt in the late Twentieth Dynasty, and the mere fact that they are documented may reflect a defensive attitude and lack of political confidence in the local officials themselves.

RAMESSESNAKHTE AND THE FAMILY GOVERNMENT OF THEBES

The food crisis at the end of the reign of Ramesses III seems to mark a significant change in the relationship between the local priesthood and the administration of the Tomb. Mention of the high priest of Amon is unusual in their documents before that date, but the high priest Ramessesnakhte—attested in office from year 1 of Ramesses IV until early in the reign of Ramesses IX—appears quite frequently in connection with food supply, control of materials and equipment, and visiting the work to commission and control the workmen. Whatever the business, he now characteristically appears in the commissions of visiting officers of state: notably the vizier, overseers of the treasury and the granaries, and royal butlers, as well as the local mayor.[144] Most interesting is a figured ostracon from the Valley of the Kings that shows Ramessesnakhte dancing (?).[145] Such ostraca are essentially votive, made and placed there by the workmen, and such an object implies a personal interest, parallel to that commonly attested in their graffiti that add the name of a vizier to their own.[146] A process by which the local authority of Ramessesnakhte de facto encroached on the administration of the Tomb seems reasonably clear, if not without tensions and confusion. In the middle of the dynasty, the chiefs of workmen seem ambivalent about his authority—for instance, objecting that the recruitment of an assistant draftsman had been referred to him, when it was their business.[147] But with the removal of the workforce to Medinet Habu, probably early in the reign of Ramesses IX, the workmen were living on ground formally inside the "House of Amon"—that is, under the authority of the high priest.[148] Perhaps as important, they were living in the compound of a temple where the family of Ramessesnakhte had always been the leading administrators (see below). Yet still in year 3 of Ramesses X, the high priest—presumably Amenhotep at this date—denies formal responsibility for the wages of the workmen,[149] although he issues orders about whether they should go to work.[150]

A journal entry from 1 *peret* of year 1 (of Ramesses V or VI)[151] records the workforce "absent in the face of the enemy" (*p3 ḫrw*). On day 13, it notes the "arrival by the two chiefs of Medjay, saying 'The people who are enemies have come; they have reached Pernebyt—giving birth in the night by Menneferemheb[152]—they destroyed all that was there, and its people burnt.' So they said. The High Priest of Amon said to us, 'Bring the Medjay of Pernebyt with those who are in the south, and those of the Tomb, and have them stand here to watch the Tomb.'" This entry and page finish with a set of work measurements from a tomb (?), but the next preserved entry resumes with "the chief of Medjay Montumose, he said to the leaders of the Tomb, 'Don't go up (to work) until you see what will happen. I will run and look [for] you, and I will hear what they say. I am the one to come to tell you to go up (to work).'" The final preserved entry still has them "absent in the face of the enemy." Both the danger of violence and the role of Ramessesnakhte, taking authority in a crisis, are striking.

The wider picture of government at Thebes and indeed throughout Upper Egypt is that of a family business under Ramessesnakhte:[153] he controlled the temple of Karnak and many of the lands under its authority; his son Usermaatrenakhte was steward of Amon and chief taxing master.[154] One son, Nesamon, may have held the high priesthood briefly,[155] while another son, Amenhotep, held office during the disorders of the late Twentieth Dynasty. A fourth son, Meribastet, was married into the family of the high priests of Nekhbet at El Kab,[156] and his daughter was married to Amenemope, high priest of Mut and third priest of Amon.[157] The family held the office of high steward of Medinet Habu;[158] indeed, it is difficult, and possibly unrealistic, to try to distinguish between the stewardships of Karnak and Medinet Habu at this date. Ramessesnakhte's father, Meribastet, had held office as steward and chief taxing master,[159] and a Ramessesnakhte appears as steward of Amon responsible for lands and grain collections in the Amiens and Baldwin papyri.[160] This text is probably to be dated to the mid-Twentieth Dynasty and is likely, therefore, to refer to another member of this extended family. In practice, the family clearly controlled the agricultural revenues of much of Upper Egypt.

The documents consistently place the actions of Ramessesnakhte under the explicit authority of the king, showing cooperation with visiting state officers: notably the vizier, overseers of the treasury and the granaries, and royal butlers. They show at least a formal subordination to the vizier in the hierarchy. Formally, the high priest carries out royal commands, but the range of his activities is very wide. Particularly striking is the role of Ramessesnakhte in a set of five letters that presumably come from his official archives at Karnak.[161] One letter, from Ramesses IX himself, carries a docket recording delivery in year 2 (2 *shemu* 13) by the hand of a Hori who was chief of *Hapati*-soldiers. It complains to Ramessesnakhte that the galena (*msdmt*) sent for making the royal eye paint, was substandard: the original commission to deal with this had been delivered by an overseer of the Treasury of Pharaoh and by a royal butler. Galena was a product of Aswan.

In a second letter, Ramessesnakhte congratulates Nubian troops for their success in protecting gold-workers of the temple of Amon, defeating and plundering foreign bedouin "of the reversed water" (*nȝ ḫrw n šȝsw n mw ḳd*) who had encroached on the land of Egypt. Ramessesnakhte is also recorded in a stela from the Wadi Hammamat as responsible for organizing the transport of stone from a major expedition to the quarries in year 3 of Ramesses IV.[162] He seems to have controlled what public works were carried out at Thebes in this period: he and his family seem to have been responsible for building works on the mortuary temple of Ramesses IV and his successors,[163] although progress seems to have been slow, and very large quantities of newly quarried sandstone seem to have been devoted to Ramessesnakhte's own monument on the Dra' Abu el-Naga.[164] While the temple of Amon had a long-standing interest in the produce of the gold mines[165] and involvement in quarry work for temple building, the overall picture seems to be one in which Ramessesnakhte acts as the overall resident authority in the south.[166] The growing frequency with which the title "royal butler" appears in the titulary of officials visiting the West Bank of Thebes in the period following the reign of Ramesses III—from the ordinary work commissions in the Valley of the Kings through to the royal commissions investigating the Tomb Robberies—reinforces the impression of a royal oversight through personal envoy and personal representative, rather than through regular and structured administrative process.

These themes are made fully explicit with the accession of Amenhotep son of Ramessesnakhte to the office of high priest. His inscription at Karnak from year 10 of Ramesses IX[167] records that the king personally ordered his courtiers to reward Amenhotep "for the many valuable monuments he made in the House of Amon-Re, King of the Gods, in the great name of" the king Ramesses IX. Consequently a commission came from the king to "praise" the high priest Amenhotep, in the Great Courtyard of Amon, for his successful administration of the temple economy: the commission included the overseer of the state treasury and royal butler Amenhotep, the royal butler and king's scribe Nesamon, and the royal butler and king's herald Neferkareemperamon. Stress on the profitability of the temple is considerable, and the lists of gifts is impressive. The inscription of this text on the temple wall and the depiction of Amenhotep on an equal scale with the king are innovations that ideologically inflate his position in a new way. Yet the actual content of the text remains the characteristic motif of the royal reward of the individual official for his performance in office and carrying out his royal (com)mission: the normal theme that the king sends officials from court, at royal command, to carry out his missions and to perform the normal tasks of government. Nevertheless, the Ramesside period may be characterized by an extensive personal enrichment of the higher priesthood, as the focus of local fiscal administration and to the decrease of status of resident "state" officers.

In parallel to this, the stress on priestly genealogy and the hereditary right to temple office receives a new emphasis. While the right to pass on religious function is a key feature of funerary or temple endowment from the earliest known examples in the Old Kingdom, and while hereditary rights of this sort are taken as a norm at all periods,[168] both the scale and manner in which this is expressed seem to indicate a quantitative and a qualitative change through the Ramesside period. For instance, the statue of Basa, a third prophet of Hathor at Dendara in the late Twenty-second or Twenty-third Dynasty, traces his genealogy back through holders of temple office, through that Neb-wenenef who was transferred to the high priesthood at Karnak early in the reign of Ramesses II, and then through another six generations beyond that at Abydos.[169] From at least the middle of the Eighteenth Dynasty, this family had controlled a priestly office, often that of local mayor, marrying within the local priestly-mayoral elite. Local continuity here lay in the temple administration. Succession of an official's son to his office is an ideal that is central to the self-identity and ambition of the Egyptian elite at all periods, but the reality and politico-administrative significance of family succession to key local office is very marked in Upper Egypt through the Ramesside period.

A similar emphasis can be seen in the development of the oracle at Karnak. An early fragmentary example records a request by a *wab*-priest of Maat, made during the festival of Maat, in the presence of the high priest Ramesses-nakhte.[170] By the Third Intermediate Period, appointment to priesthoods was overseen—controlled or manipulated—by oracle, in a manner that attempted to exclude outsiders from office.[171] Indeed, one accusation against the offending *wab*-priest of the temple of Khnum at Elephantine, found in the Turin Indictment Papyrus of the reign of Ramesses V, seems to be that he conspired with others in an agreement to fix the oracle of the god they carried, to prevent an outside priestly appointment.[172] Stress on the priestly descent of the ritualist is seen already in the wording of the daily ritual seen in the temple of Seti I at Abydos.[173] By the Saite period, Herodotus[174] stresses the existence of a distinct priestly caste and the succession from father to son of the post of high priest. By the Roman period, legislation excludes those of nonpriestly descent from temple office, a policy that, from a Roman standpoint, no doubt helped to isolate rather than integrate the temple hierarchy, while pandering to traditional native prejudices. In the Ramesside period, family continuity in local office, with control of temple and local office, provided regional stability and unity around the institutional, economic, and administrative focus of the local temples in Upper Egypt. Characteristically, the stress on personal genealogy seen in "autobiographies" of the Third Intermediate Period and later has been understood as a reflection of a "Libyan" social context—a reflection of oral traditions of tribal genealogy characteristic of the immigrant Libyan ruling elite. However, the inhabitants of Deir el-Medina were as well aware of their genealogies as the local priesthoods, and the people of the Tomb showed a strong interest in their wider family connections. These provided the context and basis for their claim to function. The genealogies of the native Upper Egyptian elite of the post-Ramesside period go back beyond any possible Libyan influence. In this respect, foreign influence may have been negative rather than positive, leading to a stress on long native and local continuity against the foreign origins of the new political power, rather than simply copying the habits of a new regime.

GRAIN REVENUES

Papyrus Valençay 1, of the reign of Ramesses XI, provides circumstantial detail for the process of revenue collection in the later Ramesside period.[175] In a letter, the mayor of Elephantine complains to Menmaatrenakhte, the "chief taxing master" (ꜥꜣ n št), who is the official responsible for collection of grain revenues at Karnak.[176] A scribe from the House of the Divine Adoratrice of Amon had arrived to demand grain from him, due on a holding of *khato*-land at Kom Ombo. He denies that he had cultivated (*skꜣ*) this plot: it is a holding of "freemen" (*nmḥw*) who pay direct (*fꜣi nbw*, literally "carry gold") to the Treasury of Pharaoh. He accepts responsibility for another plot at Edfu but insists that at that location only four *aroura* were inundated and so cultivable; he explains that he had actually put a man and plough team on this land and paid the revenues due for that small cultivable area and that he had not failed to hand over anything due.

It has never been easy either to assess or to collect grain revenues from Egyptian villages, either from the peasant working the land or from the local landholder. It is interesting to see here that the mayor of Elephantine, in principle the regional representative of the state, is held responsible for lands in the neighboring provinces of both Kom Ombo and Edfu. The land is of the category *ḫꜣ-(n-)tꜣ*. A class of royal land, this was often worked as endowment (here for the Divine Adoratrice) and administered by Karnak. In contrast, the *nmḥw* holding here is said to make direct cash payments (*nbw*) to the state treasury and not grain revenues to the state granary.

The impression here is that of a practical absence of distinction between state and temple responsibility for the collection of revenues, although clearly a potentially profitable confusion existed over land classification and, as always, over the accuracy of survey of the inundation. The Turin Indictment Papyrus[177] of the reign of Ramesses V provides an extensive list of accusations against a certain Penanqet, *wab*-priest of the temple of Khnum at Elephantine: theft, peculation, adultery, improper behavior in performance of the cult, and abuse of power. A particular theme seems, however, to be a resistance to any outside control or intervention in the administration of the temple or use of its resources. The accusations of theft and administrative malfeasance are detailed and highly circumstantial, focusing largely on Penanqet's use of temple resources to promote his own interests within a complex web of local relationships. In one accusation,[178] it is said that "they" had entered a silo under "the seal of the administrators (*rwḏw*) of the granary, who administer for the House of Amon (? *sic*)" and took 80 *khar*. More extensive are the accusations against a "transport-boat chief" (*ḥry-wsḫ*)[179] who had been appointed by a previous priest (*ḥm-nṯr*) in year 28 (of Ramesses III). Over nine years, from the beginning of the reign of Ramesses IV, it is claimed that he never brought more than a small proportion of the 700 *khar* he was due to transport each year from what appears to be an endowment (of Ramesses III?) in "the Northern District." The total deficit is given as 5,004 *khar,* although the individual annual totals actually come to 5,724. The claim is that "this transport-boat chief combined with the scribes, administrators and cultivators of the House of Khnum, and he/they defaulted with it, and they made their own use of it for their own ends." The accusation is that the failure to deliver specified revenues was simply fraudulent. In reality, in troubled years, it may well have been difficult to collect grain in the north due for payment to an endowment in the far south.

It is unclear to what extent the central regime attempted to administer agricultural land directly or to collect revenues direct from the farmers, in the Ramesside period or any other. Such administration requires land survey at the time of the inundation, by men with local knowledge, personnel to collect, and transport. There is, in fact, no clear evidence for a state bureaucracy employing the necessary personnel. It may be, simply, that the relevant documents have not survived, but the norm in Egypt has always been the practical delegation of revenue collection to a local level. The size and cost of a central bureaucracy capable of performing these functions field by field is too large. For practical purposes, irregular surveys, estimates, and attempts to enforce communal responsibility on localities and on local administrations, have been the norm. There is no evidence for tax farming in the pharaonic period. Probably the Granaries of Pharaoh focused on the delegation of revenue assessment, collection, and transport to intermediaries and worked with rounded and global estimates, without attempting to collect individual assessments itself.

The ineffectiveness of standard procedures by which the central regime collected and distributed its grain revenues is demonstrated most clearly in the Turin Taxation Papyrus from years 12 and 14 of Ramesses XI.[180] This records the collection of grain by the scribe Djehutimose of the Tomb "from ḫȝ-(n-)tȝ lands under the control of the priests [. . ., under the authority of] the fan-bearer on the right of the King, the royal scribe, general, overseer of the Granaries [of Pharaoh, the King's Son] of Kush, overseer of southern lands, the leader Panehsy of the bowmen [of Pharaoh]"[181]—that is, in the period of military occupation of Thebes. Djehutimose collected grain from a number of towns, typically from local priests or temple officials of a variety of endowments. However, actual cultivators are mentioned in some numbers, and a remarkably high proportion are titled as "foreigner" (ȝꜥꜥ).[182] Djehutimose is accompanied by "gatekeepers," and sometimes it was fishermen of the Tomb who provided the necessary transport. He delivered the grain to Thebes, where it was received mostly by Paweraa, mayor of Western Thebes.

These expeditions are partly to be explained by the way in which the officials and workmen of the Tomb provided a convenient and apparently trusted group, used for a variety of jobs other than tomb building by the military regime of the late Twentieth Dynasty. The expeditions are also likely to represent an element of self-help in obtaining the grain for their rations. That procedure was not a complete innovation. The correspondence of the scribes of the Tomb from the end of the period makes several references to collecting and transporting grain, in one case with considerable argument over variation in the size of the measures used and over excessive transport fees or wages deducted by the fishermen:[183] grain rations for the fishermen while doing the work formed a proper and standard expense. Already in years 6 and 7 of Ramesses IX, the necropolis registers refer to scribes and fishermen of the Tomb bringing grain from outside Thebes to pay the rations of the workmen, although the responsibility for normal transport arrangements in this case fell not to the chief scribe but to the scribes controlling the smdt-staff.[184]

TEMPLE ENDOWMENTS AND LAND MANAGEMENT

The growth in temple wealth in the New Kingdom, in particular the control of land,[185] was based not simply on royal gift but also on private endowments, which themselves established perpetual rights to office, function, and income for the family and descendants of the donor. The practice of creating religious foundations, particularly for funerary or temple statue cults, was ancient and normal, but the Ramesside period shows an increase in donations (both characteristic subsistence plots of three to five *aroura* and larger donations), and there is an evident stress on military as well as priestly tenures.[186]

A rather different process seems to be attested by Papyrus Berlin 3047,[187] which records a case heard in year 46 of Ramesses II by the Court (ꜥrryt) of Pharaoh at Luxor, by a tribunal led by the high priest of Amon. Two branches of an extended family had evidently quarreled over rights to shares in the income of an extensive landholding: 140 *aroura* in four separate plots, to which a list of beneficiaries—the heirs of two different women—had rights to shares. Neferabet, the scribe of the king's offering table, sued Nia, the chief of the workshop of the temple of Amon, over management of the land. Neferabet presented written evidence, and Nia conceded the case. Neferabet also testified that he donated his share to the priest (ḥm-nṯr) Wenennefer of the temple of Mut in return for the annual payment of one-third of the harvest. Wenennefer was a member of the tribunal, and at the end of the case, he formally accepted the property from Neferabet on this condition. The income is at a level that Neferabet could have expected from renting the land privately, but this does not look like a purely private transaction: the best understanding is that he was transferring the land to temple management, to avoid the trouble of dealing directly with cultivators himself and, at the same time, to minimize the potential for family dispute.

These measures imply a confidence in temple administration of land, as perpetual, reliable, and impartial—a reservoir of local management capacity as well as a reservoir of resources per se. The Wilbour Papyrus, from the reign of Ramesses V, shows the holdings of the temple of Karnak divided between ordinary and "apportioning"—literally "share" (pš)—holdings, which it managed partly for other temples and partly for named individuals. The temple income from these holdings is significantly lower than that for ordinary holdings, and the overall picture seems to be one in which Karnak was becoming not so much the direct owner of land but its controller, by providing the necessary administrative and management structures regardless of whether such land was legally "private," or a category of state land, such as ḫ3-(n-)t3. This tied the beneficiaries and primary landholders to the temple, both politically and economically.[188]

ORACLES AS ADMINISTRATIVE PROCESS

The use of oracles provides one of the most characteristic features of sociolegal behavior in Twentieth Dynasty Luxor. The principle of asking or taking advice direct from a god, as revealed through dreams or physical signs, has no beginning but is implicit in Egyptian religion at all periods.[189] A distinct oracular procedure by which individuals publicly approached a statue in procession to ask specific questions is only attested properly from the Nineteenth Dynasty[190] but appears to have been regular and normal on the West Bank at Thebes during the Twentieth Dynasty,[191] with a particular focus on use in the resolution of disputes[192] as well as in asking personal advice, often of an apparently trivial nature. In the early Twentieth Dynasty, the workmen at Deir el-Medina seem to have used the oracle for advice and mediation, in ways that more normally might have been taken to trusted leading members of the community in an Egyptian village.

The simplest explanation for this popularity of the oracle would be a marked decline in confidence in human authority and particularly in the official hierarchy, both local to Deir el-Medina and more generally. This is mediated by a marked development in the expression of a personal spirituality, faith, and direct personal address to gods through prayer, which is characteristic of the private monuments and literature of the post-Amarna and particularly the Ramesside periods. The novelty of this explicit personal piety is easily exaggerated, reflecting changes in emphasis in preserved literary genres and in tomb decoration: it is hardly surprising, for instance, that Ramesside tombs at Luxor should cease to emphasize the personal relationship of the tomb owner to the king and place greater emphasis on religious and funerary motifs, when the tomb owners were not personally courtiers—not part of the personal circle around the king—and had minimal personal contact with an absentee kingship compared to the owners of Eighteenth Dynasty tombs in this area.

The local and administrative dominance of the temple of Karnak is matched in the late Twentieth Dynasty by an ideological presentation in which the god communicated his rule directly, through oracle and in answer to direct questions. This contrasts with the presentation of kingship in the earlier New Kingdom, when the king ruled humankind as son, representative, and intermediary for Amon(-Re), whose divine approval was revealed by physical manifestations—events, including military or policy success—classed as *biȝt* performed by god as signs for the king. There is a significant change of emphasis here. Where Eighteenth Dynasty sources—notably those of the reigns of Hatshepsut and Tuthmosis III—stress the "reality" of the divine birth of the king and the choice by god as a reinforcement of legitimacy, the Twentieth and Twenty-first Dynasties lay more emphasis on the god's choice as a practical oracular process, deliberately mobilized and potentially controversial.[193] The term *biȝt* is used in the Ramesside period to refer specifically to the oracular process, and by the end of the Twentieth Dynasty it is clearly not a royal prerogative at Thebes. The theme is expressed most clearly in the literary *Story of Wenamun*, which takes place during the Repeating of Births, at the very end of the reign of Ramesses XI. Although it was probably composed a little later,[194] the core issues of its ideological discourse belong to this period.

Wenamun was sent on his mission to Byblos, to obtain timber for the divine bark of Amon, as the result of a direct order given by Amon to Herihor—that is, presumably an oracle.[195] Wenamun declares himself the human envoy of Amon-Re; the statue he carries with him—Amon of the Road—is the actual (divine) envoy.[196] The ruler of Byblos is urged to provide the timber for the god, who gives life and who anyway created and owns the world—Byblos and Syria-Palestine as well as Egypt. This is in contrast to previous pharaohs, who Wenamun agrees had bought the timber, since they were not divine and had not divine patronage to offer. In particular, he applies this criticism to "Khaemwese," whose envoys had died after spending eighteen years at Byblos. Wenamun indignantly asserts that he is not like them: "As for Khaemwese, the messengers he sent you were human, and he himself human."[197] It is difficult to see in "Khaemwese" anything but a reference to Ramesses XI by his birth name, and the comment appears to be an ideological justification for the era of Repeating of Births that marked a restoration of sociopolitical order to Luxor and the establishment of the regime of the Twenty-first Dynasty. Its founders, Herihor and Payankh, were apparently military men—quite possibly of Libyan origin—who took control of the high priesthood at Karnak.[198] Their regime probably originated in a military coup that justified itself ideologically by divine selection and, where necessary, justified its political decisions by oracle. Ideologically, theologically, and even politically, their claim to legitimacy by divine choice, approved by oracle, is identical to that made by Sethnakhte and Ramesses III at the beginning of the dynasty (see above), even if the sociopolitical makeup of the state had changed.

TOMB ROBBERY AND THE COLLAPSE OF ORDER

The direct corollary to the passage in *The Story of Wenamun* is a comment in a letter[199] from the general of Pharaoh—that is Payankh—to the scribe of the Tomb Tjaroy—that is, Djehutimose. It requires him to cooperate with Nodjmet, chief of the harem of Amon-Re, and with the (general's) agent (*rwdw*)

Payshuweben to interrogate two Medjay, to look into claims they had made, and if necessary drop them secretly in baskets into the river at night. Payankh assures Djehutimose: "As for Pharaoh, how can he reach this land?"[200] And as for Pharaoh, whose lord is he still?" Tjaroy is then also told to dispatch the money required by the general. These comments seem to mark the practical collapse of central authority over the government of Upper Egypt. In contrast, the Tomb Robbery Papyri of the preceding years assume a royal authority, mobilized for the investigation of crime.[201] In year 1 of the Repeating of Births, the vizier asks a tomb robber: "You used to be making the forays that you used to make, and the god caught you, and brought you and placed you in the hand of Pharaoh. Tell me all the people who were with you in the Great Places."[202] In year 2 (of the Repeating of Births), investigations into robberies from Medinet Habu were instigated when "the god's-father Amenmose son of To, of the Temple, reported them before Pharaoh, and One personally commissioned (*dit m ḥr n*) the overseer of the city and Vizier Nebmaatrenakhte, the overseer of the Treasury of Pharaoh, overseer of the Granary and royal butler Menmatrenakhte, and the steward and royal butler Yensa to investigate them."[203]

The basic process for these inquiries is best illustrated in the Abbott Papyrus and the Leopold Amherst Papyrus from 3 *akhet* of year 16 of Ramesses IX. Substantive reports, accusing named thieves, were investigated by a commission of inquiry: the vizier Khaemwese; the royal butler and scribe of pharaoh Nesamon; and the steward of the House of the Divine Adoratrice, royal butler, and herald of pharaoh Neferkareemperamon. The specific accusations are recorded in the name of mayor of Western Thebes Paweraa and other West Bank functionaries, apparently the officials responsible for local security.[204] Of the members of the commission, Khaemwase and perhaps Nesamon[205] can be seen as non-Theban, and their offices seem to mark them as personal representatives of the king. The specific accusations were investigated by the commission on site. The accused were interrogated, with beatings and physical force used to loosen their tongues, and their testimony was recorded. Of those interrogated, the majority confessed. These were entrusted as prisoners to the high priest of Amon. The high priest was also required to have the missing thieves from the gang brought and imprisoned, "until Pharaoh our Lord decides their punishment."[206] When no case was proved, the accused were released. In fact, the men convicted at this date were executed, by impalement. Their punishment is mentioned specifically as a deterrent in the testimony of people interrogated by the later commission of inquiry that took place at the beginning of the Repeating of Births.

These inquiries in the reign of Ramesses IX reveal a deep personal antipathy between the mayors of Thebes and of the West Bank and a blurring of responsibility in the administrative process. The Tomb Robbery Papyri almost certainly come from a deposit in an office at Medinet Habu, which is probably where Paweraa had his residence, and the writer of the documents seems to be concerned to place the best interpretation on Paweraa's actions. The role of the mayor Paser, of Thebes proper, is not entirely clear, and the interpretation put on his actions by the writer of the Abbott Papyrus is neither neutral nor favorable. Following an inspection of the Valley of the Queens on day 19, which found no evidence of damage, "the great officials let (or "caused," *dit*) the controllers (*rwdw*), leaders and crewmen of the Tomb, the chiefs of Medjay, the Medjay and all the staff (*smdt*) of the Tomb go round the West of Thebes in a great mission (*wpt*) as far as Thebes."[207] This ended in a riotous demonstration by people of the Tomb on day 20, outside the office (*at*) of the mayor Paser and in the presence of Nesamon and Paweraa.[208]

Paweraa reports the claims and counterclaims he says he heard on this occasion: Paser, as "the mayor who reports to the Ruler," objected to the behavior of the people of the Tomb and stressed that one royal tomb at least had been robbed. The workman Userkhepesh rudely—and perhaps ironically—responded that the dead kings and their families in the Valley of the Kings and the Valley of the Queens were safe: "The good plans (*sḫrw nfr*) of Pharaoh, l.p.h., their child, guards them and polices them strictly (*smty=w ḏri*)."[209] Paser responded that the scribes Horisheri son of Amonnakhte and the scribe Pabes, of the Tomb, had made accusations to him that he could not ignore and had to report to pharaoh, in order to have people of pharaoh come to investigate them. Paweraa complains that the scribes of the Tomb should not have reported to the mayor of Thebes but direct to the vizier, in person if he happened to be in town, but otherwise in writing and by messenger. Paweraa says that he is now personally making a formal report of the whole affair, to have it investigated. The initial outcome was embarrassing for Paser. He was added to the closing tribunal of the Abbott Papyrus,[210] on day 21, which took place as "the Great Tribunal of Town" at Karnak. Also present were the vizier; the high priest of Amon Amenhotep; the priest of Amon-Re and *setem*-priest of the mortuary temple of Ramesses IX, the royal butler Nesamon, who was the scribe of pharaoh; the steward of the House of the Divine Adoratrice, royal butler, and herald of pharaoh Neferkareemperamon, who was the reporter (*wḥmw*) of pharaoh; the deputy of chariotry Hori; the standard-bearer of the navy Hori; and the mayor of Thebes Paser. They interrogated coppersmiths from Medinet Habu accused by the mayor of Thebes, and his accusations were declared to be without foundation. However, Paser also sat on the tribunal of the Leopold Amherst Papyrus on day 22 or 23, which convicted the robbers of the royal tomb.

The role of the scribe of the Tomb Horisheri seems as ambiguous here as that of his father in the Turin Strike Papyrus: unable to control the workmen under stress, he is concerned with not being held responsible for their individual behavior.[211] While the royal tombs are said to be intact at this date, the private tombs are said already to be the object of regular robbery[212] and already to have been emptied, by and large, by the inhabitants of the West Bank.[213] The general picture of civil administration in Thebes at the end of the reign of Ramesses IX is one in which administrative process is not functioning well, with unclear and rival chains of responsibility and serious personal tensions in practice.

By the end of the reign of Ramesses III, the situation in the Theban area was already characterized by serious and continuing problems of public security. The following years show that even in the far south, there were significant numbers of foreigners settled in the countryside; that incursions from the deserts to the west—Libu and Meshwesh[214]—and pressures from Nubia were all a major threat to Thebes itself; and, if the correspondence of Ramessesnakhte is taken at face value, that pressures were also severe in the Eastern Desert from the Red Sea coast. Civil war is not clearly attested before the "suppression" or "war" of the high priest Amenhotep, late in the dynasty, but the threat of conflict is endemic much earlier. The picture of Thebes at the end of the dynasty, in the aftermath of that war, is one not so much of endemic bureaucratic corruption, which is itself a form of political order, but of a society conditioned by insecurity and social violence.

The precise sequence of events between year 17 of Ramesses IX (when the high priest Amenhotep was dominant in Thebes) and year 1 of the Repeating of Births (when the new military regime of Herihor and Payankh was in firm control) remains unclear.[215] The necropolis journal for year 17 contains chronic complains that the workmen were hungry,[216] and the journals of year 3 of Ramesses X record continuing difficulties and delays in payment.[217] However, most of the key references come in evidence given to the Tomb Robbery tribunals, when the testimony of those investigated for robbing in the tombs and temples makes repeated reference to the chaos and hardship of the preceding years. The period includes Libyan incursions; the "war" of the high priest Amenhotep;[218] the occasion when a robber describes how "the 3^{rc} came, and they seized the Temple (= Medinet Habu), and I was in charge of the donkeys of my father, and Pahaty, an 3^{rc}, seized me, and took me to

Ipip when one suppressed (*th3*) Amenhotep, who had been High Priest of Amon";[219] and the occupation of Thebes by the viceroy of Nubia Panehsy, referred to in the testimony of "the *wab*-priest Payseni, who had been guard (*s3w*) of the House of Pharaoh; he said 'I left (*pri*) the House of Pharaoh after Paynehsy came, and he suppressed (*th3*) my chief, although there was no offence in him.'"[220] It includes Paynehsy's rule in Thebes;[221] his campaign further north, with the destruction of Hardai;[222] and the conscription (?) and death of people from the West Bank: thieves killed in the war in the north (*m p3 ḥrw m ꜥ mḥty*) are listed against thieves whom Panehsy killed, thieves who had previously been put on the stake, and those imprisoned but still alive.[223] There were periods of starvation, such as the year of the hyenas, when people starved.[224] The robberies were justified by the fact that people needed money to get bread,[225] and very high sums were paid for a *khar* or two of grain.[226] Violence seems endemic, from foreigners—"Now when the chief of bowmen of the foreigners killed your father, they took me to interrogate"[227]—and in the conduct and sharing of the spoils of the robberies.[228] This period includes a wholesale plundering of temples on the West Bank[229] and probably also of tombs in the Valley of the Kings as well as the Valley of the Queens.[230] The final expulsion of Panehsy is not documented.[231] At some point, the king himself seems to have been in Thebes: testimony during the investigations of year 2 of the Repeating of Birth comments that "when Pharaoh our Lord came to Town, he made the *setem*-priest Hori *setem*-priest of the temple," and it says that the mayor refused to give up some timber to the merchant of a certain Tjatjawy "who was in Town with Pharaoh," in the absence of a direct order from Pharaoh.[232] The impression is not one of very effective exercise of authority. War continued during the Repeating of Births with expeditions against Panehsy in Nubia itself. This involved the people of the Tomb in making weapons,[233] feeding Meshwesh,[234] and being told to "look after the people of the army. Don't let them desert (*wꜥr*), and don't let them go hungry."[235] There is also the rather obscure matter of their scribe Djehutimose having to travel south in connection with the campaign.[236]

The general picture from the testimony of the Tomb Robbery Papyri is one of deep personal trauma and a struggle to survive in a crisis of social collapse that is marked by violence, rather than simple corruption. There was evidently a political necessity to use whatever administrative and technical expertise was available and reliable, to ensure stability and the process of government. The immediate picture in texts from early in the period of the Repeating of Births is that of a general restoration of order, and the major issue for local government was the re-creation of local economic and political stability, to which any political claims by the central monarchy in the north were now of little significance.

SUMMARY

Deficiencies in the historical record mean that any evaluation of underlying historical process is likely to be falsified by additional evidence. However, a number of specific themes seem to have become critical for our understanding of Egyptian society by the end of the reign of Ramesses III. Long-term ecological pressures in areas surrounding Egypt produced major waves of pastoralist immigration. Massive and violent invasions were probably less disruptive to the demography and settled arable economy of Egypt than chronic raiding and local inability to prevent the arrival of immigrant groups, with their herds, in the river valley. There is no clear evidence of catastrophic Nile failures at this period, although a medium-term decline in Nile heights and significant changes in the course of the branches of the Nile—at least in the Eastern Delta—seem to have had at least regional effects on settlement patterns and land use. In practice, however, the arrival of wandering herds of sheep and goats from the desert on the arable fields of Egypt is more destructive for medium-term economic health than either the immediate violence of their owners or an occasional failure of the Nile. If crops cannot be gathered securely, fields will quickly go out of grain production, and villages will depopulate and be abandoned. The occupation of abandoned fields by herding populations will produce both demographic change and differences in socioadministrative structures.

The Ramesside period is characterized by a militarization of society and government. This is different in character from the expansive militarization of the early New Kingdom, a change from an essentially imperial military regime in the Eighteenth Dynasty, with focus on the king as hero, to what was in effect an imposed military local government by the end of the Twentieth Dynasty, where authority derived from control of an army. Local survival required toughness in a very harsh world, against the horrors of endemic raiding, warfare, and military occupation. In areas of significant Libyan immigrant population, tribal-military regimes are likely to have provided local coherence, as old political structures were swept away in demographic change.

On the west of Thebes, the walled temple compound of Medinet Habu provided physical security by the late Twentieth Dynasty. It is unlikely to have been unique among the temples of Upper Egypt in this respect; indeed, Karnak on the East Bank provided similar walled security. The temple hierarchy, focused on the old capital of Thebes, seems to have provided both a socio-political coherence and a reserve of administrative capacity to maintain a degree of social security, political coherence, and economic structure. By the end of the period, the temple of Amon is left, de facto and by default, as administrator of the land regime and revenues of Upper Egypt. This may seem the culmination of earlier New Kingdom trends, as both kings and private individuals endowed the temples with lands and people to work them, but it also reflects a collapse of the penetration of central government into Upper Egypt. More significantly, it lay the foundation for long-term landholding patterns in Upper Egypt. Through the Third Intermediate Period, political control of Karnak was economically vital to any dynasty attempting to claim central authority, but it seems to have been a largely military control that was neither comfortable nor unchallenged by the local hereditary elite. By the Ptolemaic period, agricultural land in Upper Egypt is characterized by the formal status of "temple land," while lands in the north—with their extensive areas of colonist occupation—are much more varied in "legal" status.[237]

Evidently the tax base had largely collapsed by the end of the reign of Ramesses III. The building activities of Ramesses IV and his successors were severely restricted. Major building projects in the New Kingdom seem to have used immigrant populations—"captives"—to provide core labor. Building works then required a regular wage regime in terms of food supply for the laborers through at least moderately effective revenue collection. It seems reasonable to attribute the difficulties over ration payments at Deir el-Medina to problems of revenue control by the state, at least as much as to ecological difficulties and poor crops following unsatisfactory inundations, for which there is no specific evidence at this date.[238] There was hunger on the Theban West Bank in the late Ramesside period: testimony in the Tomb Robbery Papyri refers to "the year of the hyenas, when men starved," or a woman says, "Now I happened to be sitting hungry under the sycamores,"[239] or quotes an associate as saying, "Some men have found something that can be sold for bread; let us go so that we may eat it with them."[240] Robbery and extortion are explained as a reaction to hunger, a necessity to survive; but such explanations refer to the disastrous period of civil war preceding the era of the Repeating of Births, when local disasters can be explained directly by civil war and civil disorder, and not simply by failures of the harvest. Warfare is sufficient cause for the individually worst years.

It is, of course, impossible to document the extent to which local delegation of revenue collection was the norm in pharaonic Egypt. The Wilbour

Papyrus shows a pattern of local intermediaries—often themselves "cultiva-tors"—held responsible for local plots,[241] but a peasant farmer will generally not pay tax unless compelled to do so by the visit of a tax collector. The moral basis of taxation is of little interest to the ordinary farmer, who minimizes to the best of his ability the surrender of his crops—whether as rent or tax—without any sense that his practice is corrupt. The entire process of assessing and collecting grain revenues is, of necessity, characterized at all periods by negotiation and practical compromise, supported by physical force. Without a practical show of force, or at least a credible threat of force, the central regime could not expect to collect efficiently from the provinces. Without floggings, revenues have never been collectable from the peasantry of Egypt.[242]

The significance of endemic corruption in the Ramesside period is impos-sible to assess.[243] Indeed, it is not simple to provide a practical definition of corruption, or, rather, to outline the socially acceptable borderlines of ex-ploitation imposed on producers by either local or central elites. The context is one in which family relationships and local loyalties are primary, in a society built on structures of patronage and personal relationships—local, profes-sional, and kinship. There may be conflicting and erratic material demands by different levels of the hierarchy—central and local—while leakage and wastage at the margins are inherent in any revenue system based on perishable commodities. While the moral guidelines of truth and wholly impersonal ad-ministration are easily laid out in literary form—wisdom literature and auto-biography—that literature is also deeply embedded in social reality and the typical practices of government and hierarchical behavior, which are always characterized by the pressures of personal relationships, personal ambition, conflicts, and needs.

For instance, the Middle Kingdom *Instruction of Merikare* is quite ex-plicit that impartiality can only be expected from an honestly enriched elite.[244] In contrast, the early Ramesside *Maxims of Ani* urge the son to make friends with the "herald" of his locality, to give him presents, and to accept his demands, and state clearly that there is no disgrace in this.[245] Both wis-dom literature and autobiography can, in the detail of what they reject, be taken to provide an accurate picture of the normal mechanisms by which individuals profited from position and function—a clear picture of ordi-nary bureaucratic and elite attitudes, on the understanding, explicit in the school texts and *Satire on the Trades,* that the functionary (the scribe) de-mands and others pay. In that respect, a text like the Decree of Horemheb,[246] with its focus on the regulation of specific practices associated with the col-lection of revenues and imposition of services, may be taken as evidence of characteristic processes rather than simply as a special measure to reform unusual practices.

Specific accusations of corruption are difficult to evaluate in a context where both the practical basis of local authority and the root of personal prestige lie in the ability to manipulate resources and to enforce personal authority to that end. Corruption lies in the personal abuse of that authority by the visiting official or the village tyrant, using physical and moral power to the unreasonable disadvantage of individuals. This characteristic theme of wisdom literature finds its real expression in the personal antipathies and local rivalries seen in such texts as the Turin Indictment Papyrus, the earlier Papyrus Salt 124 from Deir el-Medina, and the accusations of Penanqet in the Turin Strike Papyrus. These all seem thoroughly imbued with personal spite,[247] which is not to say that their targets may not have been evil men. A degree of shrinkage in the cargo of the grain boat is to be expected,[248] as is argument over the size of the grain measure. An ostracon of year 17 (of Ramesses III) records a complaint of the chiefs of the Tomb that the *ipet*-measure used for their grain rations was undersized. It had been brought by the scribe Paser, an outside scribe who appears frequently in the documents of the period, acting as an intermediary between the crew and the outside authorities. On checking, it turned out only to contain thirty-eight of the forty *hin* needed to make up the full measure.[249] It is characteristic in any society that reduction of the revenue or shrinkage in rent payment is regarded morally as a victimless and trivial crime, particularly when there is personal and urgent need for the resources locally. The issue is one of scale. It takes a particularly strong and efficient central government to exact full demands from provincial administration without shrinkage, just as local authorities find it difficult to exact revenues smoothly and regularly from the individual farmer. The accusations against the *wab*-priest Penanqet may have been targeted more at claims that he was working against the interests of the central regime than simply at claims that he was personally corrupt in the conduct of local business.

In contrast, the pessimistic literature of the Middle Kingdom provides clear descriptions of the effects of raiding and immigration on the settled lands, with resulting warfare, which should no more be taken as merely a literary topos than should the literary discussion of administrative practice. Neferti "recalls the state of the East, when the Asiatics move in strength, and they terrorize the hearts of those who are harvesting, and seize the teams that are ploughing."[250] He describes "the flocks of the desert (*ḫ3st*) drinking at the river of Egypt," with the consequence of disorder, blood, and war through the land[251] and dispossession of the populace: "little (in quantity) is the grain; large is the *ipet*-measure, and one measures to overflowing."[252] *The Admonitions of Ipuwer* lament that "[. . . must bow (?)] on the ground because of bands, and a man goes to plough with his shield."[253] More tellingly, they report, "O, but Hapy floods, and nobody ploughs for him; everybody says 'We do not know what is happening through the land.'"[254] As its core, literature uses memories and images of personal and social crisis to discuss the human condition in general and social instability in particular. As Ani says, "The flow (literally "going downstream") of the water of last year is gone; it <is> in another channel this year. Great swamps (?) (*w3d-wr ʿ3y*) have turned into dry places, and sandbanks have turned into depths."[255] These are given contemporary flavor in the Moscow literary letter that describes the horrors suffered by a priest violently expelled from office, impoverished, and forced to wander an unfriendly and disordered country in destitution: the identification of this text as a roman à clef for the sufferings of the suppressed high priest Amenhotep is attractive but uncertain.[256] These themes provide vivid images of the reality of demographic and political change appropriate to events in Ramesside Egypt, and a context for the troubles documented in Thebes.

Whatever the final evaluation of the personal and social morality of the population of the Theban West Bank may be, the documentary record in the Ramesside period reflects poorly on the ability of the state institution to penetrate the local economy of Upper Egypt effectively. The functioning of its administrative process was at best erratic, but the background to this seems to lie primarily in the inability of the regime to maintain military and public order in ways that would protect the rural population and so the agricultural base of the Egyptian economy.

Notes

1. *KRI* V.39.11–14 = *MH* I, pls. 45b, 46: the address to the people of the entire land in the "Sea Peoples" inscription of year 8 from Medinet Habu.

2. P. Harris I.75.7.

3. P. Harris I.75.10–76.17.

4. Drenkhahn (1980); *KRI* V.671–72; Altenmüller (1982); Seidlmayer (1998). For the general situation at the end of the Nineteenth Dynasty, cf. also Gnirs (1996a) 129–31.

5. Lines 10–12.

6. P. Harris I.75.2–6.

7. P. Harris I.76.11–77.2.

8. Cf. Butzer (1979) 29–33, 97–98.

9. Cf. Snape (1998).

10. E.g., *KRI* VI.50–52; *KRI* V.36.10–12 = *MH* I.44.16–17 + *KRI* V.39.11–12 = *MH* I.46.14–15; *KRI* V.217.9–12 = *MH* IV.231.25–27, for which see Moftah (1985) 106–7.

11. Line 13 = *KRI* V.672.8–9. See also line 16 = *KRI* V.672.11. Cf. Altenmüller (1982) 108.

12. *KRI* V.340–41.

13. Eyre (1996b).

14. Grandet (1994) I.107–27 develops the fantastic theory that this papyrus was physically displayed as a public notice on a wall at Medinet Habu. For alternative explanations, see Haring (1997) 158–61. Whatever the manner of publication one might envisage, its format is essentially that of a speech at a royal audience. Its rationale is public self-justification in the manner of tomb autobiography to justify the dead and assert the heritage of his heir, whether this is targeted at a general public or a narrow political circle or simply in the normal context of tomb and temple inscription. It defines proper function as expected by men and gods.

15. Koenig (2001) stresses the nature of both the Turin Judicial Papyrus and Papyrus Harris I as "sacralisations," stressing the magico-ritual rather than juridico-political context of their composition.

16. *KRI* I.110–14; Brand (2000) 182–83, 310, 377–79.

17. *KRI* VI.17–20; Peden (1994b) 151–58.

18. *KRI* VI.20–25; Peden (1994b) 159–74.

19. Loprieno (1998) 5–8.

20. Cf. Keller (1994).

21. Line 5 = *KRI* VI.18. 4.

22. Line 13 = *KRI* VI.23.5–6.

23. Line 15 = *KRI* VI.23.8–9.

24. Line 18 = *KRI* VI.23.14.

25. Lines 35–36 = *KRI* VI.25.9–10.

26. Line 16 = *KRI* VI.19.5.

27. Lines 21–23 = *KRI* VI.19.12–16.

28. Kitchen (1982b); for the most recent reevaluation, see Leblanc (2001).

29. The treatment in Cruz-Uribe (1994) is very superficial. See Eyre (1996a); Eyre (2000); Eyre (2004).

30. See Martin (2000) for analysis of burial patterns between Thebes and Saqqara.

31. Raven (2000); note particularly the work documents P. Cairo JdE 52002 and 52003 = *KRI* III.263–68 = Posener-Kriéger (1981) and Posener-Kriéger (1996).

32. Butzer (1976) 29–33; Seidlmayer (2001) 12, 63–73.

33. E.g., *KRI* V.484, on 2 *akhet* 15 in year 22 of Ramesses III and 2 *akhet* 17 of a previous (?) year; *KRI* V.536, month and day lost, for year 29.

34. Seidlmayer (2001) 70; *KRI* VI.459.

35. Bietak (1975) esp. 215–17, 49–58, 117–39 (for the water regime in the Eastern Delta); cf. Eyre (1994b) 71–72, 78.

36. Cf. Butzer (1976) 55–56.

37. *KRI* IV.4.9–10, 14–15; Kitchen (1990) 20.

38. P. Harris I.76.8–9.

39. P. Harris I.77.4–6; cf. *KRI* V.24.2–3 = *MH* I.28.40. Grandet (1994) II.253–54 n. 929 perversely argues that this does not imply that "tribal" structures of the immigrant populations were preserved.

40. Gnirs (1996a) 193; Jansen-Winkeln (1994).

41. P. Harris I.78.8–11.

42. Gardiner (1941–48) II.32–33; O'Connor (1972) 693–95.

43. Gardiner (1941–48) II.77–82; Katary (1989) 70–72; Katary (1999) esp. 69–71, 76–80.

44. *KRI* V.270; Kessler (1975); most recently discussed in Menu (1998) 140.

45. Menu (1998) 174.

46. Gnirs (1996a) 57–65 argues that this term is of West Semitic origin but was used by this date to refer to controllers of military colonies.

47. Gardiner (1941a); cf. Eyre (1992).

48. See Butzer (1976) 76–80 for general patterns of settlement; *LÄ* III.672–73 s.v. "Kolonisation"; Eyre (1994b) 71–72; Eyre (1997) 376–77; Eyre (2004) 161–62.

49. Gnirs (1996a) 57–65, 193.

50. Tallet (2000).

51. *KRI* V.91.5–7; Kitchen (1990) 20; Gnirs (1996a) 60–61.

52. In general, see Gnirs (1996a) 37–39.

53. *KRI* V.76.3–4.

54. P. Harris I.75.1–2.

55. Lines 15–17 = *KRI* V.672.11–12; cf. Altenmüller (1982) 108–9.

56. Helck (1961–70); Helck (1975); Janssen (1975b).

57. See, e.g., the attempt in Ward (1994) for Deir el-Medina.

58. *KRI* V.12–14.

59. *KRI* V.18.

60. See Grandet (1994) I.88–91; cf. Janssen (1975b) 139–41 for the difficulty of quantification.

61. See O'Connor (1972) for general distribution.

62. Kitchen (1999b); *HO* pls. 81–82 = *KRI* III.138–40.

63. Kitchen (1999b) 236 argues that the border should lie north of Nefrusi (in the fifteenth nome) but south of Hardai (in the seventeenth nome) and probably should lay at the border of the sixteenth and seventeenth nomes, so that the area would include the nomes south of Memphis and the Fayum. At the end of the Twentieth Dynasty, the border of the Theban regime was slightly further north, at El-Hibe, while there is reference to the sacking of Hardai by the forces of Panehsy (see below), probably implying that it was a border garrison town.

64. Kitchen (1999b) 237 collects relevant data; cf. Eyre (1999a) 47. By comparison with the "tax" ratios of the Wilbour Papyrus, this figure implies cultivation of twenty *aroura* per man, a high but perhaps possible figure.

65. As a crude point of comparison, that would pay 26,545 "middle-class" employees at the rate of a Deir el-Medina workman, 5.5 *khar* a month, or 97,000 men on a subsistence minimum of 1.5 *khar* a month. Compare the figure of 62,626 people with whom Ramesses II claimed to endow Medinet Habu (P. Harris I.10.3), which Kitchen contrasts with the figure of 61,517 plus missing figures for cowherds and fishermen in O. Gardiner 86.

66. P. Harris I.16b.13–15.

67. P. Harris I.12b.3 (total for Medinet Habu and four minor Theban temples). See Grandet (1994) I.59, 90–91, for stress that the lists are only the donations of Ramesses III.

68. Implicitly Kitchen's estimate assumes, reasonably, a grain production from endowment in Upper Egypt at least twice that of Lower Egypt.

69. Lines 18–19 = *KRI* V.672.12–14.

70. Haring (1997) 272–74; cf. Tallet (1999) 419 with *RAD* 51.15–52.3 (see below).

71. Kitchen (1984a) 552–53.

72. Right-hand stela of pair, lines 21–22 = *KRI* V.245.14–16; cf. Grandet (1994) I.97.

73. Grandet (1994) I.85–88.

74. Line 19 = *KRI* V.245.10.

75. Line 16 = *KRI* V.245.3.

76. Kitchen (1984a) 551; Grandet (1994) I.94–101.

77. *KRI* V.231–34; Kitchen (1984a) 551; Grandet (1994) I.95–98.

78. *KRI* V.233.3–4.

79. *KRI* V.232.9, 233.8.

80. Kitchen (1984a) 549–50 on *KRI* IV.26.

81. Vleeming (1993); Gasse (1988); Eyre (1997) 371–77, 380, 385; Eyre (1999a) 45.

82. Cf. Haring (1997) 198–99.

83. Janssen (1975b) 181–82; Janssen (1979a); Haring (1997). For the Eighteenth Dynasty, see also Eichler (2000).

84. van den Boorn (1988).

85. Eyre (2000) esp. 25–27, 29–33.

86. P. Harris I.75.3–4.

87. P. Harris I.59.11.

88. The text describes the return of temple personnel to the temple and its functionaries, from that of a vizier, authority overall. It says nothing clear about either the background or the actual measures taken against the vizier—whether it was a purely administrative clarification or a coded reference to a major political event. Cf. Grandet (1994) II.194–96 nn. 802–5, with extensive earlier bibliography.

89. See below for the case of BM 10383.

90. Černý (1973); Valbelle (1985); Eyre (1987a) 168–80.

91. Cf. the stela of Ramesses II from Manshiyet es-Sadr, describing the terms of employment of his quarrymen: *KRI* II.360–62.

92. Eyre (1999a).

93. Cf. Allam (1997), drawing specific parallels with later municipal councils of the Hellenistic period.

94. Janssen (1975a) 460–66; Janssen (1997) 13–35.

95. Janssen (1975a) 109–11.

96. Haring (1997) 249–63.

97. Donker van Heel and Haring (2003).

98. Janssen (1997) 147–92.

99. Černý (1973) 339–83 = appendix D.

100. Graffiti 1111 and 1143 = *KRI* V.379.

101. Bruyère (1930) 14–16, figs. 10–11.

102. Černý (1973) 340–41.

103. Ibid.; *KRI* V.379–80.

104. Černý (1973) 341, 346 n. 8; Bierbrier (1975a) 39 n. 186.

105. O. Louvre N696 = *KRI* VII.320–21; cf. also P. Berlin 10496.7 and v. 8 = Allam (1973) 80–83, for Amonnakhte as "scribe of the vizier."

106. O. Berlin 10633; *KRI* V.529–30.

107. TT 106, Dynasty Nineteen.

108. But note Janssen (1997) 159.

109. *RAD* 55.15–56.7; cf. Vernus (1980) 121–24. Cf. Ostracon Oriental Institue Chicago 16991 = *KRI* V.559–60 for similar complaints in a letter to him from the scribe Neferhotep. For the Sed Festival, note also the inscription from the tomb of Setau at El Kab: *KRI* V.430.

110. Janssen (1997) 156–57; cf. Allam (1997).

111. O. Deir el-Medina 148; Janssen (1997) 156–57.

112. McDowell (1990) 217–19.

113. O. Berlin 10663; Janssen (1997) 158.

114. O. Deir el-Medina 35.9–10; cf. O. Deir el-Medina 153.16–17; Janssen (1997) 158; Kitchen (1985); Haring (1992) 79–80.

115. O. Turin 57072 recto; Janssen (1979b) 301–6.

116. See Meskell (1999) 183–212 for attempts to quantify personal wealth at Deir el-Medina.

117. See above and Frandsen (1990).

118. Donker van Heel and Haring (2003) 32, 37, 40, 67 n.106; for a general survey of the text, see Vernus (1993) 75–100.

119. Cf. Eyre (1979) 84–87; Donker van Heel and Haring (2003) 40, 72–76 (for the corpus of ostraca of the period).

120. See Frandsen (1990) esp. 192–99, although Frandsen's interpretation is doubt-less far too favorable to the character, motives, and actions of Amonnakhte himself.

121. *RAD* 52.16–53.3, 54.14, 55.7–8, 56.13–16.

122. *RAD* 54.7–8 (chief of Medjay), 56.9 (foreman Khonsu).

123. *RAD* 54.15–55.2.

124. *RAD* 54.1–3; cf. 57.3, 56.11.

125. O. Berlin 10633 = *KRI* V.529–30 (see above).

126. *RAD* 49.16.

127. *RAD* 52.16, 49.17.

128. *RAD* 54.11.

129. *RAD* 53.6 and 10.

130. Eyre (1979) 82–83 n. m.

131. *RAD* 51.15–52.3. For the role of the temples in the strike documents, see Haring (1997) 268–73.

132. Eyre (1979).

133. Donker van Heel and Haring (2003) 67 n. 106.

134. Keller (1994) 152–54.

135. Year 2, of Ramesses V or VI. O. Berlin 12654 v. = Allam (1973) pls. 14–15; Janssen (1982). In year 1, probably of Ramesses V, when a descent of "the enemy" saw

the destruction of Pernebyt, the crew could still muster 120 men. See below on P. Turin 2044.

136. P. Salt 124 = *KRI* IV.408–4. For the family, see Bierbrier (1975a) 21–23; Davies (1999) 34–39.

137. *HO* 27.3 = O. Gardiner 4 = *KRI* VI.142; McDowell (1990) 114–17, 133.

138. P. Salt 124, vs. 2.1 = *KRI* IV.414.8. For a general treatment of the text, see Vernus (1993) 101–22.

139. Černý (1973) 339–83; Bierbrier (1975a) 39–42; Davies (1999) 105–18.

140. Černý (1973) 124–27; Bierbrier (1975a) 36–39; Davies (1999) 12–30.

141. Bierbrier (1975a) 30–36; Davies (1999) 43–58.

142. For the most recent, but highly speculative, resurvey, see Leblanc (2001) 151–81.

143. Janssen (1975a) 105–9; Janssen (1975b) 156–58.

144. Eyre (1979) 81; Eyre (1984a) 205–7; Janssen (1997) 161–67. Note also the appeal for payments of the mid-Twentieth Dynasty P. DM 24 = Eyre (1987b); and note P. Bibl. Nat. 339–40 = *KRI* VI.339–40, putting the cartouches of Ramesses VI on the entrance to the gatehouse (*ḫtm*). For the relationship between Ramessesnakhte and the Tomb, see Allam (1997) esp. 1–4, 10–11.

145. O. Cairo 25030; Peterson (1973) 17–18.

146. See above, and note a single figured ostracon with the figure of a vizier, the contemporary Neferronpet: Peterson (1973) 18.

147. P. Ashmolean Museum 1958.112, vs. 4–6 = Eyre (1984a) 198, 205.

148. Haring (1997).

149. *Giornale* 55.23–56.2, 60.1–2 = *KRI* VI.694, 698.1–2 = Jenni (2000) 97, 102.

150. *Giornale* 52.12–53.21 = *KRI* VI.691.4–6 = Jenni (2000) 93.

151. P. Turin 2044, vs. 2.3–3.6 = *KRI* VI.342–43; Černý (1973) 277–78. See von Beckerath (2002) for the problem of the layout and date of the text.

152. This is evidently an interpolation, in available space at the end of the line.

153. Polz (1998) gives a recent general survey, and see esp. 283–88 for the family relationships and offices held. See also Bell (1980).

154. Gardiner (1948) 131, 165.

155. See Bell (1980) 16–27 for the problem.

156. Polz (1998) 283–84.

157. Ibid., 284–85.

158. Ibid., 282–83.

159. Ibid., 283–84; Gardiner (1948) 131.

160. *RAD* 1–13 + Janssen (1995); see Gardiner (1941b) 42–43. For the date, see, most recently, von Beckerath (1997b). Bierbrier's (1972) identification of a second Ramessesnakhte who was high priest is unsubstantiated and remains unlikely: cf. Bell (1980) 16–27.

161. Helck (1967) = *KRI* VI.517–22.

162. *KRI* VI.12–14. See Christophe (1949); Perdriaud (2002). Cf. also *KRI* VI.1–2 for inscriptions of the priest of Coptos Usermaatrenakhte and of the high priest of Montu Turoy from year 1.

163. Polz (1998) 279–81.

164. Ibid., (1998) 270–71, 291–92.

165. Janssen (1975b) 153–56.

166. Cf. *CAH*³ II.2.626–28.

167. *KRI* VI.455–58; Helck (1956) 161–78. This is the first year he is attested in office. For the relative paucity of attestations of Amenhotep, see Polz (1998) 282.

168. They are explicit in, e.g., the Coptos Decree of Nubkheperrure Antef of the Second Intermediate Period, Sethe (1928a) 98.

169. Ritner (1994).

170. Vernus (1975) = Cairo JSE91927. The subject is lost in the break at the bottom of the stela, but the assumption must be that it was the right to inheritance of property or office.

171. Eyre (1999b) 249; Kruchten (1989) 264–67.

172. Recto 1.13 = *RAD* 75.9–15.

173. David (1973) 94.

174. II.37.

175. P. Valençay 1 = *RAD* 72–73; Gardiner (1948) 205–6; Wente (1990) no. 156, pp. 130–31; Eyre (in press).

176. For the title and its holders, see Fischer-Elfert (1991).

177. 1887 = *RAD* 73–82; Gardiner (1941a) 60–62; Vernus (1993) 123–40.

178. Vs. 1.4 = *RAD* 78.8–10.

179. V. 1.7–2.14 = *RAD* 78.16–81.12.

180. 1896 + 2006 = *RAD* 35–44; Gardiner (1941a) 22–37 (but note that Vinson [1995] argues against Gardiner's explanation of difficulties over some of the figures by corruption or falsification of the accounts); Eyre (1984a) 203.

181. 1.3–4 = *RAD* 36.3–5.

182. See Gnirs (1996a) 197 for $\mathit{3}^{rc}$ people in Western Thebes.

183. *LRL* 57.7 –58.16 = Wente (1990) 174–75. Cf. *LRL* 69.16–70.2 = Wente (1990) 172–73; *LRL* 70.9–15 = Wente (1990) 202. Note also *LRL* 67.10–13 = Wente (1990) 173 for an argument over a bad joke included in a letter to the taxing master (ꜥꜣ n št).

184. P. Turin 1930/2050 + 2013 = *KRI* VI.599–603; P. Turin without cat. number—label has "27(H)"—frame "PN.109," known to me from Černý MSS 17.152.19–20, and cf. Janssen (1997) 7 n. 54.

185. Cf. Helck (1975) 240–41.

186. Meeks (1979); Eyre (1994a) 119; Haring (1997) 142–55; Menu (1998) 121–54, esp. 149.

187. Helck (1963); Baer (1962) 36–39; Eyre (1994a) 118–19; *KRI* II.803–6.

188. Eyre (1994a) 120–25.

189. Baines and Parkinson (1997).

190. Černý (1962). For a specific clear example from Abydos in the reign of Ramesses II, see *KRI* III.464–65.

191. Vleeming (1982).

192. McDowell (1990). For the following period, see Römer (1994).

193. Cf. Vernus (1995a) 122–50; Eyre (1999b) esp. 246–49.

194. Baines (1999) 210–11.

195. *LES* 69.9–10.

196. *LES* 72.13–14.

197. *LES* 72.5–10.

198. Gnirs (1996a) 195–201.

199. *LRL* no. 21; Wente (1990) 183. Cf. Jansen-Winkeln (1991).

200. But see below on BM 10383.

201. For general evaluation, see Vernus (1993) 17–74.

202. BM 10052.1.6–7.

203. BM 10383.1.2–3. Cf. BM 10052.1.45–5; P. Mayer A.1.6–7.

204. Abb. 1.7, 4.5–10; P. Leop.-Am. 1.4.

205. But see below, where his titles in the local priesthood may imply he was actually that Nesamon known as the brother of the high priest Amenhotep.

206. P. Leop. Am. 4.9–11.

207. Abb. 5.10–11.

208. Abb. 5.10–12, 5.19–6.16.

209. Abb. 6.7–8.

210. Abb. 7.1–16.

211. For primary discussion, see Capart, Gardiner, and van de Walle (1936).

212. P. Leop.-Am. 2.5, 3.5–7.

213. Abb. 4.1.

214. Haring (1992).

215. For recent treatments, see Vernus (1993) 36–40; Gnirs (1996a) 193–95. For more speculative attempts at interpretation, see Niwinski (1995); Morales (2001). Von Beckerath (2001) provides a proper caution in rejecting the more speculative attempts to reevaluate and shorten the traditional chronology of these years, for which see, most recently, Thijs (2003).

216. *KRI* VI.570–74 = *Giornale* pls. 14–17; *KRI* VI.579–80 = *Giornale* 25, although note that this is also the period of the Tomb Robbery inquiries. Cf. *Giornale* 4–7 = *KRI* VI.563–66 (year 13) and *HO* 69.1.2–4 (year 14).

217. Jenni (2000) 87–104 surveys the texts of the reign.

218. BM 10052.13.24.

219. P. Mayer A.6.4–7; *CAH³* II.2.630–33.

220. BM 10383.2.4–5.

221. Turin Taxation Papyrus = *RAD* 36.1–5; letter to him from Ramesses XI, P. Turin 1896 = *KRI* VI.734–35.

222. BM 10052.10–18.

223. P. Mayer A.13.B.1–4.

224. BM 10052.7–8; cf. 10403.3.5–7.

225. BM 10052.1.9–10, 3.4, 6.4, 6.19, 10.7, 14.6; P. Mayer A.3.5.

226. BM 10052.11.7–8; BM 10403.3.5–7; P. Mayer A.2.8–9, 9–17.

227. P. Mayer A.2.20–21.

228. BM 10052.3.16–17, 6.10–11, 12.1–8.

229. BM 10053, 10383, 10403; Abbott Dockets; P. Mayer A.

230. Aldred (1979b); cf. Jansen-Winkeln (1995a).

231. P. Mayer A.4.5–6 refers to the time Panehsy did *nꜣ mdw ꜥn* as a notably bad time.

232. BM 10383.1.10, 3.1–7.

233. *LRL* 72.8–73.4 = Wente (1990) 190; *LRL* 19.14–20.1 + 20.9–14 = Wente (1990) 192; *LRL* 21.8–10 = Wente (1990) 195–96; *LRL* 32.5–11 = Wente (1990) 193. Cf. also *LRL* 50–51 = Wente (1990) 197–98 for chariot parts and copper.

234. *LRL* 35; Haring (1992) 77–78.

235. *LRL* 8.6–8.

236. Wente (1967) 9–15; (1990) 185–201; Janssen (1991) 11–24. Thijs (1998a and 2000) provides a rather speculative re-evaluation.

237. See Manning (2003).

238. Cf. Butzer (1976) 55–56.

239. BM 10403.3.5–7.

240. BM 10052.1.9.

241. Eyre (1994a) 127, 130; Eyre (1997) 371–77; Eyre (1999a) esp. 45; Eyre (2004).

242. E.g. *LEM* 104.11–105.1 = P. Lansing 7.1–5.

243. For a general evaluation, see Vernus (1993) esp. 159–96.

244. Merikare P42–44.

245. P. Boulaq 4.22.10–13; see Quack (1994) 119 for the textual difficulty.

246. Kruchten (1981); cf. Gnirs (1989).

247. Eyre (1984b) 104–5.

248. This goes far beyond the excessive deduction of costs (see above) or the sale by the captain of a part of the cargo and arrival with a deficit, a noted trick in the "taxation" process in the Islamic period: see Frantz-Murphy (1986) 78.

249. E.g., *HO* 34.4 = *KRI* 467–68 = O. Leipzig 2. Cf. the argument in *LRL* 57.10–58.2 + Wente (1990) 174–75 about the size of measure used when collecting and delivering grain. See BM 10052.5.20 and 3.8 on use of a small measure in sharing out spoils of robbery.

250. Neferti 18–19.

251. Neferti 35–44.

252. Neferti 50–51.

253. *Admonitions* 2.1.

254. *Admonitions* 2.3.

255. P. Boulaq 4.21.8–9. See Quack (1994) 112–13 for the textual problems.

256. Caminos (1977). For recent discussion, see Niwinski (1995) 336–37.

Chapter 5

Nomads of Sea and Desert: An Integrated Approach to Ramesses III's Foreign Policy

The Aegean and Anatolia

PETER W. HAIDER

If Ramesses III wanted to be in a position to protect and to defend the Mediterranean coast of his empire, as well as the traffic in goods between Egypt and its Asiatic provinces, he had to possess an effective navy. He needed such a fleet in order to engage in active foreign relations and an export trade. For that reason, Ramesses had to build, equip, and arm a new fleet at the beginning of his reign:

> I made for thee [i.e., the god Amun] transports, galleys, and barges, with archers equipped with their arms, upon the sea. I gave to them captains of archers and captains of galleys, manned with numerous crews, without number, in order to transport the products of the land of Zahi [i.e., Palestine] and the countries of the ends of the earth to thy great treasuries in Victorious Thebes.[1]

In addition, the existence of this navy made it possible to protect the Nile Delta against the invasion of the Sea Peoples in the eighth year of the pharaoh (1176/75 BC)[2] and to defeat them:[3]

I caused the Nile mouth to be prepared like a strong wall with warships, galleys, and coasters, equipped, for they were manned completely from bow to stern with valiant warriors, with their weapons.[4] . . . countries [i.e., peoples] who came from their land in the isles in the midst of the sea, as they were (coming) toward Egypt, . . . a net was prepared for them, to ensnare them. They that entered into the Nile mouths were caught, fallen into the midst of it, pinioned in their places, butchered, and their bodies hacked up.[5]

It is an interesting fact that the appearance of the Egyptian warships manifests an apparent Aegean influence. The high bulwark, the castles, a high angular sternpost, the rigging, and the crow's nest are the elements taken over.[6] We know that "Kaftu (Keftiu) ships," vessels of Cretan type, were built in the royal dockyards of Memphis already in the time of Thutmosis III and Amenophis II.[7] But what do we know about the connections between the Egyptian royal court and the Aegean world during the thirty-two years of the reign of Ramesses III?

First and foremost, the Egyptian historiographers during his reign listed the names of the following countries or states of the Aegean and Anatolia: Alashia, Menus, Ardukka, Hatti, and Arzawa (fig. 5.1).[8] Alashia is identified with Cyprus.[9] Menus, as one of the (north)western countries known to the Egyptians, has to be localized in the Aegean.[10] It is usually named together with Kaftu (Keftiu), the island of Crete, or instead of it.[11] Its name is hardly separate from the much later Minos, the mythical king of Knossos. Ardukka is known as a land in the northwestern part of Anatolia.[12] Hatti, the core of the well-known Hittite Empire in central Anatolia, and Arzawa, a country and sometimes the name of a political coalition of smaller states in the middle of western Anatolia,[13] were the most significant lands of Anatolia at that time. However, it is hard to decide whether or not these countries or states named in the topographical lists from the time of Ramesses III are only copied from older records without any topical and historical relevance.

The absence of Kaftu (Keftiu) in the lists is very striking, because the earlier pharaohs had intensive connections with Crete from the time of the late Hyksos period through the reign of Ramesses II.[14] Moreover, Ramesses III intentionally depicted Minoan stirrup jars in a storeroom of his tomb.[15] These vessels are not imitations, as is generally thought,[16] especially by those who do not know Late Minoan IIIC pottery.[17] Therefore, the reproduction of these stirrup jars proves not only a direct or indirect contact between the Egyptian royal court and Crete but also the importance of the products

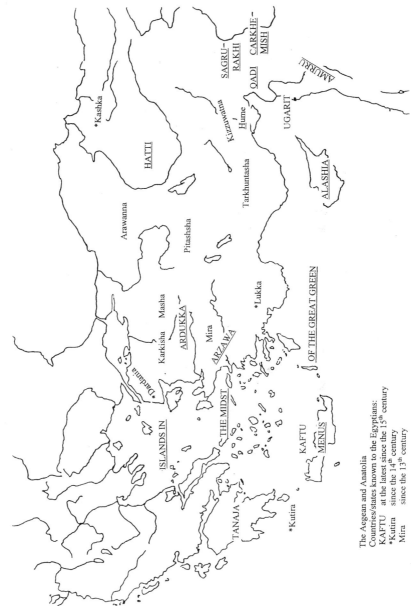

The Aegean and Anatolia
Countries/states known to the Egyptians:
KAFTU at the latest since the 15th century
*Kutira since the 14th century
Mira since the 13th century

Fig. 5.1. Map of the Aegean and Anatolia, with areas known to the Egyptians. (Drawing by P. W. Haider.)

transported by them as well as the king's pride in these goods. Since an Egyptian import was found in a Late Minoan IIIC context at Knossos on Crete,[18] I would suggest that it is possible to identify that site with Menus. The absence of Kaftu (Keftiu) in the lists becomes explainable if one suggests that it has been replaced by Menus.

The label "the islands in the midst of the Great Green" appears numerous times in different documents of Ramesses III.[19] It must designate the Aegean islands,[20] for in those days, Egyptian objects arrived at Rhodes, Cos, and Melos and at the port of Perati on the eastern coast of Attica (fig. 5.2).[21] Moreover, "the northern countries [i.e., peoples] which are in their islands"[22] are also characterized as a region connected to the Sea Peoples.[23] The groups whose men wore helmets with feathered crowns belonged to the Sea Peoples also;[24] they are portrayed in figurines on Crete[25] and are drawn on vessels from Cos and Tiryns.[26] The combination of historiographic, iconographic, and archaeological sources allows us to identify these peoples with the Danuna on the eastern Peloponnesus;[27] the Pulasti/Philistines, who probably came from Thessaly or Crete;[28] and the Zakara, who presumably are from the southern Cycladic islands.[29] The Tur(u)sha, who wore head scarfs, came probably from the islands of the northern Aegean,[30] and the Washasha can be linked by name with the Oassa/Oassassios on eastern Crete.[31] However, the countries of origin of the Shardana and Shakalusha, wearers of horned helmets, are unclear even now. They may come from northern or western Greece, rather than from the eastern Aegean,[32] and are unlikely to be from Sardinia and Sicily.[33]

The ongoing contact with the Aegean put Ramesses III into a position to consecrate splendid Minoan or Mycenaean vessels of gold, silver, and other precious material, acquired as goods, as tribute, or as gifts to Amun-Re.[34] One of those trading ships that conveyed Egyptian artifacts to the Aegean, in addition to Mesopotamian, Syro-Palestinian, Cypriot, and Anatolian objects, went down at Cape Gelidonya[35] in one of the very last years of Ramesses III.[36] This shipwreck testifies to the existence of an international maritime trade right up to the middle of the twelfth century BC. Copper, tin, and bronze were the most important raw products for Egypt.[37] For this reason, the Egyptian state could never dispense with the importation of those metals, which were brought from Cyprus and Anatolia. We find the same type of oxhide ingots both on the Cape Gelidonya shipwreck[38] and on the reliefs of Ramesses III.[39]

It is probably the continuing relation to and trade with the crude metal markets that prompted the Egyptian historiographers to enter Alashia,

The Aegean and western Anatolia

- Imported Egyptian object in an early LM/LH III C-context
x   Wreck of Cape Gelidonya
MENUS   Country/state mentioned under Ramesses III

Fig. 5.2. Map of the Aegean and western Anatolia. (Drawing by P. W. Haider.)

ARDUKKA

ARZAWA

THE MIDST

ISLANDS IN

OF THE GREAT GREEN

Cape Gelidonya

Rhodos

Cos

Knossos

Melos

Perati

Mycenae

Arzawa, Ardukka, and Hatti into their topographical lists, for they did not include the other Aegean and Anatolian countries that they could see named in the older lists. The last known information that we have reports not only on intensive and friendly relations between the Egyptian royal court under Merenptah and the king of Ugarit[40] but also on a shipment of grain to Hatti "to keep alive that land" before the fifth year of this pharaoh (1209/8 BC).[41] There are no more reports until the most momentous message, that not later than in the fifth year of Ramesses III (1179/78 BC) "all foreign countries separated from their islands. Removed and scattered in a struggle were the flat countries at one time. No lands could stand before their arms, from Hatti, Qadi, Carchemish, and Arzawa up to Alashia chopped up [at one time]."[42] After the collapse of the states in the Aegean, in Anatolia, and in parts of northern Syria during the years between 1190 and 1180 BC, only Egypt had the power to control the sea routes. It was then left to the determination of Ramesses "to transport the products of . . . countries of the ends of the earth"[43] to Egypt.

Notes to Haider

1. P. Harris I.7.8. The same information is given referring to the sanctuary of Ptah at Memphis: P. Harris I.48.6, 51a.13.

2. I am here following the chronology of Beckerath (1997a) 104–6, 190, 200–201.

3. For the textual record and illustration of the naval battle, see *MH* I, pls. 37–40, 42; Edgerton and Wilson (1936) 41–42. See also Nelson (1943) 40–45; Sandars (1978) 124–31, figs. 80–84; Wachsmann (1981) 191–96, figs. 1–9; Hölbl (1983) 131–35; Haider (1988) 54–59 with references; Grandet (1993) 195–99, figs. on pp. 198, 200, 201; O'Connor (2000) 97–99, figs. 5–6; Wachsmann (2000) 105–15, fig. 6.1–8. For critiques of the Medinet Habu records as historical sources showing the compositional dimension and the conceptual background to represent the cosmic process and the royal ideology, see Hölbl (1983) 121–38; Cifola (1988) 275–307; Redford (2000) 8–13; O'Connor (2000) 85–101.

4. *MH* I, pl. 46; *KRI* V.40.5–12; Edgerton and Wilson (1936) 54 (pl. 46.20).

5. *MH* I, pl. 42; *KRI* V.33.4–6; Edgerton and Wilson (1936) 42 (pl. 42.3–7).

6. Sandars (1978) 127, figs. 80–84; Wachsmann (1981) 191, figs. 3 and 13. For ample argumentation and discussion, see Raban (1988) 266–72, figs. 1–3.

7. For sources and interpretation, see Vercoutter (1956) 53–55 (nos. 6–7); Helck (1964) 881, 884–85; Haider (1988) 22–23; Helck (1995) 32–33; Haider (1999b) 205.

8. For *J-s-jj*, *mn-nu-w-s<u>* (*u* erroneously written instead of the determinative "foreign country"), and *J-r-t-g-w*, see *MH* I, pl. 43; *KRI* V.35; Edgerton and Wilson (1936) 44, 45 (pls. 43:30); Simons (1937) 175 (list XXX, 8.9.14); Vercoutter (1956) 169 (no. 62). Vercoutter's identifications of nos. 8, 13, and 14 are wrong (see nn. 10 and 13 below). For *H̱-t-3*, *i-r-t-w*, see *KRI* V.111 no. 38a; Simons (1937) 177 (list XXXd, 4.5).

9. The earlier identification with Asija/Asie/Asia in western Anatolia was assumed by Vercoutter ([1956] 179–81), Helck ([1983a] 29–36), Haider ([1988] 17), and Helck

([1995] 28–29). But Quack (1996) shows that *Jsjj* was the traditional form of writing from the Middle Kingdom onward. Since the beginning of the New Kingdom, the name for Alashia was also written *Jrs* in the Egyptian language.

10. All sources are collected and discussed in Vercoutter (1956) 159–70 (nos. 56–62). For an identification, he also suggested Melos, Rhodes, or Carpethos. For a new discussion, see Haider (1988) 16–18, 42–43, 46–47. Helck ([1995] 29–30) left the localization open.

11. Haider (1988) 16–18.

12. That site was named from the reign of Thutmosis III to that of Ramesses III: see Edel (1975) 58–59, 69–70. Edel demonstrated the identification with Ardukka in the Hittite texts; see Del Monte and Tischler (1978) 40 s.v. "Artuka."

13. All sources are collected and critically discussed by Heinhold-Krahmer (1977). Haider (1999b) dealt with the contacts between Egypt and Arzawa. A list of the Hittite sources is given by Del Monte and Tischler ([1978] 42–45; [1992] 14). For a recent critical view of the historical geography of western Anatolia, according to Hittite texts, see Haider (1999a) 665–75, pl. 162.3.

14. Here is not the place to discuss all the older theories of identifications, for they have become indefensible in the meantime. For references and argumentations, see Vercoutter (1956) 33–38; Wachsmann (1987) 93–99; Haider (1988) 1–47; Cline (1991) 11–71; Cline (1994) 31–47, 118–14; Leclant (1996) 613–25.

15. Fimmen (1921) figs. on pp. 209 and 215; Vercoutter (1956) pl. LIX.438–41; Buchholz (1974) 453, fig. 89c–f; Wachsmann (1987) 110, 136, pl. LIX A.

16. Fimmen (1921) 209; Vercoutter (1956) 354; Buchholz (1974) 450–51.

17. Such stirrup jars with a flat and wide base, rather straight sides, and a body covered with horizontal decorated bands of waves and zigzag lines or reticulate patterns were developed in LM IIIA and became popular in LM IIIC: see the analyses of LM/LH IIIC pottery in Schachermeyr (1979) 122–92, 201–20; Schachermeyr (1980) 64–199; Kanta (1980) 248–55; Mountjoy (1988) 1–37; Deger-Jalkotzy (1998) 114–28. Cf. the stirrup jars of Ramesses III: Schachermeyr (1979) 188–89, 208–9 (figs. 53.5–6 and 54.D9–D10, pl. 12a); Kanta (1980) 64 (fig. 28.1), 135 (fig. 122.1 and 4), 173 (fig. 66.9), 181 (fig. 68.3–4).

18. For this vessel, see Cline (1991) 31, 218, 406 (no. 279), tables 1 and 5; Cline (1994) 262 (last line). This alabastron, produced in Egypt during the Eighteenth Dynasty, was found in Knossos stratigraphically in an LM IIIC context; cf. Warren (1989) 4 (no. 14, fig. 1, 3, pl. 6). It is not clear why Cline (1994) 168 (no. 287) dates the context of this object to LM I–IIIA without any argumentation, although he is probably following Phillips (1991) 576 (no. 189). We have at Knossos the same situation as at Mycenae, where another Egyptian alabastron of the Eighteenth Dynasty was also imported during the early LH IIIC period (see n. 21 below).

19. For all nine sources with argumentation, see Vercoutter (1956) 141–46 (nos. 42–50); Cline (1991) 53–55; Cline (1994) 118–20 (nos. A.51– A.59), fig. 7.

20. Besides the literature in the preceding note, see Vanschoonwinkel (1991) 470–73; Cline (1994) 116–18 (nos. A.38–A.59); Leclant (1996) 618, 625. Redford (2000) 12 is correct to emphasize that the term *iw.w* means "islands" and does not include coastal lands, because the Egyptians had a number of words already for "maritime littoral" (e.g., *pdsw-š, wḏb,* etc.). Besides the identification with the Aegean islands, this term includes perhaps the Ionian islands also.

21. The archaeological facts have been collected and analyzed in Cline (1991) 11–17, tables 2–6, fig. 3; Cline (1994) 37–38, tables 25–28 and 30, fig. 7. At Mycenae, one Egyptian import was found in an LH IIIC context: see Cline (1991) 399 (no. 253), table 4; Cline (1994) 164 (no. 255), table 28; Cline (1995) 95, 101 (no. 35).

22. *MH* I, pl. 37, I.8–9; *KRI* V.32.6–7; Edgerton and Wilson (1936) 41; Vercoutter (1956) 142 (no. 43); Cline (1994) 119 (no. A.52).

23. *MH* I, pls. 27–28.51–52; *MH* I, pl. 37, I.8–9; *MH* I, pls. 42.3–4, 44.14–15, 46.16–18, 107.7; *KRI* V.25.4–6, 32.6–7, 33.4–5, 36.7–8, 39.14, 40.3–4, 73.9–10, 91.11–12; Edgerton and Wilson (1936) 30, 41, 42, 44, 53, 130; P. Harris I.76.7. The idea presented by Sherratt ([1998] 292–313) that the so-called Sea Peoples "were rather an economic and cultural community than primarily genetic or linguistic units" polarizes the discussion needlessly, for a cultural uniformity and economic equivalence of some population groups does not exclude the possibility that they consist of different genetic and/or linguistic units.

24. Haider (1988) 60–61, 68 with references; Borchhardt (1972) 115–18.

25. Kanta (1980) 71, fig. 24.8 (no. 18.396).

26. For early LH IIIC kraters from Cos and Seraglio, see Sandars (1978) 135, fig. 92; Schachermeyr (1979) 129, pl. 16c; Schachermeyr (1980) 157–58, pl. 34c–e; Wachsmann (1981) 200, figs. 15–16. For such kraters from Tiryns, see Schachermeyr (1980) pl. 33d; Schachermeyr (1982) 84–86, pl. 5c–d.

27. The names given for these people are *D-3-jn.nw-n-3*, "Danuna," or *D-3-jn.jw*, "Danu." The reading of *-jn.jw-* as *-nu-* has been proven since the study of Edel ([1966] 65). For that reason, the reading "Denyen" is impossible. *Danu(na)* with the ending *-na* can be linked with the later testified Danaoi as the population on the eastern Peloponnesus: see Lehmann (1979) 488; Strobel (1976) 201–4; Schachermeyr (1982) 191–93; Haider (1988) 8–9, 54, 72–73. Margalith (1994) 91–124 identifies the Danu(na) with the Danu(nim) in the Bible also. But against the opinions of Strobel ([1976] 203–4), Sandars ([1978] 162–64), and Helck ([1995] 115) that the Danu(na) went from Cilicia to Greece, see Haider (1988) 72. Emphasis should be placed on the fact that the Danu(nim) are not named in Cilicia before the eighth century BC. It is assumed that the Danu(na) coming from the Aegean settled in Cilicia after 1190/80 BC. Cf. Schachermeyr (1982) 196–97; Haider (1988) 8–9, 72.

28. The name *P-w-r-s-t-j*, "Pur/lasti," can be linked with the Pelastoi, another form of the name *Pelasgoi*, and the name of the Thessalian region Pelasgiotis, where the Mycenaean culture was also present. With references to the older literature, see Strobel (1976) 159–61; Haider (1988) 78–80; Margalith (1994) 42–43; Helck (1995) 114–15. Pelastoi/Pelasgoi are testified on Crete also by the Greek historians. The connection between Crete and the Philistines is known from the Bible (Deut. 2:23; 1 Sam. 30:14; 1 Kings 1:38; Ezek. 25:16; Jer. 47:4; Zeph. 2:5). The Philistines reached Canaan from Caphtor; the Caphtorim then settled in and around Gaza, which was then named "Minoa" and was where the Cretan god Marnas was worshiped up to the Roman era: see Faust (1969) 88–107; Strobel (1976) 214–17; Schachermeyr (1982) 211–12; Haider (1988) 43, 78–80; Vanschoonwinkel (1991) 474–94; Margalith (1994) 24–32; Machinist (2000) 54–83. The material culture of the initial phase of Philistine settlements shows their Aegean origin: see Dothan (1982) 21 passim; Dothan (1998) 148–61; Dothan (2000) 145–58; Dothan and Dothan (1992) 29–73, 92–96, 137–40, 149–57. See also

Kitchen (1973) 57–78; Strobel (1976) 77–100, 220–23; Schachermeyr (1982) 211–12, 214–28, 236–68; Singer (1988a) 239–50; Mazar (1988) 251–60; Raban (1988) 261–94. The same phenomenon is proved now in northern Israel and the Jordan Valley, where groups of Sea Peoples settled under Egyptian control: see Stern (2000) 197–212; Tubb (2000) 181–96. For their helmets and types of ship, see n. 33 below.

29. On the *T3-k3-3-r-3*, *T3-k3-(k3-)3-r-w*, *T3-3-k3-3-r-j-j*, *T3-k3-3-r*, "Zak(k)ara/u/ia, Zakar(a)," usually identified with the Teukroi of the first millennium BC, see, both with references, Schachermeyr (1982) 113–22; Haider (1988) 80. The Teukroi were a wandering group until 500 BC (Herodotus 7.75). In those days, they settled in the Troad, on Crete, and on Cyprus. Since the end of the second millennium, people on the southern Cycladic islands who wore similar Zakara helmets with feathered crowns can be identified with them.

30. For the *T-w-i-r-š3*, "Tuirsha," see *MH* VIII, pl. 600; *KRI* V.91.12, 104.14. Older writings are *T-w-r-w-š3-3*, "Turusha" (*KRI* IV.2.13), and *T-w-r-i-š3-3*, "Turisha" (*KRI* IV. 4.1). It is understood that they are the historical Tyrsenoi who lived in the northern Aegean region up to 500 BC: see Strobel (1976) 182–85; Sandars (1978) 111–12, 165; Haider (1988) 49, 53, 63–64, 75–76.

31. On the *W3-š3-3-š3-3*, "Washasha," see Strobel (1976) 208–9; Haider (1988) 54, 57, 78, with references. The Washasha could be the biblical Caphtorim who came together with the Philistines from Crete and settled at and near Gaza-Minoa; see n. 28 above.

32. The names used are *Š3-3-r-d-i-n-3*, *Š3-3-i-r-d-3-n-3*, "Shardi/ana," and *Š3-3-k3-rw-š3-3*, "Shakar/lusha," or "Shikalaju" in the Akkadian language (RS 34.129: see Lehmann [1979] 481–94). It would be fruitless to return to the many theories on the topic. For references, see Lehmann (1979) 481–94; Lehman (1983) 90–91; Haider (1988) 49, 52–53, 57–58, 74–75, 81–82; Loretz (1995) 125–40. Against the opinion that the Shardana and Schakalusha/Shikalaju came from western or northwestern Anatolia, Niemeier (1988) 45–49 showed that there is no evidence at all for western Anatolian settlement in the southern Levant. Lehmann (1979) 493–94 and Schachermeyr (1982) 39–40 plead for an Adriatic region from the origins of the Shakalusha.

33. As Vagnetti (2000) 305–26 showed, the archaeological evidence in Italy, on Sicily, and on Sardinia speaks well for the assumption that the Shardana and Shakalusha/Shikalaju were "of Aegean origin and arrived in the west during the so-called 'Dark Ages.'" They brought the toponyms attached to the two islands (but see the different opinion proffered by Cline and O'Connor later in this chapter). Like the helmets with feathered crows, the horned helmets also belong to the same sort of Aegean Zonen helmets: see Borchhardt (1972) 109–18; Strobel (1976) 251; Haider (1988) 68. For an initial origin of these two peoples and perhaps also of the Pulasti/Philistines from the northern Balkans, as indicated by the type of the double-headed "bird boats" that were common in the Urnfield cultures in central Europe, especially in the Danubian regions, see the analysis in Wachsmann (2000) 115–43 (figs. 1B, 7).

34. Vercoutter (1956) 309 (nos. 237–38), 312–13 (nos. 254a–c), 314–15 (no. 262), 316 (no. 267b), 323 (nos. 299–300), 331 (no. 336), pls. XXXVI–XXXIX, XLII, XLV, LIII; Wachsmann (1987) 59–60.

35. Bass (1967) 44 and passim; Bass (1997) 183–89; Cline (1991) 280–85; Cline (1994) 101.

36. Giveon (1985) 99–101 analyzed the scarabs found in the wreck once more and

showed that the ship went down "clearly to the time of Ramesses III . . . with a possibility of an even later date, Ramesses IV."

37. For analyses of written and archaeological sources regarding the metal trade, see Buchholz (1959) 1–40; Bass (1967) 84–121, 135–42; Muhly (1977) 73–82; Muhly, Wheeler, and Maddin (1977) 353–62; Buchholz (1988) 187–228; Muhly (1989) 298–314; Cline (1991) 54–55, 136–40, 243–303; Cline (1994) 9–106; Helck (1995) 98–102; Bass (1997) 188–89; Sherratt (1998) 292–313.

38. Bass (1967) 52–83; Helck (1995) 99–101.

39. MH V, pl. 328. Bass (1967) figs. 83–84; Helck (1995) 100. Both authors believe that these reliefs are copies from analogous scenes in the Ramesseum. But there is one such scene preserved, and even if Ramesses has copied that, an analogous picture can never be reason enough to exclude the reality of an autonomous import of such ingots by Ramesses III.

40. For Merenptah's letter to the king of Ugarit (RS 88.2158), see Lackenbacher (1995) 77–83; Lehmann (1983) 86–90. See also Yon (1989) 115–22; Helck (1995) 115; Klengel (1999) 297–98; Singer (2000).

41. KRI IV.5.3; Otten (1983) 15–16; Lehmann (1983) 88; Klengel (1999) 297–98. On the different reasons for the collapse of the Hittite Empire, see, now, Sandars (1978) 140–44; Otten (1983) 37–47; Bittel (1983) 37–47; Lehmann (1983) 91–93; Hoffner (1989) 46–52; Klengel (1999) 300–319; Singer (2000) 25–28.

42. MH I, pl. 46.16–17; KRI V.39.14–15. The translation of jrj-w šdtt as "made a conspiracy" by Edgerton and Wilson ([1936] 53), Edel ([1985] 225), and Schachermeyr ([1982] 66) is impossible. It has to be translated "they separated," as shown by Hölbl ([1983] 128–29), Helck ([1987] 131–32), and Haider ([1999b] 216 with n. 77).

43. See n. 1. See Merrillees (1989) 91 for the opinion, problematic in light of the aforementioned facts, that "Ramesses III could do no more than defend the Delta against the Sea Peoples."

Egypt and the Levant in the Reign of Ramesses III

JAMES M. WEINSTEIN

The reign of Ramesses III opened the final chapter in the history of the New Kingdom empire in western Asia. The pharaohs of the early Eighteenth Dynasty (late sixteenth to early fifteenth centuries BC) carved out an empire that reached as far north as the Euphrates River in Syria. Over the next several centuries, Egypt governed Syria-Palestine by means of a loose colonial administration that was managed through one or more regional headquarters and included the retention of local vassal princes. The principal headquarters during most of the New Kingdom was at Gaza in southwestern Palestine. Other

Egyptian administrative headquarters, attested for shorter time spans, have been proposed for Kumidi, in the Bekaa Valley of southern Lebanon, and at Sumur, north of Tripoli, along the Syrian coast. Administrators stationed at the regional headquarters, supplemented by circuit officials and tax collectors, and supported militarily by small garrisons of Egyptian troops (and, later on, by increasing numbers of foreign mercenaries) at these and other strategic points comprised the bulk of the personnel who ran the empire for the pharaoh on a day-to-day basis. When so required, the king could dispatch more substantial military forces (which he sometimes personally led) from Egypt to put down rebellions in Canaanite towns, bring troublesome non-urban groups under control, or confront any of the great powers of the Near East (Mitanni initially, Hatti later on) that might challenge Egyptian authority in the Levant.

This colonial enterprise fluctuated in strength and geographical extent over a period of some four hundred years, but it generally functioned rather well until the reign of Ramesses II (1279–1213 BC), when much of Syria slipped out of Egypt's hands following the battle at Kadesh against the Hittites in the king's fifth regnal year. After that clash, Egyptian authority gradually receded until it encompassed primarily the southern Levant and the Phoenician coast. Within Palestine, the Nineteenth Dynasty pharaohs found it necessary to expand the number of garrisons and reinforce already existing strongholds. Those actions, combined with the suppression of occasional small-scale revolts in the reigns of Sety I (1294–1279 BC), Ramesses II (1279–1213 BC), and Merenptah (1213–1203 BC), sufficed to keep the area in Egyptian hands—until political instability in Egypt and perhaps the movement of new peoples into Palestine at the end of the thirteenth and beginning of the twelfth centuries BC contributed to a loss of Egyptian hegemony over substantial parts of the highlands and fringe areas of the southern Levant and possibly also Phoenicia.[1] The early Twentieth Dynasty opened with Egyptian rule focusing on lowland Palestine to exploit its resources and protect Egypt's imperial interests against any hostile challenges.

THE INVASION OF THE SEA PEOPLES

The empire suffered a serious blow when a confederation of tribal groups known as the Sea Peoples moved out of the northern Mediterranean world in the early twelfth century BC, attacking towns at various points along the Syro-Palestinian littoral and moving south as far as the Egyptian Delta in regnal year 8 (1177 BC) of Ramesses III (1184–1153 BC). Their assault, like that of the hordes of Libyan tribesmen who attacked Egypt's western border in regnal years 5 and 11 of the king, was repelled, but the effect of the invasion and its aftermath was to hasten the demise of Egyptian rule in western Asia.

Various groups of Sea Peoples are attested in Egyptian records as far back as the Amarna period in the mid-fourteenth century BC. Sometimes they served as mercenaries in the Egyptian military. At other times they were Egypt's immediate enemies (or allies of the latter): an attack on Egypt's western border by several Sea Peoples groups was beaten back in the days of Merenptah. The records of the assault in year 8 of Ramesses III, preserved on the walls of the king's memorial temple at Medinet Habu and in Papyrus Harris I from the reign of the king's immediate successor, Ramesses IV,[2] attest to the most serious assault on Egypt's security since the Hyksos takeover of the Eastern Delta in the seventeenth century BC. According to the Egyptian accounts, the northern tribesmen—encompassing the Peleset (the biblical Philistines), Tjekeru (= Sikils), Shekelesh, Denyen, and Weshesh in the Medinet Habu account, with the Sherden replacing the Shekelesh among the invaders according to Papyrus Harris I—devastated a large part of the Eastern Mediterranean world, from Anatolia and Alashiya (Cyprus) down through Syria-Palestine, before finally being stopped at or not far from the entrance to Egypt itself. Regrettably, the laconic and bombastic nature of the Egyptian sources provide only a broad outline of the specific events of the period.

The naval and land battles between the Egyptians (and their foreign mercenary allies) and the Sea Peoples, described elsewhere in this book in greater detail, may have taken place within sight of each other near the mouth of one of the eastern branches of the Nile, or they may have taken place some distance apart. There is much debate on the setting of the land battle, with a minority of scholars arguing for an Asiatic locale—perhaps even in northern Palestine.[3] In any case, the pharaoh reports that his forces were totally victorious in all encounters and that the Sea Peoples were repulsed with great loss of life. Thereupon, the king brought the captured survivors to Egypt and enclosed them in strongholds (Papyrus Harris I.76–79).

The location of these strongholds has been debated for years. Ramesses' statement indicates that they were in Egypt,[4] and there is textual evidence for Sherden and even Peleset mercenaries being stationed in strongholds in Egypt.[5] As yet, however, the remains of these settlements have not been unearthed anywhere in the Delta or Nile Valley.[6] But there is extensive archaeological evidence for these Mediterranean groups settling down in Palestine in considerable numbers.[7] Hence, while the king probably initially confined some of the captured Sea Peoples within strongholds in the Delta or Nile Valley or both, it is reasonable to think that those captives constituted a much smaller proportion of the survivors of the year 8 naval and sea battles than the ones who settled in Palestine. Considering the propagandistic and self-laudatory nature of Egyptian war texts, it should not be at all surprising that the king would claim he settled his (defeated) enemies in strongholds in Egypt, while at the same time conveniently ignoring the much larger numbers who settled down in Palestine—despite any efforts his forces might have made to dislodge them.

The Sea Peoples' settlements along the Palestinian coast and inland on the southern coastal plain had a damaging effect on Egyptian authority in the southern Levant. We do not know whether or to what extent the Egyptians actively tried to block the Sea Peoples from settling where they did, but it is unlikely they could have succeeded.[8] There is evidence of destructions at Ashdod, Tel Miqne (Ekron), and Tell es-Safi (Gath), though not at Ashkelon, at the end of the Late Bronze Age,[9] as well as of the subsequent establishment at these sites of large Philistine centers.[10] The situation at Dor farther up the coast, which became the site of a fortified town of the Tjekeru (Sikils) during the Early Iron Age, as well as at Akko on the northern Palestinian coast, which evidently fell into the hands of the Sherden, is more murky: Dor appears not to have suffered a destruction at the end of the Late Bronze Age,[11] while the archaeological history of Akko in the thirteenth and early twelfth centuries BC is little known. Control of southwestern Palestine by the Sea Peoples would have made it more difficult for officials in Gaza to supply and communicate overland with the Egyptian military and administrative personnel to the north.[12] It has also been noticed that some of the forts along the North Sinai land route to western Asia, which previously had provided support for the Gaza headquarters, were allowed to deteriorate during the Twentieth Dynasty.[13] In addition, with the principal port facilities along the southern coast in the hands of the Sea Peoples, there was a decline in maritime trade between Egypt and southern coastal Palestine.[14]

A question we cannot answer with certainty at this point is whether the Sea Peoples took control of the Canaanite towns on their way *to* or *from* Egypt. If the former, then possibly such places served as bases for the subsequent attack on Egypt, so that after their defeat at the hands of the Egyptian military, the Sea Peoples retreated to the Palestinian towns they had already captured. If the latter, then the Sea Peoples bypassed various major towns in Canaan on their way to the gates of Egypt and only took the towns after being thrown back by the Egyptian forces. The Medinet Habu and Papyrus Harris I accounts provide only a sketchy account of the activities of the Sea

Peoples before, during, and after regnal year 8, and neither the archaeological nor textual data are sufficiently precise to establish when the Canaanite settlements were captured or settled vis-à-vis regnal year 8: this makes it difficult to link the archaeological sequence at Palestinian sites to the events recorded in the Egyptian texts and reliefs.[15] In addition, the destruction, abandonment, and/or settlement process may have taken longer and been more complex than the current data allow us to recognize.

THE EGYPTIAN STRATEGY IN SOUTHERN PALESTINE

The Egyptian response to the presence of large Philistine settlements along the coast and in the southern coastal plain was a defensive strategy designed to block Philistine expansion, as well as a plan to administer the areas of southern Palestine that remained under Egyptian control. The archaeological evidence from the second and early third quarter of the twelfth century BC suggests that the military goal was to enclose Philistia between a line of Egyptian bases and administrative centers and the sea and to prevent Philistine expansion into Egyptian-controlled territory. This policy was carried out through the construction or rebuilding of Egyptian fortresses on the northern and southern borders of Philistia as well as the stationing of Egyptian administrative and military personnel within Canaanite settlements inland from Philistia. These sites formed a geographical arc beginning at Tel Mor north of Philistine Ashdod; going inland perhaps to Gezer; then heading south to Lachish, Tell esh-Shari'a, and Tell el-Far'ah (South); and finally heading northwest back to Deir el-Balah and Gaza in the modern-day Gaza Strip.[16]

This historical picture has been reconstructed primarily on the basis of the difference between the Egyptian(ized) material culture found within Philistine territory and that found outside the area. Excavations at most southern Canaanite settlements dating to the thirteenth century BC have yielded Egyptian and Egyptian-style materials such as one might expect to find as the result of trade between two adjacent regions with close commercial ties (e.g., pottery, alabaster, and faience vessels; scarabs, beads, and amulets; and a variety of cosmetic objects). This is especially true for the sites located within what later became known as the Philistine Pentapolis (encompassing Gaza, Ashkelon, Ashdod, Ekron, and Gath). Significantly, however, anthropoid coffins (employed in Palestine for Egyptians who died abroad and likely also for some of the Sea Peoples mercenaries in their employ), Egyptian buildings and construction techniques and statuary, and large quantities of Egyptian and Egyptianized pottery that constitute the hallmark of Egyptian occupation in much of Palestine in the first half of the twelfth century BC are missing from the Pentapolis sites. It is at sites outside Philistia that such Egyptian/Egyptianized materials appear in quantity, and these sites yield little or none of the locally made Mycenaean IIIC:1b Monochrome pottery that is ubiquitous in early Philistine contexts prior to the appearance of the classic Philistine Bichrome ware.[17]

Ashdod was the northernmost of the three major Philistine towns along the southern coast. About seven kilometers north of Ashdod sits Tel Mor, which in Strata VIII–VII (thirteenth century) was the site of a fortified Egyptian structure that was 22.5 × 22.5 meters in size. Following the destruction of this building (perhaps by Canaanites) in the late thirteenth or early twelfth century and a brief period of abandonment, a new and much smaller fortress-like structure (only 11 × 11 meters) followed in Strata VI–V (first half of the twelfth century BC).[18] This building yielded Egyptian-style pottery but not the Monochrome pottery or the slightly later Bichrome ware that characterizes Philistine settlements; it was abandoned still within the twelfth century BC.[19] In view of the small size of the building from Strata VI–V, it is thought that Tel Mor supported only a small Egyptian garrison.

An Egyptian fortress (or fortresses) also sat at the opposite (i.e., southern) border of Philistia, to prevent Philistine expansion into Egyptian-held territory south of the Wadi Gaza (the so-called Brook of Egypt). One fortress has been associated with Stratum VII at Deir el-Balah, about thirteen kilometers south of Gaza, dating to the late Nineteenth and early Twentieth Dynasties.[20] Gaza, the site of the Egyptian regional headquarters in Palestine since the early Eighteenth Dynasty, was probably the location for the principal Egyptian garrison (as well as administrative headquarters) in this period, but because the ancient remains of the town lie beneath the modern city and, as such, cannot easily be excavated, little is known archaeologically about the town in the second millennium BC. Papyrus Harris I (9.1–3) refers to "The-House-of-Ramesses-Ruler-of-Heliopolis," a temple of Amun, in "the [town of?] Canaan," presumably Gaza.[21] Gaza probably remained in Egyptian hands for a considerable time after year 8 and may have become a town of the Peleset only after the death of Ramesses III.

The argument for an Egyptian garrison within the Early Iron Age town of Gezer,[22] situated east of Tel Mor and northeast of the huge Philistine city at Ekron, is based more on conjecture than fact. Excavations conducted at Gezer between 1902 and 1909 by R. A. S. Macalister uncovered Egyptian-style remains of Ramesside date, including a large architectural block inscribed with the Egyptian hieroglyphic sign for "gold."[23] Some of this material may date to the Twentieth Dynasty, but the excavation techniques and recording methods employed by Macalister make it impossible to date his discoveries with any precision. Much of the Ramesside material at Gezer could just as easily relate to the town captured by Merenptah in the thirteenth century BC (an event recorded on the famous "Israel stela" of this king). The two items found by Macalister at Gezer that actually name Ramesses III are a fragment of a faience vessel and a plaque,[24] and these objects could easily have reached Gezer in the course of commercial relations or as gifts. Recent attempts to identify various buildings excavated by Macalister as an Egyptian residency of the Nineteenth Dynasty or Twentieth Dynasty are largely speculative.[25]

Well to the south of Gezer, at Lachish, there was a substantial Egyptian presence in the early twelfth century BC (represented by Level VI). A bronze object (possibly a door fitting) from the Inner Gate area of this Canaanite town is inscribed with the prenomen of Ramesses III.[26] In addition, Tomb 570 yielded two anthropoid clay coffins (though not specifically datable to the reign of Ramesses III); one coffin contained a crude Egyptian funerary inscription.[27] Also indicative of Egyptian activity at Lachish in the Ramesside period are various alabaster, glass, and faience vessels.[28] Belonging to the early twelfth century is the Acropolis Temple, with its small octagonal columns and other Egyptian-style architectural elements.[29] Philistine Monochrome and Bichrome pottery is conspicuous by its absence in Level VI, whose end later on in the century came as the result of a major destruction.[30]

The most interesting Egyptian finds associated with Level VI are a series of small pottery bowls and fragments discovered at the center of the tell and inscribed with short hieratic texts.[31] One fragment, dating to year 10 + x, was found in the foundation fill of Palace A.[32] Three other sherds come from unstratified contexts; one is inscribed with the title "scribe."[33] There are also three ostraca that were found in rubbish attributable to the Late Bronze Age.[34] Parallels for the Lachish hieratic bowl inscriptions are known from at least four other sites in southern Palestine: Tell el-Far'ah (South),[35] Haror,[36] Deir el-Balah,[37] and Tell esh-Shari'a,[38] and perhaps Tell es-Safi.[39] Although no royal names appear in any of these inscriptions, the dates on one of the Lachish bowls (year 10 + x) and on a bowl from Tell esh-Shari'a (year 22 + x), combined with the paleographic evidence, show that Ramesses III was the king in whose reign many of these administrative texts were written. The inscriptions on the bowls mainly relate to the delivery of grain as taxes. The quantities of grain mentioned on the bowls are substantial and reflect the considerable tax burden that the Egyptians imposed on their Canaanite subjects.[40] The grain was collected to feed Egyptian administrative and military contingents in Palestine, as well as to provide offerings for the Egyptian temple of Amun in "the Canaan" (to which Canaanites also donated, according to Papyrus Harris I.9.1–3) and other Egyptian institutions in Palestine.[41]

At Tell esh-Shari'a (Tel Sera) in the northwestern Negev, Stratum IX included a three-phase brick residency with Egyptian-style foundations that had initially been constructed in the Nineteenth Dynasty.[42] Among the finds associated with the structure from the twelfth century BC were four bowls and seven sherds containing hieratic inscriptions,[43] as well as hundreds of Egyptian-style pottery vessels and various small Egyptian items (scarabs, beads, etc.). As noted above, several of the bowl texts refer to the payment of large quantities of grain. Stratum IX came to an end in a violent destruction.

At Tell el-Far'ah (South), in addition to the hieratic bowl inscriptions mentioned above, there was a brick residency constructed according to Egyptian plan and employing Egyptian construction methods;[44] a recent study of this building has concluded that it was originally constructed in the Nineteenth Dynasty and then destroyed sometime between the reigns of Ramesses III and VII in the Twentieth Dynasty.[45] Although both Egyptian and Philistine pottery was found in the ruins of this building—which has suggested to some the possibility of a working relationship between the two groups at this site[46]—the digging methods employed by the excavator back in the late 1920s were inadequate to rule out the possibility that the Philistine pottery relates to the very end of Egyptian occupation at the site or even shortly thereafter. Tell el-Far'ah (South), like Tell esh-Shari'a, evidently managed to avoid the destructions that hit so many other southern Canaanite sites at the end of the Late Bronze Age. The site also yielded four scarabs naming Ramesses III,[47] as well as several tombs with anthropoid coffins.

In summary, Egyptian personnel resided at Tel Mor, Lachish, Tell esh-Shari'a, Tell el-Far'ah (South), and Deir el-Balah along the northern, eastern, and southern borders of Philistia; a large Egyptian garrison probably also existed at Gaza prior to the establishment of Philistine control of the town. Destruction or abandonment mark the end of Egyptian activity at these sites situated along the periphery of Philistia.

THE EGYPTIAN STRATEGY IN NORTHERN PALESTINE

If the principal features of Egyptian policy in southern Palestine—defense and taxation—are clear, the rationale behind Egyptian policy in northern Palestine is somewhat less so. The primary evidence for Egyptian activity in the north in the reign of Ramesses III comes from three sites, all well inland—

at Beth Shan, Megiddo, and Tell es-Saʿidiyeh. The towns of coastal and inland Syria to the north were no longer Egyptian possessions by the early twelfth century BC: other than a statuette fragment from Byblos that contains the name of Ramesses III[48]—a royal object presumably reflecting a continuation of Egypt's long-standing and special political relationship with the port town of Byblos and its local rulers—there are few signs of an Egyptian presence in the towns of Phoenicia or the Bekaa Valley of Lebanon or in Syria to the north and east in the first half of the Twentieth Dynasty.[49]

The one Egyptian military installation in northern Palestine—the only large Egyptian garrison of the twelfth century BC excavated so far in Palestine—was at Beth Shan, which sits at the eastern end of the Jezreel Valley, overlooking the entrance to the Jordan River Valley.[50] Already by the mid-Eighteenth Dynasty (Level IX) there was an Egyptian garrison at the site.[51] Following a subsequent Egyptian garrison of the Nineteenth Dynasty associated with Levels VIII–VII, there was a somewhat ambiguous transitional phase represented by Late Level VII, which dates perhaps to the early Twentieth Dynasty,[52] and then a substantial Egyptian garrison town of the period of Ramesses III assigned to Level VI.[53] Whether the buildup of the Level VI town was initiated in anticipation of the coming of the Sea Peoples or followed the clash of regnal year 8 is debatable.

The principal Egyptian structure in Level VI was building 1500, a residential structure with a central columned hall, for the royal scribe, troop commander, and overseer of foreign lands Ramesses-Userkhepesh. This individual was the governor and senior officer in the garrison.[54] Building 1500 replaced a small fortified structure of Level VII, suggesting that Ramesses-Userkhepesh occupied the residence after the defeat of the Sea Peoples and that the Egyptian military no longer felt the need at that point to have a fortress at the site. A basalt statue, originally associated with Level VI and showing the seated figure of Ramesses III, was found in the courtyard of the northern temple in the later Level V.[55] Tombs in Beth Shan's Northern Cemetery yielded numerous clay anthropoid coffins; these held the remains of Egyptian troops and perhaps also some of the foreign mercenaries in their employ, stationed at the site in the thirteenth and early twelfth centuries BC.[56] Other Egyptian finds associated with the garrison community and tombs included stelae; ushabtis; Egyptian-style vessels in a variety of materials; reliefs;[57] and large numbers of scarabs, amulets, pendants, and other small items.[58] Moreover, although much of the pottery found during the Hebrew University excavations of the site in Levels S4 and S3 (= the earlier University of Pennsylvania Museum Late Levels VII and VI) was Egyptian in style, the bulk of this pottery was locally made but followed Egyptian techno-logical practices; squat jugs formed one of the few vessel types that actually came from Egypt.[59]

The Level VI garrison came to an end in a massive conflagration. The date and agent(s) of this destruction are unknown, but a post-Ramesses III dating is likely, based on the presence of a scarab of Ramesses IV, found in an un-stratified context on the mound,[60] as well as four faience plaques and a scarab inscribed with the name "Ramesses," written in a form regularly employed only in connection with Ramesses IV, possibly from deposits associated with a temple of Level VI.[61] The appearance of these items at Beth Shan as well as an inscribed stone fragment of Ramesses IV found on the surface north of Beth Shan (and originally taken from there?) at Delhamiya in the Jordan Val-ley near the Sea of Galilee[62] combine to show that the Egyptian garrison at Beth Shan survived at least into the reign of Ramesses IV.

Megiddo sits to the west of Beth Shan, at a point where the Wadi ʿAra (Nahal ʿIron) opens into the central part of the Jezreel Valley. This imposing mound dominates the historic route leading from Egypt through the Carmel Ridge and up to Syria. The Egyptian material from the period of Ramesses III is associated with Stratum VIIA, whose construction followed Stratum VIIB belonging to the thirteenth century BC.[63] The most impressive Egyptian ob-jects of Stratum VIIA came from the palace "treasury" and included an ivory model pen case inscribed with the cartouches of Ramesses III,[64] as well as four ivory plaques, three of which contain the private name *Kerker* ("Songstress of Ptah, South of His Wall");[65] from elsewhere on the site came a scarab of Ramesses III.[66] The pen case also contained the partially preserved name of the "Overseer of Foreign Lands, . . . mes"; this official may or may not be the same individual as a certain Thutmose, the captain of troops, whose name appears on several blocks found at Beth Shan and who was the father of the garrison commander there, Ramesses-Userkhepesh.[67] If the Beth Shan and Megiddo personages are the same individual, then there is a clear link between the two sites, though it does not explain specifically why the official was at Megiddo. Other Egyptian finds of this period include bronze, alabaster, and ivory vessels, many of which came from the Stratum VIIA palace and "treasury," as well as a limited amount of Egyptian pottery (much of it probably locally made) and numerous small items, including scarabs, pendants, and amulets.[68]

Megiddo VIIA lacks the large Egyptian structures, reliefs, inscriptions, and statuary, as well as substantial quantities of Egyptian and Egyptian-style pottery, that have been found at Beth Shan.[69] Also missing are the anthropoid coffin burials. Clearly the town played a different role in the Egyptian administration of Canaan during the reign of Ramesses III than did Beth Shan. Rather than being an Egyptian garrison town, Megiddo is a relatively wealthy, unfortified Canaanite town throughout the Late Bronze Age and the beginning of the Iron Age, ruled by a line of vassal princes but with Egyptian military officers and administrators (some bearing gifts, others bringing orders) and merchants (carrying trade goods) coming and going on a regular basis. Seen in this light, the numerous luxury goods found in Stratum VIIA may be viewed as expensive gifts and trade goods for the Canaanite prince and the local elite, as well as the personal possessions of members of the Egyptian administration in Palestine.[70] Considering Megiddo's strategic location, it is most curious that this important town was not occupied by a permanent Egyptian military contingent: instead it relied on the garrison at Beth Shan to protect Egyptian interests in the central part of the Jezreel Valley. Megiddo VIIA, like Beth Shan Level VI, ended with a destruction.[71]

Tell es-Sa'idiyeh, located southeast of Beth Shan on the east side of the Jordan River, may have had yet another type of Egyptian occupation.[72] Two structures belonging to Stratum XII of the twelfth century BC—a large residency building and the Western Palace—were constructed following Egyptian building techniques, and both yielded numerous Egyptian-style storage jars. In addition, Egyptian and Egyptianized objects were commonplace in the associated cemetery, some of whose burials even included bitumen-treated linen wrappings for the deceased (an apparent attempt at imitating the Egyptian practice of mummification). There also were various Aegean-style bronze artifacts and nonnative burial practices which the excavator (Jonathan Tubb) thinks reflect the presence of Sea Peoples at the site.[73] The rich assortment of Egyptian goods in the cemetery, together with the architecture and substantial quantities of Egyptian storage jars on the mound, suggests that Tell es-Sa'idiyeh's principal function for the Egyptians was as a trading center. The site was destroyed still within the twelfth century BC.

In summary, the Egyptian presence in northern Palestine during the reign of Ramesses III was more limited than in the south and was concentrated at a small number of sites. Archaeological evidence for an Egyptian military presence in this period in the western part of the Jezreel Valley is missing, and the hieratic bowl inscriptions relating to grain taxation, so common in the south, are absent from the north.[74] The garrison at Beth Shan presumably was not needed as a defense against any Sea Peoples ensconced along the Mediterranean coast (e.g., at Akko)—for then a major garrison surely would have been required at Megiddo—nor were there powerful enemies to the north in the Huleh Valley to defend against (since the major Canaanite town of that region, Hazor, had already been destroyed in the thirteenth century BC).[75] Perhaps the garrison at Beth Shan was adequate to protect Egyptian interests throughout the central and eastern half of the Jezreel Valley, as well as in the Galilee and the northern Jordan River Valley. Taking into account the fact that Ramesses II had found it necessary in the Nineteenth Dynasty to suppress uprisings by several Galilean towns, it would not be at all surprising if Ramesses III considered it necessary in the Twentieth Dynasty to retain a garrison at Beth Shan for much the same reason.

EGYPTIAN ACTIVITY ON THE FRINGES

During the reign of Ramesses III, Egyptian expeditions continued to go to the copper mines of the Timna Valley north of Eilat/Aqaba, as they had since at least the early days of the Nineteenth Dynasty, as well as to the turquoise mines near Serabit in-Khadim in western Sinai. Regular expeditions to the Timna mines may have been interrupted in the late Nineteenth and early Twentieth Dynasties (since the names of Amenmesse, Siptah, and Setnakht are not found at Timna among the numerous inscribed objects bearing royal names), but exploitation of the mines was revived in a significant way in the reign of Ramesses III, since we have the king named on a rock stela belonging to the royal butler Ramessesemperre as well as on a faience jar stand and possibly also on a fragment of a faience bracelet or counterpoise.[76] In addition, there is a rock inscription displaying the two cartouches of Ramesses III at Nahal Roded, south of Timna.[77] The Timna region is probably to be identified with the toponym 'Atika, the destination of an Egyptian expedition during the king's reign according to Papyrus Harris I (78.1–5). As for Serabit el-Khadim, this place has yielded a dedicatory stela dated to year 23 of Ramesses III.[78] There are also several dozen minor objects naming the king.[79]

An undated event in the reign of Ramesses III is a campaign, mentioned only in Papyrus Harris I (76.9–11), to destroy the Shasu of Seir in Transjordan.[80] This military operation was clearly a minor affair.

THE LEGACY OF RAMESSES III'S REIGN IN THE LEVANT

The focus of Egyptian interests in western Asia throughout Ramesses III's reign was the southern coast and coastal plain of Palestine, the northern Negev, the Jezreel Valley, at least part of the Jordan River Valley, and the copper-mining area of Timna. In southern Palestine, the king reinforced or rebuilt Egyptian garrisons, sometimes within Canaanite towns, and exploited the agricultural resources of the Egyptian-controlled areas through taxation. Blocking the expansion of the Philistines beyond the major towns of Philistia was a key objective of Egyptian military policy under Ramesses III. To the north, Egyptian activity was evidently limited to refortifying the garrison at Beth Shan for the Egyptian troops and their mercenary allies, maintaining a major administrative center and keeping good relations with the vassal prince at Megiddo, and exploiting the resources of the Jordan River Valley through an operation at Tell es-Sa'idiyeh.

A secondary interest of Egyptian policy may have been to keep commercial and political ties open with the major remaining Canaanite centers in the region and to defend those interests against possible threats from various nonurban groups (e.g., the Shasu, the Ammonites, possibly the early Israelites, and others). While there are no signs of Egyptian garrisons in the hill country or on the Jordanian plateau at this time, an occasional small-scale campaign against a troublesome group, combined with the presence of garrisons spread north, east, and south of Philistia as well as the garrison at Beth Shan up in the north, probably sufficed to keep things under control.

In Papyrus Harris I, Ramesses III claimed to have "extended the boundaries of Egypt," but that boast rings hollow. Egypt's military efforts in the Levant following the defeat of the Sea Peoples were principally defensive in nature: even the minor punitive operation against the Shasu can be seen in that light. Moreover, none of the king's three immediate successors— Ramesses IV, V, and VI—are known to have waged campaigns in Palestine; whatever these later rulers may have done to hold on to the empire, they did not initiate any major expansion of the existing military strongholds or build up Egyptian troop strength in the region.

With the end of the reign of Ramesses III, the demise of the Egyptian empire in Palestine was close at hand. Nothing specific can be said about Egyptian actions against the Philistines following the king's death in 1153 BC. The Twentieth Dynasty administrative and military officials attested by name at Beth Shan, Megiddo, and Timna are linked to the reign of Ramesses III and not to later pharaohs;[81] hence, Egyptian rule in Canaan is unlikely to have continued much past the death of this king. No break in Egyptian activity in Palestine is documented for the reign of Ramesses IV (1153–1147 BC). Although his name appears on less than a dozen scarabs in Palestine (at the southern Tell el-Far'ah, Gezer, Beth Shan, Megiddo, Ashdod, Aphek, Tel

Rehov, Shechem, and Khirbet Ni'ana),[82] it may be significant that five of these sites—Ashdod, Beth Shan, Megiddo, Gezer, and Tell el-Far'ah (South)—have yielded scarabs of both Ramesses III and IV, suggesting continuous Egyptian activity in Palestine from the former reign to the latter.[83]

Egyptian authority probably ended in most of Palestine within a decade or two following the death of Ramesses III. The Egyptian garrison at Beth Shan in northern Palestine went on into the reign of Ramesses IV, as did Egyptian activity at several other sites in Canaan where Egyptians were stationed, while the bronze statue base of Ramesses VI (1143–1136 BC) found at Megiddo suggests that there was an Egyptian presence at this site as late as the reign of this pharaoh.[84] Many of the sites in Palestine where Egyptians had been active during the reign of Ramesses III met their end in destruction, indicating that Egypt's withdrawal from Canaan was not a peaceful affair. As for the fringe regions of the southern Levant, Ramesses V (1147–1143 BC) is the last ruler mentioned in the area of the Timna copper mines,[85] while Ramesses VI is the last king named at the turquoise mines of Serabit el-Khadim in western Sinai.[86] Ramesses III managed to hold on to much of inland Canaan following the Sea Peoples' incursion, but within a generation, his successors lost control of all of it.

ADDENDUM

A number of publications pertinent to the present study became available too late to be included in this presentation. Among the most important are the following:

"Hoarded Treasures: The Megiddo Ivories and the End of the Late Bronze Age," *Levant* 41 (2009): 175–94, by M. Feldman.

Excavations at Tel Beth-Shean 1989–1996, vol. 3: *The 13th–11th Century BCE Strata in Areas N and S*, ed. N. Panitz-Cohen and A. Mazar. Jerusalem: Israel Exploration Society, 2009.

"Egyptian-Type Pottery at late Bronze Age Megiddo," by M. A. S. Martin. In *The Fire Signals of Lachish: Studies in the Archaeology and History of Israel in the Late Bronze Age, Iron Age, and Persian Period in Honor of David Ussishkin*, ed. I. Finkelstein and N. Na'aman, 159–78. Winona Lake, IN: Eisenbrauns, 2011.

The Philistines and Aegean Migration at the End of the Late Bronze Age, by A. Yasur-Landau. New York: Cambridge University Press, 2010.

Notes to Weinstein

1. How much impact these new groups had on Egyptian authority in these peripheral areas is debatable. For a few comments on the subject, see, e.g., Singer (1988b) 6; Younker (2003) 167–86.

2. The Rhetorical Stela of Ramesses III from Deir el-Medina also makes mention, albeit briefly, of the year 8 victory over the Sea Peoples. See KRI V.90–91; translation of Sea Peoples passage in RITA V.70. For the Medinet Habu texts, see KRI V.27–30, 32–43; translation in RITA V.24–36. Translations of the Medinet Habu texts and the historical retrospect section of Papyrus Harris I are conveniently collected in Cline and O'Connor (2003) 136–38. Peden (1994b) 23–36, 63–67, and 211–24 provides translations of all three sources.

3. Recent efforts (e.g., Singer [1994] 291; Ussishkin [1995] 263; Ussishkin [1998] 216; Ussishkin [2008] 206–7) to separate the battles geographically and place the land conflict as far away as northern Palestine—based on Ramesses III's contention that he prepared his frontier in Djahy for the invasion and also on the assumption that the most logical land route for the Sea Peoples' movement southward through the Carmel Ridge would be via the pass guarded by Megiddo, which the Egyptians would have had to defend—are not convincing. That the king claims to have reinforced defenses in Syria-Palestine does not tell us where the land battle(s) ultimately took place. As for the notion that Egyptian forces would have fought to protect their interests at Megiddo, one must consider another possibility—that the Egyptians might have abandoned towns in the face of the advancing Sea Peoples (see n. 15 below, for a possible example, namely, Ashkelon). Also, if Megiddo was considered so critical to Egyptian interests at this time, why was there no military garrison stationed there during the Ramesside period? Morris ([2005] 696–97 and n. 16) also prefers a non-Egyptian setting for the land battle but does not try to place its location more specifically. If the battle occurred somewhere in southwestern Canaan, then presumably the Egyptian forces withdrew afterward, since the Philistines subsequently settled in that area. Hoffmeier and Moshier (2006) follow the views of those who prefer an Egyptian or Sinaitic location for the conflict, suggesting that the paleolagoon into which the Pelusiac branch of the Nile opened in the northwestern corner of Sinai was the setting for the naval battle and that the land battle took place nearby. Altogether, while the evidence for the location of the battle is inconclusive, it seems more likely that the land and sea battles were fought in the region of the Eastern Delta and northern Sinai than in northern Canaan.

4. A view preferred in, e.g., Finkelstein (1995) 226–27; Finkelstein (1998b) 143; Morris (2005) 699–701, 731–35.

5. Morris (2005) 734. As already noted, the Sherden had served as mercenaries in the Egyptian military for quite some time. In an important new hieratic text, Papyrus Louvre N 3116, which probably dates to the reign of Ramesses III (but not later than the reign of Ramesses IV), there is mention of one hundred Peleset ("and we caused 100 of the Peleshe[t] to go forth") and two hundred Sherden ("of the great strongholds"), possibly in relation to a conflict with the Libyan invaders of regnal year 5 or 11. See Spalinger (2002) 359–65, p. x + 1, lines 8–9.

6. Any notion that the Philistines among the captives who were settled in Egypt quickly adopted the local culture and, for that reason, are undetectable as a distinct

cultural entity seems improbable considering the distinctive nature of Philistine material remains in Palestine. (The material culture of the other Sea Peoples groups is little known.)

7. As Stager (1995) has pointed out, Philistine cities were consistently larger than their Late Bronze Age Canaanite predecessors.

8. The rural countryside of Philistia saw a substantial decline in the number of settlements from the Late Bronze Age into the Iron I period. See Finkelstein (2000); Gadot (2006) 31. This suggests that neither the Philistines (directly, through cultivation) nor the Egyptians (indirectly, through taxation) seriously exploited the agricultural resources of this area. The archaeological evidence also argues against the Philistines being large-scale importers of goods from the Mediterranean world (Barako 2000). Hence, it seems unlikely, contra Morris (2005) 703–6, that the pharaoh would have gained much by settling the Sea Peoples in southwestern Canaan as a solution to a hypothesized "serious labor shortage" in the region and as a new source of taxes for the Egyptian colonial administration. Whatever advantage the Egyptians would have gained by employing the defeated Sea Peoples to solve some perceived labor shortage would be outweighed militarily, administratively, and economically by the loss of control over such a strategic area.

9. See, e.g., Stager (1995) 342–48. For Tell es-Safi, see, e.g., Maeir, Martin, and Wimmer (2004) 127–28. More recently, it has been concluded that there was no destruction at Ashkelon. See, e.g., Stager (2008) 1580; Stager et al. (2008) 256–57. As for Ashdod, the absence of evidence for a destruction in area H—in contrast to area G, where the "governor's residence" suffered a fiery destruction (Dothan and Porath [1993] 10–11, 53)—indicates that not all of the site experienced equal devastation. See Mazar and Ben-Shlomo (2005) 13.

10. Regarding Gaza, since it was the principal Egyptian headquarters in Canaan during the reign of Ramesses III, presumably any destruction there occurred in the reign of one of the king's successors.

11. Interestingly, commercial relations between Egypt and Dor continued into the twelfth century. See, e.g., Gilboa (2005) 54.

12. Like the author, Bietak (1991 and 1993) believes that Egypt under Ramesses III administered Canaan essentially in two different segments—one in the south and a separate one in the Jezreel Valley and northern Jordan River Valley. Bietak thinks that the northern segment was supported not overland from the south but through some coastal facility (possibly Tell Abu Hawam) in the plain of Akko. This is possible, but it is curious, then, that there is no sign of an Egyptian garrison stationed along the northern coast of Palestine to protect the supply lines that presumably would be required to support Egyptian control at the inland sites of Megiddo and Beth Shan. If there was an Egyptian support facility on the coast, it is likely to have been at Akko, inasmuch as recent excavations at Tell Abu Hawam indicate that the harbor facility at Tell Abu Hawam went out of use in the thirteenth century, with maritime trade henceforth centered at Akko. See Artzy (2006) 60.

13. Morris (2005) 711.

14. See, e.g., Master (2009) 118*. Barako (2000) emphasizes the lack of archaeological evidence for long-distance trade relations—especially with Cyprus and the Aegean world—at the Pentapolis sites, while Master's (2009) petrographic analysis of

the pottery indicates that Ashkelon's Mediterranean commerce in the Early Iron Age was oriented northward to Phoenicia.

15. At Ashkelon, the Egyptian garrison appears to have abandoned a substantial fortress from the late Nineteenth or early Twentieth Dynasty without a fight—or at least without the structure suffering a destruction—which makes it tempting to think that the Egyptian military fell back south in the face of the oncoming Sea Peoples. An alternative explanation, which seems less likely, is that the Sea Peoples bypassed towns like Ashkelon on their way to Egypt, and it was after the land and sea battles that Egyptian forces abandoned places like Ashkelon without a fight. A scarab of Ramesses III found at Ashkelon in association with the post-Egyptian occupational phase does not support any particular historical reconstruction. See Stager (2009) 211*.

16. E.g., Stager (1995) 342–44, fig. 2.

17. A good discussion of this material and its significance is found in Stager (1995) 340–44, fig. 2.

18. Barako (2007).

19. Cline and Yasur-Landau (2009) have reasonably suggested—based on the pottery and other material culture remains—that the garrison force consisted of both Egyptians and Canaanites/Shasu. It is in the subsequent Stratum IV, sometime following the end of Egyptian occupation, that Philistine Bichrome (but not the earlier Monochrome) pottery first appears. This is not the place to enter the highly contentious debate regarding the archaeological chronology of Palestine in the Early Iron Age, specifically, whether we should follow Finkelstein ([1995]; [1998a] 167–68; [1998b] 143–44) and numerous later publications in placing the initial phase of Philistine settlement in Palestine (represented by Monochrome ware) after the demise of the Egyptian empire in Palestine or, with Mazar (1997) and many other archaeologists, leave the initial settlement activity contemporary with the reign of Ramesses III.

Finkelstein's position requires two waves of Sea Peoples, the first one (that of the regnal year 8 invasion) ending with the settlement of Sea Peoples in strongholds in Egypt, and a second one later on, following Egypt's withdrawal from Canaan, resulting in the settlement of the Sea Peoples in Palestine. Finkelstein's principal line of evidence is the absence of Monochrome ware from Lachish Level VI and contemporary levels at other sites that had Egyptian occupation. Mazar and other scholars (see, e.g., Bunimovitz and Faust [2001]) explain this phenomenon as a result of Egyptian forces blocking off contact with the Philistines. A similar explanation is given for the situation at Egyptian-occupied sites in northern Palestine. More recently, high-precision radiocarbon dates have been brought into the argument, with various date series being offered to support one or the other chronological schemes. (For the radiocarbon debate, see, e.g., the papers published in Levy and Higham [2005].) The present chapter follows the conventional chronology, while acknowledging that some of the radiocarbon data are supportive of a lower chronology. (For some recent comments on the chronological debate, see Killebrew [2008] 64–65; Mazar [2008a].)

20. Killebrew, Goldberg, and Rosen (2006) 115, fig. 17b, table 5. T. Dothan ([1993] 343–45), the site's excavator, dated this building to the Nineteenth Dynasty and interpreted the twelfth-century phase as lacking architectural remains.

21. This equation follows the view of most scholars, who interpret this inscription

as referencing an Egyptian temple in the principal Egyptian town in Canaan, that is, Gaza. Higginbotham (2000) 56–59 has recently questioned this identification. Ueh-linger (1988) 11–15 proposed that a scarab from Tell el-Far'ah (South), as well as two scarabs from Beth Shemesh, which are inscribed with the word *pr*, "estate," plus the nomen of Ramesses III, refer to estates associated with the temple of Amun mentioned in Papyrus Harris I. But Brandl (2004) 59 has observed that there are no less than eight scarabs inscribed with the same text and that they probably all come from Egypt and therefore relate to an estate of Ramesses III in Egypt, not Canaan.

22. E.g., Stager (1995) 342.

23. Macalister (1912) 2:307, fig. 446.

24. Macalister (1912) 2:235, fig. 388 (scarab); 3: pl. 121.20 (plaque); *KRI* V.257.79A; translation in *RITA* V.215.

25. Singer (1986–87); cf. Dever (1993) 503, against which see Bunimovitz (1988–89) and Maeir (1988–89).

26. Ussishkin (1983) 123–24, pl. 30; *KRI* VII.259.251; Giveon (1983); Giveon, Sweeney, and Lalkin (2004).

27. Tufnell (1958) 131–32, 249, pls. 45.1–3, 46.

28. For a convenient summary of the various categories of Egyptian(ized) material at Lachish, see Higginbotham (2000) 108–11.

29. Wimmer (1998) 89–90; Morris (2005) 768.

30. Krauss (1994) sought to identify a scarab from the British excavations at Lachish (Tufnell [1958] pls. 39–40.380) as containing a defective writing of the name of Ramesses IV and thereby providing a *terminus post quem* for the destruction. Brandl (2004) 60 has challenged this identification, as well as that of several scarabs found in Palestine (at Tell es-Safi, Beth Shemesh, and Tell er-Ruqeish) that are similarly inscribed. For additional discussion on possible Ramesses IV scarabs from Lachish, see Ussishkin (2008) 210–11.

31. Sweeney (2004) provides a comprehensive discussion of the inscriptions. Wimmer (2008) 69–71 offers an up-to-date list of the material.

32. Gilula (1976); *KRI* VII.259.251B.

33. Goldwasser (1991a).

34. Černý in Tufnell (1958) 132–33, pls. 44.3–6, 47.1–4.

35. Goldwasser and Wimmer (1999). The hieratic texts have been dated paleo-graphically to the Twentieth Dynasty.

36. Goldwasser (1991b); Oren (1993a) 582.

37. Unpublished; see Goldwasser and Wimmer (1999) 41 n. 3; Wimmer (2008) 71.

38. Groll (1973b); Goldwasser (1984); *KRI* VII.259–60.252. One is dated to year 22 + *x*, almost certainly Ramesses III.

39. Two hieratic inscriptions—one in ink and mentioning a "prince," the other a single sign incised on a sherd—are associated with the late Nineteenth and early Twentieth Dynasties. See Maeir, Martin, and Wimmer (2004); Wimmer and Maeir (2007). In addition, an ostracon containing part of a nonadministrative text has recently been published from Ashkelon. See Wimmer (2008).

40. Based on the evidence noted earlier for the lack of rural settlements in Philistia, the grain probably came from Canaanite sites, not those in Philistine territory.

41. See, e.g., Sweeney (2004) 1614–15 for discussion with previous bibliography.

42. Oren (1993b) 1331; Morris (2005) 752–55. For the Egyptian ceramic forms found at Shari'a, see Martin (2004).

43. See n. 38 above for the principal sources. A recent discussion of some of the Shari'a hieratic inscriptions is in Higginbotham (2000) 61–62.

44. Petrie (1930) 17–19, pl. 54; Macdonald, Starkey, and Harding (1932) 27–29, pls. 67–69.

45. Yannai (2002). Over the years, numerous large buildings have been classified as "governors' residencies" or "Egyptian residencies" and indiscriminately linked to the Egyptian administration of Canaan in the thirteenth and early twelfth centuries BC. It is now recognized that not all of these buildings should be so identified.

46. See, e.g., Morris (2005) 749–52.

47. Macdonald, Starkey, and Harding (1932) pls. 52.126–28, 57.374; Brandl (2004) 62, pls. 2f–g, 3g–h.

48. *KRI* V.256.78; translation in *RITA* V.215. The reference in Klengel (1992) 177 (repeated in Morris [2005] 707) to a fragmentary stela of Ramesses III at Tyre is incorrect. The stela evidently belongs to Ramesses II; see Leclant (1961) 394.

49. The Syrian toponyms that appear in topographical lists found at Medinet Habu are probably anachronistic/plagiarized. See, e.g., Grandet (1993) 206–7; Kitchen (2009) 132. Cf. Morris (2005) 706–7.

50. For the levels at Beth Shan from the thirteenth and twelfth centuries BC, see, most recently, Mazar (2006); Mazar (2008b) 1619–21.

51. A summary of the evidence for an Egyptian base at Beth Shan in the Eighteenth Dynasty appears in Morris (2005) 249–51. See also Mazar (2003) 331–32; Mazar and Mullins (2007) 19–21.

52. Mazar (1997); Mazar (2002) 265; Mazar (2003) 333–35, table 1; Mazar (2006) 29, table 1.2; Mazar (2008b) 1619.

53. The site was excavated first between 1921 and 1933 by the University of Pennsylvania Museum and subsequently between 1989 and 1996 by Amihai Mazar on behalf of the Institute of Archaeology of the Hebrew University of Jerusalem. Late Level VII of the Pennsylvania excavations is equivalent to Stratum S4 of the Hebrew University excavations, Level VI to S3, and Late Levels VI(?) and V to S2.

54. For the inscriptions of Ramesses-Userkhepesh, see James (1966) 4–8, 163–74, figs. 88–99 passim; the inscriptions on the doorways of building 1500 are also published in *KRI* V.252–55.76BI–VI; translations in *RITA* V.212–14. Building 1500 was initially excavated by the Pennsylvania team, then thoroughly reexamined by the Institute of Archaeology, Hebrew University. For the latter examination, see Mazar (2006) 61–82, identifying the building as a "small palace, probably the ceremonial palace of the Egyptian governor."

55. Rowe (1930) 36, 38, pl. 51; James (1966) 35, fig. 81:3; *KRI* V.251.76A; translation in *RITA* V.212. Higginbotham (1999) has proposed that it was originally cut in the Nineteenth Dynasty to represent a god, then usurped by Ramesses III for himself.

56. The coffins are published in Oren (1973). The naturalistic-style anthropoid coffins are traditionally identified with the Egyptian personnel, while those created in the so-called grotesque style are often linked to Aegean mercenaries (generally the Sherden) in the employ of the Egyptians.

57. In addition to the reliefs from the Pennsylvania excavations, see the new relief fragment published in Sweeney (1998).

58. Among the small finds are two scarabs naming Ramesses III. See Brandl (2004) 62, pl. 2b, i.

59. Cohen-Weinberger (1998); Martin (2004); Martin (2006). Other recent discussions of the Egyptian(-ized) pottery and ceramic technology in Late Bronze Age and Early Iron Age Canaan include Killebrew (2005) 67–80 and Martin (2009).

60. Weinstein (1993) 221, fig. 165.8.

61. See Porter (1998); Porter (2008).

62. For the Delhamiya fragment, see Leclant (1982) 485, fig. 83.

63. Ussishkin ([1995] 246; [1998] 204) and Finkelstein ([2009] 113–14) have proposed a peaceful transition from Stratum VIIB to Stratum VIIA. Against the Tel Aviv excavators, Mazar (2002) 264–65 agrees with the original Chicago excavators that the VIIB palace was destroyed and the VIIA palace rebuilt along similar lines in the twelfth century BC.

64. Loud (1939) 11–12, pl. 62.377; Fischer (2007) 151–53, pls. 30–31; *KRI* V.255.77A; translation in *RITA* V.214–15; Higginbotham (2000) 67–68.

65. Loud (1939) 11, pl. 63; Fischer (2007) 164–65, pls. 39–41; *KRI* V.256.77B; translation in *RITA* V.215; Higginbotham (2000) 68–70.

66. Loud (1948) 154, pl. 152.195; Brandl (2004) 62, pl. 2a.

67. James (1966) 172–73 (nos. D-2, E-1, E-3), 175–76.

68. The finds are conveniently summarized in Higginbotham (2000) 112–13. See also Fischer (2007) 91–128 and passim.

69. Mazar (2002) 271.

70. See, e.g., Halpern (2000) 550–51. Singer (1988–89) interprets the valuables found in the "treasury" as the property of an Egyptian governor whom he would equate with the owner of the ivory pen case.

71. Finkelstein (1996); Finkelstein (2009) 113–15; Ussishkin (1995); Ussishkin (1998).

72. Morris (2005) 762–67 provides a convenient summary of the archaeological evidence, with previous bibliography, for the Egyptian presence at this site. Pritchard (1980) published the final report on the cemetery, while Tubb (1995 and 2000) has presented the evidence for Sea Peoples serving in the employ of the Egyptians.

73. Negbi (1991) has challenged Tubb's view that there were Sea Peoples (possibly Sherden) working at the site in the employ of the Egyptians.

74. A few hieratic ostraca of a nonadministrative nature come from Beth-Shan. See Wimmer (2008) 71.

75. As for Tel Dan in the Upper Galilee, the pottery associated with the remains at this site from the Late Bronze II and Early Iron Age point to trade relations with Egypt but not to an Egyptian presence at this site (Martin and Ben-Dov 2007).

76. Rock inscription: Ventura (1976); *KRI* V.257.79C1; translation in *RITA* V.215–16. Schulman in Rothenberg (1988) 143–44, Eg. cat. no. 260, fig. 52, pl. 105, with previous bibliography. Faience jar stand: Rothenberg (1988) 127, e.g., cat. no. 96, fig. 31.5, pl. 119.3. *KRI* V.257.79CII; translation in *RITA* V.216. Faience sherd: Rothenberg (1988) 141, e.g., cat. no. 216, fig. 40.5, pl. 122.9.

77. Avner (1972); *KRI* V.257.79B; translation in *RITA* V.215–16.

78. Gardiner, Peet, and Černý (1952, 1955) no. 273; KRI V.248–49.73; translation in RITA V.210.

79. Gardiner, Peet, and Černý (1952, 1955) nos. 274–88. KRI V.257.D; translation in RITA V.215–16; Lilyquist (2008).

80. Giveon (1971) 134–37; Peden (1994b) 215. The Shasu also appear among the captives in the Medinet Habu reliefs on the Sea Peoples campaign.

81. Weinstein (1992) 146.

82. See Brandl (2004) 62–63 for the corpus of Ramesses IV scarabs from Palestine. For the Ramesses IV scarab from Ashdod, see now Keel and Münger (2005) 276, fig. 6.1.4. A brief summary of Egyptian activity in the Levant during the reign of Ramesses IV appears in Peden (1994a) 18–20.

83. Brandl (2004) 61.

84. Statue-base inscription published in KRI VI.278. For recent discussions on the context of this object, see Harrison (2004) 9, 11, fig. 3; Ussishkin (2008) 204. Ussishkin is of the opinion that the Egyptian collapse took place concurrently in northern and southern Canaan (represented by Megiddo VIIA and Lachish VI, respectively) and should be dated shortly *after* the reign of Ramesses VI—since he interprets the statue base of this king found at Megiddo as indicating Egyptian control continuing through the king's reign.

85. Rothenberg (1988) 122, Eg. cat. no. 44–45, 46(?); KRI VI.221.1A.

86. Gardiner, Peet, and Černý (1952, 1955) nos. 290–93; KRI VI.279.A–D.

The Sea Peoples

ERIC H. CLINE AND DAVID O'CONNOR

For some historians, the story of the Sea Peoples is a dramatic one. In this version of their story, the Sea Peoples came sweeping across the Mediterranean ca. 1200 BC, wreaking havoc and creating chaos, leaving smoking ruins and destroyed cities in their wake. To them is attributed the collapse of the Hittite Empire, the downfall of Cyprus, the destruction of Syria-Palestinian and Canaanite petty kingdoms, and perhaps even the demise of the Mycenaeans and the Minoans. Indeed, the Sea Peoples may be responsible for the very collapse of Bronze Age civilization in the Aegean and Eastern Mediterranean and for bringing on the centuries-long Dark Ages that followed.[1]

In reality, the Sea Peoples continue to perplex and mystify historians and archaeologists of the ancient Mediterranean. During the thirteenth and especially twelfth centuries BC, they are a major and aggressive force in the Eastern Mediterranean, on which they had an impact that to some scholars seems catastrophic. Yet the Sea Peoples, on present evidence, seem to come suddenly from nowhere, cause widespread disruption, take on some of the greatest powers of the region, and equally abruptly disappear from history, save for one or two historic peoples of later times.

At the heart of the Sea Peoples mystery is a short text inscribed on the walls of the mortuary temple of the pharaoh Ramesses III (ca. 1184–1153 BC) at Medinet Habu, Western Thebes. Laconic but explicit, it is awe-inspiring in its implications.

> The foreign countries made a conspiracy in their islands. All at once the lands were removed and scattered in the fray. No land could stand before their arms, from Khatte, Qode, Carchemish, Arzawa, and Alashiya on, being cut off at [one time]. A camp [was set up] in one place in Amor. They desolated its people, and its land was like that which has never come into being. They were coming forward toward Egypt, while the flame was prepared before them. Their confederation was the Philistines, Tjekru, Shekelesh, Denye(n), and Washosh, lands united. They laid their hands upon the lands as far as the circuit of the earth, their hearts confident and trusting: "Our plans will succeed!"[2]

In hieroglyphs, the passage quoted above occupies less than three vertical columns of text, but it has generated an enormous amount of scholarly literature and public speculation since it was first published in 1844. The most recent study of the Sea Peoples is 360 pages long and equivalent to many, many columns of hieroglyphs.[3] The Sea Peoples, as modern historians call them, are the "foreign countries . . . in their islands" referred to above and have long provoked scholarly debate because the most fundamental questions about them still have no definitive answers.

Where did the Sea Peoples come from? The Egyptian sources provide the names of at least nine of them; in the text of Ramesses III (above) are listed the Peleset, Tjekru, Shekelesh, Danuna or Da'anu, and Washosh, while elsewhere the Eqwesh, Lukki, Shardana, and Teresh are identified.[4] However, these names are not easily identifiable with specific regions, whether those from which the Sea Peoples originated or those in which they resettled themselves after the events described during the reign of Ramesses III. The Peleset (later known as the Philistines) and the Tjekru we know resettled along the Levantine coast,[5] but other Sea Peoples remain more mysterious. For example, because of the similarity in names, the Shardana and Shekelesh have been associated with Sardinia and Sicily, respectively; but did they come from these islands or resettle there later, or is the coincidence in names purely accidental and without historical significance?[6]

Equally mysterious are the culture and organizations of the Sea Peoples and the degree of diversity with regard to those that might be expected when at least nine different peoples were involved. The Sea Peoples are depicted in Egyptian art and perhaps in that of various parts of the Levant and the Aegean, and Egyptian texts provide some glimpses of the Sea Peoples' political and military structure and of their material culture. Yet all in all, the data remain meager.

Perhaps most important of all—because it implies so much about the capabilities and nature of the Sea Peoples—did they achieve what the Egyptian text quoted above and others say they did? What is awe-inspiring about the Sea Peoples is that, according to the Egyptians, they created an aggressive coalition so powerful and effective that it brought about the collapse of some of the most powerful contemporary kingdoms in the Levant and aimed to invade Egypt itself, a dominant power in the region that had not experienced foreign invasion (except for some forays by the nearby Libyans) for well over four hundred years.

The states listed above as unable to resist the Sea Peoples were Khatte, Qode, Carchemish, Arzawa, and Alashiya.[7] Khatte was the imperial state of the Hittites, which had dominated much of Anatolia and Syria but was perhaps weakening at this time. Arzawa and Qode were large polities on the south Anatolian coast, extending even further east in Qode's case. Carchemish lay in modern Syria, while Alashiya probably represented all or much of the large island of Cyprus. Finally, the region in which the Sea Peoples set up their camp and that was devastated as a result was Amor or Amurru,[8] an extensive coastal reign straddling modern Syria and Lebanon. Moreover, not only did the Sea Peoples advance on Egypt, by land and sea, but the Egyptians had to fight two great battles to halt the onslaught. One took place, on land, in Djahy (roughly, modern Israel and the West Bank); the other took place in what the Egyptians call "the mouths of the river," by which term some area along Egypt's Mediterranean coast is apparently meant.

These specifics are discussed further below. What is noteworthy here is the very different opinions recent scholars have drawn from the same basic data. Redford concludes that both battles actually took place (as do many other scholars)[9] and even hypothesizes where: the land and sea battles "may have taken place within sight of each other just beyond the mouth of the Pelusiac branch" of the Nile. Drews accepts the battle at the sea or river mouths but doubts that the land battle occurred.[10] Cifola suggests that there were no large-scale battles but, instead, many lesser conflicts between Egypt and the Sea Peoples extending over a long period of time, conflicts that the Egyptian sources misleadingly telescope together.[11] In any event—whatever the specific details of the Sea People's invasion of the Eastern Mediterranean might have been—how can we reliably measure the Sea People's impact: can it persuasively be shown that, as Redford argues, "the movement of the Sea Peoples. . . . changed the face of the ancient world more than any other single event before the time of Alexander the Great"?[12]

Various Sea Peoples interacted with Egypt and other lands in times other than Ramesses III's reign as well. The most significant contact, in terms of surviving Egyptian textual data, occurred twenty-six years before Ramesses III clashed with the Sea Peoples in his eighth regnal year (ca. 1180 BC). King Merenptah's scribes recorded that in his fifth regnal year (ca. 1209 BC), Egypt's Western Delta was invaded by a Libu (Libyan) army, which had originated in, probably, the then Libyan homeland of Cyrenaica.[13] The Libyan forces were accompanied by contingents of Sea Peoples—namely, the Eqwesh, Teresh, Lukki, Shardana, and Shekelesh. Their services, as allies or mercenaries, had been solicited by the leader of the Libyans. In any event, the combined attack by the Libyans and the Sea Peoples was defeated.[14]

Below, we present two perspectives on the mystery of the Sea Peoples. First, we consider the specifically Egyptian perspective, because Egyptian textual and pictorial sources are so crucial for understanding the Sea Peoples. Though these sources—from our modern, Western point of view—are greatly distorted by the demands of Egyptian ideology, literary conventions, and symbolic representation, they contain enough actuality to open up important lines of research. Second, we consider the full range of material, Egyptian and other, that may bear on the Sea Peoples. This includes texts and pictures that record the existence of Sea Peoples and preserves their names, faces, and other details. We consider also linguistic evidence that stimulates suggestions as to where the Sea Peoples came from and where some at least eventually resettled. Finally, excavated remains must be involved: are there pottery, tools, other artifacts, perhaps even skeletons that can be identified as belonging to the Sea Peoples?

Two centuries of research and a spate of recent volumes about the Sea Peoples (see n. 3) have left us with much circumstantial evidence and many circular arguments, yet we find ourselves still asking the most basic of questions about them. Definitive answers still escape us, but in this discussion, we introduce one of the most fascinating issues of Mediterranean history: the origins, achievements, and ultimate fate of the various peoples grouped together by the Egyptians as "foreigners from the sea."[15]

BARBARIAN HORDES? THE EGYPTIAN PERSPECTIVE

For Egypt, the Sea Peoples must have seemed (along with the unruly Libyans) the barbarians par excellence of their day, the thirteenth and especially twelfth centuries BC. Later, the Greeks and Romans also feared, despised, and yet admired their often aggressive barbarians, those who spoke neither Greek nor Latin and whose speech sounded like "bar-bar-bar."[16] A similarly complex attitude is evinced by the Egyptians toward the Sea Peoples, who ironically may have included some ancestral Greeks. One, the Danuna, may be the Danaans (or Danaoi), a term eventually applied to Greeks in general,[17] while the Eqwesh have sometimes been identified with the Achaeans of Mycenaean Greece.[18]

As presented by Egyptian sources, the impact of the Sea Peoples on the civilized world of the Eastern Mediterranean in the twelfth century BC was apparently catastrophic. As we have seen, in or about the eighth regnal year of the pharaoh Ramesses III, a substantial coalition of Sea Peoples precipitated the collapse (roughly in geographical progression) of several powerful kingdoms of Anatolia and the Levant—the domino theory with a vengeance. Subsequently "devastating" Amurru, the Sea Peoples moved against Egypt, only to be defeated in two separate battles, one in Djahy and the other "in the mouths of the river."[19]

This was not the first serious clash between Egypt and the Sea Peoples. As mentioned earlier, contingents of Sea Peoples accompanied a Libyan army that invaded Egypt's Western Delta in the fifth year of King Merenptah (ca. 1209 BC). They, too, along with their Libyan allies or employers, were soundly defeated.

Texts produced for Merenptah and Ramesses III (as well as large-scale scenes carved on the latter's mortuary temple at Medinet Habu in Western Thebes) are our principal sources of information about the Sea Peoples so far as Egypt is concerned (for other texts, see the appendix). As such, these sources raise major issues about the Sea Peoples, which are matters of lively debate. Who were the Sea Peoples specifically, and where did they come from? Nine specific Sea Peoples are identified; but did they share a common culture and perhaps language, or were they much more diverse? How were the Sea Peoples or their various constituent parts organized in political, societal, and military terms; specifically, how was their preplanned, rapidly moving, and very effective invasion of the Eastern Mediterranean carried out? In fact, was the invasion really like that, or have the Egyptian scribes compressed into a simplistic narrative a process that was more diffuse, sporadic, and long

extended in time? Finally, to what extent were the Sea Peoples really barbarians and alien to the cultures, political systems, and accepted military norms
of the Eastern Mediterranean world? These mysteries are by no means
solved; but the Egyptian sources are especially important for framing the issues and pointing up specific lines of research that may, over time, bring us a
better understanding of this extraordinary agglomeration of warlike peoples.

UNIFIED SOCIETY OR AD HOC ALLIANCE?

The primary Egyptian sources on the Sea Peoples include a wall inscription,
a stela, and two inscribed columns, all celebrating King Merenptah's victory
over the Libyans and the Sea Peoples. The wall inscription occurs at the Karnak temple,[20] the stela is from Kom el Ahmar,[21] one column is in the Cairo
Museum,[22] and the other column is from Heliopolis.[23] The Ramesses III
sources comprise a series of large scenes along the external north face of his
mortuary temple at Medinet Habu (Western Thebes) and a long text with accompanying scene on the west wall of that temple's first court.[24] In addition,
Ramesses' defeat of the Sea Peoples is briefly described in Papyrus Harris I, a
document actually prepared during his successor's reign.[25]

Together, the texts of Merenptah and Ramesses III provide all known
names for specific Sea Peoples, but, strikingly, the relevant lists hardly overlap. Merenptah's sources refer to the Eqwesh, Teresh, Lukki, Shardana, and
Shekelesh, while Ramesses III's list comprises Shekelesh, Peleset, Tjekru, Danuna, and Washosh.[26] Papyrus Harris I provides an almost identical list to
that of Medinet Habu[27] but substitutes Shardana for Shekelesh and—being
less close in time to the actual events—may be in error. In addition, Sandars
notes that although the Teresh are not listed at Medinet Habu by Ramesses
III as part of the Sea Peoples whom he defeated, "a captive chief of the Teresh
is shown among his prisoners" in the pictorial reliefs there, and a later stela of
Ramesses III mentions the Teresh in the same breath as the Peleset.[28]

Why do we call these nine separate peoples, taken together, the Sea
Peoples? The answer lies in Egyptian phraseology. In Merenptah's texts,
the Shardana, Shekelesh, and Eqwesh are described as "foreign lands of the
sea."[29] The Teresh and Lukki are listed alongside the others, and all five
are described collectively as "northerners who came from every land";[30]
since the relevant texts are very fragmentary, the Teresh and Lukki, too, may
have been identified as "of the sea." The texts of Ramesses III specifically
identify all five peoples named as "foreign countries (who) made a conspiracy in their isles" and elsewhere refer to them generally as "the northern

countries who were in their isles" and as "the countries who came from their land in the isles in the midst of the sea."[31] The translation of the relevant word (*iww*) as "isle" or "island" is accepted by most Egyptologists.[32] Papyrus Harris I also refers to the Danuna "in their isles" and to the Shardana (= Shekelesh?) and Washosh "of the sea."[33]

If we look at these groups one by one, the Lukki (Egyptian *Lk*) are well known from numerous additional inscriptions, Hittite as well as Egyptian, for they were notorious pirates. Most scholars see the Lukki as originating in Anatolia. Although there is some discussion as to where exactly in Anatolia they came from, most historians agree that it was probably southwestern Anatolia, in the area later known as Lycia and Caria. They are believed to have raided Cyprus on occasion, as recorded in the Amarna Letters of the mid-fourteenth century BC, and to have fought on the side of the Hittites against the Egyptians at the battle of Kadesh ca. 1286. Unfortunately, our evidence for the Lukki in Anatolia is purely textual; no cultural remains have yet been definitely identified as belonging to the Lukki by any archaeologists anywhere.[34]

The Shardana (Egyptian *Šrdn*) appear already in the Amarna Letters of the mid-fourteenth century BC, where they are found serving as part of an Egyptian garrison at Byblos.[35] They were mercenaries and, as such, fought both for and against Egypt in various conflicts during the latter part of the Late Bronze Age. Sandars notes, in particular, a fragmentary inscription of Ramesses II from Tanis that reads, "Shardana, rebellious of heart . . . [and their] battleships in the midst of the sea," and that claims that Ramesses "destroyed [the] warriors of the Great Green (i.e. the Mediterranean), and lower Egypt spends the night sleeping peacefully."[36]

None of the texts that mention the Shardana give a homeland for them. In the Egyptian pictorial reliefs, the Shardana are shown wearing horned helmets and frequently carrying round shields, but these facts are of little help in ascertaining the origin of these people.[37] Based on the linguistic similarities between the word *Shardana* and the name *Sardinia*, scholars frequently suggest that the Shardana came from the island of Sardinia. It is equally possible that this group eventually settled in Sardinia after their defeat at the hands of the Egyptians and only then gave their name to this island, as Maspéro and others have suggested.[38]

However, in Papyrus Harris I, Ramesses III says that the Shardana (and the Washosh) were "brought as captives to Egypt," that he "settled them in strongholds bound in my name," and that he "taxed them all, in clothing and grain from the store-houses and granaries each year." This would seem to indicate that the Shardana had been settled either in Egypt itself or somewhere close enough that he could tax them every year, which would suggest an area no further away than Canaan. This location may be further substantiated by *The Onomasticon of Amenemope,* dating to ca. 1100 BC, which lists the Shardana among the Sea Peoples who were settled on the coast of Canaan.[39] If this is the case, we would be inclined to see the Shardana as originally coming from Sardinia and eventually being settled in coastal Canaan. We should also note, however, that Shardana are reportedly listed—in the Wilbour Papyrus—as living in Middle Egypt during the time of Ramesses V, which would suggest that at least some of them were settled in Egypt rather than Canaan.[40]

In terms of archaeological remains, scholars usually call attention to the ruins found on the island of Sardinia—in particular, the Bronze Age circular stone structures known as *nuraghi* whose function is still debated—and hypothesize about their relationship to the Shardana.[41] Most recently, Adam Zertal of the University of Haifa believes that an Iron Age site he is currently excavating in northern Israel—El-Ahwat—has stone architectural features that appear similar to those found on Sardinia. He hypothesizes that this site may have been one of the villages/towns/cities established by the Shardana when they were settled in Canaan by the Egyptians. If so, its existence may corroborate the references found in Papyrus Harris I and *The Onomasticon of Amenemope,* although Zertal is the first to admit that there is no identifiable "Shardana" pottery yet found at this or any other site in the region.[42]

The Teresh (Egyptian *Trš*) do not appear in Egyptian texts before the time of Merenptah, at which time they appear both in his Great Karnak Inscription and on the Athribis stela. It has been suggested that the Taruisha mentioned in Hittite texts and probably located in northwestern Anatolia (i.e., Troy) are to be linked with the Teresh, but this seems unlikely. Other attempts have been made to link the Teresh with the Greek Tyrsenoi and the Tyrrhenians of central western Anatolia mentioned much later by Herodotus. This is considered important for several reasons, foremost among which is that Herodotus claims the Tyrrhenians migrated from central western Anatolia to central Italy, where they found later fame as the Etruscans.[43] However, another link has been recently suggested—namely, that the Teresh are to be identified with Tyrsenia, said to be the original Greek name for Italy. This may be related to Herodotus's explanation, but we are left with the question of whether the Teresh came from Italy or went there after being defeated by the Egyptians.[44] There is no archaeological proof for any of these suggestions, and there are, as yet, no archaeological remains that have been identified as specifically "Tereshian."

The Shekelesh (Egyptian *Šklš*) are probably mentioned in a letter sent by the Hittite king to the last king of Ugarit, in which he refers to the "Sikilayu who live in ships." In Egyptian texts, the Shekelesh first appear in Merenptah's Sea Peoples inscriptions.[45] Based on the linguistic similarities between the word *Shekelesh* and the name *Sicily*, scholars frequently suggest that the Shekelesh came from the island of Sicily. However, linguistically speaking, it is equally possible that this group settled in Sicily only after their defeat at the hands of the Egyptians and only then gave their name to this island. As Sandars notes,[46] the colonizing Greeks of the eighth-century BC found people known as the "Sikels" already living on this island; they thought that the Sikels had migrated to the island from southern Italy after the Trojan War. Instead of migrating to the island from southern Italy, however, perhaps they had come all the way across from the final battlegrounds in the Egyptian Delta. It is also conceivable that there is no connection at all between the Shekelesh and Sicily.

As for archaeological remains specifically belonging to the Shekelesh, claims have been made for so-called Sikil remains at a number of sites in Syria-Palestine. In particular, at the coastal port city of Dor, located south of Mount Carmel in modern Israel, long-term excavations by Ephraim Stern have revealed many archaeological remains—including pottery and incised cow scapulas possibly used for divination and/or musical instruments—which he believes are to be attributed to these former Sea Peoples. Other sites on the Carmel coast that have yielded possible "Sikil" remains include Tel Zeror and 'Ein Hagit, and we should not forget the famous engravings of ships found on the rocks of the Carmel ridge, which may be representations of the ships of the Sea Peoples.[47]

The Eqwesh (Egyptian *'Ikwš*; also called the Akawasha by some scholars) are a little-known group who are mentioned only in Merenptah's Sea Peoples inscriptions. They are not mentioned by Ramesses III or in any other Egyptian inscriptions (at least by that name). Most frequently, scholars have tentatively suggested that the name of the Eqwesh might be the Egyptian attempt to reproduce the word *Achaioi* for the Achaeans, Homer's Mycenaeans, coming from the mainland of Greece, Crete, and the Cycladic Islands of the Bronze Age Aegean.[48] A possible linguistic link with the Ahhiyawa mentioned in Hittite texts has therefore also been suggested, but the identification of Ahhiyawa with the Achaeans/Mycenaeans is itself a hotly contested discussion that has been ongoing for nearly the past century.[49] There are no archaeological remains attributable specifically to the Eqwesh, especially since any suggested connection to the Achaeans and/or Ahhiyawa is, at present, unsupported.

As for the Tjekru (Egyptian *Tkr*), while they are elusive in Egyptian and other texts prior to the time of Ramesses III, they are later found mentioned in *The Story of Wenamun*, a tale the details of which may date to ca. 1100 BC.[50] As Sandars has noted, the Tjekru have long been suggested to have connections with the Teucri of the Troad and with the Greek Teucer, the legendary founder of Salamis in Cyprus after the Trojan War. Although they have a seagoing reputation, this does not help much in determining their origins, for the chronology of these connections is unclear, if the connections are even warranted.[51]

The case of the Tjekru is, in fact, an outstanding example of how scholars have gaily and glibly used all sorts of evidence coming from all kinds of chronological periods in their attempts to trace the Tjekru and other members of the Sea Peoples. Many of these so-called data may have nothing to do with each other and are quite likely red herrings. We would suggest that future scholars considering these various suggestions put the relevant textual sources into a hierarchy of relevance and likely contemporaneity. A Hittite document discussing the Lukki, for instance, could be considered both contemporary and relevant and thus be assigned a higher priority than a later document concerned with Teucer and the foundation of Salamis on Cyprus, which in turn might be assigned a higher priority than a much later Greek or Roman document, which in turn would be assigned a higher priority than a medieval manuscript of dubious authenticity, and so on.

The Onomasticon of Amenemope, dating to ca. 1100 BC, provides an additional nugget of information by listing the Tjekru in between the Shardana and the Philistines. If the details found in *The Story of Wenamun* and *The Onomasticon of Amenemope* are correct, we might suggest that the Tjekru eventually settled (or were forcibly settled) on the coast of Canaan near the Sharon Plain following their defeat by Ramesses III. Indeed, one potentially revealing line in *Wenamun* describes his travails in a harbor town in Syria-Palestine, beginning by saying simply, "I reached Dor, a town of the Tjekru."[52]

As mentioned above, Ephraim Stern has uncovered many remains at the site of Tel Dor in modern Israel that he believes are to be attributed to the Sea Peoples. Stern refers to the Sea Peoples at Dor as "Sikils" rather than as the "Tjekru," despite the reference to Dor as a town of the Tjekru in *The Story of Wenamun*. One reason for this is an intriguing suggestion that the final letter in name for the Tjekru should be vocalized as an *l* rather than as an *r*—that is, that the name should be seen as *Tjekel* rather than *Tjekru*—and that there is a linguistic connection to Sicily and the Sikels. We might then see *Tjekel* as an alternate name for the Shekelesh, since these names rarely appear together in the Sea Peoples inscriptions. Indeed, it has been suggested that the Shekelesh of Merenptah's inscriptions and the *Tjekel* of Ramesses III's inscriptions are one and the same group, just as Merenptah's Eqwesh and Ramesses III's Danuna may be two names for the same group.[53] If this is correct, we could hypothesize an origin on Sicily and a final settlement in coastal Canaanite for the Tjekru/Tjekel/Shekelesh/Sikels.

Turning now to the Danuna (Egyptian *Dnjn*), it has long been suggested that they are to be equated with the land of Danuna. If so, then they—or, rather, their land—are mentioned in Hittite letters and in the Amarna Letters as being located in southeastern Turkey in the Adana region of Cilicia, to the north of the city of Ugarit.[54] It has also been frequently suggested that the Danuna should be equated with Homer's Danaans or Danaoi—his alternate name for the Achaeans. Speculation regarding both the origin and the final settling place for the Danuna has usually involved circular arguments based on whether they are equated with the land of Danuna or with Homer's Danaans/Danaoi. To date, nothing has been agreed on, although those scholars who equate the Danuna with the Danaans/Danaoi suggest that they will have come from the Aegean region, while those scholars who equate the Danuna with the land of Danuna suggest that they will have either come from or settled down in the coastal region of southeastern Turkey or northern Syria.

Most recently, Drews has noted the similarity between the *Dnjn* of the Sea Peoples inscriptions and the *Tj-n3-jj* (vocalized as *Tanaja*) of the earlier Eighteenth Dynasty inscriptions, primarily of Thutmose III and Amenhotep III. *Tanaja* is, most likely, the Egyptian word for the Mycenaeans of Bronze Age mainland Greece. Drews suggests that *Danuna* and *Tanaja* are two words for the same place and people and that, therefore, the Danuna should be equated with Homer's Danaans/Danaoi rather than with the Hittite land of Danuna. Of further related interest, therefore, is the additional observation by Drews that the Danuna (= Tanaja/Danaoi?) of Ramesses III's Sea Peoples inscriptions have apparently taken the place of the earlier Eqwesh (= Achaoi/Achaeans?) of Merenptah's Sea Peoples inscriptions, just as the Tjekru of Ramesses III may have taken the place of the earlier Shekelesh of Merenptah.[55]

As mentioned, speculation regarding both the origin and the final settling place for the Danuna has usually involved circular arguments based on whether they are equated with the land of Danuna or with Homer's Danaans/Danaoi. It is conceivable that we should be considering an Aegean origin, with a final settlement in the coastal region of southeastern Turkey (i.e., the area of Adana in Cilicia). However, another suggestion that has found recent favor relates the Danuna to the biblical tribe of Dan, which would suggest that these Sea Peoples were also ultimately resettled or were settled by the Egyptians in Canaan. If so, some of the archaeological remains uncovered by the ongoing excavations at the site of Tell Dan in northern Israel will be relevant to this discussion.[56]

The Peleset (Egyptian *Prst/Plst*) are today perhaps the best known of all the Sea Peoples, since they are almost universally identified with the Philistines of the Bible. Indeed, there is certainly a linguistic connection between the Peleset of the Egyptian texts and the Philistines of the Bible. However, the Peleset do not appear in any Egyptian texts before the time of Ramesses III and are not readily found in many other inscriptions apart from the Bible, where they are called the Philistines rather than the Peleset.[57]

The commonly held identification of the Peleset as synonymous with the Philistines of the Bible does not help in identifying their origins, for no Egyptian text—or any other inscription, for that matter—gives any indication as to where they came from. Suggestions for their origins have ranged from Crete to Arzawa in Anatolia to Canaan, but there is no clear solution yet in sight.[58]

However, if the Peleset really are synonymous with the Philistines of the Bible, we know where they ended up—for the Bible talks at great length about the Philistine cities in Canaan. We know this from other sources as well; for instance, *The Onomasticon of Amenope,* dating to ca. 1100 BC, lists the Peleset among the defeated Sea Peoples who resettled or were settled by the Egyptians on the coast of Canaan.[59] In addition, the archaeological remains of the Philistines are numerous and may give some indication as to the origin of the Peleset after all.

Space limitations here preclude a full discussion of all the relevant archaeological material identified as Philistine—primarily pottery, but also including full-blown architecture and other material goods from sites such as Tell Qasile, Tell Miqne/Ekron, Ashdod, and Ashkelon in Israel. Perhaps most relevant is the identification of so-called Mycenaean LH IIIC:1b pottery—Aegean-inspired pottery that seems to be locally made in Syria-Palestine—and the question of whether Philistine pottery can be described as a degenerate form of Mycenaean pottery and used to support a hypothesis that at least some of the Philistines originated in the Aegean. For instance, Ann Killebrew, a specialist on these topics, has written recently:

> Thus, in my opinion, the appearance of large quantities of Aegean-inspired locally-produced Mycenaean IIIC:1b and its related wares at a number of sites in Syria-Palestine is a classic case study in material culture of the incursion of new peoples settling at several centers on

the southern coastal plain of Canaan at the close of the Bronze Age. Though the material culture has its tradition in the Aegean, these peoples, termed Philistines in the biblical account, probably originated on Cyprus, Rhodes, and/or in southern Anatolia.[60]

In contrast to the Peleset/Philistines, "of the shadowy Washosh," Sandars once said, "virtually nothing is known, unless they had any connection with the 'Wilusa' (Wilusiya) of Hittite writings, that may have lain in southwestern Anatolia, or with 'Ilios' (Troy) in the north-west."[61] We may know nothing about the origins of the Washosh, but we can make an educated guess as to where they ended up. In Papyrus Harris I, Ramesses III says that the Washosh (and the Shardana) were "brought as captives to Egypt," that he "settled them in strongholds bound in my name," and that he "taxed them all, in clothing and grain from the store-houses and granaries each year."[62] This would seem to indicate that the Washosh had been settled in Egypt itself. However, there are, as yet, no identifiable archaeological remains that can be linked to the Washosh.

According to the Egyptian sources, the Shekelesh, Peleset, Tjekru, Danuna, and Washosh were all islanders, each living on land entirely surrounded by water, and the Shardana and Eqwesh occupied territories that, at the least, had a coast fronting on the sea. The status of the Teresh and Lukki, in these regards, remains uncertain, although it is generally accepted that the Lukki are to be associated with the southwestern coast of Anatolia, in the area later known as Lycia. Moreover, again according to the Egyptian texts, the specific Sea Peoples were all "northerners" relative to Egypt, while those named in Ramesses III's texts apparently originated west of central Anatolia and Cilicia, to judge from the geographical sequence of the kingdoms that they attacked.

In these circumstances, it is not surprising that we must infer that the five Sea Peoples who collaborated in the Libyan attack on Merenptah's Egypt must have sailed to Libya to do so, because the invasion originated in the Libyan homeland—in all probability Cyrenaica.[63] The Sea Peoples in question could not have traversed the Egyptian Delta and the land route (controlled by Egyptian fortresses) to Cyrenaica. As for the almost completely different Sea Peoples involved in the invasion of the Eastern Mediterranean in the time of Ramesses III, the Egyptian texts state that they came by sea but also, more surprisingly, by land.[64] Moreover, the contingent moving by land was apparently a very large one, for Ramesses seems to have organized a large military force to deal with it,[65] and the Sea Peoples had earlier set up a substantial camp "in one place," from which base they supposedly devastated the entire and extensive land of Amor or Amurru.[66]

The Sea Peoples' advance by land may have been due to two factors, insofar as the Egyptian evidence is concerned. First, unlike the Sea Peoples involved in invading Merenptah's Egypt, those identified under Ramesses III were accompanied by women and children and presumably possessions, conveyed in heavy-looking wooden carts drawn by slow-moving zebu oxen, although the evidence for these important data are purely representational, not textual.[67] Apparently, the vessels of the Sea Peoples were not suitable for these purposes. Second, while the polities attacked by the Sea Peoples all had shipping, capable to some degree of opposing the seaborne advance of the former, they also had extensive inland territories more effectively overcome or reduced by forces moving by land.

Since the land contingent was organized specifically by peoples all identified as "islanders," a very considerable organizational effort is implied. Indeed, there is archaeological evidence for destructions at numerous sites—both inland and coastal—in the Aegean, Anatolia, Cyprus, and Syria-Palestine, all occurring within a fifty-year period from ca. 1225 to 1175 BC. The question, of course, which has been debated for the past century or more, is whether the Sea Peoples caused all of these destructions or if, in fact, they are even all related; various alternate theories proposed during the past century have included earthquakes, drought, famine, internal rebellions, and systems collapse.[68] However, that the Sea Peoples' route to Egypt went via Ugarit in northern Syria seems without question, if a letter found at that site is any indication:

> Say to the king of Alashiya [Cyprus], my father: Thus says the king of Ugarit, your son:
>
> My father, now the ships of the enemy have been coming. They have been setting fire to my cities and have done harm to the land. Doesn't my father know that all of my infantry and [chariotry] are stationed in Khatte, and that all of my ships are stationed in the land of Lukki? They haven't arrived back yet, so the land is thus prostrate. May my father be aware of this matter. Now the seven ships of the enemy which have been coming have done harm to us. Now if other ships of the enemy turn up, send me a report somehow(?) so that I will know.[69]

The Egyptian sources also raise some significant geographical issues. First, why are the two lists of Sea Peoples (Merenptah's and Ramesses III's) almost entirely different in composition? This raises the possibility that the two sets of peoples were geographically remote from each other, for example, perhaps along the eastern and western sides of the Aegean, respectively, or perhaps west of the Aegean altogether in one case. The two sets have in common only the Shekelesh and perhaps (but doubtfully) the Shardana and the Teresh. Possibly, quite different factors were at work, involving political and other relations among the various Sea Peoples rather than their geographical disposition. However, given our still very imperfect understanding of the Sea Peoples, any reasonable possibility suggested by the Egyptian sources needs to be kept in play until definitive evidence to the contrary emerges.

In some instances, the Egyptian sources display a selectivity that may be significant, but whether in relationship to the Sea Peoples themselves or to specific compositional needs (written or pictorial) is debatable. For example, two of Merenptah's documents highlight only one of the several Sea Peoples accompanying the Libyans, noting that the Libyan leader mobilized the Shekelesh and "every foreign country" involved[70]—that is, the other Sea Peoples, mentioned on the other stelae of Merenptah. Presumably, the compression was for reasons of space, but why pick the Shekelesh as the specific representative of the entire group? This singling out reminds us that the Shekelesh alone may have been involved in both of the initiatives against Egypt: was there something especially impressive about them?

A similar kind of selectivity is seen in the texts of Ramesses III. The full list of the relevant Sea Peoples is provided only twice and in different texts (Edgerton and Wilson 1936, 53, 131); all five are (except for substituting Shardana for Shekelesh) also listed in Papyrus Harris I.[71] Elsewhere in the Medinet Habu texts, when limited space or a desired compositional emphasis required that not all the Sea Peoples be listed, it is typically the Tjekru and the Peleset who are named.

For example, in a scene showing prisoners from a fifth-year campaign against Libyans and from the fifth-year conflict with the Sea Peoples being presented to Amun-Re, the compositional structure allowed only two registers. One appropriately depicts Libu, but the other only depicts "the great fallen ones of Tjekru," as if they are more significant than the other Sea Peoples or—much the same thing—can stand for all the others.[72] Moreover, in a text primarily describing the fifth-year Libyan campaign, the essentials of conflict with the Sea Peoples are reported laconically, but while the "northern countries" are specified, only the Tjekru and Peleset are named, as if the two are more significant than the others.[73]

The Peleset are singled out in other ways. In an elaborate depiction of arms being issued, both the fifth-year (Libyan) and eighth-year (Sea Peoples) campaigns are referred to, with Tjemeh (an archaic term for Libya) standing for the former, and the Peleset for the latter, as if somehow representative of the entire confederation of Sea Peoples.[74] Moreover, in the especially important and large-scale representation of the king presenting Sea Peoples prisoners to Amun-Re (west wall, first court), the text epitomizes his defeat of the Sea Peoples by referring only to the Peleset, Danuna, and Shekelesh, while the three registers of prisoners are labeled, from top to bottom, as "leaders of every country" (i.e., implicitly, all the Sea Peoples?), the Danuna, and the Peleset.[75] Finally, the Peleset are once described as "hidden in their towns" (Egyptian *dmiw*).[76] Towns are not otherwise associated with Sea Peoples in Egyptian sources.

Many of the examples concerning the Tjekru and the Peleset cited above may be due to variations in usage or misused conventional terms. However, given the paucity of evidence about Sea Peoples, the possibility that more was implied should not be overlooked.

Finally, the historicity of the textual records, both of Merenptah and Ramesses III, is an important issue. Two points are especially significant. First, are the "historical" records of Ramesses III's reign, as displayed at Medinet Habu, actually those of Merenptah, copied from his nearby and now largely destroyed mortuary temple? The case has been made[77] but is not supported by most scholars. In any event, it would simply push the issue of the historicity of the texts about the Sea Peoples back into an earlier reign, without changing the essentials.

The second, more important point is the suggestion, made by many scholars, that the demands of temple symbolism, royal ideology and, more crudely, propaganda mean that the records of Ramesses III are not to be taken at face value; doubts are less often raised about the historical narratives describing Merenptah's contacts with Libyans and Sea Peoples, although, on the same grounds, they should be equally suspect. An extreme example of this skepticism is provided by Cifola, who argued that the Sea Peoples in Ramesses III's time were not a coherent body or a confederation and that the process of their migration into the Eastern Mediterranean was not unitary but involved different groups at different times. This resulted in many small-scale clashes between Egyptians and Sea Peoples, which the Egyptians transformed into two great but nonexistent battles in the Medinet Habu records.[78]

It is good historical practice to review alternative scenarios in assessing ancient data, but in the final analysis, primary weight should be given to the actual content of that data, unless there is a strong probability, provided by other evidence, that it is not accurate. As the essential framework for continuing research into the Sea Peoples, the quite explicit Egyptian statements must be accepted at face value, at least for now. Under Merenptah, some Sea Peoples joined Libyans in a substantial, if abortive, invasion of the Western Delta. Relatively soon after, another group of Sea Peoples created an effective combined military and migratory force that moved along the southern coast of Anatolia and then down along the Levantine coast and coastal lands. The kingdoms encountered en route were unable to resist; and the process was relatively rapid, even if it involved a few years rather than a few months. Finally, the Sea Peoples offered a very substantial threat to Egypt and, as the attack on the Nile mouths indicates, intended to penetrate and settle in Egypt. The Egyptians successfully prevented this but did settle their many Sea Peoples prisoners in royal "strongholds" in Egypt and perhaps elsewhere,[79] in part as a military resource. At Medinet Habu, Sea Peoples are shown fighting on the Egyptian side in the battles against the Libyans, Nubians, and others, although, in theory, these events sometimes antedate the eighth-year victories.

For example, Sea Peoples with feathered headdresses appear fighting on the Egyptians' side against Nubians,[80] and Sea Peoples with horned helmets defend attacks on two cities in the Levant.[81] All these events are undated and may be unhistorical, included in the decorative program to fill out its cosmographic coverage. However, in the Egyptian campaign against Libyans in the fifth regnal year of Ramesses III (i.e., three years before the conflict with the Sea Peoples), several relevant scenes show Sea Peoples in feathered headdresses or horned helmets fighting on the side of the Egyptians.[82] Was this simply anachronism, since the scenes were probably designed and carved after the eighth regnal year; or did the Egyptian army include Sea Peoples before Ramesses III's conflict with the Sea Peoples? They could have been former prisoners of war of King Merenptah, captured eleven years before. This likelihood is reinforced by the fact that Ramesses III's battles with the Sea Peoples themselves included Sea Peoples with horned helmets fighting on the Egyptian side![83] Finally, in the battle against Libyans in the eleventh regnal year of Ramesses III, Sea Peoples wearing feathered headdresses and horned helmets join the Egyptians in the conflict.[84]

In Djahy, however, Egypt—while victorious in battle—was less successful in stemming or controlling Sea Peoples' settlement in the area. No surviving record after Ramesses III refers to the Danuna, Shekelesh, or Washosh (this last people, in fact, is attested only at Medinet Habu), but the case is quite different as regards Tjekru and Peleset. After Ramesses III, Egypt's domination of the area now occupied by Lebanon and Israel seems to have gradually but unceasingly contracted,[85] while the demographic and cultural composition of the region changed considerably. Sea Peoples were part of this change. As discussed above, an Egyptian text of ca. 1100 BC, less than a century after Ramesses III's victory, shows that Shardana, Tjekru, and Peleset were settled in the coastal regions of Canaan.[86] The Peleset went on to become the Philistine kingdoms of the Bible,[87] and a fictional but historically based description of an Egyptian envoy's adventures in ca. 1082 BC reveals that Dor (on the coast of modern Israel) was a "Tjekru town."[88] We have no clear indication as to where the defeated remnants of the Eqwesh, Denyon, Teresh, Washosh, and Lukki settled, but the Lukki may well have simply made their way back home to southwestern Anatolia, while the Danuna may conceivably have settled in the biblical area of Dan—in what is now northern Israel.

PICTURES WORTH A THOUSAND WORDS?

So far, this discussion has been based mainly on Egyptian textual sources, but at Medinet Habu, these are complimented by a rich pictorial record concerning the Sea Peoples. What can the pictures tell us about these mysterious peoples?

The pictorial record comprises several large-scale scenes (complemented by relatively short texts) extending along the external face of the north side of the mortuary temple of Ramesses III. Usually, the scenes are demarcated from each other by vertical dividers of text. The subject matter comprises, from west to east, the equipping of the Egyptian army; its march to or into Djahy; the land battle against the Sea Peoples; a royal lion hunt; the battle against the Sea Peoples' ships in the river mouths; and—in one instance not divided off from the preceding scene—the celebration of victory, with emphasis on the water battle. Finally, a last scene shows the king presenting Sea Peoples prisoners and Libyans to Amun-Re,[89] the Libyans referring back to scenes depicting the fifth-year conflict with Libyans, scenes that precede those dealing with the Sea Peoples and run along the west (north half) and north (western segment) external wall faces.

The other relevant scene occurs on the west wall (south half) of the first court and depicts Sea Peoples prisoners presented to Amun-Re.[90] It is balanced on the north half by the long text describing the conflict and its causes.[91] The temple proper begins at this point, with a pylon and a second court; the first court and its pylon is, functionally, an add-on.

The texts relevant to Sea Peoples at Medinet Habu contain a core of historical actuality (see above), and this should be true of the scenes as well.

Especially interesting is the appearance of the Sea Peoples warriors. Although five specific Sea Peoples are identified as comprising the invaders, all the warriors in the land battle scene (and the representations of Sea Peoples prisoners in various scenes) wear identical costumes, specifically a helmet or headdress resembling feathers and a distinctive type of kilt. Apart from their capacity for uniting into a confederation, this is the principal indication in the Egyptian sources that the Sea Peoples (at least those represented at Medinet Habu) shared a common culture to a significant degree. If Sea Peoples' costumes varied significantly from one to another people, the Egyptians were likely to have indicated that fact, a supposition made likely by the unique treatment of Sea Peoples' costumes in the scene depicting the battle in the river mouths.

Here, two types of Sea Peoples costume are carefully distinguished.[92] Some of the Sea Peoples' ships are manned exclusively by men wearing the costume described above, others exclusively by men with a similar kilt but wearing round, smooth profile helmets, each with a pair of projecting horns. In the horizontal register below, Sea Peoples prisoners of both iconographic types are mingled together, but in the actual battle scene, they operate quite separately from each other. The implication is clear: one or more of the Sea Peoples was costumed differently from one or more of the remainder, and thus there was a considerable difference in material culture within the Sea Peoples. Moreover, those wearing horned helmets associate solely with sea travel in the Medinet Habu scenes, yet a further example of differentiation.

At this point, comparative evidence is insufficient to equate specific peoples with specific costumes. Many scholars identify the wearing of horned helmets with the Shardana, with some reason,[93] but at Medinet Habu, there is no indication that Shardana were involved in the Sea Peoples' invasion. Papyrus Harris I does indicate this but is a less significant source and omits the Shekelesh, a further indication of unreliability.

The Sea Peoples as a whole are also characterized by a type of ox-drawn cart, unique among Egyptian representations (land battle only), and a distinctive type of ship, with "birds heads" at the prow and stern (battle in the river mouths). These ships were powered only by sail, not by oarsmen, conspicuous on the Egyptian ships in the scene depicting the battle in the river mouths. As an example of how ideological needs can influence historical conclusions, Shelly Wachsmann has interpreted the depiction of a capsized Sea Peoples' ships as showing that such ships had rowers' guards and hence were rowed.[94] However, it seems more likely that the ship is shown breaking up (its sail also has a huge hole torn in it) and that the "rowers' shield" is a plank separating from the vessel's body.[95]

Finally, the success of the Sea Peoples' invasion before encountering Egyptian forces suggests that they were militarily effective on land and sea and that they had some form of centralized leadership.[96] Neither of those characteristics are highlighted in the Medinet Habu scenes, which, of their very nature, must show the Sea Peoples as totally disorganized and bereft of leadership and thus fully equivalent to the malevolent yet chaotic force of Isfet, which is continually reduced to impotence by the overwhelming power of cosmic and societal order, as manifest in the triumphant Egyptian king. Moreover, the leaders of Egypt's foreign foes are typically, though not always,[97] minimized or overlooked in such scenes in general, because the enemy, if chaotic, should be leaderless and because actual leaders should not be given visual or verbal prominence since, as embodiments of leadership, their role in opposing the pharaoh, the ultimate embodiment of leadership, is so despicable.

This said, it can be observed that clues as to these aspects of the Sea Peoples are provided in the Medinet Habu scenes, within the interstices of the larger, ideologically driven compositions. For example, the land battle scene does provide indications of Sea Peoples' military capacities. It reveals the Sea Peoples' deployed chariotry as well as infantry (with no indication of the former in the texts), and the Sea Peoples warriors fleeing the carnage in the upper and lower right-hand corners do so in good order, perhaps reflective of the military discipline of Sea Peoples warriors as a whole. Visually, the scene depicting the battle in the river mouths does not provide such indications of the Sea Peoples' military effectiveness at sea; here, the described Egyptian preparations are a more significant indication of the Sea Peoples' anticipated strength: the king states, "I caused the Nile mouth to be prepared like a strong wall with warships, galleys and coasters,"[98] while a "stockade of lances" surrounded the Sea Peoples along the shore.[99]

SUMMARY AND CONCLUSION

It is hoped that this discussion will serve as a single source of information for people wishing to know more about the origins, journeys, conflicts, and ultimate destinations of the Sea Peoples. For this reason, an appendix is attached, which contains English translations of all of the relevant Egyptian texts concerned with the Sea Peoples. As with any new publication, it is hoped that this discussion will serve not only as a recapitulation of facts and theories already presented by previous scholars but will push scholarship forward in at least a few places, particularly concerning support for a westward movement of the Sea Peoples.

Appendix: English Translations of the
Inscriptions concerning the Sea Peoples

MERENPTAH

Year 5

Great Karnak Inscription[100]

[Beginning of the victory that his majesty achieved in the land of Libya] . . .
Eqwesh, Teresh, Lukki, Shardana, Shekelesh, Northerners coming from all
lands.

. . .

. . . the third season, saying: "The wretched, fallen chief of Libya . . ." has fallen
upon the country of Tehenu with his bowmen----------Shardana, Shekelesh,
Eqwesh, Lukki, Teresh, taking the best of every warrior and every man of war
of his country . . .

. . .

List of the captives carried off from this land of Libya and the countries which
he brought with him . . .
-----------[Sher]den, Shekelesh, Eqwesh of the countries of the sea, who had
no foreskins:

Shekelesh	222 men
Making	250 hands
Teresh	742 men
Making	790 hands
Shardana	--- ---
[Making]	--- ---

[Ek]wesh who had no foreskins, slain,
whose hands were carried off, (for) they
had no [foreskins]   --- ---
. . . Shekelesh and Teresh who came as enemies of Libya   --- ---
-----Kehek, and Libyans, carried off as living prisoners   218 men

Cairo Column[101]

Year 5, second month of the third season (tenth month). One came to say to
his majesty: "The wretched [chief] of Libya has invaded [with] ---, being
men and women, Shekelesh and every foreign country ------."

Heliopolis Text[102]

Year 5, second month of the third season (tenth month). One came to say to his majesty: "The wretched [chief] of Libya has invaded [with] ---, being men and women, Shekelesh and every foreign country ------."

Athribis Stela[103]

. . . Eqwesh [of] the countries of the sea, whom had brought the wretched [fallen chief of Libya, whose] hands [were carried off]   2,201 [+ *x*] men

Shekelesh   200 men

Teresh   722 [+ *x*] men

-------- Libya, and Shardana, slain   --- men

RAMESSES III

Year 8

Text Inscribed in Interior Courtyard at Medinet Habu[104]

Year 8 under the majesty of (Ramesses III) . . . The foreign countries made a conspiracy in their islands. All at once the lands were removed and scattered in the fray. No land could stand before their arms, from Khatte, Qode, Carchemish, Arzawa, and Alashiya on, being cut off at [one time]. A camp [was set up] in one place in Amor. They desolated its people, and its land was like that which has never come into being. They were coming forward toward Egypt, while the flame was prepared before them. Their confederation was the Philistines, Tjekru, Shekelesh, Denye(n), and Washosh, lands united. They laid their hands upon the lands as far as the circuit of the earth, their hearts confident and trusting: "Our plans will succeed!"

Now the heart of this god, the Lord of the Gods. was prepared and ready to ensnare them like birds. . . . I organized my frontier in Djahy, prepared before them: princes, commanders of garrisons, and maryanuu. I have the river-mouths prepared like a strong wall, with warships, galleys and coasters, (fully) equipped, for they were manned completely from bow to stern with valiant warriors carrying their weapons. The troops consisted of every picked man of Egypt. They were like lions roaring upon the mountain tops. The chariotry consisted of runners, of picked men, of every good and capable chariot-warrior. The horses were quivering in every part of their bodies, prepared to crush the foreign countries under their hoofs. I was the valiant Montu, standing fast at their head, so that they might gaze upon the capturing of my hands.

Those who reached my frontier, their seed is not, their heart and soul are finished forever and ever. Those who came forward together on the sea, the full flame was in front of them at the river-mouths, while a stockade of lances surrounded them on the shore. They were dragged in, enclosed, and prostrated on the beach, killed, and made into heaps from tail to head. Their ships and their goods were as if fallen into the water.

I have made the lands turn back from (even) mentioning Egypt: for when they pronounce my name in their land, then they are burned up. Since I sat upon the throne of Har-akhti and the Great-of-Magic was fixed upon my head like Re, I have not let foreign countries behold the frontier of Egypt, to boast thereof to the Nine Bows.

Inscription in Interior Courtyard at Medinet Habu Labeled
"The Inscription of the Year 5" but Most
Probably Recording Events from the Year 8[105]

The northern countries quivered in their bodies, the Peleset, Tjek[er and . . .]. They cut off their (own) land, and were coming, their soul finished. They were *teher* warriors on land: another (group) was on the sea. Those who came on [land were overthrown and killed. . .]. Amon-Re was after them, destroying them. Those who entered the river-mouths were like birds ensnared in the net. . . . Their leaders were carried off and slain. They were cast down and pinioned. . . .

Text (MH I, pl. 14) Inscribed within Panel XIV at Medinet Habu,
Accompanying a Scene of a Naval Battle with Vessels of Both
Egyptians and Sea Peoples, with the Pharaoh and
His Infantry Fighting from the Shore[106]

Now the northern countries, which were in their isles, were quivering in their bodies. They penetrated the channels of the Nile mouths. Their nostrils have ceased (to function, so that) their desire is <to> breathe the breath. His majesty is gone forth like a whirlwind against them, fighting on the battlefield like a runner. The dread of him and the terror of him have entered into their bodies: (they are) capsized and overwhelmed in their places. Their hearts are taken away; their soul is flown away. Their weapons are scattered in the sea. His arrow pierces him whom he has wished among them, while the fugitive is become one fallen into the water. His majesty is like an enraged lion, attacking his assailant with his paws: plundering on his right hand and powerful on his left hand, like Set destroying the serpent "Evil of Character."

It is Amon-Re who has overthrown for him the lands and has crushed for him every land under his feet: King of Upper and Lower Egypt, Lord of the Two Lands: Usermare-Meriamon.

Text (MH I, pl. 15) Inscribed in Panel XV at Medinet Habu[107]

Spoken by his majesty to the royal princes, the officials, the royal chamberlains, and the charioteers: "See ye the great strength of my father Amon-Re! As for the countries who came from their land in the isles in the midst of the sea, as they were (coming) forward toward Egypt, their hearts relying on their hands, a net was prepared for them, to ensnare them. They that entered into the Nile mouths were caught, fallen into the midst of it, pinioned in their places, butchered, and their bodies hacked up. I have caused that you see my strength, which was in that which my arm has done, while I was alone. My arrow hit the mark without fail, while my arms and my hand were steadfast. I was like a falcon in the midst of small fowl, for my talon did not fail upon their heads. Amon-Re was on my right and on my left, and the awe of him and the terror of him were in my person. Rejoice ye, for that which I commanded is come to pass, and my counsels and my plans are perfected. Amon-Re repels my foe and gives to me every land in my grasp."

Year 12

Stela at Medinet Habu to the South of the Main Gateway,
on the Face of the First Pylon, Beginning with the Phrase
"Year 12 under the Majesty of Horus"[108]

I overthrew the Tjek[er], the land of Pele[set], the Danuna, the [W]eshesh, and the Shekelesh; I destroyed the breath of the Mesh[wesh],-----, Sebet,-----, devastated in their (own) land. I am fine of plan and excellent of------ ---.

Papyrus Harris I[109]

I extended all the boundaries of Egypt. I overthrew those who invaded them from their lands. I slew the Danuna [who are] in their isles, the Tjekru and the Peleset were made ashes. The Shardana and the Washosh of the sea, they were made as those that exist not, taken captive at one time, brought as captives to Egypt, like the sand of the shore. I settled them in strongholds bound in my name. Numerous were their classes like hundred-thousands. I taxed them all, in clothing and grain from the store-houses and granaries each year. . . . I made the infantry and chariotry to dwell (at home) in my time; the Shardana and Kehek were in their towns, lying the [length] of their backs; they had no fear, (for) there was no enemy from Kush (nor) foe from Syria. Their bows and their weapons reposed in their magazines, while they were satisfied and drunk with joy. Their wives were with them, their children at their side; they looked not behind them, (but) their hearts were confident, (for) I was with them as the defense and protection of their limbs. I sustained alive the whole land, whether foreigners, (common) folk, citizens, or people, male or female.

The Onomasticon of Amenope[110]

(268) *Šrdn* (Shardana); (269) *Tkr* (Tjeker); (270) *Prst* (Peleset)

Ugarit Letters

Letter from the King of Alashiya (Cyprus) to Hammurabi, King of Ugarit (RSL 1; Ugaritica 5.23)[111]

Thus says the king (of Alashiya): say to Ammurapi, king of Ugarit: May you be well, and may the gods protect you in well-being!

Concerning that which you wrote (me): "Enemy ships have been sighted at sea"—if it is true that ships have been sighted, then make yourself very strong. Now where are your infantry and [your] chariotry stationed? Aren't they stationed with you? No? Who is sending you after(?) the enemy? Surround your cities with walls. Bring (your) infantry and chariotry into (them). Be on the lookout for the enemy and make yourself very strong.

Letter from Hammurabi, King of Ugarit, to the King of Alashiya (Cyprus) (RS 20.238; Ugaritica 5.24)[112]

Say to the king of Alashiya, my father: Thus says the king of Ugarit, your son:

I fall at the feet of my father. May my father be well! May your palaces, your wives, your infantry, and everything which belongs to the king of Alashiya, my father, be very, very well!

My father, now the ships of the enemy have been coming. They have been setting fire to my cities and have done harm to the land. Doesn't my father know that all of my infantry and [chariotry] are stationed in Khatte, and that all of my ships are stationed in the land of Lukki? They haven't arrived back yet, so the land is thus prostrate. May my father be aware of this matter. Now the seven ships of the enemy which have been coming have done harm to us.

Now if other ships of the enemy turn up, send me a report somehow(?) so that I will know.

Notes to Cline and O'Connor

1. This discussion is an abbreviated and revised version of a longer presentation coauthored by Eric H. Cline and David O'Connor that originally appeared as "The Mystery of the 'Sea Peoples'" in *Mysterious Lands,* ed. D. O'Connor and S. Quirke (London: UCL Press, 2003), 107–38. It is presented here by permission of the series editor, Peter Ucko, and the volume editors, David O'Connor and Stephen Quirke.

2. Wilson (1969) 262.

3. Oren (2000). For other recent publications, with earlier bibliography, see Nibbi (1975); Sandars (1985); Dothan (1982); Dothan and Dothan (1992); Ward and Joukowsky (1992); Drews (1993); Zangger (1994); Idem (1995); Gitin et al. (1998); O'Connor (2000); Redford (2000); Leahy (2001). On the ships of the Sea Peoples, primarily as depicted in the Medinet Habu reliefs of Ramesses III, see Raban and Stieglitz (1991); Wachsmann (1981); Wachsmann (1982); Wachsmann (1997); Wachsmann (1998); Wachsmann (2000); Artzy (1997).

4. The renderings of the names of the Sea Peoples follow Redford (1992) 251, 248 n. 34, 251, 252, 476, 483, 485, 488. An exception is *Lukki,* for which see Gardiner (1947) I:314, 316.

5. See, e.g., Redford (1992) 289–94.

6. Vagnetti (2000).

7. Following Redford (1992) 251, 473, 480, 484.

8. Ibid., 474.

9. Redford (2000) 13.

10. Drews (2000).

11. Cifola (1988).

12. Redford (1992) 243–44.

13. O'Connor (1990) 37–38.

14. Breasted (2001) 3:238–64; Iskander (in preparation).

15. Ibid., 3:255.

16. Finley (1970) 4.

17. Redford (1992) 252.

18. Gardiner (1961) 270–71.

19. On the latter, see Edgerton and Wilson (1936) 31, 41, 42, 54, 55.

20. Breasted (2001) 3:241–52.

21. Ibid., 3:253–56.

22. Ibid., 3:252–53; Edel (1961) 101–3.

23. Bakry (1973) 3–21.

24. *MH* I, pls. 29–43, 44, 46.

25. Breasted (2001) 4:201.

26. Cf. Breasted (2001) 3:239–56 with Edgerton and Wilson (1936) 30, 35, 45, 47–48, 53, 130–31.

27. Breasted (2001) 4:201.

28. Sandars (1985) 112.

29. Breasted (2001) 3:249, 255.

30. Ibid., 241.

31. Edgerton and Wilson (1936) 41, 42, 53.

32. Gardiner (1947) I:281; Faulkner (1999) 12; Lesko (1982) 21.

33. Breasted (2001) 4:201.

34. Sandars (1985) 37, 107; Bryce (1979); Bryce (1986) 1–41; Bryce (1992) 55–57.

35. Moran (1992) 201–2.

36. Sandars (1985) 50, 106. See Gardiner (1947) I:195.

37. Sandars (1985) 106–7.

38. See the detailed discussion of the various hypotheses in Drews (1993) 53–61. See also Drews (1992) 21–22.

39. Gardiner (1947) I:194–99; Sandars (1985) 133; Knapp (1992) 124.

40. Leahy (2001) 259.

41. See Knapp (1992) 119–22, 124–25. The most recent summary can be found in Vagnetti (2000).

42. Zertal (2001).

43. Sandars (1985) 111–12; Drews (1992).

44. Drews (2000) 177.

45. Sandars (1985) 112; Drews (2000) 178–80.

46. Sandars (1985) 112–13.

47. See Stern (1994); Stern (1998); Stern (2000); Raban and Stieglitz (1991) 37–38, 41–42.

48. See Drews (2000) 181–82.

49. See, most recently, with thorough earlier bibliography, Niemeier (1998).

50. Pritchard (1969) 25–29, esp. 26.

51. Sandars (1985) 158, 170.

52. Gardiner (1947) I:199–200; Pritchard (1969) 26; Dothan (1982) 4–5; Niemeier (1998) 47.

53. Drews (2000) 178–80, citing earlier bibliography, including Edel (1984).

54. Moran (1992) 238–39.

55. Drews (2000) 181–82. See Cline (1994) 114–16 (nos. A32–37) for a detailed discussion of the occurrences of Tanaja in Egyptian inscriptions.

56. Yadin (1968) 9–23; Sandars (1985) 162–64; Raban and Stieglitz (1991) 41; Machinist (2000) 67.

57. Sandars (1985) 164–66; Drews (1998) 50–61; Machinist (2000).

58. See, e.g., Drews (1993) 54–72; Drews (1998) 53–57; Niemeier (1998) 47.

59. Gardiner (1947) I:200–205; Knapp (1992) 124; Drews (1998) 50.

60. Killebrew (1998) 166. See also discussions in Dothan (1982); Dothan (1995); Dothan (1998); Dothan and Dothan (1992); Brug (1985). See, now, the various contributions in Oren (2000), including those by Killebrew, Kling, Mazar, Finkelstein, and Dothan.

61. Sandars (1985) 158.

62. Breasted (2001) 4:201.

63. O'Connor (1990) 37–38.

64. Edgerton and Wilson (1936) 30, 55.

65. Ibid., 35–39.

66. Ibid., 53.

67. *MH* I, pl. 32. See also discussion contra in Drews (2000).

68. Drews (1993); Nur and Cline (2000); Stiebing (2001). See also Sandars (1985) 83; Betancourt (2000).

69. RS 20.238 = *Ugaritica* 5.24; present translation following Beckman (1996) 27. See also Sandars (1985) 142–43 and, previously, Schaeffer (1968) 87–89.

70. Edel (1961) 101–3; Bakry (1973).

71. Breasted (2001) 4:201.

72. Edgerton and Wilson (1936) 44–46.

73. Ibid., 30.

74. Ibid., 35.

75. Ibid., 47–48.

76. Ibid., 35.

77. Lesko (1989).

78. Cifola (1988).

79. Breasted (2001) 4:201.

80. *MH* I, pl. 8.

81. *MH* II, pls. 88, 94.

82. *MH* I, pls. 17–19, 24.

83. Ibid., pls. 30, 32, 35.

84. *MH* II, pl. 71.

85. Weinstein (1981) 22–23.

86. Redford (1992) 292.

87. Ibid., 298.

88. Lichtheim (1976) 228.

89. For the entire sequence, see *MH* I, pls. 29–43.

90. *MH* I, pl. 44.

91. Edgerton and Wilson (1936) 49–58.

92. Stadelmann (1984).

93. See Edgerton and Wilson (1936) 36 n. 39a.

94. Wachsmann (2000) 105–15.

95. O'Connor (2000) 99.

96. Contra the arguments in Cifola (1988).

97. See Edgerton and Wilson (1936) 60–68.

98. Ibid., 54.

99. Ibid., 55.

100. After Breasted (2001) 3:241, 243, 249.

101. After Breasted (2001) 3:253.

102. After Edel (1961). See Bakry (1973).

103. After Breasted (2001) 3:255.

104. After Edgerton and Wilson (1936) pl. 46, lines 1 and 16–25; revised translation following Wilson in Pritchard (1969) 262–63.

105. After Edgerton and Wilson (1936) pls. 27–28, lines 51–56; revised translation following Wilson in Pritchard (1969) 263.

106. After Edgerton and Wilson (1936) pls. 37–39, lines 8–23.

107. Ibid., pl. 42, lines 1–13.

108. Ibid., pl. 107, lines 7–9.

109. After Breasted (2001) 4:201. See also Sandars (1985) 133.

110. Gardiner (1947) I:194–205.

111. After Beckman (1996) 27. See also Sandars (1985) 142–43 and, previously, Schaeffer (1968) 85–86.

112. After Beckman (1996) 27. See also Sandars (1985) 142–43 and, previously, Schaeffer (1968) 87–89.

Chapter 6

The Mortuary Temple of
Ramesses III at Medinet Habu

DAVID O'CONNOR

Two especially significant monuments survive from the reign of Ramesses III, both located on the West Bank at Thebes. One is his richly decorated tomb in the Valley of the Kings; the other is his mortuary temple. Set some distance away from the tomb, the temple had a complementary relationship to the tomb, since the temple provided for the mortuary cult that, theoretically in perpetuity, contributed powerfully to the king's capacity to benefit from the afterlife. Today called Medinet Habu, Ramesses' temple is among the few New Kingdom temples to survive relatively well preserved, alongside Karnak and Luxor on the Theban East Bank, the temple of Seti I at Abydos, and the temples of Ramesses II and Nefertari at Abu Simbel.

Ramesses' mortuary temple certainly merits a full chapter to itself. The other monuments of his reign are covered comprehensively by Bojana Mojsov in this volume. It should be noted that in my treatment of Medinet Habu, I have kept citations to a minimum in order to convey to the reader my understanding of the nature and significance of the temple. In doing so, however, I have of course built on important documentary publications and interpretive studies, which are provided in an analytical note at the end of this chapter.

Like the other Ramesside mortuary temples (Nineteenth and Twentieth Dynasties) of Western Thebes, Medinet Habu had its own unique name: "The Temple of Usermaatre-Meryamun (i.e., Ramesses III) 'United with

Eternity' in the Estate of Amun on the West of Thebes." The exact reading of this and of the names of the other mortuary temples is a matter of debate, but the being venerated in the temple was also unique, a symbiotic fusion of Ramesses III himself and a specific form of Amun unique to the temple; both were understood as "United with Eternity," with "Eternity" specified as Neheh, which has been described—in a positive sense—as "eternal stasis." However, the temple's name also refers to a larger context, the totality of the Theban temples that fell into the "Estate of Amun," the primary god worshiped in the Great Temple at Karnak. Ramesses III/Amun "United with Eternity" was a divine being whose viability depended on being a special manifestation of Amun of Karnak and was, in a sense, a product of the larger ritual cycle of the latter within the Theban region.

The identification of the deceased Ramesses III with a particular form of Amun guaranteed that he would effectively experience the endlessly repeated regenerations or rebirths necessary for his eternal well-being in the afterlife. At the root of this process was the union of Osiris and the sun god (of whom Amun was a manifestation) in the netherworld. The royal tomb was so structured, decorated, and ritually treated as to demonstrate that the mummified and entombed king was identified with these gods. When they fused together to achieve regeneration, the king took on the form of each and experienced the same rebirth.

Via his mortuary temple, Ramesses III also had another kind of relationship with Amun-Re, "Lord of the Gods," at Karnak. The mortuary temple could be personified as a goddess and called the "king's mother." Although not stated as such specifically, this evoked the goddess Hathor, an immensely important being in Egyptian solar mythology and one specifically linked emotionally and even sexually with Amun of Thebes. Mythologically, Hathor functioned as the daughter, consort, and mother of Re the sun god: as a result, she played an essential role in the repeated rebirths of the sun god and in the endless renewals of the solar cycle this made possible. The sun god's rebirth guaranteed, in turn, the survival of the cosmos itself and of all those—living and deceased—who were part of it.

These general roles of Hathor took on a special form at Thebes. Here, Hathor was also the goddess who received and nurtured the dead, a role that depended, in turn, on an annually celebrated interaction with Amun of Karnak. The rebirth of the sun god, via his relationship with Hathor, was a daily event, signaled by his ascent at dawn; so was his regeneration via union with Osiris, occurring at midnight and preparing him for the gestation and rebirth process. However, the sun god also experienced an annual cycle of rebirth and renewal, as well as cosmic rule, indicated by his annual progress along the horizons from north to south and back to north again. In this, too, interaction with Hathor would be a crucial part of the process. This latter circumstance provides a context for the annual celebration of the Valley Festival at Thebes.

The festival was structured around a ceremonial visit by Amun of Karnak to Hathor's chapel at Deir el-Bahari, on the West Bank, where they celebrated a "sacred marriage," identified with the union between Re and Hathor. Its product was an especially exalted version of an otherwise daily event, the return of a renewed form of Amun-Re from the netherworld to the realm of the living and the resumption of the orderly rule that maintained the effectiveness of the cosmos. By incorporating the royal mortuary temples into this particular festival, deceased kings and the special form of Amun with which each was identified were guaranteed this especially potent means of renewal and effectiveness.

Throughout this chapter, I use the term *mortuary temple* as one convenient for Medinet Habu and the temples of identical function on the Theban West Bank. It should be noted, however, that the appropriateness of this term is debatable. Such mortuary temples could also be called "mansions of millions of years," as were temples elsewhere in Egypt. Haeny has suggested that the application of this phrase to mortuary temples indicates that they were essentially "constructions for royal statues" connected to the king's afterlife needs and that their precursors were royal "ka chapels" (mahats) built near the temples of various deities at a variety of sites and enabling the king commemorated in each ka chapel to share in the rituals and offerings received by those deities.[1]

EVALUATING THE TEMPLE OF MEDINET HABU

Any discussion of Medinet Habu is necessarily structured around two questions. First, how important was Medinet Habu in the building program of the reign of Ramesses III as a whole? Second, how should the modern observer assess its intrinsic value as, essentially, a "work of art" (a fair term given the complex interrelationships that any Egyptian temple represents between choreographed ritual, ideological conceptions, architectural form, and "decorative" program)?

As to Ramesses' general building program, such programs—as regards the totality of structures produced—are often used by scholars to measure the relative prosperity and effectiveness of individual king's reigns. Temples, of which at least elements are likely to survive, are especially significant in this regard. However, as a criterion, temple building is an ambiguous entity: our perception of a building program is affected by the sometimes short reigns of otherwise effective kings or, more generally, by the vagaries of preservation, whether of actual structures (partial or otherwise) or simply of textual references to them.

Given these circumstances, it is not surprising to find that opinions about the building program of Ramesses III vary considerably. Grandet, an authority on the king, concludes that he had a nationwide "program of construction and re-organization of a very great amplitude;"[2] whereas Kitchen, an expert on the Ramesside period, argued that Medinet Habu "was the *sole* vast building enterprise of the reign."[3]

As to the second issue, the evaluation of Medinet Habu in modern times, it has received mixed reviews as regards both its art (the representations and accompanying texts on its walls) and architecture, in terms of both originality and intrinsic quality. Nims, for example, commented at length on the program's dependency on the mortuary temple of Ramesses II. He observed, "The scribes responsible for the design went to the older temple and made copies of what they found, then put the scenes on the walls of the temple of Ramesses III, often in exactly the same position . . . The ruined condition of the Ramesseum [the temple of Ramesses II] makes it impossible to tell just how far the copying went, but it was clearly very extensive. Often mistakes in the inscriptions of Medinet Habu arose from misunderstanding those of the Ramesseum or from careless copying."[4] Moreover, it has also been suggested that the sometimes seemingly inventive (in compositional terms) and certainly extensive scenes related to warfare and triumph at Medinet Habu were largely copied from the (now destroyed) temple of Merenptah,[5] although this suggestion has not won general acceptance.

These same battle reliefs have also attracted negative comments. In 1951, in a well-known study, Groenewegen-Frankfort noted that in these reliefs, "New Kingdom art appears to have swung full circle; it ends where it began with a paean to the divine ruler," as compared to livelier and more innovative treatments under Seti I and Ramesses II. At Medinet Habu, "even the tensest of battles are immobilized, reduced to a symbolic statement that the king's victory was absolute." There was even a degree of moral decay: "One might even sense a trace of corruption in the only efforts to stress the human side of Ramesses III: on the High Gate that formed the entrance to the temenos wall of the temple we find the dull erotic scenes . . . of Pharaoh seeking entertainment."[6] Stevenson Smith, in his magisterial survey of Egyptian art, praised the plasticity of the modeling in the reliefs of Medinet Habu but noted a decline in coherence in some of the major battle scenes, which produce "chiefly an impression of confused overlapping shapes."[7]

The mostly well-preserved architecture of Medinet Habu is usually described in relatively neutral terms, lacking, however, the enthusiasm lavished on the innovative architecture of the other relatively well-preserved and much earlier mortuary temple of Hatshepsut at Deir el-Bahari. Sometimes, however, comment can be implicitly or explicitly negative. Dieter Arnold, for example, notes that the core temple of Medinet Habu is derivative and "largely follows the plan of that of Ramesses II";[8] while Haeny has observed that "compared with earlier temples, the plan of Medinet Habu appears reduced, even congested in its layout. The side chambers of the second and third halls and the barque chambers are extremely small, and access to them is tortuous and narrow."[9]

The cumulative effect of the observations about the art and architecture of Medinet Habu, cited above, suggests that, for some observers, the temple documents a decline in creative vitality and architectural clarity that might be considered a manifestation of a political, economic, and even moral exhaustion that was beginning to affect the whole culture as the New Kingdom drew to a close. However valid such observations in general might be, I suggest below that they are not relevant to the evaluation of Medinet Habu. In important ways, its art was innovative in both general and specific ways, although obviously also a continuation of a preexisting tradition. And as for architecture, Medinet Habu is best evaluated as sharing in a complex and dynamic interplay of continuity, variation, and change that characterized *all* the surviving mortuary temples of the Theban West Bank.

MEDINET HABU AND THE WEST BANK MORTUARY TEMPLES

The suite of other West Bank mortuary temples to which Medinet Habu should be compared comprise those for which the architecture is relatively well preserved, although sometimes only as a ground plan. Before undertaking this comparison in detail, however, some general considerations as to the relationship of form to function in these temples need to be addressed.

Two primary functions are of equal and complementary significance. The first is a sequenced set of ritual acts performed on a daily basis, which involved a mortuary cult complex south of the central axis; a Re-Horakhty (or solar cult) complex north of that axis; and perhaps also a centrally placed, rear-located sanctuary between these two architectural entities. The southern complex, which may be loosely described as "Osirian," highlighted Osiris,

Sokar, and other mortuary deities; in it, the king was shown performing rituals for the benefit of his deceased self and for Osiris, with whom the deceased king was identified. In the northern complex, the king performed the rituals supporting the annual cycle of the sun god—rituals that, since they involved that god's nightly sojourn in the netherworld and his rebirth therefrom, also functioned as a kind of mortuary cult. Here, the deceased king was identified with the sun god and his capacity for rebirth.

But the deceased king was also identified with a particular form of Amun who, as a solarized deity himself, was equivalent to the sun god yet had a different personality. Hence, the rituals celebrated individually in the Osirian and Re-Horakhty complexes found their central meaning in the being celebrated in the centrally placed sanctuary, that is, the combined being of the deceased king and special form of Amun, energized and reborn via its identification with Osiris and Re-Horakhty and their fusion. A stone false door in the central sanctuary provided the means whereby the king-as-Amun could make the transition between the otherworld and this one and become ritually accessible. The architectural dispositions therefore seemed to manifest these symbolic relations, with the sanctuary dedicated to the product of the Osirian and solar processes centrally placed—bridging, as it were, the southern and northern architectural complexes.

The central sanctuary may well have been the focus of daily rituals, but it clearly gained special meaning at the time of the annual festival visit of Amun of Karnak, whose traveling shrine—supported on a boat-shaped palanquin (i.e., the solar bark)—rested within the sanctuary or within a separate chamber in front of it. The very fact that this annual visitation took place indicates that it had an essential role in guaranteeing the deceased king's afterlife, in this instance via the regenerative connection between Re and Hathor, which was paralleled by that between Osiris and his consort Isis, often identified with Hathor.

This second function—to house and facilitate the impact of Amun's annual visit—was the other primary purpose of the mortuary temple, as is evident from other features of its form. Basically, the Valley Festival involved the assembling of the bark-palanquins of Amun of Karnak, his consort Mut, and their son Khonsu on the East Bank; their transportation in three separate ceremonial barges to the West Bank; ritual visits to the contemporary royal mortuary temple and, notionally at least, to all earlier ones; and finally the progress of the three Theban bark-palanquins and those of the deceased kings from their mortuary temples to Deir el-Bahari, where the bark-palanquin of Amun was deposited in the shrine of Hathor as well as in the centrally placed chapel relating to Amun. Once the rituals associated with the "sacred marriage" of Amun and Hathor were concluded, the Theban triad returned to its East Bank temples, while the bark-palanquins of deceased kings returned to their respective West Bank temples.

The centrality of this annual visit was highlighted in the plan of the mortuary temples. Along the central axis, a series of columned halls provided an architecturally impressive approach to either a separate chamber for Amun's bark-palanquin or three for those of the triad as a whole. In some instances, the rear sanctuary and Amun's bark chapel were combined; in others, they were separately defined, the sanctuary lying behind the bark chapel.

Seen in a larger context, since the royal mortuary temples typically lay to the local south of the Hathor shrine at Deir el-Bahari (the mortuary temple of Seti I is a seeming exception, while Hatshepsut's temple is *at* Deir el-Bahari), the processional route of the Valley Festival involved both an east-west-east progression along the axes of Karnak and Deir el-Bahari and a north-south-north progression to the relevant mortuary temples and then to Deir el-Bahari. Thus, the ceremonial programs traced out both the daily course (east-west) and the annual one (north-south-north) of the sun god and rendered the mortuary temple's elements in a structure involving both the built and natural landscapes at Thebes in a representation of the two chief cycles of the sun god.

With these basic functions and forms of the royal mortuary temples in mind, I turn now to the specific layouts of Medinet Habu and the other temples and to the patterns of continuity, variation, and change that they exhibit (figs. 6.1–7). The basic continuity in form and function that runs through all the mortuary temples is best exemplified by the earliest and latest in the series (as we have it), namely, Hatshepsut's temple at Deir el-Bahari and Medinet Habu itself.

Hatshepsut's temple (fig. 6.3) is unusual in its location—at the foot of the cliffs rather than close to the edge of the floodplain—and in its terraced architecture. However, the structures on its highest terrace are analogous to later mortuary temples both in plan and in the functions the plan accommodates. The central feature is usually called a "court" by Egyptologists but might more accurately be described as a roofed columned hall with a relatively small space left open to the sky. In later mortuary temples, this particular feature is usually transformed into two or more columned halls, arranged sequentially along the temple's central axis. In these cases, however, the frontal hall is usually larger than the others and, hence, similar to the relatively large scale of Hatshepsut's hall.

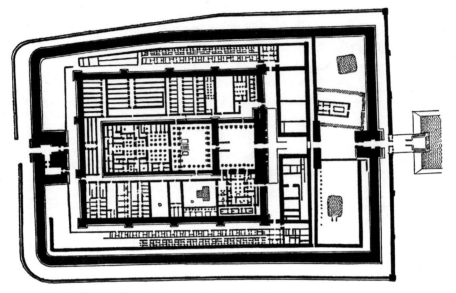

Fig. 6.1. The Medinet Habu complex. (After Baldwin Smith [1938] 140 no. 2.)

At its rear is a bark chapel, cut into the rock and intended to house the visiting boat-palanquin or sacred bark of Amun of Karnak during the Valley Festival. This festival also included boat-palanquins for Mut and Khonsu (they are depicted, e.g., on the walls of Hatshepsut's hall), but separate chapels are not provided for them until the mortuary temple of Seti I, built some 180 years later. The great significance that the Valley Festival had for the royal mortuary temples in general is especially evident from Hatshepsut's temple; its unusual overall layout, with a terraced form and columned façades, indicates that it was conceptualized as "a huge barque station raised above the plain of the Asasif Valley."[10] Similar but much smaller bark stations recurred along the processional ways in the city of Thebes, and scattered examples have been located on the West Bank as well. The mortuary temple of Thutmose III also conveyed the visual effect of a bark station, but later ones did not, perhaps because their locations—relatively distant from Hathor's chapel—made such an initiative inappropriate, whereas Hatshepsut's temple actually incorporated the Hathor chapel into the temple itself.

In addition to the rock-cut bark chapel, Hatshepsut's temple had a sanctuary behind it; if the sanctuary had a false-door stela, it could, as later, have serviced the cult of the king manifest as a particular form of Amun. In addition, large structures lay north and south of the columned hall in Hatshep-

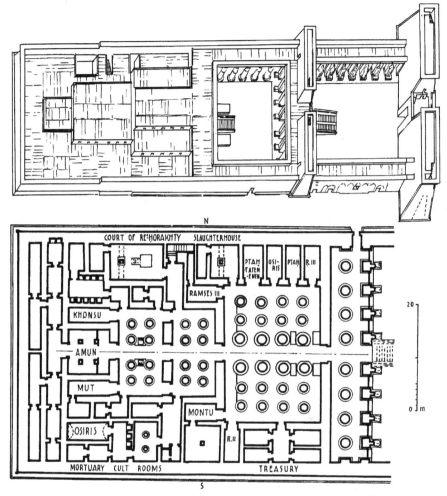

Fig. 6.2. The mortuary temple at Medinet Habu. (After Badawy [1968] fig. 185.)

sut's temple. The northern was dedicated to Re-Horakhty; the southern was dedicated to mortuary cults for Hatshepsut and her father, Thutmose I, and hence related to Osiris and his identification with deceased rulers.

The same components, similarly disposed spatially, occur 270 years later in the mortuary temple of Ramesses III at Medinet Habu, as they did in the intervening temples, in which poor preservation of the relevant scenes and texts sometimes makes their identification inferential, rather than direct. At

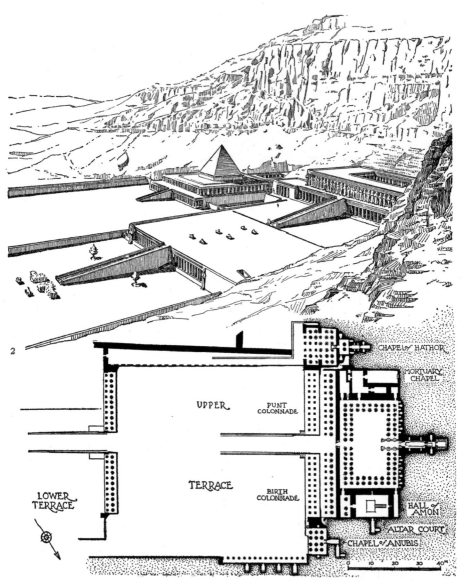

Fig. 6.3. Hatshepsut's temple, Deir el-Bahari. (After Baldwin Smith [1938] 128 nos. 1–2.)

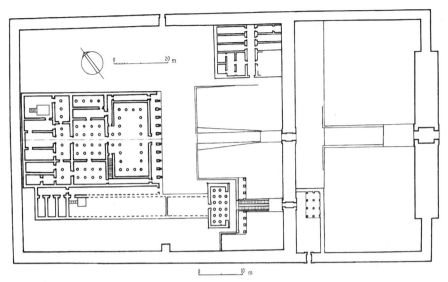

Fig. 6.4. Temple of Thutmose III. (After Badawy [1968] 336.)

Medinet Habu, Hatshepsut's single great columned hall has become threefold, but the intention is the same in both cases—to provide an impressive processional approach to the bark chapel located near the rear of the temple. At Medinet Habu, the single bark chapel in Hatshepsut's temple has become a triple-chambered one, so as to formally house the boat-palanquins or sacred barks of Mut and Khonsu, as well as Amun's. Immediately behind Amun's centrally placed bark chapel is, as at Deir el-Bahari, a sanctuary with a false-door stela, although this sanctuary at Medinet Habu also connects to a series of regularly laid-out chapels extending across the width of the temple. Finally, at Medinet Habu as at Deir el-Bahari, an Osirian complex is found south of the bark chapels, with the hall in front of them, and a Re-Horakhty complex lies to their north. The Osirian complex includes a royal mortuary cult chapel, as at Deir el-Bahari, but allots greater representational and textual reference to Osiris than was the case in Hatshepsut's temple.

Thus, Medinet Habu illustrates not only the fundamental continuity of the functions and forms attested in Hatshepsut's and the other surviving mortuary temples but also the marked capacity for variation and change within this basic template that all the mortuary temples display. This capacity is as evident in Medinet Habu as in any other temple and indicates that Medinet Habu was, in architectural terms, as creative as any other. To some degree, this creative capacity relates to traits specific to Ramesside as compared to

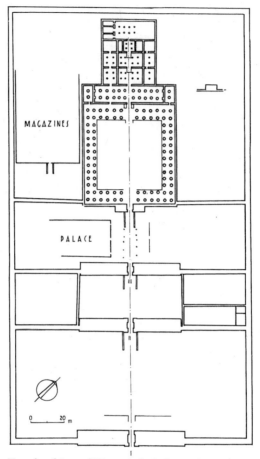

MAGAZINES

PALACE

0   20 m

Fig. 6.5. Temple of Ay and Horemheb. (After Badawy [1968] fig. 181.)

Eighteenth Dynasty mortuary temples; but it also relates to aspects unique to
Medinet Habu itself.

Thus, whereas Eighteenth Dynasty mortuary temples (those of Hatshepsut, Thutmose III and IV, and Ay and Horemheb) favor large and relatively
simply articulated entities for their various components and hence have
relatively simple plans, Ramesside ones typically multiply the numbers of
entities involved, both within the larger components and as filling for spaces
between them. Ramesside mortuary temple plans are, as a result, denser and
more complex, with more complicated systems of internal intercommuni-
cation. Simple statistics reflect the contrast. The four Eighteenth Dynasty
temples have, on average, fourteen to fifteen entities (singular ones or others

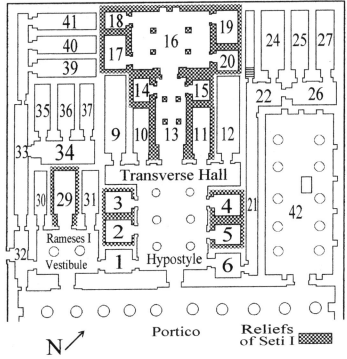

Fig. 6.6. Temple of Seti I. (After Brand [2000] plan 4.)

making up larger components), whereas three of the Ramesside temples average fifty-one entities each, although Merenptah's reverts to a simpler plan, with only twenty.

The overall proportions of West Bank mortuary temples (excluding their frontally located court or courts), as regards Eighteenth Dynasty temples compared to Ramesside ones, display both continuity and significant differentiation. Overall, Eighteenth Dynasty temples are either wider than they are deep (Hatshepsut: 2:1) or almost square (Thutmose III and IV: virtually 1:1). Only the temple of Ay and Horemheb, significantly at the point of transition to the Ramesside period, is more markedly rectangular in outline (its complex shape can be approximately described as 1:1.5). In the Ramesside period, the temple of Seti I actually follows the Eighteenth Dynasty norm, at a width-to-depth ratio of 1.2:1, but the ratios for the temples of Ramesses II, Merenptah, and Ramesses III are 1:1.44, 1:1.44, and 1:1.3, an average of 1:1.39, significantly different in visual terms from the Eighteenth Dynasty overall proportions.

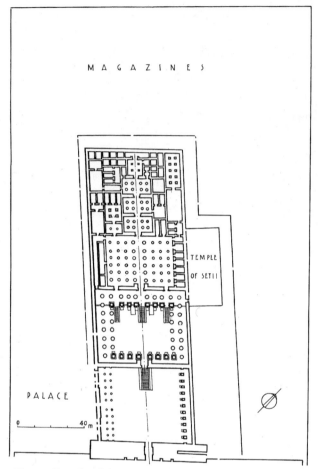

Fig. 6.7. Temple of Ramesses II. (After Badawy [1968] fig. 183.)

Yet continuity is also evident, if more subtly, in proportional data. The more elongated Ramesside proportions are the product of an evident desire for a frontally placed hall that is noticeably larger, in proportion, than in Eighteenth Dynasty temples. However, the remainder of each Ramesside temple, west of the larger frontal hall, is proportionately similar to the temples of the Eighteenth Dynasty, at a width-to-depth ratio of 1.2:1 (Ramesses II), 1.08:1 (Merenptah), and 1.14:1 (Ramesses III), an average of 1.14:1.

At a finer level of detail, while every mortuary temple follows the same basic template, not one is completely identical to any other. In every case, the advisors, architects, and others involved were free to make endless changes so far as significant details were concerned and sometimes to make more major ones, such as the three bark chapels seemingly introduced into the temple of Seti I. Even in the Eighteenth Dynasty, variations can vary from the subtle to the more obvious. The plans of the temples of Thutmose III and IV, at first glance seeming very similar, differ in various ways, such as the system of interconnections or, in the case of Thutmose IV, the expansion in width of the frontal hall. The temple of Ay and Horemheb, built some sixty or seventy years later, contrasts more boldly with earlier ones. For example, beyond the sanctuary or perhaps bark chapel, it has a rear component oriented a notional north-south, not east-west like the rest of the temple, while its frontal hall is actually wider than the rest of the temple yet extremely shallow in depth.

By the time of Ay and Horemheb, the line of mortuary temples had extended quite far to the local south of the Hathor chapel at Deir el-Bahari, some 2.7 kilometers away. However, Seti I positioned his temple close to Deir el-Bahari and next to the processional way linking it to the Karnak temple, a seeming desire for closer proximity to the Valley Festival that might be also reflected in the accommodation provided in his temple for Mut's and Amun's sacred barks as well. Moreover, the overall plan and proportions of Seti's temple are reminiscent of those of the temples of Thutmose III and IV, which are relatively close by and may have influenced Seti's advisors and builders. Like earlier mortuary temples, Seti's temple has three clearly articulated components—a central one, flanked by northern and southern ones. The northern component, dedicated to Re Horakhty, is simple in plan, as earlier. The southern component is more complex than before, but this is in part fortuitous. Linked to Osiris and housing a royal mortuary cult, the southern component had to house chapels for both Seti and his short-reigned father, Ramesses I, who did not have a mortuary temple of his own.

The central component of Seti's temple was also more complicated than earlier plans, although we should not exaggerate the degree of complexity. The increase of the latter was due in part to the innovative desire for three separate bark chapels and to the addition of flanking side chapels in the frontal hall. Overall, the plan of Seti's temple was denser than earlier ones and reflected a more complicated pattern of ritual movements. This might have been due to the addition of further deities to the temple's pantheon, but since earlier temples (apart from Hatshepsut's) are so denuded that we do not know the full roster of the deities venerated in them, it may be that Seti's temple merely provided more articulated architectural settings for preexisting cults.

While the temples of Ramesses II, Merenptah, and Ramesses III include features found in Seti's temple, such as the three bark chapels (not, however, easily identifiable in the temple of Ramesses II), they are reminiscent in important ways of the temple of Ay and Horemheb as well, to which all three are relatively close, while they are correspondingly distant from that of Seti I. The temple of Ramesses II is 1.9 kilometers distant from that of Seti I, as the crow flies, but only 1.2 kilometers away from that of Ay and Horemheb. Merenptah is even closer to the latter, while the temple of Ramesses III is immediately adjacent to it and has an angled enclosure wall so as not to intrude on a still-respected structure. That the designers and builders of the later Ramesside temples may have been influenced by that of Ay and Horemheb is suggested by the rectangular overall proportions of all of them and by the rear-lying, north-south component found at the rear of the temples of Ay and Horemheb, Ramesses II, and Ramesses III, although the details of the plans differ substantially. In general, Merenptah's temple contrasts with those of Ramesses II and III because of the relative simplicity of its plan, reminiscent of Seti's and even the latter's Thutmoside predecessors, yet a further indication of how complicated the West Bank mortuary temples can be in terms of both variations in individual plans and their formal relationships to different prototypes.

In some ways, the temples of Ramesses II and III seem similar to each other, and—as noted earlier—the latter is sometimes seen as derivative of the former and hence lacking in creative variations. In reality, however, the two temples differ significantly in detail: one might even describe the plan of the temple of Ramesses III as an improved version of that of Ramesses II, in that the later temple provides a more clearly and rationally articulated version of the seemingly overwhelming complexity of the earlier temple. Although the central component is similarly laid out in both temples, the triple bark chapels of Ramesses III are laid out more clearly than the less coherent plan provided for the same space in the temple of Ramesses II. While Amun's bark chapel in both instances gives access to a sanctuary linked to a mass of small chapels extending over much or all of the temple's width, the arrangement of the small chapels seems much less coherent in the temple of Ramesses II (although it is not as well preserved either) compared to their more regularly laid-out counterparts in that of Ramesses III.

Moreover, while the northern and southern wings of both temples are more complex in their plans than those of earlier temples were, those of the temple of Ramesses III are laid out in a more symmetrically and coherent fashion than those of the temple of Ramesses II. Reading from the frontal hall westward, the temple of Ramesses III presents similarly laid-out entities on either side of the second hall and clearly laid-out solar and Osirian entities, respectively, on the north and south sides of the third central hall and the bark chapels. In both wings, there are additional chapels between the solar and Osirian complexes and the central halls and bark chapels, but these, too, are relatively (not exactly) symmetrically related to each other. In contrast, the north and south wings of the temple of Ramesses II do not display the same high (not exact) degree of symmetry vis-à-vis each other that we see in the temple of Ramesses III. In the temple of Ramesses II, the north wing includes a recognizable solar complex but also other, relatively large chapels, while the south wing is occupied by four large chapel-like arrangements, very different in layout from those of the north wing. Finally, the large frontal hall in both temples is flanked on the north by a row of chapels and on the south by a "treasury." In the temple of Ramesses III, however, the latter has a regular, rationally organized plan, compared to a seemingly less coherent one in the temple of Ramesses II.

So far, we have been focusing on the West Bank mortuary temples and the ways in which earlier examples may have influenced later ones, but there is yet another potential source of influence or modeling that needs to be taken into account—namely, the Great Temple of Amun at Karnak. The West Bank mortuary temples were, to a degree, treated as way stations deployed along a processional route followed by the boat-shaped palanquins or sacred barks of Amun, Mut, and Khonsu during the Valley Festival. The mortuary temples also accommodated mortuary cult complexes dedicated to the royal owner and sometimes his ancestors, as well as other cult complexes dedicated to Re-Horakhty, which correlated in meaning and ritual function with the royal mortuary complex. Yet mortuary temples had a third function: to venerate the deity manifest in the temple as a mysterious union of the deceased king with a special form of Amun; that is, like Karnak, the mortuary temple was also an Amun temple. Moreover, the relevant sanctuary was central to the temple and spatially integrally related to the halls and bark chapels provided for the visiting Theban triad.

These circumstances indicate that a brief comparison between the Karnak Temple and the mortuary temples could be useful in identifying functions and models that influenced the changing forms of the latter. The Karnak Temple itself, of course, expanded and changed in form over the New Kingdom, yet another complicating factor; but for simplicity's sake, we can divide its history into an Eighteenth Dynasty phase (with specific reference to the area extending from the Fourth Pylon eastward to and including the Akh-Menu) and a Ramesside phase, initiated by the great hypostyle hall begun by Seti I and completed by Ramesses II.

At Karnak, the original Middle Kingdom temple initially continued to function as *the* temple of Amun, while the larger complex developed further to the west, due to building activities stretching from Amenhotep I to Hatshepsut. Subsequently, Thutmose III added a major addition to the east, called the Akh-Menu. It has been suggested that the original Middle Kingdom temple was by now becoming so hard to maintain (due to its age and the harmful effects of groundwater) that the Akh-Menu became the actual sanctuary of Karnak, although the repository for Amun's sacred bark continued to be maintained to the west of the Middle Kingdom temple. Generally, Karnak was on a substantially larger scale than the mortuary temples, yet the latter relate in interesting ways to specific components within Karnak.

For example, while Hatshepsut built a bark chapel for Amun in front of the Middle Kingdom temple and hence far away from the presumed sanctuary or sanctuaries dedicated to Amun at the rear of the Middle Kingdom temple (dedicated to the ruler identified with Amun), the apparent sanctuary and the bark chapel at Deir el-Bahari are immediately adjacent to each other. However, it needs to be recalled that Amun's visit to Hatshepsut's sanctuary was while he was en route to (or from) the Hathor chapel, located to the southeast. It is also interesting to note that the overall scale and proportions of Hatshepsut's temple are very similar to that of the Akh-Menu built later by Thutmose III, and the nature and functions of the basic components of each are very similar: a central sanctuary area linking Amun and the king together, a mortuary complex to the south, and a Re-Horakhty complex to the north. Here, West Bank mortuary developments may have influenced subsequent ones at Karnak. Further enriching this complexity, it should also be noted that the roofed component of the Middle Kingdom temple, while smaller in scale, was similar in proportions to the mortuary temple of Hatshepsut and the Akh-Menu. Moreover, the internal layout of the Akh-Menu can be read, if in very approximate terms, as similar to that of the roofed section of the Middle Kingdom temple.

For their part, the mortuary temples of Thutmose III and IV are similar in scale and proportions to the Karnak Middle Kingdom temple (including, however, the latter's court, which could be read as equivalent to the large frontal hall found in the mortuary temples). Their basic layout corresponds to that of Hatshepsut's temple but is evocative of the Akh-Menu as well. The temple of Ay and Horemheb, at the very end of the Eighteenth Dynasty, has a core component similar in scale and layout to the temples of Thutmose III and IV. However, its frontal hall is unusually wide, if shallow; and it has an extension on the west that may have been derived from the great mortuary temple of Amenhotep III (only a fraction of the latter's ground plan has been recovered) but also resonates with the location and proportions (3:1, compared to 2:1) of the Akh-Menu, although the specific plans, as well as scales, are very different. Overall, the result is to provide the temple of Ay and Horemheb with rectangular proportions, compared to the square proportions of the temples of Thutmose III and IV.

As for the Ramesside period, the addition of the hypostyle hall greatly increased the scale and influenced the overall proportions of the Karnak Temple. The functions and meanings of the hypostyle hall were multiple, complex, and interwoven. It was a temple in its own right, dedicated to a special aspect of Amun (identified with other deities, not any king); a cult place, or "Mansion of Millions of Years," for Seti's own *ka,* or "vital spirit"; and a gigantic "bark repository," where the sacred barks of Amun, Mut, and Khonsu assembled before embarking on the processional celebrations of the Opet Festival (East Bank only) and the Valley Festival.

As for the Ramesside mortuary temples, that of Seti I is larger in scale than its Eighteenth Dynasty predecessors but similar to them in proportions and relative simplicity of plan. It is the first mortuary temple known to have provided an architecturally defined bark repository of all three barks of the Theban triad (also emphasized in the Karnak hypostyle hall), which could also be considered to have formed a unit with the columned hall preceding it—a relatively modest one, with only six columns, yet nevertheless an impressive processional route via which the three barks would access their repositories. Moreover, Seti included side chapels in the frontal hall. The Karnak hypostyle hall does not include such chapels, but those in the mortuary temples of Seti I were dedicated to the deceased king and a form of Amun with which he was identified, as well as to Osiris, creating a complex of cultic interests reminiscent of those celebrated in the Karnak hypostyle hall. Thus, to some degree, one might suggest that the mortuary temple of Seti I gave expression to prominent features of the Karnak hypostyle hall. Merenptah's mortuary temple, as noted earlier, is similar to Seti's in plan, although little of the program has survived to indicate what cults might have been favored there.

The temples of Ramesses II and III, however, are noteworthy for their exceptionally large and multicolumned frontal halls, which increase the rectangular overall proportion so that they are reminiscent of (but certainly not identical to) the proportions of Karnak at this time (1:1.4, compared to 1:2.65). On a more modest scale, the comparatively large frontal hall of Merenptah's temple creates for it a similar rectangular form (1:1.4). In the case of Ramesses II and III, however, we may have frontal halls directly inspired by the Karnak hypostyle hall and hence indicative of a desire to render mortuary temples even more evocative of Karnak.

This is particularly true of the frontal hall in the temple of Ramesses II, which has 48 columns (the two central rows supporting a clerestory) compared to the Karnak hypostyle hall's 134, so the mortuary temple version can be considered only a miniaturization of the Karnak hypostyle hall. The frontal hall of the temple of Ramesses III is also impressive compared to most of those in the mortuary temples, but it is a pared down version of that of Ramesses II, with only twenty-four columns but also with a clerestory. It is also noteworthy that beyond the frontal halls, both temples have unusually high numbers of intermediate halls (three for Ramesses II, two for Ramesses III), perhaps evocative of the considerable distance and architectural complexity of the area separating the Karnak hypostyle hall from the sanctuary at Karnak.

MEDINET HABU AND THE WEST BANK MORTUARY TEMPLE COMPLEXES

So far as architecture is concerned, the last issue is to analyze Medinet Habu in terms of the totality of the complex of buildings associated with it, as compared to the same aspect of the other West Bank mortuary temples. This comparison is particularly valuable in that not only does the actual temple of Medinet Habu display some significant variations of its own on the basic template for mortuary temples, but the totality of its structures is particularly innovative as compared to the total complexes of the other mortuary temples.

As figure 6.8 illustrates, the total architectural complex of each temple varies considerably in size, with those of Hatshepsut, Ay and Horemheb, Ramesses II, and Ramesses III being relatively large, while of those of Thutmose III (and IV), Seti I, and Merenptah occupy substantially smaller amounts of space. However, as regards Medinet Habu, we need to note that it is unique in having a double circumvallation. All the mortuary temple complexes (with the partial exception of Hatshepsut's) are set within a walled enclosure, but Medinet Habu has a second, outer enclosure not apparently attested elsewhere. The inner enclosure is the one that corresponds to that of the other mortuary temples.

With this in mind, one can identify three categories of spatial coverage: two very large ones (Ay and Horemheb, Ramesses II—yet another connection between them), a group intermediate in size (Hatshepsut, Seti I, Ramesses III), and relatively small enclosed spaces (Thutmose III and IV, Merenptah). How-

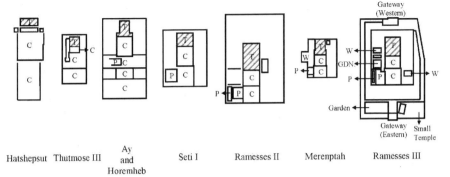

Fig. 6.8. Comparative diagram: the mortuary temples and their surrounding complexes. (Drawing by D. O'Connor and T. Prakash; all structures are at the same scale; C = court; T = temple proper; P = palace; W = well.)

ever, if we take the outer enclosure of Medinet Habu into account, the space involved is even larger (by a factor of about 1.2) than that occupied by the total enclosure of the temple of Ramesses II. Adding to the complexity is the area occupied by the actual, roofed temple (excluding courts). Here, the temple of Ramesses II is the largest by far; the next two largest are those of Ramesses III and Seti I. A third category comprises the temples of Hatshepsut, Ay and Horemheb, and Merenptah; while that of Thutmose III (and IV) is the smallest. Again, these data emphasize how variable the mortuary temples can be, each in relationship to the other.

This said, it is also important to remember that the temple of Ramesses III, while in a median size range, accommodates a much larger number of entities than the temple of Seti I. The latter consists of some forty-one units, including corridors; the temple of Ramesses II, about sixty-six units; and that of Ramesses III, about fifty-one. While presenting a more rational and clearly articulated version of the plan of the Ramesses II temple, that of Ramesses III has to still accommodate a high number of units into an area that is only a little over half the size (about 60 percent) of the temple of Ramesses II. This explains why many of the units in the temple of Ramesses III have an almost miniaturized quality, as Haeny observed. If we exclude in both temples the rear chapels, the bark chapels, and the three (Ramesses III) or four (Ramesses II) halls, then the figures for the number of individual units are as follows:

Ramesses II	Ramesses III	Ramesses II South Wing	Ramesses III North Wing
23	18	14	16

The approximate parity in numbers of units, compared to the disparity in space, indicates that in the two wings in question, units in the Ramesses III temple are typically going to be individually distinctly smaller than units in the Ramesses II temple. This is an issue to which I will return below.

To move to a more general level of comparison, one should note that with all the mortuary temples except Hatshepsut's, a significant percentage of the enclosed area was dedicated to storage facilities, a feature that expanded enormously in number and area in the complexes of Ramesses II and III. In both cases, the storage units were contained within the enclosure surrounding the temple proper, while the outer enclosure at Medinet Habu included not storage units but double rows of mostly relatively small residences on the north and south and a variety of larger and more functionally varied structures on the east. Thus, the temple of Ramesses III was innovative not only in having a second, outer enclosure but in using it to shelter residential, cultic, or other entities, rather than having storage units filling—outside of the temple proper—much of the inner enclosed space. While the staff of other mortuary temples, presumably especially that of Ramesses II, must have had residences located somewhere, they were apparently quite spatially separate from the mortuary temple complex proper. Under Ramesses III, it was decided to integrate them into the complex, a decision relating more to logistical and formal issues than to any anxiety about the security of those dwelling therein; the reign of Ramesses III seems to have been a relatively peaceful one so far as conditions internal to Egypt were concerned.

Typically, from the outset, mortuary temples were preceded by several open courts, separated from each other by walls and monumental gateways and sometimes even pylons. Hatshepsut's temple was preceded by two such courts, that of Thutmose III and IV by three (the innermost provided with a colonnade on each side), and that of Ay and Horemheb by no less than four. All the Ramesside temples have two courts, the front one always having a palace, oriented north-south (at right angles to the notional east-west orientation of the temple) on its south side. The palace was apparently introduced in the reigns of Ay and Horemheb, although it may have existed in the mortuary temple of Amenhotep III (as yet poorly known), and another version of it is perhaps seen in the small Aten temple at Amarna.

In any event, in Ramesside mortuary complexes, the palace was always a conspicuous feature, located in a similar position in each one. Each palace was provided with a central window or balcony "of royal appearance," overlooking the first court; behind the window or balcony was typically a columned hall fronting a throne room. In the mortuary temple complex of

Ramesses III, the original palace, which conformed in its basic plan to the other Ramesside ones, was replaced by a second one, with a distinctly more complex plan but still including a window or balcony of royal appearance. The second palace of Medinet Habu is usually also dated to the reign of Ramesses III, but it has been recently suggested that it replaced the earlier one at a significantly later date, between the late Twentieth and early Twenty-first Dynasties. In any event, I shall here confine my observations to the first palace. These Ramesside palaces, attached to the temples, are relatively small, although provided with a bedroom, bathroom, and latrine. In two cases, a further suite of rooms is added to the rear, separated from the rest of the palace by a corridor (Ramesses II and III). Generally, the palaces are relatively spacious, but a degree of miniaturization is evident in the later ones.

These Ramesside mortuary temple palaces are best compared to an actual palace of Merenptah at Memphis. Its hall, throne room and side chambers, and residential suite occupied 1,504 square meters. The areas of the comparable components of the mortuary temple palaces of Seti I and Ramesses II are somewhat similar, at 1,693 and 1,253.4 square meters, but those of Ramesses III occupy only 739.2 (smaller than the Memphite palace's components by a factor of 2) and those of Merenptah only 479.1 (smaller by a factor of 3.1). These data relate to an ongoing debate as to whether the mortuary temple "palaces" were actual ones, used by the living king during his lifetime, or only symbolic ones, intended for the use of the deceased king only. While those of Seti I, Ramesses II, and, more doubtfully, Ramesses III might be of a scale suggesting they were actual and used by the living king, the very fact that Merenptah's was so small and hence more likely to be symbolic opens up the possibility that even the larger mortuary temple palaces were symbolic rather than real.

This possibility is supported (though hardly confirmed) by another factor. In each mortuary temple palace, the window or balcony of royal appearance, central to the facade, is flanked equidistantly by a doorway on each side. At Medinet Habu at least, these doorways are inscriptionally identified as giving the king access to the Opet Festival (eastern side) and the Valley Festival (western side). However, the Opet Festival took place entirely on the East Bank at Thebes, and hence the mortuary temple palaces were possibly versions of an actual palace, located on the East Bank. Given that the mortuary temple palaces are always near the southeast corner of the relevant temple, a good candidate for this supposed East Bank palace was one that apparently stood near the northwest corner of the Karnak Temple itself: its actual location would have moved further west as the temple expanded over time, but it is possible that versions of this palace existed throughout most of the Eighteenth

Dynasty and all of the Ramesside period. This, then, would be yet another feature to add to others (discussed above) indicating that West Bank mortuary temples resembled that of Amun of Karnak in important ways. At the West Bank temples, the transfer of the palace to the southeast corner of the temple would be an appropriate reversal.

It is also possible that this admittedly hypothetical palace at Karnak (its existence has never been archaeologically documented, although there are possible textual references to it) was much larger than any of the West Bank mortuary temple palaces. Northwest of the small Aten temple at Amarna (which actually occupied as much space as the late Eighteenth Dynasty temple of Karnak) was a palatial complex occupying approximately an area of 244.4 × 277.8 square meters (6.78 ha), while the temple of Ptah at Memphis had, near its southeast corner (since it lay on the West Bank, not the East Bank), a palatial complex of Merenptah measuring in excess of 185 × 233.9 square meters (4.3 ha). If the Karnak palace was on these kinds of scale and if the West Bank mortuary temple palaces were supposed to represent it, the latter are more likely to be symbolic than actual.

Whatever its significance, the first palace of Medinet Habu is modeled closely on the ones in the earlier mortuary temples. But outside of the inner enclosure, Medinet Habu is completely innovative in its architecture. The structural complexity of the totality of Medinet Habu is best appreciated by working from the outermost enclosure wall to the innermost enclosure.

Around the entire complex is a high massive wall, entered by exceptionally tall gateways (called by the excavators the "High Gates") located on the central east-west axis on the east and west, respectively. Outside of the outer enclosure wall is a low perimeter wall, which at least nominally protects the approach to the former. Within the outermost wall are three further enclosed spaces. One, defined by a relatively low wall, occupies about 80 percent of the total complex. Set within it is yet a third enclosed space, that of the temple proper, its palace, and many other structures, mostly magazines and storerooms. This third enclosed space is defined by a high, massive and externally towered wall, with a centrally set and enormously scaled pylon in its eastern face. On the north and south, the area between the lower wall of the second enclosure and the high towered wall of the third is occupied mainly by small residential units. However, the second enclosed space has a wider expanse on the east, where, unfortunately, the original architecture is poorly preserved. It has been surmised that it contained accommodations for the king's bodyguard and its (chariot) horses on the south and plantations and cattle pens on the north.

The remaining 20 percent of the total complex was occupied by yet a fourth enclosed space. This was signified as an area of importance by its entryways and exits: namely, the Eastern High Gate on the east and a small but substantial pylon on the west. Running between these two features was a broad space that would have included the first stage of the processional way for the sacred barks of the Theban triad once they had entered the complex. The area to the south of the processional way was occupied apparently by a very large garden or plantation, with a substantial pool. It had its own enclosure wall and may have been accessible only from a ramp running down from the Eastern High Gate. North of the processional way was an equally large area, also enclosed—by its own wall on the west and by the high outermost wall on the other three sides. This area contained the Small Temple (described below), set within its own enclosure and located near the northwest corner of the Eastern High Gate. The rest of the area may have been occupied by gardens, plantations, and perhaps a "sacred lake."

This elaborate series of compartmentalized enclosed spaces is not articulated in the earlier Ramesside mortuary temple complexes, although the poorly preserved remains of the late Eighteenth Dynasty temple of Ay and Horemheb, immediately adjacent to Medinet Habu, did have a large but enclosed space on the east, occupying about 25 percent of the area of the entire complex. Never excavated, this might correspond in some way to the arrangements in the eastern 20 percent of the Medinet Habu complex. What might have been the reasons for the multiple enclosed entities of Medinet Habu?

Undoubtedly, one purpose was to provide a defined space for the many residences on the north and south sides of the second enclosed space, for which provision had not been made in earlier royal mortuary temple complexes. In theory, however, they could have been included in the third enclosure, which contains many magazines as well as the temple proper and its attached palace. It is hard to escape the impression that the desire for a particularly large expanse of space on the east—beyond the precincts of the temple proper and the structures traditionally associated with it—was the principal reason why Medinet Habu was provided with its unusual, outermost wall. If so (and this notion can only be a theory), why was this extension of the total complex to the east so desirable?

Perhaps it was desired that the Small Temple of Medinet Habu should be physically and conceptually integrated into the mortuary temple complex of Ramesses III. The Small Temple seems to have been built as a complement to the Luxor Temple, at the local southern end of Thebes, and was placed where it was to face toward Luxor. The Luxor Temple itself is of unique character and has been interpreted as incorporating a smaller temple for the god Amenemopet (a form of Amun) and a "much larger *Opet*-festival Annex, . . . in essence, an elaborate barque shrine for accommodating Amun-Re of Karnak and his full entourage" during his annual visit to Luxor.[11] The incumbent pharaoh at the time of each Opet Festival was at least nominally involved and often actually deeply so, for the Opet Festival was the occasion for the "annual ritual rebirth of the royal *ka*, the immortal creative spirit of divine kingship" and at Luxor the incumbent pharaoh "was worshiped as the living royal *ka*, the chief earthly manifestation of the creator."[12]

The Small Temple of Medinet Habu was intimately related to these portentous meanings, for it was, in effect, a bark shrine for the visiting sacred bark of Amenemopet of Luxor, who journeyed to it every ten days to experience a form of regeneration and to perform funerary services for a primeval group of gods, his own ancestors, buried under a mound—called Djeme—the position of which was indicated by the small roofed sanctuaries positioned behind the bark shrine. The surviving reliefs show the king performing the appropriate rituals as regards the festival, but the original focus of worship was a gigantic statue of Amun and Thutmose III seated side by side; ultimately each king likely sought an identification with or parallelism to this regenerative form of Amun, just as each did with a unique form of Amun in each mortuary temple.

To incorporate this small but incredibly potent sacred place into his own mortuary complex was perhaps seen as providing a uniquely powerful reinforcement to the regeneration of the deceased king that was normally affected through the rituals practiced in the mortuary temple itself. In part, this reinforcement may have related to the ritual life of Medinet Habu as a whole. Daily, cult was performed in the mortuary temple on behalf of the dead king and his union with the form of Amun peculiar to Medinet Habu; and once a year, during the Valley Festival, this process climaxed in the visit of Amun of Karnak to Medinet Habu and presumably a union of all three entities—Ramesses III, Amun of Medinet Habu, and Amun of Karnak—which was of especially vital force in the processes of regeneration and rebirth the dead ruler desired. However, the Small Temple of Medinet Habu was visited every ten days—that is, weekly—by the potent deity Amenemopet of Luxor, again for rites signifying regeneration and rebirth, and Ramesses III associated himself inscriptionally with this process as well.

If we assume that the total complex of Medinet Habu expanded eastward to include the Small Temple and that it was desired to maintain a symmetrical overall layout, then the expansion created considerably more space than was needed to accommodate the Small Temple itself. On the north, the plantations, gardens, and lake provided natural complements to the Small Temple itself and indeed may have existed in some form before Medinet Habu itself was built. However, as noted above, the southern half of the space created by the eastward extension was dedicated apparently to a large garden or plantation, with a pool or lake, which was linked to the Eastern High Gate, not to the Small Temple and its related entities. It should be noted that, so far as the admittedly poor remains are concerned, no other access to the enclosed southern garden was found.

This brings us to the two most intriguing and unusual aspects of the architecture of Medinet Habu, the Eastern and Western High Gates. Of the two, the Eastern High Gate is by far the better preserved, although both were essentially similar (despite the somewhat different ground plan of the Western High Gate) and were decorated with similar programs of scenes and texts. The High Gates, especially the Eastern High Gate, have attracted much debate. At the front, each had two high towers, flanking a roadway running into the solid mass of the remainder of the gateway. On each side, the gateway rose three stories high (ground, second, and third: the top of the gateway was a kind of patio, with yet a fourth story in that a chamber was built at the top of each three-storied tower), although the ground story was in fact completely solid except for the gateway, topped by the second and third stories, providing access to the interior of the complex. Although the High Gates clearly evoke Egyptian military architecture, in keeping with the massive and once crenellated outer enclosure wall, this is only part of their meaning: as regards the latter, the fortified area (rather than actual effectiveness) of the outermost wall and its gateways signify the protection against supernatural danger with which ritual has provided the entire mortuary temple complex.

Moreover, while the exterior program of scenes and texts on both gates emphasized the king's domination of the foreign foe and the presentation of foreign prisoners by the king (as well as some cultic episodes), the interior program—of which much, but by no means all, survives—is of a very different and indeed, for a mortuary monument, very unusual character. It focuses exclusively on different forms of entertainment, some of it of a ceremonialized nature, proffered to the king by young women of the royal court. Moreover, the two stories of the gate above the gateway into the complex each have a large window in the front and rear, features incompatible with a military function. There are numerous other windows in the Eastern High Gate (as there probably were in the Western High Gate), facing literally in every direction, but they are smaller and likely for the provision of light and air, whereas the central windows give the impression that they were used by the king for viewing and possibly also for presenting himself to an imagined audience.

These circumstances suggest that, as well as mimicking a fortress gateway, the two gates each evoked a feature of palace architecture. The only known archeological situation that might have catered to the interaction between the king and royal women of some kind (not necessarily queens and princesses) for the purposes of refined and ceremonialized entertainment are two sets of four suites each flanking a hall at the end of which is a royal throne room and residential suite, which form part of the palace of Amen-hotep III at Malkata on the West Bank (a palace that was likely in ruins and denuded by the time of Ramesses III). At Malkata, the structures in question are all at one level, but perhaps the rooms distributed through the two stories of the Eastern High Gate, as well as the ones on tops of the towers, represent a vertical arrangement of the recreational section of a royal palace.

Whether such multistory versions existed in reality is uncertain, but here yet another aspect of palace architecture may be involved. The Memphite palace of King Merenptah, discussed above, had in front a walled, colonnaded court and an elevated facade. The latter had a second story and a large window overlooking the court, but not a window of royal appearance in the usual sense of the word. Possibly, the second-story window had been balanced on the other side by another, in this case overlooking a more expansive vista—perhaps palace gardens and the city of Memphis beyond. The two-storied central part of the Eastern High Gate may have incorporated this concept as well yet simultaneously related to "harem suites" such as were found at Malkata.

These possibilities also relate to the large garden or plantation, with pool or lake, in the vicinity of the Eastern High Gate, for the entertainment of pharaoh by royal women was linked also to such recreational landscapes in the vicinity of a palace. For example, the story of King Snefru, which forms part of the composition called *The Tale of King Kheops' Court* (created in the Middle Kingdom), describes the king roaming through "every [chamber] of the Royal House" in an almost desperate search for distraction. Snefru's advisor recommends that the king go to "the lake of the Great House" to be rowed by "the beauties from inside your palace." There, viewing young women will entertain the king, as will the beauty of the lake's setting—"beautiful pools" and "its countryside and its beautiful banks"—all bringing "relief" to the "king's heart."[13]

Finally, among the coexistent and multiple meanings the Eastern High Gate (and presumably the Western High Gate) might have had is that of the migdol, the name of which is taken into Egyptian from the Semitic language of the Levant. What kind of a structure this might have been, both in Egypt and the Levant, is much debated, but the notion of a "tower" seems central to it, even if the word *migdol*—especially in toponyms—might be applied to architecturally quite complex entities. Indeed, at Medinet Habu itself, an actual migdol—so labeled and named after Ramesses himself—is depicted as a single tower with a large gateway or doorway, above which a window (closed and not a window of royal appearance) is set in a second story. Ramesses III himself is depicted nearby, receiving Sea Peoples prisoners captured as a result of a battle that had taken place in the vicinity. He stands on a platform, in front of which is a balustrade topped with a cushion or bolster, on which the king rests his arm. It may be that we are to understand this as a separate representation of the king actually appearing in the window of the migdol while the prisoners are paraded before him. The central rear tower of the Eastern High Gate might be itself intended to represent a towerlike migdol (and it is differentiated from the rest of the gateway in a variety of ways), particularly as the two windows (one above the other) are framed by depictions of the king leading or driving prisoners toward the windows, which are themselves settings in which the king would appear.

THE ARCHITECTURE OF MEDINET HABU: AN OVERVIEW

In retrospect, then, Medinet Habu is an impressive and sophisticated monument that is not a highly derivative version of earlier mortuary temples and that also makes use of some innovations that go well beyond anything attempted in such temples before. Like all the other West Bank mortuary temples, Medinet Habu displays its own unique variations on the various components forming the basic template. In doing so, it evokes aspects of earlier mortuary temples, including that of Seti I (which the innermost enclosed complex at Medinet Habu matches almost exactly in scale, despite the greater complexity of the Medinet Habu plan) and even, in some ways, the temple of Ay and Horemheb. More specifically, Medinet Habu certainly relates to the enormous mortuary temple complex of Ramesses II (whose mortuary image periodically visited Medinet Habu itself, where it had its own bark chapel), yet not as a simpleminded copy. Instead, the actual mortuary temple at Medinet Habu represents an improvement—almost a rationalization—of the densely patterned and, in places, even inchoate plan of the temple of Ramesses II. In doing so, the advisors of Ramesses III eschewed the reaction of the builders of Merenptah's temple to its potentially overwhelming predecessor, which was to produce a quite small, highly simplified version of the basic mortuary temple template, even though Merenptah would have had the time and resources to build a substantially larger and more complex structure. The builders of Medinet Habu, however, took on the challenge presented by the temple of Ramesses II and modified and adapted it so as to produce a more orderly and coherent plan, itself innovative in a number of ways.

More strikingly innovative, however, was the unprecedented creation at Medinet Habu of a series of enclosed spaces, in an almost nested type of structure. Only the innermost space—the temple, palace, and associated magazines—conformed to the preexisting Ramesside mode. The second enclosed space, containing residences and other structures, and the third enclosed areas in the eastern quarter were unanticipated in earlier mortuary temple complexes, as far as we can tell, as was the massive outermost enclosure wall and its extraordinary high gateways. Seemingly, here—toward the end of the New Kingdom—Ramesses III and his advisors created a new, enlarged and innovative template for the royal mortuary temple; whether his successors ever tried to emulate it is unknown, for over the remaining eighty-one years of the Twentieth Dynasty, none of eight rulers involved did more than begin the relevant mortuary temple. However, one—that of Ramesses IV—was designed to be "half again as big as his father's temple at Medinet Habu"[14] and thus was likely to follow a similar model as Medinet Habu insofar as overall layout was concerned.

FORM AND PROGRAM AT MEDINET HABU: AN INTRODUCTION

Unlike many of the other Theban mortuary temples, Medinet Habu is still an architectural form, a three-dimensional reality of visually impressive dimensions. Moreover, the temple proper and some other features are covered—on walls and ceilings—with a rich variety of texts and scenes, some still preserving the bright and variegated colors that powerfully reinforced their visual impact on the viewer. The notion of a viewer or an audience is, however, a complicated one so far as Egyptian temples like Medinet Habu are concerned: some potential viewers had greater degrees of access to the temple than other viewers and hence derived richer experiences from what they saw of its form and program. Here, I would like to examine how the plan, form ,and program of Medinet Habu was designed to provide a structured set of experiences based on variable access and hence on the varied status of different categories of viewers.

Visualizing Medinet Habu in its pristine state, with all its stone and brick

Fig. 6.9. External view of Medinet Habu temple. (Drawing by D. O'Connor and T. Prakash.)

architecture intact, we should first realize that to the majority of Thebans and visitors to Thebes and its monuments, Medinet Habu presented a potent yet starkly bare image (fig. 6.9). Its outermost enclosure wall, about 18.5 meters high, masked the entire complex (except for one important feature discussed below) and presented enormous expanses of undecorated, mud-plastered external faces. These attributes reinforced the visual impact of the stone-built double towers of the Eastern and Western High Gates—the only entrances—on which the largest, most prominent depictions were brightly colored vignettes of the pharaoh charging foreign foes in his chariot (Western High Gate) or threatening them with an upraised weapon (Eastern High Gate).

The two High Gates thus signaled to the externally situated viewer not only that this (like any temple) was a royal monument but that its external walls sheltered an intensely sacred space, which nevertheless remained virtually invisible to human eyes in general. Moreover, the aggressive images on the gateways signified that the sacred space within had been ritually provided with immensely powerful apotropaic protection. This prevented its gateways from being penetrated by destructive supernatural forces, charged with the enormously powerful but negative energy of the chaos or nullity that surrounded the cosmos on every side.

Yet one other significant feature was also intentionally made visible to the external viewer, imagined here on the floodplain or local east side of the temple complex. Behind the eye-catching towers of the Eastern High Gate rose the upper parts of the two towers of the main pylon of Medinet Habu, which stood in front of the temple proper and were about twenty-four meters high. No large-scale, symbolically stimulative imagery was visible (this, lower down on the main pylon, was hidden by the outermost enclosure wall), but the overwhelming symbolism of the pylon form was likely known to all potential viewers. It represented the mountains or "horizons" edging the peripheries of the terrestrial realm and shielding from human perception the processes of the divine world that lay beyond them. These processes involved the very survival of the cosmos, which they continually re-created, and their effectiveness was dependent on their hidden nature. Thus, the blank wall faces of the outermost enclosure signified that the temple of Medinet Habu was also a place of mysterious, hidden renewal and that the rites performed in and around it were effective because of the concealment provided to them and the context—the built forms—in which they took place.

There were some categories of humans who were privileged to pass through the outermost enclosure walls, to service the temple in various ways, and even to live within its larger complex. Nevertheless, within this complex, the architectural form and "decorative" program were so structured as to continue the processes of concealment, signification, and differentially limited access already experienced, in their simplest form, by those viewing Medinet Habu only from an external point of view. Here again, the deployment of enclosures was a primary device, as was the manipulation of decorative programs.

The Eastern High Gate was probably the primary route for ceremonial access, and except during festival celebration, its gateway was likely kept closed. The Western High Gate incorporated a kind of secondary gateway, via which supplies and approved categories of individuals could come and go under the survey of guards and gatekeepers. However, as we have seen above, the vast area defined by the outermost enclosure was, within the walls of the latter, almost entirely occupied by two further enclosures, unequal in size and with relatively thin, but comparatively high, walls.

One enclosure defined the area immediately behind the Eastern High Gate and included the beginning of the festival processional way within the complex as a whole. This processional way was provided with a pylon on its local western side, as a counterpart to the Eastern High Gate. The pylon—functioning as an entrance-cum-exit for the processional way—was relatively modest, built in mud brick and only about thirteen meters high (the Eastern High Gate in general is about eighteen meters high) and dwarfed by the enormous main pylon, twenty-four meters high, which lay only some forty-two meters further to the local west. Nevertheless, the small pylon's symbolism, as representing the "horizons," signaled a transition to a space increased in sacredness.

Immediately beyond this first, inner enclosure was the local east wall of another enclosure: also with thin (though relatively high) walls, this enclosure flanked the residences and offices locally north and south of the innermost enclosure, the large but more ambiguous structures locally east of the innermost enclosure, and the local western side of the innermost enclosure itself. Some of those residing in these zones had access to the temple proper; others—maybe the majority—likely did not. The temple was always a powerful visual presence, but again one representing concealment and strictly limited access. Towering above the offices, residences, and other structures were the largely blank-faced walls of the innermost enclosure, fifteen meters high. Its defensive and fortress-like character was emphasized by the projecting towers distributed along its entire periphery.

The ceremonial entrance was marked by the main pylon (twenty-four meters high). The external faces of each of its two towers were decorated with a large panel depicting the pharaoh seeming to smite foreign foes in the deity's presence, resonating—on a much larger scale—with the smiting scenes on the two towers of the Eastern High Gate. Again, this main entranceway would have been kept closed except on festival occasions. On each side of the main pylon, secondary, much smaller doorways gave access to the palace area (local south) and, on the local north, to a narrow roadway that separated the temple from the magazines and other features flanking it on three sides. Periodically, relatively large numbers of people would have utilized this road to provide material to the magazines, which would have also been entered on a daily basis to remove foodstuffs, liquids, and other materials and items utilized in cult, to be redistributed to provision the residents of the zones external to the inner enclosure. As for the temple proper, a single doorway on each side of the second court provided access to the priests and assistants who entered and exited the temple for ritual purposes during the day and probably during the night as well.

The roadway surrounding the temple proper on three of its sides provided visual access to the externally located large-scale, brightly colored scenes of the pharaoh's triumphs over his foreign enemies on the local north and west sides and to the enormous text covering most of the local south side, documenting the dates on which a variety of festivals were celebrated in the temple and enumerating the provisioning of each. The logic of this arrangement was perhaps that the victory scenes to the local west, north, and east (i.e., the scenes on the pylon), while apotropaic in signification, also represented the "worldwide" dominion that fed the magazines, while the calendar, on the local south wall, related to the contents of the magazines, which supported the festivals in question. However, the roadway was essentially a utilitarian feature and did not provide an area from which the externally located scenes and texts could be easily comprehended, even from the far side of the roadway. The latter was only about three meters (almost ten feet) wide, yet the scenes rose to a height of many meters above ground level.

Even on festival occasions—and there were quite a few in the Medinet Habu calendar—the experience for those involved was, in terms of visual access, relatively limited. Festival processions, when involving divine visitors external to the temple (most conspicuously, the Theban triad), moved along the central axis, with its various gates and doors open for the occasion, and involved substantial numbers of participants—theoretically, not only a large number of priests, but also the king, other royalty, members of the elite, and even representatives of "the people" (realistically, of the Theban population) at large. However, it was likely that as the procession penetrated deeper into the sacred realm, its human participants became increasingly lesser in number, with the king seemingly performing the most crucial rites alone, within the sanctuary, innermost chapels, and perhaps the bark chapels. The temple plan itself perhaps reflects this process. The relatively spacious first and second courts and the large frontal hall provided space for relatively large assemblies, which need not, however, have occupied that space in its entirety. Largeness in scale was also a signifier of the high status of the deity and of the symbolic value of the temple as a representation of the cosmos, itself occupying vast amounts of space. Beyond the frontal hall, however, spaces grew ever smaller and layouts more complex, indicative of a shrinking group of participants.

As for visual access to the temple's "decorative" program, the numbers of people so privileged would have decreased over the course of the festival progress and was relatively limited even for the most privileged. The reliefs and texts of the Eastern High Gate, the main pylon, and the first and second courts would, of course, be seen by the relatively large number of participants in the earlier stages of the festival procession, but the procession was the primary focus of attention, not the wall scenes, which were dense in composition and took time to comprehend in any detailed way. Moreover, once the procession entered the temple proper, beyond the second court, artificial means were the primary sources of illumination, and much of the program on walls and columns must have been obscure, as well as even more complex in content than those visible in the courts and on pylons and gateways. Moreover, once again, the performed rituals were the foci of attention, rather than the programs on the walls.

These observations bring us to another essential source for understanding the functions and meanings of the temple of Medinet Habu, both as an example of the generic temple type of the period and as the manifestation of a specific ruler, his life experience (as a specific exemplar of the divine institution of kingship), and his imagined afterlife needs. These functions and meanings have been extensively discussed in other contexts, so here I attempt a generalized overview, as well as specific reference to the apparent concerns of Ramesses III and his advisors and perhaps of the builders and artisans who created this extraordinary edifice.

Ancient Egyptian temples of the New Kingdom were very complex as regards the multiple meanings represented in them. For analytical purposes, we can envision each meaning, defined in terms of its basic theme, as a layer superimposed on preceding ones; in reality, each meaning—expressed via ritual, architecture, and program—is interfused with the others. Each individual ritual act and utterance, specific architectural space or form, and specific scene or text therefore conveyed in itself a multiplicity of meanings and also formed but one element making up an ordered and meaningful assemblage represented by the temple in its entirety.

Two meanings in particular were fundamental to the definition and, from an Egyptian perspective, the functions of a temple, whether dedicated to a god's or goddess's cult or to the specific needs of a royal mortuary temple. One meaning seems obvious yet is often underrated in modern overviews of Egyptian temple architecture and art: namely, ritual—the elaborately choreographed sets of actions and utterances (based on consistently maintained written traditional records, which nevertheless also reflected a continuous process of elaboration and even innovation) that each temple was meant to house. The second fundamental meaning is less obvious to us moderns but, in a sense, seems almost paramount to the Egyptians: namely, temple as artifact, as a wondrously worked and complete work of art, the perfection and beauty of which mirrors the ultimate expression of these qualities, the cosmos itself.

Many aspects of temple ritual have been studied in depth, but many remain to be analyzed in detail; the overall structure of ritual actions and of the all-important utterances (prayers, hymns, invocations, spells) that accompany them are, however, relatively well known. Yet we perhaps often insufficiently allow for the reality that the architectural form (plan and elevations) and program (scenes and texts) are a direct expression of ritual in several ways. The plan of the temple facilitates the progress of ritual activities (some daily, some—more elaborate—for periodic festival performances) involving both the chief deity and other deities whose cults were celebrated separately within the same structure. Similarly, volumetric dimensions contribute to the appropriateness of ritual, as when the roofline descends from front to rear, in concordance with a desire to render the rear-placed sanctuary relatively small and—absent artificial light—intensely dark, or when the floor level subtly increases in elevation, so the sanctuary and the shrine it contains are set on a symbolic "primeval mound," a place of cosmic creation and renewal. As for scenes and texts, these often directly mirror actual rituals performed in the temple; but they can also refer to the otherworldly realms to which the rituals relate or to this-worldly events (e.g., royal births, coronations or victories) that manifest the king's roles in the maintenance and protection of the cosmos, themes reiterated in temple ritual and utterance as well.

As for the temple as artifact, New Kingdom texts celebrating a king's renovation or expansion of an existing temple or the building of an entirely new one emphasize not the temple's complex program or rich panoply of architectural detail (the features attracting the interest of modern observers) but, rather, the temple as an artifact, distinguished especially by its scale and valuable materials, and as a symbolically correct and complete structure that is, in effect, an effective ritual implement in its entirety. In these regards, the building inscriptions of Ramesses III concerning Medinet Habu are typical of a New Kingdom genre produced in virtually all reigns of the period. For example, in one inscription, the king describes Medinet Habu as an august residence for Amun built of fine white stone, with doorjambs of pure gold, set with inlay figures made of splendid and expensive decorative stones: moreover, a myriad of statues, depicting a variety of gods and goddesses, have been placed therein. Elsewhere, in Papyrus Harris I (a near-contemporary document purporting to give the words of Ramesses III), the material aspects of Medinet Habu are provided in greater detail—the varied nature of its stone masonry (sandstone, quartzite, granite); its doors of electrum and copper; a marvelous statue of Amun himself, adorned with genuine and expensive stones; and royal colossi (now gone) flanking the entrance. Emphasized at the same time are the symbolic completeness and implicit ritual efficacy of the temple as a total artifact, especially as regards the crucial solar cycle around the cosmos and its regenerative effects. It is repeatedly noted that the temple's form is like the horizon (Akhet) of heaven, that is, the mysterious transitional zone between the otherworld, the netherworld, and this world that is concealed by the mountains at the world's edge, mountains replicated in the temple pylon itself. At the same time, the temple represents the primeval world, from whence the creation of the cosmos originated, and is the pure ground of Amun as creator and lord of the cosmos, surrounded by his ennead or supporting pantheon, embodied in the many divine statues mentioned above.

Indeed, one of the Medinet Habu building inscriptions actually refers to not only the visual but the tactile pleasure that the temple's unique beauty brings to the sun god, of whom Amun-Re was a form. Having described this great palace of the Akhet, with its stone body, golden throne, silver floor, and doors sheathed in gold, the text concludes by describing the sun rising from it, its rays caressing its splendid form and materials, and then setting, descending into the temple and touching its beauty, defined not as magnificent representational art or elaborate architecture but, rather, as silver, electrum, and expensive stones.

This consistent Egyptian vision of the temple as an artifact in itself suggests some interesting, if necessarily speculative, observations. As we have seen, the Theban royal mortuary temples varied considerably in size, with two being noticeably small as regards both the temple proper and the enclosed complex surrounding it: namely, those of Thutmose III and Merenptah. While both were functional in ritual terms, they have almost a miniaturized dimension in other ways. Other mortuary temples are noticeably larger (e.g., those of Hatshepsut, Ay and Horemheb, Seti I, and Ramesses II), especially when their total complex is included.

At first glance, Medinet Habu, in its totality, seems to correspond to the larger, more seemingly "functional" temples and their surrounding complexes. However, Medinet Habu actually includes *two* major enclosed spaces: that within the innermost enclosure and the area between the innermost and the outermost enclosure. The first spatial entity corresponds to the *entirety* of the other mortuary temple complexes, none of which have the second spatial entity found at Medinet Habu, except partially perhaps in the case of the temple of Ay and Horemheb. The impact of these circumstances on the spatial dimension of Medinet Habu are conveyed by a few basic statistics. The area defined by its innermost enclosure is similar to that of Hatshepsut's and Seti I's temples, both of which, however, are much simpler in plan. The complex of Ay and Horemheb (excluding its first court) is about 1.2 times larger and is also much simpler in plan. Finally, the complex of Ramesses II, which Medinet Habu resembles in the density of its plan, is 2.4 times larger than the area defined by the innermost enclosed area of Medinet Habu.

These circumstances suggest that this innermost area (temple, palace, magazines, etc.) at Medinet Habu, while perfectly functional in ritual terms, included a strongly miniaturized dimension, with many of its features intended for use in the otherworld, or netherworld, not by the living. This would explain the seemingly tortuous aspects of some features of the plan of the temple itself and points to the possibility that the attached palace is a small-scale version of an entity that, in actuality, would be much larger. Moreover, the seeming harem apartments of the Eastern and Western High Gates are awkwardly accessed in terms of their vertical distribution over some four stories and also display rooms that are in general considerably smaller than comparable palatial complexes used by living royalty. For example, the two "throne rooms" in the Eastern High Gate (rooms 2 and 5) each occupy 19.05 square meters, whereas the throne room in the harem suite at Malkata occupies 91.26; that is, it is almost five times larger. The High Gates might then represent vertically organized, small-scale versions of palatial complexes that, in actuality, were much larger and structured horizontally, at ground level.

If some mortuary temples—Merenptah's and to some extent that of Ramesses III—seem to include much (including even parts of the plan of the temple proper) that resembles model-like, smaller-scale versions of actually larger prototypes, then it is possible that the larger mortuary temple complexes also included much that was model-like in nature and not intended to be functional except in a nominal sense. They would have then been larger examples of the concept of temple as artifact. Evidently, this suggestion needs much more detailed analysis than can be attempted here, but it might be worth pursuing in the future.

Yet a third meaning applicable to temples, like elite tomb chapels, involved their role as documentation, a kind of certification covering several interrelated issues. On the one hand, by quoting, describing, and depicting the correct performance of all rituals associated with temples—from the founding process to the performance of established cult on a daily basis and during festival occasions—the program of the temple attested that it was a fully perfected and fully protected entity. On the other hand, the chief and symbolically only ritualist was the king, so the temple as document had to further document, via its program, that the ruler in question had acceded to the throne legitimately and—both prototypically and in terms of his specific biography—had carried out all the responsibilities of that office, including its ritual ones, to perfection. Memorializing this information was intended to attract, reassure, and placate the temple's chief deity and others represented therein, so that they would respond to ritual, become embodied in their statues and other images, and interact productively with the king and, via him, the world. The perfection of the temple as document was thus part of its irresistible beauty, almost compelling the deities to enter it and become manifest; but it also attested to them that the temple and its ritual were effective and legitimate in every respect, hence providing no opportunity for chaotic or negative forces to become active in the temple and threaten harm—even destruction—to its divine inhabitants or visitors. Any sense that such dangers might be possible, because of some flaw in the temple's perfection, would stimulate the anger and aggression of the deities, directed against—in the first instance—the king who had founded the temple and dared to perform its cult.

In a royal mortuary temple, of course, there was an added dimension to these concerns, in that there was a specific focus on providing ritual attentions to the deceased ruler—and the form of Amun with which he was identified—that would make manifest the processes whereby he was experiencing endlessly repeated revitalizations: full capacity for enjoying the extraordinary qualities of the divine world he had entered and full protection against the harm and even destruction that chaotic force repeatedly launched against that divine world. To us, it might seem strange to see, in the temple program, the king ministering to his own mortuary cult, but in this regard, the specific king in question was enacting the fundamental, prototypical responsibility of all kings to tend to the mortuary cults of their ancestors. Here, the king, performing his own cult, stood in for his successors who, theoretically at least, would maintain it.

These three fundamental levels of meaning—temple as ritual arena, irresistibly beautiful artifact, and legitimizing document—are associated with the other significations presented by mortuary and other temples of the New Kingdom. These were cosmotopographical in nature and expressive of the notion that the essential features and processes of the cosmos as a whole were replicated at several different levels of Egyptian experience and perception. For the Egyptians, the cosmos was a perfectly functioning entity—comprising celestial, terrestrial, and netherworld dimensions—surrounded by an endless expanse of utterly dark, seemingly liquid formlessness or chaos, which continually tried to reabsorb the cosmos and reduce it to formlessness, even exercising aggressive and destructive force to do so. The solar cycle, involving repeated revitalizations of the cosmos that transformed the negative but life-giving energies of chaos into the positive processes of the cosmos, was the chief guarantor of the cosmos's survival and, at a personal level, of the afterlife survival of both deceased pharaohs and their subjects.

For the Egyptians, the cosmos—as thus envisaged—manifested itself in a series of nested entities, as well as in the form and program of individual temples. The city or town in which the temple stood and its surrounding region was one such entity—the cosmos replicated at the regional level. Egypt, the image of the perfect land and its society, hemmed in by arid deserts and the salty seas, was another. And a third was the entire world, as known to the Egyptians, with Egypt as its orderly center and with foreign lands and peoples acting out the roles of chaos yet, when passive subjects, signifying the transformation of negative energy into positive force. The totality of the cosmos itself, the actuality of its three full dimensions directly apprehended (not perceived from a terrestrial point of view), was the ultimate image affecting the form and program of the temple. Here, the two primary processes of the cosmos could be manifested: first, its creation, the cosmogony brought into being by a unique, inherently solar creator god; and second, the renewal of that creative process generated daily (and, from a different perspective, annually) by the solar cycle—the daily role of the cosmos, the solar descent and seeming death, the netherworld revitalization via Osiris and the solar rebirth, paralleling the first sunrise that activated a cosmos that was already fully conceptualized yet inert, if potent, until brought to life by the energizing and beautifying rays of primeval sunrise.

Why was the evocation of the cosmos, with reference to these several nested manifestations of it, so important to the concept and form of the Egyptian temple? In part, it was because Egyptian temple ritual was saturated—in utterance, act, and image—with reference to the cosmogony and the recurrent solar cycle, because of their fundamental significance in the Egyptian worldview. Temples rich in cosmological symbolism functioned as a material embodiment of the cosmological concepts expressed in the ritual, much as the latter also found expression in the multiple, ever-varied scenes of cultic performances depicted on temple walls. Moreover, as the cosmos, the temple projected—like the cosmos—a tremendous apotropaic aura that protected it and its august denizens from harm and provided them with the power to defeat their chaotic enemies. But perhaps the most significant aspect of cosmological symbolism brings us back to the concept of temple as artifact, incredibly attractive to the deities, incredibly effective in servicing the cults that delighted and placated them and ensured a productive interrelationship between the divine and human worlds. The cosmos itself was the ultimate expression of beauty—in its order, vitality, and richness—and hence was the ideal form on which the temple, the quintessential gift to the deities, should be modeled. This issue brings us back to the building inscriptions in which the artifactual nature of the Egyptian temple is most evidently displayed. Not only do these texts repeatedly correlate the temple with the most fundamental cosmological processes and forms, particularly the Akhet, the region of rebirth and revitalization; they also emphasize the essential components of the cosmos, which in Egyptian belief extend into the worlds of deities, living humans, and the dead.

The essential bones of the cosmos are represented by stones and metals; the surfaces of the cosmos—earth, water, and vegetation—are reflected in the pools, gardens, and plantations mentioned in building inscriptions; and the cosmos's sinews—its living populations—are embodied in the thousands of Egyptians and foreign prisoners dedicated to temple service and estates and the vast herds and flocks provided as well.

PROGRAMMATIC ASPECTS OF MEDINET HABU

It is against this background of the patterns of signification typical of Egyptian temples that we must consider the general structure and specific aspects of the program of Medinet Habu and their relationship to the architectural form of the temple and of the complex surrounding it. This program, the carefully structured and organized system of scenes and text covering much of the walls and also much of the ceiling and columns of Medinet Habu, has not yet received the in-depth analysis—hall by hall, chamber by chamber, and court by court—that it merits, but most of the program has been published in detail by the Oriental Institute of the University of Chicago. Moreover, William Murnane's invaluable guide to Medinet Habu provides descriptions of the program and interpretations of its meaning that are more detailed and stimulating than is usually the case.[15]

To discuss in any detail the entire surviving program of the temple of Medinet Habu (in some parts of the temple, it has been largely destroyed by later reuses of the structure) would be impossible in a context such as this chapter. Instead, I focus on the general organization of that program and on certain parts of the temple in which the program is better preserved than it is in other areas. To this end, I have provided a diagrammatic representation (see fig. 6.11 below) to provide some guidance to the reader in making his or her way through the following discussion.

There are two most important points to keep in mind. First, in terms of its program, Medinet Habu follows a basic template evident in other and earlier New Kingdom temples; but, as with its plan, it also displays some significant individual variations on that template. Second, interwoven with the generic features of the program at Medinet Habu are specific references to and evocations of Ramesses III himself and of his individual experiences and achievements as a specific, historical king. As in other temples, these aspects of the program specifically identify the king involved in the creation of this temple, so the deities' reciprocal gratitude will be lavished on the appropriate person, and they also demonstrate that through his specific and historical experiences,

Ramesses III carried out perfectly the prototypical responsibilities of kingship. Hence, Medinet Habu is free of any taint of illegitimacy, and the security of its divine inhabitants and effectiveness of the cult proffered them are guaranteed. At the same time, Medinet Habu—unlike many other temples—is dedicated in large part to the mortuary cult of Ramesses III (albeit identified with a form of Amun specific to the temple), a factor that strongly influenced the program in important ways.

In my analysis, I am, in general, following lines of interpretation and modes of analysis as regards temple programs that have already been discussed in the relevant scholarly literature, applying them to this particular and individualistic example of such a program. However, the program at Medinet Habu brings out a feature of temple programs that has been less intensively analyzed: namely, that not only were the components of such programs conceived of as an integrated whole throughout the entire temple, but the patterns of interrelationships constructed are more detailed and subtle than we perhaps realize. In particular, I think there are points of conjunction between the "external" program, displayed on the temple's external walls, and its "internal" program, displayed on the walls of its courts and throughout the roofed area of the temple. A thorough analysis of such a possibility would require an entire monograph and cannot be entered upon here.

Before the temple proper, the Eastern High Gate and its program first requires discussion. Like the less well-preserved Western High Gate, the Eastern High Gate programmatically is a self-contained conceptual entity, separate from the program of the mortuary temple itself. Yet the Eastern High Gate's program resonates powerfully—and seemingly intentionally—with the multiple meanings manifested by the temple's program.

The Eastern High Gate has as its central feature a migdol, in its simplest form of a single, towerlike structure. The migdol is incorporated into a massive gate, modeled on gates of contemporary Egyptian fortresses. Levantine fortified gates are sometimes suggested as the model, but would be inappropriate, evoking the despised foe whose defeats at Egyptian hands are several times celebrated in the temple's program. The point of the nonfunctional fortress gate is to reinforce the apotropaic significance of the pseudofortified outermost enclosure as a whole.

Moreover, the Eastern High Gate also incorporates elements of palatial architecture, that is, a suite of vertically structured harem apartments, with the centrally placed and largest two rooms—one above the other in the migdol—representing the throne room found at one end of the harem apartments in the palace of Amenhotep III at Malkata. This harem suite, with rooms notably small in area (i.e., semiminiaturized), may have been non-functional, intended for its otherworld use by the pharaoh and his women. If so, it makes the popular idea that the well-documented assassination attempt on Ramesses III occurred in one of the two gates unlikely.

Functionally, the Eastern High Gate's primary role was to permit festival processions, such as that for the Valley Festival, to enter and exit the mortuary temple complex. Otherwise, the actual gate itself—set in the east facade of the migdol—was probably kept closed. The program of scenes and texts displayed on the walls of the Eastern High Gate therefore likely gained much of their meaning from the periodic passage through it of festival processions, mimicking the solar cycle and its rejuvenating potential.

Was the Eastern High Gate also used for the passage of prisoners of war into the temple complex so the pharaoh could present them to the temple's deity as part of the thanks offerings kings habitually performed for deities after a victorious campaign abroad? The king is shown leading or presenting such prisoners to Amun at the opposing eastern ends of the gate's roadway, on the south side of the actual gateway (under the migdol), and on the west face of the migdol. Yet similar scenes occurred on the Western High Gate, functionally much less suitable for such a purpose than the Eastern High Gate, so in both cases, the representations may be symbolic, rather than depicting actual events occurring within the Medinet Habu complex.

More significant for our understanding of the Eastern High Gate is the circumstance that its program is organized like that of a temple and is focused on a symbolic celebration of the king's rejuvenation, an apparent evocation of the actual rejuvenation achieved for the king-as-Amun in the sanctuary of the temple itself. The gate's access to the Valley Festival is also relevant here, for this annual event—again within the temple proper—seems to have been the climax of the king's repeated processes of rejuvenation.

As in a temple, the most obviously external faces of the Eastern High Gate refer to the king's divinely authorized defeat and capture of foreign foes, in the form of smiting scenes on the faces of its eastern towers and, on the gate's west facade, repeated depictions of the presentation of foreign prisoners by the king to Amun and, seemingly, to himself (on either side of windows in which, notionally at least, the king himself or his statue would have appeared). Moreover, in a temple, scenes of cult were displayed not on external faces but, to some degree, on the internal faces of courts and more especially throughout the roofed part of a temple. Similarly, in the Eastern High Gate, cult scenes are found on the wall faces overlooking the roadway leading to the actual gateway, a location shielding them from the view of externally located viewers.

However, the actual roofed area of the gate—the symbolic harem apartments—depict not cult but the recreational, though ceremonialized, attentions provided to the king by members of the harem or, better, female collectivity that had surrounded him in life. Yet perhaps the point was that the rejuvenating effect the harem women had on the king was analogous to the rejuvenating effect temple cult had on the deities actively embodied in their statues in the temple's sanctuary and chapels.

This last suggestion is supported by an analysis of the Eastern High Gate's program that leads to a similar conclusion: namely, that the entire program is intended to celebrate the rejuvenation and, indeed, rebirth that the mortuary temple and its cult provides the king-as-Amun and to emphasize that this process is analogous to or identical with the daily experience of solar rebirth that signals the repeated renewal of the cosmos and its order. In such a context, the ministrations that harem women provide the king, to ensure the stability of his personality and effectiveness, are equated with the services that Hathor and other goddesses provide to the sun god, for the same purposes. The resulting analogy between sun god and king celebrated iconographically in the gate would be reinforced yet further by the repeated progress through it of processional festivals, which mimicked the sun god's descent into the west (a "rebirth" into the netherworld) and ascent into the east (rebirth into the celestial world). Architecturally, in fact, the Eastern High Gate could have been read as a depiction of the Akhet, the liminal zone between this world and the other, or divine, world in which the birthing process of the sun god culminated—a circumstance suggesting that the king-as-Amun, owner of the temple to which the gate gave access, would undergo the same experience.

To an external viewer, only the two towers and, framed between them, the migdol at the rear would be the visible features of the gate. The towers were higher than the migdol in height, so in combination, all three would resemble the hieroglyph for Akhet, two mountains with a depression between them. The mountains, set at the periphery of the world, signified the Akhet behind them and the mysterious processes within it that had to be hidden from the sight of the living in order to be effective. This Akhet-like form imparted to the gate would be further emphasized by the two towers (also representing the mountains of the Akhet) of the main pylon, which, visually, would seem to immediately rise behind—and extend beyond—the Eastern High Gate. The identification of the latter with the Akhet was further reinforced by the gate's program. The smiting scenes on either tower face refer to the defeat of the chaotic forces that attempt to abort every sunrise (i.e., every rebirth of the sun god) and thus to bring the cosmos to an end. Moreover, the centrally located program, on the east face of the migdol, can also be read (see below) as identifying the "resurrection" of the king with the rebirth and reappearance of the sun god, emerging in the depression between the two mountains. Indeed, the hieroglyphic representation of the Akhet always includes the sun disc rising between the two mountains.

More specifically, on the migdol's east face, the actual gateway, at its base, is flanked and surmounted by representations of the king performing cult for Amun. This action would take place in temples, representing the interface between earth and heaven. Thus, the scenes set above those flanking and immediately surmounting the gateway can be read as set in the celestial realm, a notion supported by the depictions above each of the two windows. These depictions seem to show the king experiencing the same processes of rebirth and ascent experienced by the sun god. In analyzing this possibility, we must remember that notionally at least, each window framed the living king, although in actuality it might have been a statue that was thus displayed.

The space above the lower window is filled with an enormous vulture, wings outspread. She is identified as Wadjit, a tutelary goddess of kingship. The other such goddess was Nekhbet. Wadjit was considered the younger of the two, and is featured here in reference to the young harem women depicted in the rooms of the Eastern High Gate.

Again assuming that the royal person or image was also displayed in the upper window, the space above it, coinciding with the window's width, is filled with enormous hieroglyphs spelling out, in compressed mode, the king's two chief names, displayed twice, in the form of a mirror image. Reading from the center outward, the two names can be translated as "Re is overflowing with Maat, who is [beloved] of Amun" (*Usermaatre MeryAmun*) and "Re, the ruler of Heliopolis, is the one who has caused him (the king) to be born" (*Ramesses Heka jwnw*). In the text, the hieroglyph used to represent the word "birth" (*messes*) also represents the "ruler" of Heliopolis. The hieroglyph represents, in the former capacity, the solar child, with a solar disc above (i.e., the infant sun god), and, in the latter, a royal child, holding the regalia of kingship (i.e., Ramesses himself). Thus, the ascendant sun and the revivified pharaoh are emblematically indicated to be the same being.

The richness of the Eastern High Gate's program, as regards the issue of royal rejuvenation, becomes further evident if we turn to the scenes and texts displayed along the "inner" faces of the gate, that is, those extending from the frontal towers, then along the roadway and through the actual gateway, and concluding with the facing jambs at the western end of that gateway. In terms of the size and locations of each unit or scene, there is

WEST FACADE
(MIGDOL)
Amun

SOUTH   NORTH

GATEWAY

Amun,   Amun,
Khonsu   Thoth

EAST FACADE
(MIGDOL)

Amun

ROADWAY WALLS

	LOWER REGISTER	UPPER REGISTER	UPPER REGISTER	LOWER REGISTER
1		NA	NA	
	Amun, Mut, Thoth			Amun, Atum, Montu
2		Ioh-Thoth, Nehemetawy	Atum, Iusaas	
	Ptah, Sekhmet			Shu-Sire-Onuris, [Mehit]
3		Amun-Re-Horakhty, Maat	[Seth,] Nut	
	Amun			Amun

EAST FACADE
(TOWERS)

Amun   Re-Horakhty
(Libyans, Nubians)   (Levantines, Tjekker, Sherdan, Shasu, Tiwresh, Peleset)

Fig. 6.10. Deities represented in the East High Gate. (Table by D. O'Connor and T. Prakash.)

exact, mirrorlike positioning along the entirety of the opposing (i.e., respectively northern and southern) wall faces, a circumstance suggesting that the scenes on both faces form an interrelated program. The subject matter of each scene is different from that of the others in specifics but similar generally, in that most depict either cult scenes or royal ceremonies such as coronation, which also always involve the presence of deities. Taken as a whole, these deities form a complex yet related pattern, in part structured by oppositional relationships, from one wall to the other (fig. 6.10).

At first glance, the deities represented seem an intriguing but puzzling mixture of major deities with others who are more obscure and unlikely to be displayed prominently on a major royal monument: these more obscure deities include the god Ioh-Thoth and the goddesses Nehemetawy, Iusaas, and [Mehit]. Closer examination, however, indicates that in their totality, the deities evoke a complex set of related meanings, which relate, in turn, to the fact that the inner chambers of the gate depict not the king performing cult for deities but, instead, harem women providing recreation for the king. Sacred and "secular" alike, the total assemblage of scenes bear on the essential message conveyed by the program: namely, that within the temple that lies beyond the gate, the deceased ruler experiences repeated rebirths, accompanied by a complete renewal of his intellectual, emotional, and physical capacities, via processes analogous to or identical with the restoring to wholeness and subsequent rebirth of the sun god. The totality of the gate's architecture reinforces this programmatically conveyed message in that it is a representation of the Akhet, the hidden, liminal zone lying behind the mountains at the world's edge, in which these miraculous processes take place.

The relationship of the program to this basic message is evident in a variety of ways. First, the majority of the deities relate either to the sun or to its equivalent, the moon, which is also solar in meaning: this includes Amun(-Re), Re-Horakhty, Atum, Shu (sunlight), Iusaas (a solar consort), Seth (defender of the sun god) and Nut ("mother" of the sun god), Khonsu, Thoth, and Ioh-Thoth. This circumstance is congruent with the emphasis on solar rebirth and the integrity of the solar cycle of which it is a product. Moreover, some of these deities deploy exceptional apotropaic powers, which relate to the need to protect the Akhet and the solar rebirth it generates, against chaotic and demonic forces trying to injure or terminate the solar cycle and hence the cosmos itself. Particularly relevant in this regard are Khonsu, Thoth, Mut, Montu, Sekhmet, Shu-Onuris, and Seth; these deities are distributed throughout the entirety of the gate and represent the defense of the Akhet and its products, the revived forms of the sun god and of the king-as-Amun.

Given that these two entities—sun god and king—are restored to wholeness and complete reintegration of their faculties by the rebirthing process and its antecedents, it is noteworthy that some of the deities in the program are associated with the healing of damage or estrangement experienced by the interrelated entities of the solar disc (or "eye") and lunar disc, such as Shu-Onuris, Ioh-Thoth, Thoth, Mut, and Khonsu. Thus, they guarantee that the necessary wholeness will be secured. Moreover, a specific version of the regaining of solar wholeness—myths about the "Distant Goddess"—is given special prominence in the program and explains the presence of the more obscure deities. The "Distant Goddess" is the daughter or "Eye" (disc) of Re, who departs from him for a sometimes extended period and causes a potential breakdown in solar integrity that would be disastrous for the cosmos. Because of either an estrangement from Re or a seemingly uncontrollable aggression, the "Distant Goddess" has to be placated or restored to an orderly status (via various deities and methods) and must seek reunion with Re and a return to cosmic stability. Specific embodiments of the "Distant Goddess" vary but include Mut, Sekhmet, [Mehit], and Nehemetawy, all represented in the Eastern High Gate's program; in fact, the last three goddesses "face" each other on opposing wall faces, as if to emphasize the significance of their presence.

The programmatic themes outlined above may relate to the depictions of the activities of women of the royal harem—another major component of the program—in several ways. The recreation these women provided to the king not only was a source of pleasure but was of fundamental ideological importance, in that it maintained or restored his emotional stability and balance and even his physical capability, all essential if the king was to function effectively as ruler, responsible not only for the stability of this world but also for its productive interaction with the divine world. In performing this role for the king's benefit, harem women duplicated the identical benefit brought to the sun god by divine women, that is, goddesses. Prototypical here is Hathor, the sun god's daughter, consort, and mother, who in some myths herself becomes a "Distant Goddess"; but other examples of the latter, by reuniting with the sun god, essentially also provide him the wholeness and balance he requires. Hathor's relationship with the sun god involves sexual contact as well, and the erotic appeal of harem women was also clearly appreciated and may have involved sexual relations with the king. Perhaps for this reason or simply because of her connection with the creation and then repeated regenerations of the cosmos by the sun god, yet another solar-related goddess was included in the program. Iusaas occurs in the same cluster of scenes as the "Distant Goddesses" Nehemetawy, [Mehit], and Sekhmet. Iusaas represents the "hand of the god" with which Atum masturbated in order to begin the generative process leading to the creation of the cosmos, and by the New Kingdom, she had become personified as the god's sexual partner.

Finally, as we have seen above, Egyptian temples were also intended to evoke or correspond to the cosmos, manifest at several different cosmotopographical levels—the entire cosmos, the world, Egypt, and specific cities and their regions. The Eastern High Gate's program and architecture forms a self-contained entity in which this structuring is also evident. Indeed, the cosmotopographical structure within the gate follows the same locational structuring exemplified in Hatshepsut's prototypical mortuary temple.

In the latter, the program of the lowest colonnade refers to the foreign lands (northern differentiated from southern) surrounding Egypt; to northern and southern Egypt, representing unity in duality; and to Thebes itself. In the middle colonnade program, reference is made to foreign lands (Punt and others) and to southern and northern Egypt, but the greater part of the space is allocated to Thebes (south half) and seemingly to Memphis and Heliopolis (north half). Finally, on the upper terrace, the program of the columned court or semihypostyle hall focuses on Thebes itself, as defined by the two festivals (Opet and Valley) that traverse and define its principal components—the East and West Banks and their temples.

A similar cosmotopographical structuring is evident in the Eastern High Gate program, utilizing, however, emblematic and cultic imagery, rather than the narrative sequences deployed in Hatshepsut's temple. On the gate's eastern exterior (corresponding to Hatshepsut's lower colonnade), the foreign lands and southern and northern Egypt are highlighted, with little direct reference to Thebes itself. On the south tower, southerners and westerners (Nubians and Libyans) venerate the pharaoh, while Amun signifies Thebes and embodies southern Egypt, centered on that city. On the north tower, easterners and northerners (Levantines and Sea Peoples) venerate the pharaoh, and Re-Horakhty signifies Heliopolis and embodies northern Egypt.

In the program along the roadway (corresponding to Hatshepsut's middle colonnade), the emphasis is on Egypt as a whole and its central places at Thebes and Heliopolis. The relevant topographical references are provided by their association with the specific deities represented: for southern Egypt, Amun (Thebes), Seth (Ombos), and Onuris (Thinis); for northern Egypt, Ioh-Thoth (Hermopolis), Nehemetawy (Herakleopolis), Ptah and Sekhmet (Memphis), and Atum (Heliopolis). The rear section of the gate (the migdol, the gateway below it, and the immediately adjacent scenes) corresponds to the court or semihypostyle hall on Hatshepsut's upper terrace. The deities represented in this part of the gate seem to correspond to Thebes itself, with implicit reference to the Opet and Valley festivals, in that it is the Theban triad—Amun, Mut, and Khonsu—that is highlighted. In addition, the Theban region, in its larger sense, is evoked by the presence of Montu, who is associated with Armant, Tod, and Medamud.

The program of the mortuary temple, discussed below, cannot be treated in the detailed way I have used to analyze the Eastern High Gate and its program. The latter, however, merit this extended discussion because they are among the other innovative features indicating that Medinet Habu was not a noncreative mélange of earlier mortuary temples but, rather, one of the most interesting of them ever built. For the program of the mortuary temple itself, the reader should refer to figure 6.11, a schematic and selective representation

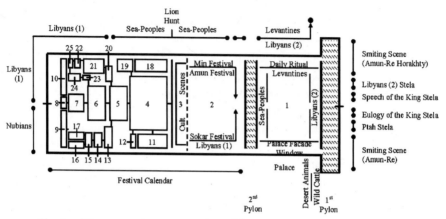

Fig. 6.11. Diagrammatic representation of the programmatic organization of Medinet Habu. (Drawing by D. O'Connor and T. Prakash.)

of some major components of that program. The issues of Medinet Habu as a ritual space and a beautiful artifact have been dealt with above; however, the documentary aspect of the program merits further discussion.

Following earlier paradigms of temple programs, that of Medinet Habu attests to the legitimacy of the cult and its supporting economic and administrative institutions and to the purity and security of the temple itself. Many of the scenes and their accompanying texts are correspondingly generic as regards themes—the defeat of foreign foes (equated with the defense of the cosmos against chaos) and the king's performance of cult for a myriad of deities (equated with the orderly functioning of the cosmos). Nevertheless, the temple as document refers not only to the successful execution by Ramesses III of the prototypical responsibilities of kingship but also to his specific and individualized manifestations of that success. As such, the program is a biography of the king himself, necessary for two reasons. The program reassures the deities of the temple that Ramesses III is specifically a legitimate ruler and capable ritualist and hence that he brings only benefit and not danger to those deities. Moreover, the king's biography shows that he is an appropriate, meritorious recipient of the temple's primary purpose, the provision of mortuary cult to the deceased king-as-Amun.

The specificity of Ramesses III as a historical individual is documented in many ways throughout the temple program. Most important is a seeming banality, the endless repetition of his names and titles literally hundreds—

maybe thousands—of times throughout the temple. These manifest his specific royal identity and convey the impression that the temple itself—an image of the cosmos—is a form of Ramesses III, much as the cosmos was a manifestation or embodiment of the creator god. In this way, the temple and the king's identity were fused together. Other biographical elements, however, were much more focused on Ramesses the individual person.

For example, the entrance to the temple proper, the doorway of the first or main pylon (fig. 6.11), was flanked by two stelae that, given their location (instantly available to the visiting Theban triad on festival occasions but also to externally located viewers), were of special significance. The text on the southern stela celebrated Ramesses' victories over foreign foes and his acknowledgment of the deities' sponsorship of these victories through the extraordinary beauty of the temple that, seemingly literally, he had built for them. The text of the northern stela quotes a speech given by Ramesses to his officials and army leaders in which he stresses the legitimacy of his kingship and his achievements as ruler.

Other examples of historical specificity as regards Ramesses are associated with the representations and descriptions of campaigns against foreign foes covering much of the temple's exterior and the walls of its two courts (fig. 6.11). While some campaigns (against the Nubians and the Levantines) are treated in generic and generalized terms, the representation of others (two against Libyans, one against Sea Peoples) include specific regnal dates and specific historical narratives, some (for the second Libyan campaign) of considerable extent. Absent any evidence to the contrary, this historical information must be taken at face value, as a direct record of Ramesses' own experience. A different kind of personalized veracity is provided by the enormously long festival calendar on the southern external face of the temple; this records in great detail the specific support Ramesses has provided for the many festivals celebrated at Medinet Habu, accurate data once again documenting Ramesses' individual actions.

Turning from its documentary dimension to the overall program of the temple of Medinet Habu, we need to recognize that it represents a coherent and predetermined composition, conceived of at an enormous scale and with great complexity of structure, yet flexible enough to incorporate new material until the temple was finally completed, during the twelfth regnal year of Ramesses III. In particular, when the temple was begun, in regnal year 5, important foreign campaigns (against the Sea Peoples in regnal year 8 and the Libyans in regnal year 11) had not yet taken place, yet they form very large and well-integrated components of the overall program. There may have well been other programmatic adjustments over time that are less obvious to us.

We need to recognize that the temple's program not only includes some distinctively innovative features, discussed below, but also manifests more subtle examples of innovation or variation even when more traditional proto-types are seemingly being followed. Adherence to prototypes at Medinet Habu is, of course, not surprising. On the one hand, Medinet Habu was similar to earlier temples in its basic functions; on the other hand, adherence to exacti-tude in the content and performance of the rituals depicted, which extended back to their origins in "primeval time," was also important. Yet at Medinet Habu, the deployment of these concerns led not to exact duplication but, rather, to specific variations of preexisting templates.

Unfortunately, the programs of the smaller hypostyle halls and of the triple-chambered bark chapel (fig. 6.11: 5–7) at Medinet Habu are too de-stroyed to be usefully compared with similar areas in earlier mortuary temples, which, in any case, are usually not well preserved either. However, the Osirian and solar complexes at Medinet Habu (attested prominently in mor-tuary temples since at least the reign of Hatshepsut) do provide important and revealing comparative data.

The solar complex (fig. 6.11: 20–22) is roughly similar in plan to the solar complexes of Seti I and Ramesses II, but its program may have been richer and more complex than those of its predecessors. In particular, although its lower registers consisted of relatively conventional offering scenes, the upper regis-ters traced out the entire solar cycle. On the east wall, the sun's ascent and re-birth was celebrated textually, while along the north and south walls, texts and images evoke the protective powers gathering around the sun god as he ap-proaches the danger-filled netherworld. The west wall, the location of the sun god's descent into that netherworld, has a colonnade in front, supporting an architrave depicting the night bark of the sun god in which he traverses the netherworld and referring also to his triumphant rebirth as a result. On the west wall itself, the sun god is further empowered to overcome the dangers awaiting him in the netherworld, while one text specifically identifies the de-ceased Ramesses III with the sun god, so that he, too, will experience the same regenerative and protected process. As for earlier examples of this highly artic-ulated representation of the solar process, the program in the relevant area of the mortuary temple of Ramesses II has not survived, but some of the pro-gram in the solar complex of Seti I has and seems—perhaps misleadingly (since it is incomplete)—to be much more limited in subject matter.

The Osirian complex of Ramesses III is more definitely innovative in plan than its predecessors and possibly more innovative in its (relatively well-preserved) program (fig. 6.11: 13–17). Generally, this particular part of earlier mortuary temples was occupied by a set of chapels that were relatively conventional in plan. Usually, such chapels were structured on a central axis that defined the ritual path, and they had one or two small-scale halls and typically a tripartite sanctuary or perhaps a bark shrine.

The Osirian complex of Ramesses III (fig. 6.11: 13–17) is not entered frontally (as earlier examples usually were) and is structured around a convoluted ritual path, not the axially direct one found in earlier Osirian complexes. Instead, it requires a right-angled change of direction to get from the vestibule (fig. 6.11: 13) to a columned hall (6.11: 14), a further right-angled change to move from the first columned hall to the second hall (6.11: 15) beyond it, and yet another right-angled turn to get from the second hall to a chamber specifically dedicated to Osiris (6.11: 17), the larger and seemingly more important of the two chambers accessed from the second hall (i.e., fig. 6.11: 16 and 17). Moreover, although chapels concluding in two chambers (others have three) are found in earlier Osirian complexes, such as that of Ramesses II, none of the earlier pairs are subdivided, whereas one in the Osirian complex of Ramesses III (fig. 6.11: 16) is.

The Osirian complex of Ramesses III may have been innovative in its program as well as in its plan. Generally, little survives of the programs in earlier Osirian complexes, except in the case of that of Seti I, where only relatively conventional cult scenes are involved. This circumstance, as well as the seeming innovation of its plan, suggests that the program in the Osirian complex of Ramesses III may have included major components not found in earlier ones.

To summarize what is in actuality a complex program, that in the vestibule (fig. 6.11: 13) seems to focus on the king as an appropriate recipient of a mortuary offering cult. The "menu" of such a cult is displayed on the east wall, the king's legitimacy as ruler is stressed on the southern, and an image of the king as a mortuary statue is displayed on the west wall. From this point on (fig. 6.11: 14 and beyond), the program seems to cover the triumphant aspects of the king's traverse of the netherworld: namely, his transformation into a fully redeveloped king (fully sustained by the rich abundance of the netherworld) and his identification with Osiris as well as the sun god, an essential element in his regeneration. All these circumstances identify the king as fully meriting the mortuary cult highlighted in the entry vestibule (fig. 6.11: 13) but, in terms of actual ritual performance, presumably occurring throughout the entirety of the Osirian complex.

Thus, the program in the first hall (fig. 6.11: 14) highlights the actual (re)coronation of the deceased king (west wall). The next hall (fig. 6.11: 15) was apparently used to display offerings for the beings venerated in the double-roomed chamber 16 and its larger counterpart, chamber 17. In chamber 16, while reference is made to the king's triumphant progress through the netherworld and his overcoming of the dangers opposing his progress, the primary emphasis is on the exalted condition he achieves as a result. In the eastern of the two chambers, chapter 110 of the *Book of the Dead* is utilized to recount the king's successful progress and celebrate its product, his emergence as a fully sustained king (south wall). On the north wall, the central vignette shows the king actually active in the netherworld's source of sustenance, the agriculturally rich "fields of Iaru." He plows the soil and reaps the crops, evidently a symbolic signification of his access to these resources, rather than actions he actually performs. In the western room, chapter 148 of the *Book of the Dead* is displayed, along with appropriate vignettes, to celebrate the support he receives and even coerces from deities associated with the sun god. Finally, chamber 17 is ostensibly dedicated to the cult of Osiris himself, the ruler of the netherworld, and the king is shown performing cult for Osiris on the north and south walls, although also to Amun. A double-leafed false door at the rear indicates that a deity—namely, Osiris—will enter this chapel and occupy a statue set in it so as to receive the cult; but a physically intimate interaction between Osiris and the king (the latter supports the former) shown twice on the entablature above the false door hints at a merging or identification of these two beings. Indeed, as a whole, the program in chamber 17 may refer to the identification between the king-as-Amun (the deity venerated at Medinet Habu) and Osiris, an experience that actually takes place in the netherworld and guarantees the king's eternal existence.

Unusually, the chamber dedicated to Osiris has a vaulted roof, on which an elaborate map of the heavens is displayed, organized so as to emphasize regular progressions in time. The latter were significant to deceased Egyptians in that their repeated experiences of regeneration were structured according to these repetitive temporal patterns; but the celestial map may also have been important as a guide to the king and others so they could successfully traverse the complicated routes involved in a successful traverse of the netherworld. Indeed, the unusually convoluted ritual path of the Osirian complex of Ramesses III might also be an intentional reflection of the complexity of those routes, which the dead had to master to achieve eternal bliss.

As I noted earlier, the central sanctuary and bark chapel of royal mortuary temples were integrated into a tripartite symbolic structure involving the north-located solar complex and the south-located Osirian complex as well. In this arrangement, the location of the solar complex correlates with the celestial realm, cosmologically equated with the north, and the Osirian complex correlates with the earthly/chronic realm, cosmologically equated with the south. The sanctuary bridges both realms, equivalent to the larger entity, that is, the temple that binds together heaven and earth. Programmatically and in plan, the solar complex and the Osirian complex of Ramesses III indicate an even richer frame of reference than these two complexes usually signal in earlier mortuary temples. At Medinet Habu, the program of the solar complex highlights the sun god's entrance into the netherworld but only anticipates his progress through it; the Osirian complex program highlights the result of the sun god's traverse of the netherworld but not the traverse itself. Thus, a major component of the experiences that lead to the regeneration and rebirth of the king, seen as analogous to the sun god, seems omitted from the conceptual world of the mortuary temple. However, since Medinet Habu *is* a mortuary temple, it has an essential ritual and conceptual relationship to the actual royal tomb of Ramesses III, located in the Valley of the Kings and separate from the mortuary temple. The program of the royal tomb corresponds, in large part, to the "missing" component—the actual traverse of the various regions of the netherworld by the sun god (with whom the king is identified)—which unfolds along the walls of the tunnel-like tomb. Thus, the sanctuary of Medinet Habu is central to a nexus of a widespread set of correlations, extending from the solar complex to the royal tomb and from thence to the Osirian complex. This set of relations might have been implicit or subtly expressed in earlier mortuary temples, but at Medinet Habu, it found, perhaps innovatively, a richer form of expression. Indeed, the Osirian complex of Ramesses III is actually reminiscent of the royal tomb itself. The deployment of *Book of the Dead* is usual in Ramesside royal tombs, and the chamber of Osiris (fig. 6.11: 17) is reminiscent of a royal tomb chamber in its unusual vaulted form and incorporates a sky map that is also commonly found in the royal tombs.

Turning to aspects of the overall program of the mortuary temple, its display of conflict with the foreigner on external wall faces and those of courtyards, of festival scenes on court walls, and of the less publicly accessible cult scenes on the walls of the roofed areas of the temple correspond to what became the paradigm for major temples in general in the New Kingdom. Nevertheless, the program at Medinet Habu represents an especially elaborate, perhaps especially carefully designed version of this paradigm and also includes within it some strikingly original elements.

The New Kingdom temple, as noted above, was envisaged as a complete image of the cosmos, both in itself and as manifest at different levels of Egyptian experience—the world of humankind and nature, organized in terms of Egypt and foreign lands; Egypt itself and the two components of which it is composed; and the immediate region and central place of the temple's location (in this case, Thebes and its region). The cosmological form of Medinet Habu is evident in the iconography of its program, as well as the architectural and programmatic aspects that link it to the Akhet. In this context, ceilings represent the sky and the heavenly or celestial realm; the floor represents the earth and, implicitly, the chthonic realm beneath it. A further indication of this distinction is provided by the wall enclosing the roof terraces, that is, the highest and most celestial elevations (apart from the pylons) of the temple. These walls displayed representations of many of Egypt's deities, posed in their celestial realm, from which they dispatch their *bas* or mobile entities down into earth's temples, in response to the rituals proffered there.

As for other manifestations of the cosmos, between the ceiling/sky and the floor/earth, the temple itself, especially in its lower reaches, represents the world occupied by humankind, that is, Egypt and the foreign lands. The program of Medinet Habu traces out this concept with considerable elaboration and even exactitude. On the main pylon, emblematic smiting scenes and lists of foreign countries and peoples represent the foreign lands; the association of the southern wing with Amun-Re (a Theban god) and the presence of the white (southern) crown suggests it signifies southern Egypt; and the association of the northern wing with Re-Horakhty (of Heliopolis) and the presence of the red (northern) crown alone suggests that northern Egypt is signified here. Much of the externally located program of the rest of the temple elaborates on this distinction between Egypt and the foreign lands, following a cosmography that has seemingly intentional topographical correlates.

A campaign located in Nubia, to the south, is placed to correspond to the notional southeast quadrant of the temple. The first campaign against the Libyans flows around the northwest quadrant, corresponding to the Libyan homeland (Cyrenaica), located both north and west of Egypt. Much of the northern external face of the temple is covered by representations of the clash with the Sea Peoples who were of northern origin (the Aegean and Anatolia), even if the Egyptian conflict with them occurred in the southern Levant and along the Egyptian shoreline. The second Libyan campaign occurred some three years later than the conflict with the Sea Peoples and, perhaps for that reason, is located inappropriately from a topographical point of view, adjacent to the northeast quadrant of the temple, although the actual position of Libya/Cyrenaica vis-à-vis most of Egypt can be described as northern, as much as western. On the same wall face is a register depicting conflict with Levantines, possibly unhistorical but desirable for the creation of a programmatic "map" covering the totality of the foreign world. Here, actual and symbolic topography again coincide, in that the northeast quadrant of the temple corresponds to the northeast position of the Levant vis-à-vis Egypt.

The other externally located component of the program is more unusual in such a location: a long list of festivals performed at Medinet Habu and the resources made available to each covers most of the south external face of the temple except for the area occupied by the palace. Despite its location, its primary audience was composed of Amun and other relevant deities, rather than an externally located human audience. Why was it incorporated into the external program, which refers to Egypt on the pylon towers and to various foreign lands or peoples elsewhere? Two reasons are possible. The simplest is that the list is so lengthy that the external face offered the best location, uninterrupted by cross walls or other features. However, it may also present the festivals and their support as Ramesses' grateful recognition that his victories over foreigners and domination of Egypt—both celebrated on the other external faces—were gifts from the deities, with his dedication to their festivals an appropriate reciprocity, recorded in a similarly external location.

To return to the cosmotopographical aspects of the temple, if the exterior corresponds to Egypt (and its twofold division) and the foreign lands or peoples around it, the rear part of the temple, like the rear-placed upper-terrace structures of Hatshepsut's temple, likely were intended to highlight Thebes itself. The city was most obviously evoked by the chapel housing the visiting Theban triad, the quintessential representatives of the city, and associated with both Karnak and its environs on the East Bank and the mortuary temple itself on the West Bank. Yet further expansions of this notion might involve the solar complex (paralleling the important one on the north side of the Karnak Temple itself) and the Osirian complex, which has features reminiscent of a royal tomb, the latter being a monumental manifestation typical of the West Bank at Thebes. Finally, to the west of the solar complex is a unit comprising three chambers dedicated to deities making up the ennead, or corporation of deities "residing (under Amun's leadership) in Karnak," that is, a typically Theban entity. Moreover, this ennead included deities embodying places near Thebes (Montu, two goddesses of Armant, and a form of Sobek venerated to the south of Thebes), who thus evoked the Theban region as much as Thebes itself.

The contrast between the cosmotopography of the external faces of the temple and that of the rearmost inner section suggests that the area between the latter and the main or first pylon in some way represented the totality of Egypt. This would perhaps be most evident in the first two hypostyle halls and the structures flanking them and might have been conveyed by certain cosmotopographical patterns represented by some of the many deities depicted in these areas. However, to investigate this possibility would require an in-depth and perhaps inconclusive analysis inappropriate in the context of this chapter.

Finally, the program displayed in the two courts of the temple are particularly complex. They combine themes to be expected in such locations—particularly representations of festival processions, for which such courts provided the route to be followed after entering the temple or leading to their exit from the temple—and other themes, relating to the defeat of foreign foes, which more usually are restricted to the external faces of temples. In fact, representations of this type in the courts are restatements of the two Libyan campaigns, the campaign against the Sea Peoples, and the more generic conflicts with Levantines—all of which are also depicted externally to the temple.

To understand this situation better, the differentiation between the two courts should be noted. The first court functioned in terms of the temple, since it was fronted by the temple's main pylon and was utilized by processional festivals. At the same time, it served as the court of the palace located on its southern side, the facade of the palace being decorated with elaborate and symmetrically structured emblematic representations of the king's domination of foreign foes, appropriate enough for a palace facade. Facing the palace, on the opposite (north) side of the court, are seven piers, each fronted by a royal colossus representing an archetypal divine king. Thus the entire court was linked to the palace as much as the temple itself, and hence depictions and descriptions of the second Libyan campaign along its east wall, the Sea-Peoples' conflict along its west wall, and battles against Levantines along the north wall (lower register) can all be considered appropriate in such a setting. The only discordant theme occupies the upper register of the north wall, in which episodes characteristic of the daily rituals performed in every temple are depicted. This would seem to relate to the functions the court served for the temple proper. But its relatively minimal spatial allotment should be noted. Moreover, its positioning behind the royal colossi may be meaningful, for perhaps it signified one primary role of the king, servicing the cult of the deities, while the rest of the program in the first court signified, much more emphatically, kingship's other main function, the defeat and domination of the foreigner and the suppression of chaos at a terrestrial level, parallel to the deities' defense of the sun god against chaos at the celestial level.

The most prominent theme in the second court are episodes relating to three festivals: that of Sokar (beginning on the south wall and culminating along the southern half of the eastern); that of Min (beginning on the north wall and culminating along the north half of the eastern); and one of Amun (briefly depicted on the north wall), not the Valley Festival. Such festival depictions were appropriate in a temple court, and it is the second court, entered via the second pylon, that is more specifically that of the temple. Sokar, a deity of chthonic significance, actually had a bark shrine on the north side of the frontal hall, and his festival procession apparently originated in Medinet Habu itself. Min seemingly did not have such a shrine, and the elaborately developed representation of his festival has intrigued scholars as to the reason for its presence. However, a festival of Min was very important at the Luxor Temple, which was ritually and conceptually linked, in turn, to the Small Temple at Medinet Habu. Since Ramesses III and his advisors went to great pains to ensure that the Small Temple was integrated into the Medinet Habu complex, this connection with Luxor might be the reason the Min Festival is highlighted in the second court of the temple.

If the daily ritual episodes seemed a discordant theme in the first court, equally or even more discordant in the second court was a representation of the first campaign against the Libyans that occupied the lower register of the south wall (under the Sokar festival) and the south half of the east wall. This seems less appropriate to this court and perhaps was placed here because there was insufficient space for it to occupy in the first court.

Why was there repeat reference to the foreign campaigns in question (already represented on the exterior of the temple) in the temple courts? Here, one point is worth noting: while the external representations are accompanied by relatively terse inscriptions, those relating to the Libyans and the Sea Peoples in the courts include long texts with relevant historical narratives as well as extended eulogies of the king. Thus, they function partly, on a monumental scale, as illustrated written reports to the temple's deity, and they are perhaps a monumentalization of an existing custom. The latter might have involved the depositions of written reports about royal campaigns, on leather or papyrus rolls, in the archives of temples, although some consider the clearest example (dating to Thutmose III) to be unique.

Finally, the program of Medinet Habu provides some significant innovative aspects that need to be briefly noted here. The representations of wars against the foreigners, around the exterior of the temple, are laid out in long continuous registers, sometimes single ones, sometimes one above the other. This system was common in earlier temples and, in itself, is not innovative. However, within the Medinet Habu deployment of this system are some striking set pieces that involve novel elements. This is particular clear in the representation of the conflicts with the Sea Peoples on the temple's north external face. Between the end of the First Libyan War representations and a scene showing the king presenting both Libyans and Sea Peoples as prisoners to Amun, the Sea Peoples' representations extend from points equivalent to the west wall of the second hypostyle hall (fig. 6.11: 5) to the east half of the second court (fig. 6.11: 2). The vignettes making up the representations are centrally divided from each other by a striking but seemingly irrelevant depiction of a royal lion hunt. The special status of the latter is indicated not only by its context but also by its placement being equivalent to the front of the temple proper, that is, the west wall of the second court (fig. 6.11: 2). In fact, the lion hunt seems to symbolize the defeat of the Sea Peoples at Ramesses' hands and provides a symmetrical structure to the entire set of representations.

To the west side of this central scene, several episodes are depicted: preparations for war in Egypt, an advance into the Levant, and the defeat of the Sea Peoples in a land battle there. To the east of the hunt is, however, a much more unified composition, albeit one involving several successive episodes. In its upper and largest register, at the far left and right ends, the composition is framed by the king's magnificent chariot horses, both pairs facing outward so as to create a formal, symmetrical effect. Left of the right pair, a superhumanly scaled Ramesses, facing left, shoots arrows into Sea Peoples involved in a battle, in ships, with Egyptian naval forces. Right of the left pair of horses, an equally superhuman Ramesses faces right, as he receives prisoners presented to him by his officials. Overall, the formality of what is a single composition occupying the area east of the lion hunt compares strikingly with the more episodic structure of the scenes occupying the equivalent space west of the hunt. The intention seems to be to signal that the episode of the battle on water and subsequent events had a special character that marks it off from the earlier episodes.

Episodes involving a land-based campaign were traditional in content, but a waterborne conflict with foreign foes had never been recorded in Egyptian art before and perhaps also had a special quality as a highly unusual historical event. Corresponding to these observations is the compositional structure of the waterborne conflict itself, which literally depicts, in real-world yet richly symbolic terms, the ships of the enemy and their occupants descending into chaos. In the uppermost section, the enemy ships are under threat; in the middle section, one has been grappled; and in the lowest section, a completely overturned enemy vessel signals the effectiveness of Egyptian techniques, but its upside-down occupants recall the upended demons experiencing punishment in the realms of the netherworld.

The battle scenes of Medinet Habu are often compared unfavorably with the depictions of a battle at Kadesh displayed in several temples of Ramesses II. The depiction of the battle at Kadesh is unusually topographical in structure and in the fluidity of its composition. The representations at Medinet Habu are certainly more formalized than the Kadesh scenes, yet the composition discussed here is not without a certain topographical ambience. The episode of the waterborne battle evokes, if it does not literally represent, the body of water involved, while Ramesses' reception of prisoners takes place near a carefully rendered migdol (inscriptionally identified as such), which in effect forms part of a landscape.

Moreover, the depiction of animal hunts is very rare in Egyptian temple art, although it was clearly a popular motif on palace walls, furniture, and other artifacts. It is therefore something of an innovation that no less than three such hunts are depicted, on very large scales, at Medinet Habu (fig. 6.11). The lion hunt signifies the enemy Sea Peoples; a wild bull hunt, the Levantines; and a hunt of desert animals, the Libyans.

Much remains to be said about the program of Medinet Habu. It merits much more detailed analysis than it has so far received, which must be left to future occasions. Like the plan and architecture of the temple and its complex, I believe the program attests to an extraordinarily creative monument, which itself reflects the cultural strengths Egypt still manifested in the reign of Ramesses III.[16]

Notes

1. Haeny (1997) 86–90, 123–26.
2. Grandet (1993).
3. Kitchen (1972); Kitchen (2004) 245.
4. Nims (1964) 159–60.
5. Lesko (1989) 151–56.
6. Groenewegen-Frankfort (1951) 139–41.
7. Stevenson Smith (1958) 217.
8. Arnold (1992) 150.
9. Haeny (1997) 122.
10. Arnold (2005) 137.

11. Bell (1997) 179.

12. Ibid., 179.

13. Parkinson (1997) 109–10.

14. Hayes (1959) 371.

15. Murnane (1978).

16. Medinet Habu documentation: Hölscher (1934–54); Epigraphic Survey 1930–70 = *MH* I–VIII. Medinet Habu overviews: Grandet (1993) 97–141; Murnane (1978); Porter and Moss (1972) 460–527. Theban temples and festivals: Aufrère, Golvin, and Goyon (1997) 77–184 ; Badawy (1968) 225–66, 324–60; Bell (1997) 127–84; Blyth (2006); Haeny (1997) 86–126; Nims (1964). New Kingdom palaces: Lacovara (1997); O'Connor (1991) 167–98; O'Connor (1995) 263–300. Mortuary temple palaces: Kemp (2006) 351–53; Stadelmann (1973) 221–42; Uphill (1972) 721–34; Vomberg (2004) 226–70. The Eastern High Gate at Medinet Habu: Cavillier (2008); Haeny (1967) 71–78; O'Connor (2005) 439–54; Seguin (2007). Symbolism of the Egyptian temple: Arnold (1992) 40–44; Finnestad (1997) 185–237; Spence (1997); Wilkinson (2000) 54–81. Aspects of the program at Medinet Habu: van Essche-Merchez (1992) 211–39; van Essche-Merchez (1994) 87–115; O'Connor (2000) 85–102; van Essche (1979) 7–24.

Chapter 7

The Monuments of Ramesses III

BOJANA MOJSOV

Ramesses III built ambitiously and extensively. The iconography of his monuments indicates that he set out on a carefully considered program of art and ideology from the beginning of his reign; a number of images suggest that he even had himself deified before regnal year 2. In so doing, he deliberately emulated his predecessors, especially Ramesses II. He commissioned a royal tomb in the Valley of the Kings (fig. 7.1), six tombs of princes (one in the Valley of the Kings and five in the Valley of the Queens) (figs. 7.4–8),[1] the temple and palace at Medinet Habu, and two temples at Karnak (figs. 7.9–11). He also added reliefs to the temple of Khonsu at Karnak and put up statues and stelae all over Egypt.

Despite his ambitious building program, the monuments he left behind indicate that his reign was anything but prosperous. Even though contemporary inscriptions give long lists of monuments he planned to build all over Egypt (Papyrus Harris I), there is little evidence of his building activity outside the Theban area. At times he even ran out of funds: we have papyri that describe rebellion and social unrest in year 28. He encountered difficulties in completing the buildings he began—their construction was often hasty and even careless. The stone used was generally of poor quality, a rule to which even Medinet Habu, unquestionably the most ambitious of the king's projects, was no exception. Additional problems were caused by the inept employment of reused blocks of stone, seen in the Karnak Temples, where numerous pieces shifted out of place soon after the temples were built. Thus, it was shoddy construction that caused the early collapse of the temple in the precinct of Mut.[2]

Usurpation of other monuments was widely practiced: the funerary temple of Amenhotep III at Kom el-Hetan was used as a quarry for sculpture, relief, and stone blocks. The reliefs added to the temple of Khonsu employed reused blocks from the funerary temples of Thutmose IV, Amenhotep III, Amenhotep son of Hapu, Horemheb, Seti I, and Ramesses II.[3]

The sculpture displays the same disparity as the king's architecture. The inscribed sculpture lends itself to a definition of a recognizable style with some difficulty. Extensive usurpation and reworking of other people's sculpture may have contributed to artistic mediocrity and to the lack of an easily definable and inspired sculptural style. It has been noted that the two dyads facing each other in the center of the hypostyle hall of the roofed temple at Medinet Habu were usurped from Amenhotep III.[4] The colossi in front of the third pylon, of which only the feet and pedestals remain today, also exhibit reliefs done in the style of Amenhotep III, and it is likely that they, too, originally belonged to Amenhotep III. Some scholars believe that all the sculptures at Medinet Habu were taken from Amenhotep III.[5] At Karnak, the four colossal statues that stand in front of the first pylon of both temples are also reworked statues of Amenhotep III. Even the sarcophagus of Ramesses III, found in the king's tomb in the Valley of the Kings, was probably usurped from another king of the Nineteenth Dynasty, possibly Amenmesses.

In contrast to the sculpture, the relief exhibits some originality. A specific style characteristic of a workshop of artisans from Deir el-Medina is easily recognized.[6] An ostracon in the Egyptian Museum in Turin (no. 17 below) may be a sculptor's model from this workshop. Although this piece is representative of the highest quality of craftsmanship, much of the large-scale material, particularly at Karnak, did not achieve this level, suggesting that other Theban workshops of varying degrees of skill were also active at this time.

The study of the monuments leaves one with the impression of artistic incongruity. The highest achievements of this age are the temple complex at Medinet Habu and the princes' tombs, both displaying mature artistic vision and good craftsmanship. By contrast, the Karnak Temples, the royal tomb, and much of the sculpture are imitative and second-rate, leaving the impression of decline and deterioration of the arts.

It would appear that the king's ambitious building plans reflected his desire to impress his subjects and create the illusion of a prosperous reign. The results were uneven. Medinet Habu struck a final glorious note in a rapidly declining Thebes. As territories and wealth were being lost, the final fortification of Medinet Habu marked the empire closing in on itself. Ironically, the fortified gate at Medinet Habu was where the king met his end at the hands of his own family and household. His successors, all bearing the name *Ramesses*, fought for the throne and ruled briefly with ever-lessening prestige and power. As the tombs of the great kings of the New Kingdom were being looted and despoiled,[7] the empire they had conquered was falling to ruin. After the disappearance of the short-lived and shadowy Ramesses XI, the Twentieth Dynasty came to a close, and the high priest of Amun took control of Medinet Habu and the Royal Necropolis.

THE TOMB OF RAMESSES III (KV 11)

As a location for his tomb in the Valley of the Kings, Ramesses III chose a tomb[8] begun by his father, Setnakht. The latter had abandoned work on the tomb after his workmen accidentally broke through the roof of the burial chamber of a forgotten tomb while excavating the fourth corridor. The forgotten tomb, later identified as that of the deposed king Amenmesses,[9] had been left unfinished. Seeing that the descending axis of his tomb had to be moved and adjusted, Setnakht stopped the excavation and decided to usurp the tomb of Queen Tausert instead. The cartouches and inscriptions of Setnakht can still be seen in the first four corridors.[10]

Ramesses III resumed the construction of the tomb, realigning the axis of descent (fig. 7.1). The descending corridor was moved 4.50 meters to the east, and the tomb was completed at 125 meters, with an additional corridor of 15 meters extending further into the bedrock behind the burial chamber.[11]

The tomb of Ramesses III was similar to Queen Tausert's tomb in plan and layout, adding 15 meters to the length. With the addition of the side rooms in the first two corridors, the tomb became one of the largest and most elaborate of all in the royal valley. The plan followed the tradition of straight-axis tombs introduced in the royal tomb at Amarna and continued by Horemheb and Seti I. While the plan of the tomb of Ramesses II had ninety-degree angles like the earlier tombs of the Eighteenth Dynasty,[12] Merenptah reverted to the straight-axis plan that may have been inspired by the Old Kingdom pyramids. The plan was outlined following the idea that the straight axis represented the sun god's western descent into the tomb and his rising in the east.[13] The inclusion of colonnaded halls produced the effect of monumentality that enhanced the plan, adding elements of temple architecture. Introduced at Amarna, this tradition was followed in all the royal tombs of the Nineteenth and Twentieth Dynasties. In the tomb of Ramesses III, the straight axis was interrupted only to accommodate the necessary adjustments required to bypass the tomb of Amenmesses.

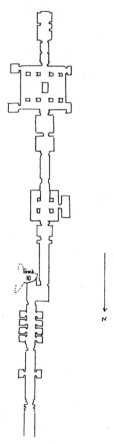

Fig. 7.1. Plan of the tomb of Ramesses III, Valley of the Kings, no. 11. (After Porter and Moss [1964] 518.)

The presence of Greek graffiti recorded by the early travelers suggests that the tomb was at least partly open and accessible since antiquity. James Bruce first drew attention to it with copies of harpists from a side room.[14] From 1893 to 1895, the tomb was partially cleared, the stairs excavated, and the doorway closed with an iron gate by the Service des Antiquities. The section at the entrance is now partly covered by modern steps.

Although the decoration is "not of the best style," in Belzoni's words, the tomb is monumental and in many ways as complete as the king's temple at Medinet Habu.[15] In the first corridor, Ramesses III is represented facing Horus, the god of the Western Mountain, who escorts him to the kingdom of his father, Osiris. Behind this scene begin the introductory verses of the Litany of Ra. On the left wall, the texts are facing in, going into the tomb, while on the opposite wall, they are facing out, "stepping forth" from the tomb.

The first two descending corridors have five parallel chapels on each side. The corridors were excavated by Setnakht, but the nichelike side chambers (each with a pit of uncertain purpose)[16] were probably added by Ramesses III, because their entrances were cut through the finished inscriptions on the corridor walls.[17] It was then that the fourth corridor, which had penetrated into the adjacent tomb of Amenmesses, was transformed into a small room with a high floor that turned 4.50 meters to the east. The fifth corridor descends to a very small and shallow well room without a shaft[18] and to a pillared hall[19] with a side chamber.[20] The sixth corridor descends to two anterooms and the burial chamber, where the sarcophagus originally stood along the tomb's main axis. Like in the tomb of Merenptah, the four side rooms of the burial chamber were placed symmetrically at the corners.[21] A corridor behind the burial chamber extends the length of the tomb for another 15 meters.[22]

The first three corridors, decorated by Setnakht, have representations of the Litany of Ra. In the third corridor and the well, there are images of the king facing various deities on his journey through the netherworld. The fourth corridor was decorated with texts from the fourth and fifth hours of the *Amduat,* the pillared hall with scenes and texts from the *Book of Gates.*[23] Before the anterooms and the burial chamber, there are two representations of the ceremony of "Opening the Mouth for Breathing." The burial chamber has scenes from the *Book of Gates* and excerpts from the *Book of the Heavenly Cow.*[24] There are no astronomical decorations on the ceiling. The burial chamber has suffered from water damage, no doubt because of the shallowness of the well.[25] On the back wall are two representations of the Judgment of Osiris. The corridor behind the burial chamber has three niches on one side and two on the other. Gods of the netherworld are represented on their back walls; the back wall of the last niche has an illustration of the expulsion of Seth turned into a pig after the Judgment of Osiris.[26] The placement of this scene is unique.

Though monumental in its proportions, the tomb has a low overall descent, and the extreme shallowness of the well (the deepest chamber in other royal tombs) leaves the impression of an ornamental plan that mechanically copied other royal tombs. The same is true of the corridor behind the sarcophagus chamber, an element dramatically introduced in the tomb of Seti I, where this passage extends some 136 meters further into the bedrock and descends 100 meters below the tomb entrance; here in Ramesses' tomb, the corridor has no descent and is mostly ornamental.

Although following in the footsteps of other great royal tombs, both the architecture and the decoration leave the impression of a dutifully pious, rather than profoundly religious, experience. However, the content of the reliefs is exceptionally varied, with unique secular scenes in the side chambers, including representations of bakers, cooks, butchers, sailing boats, blind harpists (popularized by Bruce), and many luxury objects, some of them imports from the Aegean.[27] The four pilasters with Hathor heads at the entrance are also unique.

No dates are given anywhere in the tomb. Abitz tries to date the inscriptions by distinguishing four variants of writing the king's cartouches.[28] The first two appear consistently in the corridors; the other two are found in the pillared hall and in the burial chamber. However, any definitive conclusions are complicated by the fact that in the princes' tombs, all the four variants are often written side by side.

After the tomb was completed, wooden doors were installed at the entrance. While serving as protection against illicit entry, the doors could also be opened for routine inspections by the Medjay, the special police corps entrusted with guarding the royal tombs. An ostracon in the Cairo Museum (25553, recto 4) refers to a possible inspection of the tomb in the king's regnal year 12, while another mentions the visit of the Medjay in regnal year 16.[29]

References to the tomb and to the king's burial are useful in helping us discover details about the assassination plot against the king and his death some three weeks later. The evidence gathered by Schaedel[30] and Černý[31] has been supplemented by Goedicke,[32] who quoted lines from the Lee and Rollin papyri (two fragments of the same scroll), Papyrus Turin 1949+1846, and Papyrus Harris 1, in the aim of establishing the cause of the king's death and the date of his funeral. The first date given in the papyri is regnal year 32, 2nd of Shemu, day 15—the day of the Feast of the Valley and of the execution of the plot against Ramesses III. The next date, 2nd of Shemu, day 29, probably refers to the opening of the tomb of Ramesses III in anticipation of his death. The date of the death of Ramesses III is given as 3rd of Shemu, day 6. The announcement to the workmen of the necropolis is mentioned on the 3rd of Shemu, day 16, in the following way: "One said: 'The Falcon has flown to the sky.'" The Turin Papyrus records the same day as the date of accession of Ramesses IV. On the 1st of *akhet*, day 4, the tomb equipment reached "the Great Field"—the necropolis.[33] The king's burial is recorded on the same ostracon on day 24. All the evidence implies that Ramesses III died less than three weeks after the assassination attempt and that he was buried shortly after the completion of the traditional seventy-day period for embalming.

FINDS FROM THE TOMB

The principal find from the tomb was the king's red granite sarcophagus, placed in the middle of the burial chamber. Costaz, a member of the French commission, records finding the box and notes the absence of the lid.[34] The enterprising Belzoni had taken the lid from the tomb and sent it to Alexandria. From there, it was shipped to Europe by Athanasi, who writes that Belzoni had broken the piece in two while removing it from the tomb.[35] The box was sold to the king of France and eventually went to the Louvre in Paris. Eventually, the Fitzwilliam Museum in Cambridge acquired the upper part of the lid.[36] The lower fragment is still missing.[37] The lid is better preserved than the box, "owing to it being reversed"[38]—that is, lying on its back in the ground. It had been forced open in antiquity.

The box is inscribed with texts from the *Book of Gates,* and the lid is decorated with the figure of the king as Osiris in high relief (fig. 7.2). Both the iconography of the figure on the lid[39] and the texts on the box suggest that the sarcophagus was made in the Nineteenth Dynasty. The analysis of the texts by Dodson implies that they were closer in date to Merenptah than to Siptah and Tausert, who preceded Ramesses III.[40] Two kings ruled between Merenptah and Siptah—Amenmesses and Seti II. It seems that Amenmesses preceded Seti II, because an alabaster sphinx in the hypostyle hall at Karnak has the cartouches of Seti II imposed over those of Amenmesses.[41] The head of the sphinx is now in the Metropolitan Museum of Art (34.2.2). The reign of Amenmesses seems to be rather short.[42] We have no certain dates of his rule. The only sizable monument he left is his unfinished tomb in the Valley of the Kings—the same tomb that collided with the tomb of Ramesses III.

From a relief at Medinet Habu, we know that Ramesses III considered Amenmesses a usurper. In the second court of the Great Temple there is a representation of royal statues of those Nineteenth Dynasty kings whom Ramesses III considered as his legitimate predecessors.[43] On this relief, Merenptah is immediately followed by Seti II, while Amenmesses, Siptah, and Queen Tausert have been excluded, although they are known to have ruled for a total of nearly twenty years and left large tombs in the Valley of the Kings. It has also been recorded that Ramesses III usurped inscriptions of Amenmesses in the New Kingdom temple at Amara West in Sudan.[44]

The image on the lid is different from any other sculpture of Ramesses III, and it is almost certain that the sarcophagus was made for another king. The accessibility of the tomb of Amenmesses and the similarity of the face on the sarcophagus lid to the head of Amenmesses in the Metropolitan Museum of

Fig. 7.2. Head on the sarcophagus lid from the tomb of Ramses III, Cambridge, Fitzwilliam Museum, E. 1.1823. (B.V. Bothmer Archive, courtesy of N. J. Bothmer.)

Art (fig. 7.3) suggest that the sarcophagus may have originally belonged to Amenmesses.

Other finds from the tomb include five shawabtis solid cast in bronze, two in the Louvre and three in the British Museum, Museo Egizio in Turin, and the Oriental Museum in Durham.[45] Daressy discovered the badly damaged coffin box of Ramesses III in the tomb of Amenhotep II. The box of Ramesses III was covered by the lid of the coffin of Seti II. It contained the mummy of Amenhotep III.

The mummy of Ramesses III was found together with other royal mummies in the cache tomb at Deir el-Bahari, where it had been reburied during

Fig. 7.3. Statue head of Amenmesses, Metropolitan Museum of Art, 34.2.2. (Courtesy of the Metropolitan Museum of Art.)

the Third Intermediate Period. Inscriptions on the mummy bandages confirmed the king's re-"Osirification."[46] The mummy was deposited together with that of Ahmose Nefertari in the queen's large wooden coffin. The mummy of Ramesses III is now in the Egyptian Museum in Cairo. It has not been visibly damaged. The human remains found in the royal tomb seem to be of Third Intermediate Period date and unrelated to the king.

TOMBS OF PRINCES (KV 3; QV 42, 43, 44, 53, 55)

Traces of the names of Ramesses III are still visible in the first corridor of tomb no. 3, located immediately to the east of the modern entrance to the

Valley of the Kings. The tomb is distinguished by its nonroyal plan. It consists of two corridors, a pillared hall with a side room on the north side, and two anterooms leading to a vaulted sarcophagus chamber. Like tomb no. 11, it has a shallow descent.[47] The reliefs have perished entirely, though in the 1840s, Lepsius described the painted decoration on the ceiling of the burial chamber and in the first corridor.[48] In the Coptic period, the tomb was used as a hermit's retreat, a chapel, and a stable. The painted walls have suffered from flood damage and fire.

The tomb was discovered by James Burton and subsequently cleared by Harry Burton. It yielded no finds, which suggests that it never contained a burial. The most likely owner of this tomb is found on Berlin ostracon P10063. This text records that a group of workmen "founded the tomb of a prince of His Majesty in year 28 of Ramesses III."[49] The location of this tomb in the vicinity of the royal tomb may point to a special position enjoyed by the prince.[50] One of the ancient graffiti in the tomb, recorded by Champollion, mentions the name of Butehamun, the necropolis scribe, who directed the "re-Osirification" of Ramesses III in year 13 of Pinnodjem I.[51]

An ostracon in the Oriental Institute of Chicago, also dated to year 28 of Ramesses III, records the commissioning of the princes' tombs in the Valley of the Queens.[52] Five of these tombs have been discovered on the southwestern side of the main wadi. Schiaparelli excavated four between 1903 and 1920.[53] The fifth was found in 1958 by the joint Mission Franco-Egyptienne.[54] Five tombs excavated thus far belong to the following princes: QV 44—Khaemwaset (fig. 7.4); 55—Amunhorhepeshef (fig. 7.5); 43—Seth-horhepeshef (fig. 7.6); 42—Paraherwemenef (fig. 7.7); 53—Ramesses (fig. 7.8).

Schiaparelli found at least forty coffins with mummies and funerary equipment from the Twenty-second Dynasty in the tombs of Khaemwaset and Seth-horhepeshef. These tombs must have been easily accessible in antiquity. Evidence of recarving can be seen in the tomb of Paraherwemenef, where a scene of an unknown queen standing before Osiris had been added at a later date.[55] Yoyotte also recorded some recarving in the tomb of prince Ramesses.[56] Both additions probably took place during the Third Intermediate Period and were not related to the burial of the princes.

The reliefs are well preserved only in the tombs of Khaemwaset and Amunhorhepeshef. They are in excellent condition, the colors still bright and vibrant. Distinguished by elegant style and masterful workmanship, they are regarded as the great masterpieces of the Twentieth Dynasty.

Only the tomb of Khaemwaset is completely finished. The name of the prince is the same as that of the famous son of Ramesses II, as is the title,

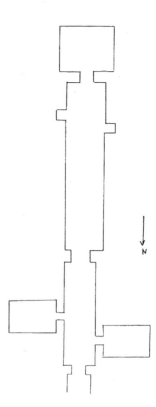

Fig. 7.4. Plan of the tomb of Khaemwaset, Valley
of the Queens, no. 44. (After Porter and Moss
[1964] 752.)

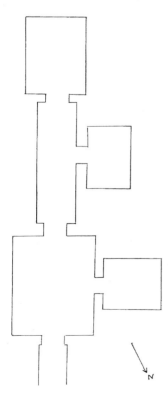

Fig. 7.5. Plan of the tomb of Amunhorhepeshef,
Valley of the Queens, no. 55. (After Porter and
Moss [1964] 752.)

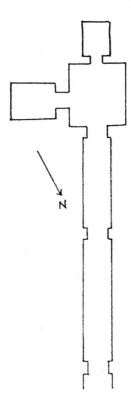

Fig. 7.6. Plan of the tomb of Seth-horhepeshef, Valley of the Queens, no. 43. (After Porter and Moss [1964] 759.)

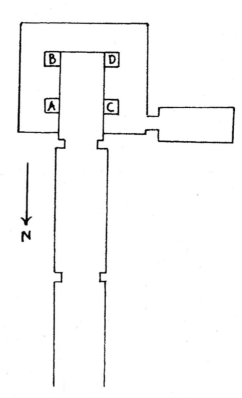

Fig. 7.7. Plan of the tomb of Paraherwemenef, Valley of the Queens, no. 42. (After Porter and Moss [1964] 759.)

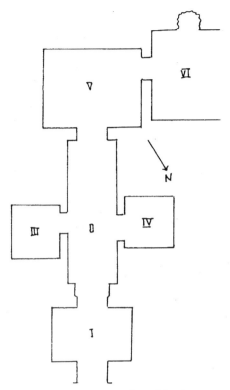

Fig. 7.8. Plan of the tomb of Ramesses, Valley of the Queens, no. 53. (After Porter and Moss [1964] 761.)

"*sem*-priest of Ptah." The plan of the tomb consists of an inclined corridor with two asymmetrical side rooms that descend to a rectangular sarcophagus chamber. Only a fragment of a sarcophagus lid was found here (Turin 5216), along with two canopic jars (Cairo JE 4085a and b). The sarcophagus fragment is inscribed with a cartouche of Ramesses IV—Khaemwaset was probably buried during the reign of this king.

The tomb of Amunhorhepeshef was clear of sarcophagi and debris when found. It is unfinished—only the first chamber and corridor are decorated with relief. The titles of the prince found in the tomb are "royal scribe" and "master of the horse"; an inscription in the first corridor also gives the title "hereditary prince."[57] The plan of the tomb is simple and straightforward. An inclined corridor follows a wide, rectangular room, leading to a small sarcophagus chamber. Two side rooms seem to be later additions.[58] Schiaparelli found a red granite sarcophagus in the tomb in 1904, but it disappeared soon after its discovery.[59]

The tombs of Khaemwaset and Amunhorhepeshef appear to have been built in succession. This is suggested by the complementary sequence of the names of gods dwelling in the fields of Iaru, known from chapter 145 of the *Book of the Dead*. The mummies of Khaemwaset and Amunhorhepeshef were found in the cache tomb at Deir el-Bahari.

Schiaparelli recorded finding no evidence that the tomb of Seth-horhepeshef had been used for burial until later in the Twenty-third and Twenty-fourth Dynasties.[60] The plan of this tomb is similar to the tomb of Khaemwaset. A long corridor descends into a central rectangular chamber with two side rooms. The reliefs are badly damaged. The titles of the prince are "royal scribe" and "charioteer of the great stable."[61]

The tomb of Paraherwemenef is immediately adjacent. This tomb has an inclined corridor leading to a chamber with four pillars and a side chapel. A red granite sarcophagus was found broken into several fragments in situ between the columns (Turin 5435). Both the reliefs and the inscriptions on the sarcophagus have been interpreted as those of a queen.[62] The addition of a female figure on the east wall of the sarcophagus chamber also suggests that an unknown queen usurped the tomb during the Third Intermediate Period.

Only two decorations remain in the tomb of Ramesses—figures of Nephthys in the first corridor and of Anubis in the sarcophagus chamber. A fragment of an inscription enabled Yoyotte to identify the owner as Ramesses. The titles of the prince are not known. The tomb has a rectangular plan followed by a corridor with two square chapels on either side. It leads to a rectangular room with a small sarcophagus chamber on the west side.

There is no uniformity of plan in the princes' tombs—each one is slightly different from the other. According to Abitz, all the side rooms were later additions, judging by the surface of the plaster where they join the corridor.[63] This excludes the possibility that the tombs were made after the princes had died, since it would leave no time for corrections and additions. The masterful reliefs as well as traces of reworking of the surface finish in QV 42, 43, and 55 indicate that considerable time and attention were devoted to them. This would have been possible only during the king's lifetime.

The relief representations and the inscriptions identify the princes with the sons of Horus, the living king. It is Ramesses III who leads them past the gates of the underworld and faces the gods on their behalf—a task usually performed by a god rather than a living ruler. The theme of the king's sacredness is reiterated once more. It seems that the princes' tombs fulfilled a function in the cult of Ramesses III.

Abitz explains the lack of decoration in the side rooms by the simple, straightforward religious program that was fulfilled in the corridors and the sarcophagus chamber.[64] It is also possible that since the side rooms were later additions, no time was left to decorate them—after the king's death, all work on the tombs was probably abandoned. Except for the tomb of Khaemwaset, none of the tombs were used for burial at the time.

On a relief at the temple of Medinet Habu, thirteen sons of Ramesses III are represented in procession on two sides of a doorway. All the princes bear the common title of "standard-bearer to the right of the king." At some later date, personal names and other titles were added in front of the first ten figures, providing duplicate lists of ten princes. The names of the first four princes were enclosed in cartouches, and royal *uraei* were added to their brows. The remaining six princes were given titles and names but neither cartouches nor *uraei*. Eight of them have the prenomen *Ramesses* and two the name *Amunhorhepeshef*.

In the north temple at Karnak, two princes are shown behind Ramesses III as part of the procession of the festival of Min. Their names are Ramesses and Amunhorhepeshef, respectively. The same two names are found on some other monuments. A door lintel in Florence has the name of Prince Ramesses with the same unusual military title as the first figure in the Medinet Habu procession. A fragment of a stele found by Bruyère at Deir el-Medina has an image of a boy with the side-lock of youth and the inscription "Hereditary Prince Amunhor."[65] In a chapel at Deir el-Medina dedicated to Ptah, Bruyère found another fragment of a stele giving the name and title "Amunhorhepeshef, Hereditary Prince."[66]

It is tempting to identify Prince Ramesses with Ramesses IV and Prince Amunhorhepeshef with Ramesses VI, as the latter king is called Amunhorhepeshef and seems to be the son of Queen Isis. The title "hereditary prince," however, implies that Amunhorhepeshef was older than Ramesses. Furthermore, the mummy of a prince called Amunhorhepeshef was found in the royal cache tomb at Deir el-Bahari. Thus, it is not entirely clear who is who at the end of the Twentieth Dynasty, and the identity of the successors of Ramesses III remains one of the more hotly debated subjects in Egyptology.

The father of Ramesses III, Setnakht, ruled for at least two years.[67] Queen Tiy Mereniset seems to be the mother of Ramesses III.[68] She is represented seated behind Setnakht on a stele in Cairo (no. 13 below) and with Ramesses III on two blocks from Abydos (no. 14 below). There are no titles next to her cartouche.

The length of the reign of Ramesses III is recorded on Papyrus Harris I and the Lee and Rollin papyri—the king died shortly after the celebration of the annual festival of Amun in his thirty-second regnal year.[69] Queen Isis was a wife of Ramesses III. She is represented on the side of the eastern colossus in the precinct of Mut and is the owner of tomb no. 51 in the Valley of the Queens, where she is called "mother of the great king." Since the tomb was built as "a favor of King Ramesses VI," it seems to follow that she was his mother and that she was buried during his reign.[70]

Judging by the last paragraph of Papyrus Harris I, there is no doubt that Ramesses IV succeeded Ramesses III. The length of his reign is recorded on Turin Papyrus 2070 as six years. He may be identical with the first figure in the Medinet Habu procession and possibly also with Prince Ramesses of QV 53. Although seven more kings called Ramesses ruled after Ramesses IV, it is not clear if and how they were related to the princes represented in the procession at Medinet Habu and mentioned on the other monuments.

THE NORTH TEMPLE, KARNAK

It was Legrain who first cleared the two temples built by Ramesses III at Karnak in the 1890s.[71] Chevrier continued the excavation and reconstruction of the north temple (fig. 7.9), publishing the records in 1933. The reliefs in both temples were documented by the Epigraphic Survey of the Oriental Institute of Chicago in 1936.[72]

The north temple was built opposite the three chapels of Seti II in the first court of the temple of Karnak. Seti's chapels were repository stations for the barks of Amun, Mut, and Khonsu, carried in procession during the annual festival, in and out of the inner temples of Amun, Mut, and Khonsu. This may have been the place where the barks came together before leaving the temple of Karnak. The temple of Ramesses III was an enlarged replica of Seti's structure, adding three more chapels on the other side of the court. It served the same purpose as the building of Seti II, providing a place of repose for the processions carrying the sacred barks. Possibly one building was used on the way out and the other on the return. Both were associated with rites related to the annual festival of Amun, "the beautiful Feast of the Valley," when the divine barks left the sacred precinct in order to visit other Theban temples.

At this time, the facade of the temple of Karnak was the pylon built by Ramesses I, now the second pylon. The buildings of Seti II and Ramesses III were originally outside the temple walls, set perpendicular to the pylon and to the main axis of the Karnak Temple. While the structure of Seti II was small, the much larger temple of Ramesses III spoiled the symmetry and ob-

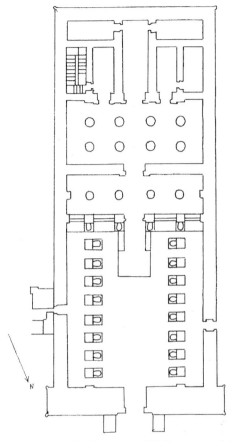

Fig. 7.9. Plan of the temple of Ramesses III, first court of the Amun temple, Karnak. (After Porter and Moss [1972] plan VII.)

scured the view of the pylon. This may have prompted the building of another court around the two temples, as well as the addition of one more pylon in the Twenty-second Dynasty.

The north temple was designed as a small replica of standard New Kingdom temples. It contained all the traditional elements except for the sanctuary, as the divine barks only passed through it once a year. The two colossal statues in front of the first pylon were probably usurped from Amenhotep III. The preserved head on the eastern statue exhibits the features of this king.

The upper part of the pylon is missing, and it is not entirely clear if it consisted of a straight top or two piers; Chevrier suggests two possible reconstructions.[73] A single wooden door was hinged on the right side. The pylon leads to a court with Osiride pillars on the north and south sides, with red and white crowns, respectively. The back of the court also has Osiride pillars, two with the red crown on the north and two with the white crown on the south. Short screen walls connect the four pillars, with a cornice and a frieze of *uraei* at the top. They seem to be later additions, since they cover the inscriptions written on the sides of the pillars.

Through the portico, one enters the hypostyle hall with eight columns, leading to three chapels in the back. The central chapel is the largest. It has two subsidiary rooms in the back without any decoration. They may have been used for storage. All three chapels have repository stones for the sacred barks. The doorway lights the central chapel; the two side chapels have clerestory windows.

The ceiling is built in three levels. The highest is above the portico and the hypostyle hall. It is somewhat lower in the central chapel of Amun and still lower in the two flanking chapels. A staircase adjacent to the eastern chapel provides access to the roof.

The temple is built of sandstone from Gebel Silsilah, except for the door lintel of the pylon, made of granite. Many aspects of the construction show signs of hastiness. The stone blocks are not of the same thickness and are often repaired with smaller pieces. The joins are irregular both horizontally and vertically. Holes in the masonry were sometimes mended with plaster that fell off shortly after the temple's completion.[74] As a result, many blocks shifted out of place.

All the walls were originally painted—the colors can still be seen at the top. On the outside walls, inscriptions were painted with yellow to suggest gold. Because of crevices in the masonry, figures on adjacent blocks often do not fit exactly. These lacunae may have been filled with plaster and the reliefs amended in paint when the temple was newly finished. Some reliefs show signs of alterations, and as the plaster has fallen off, the original and the alteration overlap. It is not always clear why changes were made. For example, a scene of the coronation of Ramesses III by Amun shows two different positions of the god's arm. It is difficult to determine which of the two drawings was primary and which secondary. The single war scene of Ramesses III in battle with the Syrians exhibits numerous corrections. The inscription is copied from Seti I. Even though it refers to the king's Syrian campaign, the foremost captive is a Libyan, while the captive in the middle wears a Syrian garment combined with a Libyan penis sheath.[75]

Four dates are recorded in the temple. Three mark the king's gift of cult objects to the temple of Amun in year 20, and the fourth mentions the pres-

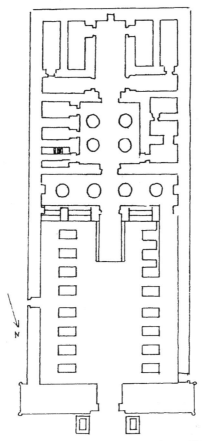

Fig. 7.10. Plan of the temple of Ramesses III, precinct of Mut, Karnak. (After Porter and Moss [1972] plan XXIV.)

entation of a tablet of precious metal in year 22. The metal tablet is also mentioned in Papyrus Harris I.[76]

THE SOUTH TEMPLE, PRECINCT OF MUT

Pillet published the excavation and reconstruction of the south temple (fig. 7.10) in 1922. Like the north temple, it was dedicated to the Theban triad as well as the cult of Amun in the form of Amun-Ra-Kamutef. The temple was made of sandstone, but unlike in the north temple, where newly carved stone was used, all the blocks were reused and recarved. The reliefs have suffered almost complete destruction.

The south temple was approximately of the same size and plan as the north. A pylon with two colossal statues led to a court with eight Osiride pillars. A ramp ascended through a doorway to a portico and hypostyle hall with three chapels in the back. Just like in the north temple, the eastern chapel had a staircase that led to the roof. Almost all of the walls are now badly destroyed. Pillet recovered only fragments of the original construction and rebuilt two colossal statues flanking the first pylon from fallen pieces, but only up to shoulder level. The head of the eastern colossus is now in the Boston Museum of Fine Arts (no. 10 below). Judging by the style, these statues were also usurped from Amenhotep III.

No dates are found anywhere in the south temple. The only preserved reliefs on the exterior west wall represent the king in triumph at the end of the Libyan war of year 11. They were copied from Medinet Habu.[77] It is possible that the temple was built some time during the king's second decade of rule, not long after the completion of the Medinet Habu relief. Other surviving reliefs on the west wall were copied from the southern enclosure wall of the Karnak Temple.[78] They represent Ramesses II and the battle of Kadesh. The sculptors did not notice that the inscription they were copying referred to the famous single-handed battle of Ramesses II against the Hittites and could have no possible application to any achievement of Ramesses III. Thus, monuments of Ramesses II were copied even when inappropriate.

RELIEFS IN THE TEMPLE OF KHONSU, KARNAK

The temple of Khonsu (fig. 7.11) was probably begun during the reign of Amenhotep III.[79] It was built from back to front. Ramesses III added reliefs as far as the hypostyle hall, decorating three of the side rooms and the chapel of the sacred bark. Although newly quarried stone was used in some of the rooms, much of the material was taken from other buildings. The earliest reused block dates to the reign of Thutmose IV—it forms part of the lintel over the east doorway in the hypostyle hall.[80] Other blocks from the Eighteenth Dynasty, usurped from Amenhotep III and Horemheb, are found in the forecourt and on the south doorway of the hypostyle hall.[81] Columns in the courtyard were made of several drums usurped from the funerary temple of Horemheb that once stood to the north of Medinet Habu. On a column in the forecourt (easternmost row, third from the south), two cartouches of Horemheb can still be seen.[82] Blocks of Ramesses II have been reused in the portico on the north side of the forecourt and in the hypostyle hall.[83]

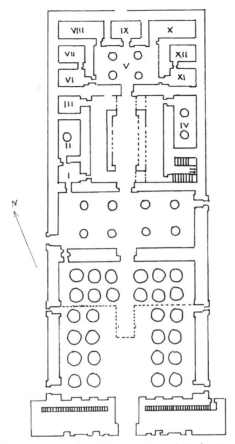

Fig. 7.11. Plan of the temple of Khonsu, Karnak. (After Porter and Moss [1972] plan XXI.)

Reliefs usurped from Amenhotep III probably come from the king's funerary temple at Kom el-Hetan.[84] Over forty-eight of them have been added all over the temple—they represent the Heb Sed Festival of Amenhotep III, celebrated in year 30 of his reign.

The temple of Khonsu was completed by the high priest of Amun, Herihor. Official dedications on the architrave attribute the building to Ramesses XI in accordance with conventional form, maintained since the Old Kingdom. Around the base of the walls, however, we find the name of Herihor accompanied by the titles "commander in chief of the armies of the south and north, viceroy of Kush, overseer of the double granary," indicating that he was by far the most important figure in the kingdom. Finally, traces of the last Ramesside king disappear about twenty-seven years after the death of Ramesses III. The high priest's supreme position was confirmed by an oracle at the temple of Khonsu, which was followed by an approval of Amun.

This event is recorded in an inscription written in the thickness of the doorway that leads from the inner hall of the roofed temple to the outer forecourt, the final addition to the temple of Khonsu. On the architrave of the forecourt, the name of the high priest stands alone enclosed in a royal cartouche. As was the case with Medinet Habu across the river, a building of Ramesses III served as a witness for the most significant political changes in Thebes long after his death.

OTHER BUILDINGS AND RELIEFS

Ramesses III added eight reliefs, which represent him offering to the gods, to the north facade of the eighth pylon at Karnak, built by Hatshepsut and Thutmose III. He also dedicated three reliefs in the rock-cut chapels at Deir el-Medina to the goddess Meret Seger of the Western Mountain, "she who loves silence." Chapels B and C each contain one stele; the lintel of the door to chapel D has an additional relief. [85]

Outside of the Theban area, there is little evidence of the king's building activity. The base of a pylon of a small temple still remains at Edfu. Although Papyrus Harris I mentions temples in the Delta, we can find only scant traces of them. Petrie found two statues with the cartouches of Ramesses III near the "Hyksos monuments" at Tanis. [86] He also found remains of a fortification, similar in plan to the fortified gate at Medinet Habu and possibly dating to Ramesses III, at Tell el-Yahudeya. [87]

STATUES

The sculpture of Ramesses III follows several traditions of the New Kingdom. From a stylistic point of view, it displays outstanding diversity and reflects the eclecticism of the age. While the extensively usurped statues of Amenhotep III inevitably recall the Eighteenth Dynasty, the favorite model for the original sculpture is the late work of Ramesses II. The colossal statues of this king—with broad faces, high crowns, and massive legs that create the impression of physical mass and strength—are imitated on every scale. Such is the almost life-size standard-bearing statue in Philadelphia (no. 5 below), stylistically the most notable piece among the inscribed sculpture. The

Osiride colossi at Medinet Habu have the king's name written in the form of a rebus, just like on the sculpture of the deified Ramesses II.[88]

The motif of the large scarab carved in high relief on top of the king's head on the cult statue from Almaza (no. 8) is found on four other royal statues, all of them Ramesside.[89] It may be related to a cult of the deified king practiced in the Ramesside period. The magical inscriptions on this statue are similar to those on the Wilbour Papyrus.[90] The formula intended to protect against scorpion bites is also found on Horus Zippus stelae of the Late Period. This statue may be a forerunner of the healing statues of the Late Period.

The sculpture of Ramesses III is the last to employ the technique of inlayed eyes in the New Kingdom (no. 6). Based on this stylistic detail as well as on the similarity of the facial features, I have attributed an unidentified head from Abydos (no. 14) to Ramesses III. The attribution of the other four sculptures without inscription (nos. 13, 15, 16 and 17) is based both on provenance and on stylistic similarities to the inscribed sculpture.

Inscribed Sculpture

1. Statue group with Horus and Seth. Cairo, Egyptian Museum, CG 629
Red granite, height: 1.69 m
From Medinet Habu

Only the fragments seen on Borchardt's pl. 116 are ancient. The feet, part of the base, and the upper part of the face have been restored. This is the only example of a coronation scene represented in the round.

Bibliography: Bissing (1914) no. 55, n. 1; Maspéro (1915) 78; Borchardt (1936) 176–77, pl. 116; Roeder (1960) pl. 5; Hornemann (1966) pl. 1365; Porter and Moss (1972) 526; *KRI* V.296; Aldred (1979a) 195; van Dam (1988) 34.

2. Standard-bearing statue, Cairo, Egyptian Museum, CG 42150
Gray granite, height: 1.40 m
Found in the Karnak Cachette in 1904

According to the inscriptions on the standard, the statue was dedicated in the temple of Karnak on the occasion of the annual festival of Amun. It may have stood in the north temple of Ramesses III.

Bibliography: Legrain (1906) 14–15; Maspéro (1915) 182, 183 (no. 674); Jequier (1933) 15, fig. 21; Leibovitch (1938) 39, fig. 27; Hornemann (1951), no. 199; Müller (1961) pl. 156; Porter and Moss (1972) 142; *KRI* V.287; Chadefaud (1982) 69; Saleh (1987) 225.

3. Bust, Boston, Museum of Fine Arts, 29.733
Red granite, height: 0.46 m
Provenance not known
Bibliography: None

4. Head, Strasbourg, Collection Universite de Strasbourg, 986
Brown quartzite, height: 0.15 m
Bought in Luxor in 1898, said to be from Karnak

Bibliography: Spiegelberg (1909) 12–13, fig. 5 on pl. IX; Buecher and Leclant (1956) 106; Porter and Moss (1972) 292.

5. Standard-bearing statue, Philadelphia, University Museum, E 15727
Yellow-brown limestone, height: 1.25 m
Provenance not known

The lion-headed standard is that of the goddess Mut, and the inscription on the standard refers to the king as "Great of Heb Seds." This statue may have been dedicated in the south temple of Ramesses III in the precinct of Mut on the occasion of the king's Heb Sed Festival, celebrated in year 29.

Bibliography: Ranke (1950) 54, fig. 31; Vandier (1958) 400, 406, 408–9, 411, 420–21, pl. CXXX (6); Monnet (1965) 231; Chadefaud (1982) 67–68.

6. Striding statue, Cairo, Egyptian Museum, CG 1104
Red granite, height: 1.30 m
Provenance not known

This is the last inscribed statue to employ the technique of inlayed eyes in the New Kingdom.

Bibliography: Borchardt (1936) 58, pl. 162; Vandier (1958) 401, n. 3.

7. Seated statue, Jerusalem, Rockefeller Archaeological Museum, PAM 2
Gray basalt, height: 1.48 m
From Beth Shahn, found outside the north temple of Ramesses III

The statue was found in fragments during the excavation of the University of Pennsylvania and restored to its present state.

Bibliography: Rowe (1930) 51; Rowe (1940) 29, pl. iii; Porter and Moss (1951) 379; *KRI* V.251.

8. Seated group, Cairo, Egyptian Museum, JE 69771
Red quartzite, height: 1.55 m
From Almaza near Heliopolis

The small chapel where the statue was found seems to have been a shrine on the caravan route leading to Canaan. The group is inscribed on the base with ten magical formulae intended to offer protection against snake and scorpion bites as well as other perils of the desert journey. The king has a figure of a scarab on top of the head, explained in the seventh magical formula, where he is identified with Khepri. This statue was deliberately destroyed in antiquity.

Bibliography: Drioton (1939) 57–89; *KRI* V.261–68; Bianchi (1988) no. 99.

9. Standard-bearing colossus, Cairo, Egyptian Museum, CG 42149
Pink granite, height: 3.80 m; crown (since removed): 0.98 m
From the Karnak Cachette

The inscriptions on the standard call Ramesses "Great of Heb Seds like his father Amun." This statue seems to have been dedicated in the temple of Amun on the occasion of the king's Heb Sed in year 29. It is modeled on similar colossi of Ramesses II, such as Cairo CG 42754, 42755, and 42668, all eventually stored in the Karnak Cachette. The colossal size of the statue suggests that it stood in an open court, possibly in front of the eighth pylon, to which the king made some additions.

Bibliography: Daressy (1902) 10 (no.7); Legrain (1906) 14, pl. XII; Vandier (1958) 401, pl. CXXXI (1); Barguet (1962) 272, n. 1 on p. 279; Vandier (1963) 156, n. 16; Porter and Moss (1972) 142; Chadefaud (1982) 65.

Usurped Sculpture

10. Colossal head, Boston, Museum of Fine Arts, 75.10
Red granite, height: 0.62 m
From the eastern colossus, south temple, precinct of Mut

This head is in the style of the late Eighteenth Dynasty. It was probably usurped from Amenhotep III.

Bibliography: Nelson et al. (1936) pls. 79, 124; Vandier (1958) 402, 615, pl. CXXX (2); Černý (1958b) 31; Porter and Moss (1972) 273.

11. Head from a group, Cairo, Egyptian Museum, JE 54477
Pink granite, height: 0.70 m
From Medinet Habu, third hypostyle hall

It has been noted that the inscriptions on the back slab of the lower part of the statue, in the third hypostyle hall at Medinet Habu, have been erased and reinscribed for Ramesses III.[91] The head in Cairo has the facial features of Amenhotep III, somewhat reworked around the eyes.

Bibliography: *Medinet Habu* VII (1964) pls. 483, 484, preface; Hornemann (1957) pl. 368; Porter and Moss (1972) 512.

12. Sarcophagus lid, Cambridge, Fitzwilliam Museum, E. 1.1823
Red granite, Length: 2.99 m
From the tomb of Ramesses III, no. 11, Valley of the Kings

Judging by the inscriptions on the box (Louvre D1) as well as by the iconography and style of the sculpture on the lid, the sarcophagus was originally made for a king of the Nineteenth Dynasty. It is stylistically similar to the head of Amenmesses in the Metropolitan Museum of Art (34.2.2).

Bibliography: Athanasi (1836) 52; Budge (1893) 1–4; Aldred (1961) 58; Porter and Moss (1964) 526; Dodson (1986) 196–98.

Sculpture Attributed to Ramesses III

13. Bust, Cairo, Egyptian Museum, CG 601
Gray granite, height: 0.50 m
From Medinet Habu?
This face of this sculpture is similar to the Osiride colossi at Medinet Habu.

Bibliography: Petrie (1925) 376, fig. 155; Murray (1930) 167–68, pl. XLIV (4); Borchardt (1936) 153, pl. 108.

14. Head, Cairo, Egyptian Museum, CG 599
Gray granite, height: 0.25 m
Abydos, south section

This statue has the same headdress as the standard-bearing statue from the Karnak Cachette (no. 2) and inlayed eyes like the striding statue (no. 6), the last to employ this technique in the New Kingdom.

Bibliography: Borchardt (1936) 151–52, pl. 108.

15. Statue of the king as Geb, Cairo, Egyptian Museum, CG 38234
Terra-cotta, height: 1.16 m
Found under the floor of room 46 at Medinet Habu

The provenance of this statue suggests its attribution to Ramesses III. The broad face is similar to the standard-bearing statue in Philadelphia (no. 5).

Bibliography: Daressy (1905) 68, pl. XIII.

16. Fragmentary head, Glasgow, Art Gallery and Museum, 9br–'12
Red quartzite, height: 0.72 m
From Heliopolis
The facial features recall the king's inscribed bust in Boston (no. 3).
Bibliography: Vandier (1958) 409, n. 1.

17. Head of a sphinx, private collection
Black granite, height: 0.18 m
From the precinct of Mut, Karnak

This fragment comes from the excavations of Margaret Benson. It may belong to one of the two sphinxes mentioned by Porter and Moss. Stylistically it is similar to the head in Strasbourg (no. 4).

Bibliography: Benson and Gourlay (1899) 42, 61, 236, pl. VII, fig. 1, facing 323; Christie's (London) Sales Catalogue of December 5, 1972, no. 2; Porter and Moss (1972) 259.

STELAE

Seven of the stelae are dated. The earliest two come from the temple of Amara West in Sudan (nos. 1 and 2). They were inscribed by Hori I and Hori II, the viceroys of Kush. The stelae from Serabit el-Khadim and Koptos (nos. 4 and 6) were probably dedicated on the occasion of the king's Heb Sed Festival. The text on the stele recorded in a photograph of the Pennsylvania University Museum (no. 5), mentions the donation of a cult statue of Ramesses III to the temple of Merenptah in Memphis. The event was recorded on the twenty-fifth day of the ninth month of year 24. We have the death of Ramesses III mentioned on the stele from West Silsileh (no. 7). Dated on the festival of the Nile god in year 31, the text describes the king as *ma'a hrw*— that is, deceased.

Three rock-cut stelae at Kahzindariya, Siriya, and Tihna (nos. 10, 11, and 12) marked the quarry sites of stone for the king's buildings. The private stele dedicated to Ramesses III by the priest Meresitef (no. 13) represents Queen Tiy Mereniset as the consort of Setnakht and the mother of Ramesses III. Tiy Mereniset is also found on the relief fragment in Brussels (no. 14), where she is shown shaking *sistra* behind Ramesses III. The fragment in Edinburgh (no. 15) is one of the finest representations of the king, reminiscent of the best work at Medinet Habu. Three ostraca (nos. 17, 18, and 19) are probably sculptors' models used in the decoration of the tombs. The Turin ostracon is the finest of all and, in my opinion, to be attributed to the artisans of Deir el-Medina who decorated the princes' tombs in the Valley of the Queens. The other two may have been used in the decoration of the royal tomb in the Valley of the Kings.

1. Khartoum, National Museum, no. 3061
Sandstone, round-topped

From Amara West; dated to year 5 of Ramesses III. Dedicated by Hori, the viceroy of Kush.

Bibliography: Porter and Moss (1951) 162; Fairman (1939) 143.

2. London, British Museum, no. 1784
Sandstone, round-topped

From Amara West; dated to year 11 of Ramesses III. Dedicated by Hori II, the viceroy of Kush.

Bibliography: Porter and Moss (1937) 135; Fairman (1939) 143, pl. XV (2).

3. Qus, in situ
Gray granite, round-topped

The inscription dates the stele to year 12 of Ramesses III. The king is represented leading prisoners. Judging by the date, the scene may represent the war with the Sea Peoples.

Bibliography: Porter and Moss (1937) 135.

4. Serabit el-Khadim, in situ
Granite, round-topped

Found by Petrie in the excavation of the New Kingdom temple. Petrie translated the text as dating to year 23. The inscription mentions the king's Heb Sed Festival that took place in year 29. A reexamination of the surface reveals a lacuna at the end of the number that leaves room for six more lines.

Bibliography: Petrie (1906) 76; Porter and Moss (1951) 350; Gardiner, Peet, and Černý (1955) 186–87; *KRI* V.248.

5. Present location not known; Pennsylvania University Museum, no. 2882
Limestone, round-topped
From Memphis

The stele is known to us only from a photograph taken by the Pennsylvania University Museum. It is broken at the top and bottom, and only fifteen lines are preserved. The text records the presenting of a statue of Ramesses III to the temple of Merenptah in Memphis and the assignment of two purification priests and two priestesses to maintain the cult of the statue. The event was recorded on the twenty-fifth day of the ninth month of year 24.

Bibliography: Schulman (1963) 177–84; Helck (1966) 32–41; *KRI* V.249–50; Porter and Moss (1981) 858.

6. Cairo, Egyptian Museum, JE 3077
Red granite, round-topped
From Koptos; dated to year 29

Bibliography: Petrie (1896) 16, pl. XVIII (2); Porter and Moss (1937) 129; *KRI* V.250–51.

7. West Silsileh, in situ
Granite, round-topped

Dated to year 31, dedicated on the festival of the Nile god. The names of Ramesses III are followed by the phrase *ma'a hrw*, "deceased."

Bibliography: Porter and Moss (1937) 213; Rosselini (1977) XXXI (4).

8. Cairo, Egyptian Museum, JE 33903
Sandstone, round-topped
From Medinet Habu; not dated
Bibliography: Porter and Moss (1972) 526.

9. Hildesheim, Das Pelizaeus Museum, no. 379
Limestone, round-topped
From Horbeit
Bibliography: Porter and Moss (1934) 26; Steindorf (1917) pl. 12.

10. Khazindariya, in situ
Rock-cut, limestone
Probably carved to mark the quarry site; this site in Middle Egypt is known for its variety of stone.
Bibliography: Habachi (1974) 69–75, pl. XI; *KRI* V.270.

11. Siriya, in situ
Rock-cut, limestone

Carved on the outer face of the southern side of the chapel of Merenptah

Bibliography: Porter and Moss (1934), 127; Habachi (1974) 69–75, pl. XI; *KRI* V.270–71.

12. Tihna, in situ
Rock-cut, limestone
Carved at the quarry site
Bibliography: Habachi (1974) 69–74; *KRI* V.271.

13. Cairo, Egyptian Museum, JE 20395
Sandstone, round-topped
From Abydos, excavated by Mariette; a private stele, dedicated by the priest Meresitef.
Bibliography: Porter and Moss (1937) 51.

Reliefs in Museum Collections

14. Brussels, Musee Royaux d'Art et d'Histoire, E. 584
Sandstone

From Abydos, discovered by Petrie in the excavation of a chapel of the Twenty-sixth Dynasty, together with another inscribed fragment that was sent to the Cairo Museum. Both were found with the face turned down, reused as part of the pavement in front of the chapel. The relief represents Ramesses III with his mother, Queen Tiy Mereniset, behind him. The other fragment is not recorded in the catalog of the Egyptian Museum in Cairo.

Bibliography: Porter and Moss (1934) 127; Habachi (1974) 69–75, illustration on pl. XI; *KRI* V.270–71.

15. Edinburgh, Royal Scottish Museum, 1908.229.1
Sandstone
Provenance not known

One of the finest representations of the king, this relief fragment is similar to the early representations at Medinet Habu.
Bibliography: None

16. Hannover, Das Kestner Museum, 1925.227
Limestone
Provenance not known
Bibliography: Woldering (1955) pl. 35.

17. Turin, Museo Egizio, 7051
Limestone
From Western Thebes

The ostracon is most likely a sculptor's model, possibly from Deir el-Medina. It exhibits a highly refined style, reminiscent of the reliefs in the tombs of Khaemwaset and Amunhorhepeshef (QV 44 and 55).

Bibliography: Scamuzzi (1965) pl. 65; Mysliwiec (1976) 125–26, pl. CXXIV.

18. London University College, 14220
Limestone
From Thebes

This ostracon was probably also used as a sculptor's model. The face of the king is stylistically similar to the reliefs in the royal tomb. It may have been used by the workmen in the Valley of the Kings during the decoration of the royal tomb.

Bibliography: Petrie (1909) fig. 88; Mysliwiec (1976) 125, pl. CXXV.

19. Warsaw, Muzej Narodnowe, MN 141274
Limestone
From Western Thebes

Similar to the ostracon at University College, London, this fragment was probably another sculptor's model used in the decoration of the royal tomb.

Bibliography: Mysliwiec (1976) 125, pl. CXXVI.

Notes

1. It is possible that there are more tombs of princes still awaiting discovery. In a relief at Medinet Habu, thirteen princes are represented in procession, ten identified by name.

2. Pillet (1922) 258.

3. Johnson (1998) 73–74 and n. 63.

4. Haeny (1981) pls. 31a–b, 33a.

5. Johnson (1998) 73 says that "every (statue) that this author has seen, either in or from the Ramesses III precinct, is unquestionably usurped from his predecessor, Amenhotep III."

6. The Deir el-Medina artisans are mentioned on Chicago Ostracon 16991.

7. All the royal tombs in the Valley of the Kings, except for those of Tutankhamun and Amenhotep II, were robbed at this time.

8. Porter and Moss (1964) 518–27, no. 11.

9. Ibid., 517, no. 10.

10. Ibid., 532.

11. See Weeks (2000) sheets 26–72 (exact measurement of the tomb) and p. 12 (grid coordinates and elevations at the entrance to the tomb).

12. Most royal tombs of the Eighteenth Dynasty have axes with ninety-degree turns or with spiral descents. The latter may follow Middle Kingdom monuments, such as the spiral chambers of the cenotaph of Senwosret II at Abydos. Sometimes there are two right-angle turns that form a U shape (tomb of Thutmose IV), reminiscent of the pyramid of Amenemhat III at Hawara and that of Khendjer at Saqqara. Other Eigtheenth Dynasty tombs contain only one right-angle turn (tombs of Thutmose III and Amenhotep II) or two turned into a dogleg (tomb of Amenhotep III).

13. Allen (1989).

14. As a result of Bruce's publication, it was often called "Bruce's Tomb," see Porter and Moss (1964) 518.

15. Thomas (1966) 126.

16. Wilkinson (1835). No search of the pits has been made thus far.

17. The niches in the first corridor may have had their functional origin in the steeply inclined tombs of the Eighteenth Dynasty, where they helped lower the sarcophagus into the burial chamber. This function became obsolete as the angle of descent of the tomb leveled out.

18. The purpose of the well was to trap water in the rare but devastating flash floods that occur in Western Thebes. It was an integral part of royal tombs from the time of Thutmose III onward.

19. Probably the chariot hall with its annex. The chariot hall contained the equipment needed by the king to live an ordinary life and perform kingly duty once reborn—actual chariots, beds, clothing, and even a frieze of beheaded enemies (Romer [1981] 28). It was a chamber of eternal royalty, a kind of "living room"—the opposite of the burial chamber with its funerary equipment. Although such "living rooms" did not exist in the pyramids of the Old and Middle Kingdoms, the chariot hall had taken on a ritual function in the New Kingdom. It was usually the first large chamber in royal tombs, often embellished by four columns.

20. The side room, or "annex," of the chariot hall was first introduced in the tomb of Seti I. It was employed in all the tombs of the Nineteenth Dynasty, except for the unfinished tomb of Seti II, reappearing subsequently in the tomb of Ramesses III.

21. The sarcophagus chamber with its four side rooms symbolized the four parts of the world to which Isis had to travel to assemble the scattered remains of the body of Osiris. Her search seems to parallel the sacred pilgrimage to cities in the Delta described as one of the ritual acts of the funeral. One of the rooms off the burial chamber contained the canopic furniture. Representations of canopic beds decorating the side rooms in the tombs of Seti I and Ramesses I match the real canopic beds found in the tomb of Tutankhamun. Another side room has been found to contain shawabtis in the tomb of Thutmose IV, so perhaps this was the "shawabti place" of the ancient texts. If it were possible to imagine where the equipment found in Tutankhamun's tomb would have stood in a complete royal tomb, it would be easier to understand the symbolic function of many rooms.

22. In the tomb of Seti I, this corridor symbolized the passage to the primeval waters of Nun.

23. All the texts are recorded in Abitz (1984) 80–83, 289–97.

24. For the *Book of Gates* in the tomb of Ramesses III, see Andrejewski (1962).

25. In the Twentieth Dynasty, the angle of descent of the tombs had leveled out. This made them less vulnerable to water damage, and wells with deep shafts were practically eliminated. Even tombs that stood open from ancient times, like those of Ramesses III and Ramesses IV, suffered less damage than the steeply inclined tomb of Seti I after Belzoni had filled up its deep well. This indicates that the principal function of the well was practical, though a symbolic meaning may have been attached to it as well. The shallow well of Ramesses' tomb failed to protect the burial chamber from torrential rainwater; as a consequence, it is the most badly damaged room in the tomb.

26. Room Z (66); Porter and Moss (1964) 526.

27. For a study of the technique of the wall decorations, see Marciniak (1982).

28. Abitz (1986) 139.

29. Hayes (1959) II: 369.

30. Schaedel (1936).

31. Černý (1936).

32. Goedicke (1963).

33. This supports the evidence that some funerary equipment was placed in the tomb before burial.

34. Commission des monuments d'Egypte. Antiquites: Descriptions, III, 196; quoted in Thomas (1966) 127.

35. Athanasi (1836) 52.

36. Birch (1876).

37. Could it still be somewhere in the tomb?

38. Belzoni (1820) 373.

39. *LÄ* V.476.

40. Dodson (1986) 197.

41. Cardon (1980).

42. Beckerath (1984) 162, "1202–1199 BC."

43. *MH* IV, pl. 203; Porter and Moss (1972) 499–500 (98).

44. Fairman (1939) 142; Porter and Moss (1951) 161.

45. Clayton (1972).

46. The status of deification or "Osirifying"—becoming one with Osiris—was attained by the king during the funeral ceremony. It had to be repeated for the reburial.

47. Porter and Moss (1964) 752–55, 759–61.

48. For a transcription of the text, see Thomas (1966) 257.

49. Thomas (1966) 150.

50. Wente (1973) 223.

51. Quoted in Thomas (1966) 251.

52. Wente (1961).

53. Schiaparelli (1924).

54. Yoyotte (1958).

55. Abitz (1986) 101.

56. Yoyotte (1958) 27.

57. Abitz (1986) 24, 127; *KRI* V.369–72.

58. Abitz (1986) 101.

59. Schiaparelli (1924) 43.

60. Ibid., 124.

61. Abitz (1986) 129; *KRI* V.373–74.

62. Porter and Moss (1964) 753; *KRI* V.367–68.

63. Abitz (1986) 101.

64. Ibid., 102.

65. Bruyère (1930) 55.

66. Ibid, 47.

67. Hornung (1964) 108.

68. Černý (1958b).

69. Goedicke (1963).

70. Černý (1958b) 31.

71. Legrain (1929).

72. Nelson (1936).

73. Chevrier (1933) pls. IIIa–b.

74. Ibid., 19.

75. Nelson (1936) I: pl. 83C.

76. Seele (1935).

77. Nelson et al. (1936) I:vii.

78. See Anthes (1930) 26–29.

79. See Kozloff in Kozloff and Bryan (1992).

80. Epigraphic Survey (1981) pl. 178.

81. Ibid., pls. 117A, 118A, 116B, 121A, 122A.

82. Ibid., pl. 207.

83. Ibid., pls. 141, 142B, 144C, 202B–D.

84. Borchardt (1926); Siclen (1937).

85. Bruyère (1930).

86. Porter and Moss (1934) 17.

87. Petrie (1906) 30, pl. XXXV; also see *KRI* V.259.

88. See Habachi (1969).

89. Cairo CG 42145—Ramesses II, Cairo JE 27635—Ramesses IV, Marseille 209—Ramesses IV, Toledo (Ohio) 06227—not inscribed, Ramesside in style.

90. Goyon (1971).

91. Haeny (1981) pls. 31a–b, 33a.

Chapter 8

The Literary Environment of the Age of Ramesses III

OGDEN GOELET, JR.

DEFINING THE LITERATURE OF THE AGE OF RAMESSES III

By any standard, there was a great flowering of Egyptian literature during the New Kingdom. The Ramesside period is critical for our understanding of a vast sweep of Egyptian literature; it is fair to say that writing stands out as one of the greatest cultural accomplishments of that era. Not only did Ramesside scribes produce a vast corpus of works in a new dialect, but we also owe much of our knowledge of the literature of the Middle Kingdom to their efforts to preserve the older "classics."

Dynasties Nineteen and Twenty provide us with the clearest insights into the role of literature in Egyptian society, as well as how and why it was written. The number, scope, and creativity of the works in the first two volumes of Lichtheim's magisterial *Ancient Egyptian Literature* alone bear witness to these facts.[1] Yet even though it would be possible to write a literary history limited to the reign of Ramesses III and early Dynasty Twenty in a few pages, the end result would have insufficient historical context to help us understand what contemporary Egyptians thought about literature and the role it played in their society. At the end of such a basic, descriptive approach, one could legitimately object that we have simply superimposed our views of literature on the Egyptians.

For that matter, as far as the language itself is concerned, it is unrealistic to expect that dynastic divisions and changes in the Egyptian language and its literature necessarily coincide.[2] One thing, however, is certain—because the primary means for preserving what we consider Egyptian belles lettres was the delicate, highly perishable medium of papyrus, only a pitiable proportion of Ramesside literature has survived.[3]

Instead of confining ourselves to what can be dated to Ramesses III's reign, my approach here has been first to describe the Ramesside literary climate as a whole, then to focus on what can be reliably connected with the early part of Dynasty Twenty. Unfortunately, with the possible exception of the poem known as *The Encomium of the Sages*, there are no Egyptian accounts of their attitude toward literature, let alone a Ramesside equivalent of *The Lives of the Poets*, to guide us in this effort.

Recently, the appearance of *Ancient Egyptian Literature* under A. Loprieno's editorship provided literary historians with an invaluable collection of essays on a wide range of approaches to this subject, one of Egypt's cultural achievements.[4] In addition, at the 2001 International Conference of Egyptologists in Cairo, J. Baines presented an overview of past and present research on Egyptian literature; both he and the respondents to his paper offered some important opinions that touch on Ramesside literature.[5]

The present chapter is, primarily, a survey of Ramesside literature as a whole and, secondarily, a discussion of some of the important theoretical issues raised in these two milestone publications. Of course, these hardly exhaust the repertoire of recent studies on Egyptian literature.[6] However, there is so much currently available on the subject that I am often forced here to refer only to a narrow selection of studies in the annotations—I make no claims to comprehensiveness. Unfortunately, I cannot give many of the subjects discussed here the detailed attention that they deserve. This chapter is intended primarily as a survey. Some subjects—love poetry, for example— easily merit a treatment far longer than this entire contribution.

Certain problems arising from the dating, attribution, production, and classification of material continually vex literary studies in Egyptology. The problems of when an individual text may have been originally composed and when it came to be written down on a given papyrus or ostracon unavoidably complicate our attempts to place sources in their proper historical and intellectual relationships. Similar chronological questions have long been central issues in the interpretation of Middle Egyptian literature and remain equally important for our assessment of Ramesside literature. As far as questions of genre and classification are concerned, furthermore, modern approaches in literary studies can oversensitize us to the difficulties inherent in viewing the works of a culture so distant in time and so distinctly non-Western in outlook. We can easily become bogged down in a definitional morass and be tempted to sidestep such issues entirely.

This survey can only hope to engage only a small sampling of modern theoretical approaches to Egyptian literature in the space allotted here. The recurring suspicion underlying many of these studies is that Egyptian and modern views concerning the written word and its place in society are often fundamentally incompatible. This opinion certainly must have some validity, but, at the same time, it may be unduly pessimistic. In reality, the Egyptians left many valuable clues as to their attitudes and taste in literary matters. These indications are of far more than merely theoretical in nature—they can help greatly in defining Ramesside literature and its genres.

From a literary perspective, the works of this period were not just a continuation of earlier traditions and types. We can begin our search for definitions with an observation concerning the various dialects used for the Ramesside texts that we will be examining here. Early in Dynasty Nineteen, a new form of the Egyptian language, Late Egyptian, became the acceptable language for both literary material and many parts of royal inscriptions as well. Thus, Ramesside literature represents more than a construction of modern scholarship—a substantial part of the written language was now marked by a distinct change in grammar, vocabulary, orthography, and even linguistic decorum. The validation of what had previously been considered dialect brought with it a demand for a completely revised curriculum, since, in addition to this new dialect, the obsolete Middle Egyptian dialect continued to enjoy a widespread use in many facets of life and literature. The existence of two disparate varieties of written language side by side, or diglossia, heightened the influence of register and even script form on all types of compositions.

As so often happens, the new forms simultaneously increased the need for knowledge and preservation of traditional language among some segments of the literate population. In light of the influences from these two conflicting yet interrelated trends, any survey of Ramesside literature must deal at length with issues of copying, training, and didacticism in general. Scholars looking at Ramesside literature may thus inevitably confront many of the same questions that vex the study of Middle Egyptian literature, but distinctions between old and new are nevertheless easier to make.

Because of the many problems inherent in circumscribing the subject, I shall adopt a rather generous definition of the literature of Ramesses III for the purposes of this study, a definition that encompasses a wide range of literary endeavors during Dynasties Nineteen and Twenty. I shall follow the same broad guidelines that Lichtheim outlined in the introduction to the first volume of her great anthology, which recognized, above all, that most ancient literature is, in her words, "purposeful."[7] Thus, according to her standards, virtually all texts other than "the merely practical (such as lists, contracts, lawsuits, and letters)" might have literary qualities in their ancient environment. This led her to include texts written in contexts other than the papyri and ostraca traditionally associated with literature—texts on stelae and tomb and temple walls (i.e., inscriptions in the strict sense of the word) that had been largely ignored in prior anthologies.[8]

Lichtheim's criteria resulted in a selection that coincided largely with what the Egyptians themselves may well have actually considered belles lettres: literary tales; secular and religious poetry; school exercises and other didactic texts; sections of royal and private monumental inscriptions alike; and, characteristically for the Ramesside period in particular, some *opera minora*—short compositions found on papyri and ostraca that often seem to have been produced primarily for the pleasure of the author and/or his audience. As we shall see, the Ramesside period added literary forms of the normally "purposeful" category of letters to this list of genres.[9] Inscriptional praises of the king developed into yet another Ramesside specialty, giving rise to numerous "rhetorical stelae," which exhibit a highly polished use of imagery and vocabulary that, in any other context, we would not hesitate to label as poetry.[10] Another form of belles lettres, religious literature, especially hymns and prayers, will receive only a brief and general treatment here; a more detailed study of that material, especially in relation to its theological content, belongs elsewhere in the current volume.

Some recent studies of Egyptian literature have proposed that, for definitional purposes, we might demark what is literary by holding texts up to a somewhat broad and hard-to-define standard of fictionality, as proposed by Moers.[11] To be sure, this is a more subtle distinction than the term *Fiktionalität* appears to express at first glance, yet there remain two main difficulties with such a criterion. The first problem is that it seems to circumscribe the scope of what might be considered literary excessively, leaving too many "cultural works," such as didactic literature, out of consideration or in a secondary status. The second (and my major) objection is that his argumentation appears to rely excessively on discussions that are centered on current problems in the literary theory of the modern Western tradition, a tradition in which literature occupies a radically different place in society than it did in ancient Egypt. It was for that reason that Lichtheim included "purposeful" works in her anthology.

The beginning sections of the present study examine three major aspects of Ramesside literature and its genres. First comes the oft-discussed question of what degree of validity our modern literary genres have in the study of Ramesside literature. Second, I sketch briefly the process by which dialect developed into a versatile official language alongside more conservative forms of writing, as well as the important role that the royal house played in this development, a role that has interesting parallels in the ideological use of literature by the Middle Kingdom monarchs. Third, I attempt to show how the Ramesside kings, their officials, and their more humble subjects employed several forms of language.

THEORETICAL CONSIDERATIONS ON RAMESSIDE LITERATURE: INTERTEXTUALITY, DIDACTICISM, AND ANCIENT GENRES

The first task of this chapter—the discussion of the validity of modern literary genres in ancient contexts—requires an investigation into how the Egyptians themselves categorized texts and what they may have considered literature. These undertakings are complicated by the presence of three tightly interwoven themes in Ramesside literature that are normally be treated as loosely related, but ultimately distinct, aspects of Western literature. The themes in question are intertextuality, didacticism, and genre, which together reveal fundamental differences between modern attitudes and those of the Egyptians in respect to the importance of creativity and individuality in art.

The Role of Creativity and Intertextuality

The study of any body of literature must inevitably confront the problem of genres: has modern scholarship inappropriately imposed modern Western intellectual categories on ancient sources? Of course, applying the literary genres of one culture to another involves almost as many pitfalls as defining literature itself, but it would be equally wrong to avoid this definitional problem altogether. At the same time, it would be helpful to realize at the outset that constructing "airtight" genres is an unattainable ideal.[12] Many literary compositions, especially high-quality works, skillfully blend themes and represent several different genres simultaneously. This is to be expected when one engages with any endeavor in which creativity and imagination play central roles. High-quality literary works are famously those that transcend boundaries.

Despite the undeniable originality and creativity in many aspects of Egyptian intellectual life, their evaluation of the importance of creativity and imagination is probably the greatest area where they differ from the modern Western approach to the fine arts. We can begin with the fact that producing literature for its own sake—*ars gratis artis*—was not really a primary objective among the Egyptians. Concerns such as didacticism, tradition, ideology, and self-presentation all greatly outweighed any creative impulse. In the few instances when the Egyptians explicitly recognized some works as belles lettres, their descriptive terminology usually does not overlap very well with ours, even though they did recognize a genre called *r3w nw t3 sḥmḫt-jb ʿ3t*, literally "discourses for greatly distracting the heart," more freely rendered "entertainment texts,"[13] a term in which we can hear the faint echo of "art for its own sake." When Ptahhotep states that "the limits of art are not reached," the term he employs for "art" is *ḥmt*, a word that essentially means "skill," that is, the same type of craftsmanship used to make furniture or stone vases.[14]

Other than such obvious and predictable differences in terminology, there is the more important fact that a writer, as we conceive of the occupation, existed on a considerably different plane among the Egyptians. The independent author, the writer free of institutional support or patronage, almost certainly did not exist in pharaonic Egypt. As it was with other creative people, such as sculptors and artists, authorial anonymity or pseudonymity was by far the norm. The pseudepigraphy of so many texts, wherein the real writer conceals himself behind the name of a famous personage of the past, is really only a special form of anonymity.

Information from titles, rubrics, colophons, the copying of texts, and related practices can offer valuable insights into the Egyptian mindset toward a wide variety of texts. Above all, the distinctly different processes employed in writing a literary ostracon or papyrus as opposed to documentary texts show that scribes were very much conscious of a literary register.[15] Nonetheless, the degree to which they were aware of the "intertextuality" of such materials, evident in the large number of apparent quotes from a standard literary canon of such materials, is far less certain.[16]

When approached from a practical standpoint, intertextuality seems less of an issue than it is sometimes made out to be. Given the strong influence exercised by didactic and ideological purposes on the *creation* of Egyptian literature—especially since the reproduction of model texts was central to the Egyptian learning process and its associated curriculum—why should one be surprised to find a high degree of intertextuality? After all, student scribes most emphatically had to be intertextual unless they wished to fail in their training and revert to one of the professions that the *Satire on the Trades* and the *Late*

Egyptian Miscellanies so invidiously described. When a substantial component of one's education consisted of imitating the formulaic expressions found in epistolographic texts and similar elevated diction, we should not be surprised that eventually some of those stock phrases should be transported, consciously or unconsciously, into the daily life of letters and inscriptions. To a certain degree, intertextuality in Egyptian texts attests to the effectiveness of their educational process. Above all, we should admit that it is impossible for us to gauge how conscious some Egyptian citation might have been. All discourse, ancient or modern, is filled with tag phrases whose origins are lost or forgotten. For example, how many of us today, when we use the expression "signs of the times," are actually aware that we are quoting Matthew 16:3?

It would be a signal misinterpretation of the Egyptians' character to attribute the prevalence of intertextuality simply to a timorous attitude toward originality. Tradition always exerted a profound influence on all aspects of Egyptian society, not the least on literature. Pharaohs and commoners alike had to demonstrate their respect for the past and its achievements. This was not a characteristic of the high elite, since there was a remarkable knowledge and awareness of the past within the workmen's community at Deir el-Medina.[17] What modern observers are sometimes apt to dismiss as mere imitation of traditional styles would probably have been viewed by the Egyptians as evidence of their respect for tradition and continuity.[18]

Consequently, intertextuality, especially in its aspect of adherence to form, was always a cardinal virtue throughout Egyptian intellectual life and arts, including the figurative. In respect to intertextuality, Ramesses III, the focus of this study, could justifiably be called "the intertextual king." Not only did the scribes of his chancellery copy and adapt many inscriptions of his namesake and role model Ramesses II, but there was considerable reuse of texts of other predecessors, such as Merenptah.[19] The phenomenon of "archaism" in the plastic arts of the Late Period in particular might be considered yet another form of intertextuality. An admiration for tradition rather than conscious intertextuality is more likely the inspiration for the frequent pseudepigraphical mode of Egyptian texts of all types as well as the motivation behind the closely related genre of pious forgeries, such as the Memphite Theology[20] or the Sehel Famine Stela.[21]

Didacticism, Reproduction, and the Submersion of the Author

This is not the place to rehearse the well-known, central role that various aspects of didacticism played in the history of Middle Kingdom literature.[22] Suffice it to say that, if anything, the importance of the Egyptian educational system in preserving as well as producing literature increased during the Ramesside period. Within the wide range of materials employed for teaching purposes, probably the most significant compositions were those we have named wisdom or didactic literature.

Of the two alternatives, the term *didactic* is closer to the mark than *wisdom*. Unfortunately, the word *didactic* connotes something dryly pedantic, which, alas, is frequently the way modern audiences are apt to perceive these texts today. Didactic literature was intended to do more than train scribes in the skills connected with their adopted profession; it was also meant to reinforce the Egyptians' ethical code and their value system. Some of the exaggerated tone that characterizes parts of these texts may have been done with humorous intent. Since they were connected to a long-standing literary tradition, they also represent what one might call "texts of tradition" or "cultural texts."[23]

Perhaps it would more productive to see this genre as the Ramesside equivalent of the discipline of rhetoric within our modern concept of a liberal or classical education. They used these texts to practice all the essential elements of the elevated speech of a well-educated Egyptian—style, vocabulary, and phraseology. This was more than didactic literature; its intent was to provide students with texts as models to emulate in their style and vocabulary, especially in the case of material written in the new Late Egyptian dialects. Thus, we could justifiably speak of "emulative literature" rather than didactic or wisdom literature, but I think it better not to introduce new terms into a field already overburdened with terminology.

We should not allow the didactic tone of these texts to mislead us about the level of skill and the status of the students for which they were intended, however. Recent, closer examinations of "student" materials done by Gasse, McDowell, and Janssen all point to the same surprising conclusion. These studies convincingly demonstrate that the scribes writing out these exercises on papyri as well as ostraca were by no means always the unskilled beginners we have usually imagined them to be. We have been too easily misled by their numerous errors in orthography, forgetting that this is a feature of even the best-quality hieratic documents and overlooking as well the additional complications arising from the old-fashioned Middle Egyptian dialect employed in some texts. To the contrary, the careful yet rapidly executed forms and the fluid ductus of the hieratic script generally present in these didactic documents seem to reflect the confidence of experienced scribes.[24]

Therefore, on closer inspection, what had formerly been thought to represent the beginning stages of writing instruction now seems much more likely to have been the products of the later stages of scribal training, which emphasized the quality of the handwriting over the quality of the text. Furthermore, recent finds have revealed the existence of many exact or reasonably close parallels from a wide range of didactic texts at both Memphis and Thebes. We can no longer believe that schools in the two capital cities of Egypt employed distinctly different teaching materials or that each region used distinctly different teaching methodologies. Herein is an excellent example of how, in the past, accidents of preservation probably have significantly distorted our impression of how Ramesside literature developed.

Many of the works which the Egyptians attributed to great writers of the past may be largely pseudepigraphical, a description that, it should be emphasized, does not preclude the possibility that the purported author may have composed part of the original text or otherwise inspired it. A similar combination of a sense of history and important individuals whose character one should emulate also gave rise to Egyptian "saints," or culture heroes.[25] Yet, despite this, there were some greatly admired personages of the past who were considered both wise men and authors much in the same sense that we take the word, as the *Encomium* and two depictions of several of the same personages on a relief in a Saqqara tomb and in a papyrus in Athens all show.[26] One of the many things that emerges from this remarkable composition is the remarkable similarity in Egyptian and modern sensibilities expressed in the notion that an author can become an "immortal" through his writings.

A key characteristic of both the intertextuality and the diglossia evident in so many Ramesside compositions is that these phenomena are connected less with registers of speech—"high" and "low" dialect, for instance—and more with the ultimate use of a text. Furthermore, separate segments of a given text might have differences in dialect, grammar, and vocabulary.[27] The most common practical reason for the production or reproduction of a sizable proportion of all Ramesside literary compositions was their use for instructional purposes. Since instruction in writing per se must inevitably involve copying, this brings to the fore a valuable distinction that Assmann has introduced into our textual studies. He noted that some material, particularly that of a religious or funerary nature, was apt to be copied more or less verbatim and thus belonged more to what might be described as a "reproductive" stage of development. Putting aside their frequent association with the copying inherent with the scribal training practices, literary works in Late Egyptian generally tended to be more innovative and more closely connected to what should be characterized as the "productive" stage of a text or a corpus of materials.[28] As we shall see, material written both in Middle Egyptian and Late Egyptian during the Ramesside era could sometimes belong to each of these categories at the same time.

Strikingly enough, the fact that a composition was pseudepigraphic and assiduously copied out by generations of students did not necessarily relegate the work to the reproductive stage of textual development. During the Ramesside period, a number of old didactic texts were reedited, so to speak, and given a new life.[29] This practice of adaptation and renewal of certain classics is discussed at greater length below. Needless to say, this raises suspicions as to the actual integrity of certain Middle Kingdom texts known primarily from Ramesside evidence.

Egyptian Remarks in Texts and the Function of Reproduction

The titles, colophons, and similar textual notations discussed above do more than merely inform us that some material was extensively copied—such marks confirm that certain works had been selected and valued as documents for careful transmission from generation to generation. It is remarkable how often such devices appear in connection with instructional works. When one collects the material that was copied as school exercises and other compositions in which these remarks occur, a rough impression of what the Egyptians may have considered "classics" of their literature emerges.[30]

Rubrics representing either the title headings or incipits of texts, along with the opening sections of many works, also express, in the Egyptians' own words, Egyptian attitudes toward a wide range of texts, literary or otherwise. In the first place, it is obvious that rubrics were intended to draw the reader's attention to the introduction of new or special topics. Appearing at the beginning of long or short works, Egyptian titles frequently presented the mise-en-scène: the name and titles of a purported author, his intended audience, a characterization of the contents, and sometimes even the very aim of the piece.

For example, Loprieno's observation about the shift toward a more bourgeois or "demotic" point of view in Egyptian literature as it moved from the Middle Kingdom to the Ramesside period[31] seems borne out in a comparison of the rubricized title of *The Instruction of Ptahhotep* with that of *The Instruction of Ani*. Whereas the author of *Ptahhotep* presents himself as a vizier whose aim is supposedly the education of the upper levels of the administrative elite, Ani, the purported author of the later work, operates from the perspective of what we might describe as a "middle manager" in the New Kingdom temple bureaucracy and desires to instruct a much broader (and probably much lower-status) audience. In addition, the introductory rubrics occasionally contain the Egyptian descriptive terminology, the genre name, for the work in question.

It is both striking (and comforting) to find that, from time to time, the Egyptians use words in the titles of compositions that closely approach our modern English terminology for the same genres. Certainly the term *sb3yt,* "instruction," that appears in the titular rubric of several instructional texts conforms to our natural estimation of that genre.[32] Similarly, the titular rubric for the love poetry in Papyrus Harris 500 uses the expression *hswt shmh-jb,* which roughly translates as "entertainment song." As with the case of indications of copying, not all material with titles are literary. For instance, rubrics abound in that large class of texts known as "magico-medical texts." Many literary texts, be they religious materials or stories, are apt to begin in medias res, without any introductory title.

Our study of rubrics leads naturally to the other indications of the copying of texts and the implications of copying generally. In many ways, our creation of a genre called "didactic literature" overlooks the fact that, on the basis of transmission process alone, one could consider virtually all Egyptian literary texts as technically didactic; the Egyptians, just as we do today in our grammar and high school study of English, employed their literary classics as the cornerstones of language instruction. Already during the Middle Kingdom, there are indications that a degree of canonization of these texts was taking place. Scribes copying certain material, such as *The Tale of Sinuhe* or religious texts, were careful to assert the integrity, completeness, or accuracy of their work by concluding with such notations as "it is finished" or "its beginning has come to its end as it was found in writing."[33] As Quirke has astutely observed, such notations never appear before the generally accepted end of a text.[34]

The practice of ending a literary text with a colophon continued in full force during the Ramesside era, but then usually without any specific indications that the document had been copied. The usual form now became some variant of the phrase "it has come well and in peace for the [title and name of the teacher-scribe], [the title and name of the student, often with a patronymic]."[35] On two occasions, student scribes invoked divine punishment against anyone who might "speak against" the text, presumably referring to any challenge as to the accuracy of the transmission.[36] Additionally, students were sometimes apt to insert dates indicating their progress within a papyrus or a group of ostraca, some of which may hint that student scribes may have been given a *pensium,* or daily quota, of material to prepare for their instructor.[37]

It is not surprising that scribal attestations about the accuracy of their work occur in religious material alongside pseudepigraphical attributions to gods or well-known monarchs.[38] Although a very high proportion of the material copied for one reason or another was connected with the didactic process, it would be a mistake to assume that texts were not transcribed for other reasons as well, such as the desire to have personal copies of sources that were considered classics or to lend the owner the reputation of being cultivated.[39] Indeed, the possibility has even been raised that a similar motivation, the creation of the ancient Egyptian equivalent of "paperback editions," led to the copying of many ostraca that we have often been quick to dismiss simply as "student ostraca."[40]

Egyptian and Modern Literary Genres—in Summation

In summation, even though our cognitive/intellectual categories often do not quite coincide, the Egyptian and our views of literature probably have more affinities than we are usually wont to admit. Two major exceptions to this generalization perhaps really involve issues of differences in taste rather than genre, that is, our estimation today of Egyptian royal inscriptions and religious literature, two related genres whose highly rhetorical and ideological nature can easily blind the modern observer to their qualities as literature. These conceptual problems arising from royal and religious texts are accordingly treated below, in this chapter's overview of literature. The discussions of genres above reveal another significant disparity in our views about what constitutes good literature. The ancient scribes, Egyptian and otherwise, operated in an environment where literature was normally read aloud, so they developed a markedly different attitude toward important external features of style, such as repetition and originality, than we have today. In these respects, we Westerners today are very much the descendants of the Greeks.

THE EVOLUTION OF THE DIALECTS AND SCRIBAL CURRICULA OF RAMESSIDE LITERATURE

Having discussed genre and other definitional problems, we can better assess the impact of the language itself, for this is certainly one of the salient characteristics of a large proportion of Ramesside texts. Of course, we must acknowledge that in the background of any such discussion is the inescapable fact that only a small percentage of the Egyptian populace—perhaps between

2 and 5 percent—could read or write.[41] In any case, one would expect that the arrival of the new Late Egyptian dialect would in effect supply a ready-made, a priori definition of Ramesside literature.

However, as I stated at the beginning of this study, the existence, side by side and in varying mixtures, of two main dialects—Middle Egyptian and Late Egyptian, each representing its own separate and vital literary tradition—considerably complicates our picture of the Ramesside literary world. Although, technically speaking, Middle Egyptian had become an obsolete dialect by the reign of Ramesses III, not only did it remain a vital part of the scribal curriculum, but there even was an efflorescence of newly created Middle Egyptian compositions. Alongside literature written in the new vernacular, there was also a body of texts written in an antiquated, scholarly language, but one enjoying high prestige, roughly akin to the role of Church Latin during the Middle Ages; any discussion of Ramesside literature must deal equally with both dialects as part of the same tradition.[42] This means that we must also bear in mind the influence exerted by several script forms during this period, writing styles that enhanced the effects of decorum and register.[43] Finally, we should acknowledge the extent to which our image of Ramesside literature has been influenced by the simple fact that the texts created for mortuary or religious purposes were more likely to survive than the material from daily life.

In the past few decades, our image of the development and use of the Late Egyptian dialect between the Middle Kingdom and the Ramesside period has been greatly clarified by a series of important studies by Kroeber,[44] Silverman,[45] Junge,[46] Jansen-Winkeln,[47] Groll,[48] and Kruchten,[49] among others. I shall not attempt to recount here the rather lengthy and erratic evolutionary history of the Late Egyptian dialect, except to note where that development may have a direct bearing on the linguistic situation at the time of Ramesses III. I shall concentrate more on the interaction of Late Egyptian with Middle Egyptian in the written record, since this illuminates many aspects of Ramesside literature.

In any case, the shift from Middle Egyptian to New Egyptian was never total—the old dialect had, as we shall see, extensive usage throughout the Ramesside period, a usage strongly affected by register.[50] Consequently, one can seldom speak in terms of either a pure Middle Egyptian or pure Late Egyptian but, rather, must speak of a spectrum of dialects. Junge described this fluid situation well in the introduction to his grammar. To quote Warburton's translation of Junge's *Late Egyptian Grammar*:

The texts which are culturally most significant—by definition the most conservative—show the highest proportion of Middle Egyptianisms; from the everyday texts, through literary to ideological and theological works, the proportion of Middle Egyptian elements increases constantly—or rather these have been maintained longest in the linguistically more protected higher registers of the hierarchy of textual expression.[51]

Junge's incisive observation is fundamentally correct, but the degree to which it is true clearly must depend on what one means by "der kulturell bedeutsamsten Texte." Since materials associated with temple contexts and the funerary register were much more apt to survive than texts connected with daily life, Junge's observation must be unavoidably distorted by accidents of preservation. Yet the essential validity of his description remains and forms the basis of much of the discussions to follow. Junge further distinguished no less than four other types of Egyptian during this period: "Spätmittelägyptisch," "Medio-Neuägyptisch," "Neuägyptisch," and "Neo-Mittelägyptisch," forms of the language that have been more or less accepted by other scholars as well.[52] In light of this situation, French scholars have developed a fitting term to describe the use of Middle Egyptian in postclassical times—"égyptien du tradition."[53]

It should be emphasized, however, that these shades of dialect usually represent styles or registers of language, rather than successive stages of development. In estimating where a given text should be placed along this scale between Middle and Late Egyptian, we should consider a particularly appropriate sense of the term *dialect,* that is, a less proper, *unofficial* form of speech or writing. This critical nuance of the term *dialect* as nonstandard, "popular" speech has, for instance, apparently influenced some descriptions of the Amarna Boundary Stelae, which many consider as important milestones in the development of Late Egyptian. Some commentators have theorized that Akhenaten's choice of a more colloquial dialect for these inscriptions may have been motivated both by his desire to signal yet another break with the past and by a personal need to speak more like the common man in his brave new world at Amarna.[54] Significantly, an affirmation of the validity of Junge's remarks about the effect of register on language can be found in the fact that the two Hymns to the Aten, both representatives of the more conservative religious sphere, were written in what might be best described as Late Middle Egyptian, not Late Egyptian.

A problematic and often neglected document in the history of the appearance of the Late Egyptian dialect is the fragmentary literary narrative *Astarte and the Sea,* which has been dated to the end of Dynasty Eighteen, possibly in the reign of Horemheb.[55] Gardiner characterized its language as "Late-Egyptian in its oldest and most correctly spelt form."[56] Although we might describe *Astarte and the Sea* as a mythical and allegorical work, the story has the distinct tenor of a folktale, and given its subject matter, it likely had a Levantine origin. The mixed nature of the composition leaves one undecided whether its Late Egyptian dialect reflects the vox populi or whether the work's literary nature required a more refined level of speech.[57]

I would like to inject two final, but key, qualifications into Junge's view of the relationship between the various forms of language during the Ramesside period. Different portions of a given document can represent different registers of language. A royal stela, for example, may begin with an elaborate protocol written in Middle Egyptian, then continue with a section written in some form of Late Egyptian. It is not uncommon for a lengthy text to be a compilation, a pastiche of several shorter texts, each written in its own style. Especially in the royal sphere, an essentially Late Egyptian administrative inscription can appear within various framing devices derived from Middle Egyptian "decorum elements" and other royal protocol, or else it may be integrated into strings of narrative formulae.[58]

For example, the largely legal/administrative content of Seti I's Nauri Decree is preceded by a lengthy literary mise-en-scène remarkably reminiscent of the *laus urbis* found in literary papyri such as the *Late Egyptian Miscellanies.* Equally prominent is the praise of the monarch himself implicit in the "Königsnovelle,"[59] a narrative device that occurs not only in battlefield narratives but in disparate texts such as building inscriptions or Ramesses II's Quban stela.[60] Even literary papyri like the *Miscellanies* contain sections in which pastiches of widely varying styles are stitched together by formulaic (and largely fossilized) narrative or connective devices.[61] For these reasons, it is frequently best to avoid the temptation of assigning a given text to just one dialect or another—we often encounter a *mixture* of dialects and registers.[62]

The other qualification that I would bring to Junge's concepts of Ramesside dialects involves a historical development that probably had a considerable influence on both the language and the literary genres of Dynasty Twenty in particular. One of the most interesting and enigmatic aspects of the latter half of Ramesses III's reign was the virtual abandonment of the northern capital in the Delta and the apparent removal of the royal court to the West Bank of Thebes. This event brought Deir el-Medina, the source of so much of our textual evidence for Late Egyptian, into close proximity with the royal court and its attendant intellectual activity. One can only imagine how much influence the royal scribes of Medinet Habu must have on both the language and literature of Thebes during this pivotal reign of Dynasty Twenty.

Indicators of Late Egyptian Dialect

Although there is a distinct shift in the verbal system from the predominantly "synthetic" tenses of Middle Egyptian to the "analytic" tenses of Late Egyptian, the most immediately noticeable feature of any Late Egyptian text is the extensive and regular use of the definite article that was historically derived from a series of demonstrative adjectives: *pꜣ* (m.), *tꜣ* (f.), *nꜣ* (c. pl.). Equally noticeable and parallel to this development (but appearing much more sporadically) was the substitution of the possessive article series *pꜣy.f, tꜣy.f, nꜣy.f,* and so on for the suffix pronoun.[63] Actually, the use of a definite article that is so characteristic of Late Egyptian is a feature of the Egyptian language that can be traced back long before the New Kingdom.

What is easily overlooked about this use of *pꜣ* is that it was once regarded as dialect, in that term's sense of nonstandard language. During the Middle Kingdom, an official could demonstrate his command of the best, correct diction—what we might lightly call "the pharaoh's Egyptian"—by proudly asserting on his funerary stela, "I am one who speaks after the manner of officials (*srw*), free of speaking *pꜣs*."[64] This is not the place to detail the increasing appearance of the Late Egyptian definite article from the Middle Kingdom into the Ramesside period, but it is important to take into account that, for a long time, the Egyptian elite probably associated the use of *pꜣ* as well as many other features of Late Egyptian as markers of low-class speech. One might say, then, that the use of the article was quite sensitive to the effects of register.

Since Ramesside literature is distinctly connected with the development of Late Egyptian as a dialect, a nonstandard form of speech, we have some major blank spaces in our understanding of that literature, due to the scarcity of all types of hieratic nonadministrative documents during much of Dynasty Eighteen, whether literary papyri[65] or letters.[66] The dearth of letters is particularly unfortunate, since we are interested in the development of dialect, a linguistic phenomenon normally more visible in the more colloquial register of informal communications.[67] A few Dynasty Eighteen letters can be dated to the reign of Hatshepsut, but it is not until the Amarna period that we have enough correspondence to gain a picture of the new nonofficial dialect.[68] Before then, ironically, most of the texts manifesting Late Egyptian traits come from the unexpected source of royal stelae—where one would normally expect to encounter more archaizing features[69]—and from one frequently overlooked literary tale.[70]

Contrary to what one might expect, the period following the Amarna episode until the end of the reign of Seti I has yielded little in the way of documents in the Late Egyptian dialect. At this time, even lengthy legal texts, such as Horemheb's decree or Seti I's Nauri inscription, exhibit not many features of the new dialect. It is hard to say whether the apparent reluctance to use Late Egyptian was due to a spirit of conservative reaction or simply a reflection of accidents of preservation.

Another tendency that has clouded our view of how Late Egyptian and its related literature developed is that most historical studies of the dialect tend to overemphasize the verbal system at the expense of other aspects of grammar and diction. From a practical standpoint, the employment of the definite article and the possessive adjective actually can be more readily noticed than some of the more subtle aspects of verbal tenses and negative constructions. Similarly, anyone translating Ramesside material after working with Middle Egyptian texts will also be quickly struck by the differences in vocabulary, epigraphy, and orthography.[71]

The language of the Ramesside period is marked by a much greater prominence of Semitic roots and loanwords,[72] which reflects Egypt's increased international contacts and plays an especially prominent role in *The Satirical Letter*, discussed below. Foreign words are by no means connected with just "elevated" speech but occur regularly in materials ranging from royal inscriptions to the most colloquial ostraca.[73] The literary language, above all, shows a great expansion in size during this period. In the *Wörterbuch*, one finds the notations "Nä. lit." next to a surprising number of words that either have no Middle Egyptian equivalent or are rare in the earlier dialect. To be fair, it is hard to envision how systematic comparison of the literary vocabulary of Middle and Late Egyptian might be accomplished, except by a process of "solution by successive approximations." A similar, if unacknowledged, methodology is employed by Egyptologists in the creation of grammars.[74] Nevertheless, it is still remarkable that there are no comprehensive studies available on the lexical content of Middle Egyptian versus Late Egyptian.

In describing the development of Late Egyptian, one should follow Goldwasser's lead and think in terms of a long-term struggle for the legitimization of the standardized "low variety" of Late Egyptian.[75] The reign of Ramesses II seems to have marked a watershed in this slow acceptance of

Late Egyptian. There is a noticeable increase in features of the new dialect in hieratic letters that can be ascribed to this reign, as well as in the ostraca from Deir el-Medina. It is obvious that Late Egyptian had achieved widespread approval for both official and unofficial correspondence by this time. Unfortunately, precise dating of such evidence is always fraught with difficulties.

This is not the case, however, with three unexpected (and understudied) monuments in the development of Late Egyptian: the Treaty of Ramesses II and Hattusilis, the legal inscription in the Memphite tomb of Mose, and the Second Marriage Stela of Ramesses II. These texts can all be placed unquestionably in the period from the early to the middle of Ramesses' reign. Each, in fact, conforms fairly closely to the standards of "documentary" Late Egyptian of Dynasty Twenty as established by Junge, Groll, Grieg, and others.[76] Yet the extent to which these three documents are representative Late Egyptian compositions has not been recognized in recent studies of the development of the dialect.[77]

One reason for this oversight may have been the remarkable and unexpected form of these texts—they were essentially *inscriptions* at a time when we would expect texts written in this manner (and register) to employ the more formal (and aptly named) Late Middle Egyptian dialect. The dates of the first two texts in this trio are also quite significant, since they provide a firm chronological point for the *official* adoption of Late Egyptian, even at the highest levels of society, that is, somewhere near the beginning of Ramesses II's third decade, if not sooner.[78] The Second Marriage Stela additionally demonstrates that the royal chancellery was willing to adopt both the language and new rhetorical devices of literary Late Egyptian.[79] Given their subject matter—two legal texts and a royal wedding announcement of sorts—it would certainly be something of a stretch to characterize these documents as "Alltagstexte."

The regular use of Late Egyptian in both official and unofficial documents of the reign dovetails nicely with evidence that a new curriculum to address the need for training in good Late Egyptian diction had been developed during the reigns of Ramesses II and his successor Merenptah. By means of internal evidence, the composition of one of the most popular of the new didactic works, called *The Satirical Letter,* can be confidently fixed in the early part of the reign of Ramesses II.[80] The approximate date when some of the new didactic pieces may have been first composed remains unclear, but this fact is not really important for the purposes of this discussion. More to the point is that a revised curriculum that instructed scribes in all aspects of Late Egyptian grammar, style, and vocabulary was being employed throughout Egypt in this period. Notwithstanding, to judge from the sizable proportion of Middle Egyptian material among the ostraca, papyri, and other didactic materials of the Ramesside period, these Late Egyptian compositions had by no means replaced the older, more traditional texts in Middle Egyptian. Ironically, the Late Egyptian dialect and its associated literary corpus fell rapidly into desuetude soon after Dynasty Twenty, whereas the Middle Egyptian dialect apparently continued to find favor as the "classic" form of the language.[81]

THE IMPLICATIONS OF LITERARY AND SCRIBAL TRAINING IN THE RAMESSIDE PERIOD

The question of how and with what texts scribes learned to write either dialect of Egyptian have profound implications for Ramesside literary history. Intriguingly, much of the answer lies in the various forms of writing employed at this time. There was a rough hierarchy of prestige and expense among the various Egyptian scripts, most likely based on the time required to write out the texts—hieratic was the cheapest and most rapid form; then came the more costly cursive hieroglyphs and, finally, the expensive, laborious, and prestigious hieroglyphs (fig. 8.1).[82]

As far as acquiring basic writing skills was concerned, it is important that we consider that, unlike our university practice with the Egyptian language today, ancient students learned hieratic first and foremost[83]—knowledge of hieroglyphs or cursives, if acquired at all, were rather specialized skills left to later stages of training.[84] Those who learned hieroglyphs or cursives would do so primarily with the aim of producing materials used in mortuary and religious contexts. It is not surprising that the cursive hieroglyphs were often the script form chosen for materials that the Egyptians may have considered arcane or recondite.[85] Additionally, cursives occasionally served as an intermediary step when laying out hieroglyphic tomb texts.[86]

As mentioned previously, two other notable texts in the development of Late Egyptian, especially in the all-important didactic realm, were the *Late Egyptian Miscellanies* and *The Satirical Letter* of Papyrus Anastasi I. It would be very difficult to pinpoint where any text might have been placed within the Ramesside curriculum, but once the student scribes knew how to write hieratic characters and groups of signs, it seems likely that the *Miscellanies* and *The Satirical Letter* would have been among the first texts studied. These two new compositions were, after all, written in a dialect closer to what students were apt to use in their everyday life than the language in the traditional Middle Kingdom didactic texts.[87]

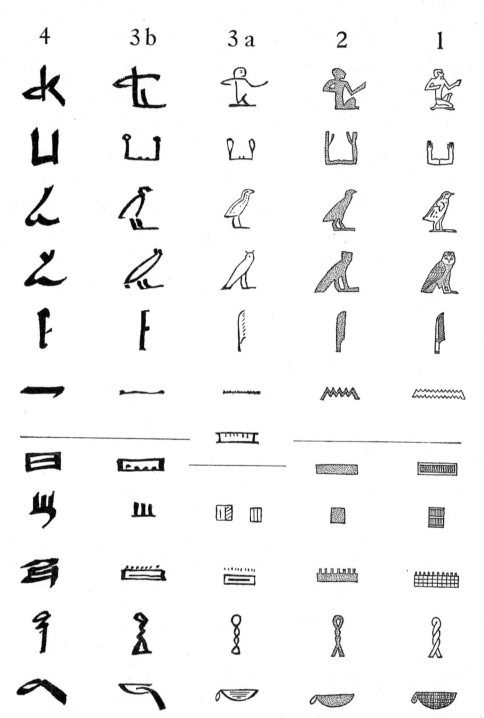

Fig. 8.1. Egyptian writing forms: *from right to left,* painted hieroglyphs, incised hieroglyphs, incised cursives, written (*Book of the Dead*) or painted cursives, and hieratic. (Originally published in Fischer [1976b] fig. 4, facing p. 40. Courtesy of the Metropolitan Museum of Art, New York.)

The old theory that ostraca texts reflected a Theban tradition, whereas the material appearing on papyri were exemplars of a Memphite curriculum is a notion most assuredly based on accidents of preservation.[88] Not only is there a major papyrus exemplar of *The Satirical Letter* from Thebes, but there are also enough Deir el-Medina ostraca quoting passages from the *Late Egyptian Miscellanies* to demonstrate that the curriculum was fairly uniform for north and south.[89] This shared curriculum may well have been formed around the same time that official texts had begun using Late Egyptian. Based on the inscriptional evidence mentioned above, the curriculum may well have been established during the reign of Ramesses II, even though many of the relevant papyri date to the reign of Merenptah and later. This is not to say, however, that each of the capital regions might not have developed a few didactic pieces of a more local character. Certainly the dearth of a large corpus of student ostraca comparable to the evidence from Deir el-Medina complicates our assessment of how the scribal curriculum in the Memphite region may have compared with its southern counterpart.

Judging by the types of errors on papyri and ostraca, both Erman and Brunner concluded that students began by learning to write hieratic texts in both Late and Middle Egyptian. In either case, the hieratic script would normally, but not always, conform to contemporary Ramesside standards.[90] According to their reconstructions, the students would first practice short excerpts chiefly on ostraca; then, once they had become more adept, they would eventually move on to write out more extensive passages, even entire works, on the more expensive medium of papyrus. However, some recent studies on the problem of Deir el-Medina literary materials have shown that this notion must be modified extensively, if not altogether discarded. These reinterpretations were begun by Posener, the great doyen of Deir el-Medina literary ostraca, and have now been expanded and sharpened by the observations of Gasse, Janssen, and McDowell, summarized briefly in the following paragraphs.

Gasse observed that a scholar sorting ostraca into literary and nonliterary examples quickly learns to make an a priori selection based on appearance—the handwriting, line spacing, and format of the texts alone—before even attempting to translate the text.[91] One might say that in this instance, register and script largely coincide. After examining a great number of published and unpublished ostraca, Gasse was able to make a list of the six most commonly attested literary works, roughly in descending order of their frequency: *Satire on the Trades* (*The Instruction of Dua-Khety*), *The Instruction of Amenemhat I,* the *Kemyt, The Satirical Letter* (Papyrus Anastasi I), the *Hymn to the Inundation,* and *The Loyalist Instruction.*[92]

One additional text, *The Instruction of a Man to His Son*, should be added to Gasse's list, although it is difficult to assess its frequency in relation to the other compositions. Fischer-Elfert has convincingly suggested that the latter work was part of a standard tripartite sequence of didactic compositions— *Satire on the Trades, The Instruction of a Man,* and *The Loyalist Instruction*— used extensively for scribal training during the Ramesside period.[93] Once again, it is significant that these three were all Middle Egyptian works. Remarkably enough, only one text on Gasse's list, *The Satirical Letter,* is in Late Egyptian.

Various selections from the *Late Egyptian Miscellanies* also appeared on ostraca, providing further evidence of the importance of the more contemporary component of the Deir el-Medina curriculum. More recently, Fischer-Elfert has noted a conundrum. The list of venerated authors of the past mentioned in *The Satirical Letter,* the *Antef Song,* and *The Encomium of the Sages* may imply a curriculum of classical literature that a learned scribe was expected to know, yet several of these texts are rarely attested among the didactic materials found at Memphis or at Thebes.[94]

As noted above, Janssen and Posener have demonstrated that the script on the so-called student ostraca is far more confident and adept than previously estimated. This observation is quite significant, since it alters considerably our conceptions of where these texts should be placed within the Ramesside curriculum. Indeed, sometimes the script on literary ostraca, such as the uncommon examples of *The Tale of Sinuhe,* can be described as calligraphic in their execution, certainly comparable with the more careful papyri.[95] In short, the *handwriting* seems experienced, even if the result, the texts themselves, are full of errors in grammar and orthography.[96] This important observation casts new light on the position of the Middle Egyptian didactic texts within the overall curriculum.

Janssen has made the plausible suggestion that at least some of these instructional ostraca may in reality provide us with evidence of an appreciation of literature for its own sake among the scribal community at Deir el-Medina, the equivalent of sporting a "classical education" in today's society.[97] Once more, this would imply a level of skill far beyond that of beginners. As we know from the words of *The Encomium of the Sages,* literature, literacy, and familiarity with the great authors of the past all enjoyed high prestige. Ostraca, as a plentiful natural by-product of tomb construction and similar activities, would have provided the ideal material for the cheap "paperback editions" of their day.

Returning for a moment to the Late Egyptian literary school papyri, Mc-

Dowell and Janssen have shown that the commonly held notion that papyrus was considerably more expensive may be based on false premises. Several of the *Late Egyptian Miscellanies* were written out on reused documentary papyri, which could be purchased cheaply, so that such works need not have been relegated to just the very end of a scribe's training.[98] The *Miscellanies* certainly seem to have been written out by well-trained students.[99] One could very well use Ennene's scribal hand as a model for instructing modern students in a fine hieratic script.

However, the skillful writing on these papyri should not be used as evidence that use of ostraca necessarily indicates the work of a beginner.[100] There is frequently nothing in the slightest that we could call "clumsy" or "awkward" in some of these hieratic hands,[101] which can occasionally be every bit as elegant as the script on the beautiful Harris Papyrus, a document that presumably was executed by a royal scribe at the very highest levels of his profession. If we put the numerous errors in the Middle Egyptian dialect in their proper perspective—either the student scribes hardly knew Middle Egyptian, or else they were copying from imperfect models—this evidence indicates that the school ostraca might actually represent the advanced part of the curriculum.[102] In this respect, it is also important to bear in mind that when one speaks of a scribe "writing" didactic material, on either papyrus or an ostracon, "copying" or "writing from memory" would actually be a more accurate description of the underlying process.[103] The work of true beginners seldom appears in the evidence, perhaps because it was mostly confined to the easily erasable medium of writing boards or perhaps just scratching in the dirt, as Dr. Deborah Sweeney has suggested to me.

Since some of these arguments are ultimately concerned with the relative expense of materials and the reuse of materials, a brief observation is in order. In quite a number of other cases, the juxtaposition of two different texts on a single writing board or papyrus simply represents nothing more than an expedient reuse, as seems to be the case with the Louvre papyrus containing *The Loyalist Instruction* and with some of the *Late Egyptian Miscellanies*.[104] The appearance of the Leiden Amun Hymn and *The Admonitions of Ipuwer* on the same papyrus is another case in point—here we have a partially reused scroll containing a rather literary religious text of the Ramesside period and a Middle Egyptian didactic composition, but it also indicates that some hymns may well have been considered to have both literary and religious qualities at the same time.[105] Of course, this odd juxtaposition could have been motivated simply by the need to reuse some relatively expensive material. A similar motivation seems at hand in the case where part of a didactic papyrus was reused for the "Diary of a Border Official." There are, however, a few instances when the juxtaposition of two similar texts may be evidence for a thematic or didactic unity.[106]

The *Kemyt* and the Ramesside School Curriculum

The preceding thoughts on script and the didactic process lead to some reflections of my own on the *intention* of the Ramesside school curriculum. I hope that the observations to follow can link some of the major themes developed thus far and show how register, prestige, dialect, and script all interacted.[107]

One source stands out among all other instructional material—the *Kemyt* (perhaps "the compendium" or "compilation"), a didactic text first composed in the Middle Kingdom that was to enjoy an enormous popularity during the Ramesside period.[108] As is the case with other Ramesside didactic material, it is uncertain once again how much of the version found on Deir el-Medina ostraca represents an original Middle Kingdom text and how much might be later accretions and adaptations. The text itself seems to be a pastiche of three or four poorly related topics.[109] Although traces of the formulaic introduction can be traced back to earlier times,[110] no portions of the main body of the text have been found that can be dated before the second part of Dynasty Twelve.[111]

Judging from the large number of its exemplars, the *Kemyt* was certainly one of the most important texts in the Ramesside curriculum.[112] As such, it was a rather odd choice. Not only was it written in Middle Egyptian, but its very writing entailed more archaic practices than other compositions. When sorting ostraca or browsing through a publication of such material, the *Kemyt* ostraca appear noticeably different—strikingly so, even to someone unfamiliar with hieratic (fig. 8.2).

To begin with, the *Kemyt* was always written in columns, a format that immediately distinguishes it from the other texts on Gasse's list. Often, these columns appear to have been marked off by lines before the text was written in.[113] By this point, columnar text had the air of the antique and was largely confined to religious and mortuary texts in tombs, occasional royal inscriptions, or papyri. Switching from the normal horizontal format of New Kingdom hieratic to the vertical columns of the *Kemyt* must have been quite a difficult experience for students. They had to develop a feel for positioning text within columns, a considerably different manner of dividing words into sign groups, and a new rhythm of ligatures and baseline alignment.

Yet the columnar format is only the most obvious of the peculiarities pre-

Fig. 8.2. A typical *Kemyt* ostracon. (After Posener [1951b] pl. 24 [1110].)

sented by *Kemyt* ostraca. On closer examination, the script adopted for *Kemyt* texts significantly differs from contemporary Ramesside hands of other instructional texts from Deir el-Medina. It was so different, in fact, that a few examples indicate that the student has awkwardly traced over with black the teacher's model in red.[114] A closer examination reveals why—the *Kemyt* ostraca employed a rather simplified, deliberately archaic hand in which ligatures occurred much less often.[115] It was, in fact, as Brunner noted,[116] an awkward imitation of early Middle Kingdom hieratic, whose forms were ultimately not far removed from cursive hieroglyphs. Some observers have suggested that these ostraca are so much alike in both the form and disposition of their signs that it seems as if the student scribes were carefully copying the text sign by sign from the same model papyrus or ostracon.[117]

The model ostraca seem to have remained remarkably constant over the years. Significantly, of the six texts on Gasse's list, only the *Kemyt* has exemplars written in cursives and even some rare instances in fully formed hieroglyphs.[118] Unlike the other compositions, the *Kemyt* is preserved exclusively on ostraca—no New Kingdom examples appear on papyri.[119] At this time during the Ramesside period, the closest comparable material, particularly in the form of the cursive script as well as the heavy use of rubricized text,[120] would be the *Book of the Dead*[121] and the Coffin Texts. The latter corpus, which we know largely from the cursive hieroglyphic texts inscribed on the insides of Middle Kingdom coffins, was actually used much more often than one might think during the New Kingdom—for instance, there is a long inscription composed of selections from the Coffin Texts in a subterranean portion of a Dynasty Eighteen tomb.[122] The Coffin Texts were, in addition, the source materials on which many parts of the *Book of the Dead* were based.

When all is said and done, the obvious question that we all seem to be leaving unanswered is *why* Middle Egyptian was so prominent among Ramesside didactic materials. Why was there this emphasis on an obsolete dialect? Even if some scribes wished to display their erudition or demonstrate their fealty to the great traditions of the past, the Egyptians ultimately were, after all, a notoriously practical people. Much of the answer to this puzzle lies, literally, in the location of Deir el-Medina and Medinet Habu—right in the midst of the Ramesside mortuary industry of the Theban West Bank. We can ask what other texts in this environment shared these characteristics of the *Kemyt:* Middle Egyptian dialect; predominantly columnar format; and an archaic, if not arcane, script. The answer is quite important and underscores how Middle Egyptian retained its vitality and had an important purpose that went far beyond copying didactic literature.

During Dynasties Nineteen and Twenty, Middle Egyptian or, at least, a form of it was used for a high proportion of the texts belonging to the private "religious" or "mortuary" register, for example, the great majority of inscriptions on contemporary tomb walls,[123] most funerary stelae, copies of the *Book of the Dead*,[124] and inscriptions on funerary equipment. In the royal domain, the great majority of "historical" texts and religious inscriptions in temples and the underworld books in the New Kingdom royal tombs (some also in columnar format and in cursive hieroglyphs) also used a form of Middle Egyptian, with some of the latter group even written in cursive hieroglyphs.[125] Though they may have been archaic and fossilized, this dialect and script were still prestigious, having acquired an aura somewhat like we are apt to accord to the equally fossilized language and italic script employed on diplomas and official proclamations in modern society.

The categories of texts just mentioned, not incidentally, are the same types of texts that seem to be preserved on a much-neglected genre of ostraca, namely, hieroglyphic ostraca. The preponderance of these objects is likewise written in a columnar format, often with the lines marked out. Many hieroglyphic ostraca contain real or imaginary titularies,[126] some with accompanying figures, as if the scribes were either practicing a decorative genre or else making preliminary drafts for tomb inscriptions.[127] A few other hieroglyphic ostraca contain passages from magical texts[128] and other religious material in Middle Egyptian.[129] Some of these may be copies of funerary material that a student or practiced scribe encountered in his work. As one can see by the script in these examples, by "hieroglyphic," I often really mean cursive hieroglyphs.

When we consider the texts in Kitchen's vast corpus and add to those the almost innumerable lesser inscribed objects in museum collections that he did not include, then the great preponderance of all preserved Ramesside textual material in hieroglyphs would fall into the categories just mentioned above. Finally, we should note in passing that we almost certainly have recovered only a small percentage of all the copies of the *Book of the Dead* produced during the New Kingdom, a potential "cash cow" for any funerary workshop employing scribes skilled in Middle Egyptian dialect and cursive hieroglyphs. Many scribes, particularly those working at Deir el-Medina and other places in Western Thebes, may well have earned a sizable proportion of their livelihood by producing and/or performing texts in Middle Egyptian connected to the vast mortuary "industry" in those parts.[130] Thus, in terms of use, Middle Egyptian was hardly a dead language during the Ramesside period. For those scribes who were not fortunate enough to obtain a position with "the Gang" at Deir el-Medina, skill in Middle Egyptian dialect and the script styles associated with it would have offered a backup source of employment.

The Nature of the Middle Egyptian
Literary Tradition during the Ramesside Period

It would be a mistake to associate the Middle Egyptian literary tradition solely with the "reproductive" mode of text creation during the Ramesside period. There was a dynamic, "productive" aspect as well, which is only now becoming evident to literary scholars. Although, as noted above, there is a remarkably high proportion of Middle Kingdom works among literary papyri from Dynasty Eighteen to the end of Dynasty Twenty, closer examination of the actual contents of these documents reveals that their relationship with the earlier tradition might not be what has been previously assumed.

Perhaps the key composition in this respect is *The Loyalist Instruction*, especially since its principal Middle Kingdom example is a stela firmly dated to the reign of Amenemhat III.[131] In later times, this composition enjoyed great popularity, with portions appearing on three papyri, one writing board, and a large number of ostraca. This text, as noted above, figures prominently on Gasse's list of the most popular of didactic compositions among the Deir el-Medina ostraca.[132] There are two distinct versions of this work, which has led to a widely held supposition that the text as it appears on the stela represents an earlier *abrégé*, an abridgement of the more complete original text now known only from post-Middle Kingdom exemplars. It is unsettling, however, that fully half of the entire composition is attested only in those documents dating to the New Kingdom.

Schipper's recent reexamination and comparison of the two traditions of *The Loyalist Instruction*—stela and papyrus—put forth a convincing argument that its later, longer version contains numerous interpolations and additions that thematically belong more closely to New Kingdom loyalist literature.[133] He concluded that the version previously considered the complete edition is more likely a major reinterpretation and reworking of the original Dynasty Twelve text—to the extent that Schipper proposed we should consider these as two closely related but separate compositions, *The Instruction of Sehetep-ib-Re* and *The Loyalist Instruction*.

An immediate analogy might be made here with the relationship between the Middle Kingdom *Satire on the Trades* and the Ramesside rewriting of the same themes found in the *Late Egyptian Miscellanies*. Although there is certainly a danger of making a series of arguments from silence, Schipper's approach and its underlying methodology might well be applied equally to *Satire on the Trades*, *The Instruction of Amenemhat I*, the *Kemyt*, the *Hymn to the Inundation*, and *The Instruction of a Man for His Son*, in addition to several other Middle Egyptian compositions that were widely employed as teaching materials during the Ramesside period. These ostensibly Middle Kingdom "classics" are likewise either virtually unattested prior to Dynasty Eighteen or else have long portions that are unknown except on the later papyri, ostraca, and writing boards of the New Kingdom.

If only one or two of these important ostensibly Middle Kingdom sources—all of which were so important to the Deir el-Medina curriculum—possessed no demonstrably Dynasty Twelve exemplars, it would be easy to ascribe this state of affairs to accidents of preservation. However, the lack of Middle Kingdom originals for *all* of the most common didactic works on Gasse's list, with the exception of the *Kemyt*, should certainly give us pause. *The Instruction of Ptahhotep,* for example, seems to possess two beginnings and two conclusions, already perhaps evidence of later accretions to the original composition by the time of its appearance in the Middle Kingdom.[134] Nevertheless, not only would it be very hard to ascertain the dates at which additions may have been made, but it would also be difficult to decide which version represented the original text.

The evidence, therefore, means that we should seriously entertain the possibility that many of those Middle Kingdom didactic texts or, at least, substantial sections of them could have been composed at a date subsequent to the Middle Kingdom proper. Of course, even if this should prove to be the case, it would be unwise to ascribe much of this possible "reedition" of earlier works to the Ramesside period alone. After all, the high level of competency in Middle Egyptian encountered on well-dated royal and private monuments of Dynasty Eighteen led Gardiner to include many examples from the Thutmoside period in his estimable *Egyptian Grammar.*[135] At some point during the New Kingdom, other Middle Egyptian didactic pieces—*The Instruction of Ptahhotep* and *The Instruction for King Merikare,* for example—may have undergone the same types of modifications that *The Loyalist Instruction* did, but probably to a much lesser degree.

In the final analysis, we should entertain seriously the possibility that some skilled Dynasty Eighteen and Ramesside *compositors* created several new texts in the Middle Egyptian language and style. Most likely, we have not realized this because we have been overly influenced by the rather tenuous abilities of later student *copyists* in their attempts to reproduce those materials accurately. On occasion, furthermore, these students may have been faithfully copying the faulty editions of their scribal masters. In short, we should keep the activities of original authors and later students more distinct in our minds. At the very least, it seems advisable to make a distinction between works that are "Middle Egyptian" and "Middle Kingdom."

LITERATURE AND THE LITERARY ENVIRONMENT OF THE REIGN OF RAMESSES III—A SURVEY

The observations at the end of the preceding section have fundamental consequences for a comprehensive assessment of the literary achievements of the

Ramesside period. Those discussions underscored the fact that there is no need to treat the Middle Egyptian and the Late Egyptian compositions of the Ramesside period as separate genres—we may consider both to be "Ramesside" in a general sense. Indeed, many of the texts that we have considered in the past as Middle Egyptian may yet prove to be largely creations or substantial reeditions of the New Kingdom.[136] These are important issues—perhaps even the key issues—when assessing the role of a large category of literary works in Ramesside literary life.

First of all, those compositions that we can ascribe to the Middle Kingdom continued to play a major part in contemporary literary life, as their many copies on papyri and ostraca alone shows. It ultimately matters little whether the primary motive for their preservation was didactic or whether those texts were appreciated as literary classics. Strikingly enough, *The Encomium of the Sages,* which is preserved amid a collection of didactic texts, demonstrates that the Ramesside scribes also knew and venerated the authors of many of the Middle Kingdom compositions they copied. Secondly, in addition to the well-known didactic works of the past (if they really are such), many new and original compositions of Dynasties Nineteen and Twenty were deliberately written in the Middle Egyptian dialect, a form of the language that one might have expected at this point to have been relegated entirely to the "reproductive" aspect of text production.

In the discussion to follow, I hope to describe the literary works that would have formed the literary environment of a literate man during the reign of Ramesses III—belles lettres used to instruct, to celebrate the king or a god, and to entertain the reader or an audience. To be honest, it is often impossible to state confidently whether a given work would have been familiar to a scribe or a student during that time, dating problems being what they are. Yet, at the same time, it is equally inescapable that a high proportion of the Ramesside literary manuscripts, especially ostraca, date to the early part of Dynasty Twenty. For these reasons, I have chosen rather broad definitions, in terms of both dating and genres, for this portion of this chapter.

Royal Inscriptions and Religious Literature in the Reign of Ramesses III

As categories, religious and historical texts share many thematic and compositional features, not the least of which is that they represent those works that one can most confidently ascribe to the reign of Ramesses III. They frequently bear a date or occur in a datable context, such as a tomb or temple, and thereby are more reliably datable than most private inscriptions or documents on papyrus. Unfortunately, a comprehensive examination of either royal religious or historical texts cannot be undertaken in this chapter, not only because of the vast amount of material available, but also because more detailed treatments would necessarily impinge on other contributions to this volume. Some general remarks are nevertheless in order, as long as they are largely limited to these texts' qualities as literary works, leaving their historical validity or theological import to other studies.

Modern and ancient literary tastes are perhaps most widely divergent concerning historical inscriptions than with any other textual genre. Three reasons for this difference of opinion become especially prominent during the reign of Ramesses III. First, a question of originality arises out of what one might politely describe as frequent "borrowings" or "intertextuality" in that king's texts. As noted previously, Ramesses III could be justly called "the intertextual king."[137] In addition, there is a strong—almost instinctive—modern reaction against a form of literature so palpably ideological, which results in a tendency to dismiss Egyptian royal inscriptions as being primarily political-rhetorical exercises rather than literary works. Finally, the Egyptians had a need, almost amounting to a compulsion, to demonstrate a continuity with the past in virtually all their creative endeavors. The question of originality and the Egyptians' close connection with their past are intertwined and will be examined here first.

As shown by his name alone—closely modeled on that of Ramesses II, "the Great," his famous predecessor of Dynasty Nineteen—Ramesses III consciously patterned many aspects of his rule after that of his well-known namesake. Since history was now officially repeating itself, it is hardly surprising that his chancellery should closely and deliberately follow the phraseology of the texts of Ramesses II and Merenptah. In all likelihood, when Egyptian royal scribal chancelleries reused texts of former kings, they approached the matter in much the same spirit as when they reinscribed statuary and other monuments with the name of the ruling king. These "usurpations," as we are apt to view them, were quite another matter in the eyes of the Egyptians. They apparently regarded such actions simply as a form of reuse justified by the current monarch's connection with a theoretically unbroken chain of kingship.[138]

This attitude would have been reinforced by a scribal training process in which copying of texts played a central role.[139] This frame of mind was further reinforced by a marked tendency of Egyptian historical inscriptions to demonstrate solidarity with the past through imitative phraseology. In short, our modern emphasis on originality as an essential characteristic of "true" literature can be especially inappropriate when applied to royal inscriptions. In the case of Ramesses III, his chancellery's historical erudition and his self-conception as a great reviver of Egypt's past glories have combined to create his reputation—unmerited in my opinion—of being a mere copycat or a plagiarist of sorts.

The imitation of royal rhetoric occurred in private contexts as well. The Carnarvon Tablet certainly confirms the impression that the Egyptians considered royal inscriptions as a form of belles lettres that student scribes might profitably imitate.[140] This writing tablet preserves an excerpt from a Middle Kingdom literary text (*The Instruction of Ptahhotep*) on one side, while the other side contains the introductory lines of a late Dynasty Seventeen royal inscription, the so-called First Kamose Stela.[141] The juxtaposition of both textual genres on a writing tablet is a good indication that some ancient Egyptian teacher believed that the royal narrative inscription was written in an admirable literary style, even though the text may have included a few unacceptably dialectal features for a contemporary royal inscription. Later, during the reign of Ramesses II and after, the Kadesh texts provide us with an even clearer example of royal inscriptions that were employed in the scribal curriculum, albeit in a modified fashion.

These are but a few examples of the major role played by solidarity with the past in Egyptian historical literature, a tendency certainly present in other genres. For this reason, above all others, our modern emphasis on originality as an essential characteristic of "true" literature can be especially misleading. Our conceptual problems with a palpable reverence for tradition that is prevalent in every form of Egyptian art have a parallel development in our tendency to underestimate Egyptian sculpture as "static" or "unchanging," without giving thought to why this should be so. These modern critiques often fail to realize that precisely because of the religious context of much Egyptian plastic art, certain unchanging cultic functions had to be maintained over any aesthetic considerations, a situation that seldom plays a role in modern Western sensibilities. Some of the same considerations carried over into the realm of Egyptian literature as well. It is ironic that the *Sitz im Leben* of much Egyptian art and writing was the funerary or the religious spheres, the most conservative areas of human life.

Nevertheless, the observations above about various forms of reuse by Egyptian monarchs, particularly in connection with Ramesses III's inscriptions, still do not address the problem of whether the events narrated in his texts actually happened in the manner described or even occurred at all.[142]

The question of the historical accuracy of Ramesses III's inscriptions is a matter properly handled elsewhere in this volume.

Now we should turn our attention to the style and language of Egyptian royal inscriptions, material that seems nonliterary according to most modern standards of taste. As noted in the introduction to this chapter, one of the major advances of Lichtheim's anthology was her recognition that the "purposeful" nature of many "historical" royal inscriptions should not preclude treating them as literary compositions.[143] Kitchen's recent anthology *Poetry of Ancient Egypt* likewise includes a large number of royal inscriptions, rightfully so.[144]

Given the debased quality of political rhetoric today, we are apt to forget that political figures such as Churchill and Lincoln wrote in beautiful, often poetical English style. Similarly, many Egyptian texts that one might be initially tempted to dismiss simply as "historical," "propagandistic," or "ideological" reveal, on closer inspection, those characteristics that one would normally associate with the best Egyptian nonroyal literary works—elegant parallels, complex composition, richness of expression, and refined vocabulary, all of which might be subsumed under the rubric of "rhetoric."[145] At the risk of making a circular argument centered on the last point, it is remarkable how often one finds that the rare, more unusual vocabulary of a Ramesside royal historical inscription is otherwise attested only in contemporary "literary" sources.

There is a simple explanation for the close relationship between the two genres. Since the pharaoh apparently was able to hire the nation's best artisans in the plastic arts, it is only natural that the royal chancellery would likewise command the services of the most highly skilled "wordsmiths," to use a modern journalistic expression. From our point of view, these texts have passages that could be described as rather flowery[146]—a less charitable assessment would call the writing orotund or bombastic. This inscriptional genre perhaps reached its acme during the reign of Ramesses II with the compositions known as "rhetorical stelae,"[147] short texts devoted to the praise of the monarch. These texts, strangely enough, are relatively uncommon among the texts of Ramesses III,[148] who apparently preferred lengthier inscriptions of the same sort. The longer royal compositions, by contrast, tend to be more purposeful, as Lichtheim would put it, with the result that they are often composites of several genres and registers and draw on other royal texts.[149] Many Ramesside royal inscriptions, including those of Ramesses III, began with a section of extensive praise of the king before introducing the main subject of the text with the particle *ist.*[150]

It is probably better to employ the term *ideological* rather than the time-honored term *propaganda* to describe the tone of most royal texts.[151] Not only is *ideological* more neutral to the ears of a modern reader, but it is a more accurate term in the ancient context. *Propaganda* normally implies political communications directed at a mass, nationwide audience, conditions generally lacking among the predominantly illiterate and nonurban populace of ancient Egypt. Although the heroic, greater than life-size images that accompany so many of Ramesses III's inscriptions at Medinet Habu are reminiscent of twentieth-century propaganda posters, the audience, just for those temple representations alone, would have been quite limited, even among the Theban population. By modern standards, the language of Ramesside royal inscriptions may frequently sound excessively fawning and obsequious, recalling the "cult of personality" that surrounded modern tyrants such as Mao and Stalin. Despite this, describing royal texts simply as "propaganda" or "ideological" would be overlooking the influence of the all-important religious component of Egyptian kingship and the pharaoh's central function as the semidivine nexus between the divine sphere and humanity. At the same time, most modern observers would hardly find the language of royal texts excessive if they encountered similar diction in a hymn of praise to a deity.

When describing Ramesside historical and biographical inscriptions in funerary contexts, whether royal or nonroyal, the expressions "self-presentation" or, less charitably, "self-promotion" hit closer to the mark.[152] Despite the fact that they were mostly written in the third person (rather than the first), the texts narrating the deeds of Ramesses III on the walls of his mortuary temple are essentially self-presentations much in the manner of private biographical inscriptions on tomb walls. Contemporary private texts of this sort often bear the marks of royal sponsorship rather prominently, because the monuments on which they appear were constructed with extensive support from the pharaoh. Accordingly, some of these ostensibly funerary texts read much like high-quality literary compositions, a point further addressed below.

Although it was written shortly after the death of its supposed narrator, Ramesses III, the lengthy "historical section" of Papyrus Harris I is, at heart, another example of a postmortem self-presentation.[153] The so-called *Königsnovelle* was a common motif added to royal inscriptions in order to enliven the account while injecting a degree of dramatic tension into the narrative. Loprieno defined this topos succinctly as "a form of Egyptian narrative which focuses on the role of the king as the recipient of divine inspiration or as the central protagonist of the ensuing decision-making process."[154] The intent is not simply to valorize the king but to reveal his position within society as a whole or to explore his role as the intermediary between the divine sphere and humanity. The *Königsnovelle* expresses its literary nature in its deliberate preference for interaction, episodic presentation, and dialogue over straightforward description of bare facts.

Ramesses III's texts at Medinet Habu comprise a virtual anthology of the styles and themes of Ramesside historical compositions in various combinations. Like all royal inscriptions, his texts are composites, frequently containing many decorum elements such as titulary, datelines, and mention of tutelary deities, in addition to the central, more narrative (and innovative) content of the text.[155] They exhibit an unusually rich vocabulary that combines the stereotypical and often bombastic terminology of Ramesside royal inscriptions with a large number of foreign words and rare terms that may represent colloquialisms.[156]

Narrative devices of this sort are attested in the Medinet Habu inscriptions. While displaying a currency with normal Ramesside epigraphy, these inscriptions, strangely enough, also maintain solidarity with the practices of a distant past by their marked preference for the obsolete columnar format, as if they were reproducing excerpts from the *gnwt* "archives" of ancient times. This columnar format was also consciously imitated earlier in Thutmose III's Karnak "annals."

In the case of the great First Libyan War inscription of year 5,[157] the antique nature of this text format was further enhanced by the retrograde direction of the inscription, perhaps employed here so that the movement of the text would cohere more closely with the narrative flow of the accompanying battle reliefs. Both this inscription and other Medinet Habu texts reflect a dialect that would be more accurately characterized as being Late Middle Egyptian than as literary Late Egyptian. For example, the use of the Late Egyptian definite article and the pronominal adjective are sporadic, and the *sḏm.n.f* appears fairly often.[158] Yet, at the same time, these texts employ an elevated vocabulary replete with those new rare words and foreign expressions that we normally associate with literary Late Egyptian and that were not attested in the earlier dialect.

Two texts on the exterior faces of the first pylon at Medinet Habu were probably inscribed to mark the completion of this massive temple: the Blessing of Ptah[159] and the double "rhetorical stelae," both of which were dated simply to year 12, without further specifying either month or day.[160] The Blessing of Ptah, a fascinating dialogue between the king and the deity describing an exchange of benefactions, is perhaps the prime example of intertextuality among his inscriptions, since the text closely parallels an original composition of his great paragon Ramesses II. Nevertheless, we should emphasize that Ramesses III's version was by no means just a slavish copy of the model but, rather, a careful phrase-by-phrase reedition and, in several places, reinterpretation of the original text. For instance, a lengthy passage connected to Ramesses II's first Hittite marriage was edited out of the later version entirely since the circumstances were no longer appropriate.[161]

Private Inscriptions and Religious Literature in the Reign of Ramesses III

Discussion of both private (auto)biographical and religious texts are best left to elsewhere in the present volume—only a few general remarks will be given here. As examples of literary works, there is often little to distinguish private and royal inscriptions, except for their length and complexity; the same holds true for the related genre of religious texts. In a polytheistic context where there was no centralized religious authority, true expression of religious feeling could come from either realm. Some thematic differences arise out of the special role of the king in Egyptian society, but, beyond that, when it came to expressing themselves, both ruler and subject operated under strong ideological restraints.

Like royal inscriptions, private biographical texts are "ideological" because they are really idealized portraits, or "self-presentations" in which the stela or tomb owner describes his societal virtues. For the same reasons, private inscriptions sometimes display a certain degree of intertextuality with didactic texts.[162] The ideological nature of private narrative texts leads them to be less innovative and hence less literary as well. A high percentage of private inscriptions are connected with the mortuary/funerary context, which acted as a further brake on any creative impulses their compositors might have felt.[163] The higher-quality stelae and the more elaborately outfitted tombs were probably done with some degree of royal support and therefore have a direct relationship with contemporary royal texts.

Over the course of the Ramesside period, the themes of both private tomb decorations and other inscriptions shifted rapidly away from daily life to concerns about the gods and the afterlife. Whereas a Dynasty Eighteen official might proudly describe his official career and related duties, his counterpart in Dynasty Nineteen or Twenty would probably prefer to decorate his tomb walls with scenes and text from the *Book of the Dead* or similar religious material. Consequently, the private biographical inscription had become a relatively uncommon genre by the reign of Ramesses III.

Comparatively speaking, the genre of private biographical texts tends to be less literary than royal inscriptions overall. The requirements of the mortuary context meant that much more effort (and wall space) had to be expended on a repertoire of texts such as the offering formula, divine hymns, and excerpts from the *Book of the Dead*, which were deemed necessary for the afterlife of the tomb owner. Even the more strictly biographical texts were often reduced to strings of laudatory epithets that possessed only a quasi-narrative quality.

Under these circumstances, material of a more literary quality occurs rather spottily within a sizable corpus. Yet there are some notable exceptions to the generalizations and observations in the discussion immediately above: for example, the Harpers' Songs, the monuments of personal piety, and the biographical inscription of Sa-mut called Kyky. The monuments of personal piety will not be discussed in the present chapter, since they more properly belong in this volume's study of other religious texts of the era. Strikingly enough, several of these religious inscriptions were written in Late Egyptian or a form of Middle Egyptian with more dialectal features than usual, distinguishing them somewhat from other religiously oriented texts.

Nonroyal Literature in the Reign of Ramesses III—Introductory Remarks

We can now move to literature in the normally understood sense, that is, narrative tales and poetry. The main reason why modern observers feel that the nonroyal sphere produced material that is more recognizably literary is that private texts generally had a much smaller ideological burden to carry than royal inscriptions and so are closer to our tastes. At the same time, however, private texts pose special difficulties for literary historians because they frequently lack precise indications of their date, especially when written on papyri and ostraca—their traditional venues. Dating problems are, however, less of a handicap than they seem at first blush.

On the whole, the corpus of material that can be ascribed to early Dynasty Twenty does not significantly differ in tone and type from what can be firmly associated with Merenptah's reign and before. This is especially true in connection with the most common genre of all private texts—didactic works. As noted at several junctures above, there is virtually no difference in the genres employing the Middle Egyptian and Late Egyptian dialects, so there is little profit in considering Middle Egyptian apart from Late Egyptian in terms of subject matter and creativity. Of course, this was not true of the more purposeful sorts of writing, that is, personal letters and documents where Late Egyptian clearly predominated. In the pages to follow, I present a survey of the large and varied corpus of private texts of the Ramesside period.

Didactic Literature in the Ramesside Period

Didactic literature was unquestionably the most influential of all literary forms during the Ramesside period. Even if its preachy tone often makes Egyptian wisdom unpalatable to modern audiences, it undeniably remains one of their greatest literary achievements. This was the means by which scribes acquired their skills, and at the same time, it provided them with moral and professional guidance. Scribes, especially those with a creative bent, transferred the phraseology and literary techniques learned during their apprenticeship into other aspects of their life and used them as the inspiration for works of their own.

For example, the well-polished business letter or an exchange of letters between colleagues, whose creation was one of the main objectives of scribal education, eventually inspired *The Satirical Letter* and became a new means for framing narrative tales as well. The influence of the letter or document format can be seen not only in *The Satirical Letter,* the *Late Egyptian Miscellanies,* and the *Kemyt* but, later, in *The Report of Wenamun* and *The Tale of Woe* as well.[164]

In this section of this chapter, I have attempted to limit the discussion to those pieces that Egyptologists have recognized as *sbȝyt,* "instruction," in their traditional format or to closely related materials that were clearly used in the instructional process. This definition is not without its difficulties. For instance, the *Hymn to the Inundation,* though clearly not an "instruction," was one of the most important of all students' exercises. The same holds true for a large proportion of Middle Kingdom narrative literature that has been preserved in Ramesside student copies. Although not "instructions" in the literal sense, they were clearly used to teach.

Since a large number of the original documents are written with verse points, red or black dots above the baseline of the text that may or may not indicate poetical units,[165] their presence hints at an unresolved relationship between didactic literature, narrative tales, and even poetry in the Egyptians' minds. Didactic papyri and other genres of literary papyri together have a number of other features that frequently allow one to distinguish them from documentary materials by their rather distinctive outward appearance alone, for example, the heavy use of rubrics or the "division marker"——▪ *grḥ,* "end"—to break either the narration or the papyrus itself into smaller divisions.[166] These characteristics are yet more evidence that a scribe consciously entered a different frame of mind when dealing with the literary register. A literary manuscript involved more than just a different style of writing—it seemingly required a different mindset as well.

At the risk of some repetition, I will begin by retracing a few points already covered in previous discussions of dialect, intertextuality, and scribal training. First and foremost, we should not let the apparent diglossia of didactic literature mislead us about the underlying practical reason for this state of affairs. To be sure, the Egyptians treasured their cultural heritage greatly and could acquire a certain amount of prestige by learning (and even collecting) ancient texts.[167] However, unlike modern students who may briefly immerse themselves in the language of Chaucer or the *Niebelungenlied* for the sake of a "liberal education" and probably never use the antiquated dialect again in their daily life, it was possible for a Ramesside student scribe eventually to derive a substantial proportion of his income from copying out religious/mortuary texts written in Middle Egyptian.[168] Since the later works have many passages that are clearly based on their Middle Kingdom forerunners, there is a natural general thematic, but not textual, relationship between the two groups.[169] In discussing this material, it is probably advisable to maintain a distinction between Middle Egyptian as a dialect and Middle Kingdom as a compositional date.

The purpose of the Ramesside material, in any case, remained the same—to train the scribe in writing, style, and vocabulary while inculcating him with pride in his chosen occupation as the best of all possible professions. Rather than limiting this discussion to what was actually composed during Ramesside times, I shall consider here the literary environment as a whole. From that point of view, Middle Egyptian didactic texts were a cornerstone of contemporary literary life. The didactic works employed in this period can be divided into two major categories: compositions patterned after the *Satire on the Trades* and life instructions[170] in the manner of *Ptahhotep*.

The first group consists mainly of two works—the largely noncanonical collections of short texts known as the *Late Egyptian Miscellanies*[171] and the numerous ostracon copies of the original *Satire on the Trades* ascribed to Khety.[172] Despite its Middle Egyptian dialect, this latter composition was the most frequently copied of all literary texts at Deir el-Medina, an indication of the high status enjoyed by this and other didactic "classics" in the older idiom. Thematically, the *Miscellanies* owed much to this earlier work, but the dialect, vocabulary, and grammar are all distinctly Late Egyptian. A major objective of both Middle Egyptian wisdom literature and the *Miscellanies* was to stress the easeful nature and relative mobility of the scribal profession—other occupations reduced humans to a (literally) beastly state, yet a scribe could enjoy an unusual degree of autonomy. He was, as the expression goes, his own boss, an assertion implying that most individual Egyptians were essentially creatures either of the state or of their employer.[173] Underlying the entire genre was a snobbish attitude toward manual labor. These texts may leave us with a rather invidious impression of a highly stratified, class-conscious society, yet, at the same time, they convey its complex vitality.

At the outset, we should admit that despite much speculation about scribal instruction during the Ramesside period, the actual curriculum still remains largely a scholarly construct or, better put, a scholarly reconstruction based on ostraca and papyri that we have identified as didactic exercises. One reason for this is that once young students had acquired the rudiments of hieratic, the rest of their education probably took place in the framework of a rather fluid apprenticeship relationship. At the same time, there was a more theoretical curriculum, judging from *The Encomium of the Sages*, which extolled the authors of the past who had supposedly composed the didactic texts that students practiced. One might call this list of scribal heroes an implied curriculum, but it seems implied only, since there is a disparity, in many cases, between the writers on this idealized list and the actual works preserved on student exercises.[174] Perhaps if we were to recover a broader range of student exercises from the Memphite region, this picture might change considerably. Our perception of the curriculum is based too heavily on Theban evidence, especially the situation at Deir el-Medina.

Within the corpus of Late Egyptian literary works, the language of the *Miscellanies* is, on the whole, closer to documentary Late Egyptian than to what appears in the literary tales of the New Kingdom. Formerly, there was a tendency among scholars to view the *Miscellanies* as the province of more advanced student scribes, because these texts had at one time been attested almost exclusively on the supposedly more expensive medium of papyrus rather than on ostraca.[175] Over the years, the steadily growing number of exemplars of portions from the *Miscellanies* among Deir el-Medina ostraca and papyri has proven that theory untenable.[176] Although many passages employ a mixture of flattery and effuse glorifications, the grammar, vocabulary, and phraseology are still distinct from what one encounters in the historical inscriptions of Ramesses III. Not only has the dialect of the *Satire* been changed, but its Middle Kingdom topoi have also been modernized, so to speak, in order to fit the greatly changed social fabric of an imperial Egypt. The satirical intent remains,[177] of course, but a number of new professions now receive the brunt of the mockery: stable master, charioteer, soldier, and priest.

The age of the (captive) student audience—teens to early adulthood—may be gauged by the frequent warnings against drinking and wenching. In addition, there was another distraction that could seduce young men away from the scribal profession. With frequent campaigning and adventures abroad, the military had come to occupy a place of pride within the society of Dynasties Nineteen and Twenty. It is no wonder, then, that soldiering is disparaged more frequently than any other occupation in the *Miscellanies;*[178] no effort is spared in describing the onerous tasks and dangers of military life,[179] which, as glamorous as it may outwardly seem, eventually turns even a charioteer into little more than a pack animal.

Satires on trades are by no means the only subject matter of the *Miscellanies.* These papyri, as their very name suggests, are pastiches of short texts that cover a much more diverse range of educational subgenres than their earlier antecedents did. Model letters, formerly an entirely separate didactic type during the Middle Kingdom, were now juxtaposed with hymns, prayers, royal encomia, praises of the teacher, admonitory addresses to the student, and glorification of the scribal trade, in addition to the satires on professions. In fact, the mélange of themes and genres is one of many factors that have raised legitimate doubts about the true nature of the *Miscellanies.* Are these works really scribal exercises, as Erman and others have supposed, or are the *Miscellanies* collections of more serious literature assembled by scribes in the early stages of their careers?[180]

Hagen has shown that the contents of the individual *Miscellanies* papyri vary widely. Some seem to be largely composed of model letters, while other manuscripts have a distinctively religious tone to their contents. From this and other evidence, Hagen has made a good case that it would be too reductive to force this athematic collection into the single rubric of student practice. Furthermore, many of the individual texts also have features of reference works or entertainment literature. Hagen also suggested that the frequent use of letters to scribal superiors as framing devices has probably contributed to our misunderstanding of the character of these papyri.[181]

These are all valid objections against dismissing the *Miscellanies* simply as schoolwork, a classification that might easily lead one to underestimate their worth. Hagen's arguments cannot be addressed in their entirety in this chapter; however, the evidence seems stronger for continuing to see these documents as integral parts of scribal training. First of all, the fact that the material was being copied as exercises, even as exercises often focused on calligraphy, need not have any bearing on the quality or even the intent of the contents. A student can practice his handwriting by mechanically copying belles lettres just as easily as dull rote pieces, but if he should concentrate on models with a fine style or useful information, he will come away with something worth preserving. A work can be didactic and humorous at the same time, as the oft-repeated admonitions to inattentive student scribes seem to be, with their exaggerated descriptions of idleness, stupidity, drinking, and debauchery— themes that would have great appeal to young men. The differences between these documents are outweighed by their similarities, enough that the internal evidence overall indicates that they came from an archive or a library, which would comport well with a school-like environment. Finally, even if the sorts of orthographical errors in these texts are hardly absent from the best professional documentary papyri, the frequency and types of mistakes in the *Miscellanies* mitigate against these being the products of experienced scribes much advanced in their careers.[182]

An interesting new genre is the *laus urbis*, lavish descriptions and praise of the chief cities Thebes, Memphis, and Per-Ramesses.[183] The school milieu and the figure of the instructor are much more in the foreground here than in the Middle Kingdom antecedents. When we read the actual correspondence of the New Kingdom, it is not hard to see the influence of this sort of scribal training in the laudatory rhetoric addressed to superiors or in the querulous scolding of colleagues and subordinates. Some of the admonitory passages in the papyri have the ring of punishment exercises given to the student for some classroom infraction. We have more direct evidence of the educational background of the corpus in the numerous parallel passages (a few nearly verbatim) found scattered among these papyri. Here is intertextuality in its most important and fundamental form—texts transmitted from one source to another as part of a curriculum.

The Lansing Papyrus attests to the essential stability and uniformity of these compositions and the didactic practices underlying them. Although it was probably written in Thebes toward the end of Dynasty Twenty,[184] more than a century after the reign of Merenptah, when its earlier Memphite parallels—Papyrus Anastasi IV, Papyrus Anastasi V, and other Dynasty Nineteen papyri—were created, the Lansing Papyrus adheres quite closely to the text of the earlier versions, sometimes surpassing them in accuracy. In fact, the seeming carelessness in the Lansing Papyrus's frequent omission of prepositions in the Late Egyptian First Present, an emendation that Gardiner frequently suggests in his marginalia, is really a manifestation of a change in this verbal form that accelerated during the reign of Ramesses III.[185]

The second major group of Ramesside didactic texts, the life instructions, when read alongside their Middle Kingdom antecedents, provide us with most of our knowledge of Egyptian moral philosophy, combined, of course, with a healthy dose of advice on much more practical concerns. The life instructions can be further divided into three subcategories. The first subdivision is made up of three interrelated pieces whose composition dates are usually ascribed to the Middle Kingdom; their dialect is certainly Middle Egyptian: *The Loyalist Instruction*,[186] *The Instruction of Amenemhat I*,[187] and *The Instruction of a Man for His Son*.[188] The second subdivision consists of three long works in some form of Late Egyptian: *The Instruction of Ani, The Instruction of Amenemope,* and Papyrus Chester Beatty IV. Of these, only Papyrus Chester Beatty IV and *Ani* can be confidently dated to the Ramesside period; *Amenemope* exists only on copies dating to the Third Intermediate Period and later, yet its language and its sensibility have a distinct Ramesside quality, so it has traditionally been dated to this era.[189]

To this list of five well-known didactic works, we should add the third and smallest subdivision, three short instructional pieces from Deir el-Medina written in Late Egyptian: *The Instruction of Amennakhte*,[190] a work whose author was apparently a well-known figure at the workmen's village, a remarkable departure from the normally anonymous or pseudepigraphical nature of this genre; *The Instruction of Hori*, written by a colleague of Amennakhte;[191] and *The Instruction of Menna*.[192] The last two works are each known only from a single ostracon found at Deir el-Medina; they show that the village scribes were not limited to the reproductive aspect of didactic literature but could create imaginative works of their own.

Whatever the composition dates of *The Loyalist Instruction, The Instruction of Amenemhat I,* and *The Instruction of a Man for His Son* may have actually been, these three Middle Egyptian works were quite popular as didactic works during the Ramesside period and apparently even formed a three-part sequence within the scribal curriculum.[193] They are unified by a conspicuous interest in the theme of loyalty toward the king. In many instances, this motif appears to conflict in spirit with the strong undercurrent of "personal piety" visible in so many facets of Ramesside society. Some have suggested that one purpose of these more loyalist-oriented works may have been an attempt at reconciling personal piety with the demands of loyalty by blurring the distinction between the anonymous deity and the king, who always stood at the border between the human and divine spheres.[194]

The title of *The Instruction of a Man for His Son* reflects another important tendency of New Kingdom didactic texts—an embourgoisement of the intended audience for literature in general.[195] The protagonists of several New Kingdom didactic pieces are no longer the kings and viziers of the earlier works but now appear as middle-level officials, local scribes, or the average, anonymous "man" who instructs his "son." This trend demonstrates the increasing status of the individual within the intellectual and religious environments of the Ramesside period, if not elsewhere. Interestingly enough, the contemporary instructions in Late Egyptian dialect do not stress loyalty to the king.

A belief in the paramount importance of an individual's relationship with his personal god plays a prominent role in two important moral instructions of this era, *The Instruction of Ani* and *The Instruction of Amenemope,* both of which are reminiscent of the classical example of Middle Kingdom didactic literature, *The Instruction of Ptahhotep.*[196] *Amenemope* shows its literary affinities in its structure—the text is divided into sections called *hwt* (literally "houses, estates," but better rendered "chapters"),[197] an organizational principle encountered in poetry and religious literature as well. Unlike the works with a loyalist orientation, these two Ramesside compositions offer instructions more centered on an individual's moral behavior in a broader sense and his or her relationship with society as a whole. The somewhat contradictory roles of the gods and the various forms of "fate" in human affairs play a central role in *Ani* and *Amenemope.*[198] In addition to the age-old deities of Egypt's past, these two texts mention an anonymous "god" (in the singular) who is also familiar to us from the monuments of personal piety. In light of such features that seem remarkably attuned to what one might call a Judeo-Christian sensibility, it is not surprising that passages from the biblical Proverbs should exhibit some knowledge of, if not occasional inspiration from, *Amenemope.*[199]

An especially personal figure in Late Egyptian life instructions, particularly in *Amenemope,* was the *grw,* "the silent man," a person who plays a central role in personal piety as well.[200] As an Egyptian virtue in wisdom texts and biographical inscriptions, silence underwent a slow change between the Middle Kingdom and the Ramesside period. At first, the silent man was a measured individual who was endowed with great self-possession, whose every action was considered and deliberate; he was aptly contrasted with the *šmw,* "the heated man," a creature of his momentary, ill-considered passions. Armed with these qualities, the *grw* of the earlier instructions was at the very center of official life, a successful man whose advice was sought at every turn.

At the risk of doing a great disservice by oversimplifying both Egyptian and sixteenth-century CE religious thought, one might say that *Ptahhotep* adopts a Calvinistic attitude toward wealth and status, which, to the vizier-protagonist, are signs of divine approval. *Ptahhotep,* as a man at the pinnacle of Egyptian officialdom, is certainly not one to question the fairness of his society and its class structure. By the Ramesside period, the silent man who appears in *Amenemope* and on a number of the contemporary monuments of personal piety has become quite a different person. He is still a patient man with admirable self-possession, but more often than not, the narrator of *Amenemope* seems to consider mundane affairs as vain pursuits in the face of fate's vagaries. The narrator's stance toward life seems to have been strongly influenced by the numerous priestly offices with which the piece's prologue credits him. In the eyes of this Ramesside *grw,* wealth and worldly success are ephemeral and can disappear in an instant; it is far better to live an inwardly directed, honest life in peace with one's god, a deity whose intentions are not quite fathomable.

Even a pious life, however, will not guarantee earthly rewards—such matters are in the hands of both fate and the deities, both named and anonymous. *Amenemope*'s attitude toward contemporary society and its concerns bears some remarkable parallels with the mentality among German pietists in the face of late eighteenth-century absolutism, which has been described as a "very grand form of sour grapes."[201] Oddly enough, although both *Amenemope* and *Ptahhotep* admit that life may not always be fair and that the virtuous are not always rewarded, neither author questions whether Egyptian society itself is righteous. Both texts, in fact, even promote a form of "situational ethics" in which a person's social status has a profound effect on how one should behave toward others.

The Instruction of Ani is less familiar to modern audiences, perhaps because its language is often quite obscure, the sense of several passages remaining rather tentative.[202] *Ani* appears to have been part of the scribal curriculum and thus can be firmly dated to the Ramesside period. However, unlike other instructions, this work does not seem to have had a canonical form; the preserved versions of the text were different enough for one editor to treat them separately rather than as normal parallels.[203] Many passages in this composition appear to have *comparativa* in a wide range of contemporary and earlier didactic literature, as well as the ideal tomb biography—certainly more than is the case with *Amenemope*.[204]

Ani has an unusual epilogue in which the author-father Ani and his son Khonsuhotep debate the value of the instruction and learning in general. In this respect, *The Instruction of Ani* shows a slight affinity with *The Satirical Letter.* Although, like *Amenemope,* the protagonist of *Ani* might be described as "middle management" within a religious institution, this composition adopts the normal stance of didactic literature. There are the expected warnings against trusting in worldly goods and one's (temporary) good fortune, yet, in the end run, *Ani* firmly embraces the goals of a good career, pursuit of success, and status in society. Although the subject moves us somewhat beyond the scope of this study, it should be mentioned that *Ani* enjoyed the unusual distinction of being used in later times as a basis for learning how to translate Late Egyptian texts into other dialects.[205]

The fragmentary work known as Papyrus Chester Beatty IV[206] is something of an oddity among the longer didactic instructions. It is really a miscellany of sorts, yet it addresses its audience in quite a different tone than the other instructions. It seems more sophisticated, lofty, and literary than the *Miscellanies*. It does not appear to have been copied in the manner of a student papyrus and has been characterized as a private commonplace book or as a collection of model compositions that a master might draw on when creating practice exercises for his charges. The work is essentially an anthology of wisdom stitched together by the repeated phrase "If you do but this, then you are versed (*sbȝyt*) in writing," employing a noticeably favorable term never applied to students in the *Miscellanies*. There is the expected negative description of the soldier's life, but the usual exhortations aimed at inattentive apprentice scribes are missing. The language is distinctly poetical at points, while the didactic elements are more theoretical and thoughtful than usual, occasionally philosophizing at a level rarely encountered in other didactic works.[207]

The most famous excerpt from this collection is *The Encomium of the Sages* (Chester Beatty IV, vv. 2.5–3.10),[208] praising the great writers of the past—one of the few passages that offers us an insight into the Egyptians' literary sensibilities in their own words. I treat this text here, rather than as an example of Ramesside poetry (the genre to which it really belongs), because of its thematic affinity with the didactic portions of the papyrus and its use of a key theme of wisdom literature.

The text expresses a somewhat subversive view of the afterlife from the point of view of the scribal class, who dwelt at the lower margins of the Egyptian elite and could only afford the simplest of burials. The message is simple: all the monuments of the high and mighty eventually crumble away and are forgotten, but great authors can live eternally through their writings. It ends by praising a list of famous scribes whose works had made them literally the "immortals" of Egyptian literature. Not coincidentally, each of these writers was associated with a *sbȝyt*. Whether any of these men were famous for other types of compositions—narrative tales, for instance—remains unanswered.

This passage strongly echoes the sentiments of the Harpers' Songs, a text genre whose most eloquent exemplar, the *Antef Song*, is similarly part of a Ramesside anthology papyrus and expressed a similar skepticism toward the afterlife, the value of tombs, and elaborate funerary goods.[209]

Amenemope, the Harpers' Songs, and the *Encomium* all, in effect, debate what life's real end might be, in the sense of both ultimate purpose and conclusion. The *Encomium* promotes little of the cynical hedonism of most of the Harpers' Songs and has an attitude toward worldly goods and status much closer to that of *Amenemope*. The praise of the great sages may have partially inspired the well-known biblical passage from the Wisdom of Ben Sirah (Ecclesiastes) that begins "Let us now praise famous men . . ."[210] The *Encomium*'s idealization of writing is echoed in a passage from the Lansing Papyrus that extols "the papyrus scroll and the palette" as personifications of learning and the ideal form of inheritance.[211]

It is difficult to fit one of the most important of all Late Egyptian didactic works, *The Satirical Letter* (Papyrus Anastasi I), into the categories above.[212] It certainly is not a life instruction, but neither does it quite fit the pattern of the *Miscellanies*, even though it expresses similarly negative opinions about the nonscribal professions. *The Satirical Letter* is likewise a collection of several short didactic compositions, but it is more coherent and organized than the *Miscellanies*.

The Satirical Letter most likely was composed sometime in the reign of Ramesses II,[213] when the Late Egyptian dialect became officially acceptable, so that a new scribal curriculum had to be developed. The work purports to be a lengthy letter in which the scribe Hori criticizes the abilities of a colleague and challenges him to prove which one of the two is the better trained *maher*, a Semitic term meaning roughly "specialist scribe" or perhaps "military scribe"— in any case, a man endowed with a wide range of professional knowledge about Syria-Palestine.[214] Granted that its main theme is knowledge of life abroad, this work still remains striking evidence of the large number of foreign words that had become part of the vocabulary of the Ramesside bureaucracy.

Because of *The Satirical Letter*'s letter format, it is not a *sb3yt*, "instruction," strictly speaking, but its didactic intent is unquestionable. A thematic undercurrent of the text appears in the not-so-subtle negative descriptions of the difficulties and dangers of military life abroad. Not only does *The Satirical Letter* have papyrus exemplars from both Thebes and Memphis, but it was, significantly, also one of the five most copied of all texts found on Deir el-Medina ostraca. Of all the compositions on Gasse's list, moreover, this was the only one written in Late Egyptian. Since one of the chief objectives of scribal training was teaching students how to write a good "business letter," it is hardly surprising that letters should develop into a major instructional tool and eventually into an important literary form in their own right.

These are the most important *sbȝyt* of the Ramesside period; they formed the basis of the standard curriculum during the time of Ramesses III. In addition to these works, a number of shorter pieces have emerged among the Deir el-Medina ostraca, one of which, *The Instruction of Amennakhte,* has now been attested on no less than fifteen different ostraca and can be confidently dated to this period though its author.[215] Amennakhte, son of Ipuwy, was one of the most important figures at Deir el-Medina during this reign, surviving until Ramesses VI. He was active both as a scribe and a teacher and may have possessed a sizable library. In fact, it was this same Amennakhte who apparently drew up the Turin Strike Papyrus, which records one of the most dramatic events of Ramesses III's reign.[216]

Deir el-Medina ostraca are also the source of two other brief didactic pieces, *The Instruction of Hori*[217] and *The Negative Precepts,*[218] further proof, if any was needed, that the scribes of this village were far more than mere copyists and could create independent works suited to their own curriculum. These two texts are but a small sample of a fairly large corpus of what might be called *opera minora* that appear among Ramesside ostraca. Stylistically, *The Negative Precepts* puts forth a list of maxims in the form of negative commands, an underappreciated form of Ramesside rhetoric. The most obvious parallels are the "Negative Confession" of chapter 125 of the *Book of the Dead* and the string of negative statements that comprise a large "poetical" section of Ramesses II's Second Marriage Stela, a text also written in Late Egyptian.[219]

Although the *Kemyt* was certainly one of the most important instructional works or the Ramesside era, it is difficult to decide whether to include it among these *sbȝyt* at all. There seems to have been an entirely different rationale underlying the *Kemyt*'s popularity as an instructional text; it apparently was an exercise intended primarily for learning the mechanics of a certain script style, along with its columnar format, rather than for didactic purposes in the broader sense.[220] Unlike the model letters in the *Miscellanies,* no effort seems to have been made to update the *Kemyt*'s antiquated epistolary formulae and themes or even its script.

Narrative Tales of the New Kingdom

During the Ramesside period, the narrative tale[221] was a form of literature in which originality prevailed, so that scribes do not seem to have been as indebted to past models as with other genres. Lichtheim aptly classes this genre among "works of the imagination."[222] Compared to the large number of Middle Kingdom didactic texts on Quirke's list of literary manuscripts dating to Dynasty Eighteen and later, there is a remarkable paucity of Middle Egyptian tales among Ramesside sources, with the exception of *The Tale of Sinuhe,* which was apparently extensively copied for didactic purposes.[223] In fact, judging from the small number of Ramesside copies of stories in either Middle Egyptian or Late Egyptian dialect, narrative literature seems not to have been associated with the instructional curriculum to the degree that other literary genres were.[224]

The Tale of Sinuhe may have enjoyed its continued popularity perhaps not only because it is such an excellent example of good Middle Egyptian style but also because this great tale's loyalist theme fit in well with the same loyalist motif that is so important in Ramesside didactic texts on ostraca. Nevertheless, the new Late Egyptian tales attest to a pattern whereby each new era created its own new corpus of literary narratives. Just as only one Middle Egyptian literary story survived in the Ramesside period, so, too, almost none of these new Late Egyptian tales were attested in the Third Intermediate Period and beyond.

Some narratives appeared as part of students' miscellanies, like Papyrus Sallier I,[225] while other stories were included in collections of poetry and entertainment texts, such as Papyrus Harris 500.[226] This did not mean, of course, that narrative fiction did not continue to be an important means for conveying moral, societal, or religious principles. There is one aspect of the genre of narrative literature that distinguishes it sharply from didactic texts—nearly all of the Late Egyptian tales are singletons, preserved in only one source. Consequently, we can be far less certain whether a work such as *The Tale of the Two Brothers,* known from only the D'Orbiney Papyrus and copied down to the reign of Merenptah,[227] might have been still *au courant* during the reign of Ramesses III. Some of the stories collected by Gardiner in his *Late-Egyptian Stories* have a colophon at the end, but this is by no means a reliable indication of student work.[228] A large proportion of the Ramesside didactic corpus in both its Late Egyptian and Middle Kingdom forms, by contrast, seems to have been copied throughout Dynasties Nineteenth and Twenty, if only in fragmentary pieces on diverse ostraca and papyri.

Despite this drawback, literary manuscripts—and narratives more than didactic material—usually have a variety of external features that immediately distinguish them visually from documentary papyri.[229] These differences are generally more acute in the case of narrative literature than with other genres, so I have decided to discuss these features in the present section rather than elsewhere.

First, there is a most helpful difference in the relationship between the direction of the script and the arrangement of the papyrus fibers. On a typical literary papyrus, the script ran in the same direction as the horizontal fibers of the sheets, whereas with a letter or an official document, the scribe rotated the papyrus roll ninety degrees before writing, so that the fibers and writing would be at right angles to each other. There are other diagnostic features of literary papyri that are immediately obvious, even before one has attempted any transcription of the hieratic.[230] As with ostraca, there seems to have been a slight distinction in literary and documentary hands on papyri; a more deliberate, ornate hand seems to have been deemed more suitable for literary materials. It was likely that the pace of writing out literary materials would be more leisurely than with official documents.[231]

As with their Middle Kingdom counterparts, literary tales in Late Egyptian were often punctuated by the problematic verse points, so it is possible that some works may have actually been long poems rather than prose narratives.[232] Thus, register and script style had a close relationship with each other and provide us with some a priori criteria for distinguishing literary and nonliterary papyri. Gasse has demonstrated that a similar state of affairs prevails with literary and nonliterary ostraca.[233] The presence of such diagnostic characteristics, shared by narrative and didactic papyri alike, as well as analogous traits that set literary ostraca apart from those with documentary content, confirm that both we and the Egyptians seem to have roughly similar aesthetics when separating the works of the imagination from those of everyday life.

Second, there are some more subjective criteria by which one might separate literary and documentary materials. One such standard might be the vocabulary of the narrative tales, which is, for lack of a better term, more "elevated" than what one might encounter in personal correspondence; but finesse in diction is really a universal characteristic of elite language. The grammar of the Late Egyptian narrative tales additionally exhibits some distinctive (but otherwise obsolete) constructions that set these works apart from the documentary Late Egyptian of everyday use.[234] These archaic grammatical phrases, however, are confined almost entirely to the framing devices that provide frequent, mechanical transitions between parts of the stories. These stock phrases are normally rubricized and thus contribute much to the distinctive appearance of literary manuscripts. Such fossilized verbal formations seldom occur in other genres of texts, even in historical inscriptions and religious texts, thereby supplying what might be considered another objective criterion for separating literary tales from other material.

Since Late Egyptian literary narrative seems born of a desire to entertain more than to instruct, it has a distinctly more otherworldly outlook than its Middle Kingdom counterparts. On the whole, Ramesside narrative appears inextricably intertwined with the mythical and magical realm. Myth is notoriously difficult to define under the best of circumstances, a problem that is far beyond the scope of this chapter.[235] In the present context, a workable, though imperfect, definition might be "tales about the gods." Since several narrative tales are preserved alongside love poetry and other entertainment literature on the same papyri, this definition of myth fits these stories well. Like Greek myth, the deities of Late Egyptian stories often appear in an unflattering light, or else they seem to exist there as personifications or for their allegorical qualities more than for their divinity per se. Like some Greek myths, Late Egyptian tales are essentially etiologies, yet their connection with religious literature remains problematic. In the descriptions below, I will present only a brief summary of the plotlines of these various tales.

One of the earliest examples of the Late Egyptian dialect we possess is a narrative mythical tale called *Astarte and the Sea,* a work that has a particularly strong folkloric quality.[236] Since the *Astarte* papyrus probably belongs to the end of Dynasty Eighteen, at a time when Late Egyptian most likely would still have been considered dialect, that may lend support to the theory that the genre of Ramesside narrative tales may have sprung largely from nonelite origins—particularly so because many stories exhibit a less than reverent attitude toward the king and the gods. The tone of most Ramesside narratives, ranging from naïveté to cynicism, has much in common with *Märchen,* to use a German term. This raises further questions about their relationship with folktales—a fascinating subject, but one far beyond the scope of the present study.

It is in Late Egyptian tales that we find humans confronting the miraculous in the sense of impossible natural phenomena—talking animals, the transformation of characters into other beings or inanimate objects, children conceived by wondrous means, and the physical intervention of deities. This magical and miraculous aspect also occurred in Middle Egyptian narrative and became yet more important in subsequent eras, as the Ptolemaic cycle of Setne Khaemwas stories demonstrate. The Late Egyptian narrative tales can be conveniently divided into two, somewhat overlapping groups—romances involving nondivine figures and mythical-allegorical stories centered around deities or personifications. The state of preservation varies, but, on the whole, many narratives are only partially preserved in a single copy. Another oddity of Ramesside narratives is that they, unlike their didactic counterparts, do not seem to have title lines identifying the works in Egyptian terms—all the names of these works are modern constructs.

Three manuscripts record what we would consider historical romances, that is, tales based on historical personages and events. *Thutmose III and the Taking of Joppa*[237] describes how that famous monarch managed to seize Joppa by smuggling his soldiers into the town in jars, a ruse perhaps with distant echoes in "Ali Baba and the Forty Thieves" from *The Arabian Knights*. *Apophis and Seqenenre*[238] is another tale based on historical figures and also contains an outlandish and amusing element—the Hyksos monarch's claim that he had been discomforted by the sound of hippopotami braying in a pool presumably located near Thebes. This story is based on an exchange of correspondence between the two rival monarchs, further evidence of the important role that letters had achieved as a vehicle for Late Egyptian literature. The central theme in both stories, fantastical tales based on famous pharaohs of the distant past, is attested in Middle Kingdom literature and is no Ramesside innovation.[239] Unlike the great majority of Late Egyptian narratives, these two historical romances have no verse points, but it is uncertain how significant that omission might be. Both texts are only partially preserved and form part of student or entertainment miscellanies.

A different and more complex problem is posed by another, more down-to-earth work in this genre, *The Tale of Neferkare and General Sasenet*. The work is known from a number of papyrus fragments of varying length, dating from Dynasty Eighteen to Dynasty Twenty-five, so that we are uncertain whether this represents a single work or a cycle of stories that grew up around the figure of a Dynasty Six general whose existence is otherwise known only from this material. The most complete section is preserved on a papyrus from Deir el-Medina[240] and written in late Middle Egyptian, a rarity for literary narrative of any sort during the Ramesside period. The tale also has a unique and astonishing theme. It recounts how the high steward observed King Neferkare (probably Pepi II) visiting Sasenet over several nights, covertly clambering through a window, presumably into the general's bedroom. The image of the king conducting a surreptitious homosexual affair takes us a long way from the idealized, ideological portrait of the godlike monarch present in nearly all other contexts.

The mythical/allegorical category of narrative tales is more difficult to discuss because the evidence is both diverse and mostly lamentably ill-preserved. The criterion for "myth" suggested above—"tales about the gods"—

unites these texts, but to a certain degree, divine beings have an important role in other forms of narrative literature and play an active part in the human affairs in many royal and private inscriptional texts as well. The best-preserved tales, *The Contendings of Horus and Seth* and *The Blinding of Truth by Falsehood*, are typical of the genre in their depiction of deities with very human failings and less than exemplary behavior.

The Contendings of Horus and Seth is the longest of all Late Egyptian stories, occupying most of Papyrus Chester Beatty I, which can be confidently dated to the reign of Ramesses IV or later.[241] The sophisticated use of language and the presence of love poetry along with other entertainment literature on the same roll probably indicate the nonreligious and nonfolkloric contexts of the tale. The story, as the title informs us, is a retelling of the mythical cycle surrounding the struggle between Horus and Seth over who should rule Egypt. The composition is episodic yet not disjointed. The tale may be set entirely in the divine sphere, but its often humorous tone as well as the deities' deportment at points have led some scholars to suggest that the tale may be partially a burlesque based on contemporary figures at Deir el-Medina, an ancient Egyptian *roman à clef*.[242] Tales in which all-too-human gods maim, trick, betray, plot, dither, and lie are hardly unknown elsewhere in the ancient world, however, so we need not look for disguised political satire here.

I shall treat *The Destruction of Mankind* briefly here for the sake of convenience more than anything else, since it belongs more to the realm of religious literature.[243] This short etiological myth, also known as *The Book of the Heavenly Cow*, stands apart from other Ramesside narrative tales in many respects: it is the only Ramesside narrative composed in Middle Egyptian; it is essentially canonical; it was written in hieroglyphs using the archaic columnar format; and it is attested not on papyri or ostraca but, rather, solely on the walls of five royal tombs, including that of Ramesses III. This tale relates how Re decided to destroy all people when he learned that they were plotting against him. He relegates this murderous task to Hathor. Fortunately, Re eventually relents, and humanity is saved through a ruse in which the goddess becomes intoxicated and is diverted from her slaughter. Thus we learn the origin of the beer-drinking rituals during the Hathor Festival. The tale is actually just the first part of a longer narrative that continues with a description of how the aging Re retired, leaving the governance of the universe to the other major deities.[244] *The Book of the Heavenly Cow* is of great theoretical interest since it is one of the few narrative myths attested in pharaonic literature before the Greco-Roman era.

There were a few other mythic tales that brought the world of the gods and humanity together, the most famous of which is *The Tale of the Two Brothers*.[245] The D'Orbiney Papyrus, the beautifully calligraphed work of the ever-industrious Innene, is not only complete but also, without a doubt, the prime example of a Ramesside literary papyrus preserved today. Although it has many connective phrases in rubrics, the red verse points so characteristic of other literary manuscripts are absent. The two ostensibly human protagonists of the tale, Anubis and Bata, are also known as the chief deities of the seventeenth nome of Upper Egypt, so that allegorical allusions running closely beneath the surface must have been readily understood by a well-educated audience. At the same time, there is an innocent charm inherent in this work that recalls a folktale or fairy tale that would appeal to a wider audience. The incident in which the older brother's wife attempts to seduce Bata, the younger brother, and then falsely accuses him when spurned provides a markedly close parallel to the story of Potiphar's wife in the biblical tale of Joseph.[246] Other parts of the story are interesting from the perspective of religious history, but those aspects belong to another section of this volume.

One of the most interesting of all Ramesside stories, *The Prince Who Knew His Fate,* is unfortunately missing its ending,[247] which would have probably provided some interesting perspectives on contemporary attitudes toward the role of fate in human affairs. In the opening section of the tale, a group of female deities. the Hathors, attend the prince's birth and predict his fate. An alternate title that is sometimes given to this tale, *The Doomed Prince,*[248] is unwarranted, since the ending is missing, and it is quite possible that the hero somehow avoided a bad outcome. In addition to divine participation in human affairs, *The Prince Who Knew His Fate* shares other themes with *The Tale of the Two Brothers.* The protagonists of both tales leave Egypt to seek their fortunes abroad in the exotic lands to the north.

As we have seen above in the discussion of *The Satirical Letter,* travel through Syria-Palestine is an important topos in Ramesside literature. The theme is hardly just a Ramesside concern but one several centuries old, for it was the central theme of *The Tale of Sinuhe* from the Middle Kingdom. Interest in this topos may be one of the reasons why the latter "classic" is the sole Middle Kingdom narrative to be attested among Ramesside ostraca and papyri.[249] *Sinuhe* was as much a part of the Ramesside literary environment as the revived works of Middle Egyptian wisdom literature, although we cannot be as sure that its *Sitz im Leben* was necessarily within the didactic curriculum. Oddly enough, other important narrative tales of the Middle Kingdom, such as *The Eloquent Peasant*, have not been attested during the Ramesside period.

Khonsuemhab and the Ghost, the only Late Egyptian tale that was copied as a didactic text, is appropriately attested only on ostraca and found at Deir el-Medina alone.[250] A few examples appear to have been numbered,[251] another indication that scribal training may have involved a *pensium*, or daily quota, of text lines that a student was expected to produce for his teacher. The story provides evidence for what may be a "folk" belief in revenants—or ghosts, as they are popularly conceived today.[252] According to the slightly more formal contexts of letters to the dead and other sources, however, contact with manifest spirits of the deceased seems to be confined elsewhere to visions or dreams, much unlike the waking contacts with an unhappy spirit narrated in this story.

Two of the most interesting (and problematic) of all works of Late Egyptian literature are *The Report of Wenamun*[253] and *The Tale of Woe*.[254] From a chronological point of view, unfortunately, both texts were written too far beyond the reign of Ramesses III to merit detailed consideration here. In the case of *Wenamun*, the work is explicitly set in the "renaissance era" at the end of Dynasty Twenty. *The Tale of Woe* was found in a large jar together with *Wenamun* and *The Onomasticon of Amenemope*, probably in a Third Intermediate Period context at El-Hibe.[255] All three papyri are written in similar hands and were probably the product of a scribal school located at this provincial town at the northern limit of the political control of the high priest of Amun at Thebes.

Rather than appearing in the normal narrative format, both *Wenamun* and *The Tale of Woe* have adopted the form of official documents, reports or letters to superiors. *The Tale of Woe* is unquestionably a fictional work, as shown by many of its features, including a passage that is adapted from the *Kemyt*. However, in the case of *Wenamun*, the format, use of rubrics, text-to-fiber orientation, grammar,[256] vocabulary, and phraseology are so close to that of the nonliterary private ostraca and the official papyri of late Dynasty Twenty that one must seriously consider whether this might not be a copy of an actual report of a series of misadventures abroad instead of a fictional narrative. There are many rather lively and slangy interchanges in the dialogue, to be sure, but that does not necessarily mean that an actual official named Wenamun had not attempted to present a colorful report of his trip abroad for the delectation of his superiors.[257]

Ramesside Poetry—General Remarks

As with the other major genres of Egyptian literature, poetry is divisible into three rather broad categories: secular, religious, and royal. Of all the genres of literature studied in this chapter, poetry is undoubtedly the hardest to define with any confidence. Our difficulties in identifying poetry go beyond our usual (and perhaps predictable) inability to find adequate equivalents for such fundamental terms as *poetry* or *prose* in the Egyptian language.

The fact remains that we are uncertain about what constitutes poetry within our own modern literary traditions as well. To a great extent, defining poetry ultimately involves many subjective judgments. Even though religious poetry comprises a substantial proportion of all preserved Egyptian poetry, particularly in the Ramesside period, that material must be left largely to another part of this volume; for much the same reasons, I also limit discussion here of the poetical aspects of royal inscriptions. It is to the Egyptians' credit that they could successfully use poetry as a vehicle for conveying complex theological concepts, but too many aspects of the discussion would necessarily touch on religious issues that would force us far beyond the scope of this chapter. Only cursory treatment of religious poetry shall appear below, along with a discussion of poetical works dedicated to the king, a type to which religious verse is related, both genres representing specialized forms of official or ideological literature.

Assuming that there are objective means for reliably distinguishing poetry from other forms of writing—a question I shall address shortly—the evidence indicates that the Egyptians considered poetry as something that formed an integral part of a person's education, a sensibility quite close to ours. Like other literary forms, verse played an important part in the scribal curriculum, likely because of poetry's well-known value as a mnemonic device. An interesting case in point was the "Kadesh Poem," which shows how verse could sometimes exist simultaneously within the boundaries of the didactic, ideological, and poetical genres.[258]

Assiduously copied by several scribes, the Kadesh papyri followed fairly close to their inscriptional counterparts on the walls of Ramesses II's temples but, at the same time, slightly modified the text in practically every section of those original versions, mostly by changing vocabulary and replacing some grammatical formations with the more modern forms of the Late Egyptian dialect. Once again, there is no definitive evidence to show whether the Kadesh text was still in either the literary canon or the school curriculum by the reign of Ramesses III, but given its picture of the heroic king in battle, both versions of the text assuredly had some influence on similar texts of Ramesses III at Medinet Habu.

On the whole, Ramesside poetry was more closely associated with entertainment and ideological concerns than modern verse tends to be. The texts we generally consider poetry certainly emerge as the best demonstrations of the Egyptians' sophisticated ability with their language, more than any other aspect of their literature. The entire battery of their literary skills was brought into play, from the forms of the poems to the use of the vocabulary in wordplay, alliterations, metaphors, and similes. Of course, given our imperfect knowledge of both the vocabulary and the sounds of the language, we can ultimately get only a dim appreciation of what they accomplished.

Verse Points and Theories about Versification in Egyptian Literary History

All the preceding remarks are predicated on the assumption that we can reliably separate Egyptian prose and verse. A recurring question among literary historians has been whether or not some hymns, prayers, narrative texts, and didactic literature might have been intended primarily as poetical works.[259] Influenced by Western literary traditions, many Egyptologists often seem overeager to regard a large proportion of Egyptian religious texts as hymns or poems. At the same time, some of these assessments often seem entirely reasonable and even inescapable—for instance, when we encounter descriptive terms such as *ḥs(w)t* or *šmꜥ*, "song," in the introductory lines of a given text.[260] Certainly, many Egyptian hymns appear to have been structured by means of anaphoric phrases, even choruses, that would readily lend themselves to chanting or singing.[261] If works of this sort were actually sung or recited, it is hard to imagine that they would have been devoid of those metrical or rhythmic patterns that we associate with poetry in its simplest forms.

The attribute of poetry most commonly used to distinguish it from prose is its special sound, often enhanced by rhythm, or, more technically, meter. Despite attempts at reconstruction, the sound of Egyptian poetry lies largely beyond our reach today. Due to the lack of vocalization in the writing system, setting out to reconstruct the sound of the poetry would be as if we set out to reconstruct a brightly feathered macaw based solely on its skeletal remains. In addition, the format of some works and textual notations in other sources might provide other objective criteria, just as fiber-to-script orientation could do in distinguishing between literary and documentary manuscripts. Indeed, special formatting—the visual appearance of the text itself—can frequently set poetry apart from prose in modern contexts as well. Good examples of such visual patterning in Egyptian usage would be the *Hymns to Senwosret III* and the *Poetical Stela* of Thutmose III.[262] Literary historians have long believed that, in fact, the Egyptians did signal the presence of poetry by other means as well, namely, through verse points, those red or (less often) black dots that appear above a horizontal line of text on papyrus. These marks have played such an important role in the theories of Egyptian poetry that I wish to discuss them at some length.

Verse points provide some of the rare indications of punctuation in Egyptian writing,[263] since they appear to function as diacritical marks that divide texts into separate lines or, more often, smaller units of verse or prose.[264] In many, if not most, cases, the dots might represent some form of metrical division, but there remain a good number of instances where other explanations seem equally plausible, so the more neutral term *division markers*, proposed by Morenz, might be more appropriate overall. Despite the difficulties that verse points might pose, they remain the fundamental elements on which several theorists have based their reconstructions of the rules of Egyptian versification and "metrics."[265]

One major school of thought, led by Fecht[266] and his followers, believes that the Egyptians employed metrical systems extensively in their verse as well as in a rather wide range of other text genres, including biographical narrative and even titularies.[267] Although Fecht's theories are based heavily on verse points—and though he lately seems to replace the word *metrical* with the more general *rhythmic*—his observations extend to material without them. Other literary and linguistic scholars, such as Schenkel[268] and Lichtheim,[269] have held that these metrical schemes may well lie largely in the believers' imagination or, at the very least, may mark nonmetrical divisions that could be grammatical or topical in nature.[270]

It is my belief that the concept of "thought couplets" as proposed by Foster comes closer to the mark.[271] However, I (and others) would extend his theory to include larger units from time to time.[272] By dividing poetical texts according to parallel pairs (or larger units) of ideas or phrases, Foster's more moderated theories have the major advantage of not relying heavily on the rather erratic usage of verse points or on our tenuous knowledge of the language's possible vocalization. Burkard has taken a middle position on this controversial subject in his survey of Egyptian poetical forms.[273] In his recent anthology of Egyptian poetry, Kitchen[274] likewise chose an expanded form of the "thought couplet" as the basis of much of his form analysis.

The difficulties posed by the verse points themselves are manifold. Tacke has shown that verse points are employed rather irregularly. Appearing in *Miscellanies* exercises that are certainly nonliterary in content, they also may be employed in one copy of a passage while a version of the same text in another manuscript leaves out the dots entirely. Most important of all, Tacke has demonstrated convincingly that the dots sometimes appear rather imprecisely and not where a division should theoretically appear. Furthermore, the marks were hastily inserted *after* a given text had been transcribed— whether by the student or his instructor is unclear.[275]

As another counterexample, dots of this sort also occur in accounts papyri or other documentary materials, where they sometimes served simply as check marks when the scribe had to work his way through a long list of items.[276] This might be particularly the case when the scribe wished to ensure that every item on some original "master" source had been copied, as seems to be the case with the late Dynasty Twenty Tomb Robbery Papyrus, which was explicitly a "copy" of a larger document, now lost, detailing the large number of things that a thief had stolen.[277]

Since much of the literary work containing verse points actually represents copies or student exercises, an equally convincing explanation for these marks is that they might be a similar form of scribal aide-mémoire signaling the presence of verse. Brunner pointed out that the Prisse Papyrus, the earliest version of *The Instruction of Ptahhotep*, has no verse points, yet nearly all the New Kingdom papyri and ostraca exemplars of this didactic text employ dots liberally.[278] These observations could be extended to several other text genres that are even less likely to be poetical, such as model letters and the *Kemyt*.[279] One could thus make a strong case that the presence of verse points is perhaps more likely to signal a work's didactic nature than its poetical qualities.[280]

In short, the presence of verse points within a text can be ambiguous. Does their presence on two Akkadian "scholarly" tablets from Amarna containing the Adapa and Erishkigal epics indicate that an Egyptian scribe wanted to denote the poetical nature of the mythical text, or, as is much more likely, do those dots merely show that he wanted to apply a standard Egyptian didactic technique to his Akkadian language instruction?[281]

Perhaps the most telling evidence of these marks' true nature might come from their earliest attestation to date—an odd, late Dynasty Twelve instructional piece known as *The Maxims of P. Ramesseum II*.[282] This text appears to be a selection of largely unrelated adages that a student scribe had excerpted and transcribed in no particular order from a master papyrus. The model papyrus (or papyri), now lost, was most likely a collection of proverbs roughly like *The Maxims of Onchshesonqi*,[283] a later didactic work written in demotic during the Roman era.

In nearly every case, the Middle Kingdom apprentice has written each adage separately on its own line(s), and in most cases, he has ended it with a verse point; in the second section of the text, the adages are written continuously and without intervening marks. Since most sayings in the first section appear by themselves on a line, surely this student scribe could have hardly been attempting to remind himself where metrical units fell—no metrical pattern could possibly apply here. His actions are far more reminiscent of someone checking off items against a master list, such as one might encounter on an accounts papyrus.

In this and several other instances, then, the evidence points to a conclusion that, in most instances, verse points actually serve as reminders, or some manner of control marks, for those copying texts. This would explain the great frequency of verse points in otherwise rather prosaic didactic texts. By the same token, Ramesside love poetry, another major venue for verse points, often appears—so titular rubrics significantly inform us—as parts of "collections," a term that similarly implies transcriptions from other sources.

It would be unreasonable to assume that the only place Egyptians were poetical or needed to indicate poetry was on papyrus. All modern anthologies of Egyptian literature have recognized that a number of religious and historical inscriptions—in the most literal sense of that medium, texts inscribed on stone—are poetical in nature. Following the model of texts on papyrus, one might then expect that verse points or some similar means would be employed to mark poetical inscriptions on stelae or on painted surfaces such as tomb walls, especially in view of the practice of imitating the yellowed surfaces of old papyri by occasionally giving tomb walls a similar background color. Unfortunately, nothing comparable is forthcoming, even in the case of the Harpers' Songs, where, in addition to appearing on a tomb wall, one song is preserved as well in an Egyptian papyrus anthology of assorted literary pieces. Verse points, it seems, represent a manuscript practice that was applied somewhat inconsistently and never intended for inscribed material on stone. In the final analysis, it might be wise to adopt Morenz's more neutral term *Gliederungspunkte*,[284] roughly "division points."

Anaphora and Other Modes of Versification

There were other poetical techniques available to Egyptian authors that went beyond metricizing texts. The Egyptians could also signal a composition's poetical nature either through patterns in a text's physical layout or by re-peating words or phrases. As noted above, songs, poems, and hymns frequently use anaphoric phrases to structure a text.[285] Occasionally both methods could be used in conjunction; graphical or visual patterns in the presentation of a text could signal its rhythmical structure.

The most extreme of all formatting schemes can be found in the "crossword" hymns of the New Kingdom, in which a hieroglyphic text was written into a grid work of small incised rectangles in such a manner that the hymn may be read either as horizontal or columnar text. The modern observer might alternate between admiring the result as a tour de force and viewing the entire exercise as borderline madness. In any case, the resulting hymn is so strained that it can hardly be described as religious poetry.[286]

The simplest form of indicating verse through format is familiar to us in our modern poetical traditions—placing each thought or clause of a text in its own line (or column).[287] This basic form of text arrangement, the stichic, or monostichic, line, is quite noticeable within the Egyptian context, where the rule was to write texts in an unbroken, unpunctuated stream of characters, line segueing into line, without indicating word divisions, let alone clauses or sentences. Before the Late Period, monostichic line structure is uncommon; the preponderance of examples of such linear formatting occur on ostraca and, more rarely, on stelae, media that lend themselves well to this format.[288] Most poems of this type are addressed to the king or to deities and therefore could be more properly categorized as hymns or prayers rather than as poetry.[289]

The Study of Love Lyrics and Other Secular Lyric of the Ramesside Period

By most estimations, Ramesside love poetry presents the Egyptian literary spirit at its highest level of imagination and skill. Of all Egyptian literary genres, love lyric is easily the most accessible to a modern audience, the crown jewel of Egyptian literature. Proof of its widespread appeal can be found in the number of people both inside and outside the field of Egyptology who have had their hand at translating these works. The bibliography is accordingly formidable, so my discussion of the genre shall draw mostly on the more recent and lengthy treatments of love lyric by Lichtheim,[290] Foster,[291] Fox,[292] Meeks,[293] Kitchen,[294] Mathieu,[295] Vernus,[296] and Sweeney.[297]

Love poetry is especially pertinent to this survey of Ramesside literature, because so much of the evidence apparently dates to the early part of Dynasty

Twenty. Love lyric was unquestionably an integral part of the literary environment during the reign of Ramesses III. However, as with several other aspects of Late Egyptian literature, our literary-historical perception is certainly distorted by the exclusively Theban provenance of the material, owing to the presence of the royal court at Medinet Habu for a substantial part of the reign. In addition, there are occasional parallels in the largely Memphite miscellanea that confirm that love lyric was most likely far more widespread than accidents of preservation have led us to believe. It seems highly unlikely that subjects with such universal appeals as love and eroticism would have been popular at just one of Egypt's metropolises.

In sum, there will always remain questions as to whether descriptions such as "poetry" and "lyric" are legitimate or have been assigned simply because of our modern expectations of what the texts should represent. As I attempted to show above, perhaps the best indicators might be the titles of the collections themselves. Other criteria, such as the presence of verse points, seem inconsistent and unreliable. Nevertheless, basing his studies on verse points and metrical patterns, Mathieu has proposed that the dominant metrical scheme is a form of heptameter, a rhythmic allusion to Hathor, who was strongly associated with the number seven. Other authors, however, are quite hesitant on associating any single metrical pattern with love lyric, particularly when one takes into consideration the shorter works on ostraca—love lyric and otherwise. These hardly would fit into a heptametric scheme.

The Origins of Love Lyric, Its Social Background, and Its Relationship to Other Genres

All in all, Kitchen's more broadly defined supercategory of "secular and lyric" serves as a better description of love lyric as a genre. Kitchen's terminology accords well with both the very titles that the Egyptians gave the collections of love lyric and the nature of the other works occurring on the same papyri. Significantly, the longer poetical collections do not preserve love lyric in isolation. Alongside the love lyric, there are other works that appear to be poems but lack erotic motifs, such as the Harpers' Songs, in addition to narrative tales, which together could fall under the rubric of "entertainment literature." In addition, one can readily find similarities in technique and vocabulary used in the praise of the beloved and some aspects of royal and divine encomia.[298] As with virtually all aspects of Egyptian literature, not only are there phraseological connections between love poetry and didactic literature, but the two genres also sometimes appear together on the same papyri.[299]

As a literary genre, the first compilations of love poetry appear in Dynasty Nineteen, although Guglielmi has raised the possibility that the origin of the genre may lie further back, in late Dynasty Eighteen.[300] Their *Sitz im Leben* is most likely the public performance. As Eyre remarked,[301] Egyptian literature was not intended for "silent reading," a practice that probably did not exist in that culture. Based on the titles of poems as well as the entire collections, Fox and others plausibly associate love lyric with recitations at banquets or other social gatherings.[302]

The actual social milieu in which these works originated is hard to judge from the poems themselves. The lovers are not married, yet their love is not chaste. Deir el-Medina figures prominently as a manuscript source, supplying all the material with provenance thus far.[303] This is somewhat odd, since the poems' protagonists often seem to represent a *junesse dorée* among the elite, as Meeks has observed.[304] Most of the lovers in these poems live in a distinctly wealthy environment of large houses with gardens and servants; they consort with princes and wear beautiful costumes; they can afford doctors; they know about foreign lands, their landscapes, and products. Although love lyric is not likely to have been solely a "courtly" literature, this refined and luxurious background probably reflects the strong influence that Ramesses III's royal residence at Medinet Habu must have exerted on Thebes and, especially, on the intellectual life of the nearby village of the tomb builders, which was so dependent on royal patronage for its livelihood.

Not incidentally, love poetry provides us with a view of women as individuals that is the most sympathetic to emerge from this heavily male-dominated society. The voice of the female narrators is prominent, either in interior monologues or in dialogue with their male lovers. The men often describe their beloved as an independent individual, free to make her own choices, unless she is still a young girl. Those verses that are told entirely from the woman's point of view might conceivably be the work of anonymous women authors. After all, tomb paintings and the minor arts especially inform us that women played an important role in singing and music. This positive image is only fitting, since Deir el-Medina was, in fact, a settlement where women enjoyed unusual independence and powers within their households.

The Language of Love Poetry

These poems mark a distinct departure from Middle Egyptian influences felt in many other areas of Ramesside literature, by adopting a form of literary Late Egyptian. That poetical language, in turn, differed from the language of the narrative tales and didactic texts that are part of the same papyri. The dialect bears only a passing resemblance to the language used in contemporary inscriptions.

As can be expected with poetical compositions, these works employ a more flowery vocabulary,[305] literally and figuratively, than contemporary letters and official documents. Imagery based on flowers, the animal world, and nature generally abounds and is used extensively to describe the beloved. The choice of words is, for lack of better terms, more "literary" and "elevated" than usual; we can hardly describe it as folk language, especially when compared with the less self-conscious diction of letters. The poetry demonstrates exceptional skill in the use of a wide range of its forms and rhetorical devices.

This does not mean, however, that these poems were necessarily products of a "courtly" literature, as were its medieval counterparts (*Minnesang*), an intriguing comparison that Guglielmi makes.[306] Further comparisons could be made between the praise of the beloved and similar themes in religious and royal encomia. Whenever we can trace provenances, a surprising proportion of the manuscripts seem to derive from Deir el-Medina, that is, the lowest level of the elite, who probably created these works independently, without any obvious debt to some other model.

Guglielmi seemingly would place love poetry in the midrange of three levels of poetic compositions. From the Egyptian point of view, the highest form of poetry was perhaps religious works or poetry dedicated to the praise of the king.[307] In the middle would stand their love poetry. Finally, the third level of poetry would be a number of works that are seemingly more popular in nature—they are quite brief and appear on ostraca. From high to low, however, there is one generalization that holds—the obscene seems rather rare among written materials from ancient Egypt, unlike the situation with the figurative arts.

Given its subject matter and what seems to be a distinct preference for euphemism or allusion over crude language, love poetry appears to have been created largely for public consumption. At the same time, we can be certain that many allusions and colloquialisms connected to the themes of love and sex probably escape us entirely today. Slang is the most distinctly idiomatic form of all language, and vocabulary remains the weakest aspect of our knowledge of Egyptian. Nevertheless, some sexual allusions are obvious in any language, such as the verses "The mansion of my sister / with a door in the center of her house / Its door-leaves are open."[308] Here the two-leafed doorway suggests a woman's sex, a theme well known in classical literature.

Similarly, when we encounter a lengthy description of the beloved's body, we can be sure that there was more than an aesthetic pleasure involved.

The Themes of Love Poetry

Interestingly enough, Egyptian love lyrics almost always appear in collections of several verses within their manuscript, and the poems are usually grouped according to a shared theme. Indeed, most love poetry revolves around a group of frequently used topoi. It can normally be distinguished by the lovers' terms of endearment, such as *sn*, "brother"; *snt*, "sister"; and a few others.[309] It is not surprising to encounter abundant references to Hathor and Hathoric themes, since she was the patroness deity of love and music in ancient Egypt; one could justifiably call her the muse of Egyptian love lyric.

Love lyric exhibits a great degree of originality, in that we do not encounter duplicates or close parallels within the corpus. This is not to say, however, that many themes and images do not reoccur.[310] Many topoi in love poetry are accessible to us because of their similarity to our own love poetry and our popular (country and western) love songs.[311] Egyptian love poetry tends toward unabashedly sentimental themes: separation, love from afar, and a wish for a transformation that would bring one closer to the object of one's desire ("I wish I were . . .");[312] the unaware or uncaring lover ("If only he/she knew . . ."); departure and greeting; comparisons of the beloved to flowers or wild animals; allusions drawn from the hunt (as seen in the biblical Song of Songs); love as an ailment; obstacles (river, doorway, family).

Fox has made an extensive study of the parallels between Egyptian love lyric and the biblical Song of Songs, illuminating their similarities as well as their differences.[313] As with all comparisons between Egyptian love lyric and its counterparts in other cultures, one ultimately feels that even though one hesitates to ascribe "universality" to any literary form, the vagaries and psychology of love affairs probably come closer to providing an exception than anything else in literature, society, and life.[314] Strangely enough, despite that universality, love lyric virtually vanishes from the Egyptian literary scene following the Ramesside period.

The Authors and Collections of Love Poetry

In the final analysis, it is probably impossible to ascertain whether any of the major collections of love poetry might have been copied or excerpted from longer manuscripts devoted to love lyric alone. Two of the longer manuscripts—nos. 1 and 2 in the list below—are compilations (and probably transcriptions) of literary works without strict regard to genre, other than a vague category of "entertainment." The poetry does not appear en bloc in these manuscripts. All these poems seem to be original in the sense that there are no repetitions or close parallels among the examples, contrary to what one might find with collections of didactic material, for instance. Perhaps their originality is reflected in the fact that, with one exception—a certain Nakht-sobek, a mere "scribe" whose authorship is generally doubted—no one is credited with this verse.[315] In other words, unlike nearly all didactic material, these are not pseudepigraphical works.

I shall close my discussion of love poetry by briefly reviewing the sources in the approximate chronological order in which the manuscripts themselves were written, rather than attempting to sequence them according to their probable compositional dates. Both Guglielmi and Kitchen have adopted this approach, although they arrived at different datings. In the summary below, I have attempted to mention the more interesting forms, themes, or rhetorical devices, rather than to embark on an elaborate piece-by-piece analysis of this sizable body of literature.[316]

(1) Papyrus Harris 500 (British Museum EA 10060).[317] The recto of this damaged papyrus starts with a poem now considerably damaged at the beginning, followed by three collections (or cycles) of poems, preserved in their entirety, each starting with the rubricized phrase *ḥȝty-ꜥ m ḥswt sḥms-jb (a3)*, "beginning of the song of (great) entertainment."[318] In addition to the love lyrics, the roll also contains one of the Harpers' Songs, known as the *Antef Song*, as well as two narrative tales, *The Prince Who Knew His Fate* and *Thutmose III and the Taking of Joppa*. The *Antef Song* appears between the second and third groups of love poems, so these do not form a unified block on the manuscript. The lyrics' introductory phrases and juxtaposition of genres indicate that the roll as a whole was intended as a collection of entertainment literature. Verse points, however, are absent throughout the manuscript.

The poems are predominantly in couplet form. The patterns vary slightly from collection to collection, without any particularly striking metrical schemes and with sparse use of parallelisms, unusual for Egyptian belles lettres of any sort.[319] The first group of poems has the lyric "On the Memphis Ferry" among the love poetry. Although this poem belongs to a genre of praises of residential cities, the *laus urbis*, its presence here is explained by its nature as a love poem to a city and its gods.[320] Equally interesting from a topical point of view is a cycle of poems in the third group in which a woman narrator offers her lover a different flower in the first line of each poem. These poems perhaps allude to folk medicine or love magic connected with the special properties of each plant.

(2) Papyrus Chester Beatty I (British Musem EA 10681).[321] This is another lengthy anthology manuscript and the best preserved of our papyrus sources. It can be dated with reasonable certainty to the reign of Ramesses V by an encomium to that monarch that concludes the verso. The papyrus is the best preserved of all the manuscripts on this list, containing three collections of love poems on both the verso and recto, in addition to the lengthy and often burlesque *The Contendings of Horus and Seth*. The poetry appears in widely separated groups, which are introduced by the rubricized phrase *ḥȝty-ꜥ m rȝw nw ȝ sḥmḫt-ib ꜥȝt*, "beginning of the sayings of (great) enjoyment (or "entertainer")," almost identical to the phrase in the titles of Papyrus Harris 500. Verse points appear in some, but not all, the poetry and are absent in the tale. The treatment accorded poetry and prose could lend some weight to the argument that the points were employed to indicate poetry, but the situation is not clear-cut by any means.

One of the finest and longest poems on the manuscript is composed of seven shorter lyrics, an allusion to the goddess Hathor, who was associated with that number. The poems are each headed with the word *ḥwt*, "house," thus supplying us with the Egyptian word for "stanza."[322] It is a dialogue poem, with the male and female speakers alternating.[323] A remarkable feature of the poem is that each stanza begins with an ordinal number—*tpy*, "first"; *sn*, "second"; *ḥmt*, "third"; and so on—and closes with a play on that word, surely a poetical tour de force.[324]

(3) The Cairo Love Songs; Ostracon Deir el-Medina 1266 + Ostracon CGC 25218; the "Cairo Jar."[325] This collection of two groups of poems appears on what amounts to a very big ostracon in the traditional sense—it was written out on a large pottery jar found at Deir el-Medina that has been almost completely reassembled. It now preserves two poetry collections but may have contained more. Whether there was any connection between the jar's practical use and the poetry is unknown. The second group of poems apparently is based entirely on the travesty motif, each verse beginning with the phrase "I wish I were . . . ," all spoken by the male narrator. This group is permeated by a certain degree of exoticism. Several foreign territories are mentioned, as well as a wide variety of plants and flowers. No verse points were employed, but the individual poems were separated by rubricized *grḥ*-signs.

(4) Papyrus Turin 1966.[326] This badly damaged papyrus apparently contains a collection solely of love poetry. There are only two fully preserved pages, which are supplemented by a number of smaller fragments. These are perhaps all derived from a single papyrus, but that is not certain. The larger fragments present poems that are thematically connected by a tree motif. Each poem begins with a tree speaking, relating how it has helped the lovers by supplying fruit or shelter. Verse points were employed throughout the manuscript.

(5) Miscellanea, consisting mostly of ostraca[327] along with occasional short works on papyrus,[328] both media that include many examples of nonamatory poetry as well. Where their provenance can be determined, the ostraca all come from Deir el-Medina. Kitchen has aptly described these minor works as "lyric fragments." These shorter works may well be original creations rather than material gathered from larger collections. In this respect, they speak to a spirit of literary creativity at the workmen's village. As with the longer manuscripts, verse points are employed erratically among these miscellanea. Poems with monostichic lines are particularly common among these ostraca, perhaps because space-saving considerations would not play as important a role as they do on the more expensive papyri.[329]

Harpers' Songs

The Harpers' Songs are an old and enduring poetical genre that dates back to short verses on Middle Kingdom stelae.[330] The first examples of these poems clearly describe the tomb and the afterlife as places of rejoicing, for the deceased had gone on to an eternal and better existence. These earlier versions lack the skeptical tenor of most of the exemplars from the New Kingdom, when these verses reached the peak of their popularity.[331]

Perhaps our impression has been distorted by accidents of preservation, but these later versions also have a distinct connection with mortuary contexts and stem predominantly from elite tombs, with the exception of the most famous example, the *Antef Song,* found on Papyrus Harris 500, the collection of Late Egyptian entertainment literature described above. This poem is supposedly from the tomb of a king named Antef, but given the absence of such worldly subjects in royal tombs of all periods, the attribution seems quite improbable, as does any date in either the First or Second Intermediate Period.[332] The poetical intent of the genre is clear in the chosen narrator, a harpist who is illustrated in the tomb paintings as he sings before a banquet audience.

Thus, even more than love lyrics, the Harpers' Songs were directly connected with banqueting and entertainment. Their skeptical, hedonistic message at times seems deliberately at variance with their mortuary context. There are numerous allusions to afterlife sex and regeneration in the accompanying scenes, enhanced by the juxtaposition of the elegantly attired young guests, scantily clad female entertainers, and drink that supposedly would inspire the deceased and assist him in reproducing himself.[333] To that end, the very instrument the musician plays may also involve an allusion to sexual intercourse.[334]

As a poetical genre, the Harpers' Songs are unusual because exemplars are found both on papyri and tomb walls. There is a marked intertextuality among the examples, some phrases appearing verbatim.[335] In fact, these poems seem to debate one another explicitly concerning their central themes—tombs versus life and the validity of afterlife beliefs, both undeniably fundamental issues.[336] An interesting aspect of this theme is that the word *Kemet*, often translated simply as "Egypt" or "the Black Land," here takes on the additional nuance of "the land of the living," contrasted with the necropolis.[337] On the whole, the versions occurring in tombs present a more positive opinion of the value of funerary monuments as a means of commemoration. In most instances, the same tombs in which the poems appear also contained standard expressions of normative afterlife concepts, such as chapters from the *Book of the Dead*, a work whose Egyptian title, "The Chapters of Going Forth by Day," implied that survival in the next world was possible. Unlike nearly all other particularly Ramesside genres, the Harpers' Songs and their themes persisted into the Late Period[338] and possibly the Ptolemaic era as well, if Ben Sira can be included among them.

To some degree, the genre is an expression of a nonelite, "subversive" view of the relationship between one's burial goods and the quality of one's afterlife, revealing a long-existing tension within Egyptian religious thought that might also be connected with personal piety. The majority of these lyrics emphasize that no one comes back from the next world to inform us of what lies beyond, so instead of dwelling on our inevitable fate, we should all "make holiday," the Egyptian equivalent of the Latin *carpe diem*.[339] Yet any tomb text, by virtue of where it was located, necessarily acquired a religious significance. That being the case, one could go a step further and note that in the Egyptian context, a debate on the prevailing afterlife beliefs would be almost like questioning whether there was a god.[340]

This pessimistic view of the afterlife seems to run counter to a widespread popular practice of writing letters to the deceased in the belief that they could communicate with the living from the beyond. *The Encomium of the Sages* presents a particularly scribal point of view on the importance of funerary equipment.[341] It extols written works rather than tombs as the ideal means of afterlife survival through commemoration[342] and is thus clearly a variant of this genre, despite the absence of the central figure of the harpist. This religious skepticism probably arose out of the events of the Amarna period, when the royal house itself appears to have called the Osirian concepts of the next world into doubt. Significantly, the inscriptional variant of the *Antef Song,* perhaps also the earliest datable example of the New Kingdom genre, derives from this period.[343]

Royal Encomia and Religious Poetry in the Ramesside Period

Royal encomia and religious poetry are topics that more properly belong to other chapters in this volume. Nevertheless, both genres unquestionably meet the most basic criteria of belles lettres, since they were royal in nature and therefore among the most carefully written of all Egyptian texts. I will offer only some brief remarks here, confining myself to their literary aspects.

For all the literary skill royal encomia and religious prayers and hymns exhibit, they still remain in a gray area between poetry and ideology, a point that I have already made above in connection with the historical texts of Ramesses III.[344] These genres often have much in common because, ultimately, there was not a great difference between praise of a god and a king in ancient Egypt. From the point of view of technique and vocabulary, they also recall love lyric in the manner in which the beloved—a king or a god—is praised.

Since the language of Egyptian religious texts always exhibited a strong tendency toward conservative and archaic forms, there are few internal features that can set them apart from the works of previous periods. The language of the afterlife texts in the tomb of Ramesses III, for example, is quite old-fashioned when compared with his historical inscriptions at Medinet Habu. Nonetheless, we should not ascribe the choice of dialect simply to the more official environment of royal tombs and temples. Works such as the great Leiden Amun Hymn (P. Leiden I 344, verso)[345] or a collection of royal encomia on a papyrus in Turin (P. Turin 54031)[346] employ the Late Middle Egyptian dialect for the most part. This choice is interesting, since, as we have seen at numerous junctures above, papyri normally tended to be more linguistically innovative than inscriptions.

Use of Late Middle Egyptian, however, tells us little about when the works may have actually been composed, a point I have made several times above in connection with texts in that dialect during the Ramesside period. For example, the *Book of the Dead* is basically written in classical Middle Egyptian, yet no examples of this important religious corpus appear until well after the Middle Kingdom,[347] leading us to the conclusion that these texts were mostly composed following Dynasties Twelve and Thirteen. However, one occasionally encounters such works as a thirty-line poem on the occasion of Ramesses III's Sed Festival, written on ostracon from Thebes, that has such innovative features as a monostichic structure and verse points and shows features of Late Egyptian.[348] One possible means of judging when a religious text may have been composed would be to assess the degree to which its theological content seems to conform with similar material of the period. This approach, unfortunately, involves religio-historical issues that are best left to other parts of this book.

If one considers these religious works from a strictly stylistic point of view, they show a great amount of technical sophistication. As Assmann has convincingly demonstrated, the skillful use of rhetorical figures and patterns encountered in love poetry is equally present in hymns, prayers, and encomia.[349] The use of verse points in such material is irregular, whereas use of the *grḥ*-sign as a marker of cola and stanzas is more common. Just as the sculptures, reliefs, and paintings produced on behalf of the temples or the king were of the very highest quality, the same would hold true when either of these two sectors of Egyptian society commissioned texts on behalf of a monarch or a god.

THE LITERARY ENVIRONMENT OF RAMESSES III—CONCLUSIONS

For this chapter, I adopted a rather broad definition of literature and attempted to describe its social environment, its *Sitz im Leben*. Taking what I sensed to be signals from the Egyptians themselves, I preferred a loose concept of belles lettres over definitions based on more specific criteria, such as "fictivity." Among the Egyptians, what we consider "literature" seems to have been referred to as simply "writing" or "beautiful words" or in similar general terms. Perhaps we should follow their lead. The fact that they lacked the repertoire of technical terms by which we identify types of literature certainly did not prevent them from using a wide range of genres. They recognized that some writing was more elegant than the rest and ought to be emulated. The Egyptians seem to have had little or no place for silent reading in their culture, so they placed a greater value on the performative than we do.

Yet, for all these constraints, the Egyptians appear to have considered essentially the same things as literature as we do. However, their genres tend to be as nameless as their authors for the most part, so we will always have to fall back on our own terminology to describe what they wrote. The forms their genres took, naturally, were not the same as ours, and more important, their hierarchy of these forms were different. Of such is taste.

We know but few facts about the social environment—the audience—of Ramesside literature. The *Sitz im Leben,* in that phrase's most literal sense, for a sizable proportion of literary works during the Ramesside must have been the classroom. Although today we read, rather than copy, literature, we, too, use belles lettres as an integral part of our educative process. Yet these observations explain little about the social status of the student audience. We should not assume that what the subelite at Deir el-Medina learned was confined to the workmen's village. It is likely that students with greater social rank were taught the same materials and that there was little difference between the curriculums employed at Memphis or Thebes.

Since literacy marked an individual as special, a person somewhat comparable to an intellectual in modern society, that special skill probably created certain common bonds across class lines among those who could read and write. The very concepts of "employment" and "patronage," furthermore, meant always that the values and aims of the upper elite influenced those below them. Those values could be communicated through literature of all types.

It is not hard to image the impact that the court of Ramesses III at Medinet Habu must have exerted on all aspects of intellectual life in the entire West Bank of Thebes during the first part of Dynasty Twenty. That influence must have been especially important for the poetical compositions of the age, whether they were love lyrics, royal texts, or divine encomia. The strong current of entertainment and the performative that flows through Ramesside poetical and narrative texts implies a wide audience, high and low, male and female, as well as providing a way to spread the enjoyment of literature beyond the literate few. Works that can be performed or read aloud address the imagination, allowing people to share experiences that might be otherwise absent in their lives.

Because I sought to describe a literary environment rather than examining literary works by themselves, this study has had a far broader chronological focus than just the reign of Ramesses III. Part of the reason for this approach was the enormous difficulty of assigning dates to the great majority of the evidence. Even in the few instances where manuscripts can be dated with relative certainty, the date when a text was written has little bearing on when it might have been composed. The literary world of Ramesses III certainly was never confined to contemporary creations but was revived and borrowed from the literature of previous ages. The subjects of his age thus partook of a range of literary traditions and new creations that was perhaps unsurpassed in Egyptian history.

An immediate difference in the attitude toward writing in our two cultures lies in the relative importance that we and the Egyptians seem to ascribe to the author, creativity, and originality. There is a great gap between Egyptian aesthetics and ours over these points especially. Much of that difference arises from the purposeful, didactic nature of the Ramesside literature that has survived and its twofold nature. To understand Ramesside literature, one must accept that the literature of the Middle Kingdom was very much a part of the literary world in the age of Ramesses III.

At first glance, the two minds of Ramesside literature manifest themselves in an extensive diglossia—many texts in the now antique Middle Egyptian dialect enjoying a new life alongside new works written in Late Egyptian. Yet that diglossia certainly only existed in written materials and was primarily an expression of the disparate aims of their scribal curriculum. Particularly for those students who lived in the Theban necropolis, the center of a great funerary "industry," there was a need to produce texts written in the conservative Middle Egyptian dialect. At the same time, there was always a more immediate need to conduct business in the here and now, the affairs of everyday life. For that aspect of his work, the student scribe had to be able to produce documents in the Late Egyptian dialect.

Whether written in Late Egyptian or Middle Egyptian, this was not simply didactic literature; these were *emulative* texts—they provided models phrases, diction, and style that carried over into the scribes' occupations, consciously or unconsciously. In the case of Middle Egyptian works, the Egyptians' great respect for tradition also played an important role, giving those texts a status sometimes akin to that held by canonical or classical literary works in our society today, perhaps also being admired and maintained in private collections as achievements of a great past.

A critical difference between these works and the classical literature of our literary canon is that the Middle Egyptian texts may well have been the creations of a much later time than they purport to be, perhaps early Dynasty Eighteen, with its reorganization of a resurgent Egyptian state. For that reason, this chapter has focused on describing the Ramesside literary environment as a whole, rather than attempting to limit the discussion to just the literary works themselves. Similarly, it would be wrong to consider only those texts that are demonstrably Ramesside in date. The new works in Late Egyptian, even if many were intended as teaching texts, show that this was hardly an era devoid of creative impulse. By contrast, we would be most reluctant to count our textbooks among the literary works of our age. The fruit of their scribal training can be seen in new and original compositions such as Ramesside love lyric, surely one of the prime literary achievements of Egyptian history.

The freelance, self-supporting author does not appear to have had a place in Egyptian society. Herein lies another conceptual gap in our two concepts of literature and its place in society. In as much as professional writers existed in any form in ancient Egypt, they remained nameless and enjoyed little of the status that they have in our society; they would have been employees of a temple or of the royal chancellery. The author's cloak of pseudepigraphy reinforced the influence of tradition in both style and thought. Copying had both a greater need and a higher value than it does for us. Because of a tendency to underestimate the significance of didacticism in Egyptian literature, many modern scholars have thus overestimated the importance of intertextuality. The reproduction of stock phrases was a necessary part of scribes' training and their later work in society. In all their artistic endeavors, whether in the plastic arts or in writing, the Egyptians put a much higher value on adherence to traditional forms, something we, to the contrary, are apt to consider a hindrance to imagination and innovation.

My emphasis on the literary environment arises out of a conviction that we are apt to forget that during the first part of Dynasty Twenty, the reign of Ramesses III, his court at Medinet Habu must have exerted a significant influence over all works of the imagination, literary or otherwise. We should bear in mind that throughout history, literature has always been dependent on patronage, and we should expect that this would lead to the same results in Egypt—that is, works strongly affirming the status quo. It is also important to remember that this was an environment where literacy was rather uncommon, even among the elite. For these reasons, orality and public entertainment were much more important to Egyptian literature than in works from later societies, such as the Romans and the Greeks.

Although the suppression of the author and didacticism are certainly striking aspects, the chief differences in our literary environments are the roles that belle lettres played in their society. The Egyptian aesthetic appears to have focused first on literature's practical applications and then on its ability to entertain. Even though literature was certainly a form of entertainment, the enjoyment it provided was clearly more closely related to the purposeful. Ideological and religious themes are, to be sure, not absent from our literary world, but in Egypt, they were prime concerns. According to our aesthetic concepts, religious or political literature exists only on the margins of the acceptable. Lacking works that could serve as national foundation epics or the equivalent of a Bible, literature among the Egyptians necessarily took on a key role in reinforcing social and political norms. If Egyptian didactic writing or fulsome praise of the king sometimes grates on modern literary sensibilities, we should remind ourselves that even in our world, one man's agitprop can be another man's socially conscious writing.

All these literary threads came together in the reign of Ramesses III to form a new tradition that stands as one of the great cultural achievements of the age.

Several additional literary studies that are relevant to a key issue, namely the dating and nature of the large corpus of Middle Egyptian texts, appeared while this volume was in its long gestation period, including Fischer-Elfert (2003), the essays in Moers (1999b), and especially the unpublished papers presented at the recent conference, "Dating Egyptian Literary Texts," held at Göttingen in June 2010. I regret not being able to take those papers fully into consideration here, but doing so would have entailed an extensive rewriting of some sections of this contribution. Nonetheless, I feel that I stand by my original conclusions in the paper as it appears here.

Notes

1. Lichtheim (1973); Lichtheim (1976); Lichtheim (1980a).

2. Goldwasser ([2001] 123–24) has recently observed that our division between Dynasty Nineteen and Dynasty Twenty is largely an artificial one in view of the actual development of the language itself. Generally speaking, Egyptologists tend to overestimate the ability of a change in dynasties to produce corresponding changes in the language.

3. Kitchen (1999c) 315 estimates that 98 percent of all papyrus-based documents have been lost.

4. Loprieno (1996a).

5. Baines (2003). This lecture was the keynote speech in the conference's "millennium debate" on the status of research on Egyptian literature. The respondents' works will be cited below as necessary.

6. I would note here, e.g., several sets of recent conference papers: Assmann and Blumenthal (1999), Moers (1999a), and Moers (1999b).

7. Lichtheim (1973) vi–vii. Particularly salient is her observation "To define literature narrowly as non-functional works of the imagination would eliminate the bulk of ancient works and would introduce a criterion quite alien to the ancient writers" (vi).

8. Lichtheim's definition is quite close to that recently proposed in Goldwasser (1999) 314: "I call here 'literary' any text that is not written for every-day private use, from administrative exercises, through historical inscriptions to hymns, songs and so forth."

9. On this point, see *Didactic Literature in the Ramesside Period* below.

10. Since the criteria are largely based on flowery language and lavish praise of the king, this is a rather vaguely defined genre. The most typical examples date to the reign of Ramesses II, for which see Spalinger (1986) 136–64 and the numerous examples collected by Kitchen ([1999c] 183–92; *RITA* II.118–60; *RITANC* II.173–89).

11. See especially Moers (1999a) and Moers (1999b) and the discussion of Moer's criteria in Baines (2003) 5–6 and Haikal (2003) 30. On this aspect, perhaps we might add the comments of Simpson (2003) 45–47, even if Simpson adopts a more conciliatory attitude.

12. This is a point Baines also made in discussing several proposed definitions for Egyptian literature, noting that the distinctions scholars make in such exercises usually result in demarcations that are not mutually exclusive. See Baines (2003) 4.

13. Texts in this Egyptian genre seem to be mostly poetry and mythical tales. See *The Origins of Love Lyric* and *Harpers' Songs* below.

14. P. Prisse 55; Lichtheim (1973) 63.

15. There are some objective criteria for distinguishing literary from documentary materials for both ostraca and papyri; see *Harpers' Songs* and *Narrative Tales of the New Kingdom*. The grammar can also be an indication; see *Evolution of the Dialects*.

16. In many ways, the locus classicus for the treatment of apparent quotes from didactic literature in other genres of texts remains Brunner (1979b). For some more recent observations on this subject, see also Loprieno (1996d); Vernus (1995b); Eyre (1990).

17. See McDowell (1992); Fischer-Elfert (2003).

18. These issues become even more important in the study of Late Period art forms in general. See Jasnow (1999).

19. For more on imitations and the style of the historical inscriptions of Ramesses III, see nn. 20–21 and *Royal Inscriptions and Religious Literature* below.

20. The epigraphy, vocabulary, and other features of the text indicate that this was not, as Shabako claimed, an actual composition of the Old Kingdom. See Junge (1973).

21. See Lichtheim (1980a) 94–103.

22. On this much-discussed topic, see, most recently, Parkinson (2002) 235–77 with references.

23. On the subject of "cultural" and "literary" texts, see Assmann (1995c); Baines (2003) 4–5; Junge (2003) 154–59. Haikal (2003) 29–30 notes that a particular problem arises when such texts are revived. If a text is later reused outside of its original historical context, should one then consider it to have passed from the realm of belles lettres into that of "cultural texts"?

24. An overview of the work of Gesse, McDowell, and Janssen on student papyri appears below. For some recent discussions of the significance of the contrast between the level of skill in the script of student papyri and the accuracy of the text, see Goelet (2008) 102–10; Hagen (2006) 84–99; Hagen (2007) 38–51.

25. The subject of deification of private persons in Egypt has been extensively studied. See particularly Habachi (1969); Quaegebeur (1977); Wildung (1977); Goedicke (1986).

26. *The Encomium of the Sages* (P. Chester Beatty IV, vv. 2.5–3.10) is discussed at length below in *Harpers' Songs*. Many of the same scribal heroes of the *Encomium* appear on the so-called Daressy relief, a fragment of wall decoration taken from an unidentified Dynasty Nineteen tomb at Saqqara (see Fischer [1976a] 63–67) and on a papyrus in the National Library of Athens (P. Athens 1826). These three sources are discussed together in Fischer-Elfert (2003) 123–31.

27. An important aspect of examining diglossia in a wide variety of New Kingdom texts is to realize that many texts, both literary and otherwise, are not uniform in their language or register. See Goldwasser (1999); Jansen-Winkeln (1995b) 85–115.

28. For a discussion of the "productive" and "reproductive," stages of a language, a concept that is invaluable in understanding the mechanisms of the transmission and canonization of Egyptian religious texts, see Assmann (1995) 1–11. Needless to say, this is a distinction that can be usefully extended to other varieties of compositions as well and perhaps could even be justified in treating the plastic arts.

29. On this important aspect of Ramesside literary life, see *Harpers' Song* below.

30. There have been many studies on this question, see, e.g., Kaplony (1977); Simpson (1996); Assmann (1985).

31. Loprieno (1996c).

32. However, exact nuance between the term *sb3yt-mtrt*, used at the beginning of *The Instruction of Amenemope* and *The Instruction of Ani* as well as in some shorter ostraca texts and meaning roughly "testimonial instruction," and the term *sb3yt-šꜥt*, from Papyrus Sallier I's copy of the *Teaching of Amenemhat I* and translating roughly as "documentary instruction," is hard to discern, unless the distinction lies in that the former type of instruction was originally intended to be delivered in an oral form, whereas the second type primarily occurs in archived texts on papyri and ostraca. On the two terms, see Schott (1990) 302–4, 507, where they are translated as "Erziehungslehre" and "Schriftliche Lehre," respectively. Junge (1996) 310 suggests "Brieflehre" for *sb3yt-šꜥt*. See also Fischer-Elfert (1986b) 2 n. a, translating *sb3yt-mtrt* in line 1 of Ostracon Gardiner 2 as "Erziehungslehre."

33. Quirke (1996a) 380. For this and similar phrases, see Schott (1990) 75–76 (no. 131).

34. Quirke (1996a) 380. For additional discussion on the forms and significance of colophons in New Kingdom literary papyri, see Hagen (2006) 88–92.

35. Quirke (1996a) 380; McDowell (2000). Interestingly enough, a Ramesside ostracon containing the concluding lines of *The Tale of Sinuhe* (BM EA 5629) uses a more modern form of a colophon: *jw.s pw nfr m htp(w)*, "it has arrived (at its end) happily and in peace"; see Koch (1990) 81. This object is illustrated in Parkinson and Quirke (1995) 21 (fig. 9).

36. P. Sallier IV, v. 16.2: see Caminos (1954) 366–67, and compare the nearly identical curse formula by well-known "student" scribe Innene at the end of *The Tale of the Two Brothers* (P. D'Orbiney 19, 9–10); see Gardiner (1932) 29.

37. Fischer-Elfert (1993) 32–34; Posener (1975) 105–12; McDowell (1996) 606.

38. Luft (1976).

39. Pestman (1982).

40. Janssen (1992).

41. See Baines and Eyre (1983). By all accounts, the rate of literacy must have been higher in the royal workmen's village of Deir el-Medina; see Janssen (1992) and Dorn (2006). However, these studies do not address the subtle issue of intermediary stages of literacy—the ability to spot certain signs and groups of letters—for which see Der Manuelian (1999).

42. I heartily endorse the following statement from McDowell (2000) 223: "The fact that Middle Egyptian literary texts and Late Egyptian Miscellanies are published separately obscures the relation between them."

43. On the complex interaction between script forms, dialect, and register in the Ramesside period, see Goelet (2003) 1–21; Goelet (2008) 102–10; Goelet (2010).

44. Kroeber (1970).

45. Silverman (1991).

46. Junge (1996) 13–22; Junge (1985).

47. Jansen-Winkeln (1995b) 85–115.

48. Černý and Groll (1994) liv–lxviii; Groll (1986); Groll (1973a). The last of these articles makes some very important distinctions between textual framing devices and the actual narrative content.

49. Kruchten (1999); Kruchten (1998).

50. Here we might note an observation of A. Roccati (2003) 43: "Late Egyptian was not the language of the people replacing the outdated former Middle Egyptian in the higher registers."

51. Junge (2005) 22.

> daß sich die Neuen-Reichs-Texte vor allem darin unterscheiden, wie hoch ihr Anteil an noch mittelägyptischen Sprachformen ist: In den Registern der kulturell bedeutsamsten Texte—den sprachlich konservativisten—ist ihr Anteil am höchsten, er steigt von den Alltagstexten über die literarischen und staatsideologischen zu den theologischen Texten kontinuierlich an—oder besser: wird in ihnen am längsten bewahrt.

Similar observations appear also in Jansen-Winkeln (1995b) 92–102.

52. Junge (1996) 20–22. For some modifications of this basic scheme of classification, particularly in respect to Middle Egyptian, see Jansen-Winkeln (1995b) 92–102.

53. For a brief discussion of the term, see Loprieno (1996e) 522–24.

54. For a comprehensive treatment of the several variations of the text of these stelae, see Murnane and Van Siclen (1993). Unfortunately, the language of the texts themselves is not discussed at any length. The contrast between the language of the Boundary Stelae and that of other texts found at Amarna has been described briefly in Jansen-Winkeln (1995b) 91.

55. This is one of the Amherst Papyri, now in the collection of the Pierpont Morgan Library of New York. See Gardiner (1932) 76–81.

56. Gardiner (1932) xii. However, it should be noted that the text also contains such eminently literary Middle Egyptian elements as the preference for the preposition $ḥnꜥ$ (rather than jrm) and the constructions $sḏm\ pw\ jr.n.f$ and $ꜥḥꜥ.n\ sḏm.n.f.$ Despite its

early date, *Astarte and the Sea* goes virtually unmentioned in the articles discussing the development of the Late Egyptian dialect that are cited in the next few notes. The text has recently been reexamined in Collombert and Coulon (2000) 193–242.

57. For a further discussion of this work and its relationship with Ramesside tales of a similar type, see *Narrative Tales* below. For a treatment of the Levantine background of the tale and its influences on Egyptian, classical, and other mythical traditions, see Redford (1990).

58. On this point, see Kruchten (1999) 55; Groll (1973a); Jansen-Winkeln (1995b).

59. Loprieno (1996b) 277–95.

60. This narrative device is discussed in greater detail below, in *Royal Inscriptions*. For the Quban stela, Grenoble Museum I, see *RITA* II:353–60. A recent translation of the stela accompanied by a transliteration has been published in Davies (1997) 232–43; for additional bibliography, see also *RITANC* II:214–15. The mixture of rhetoric and style in these and similar texts has been examined in Spalinger (2006) 415–28.

61. Groll (1973a).

62. In this respect, it is particularly interesting to note that Vernus uses the term *microcontexte* in describing the variable use of certain Middle Egyptian and Late Egyptian negative particles in the Ramesside private tomb of *S3-Mwt,* named *Kyky.* See Vernus (1978) 140 n. 143.

63. In connection with this point, it is significant that Silverman ([1991] 305) begins his discussion of the quality of the Late Egyptian in a group of letters attributed to the Amarna period by noting, "In a Late Egyptian text, one would expect to find the consistent use of the definite article and the possessive article."

64. Stela of Monthu-weser; Sethe (1928a) 79.17–18. See particularly Allen (1994) 11; Loprieno (1996e) 519; Goldwasser (1999) 316. By way of confirmation of the status of *p3,* we should point out that this use of this demonstrative pronoun (or definite article) occurs in a number of Middle Kingdom letters (Hekanakht archive and Letters to the Dead) and in the magical tales in the Westcar Papyrus. It occasionally appears in model letters emanating from the Dynasty Twelve capital at Lahun (see Grdseloff [1949]) but seems largely absent in official documents until the Kamose stelae, on which see n. 69 below. Allen, however, has recently revised his opinion on the Monthu-weser stela; see Allen (2009).

65. It is remarkable that of the list of nineteen hieratic papyri attributable to Dynasty Eighteen compiled by Quirke ([1996a] 388), only three are known New Kingdom compositions. In the case of one of these three—Moscow Pushkin MFA, *The Sporting King* and *The Pleasures of Hunting and Fowling*—we are dealing with a text that may actually have its roots in the Middle Kingdom. However, the degree to which most of the remaining papyri on this list—nearly all Middle Kingdom didactic literature—can be said to be entirely "Middle Kingdom" is problematic. On this important question, see *Didactic Literature* below.

66. Wente (1990) 89: "It is remarkable that so few letters of the Eighteenth Dynasty are extant." A possible addition to Wente's small corpus might be the letter of Amenophis II to his vizier preserved in hieroglyphs among the tomb inscriptions of *Wsr-S3tt* (*Urk* IV.1344), a text that displays a number of Late Egyptian characteristics; see Goldwasser (1999) 316.

67. Baines (1996a) 166 has also raised the possibility that our reconstruction of the

development of Late Egyptian has most likely been distorted by accidents of preservation, particularly in respect to letters.

68. Silverman (1991).

69. The texts in question are the victory stelae of King Kamose (see Gardiner [1916]; Helck [1983b] 82–97; Habachi [1972] 198–201 with pl. 1) and the boundary stelae of Akhenaten (see Murnane and Van Sicklen [1998]). For the quality of these two sources as examples of Late Middle Egyptian and Late Egyptian, see Kruchten (1999).

70. *Astarte and the Sea;* see *Narrative Tales* below.

71. As a language instructor, I am often amused by the astonishment of students well-versed in Middle Egyptian when they discover the extent to which their old friend, Faulkner's *Concise Dictionary of Middle Egyptian,* is of little help in dealing with Ramesside material.

72. The question of Semitic vocabulary in New Kingdom texts has been studied at length. At present the most thorough examination of this problem has been provided in Hoch (1994). The origin of the bulk of the vocabulary is discussed there on pp. 479–86. For some methodological objections, see Meeks (1997).

73. The presence of a good number of foreign words and colloquialisms are features particularly noticeable in the inscriptions of Ramesses III. See B. Cifola (1991) 10.

74. See the description in section e of the introduction in Černý and Groll (1993) li–lii.

75. The distinctions between literary and nonliterary usages asserted in dictionaries and grammars might not be as clear-cut as they seem. Goldwasser ([1999] 312) has recently pointed out the difficulties, if not the impossibilities, faced by any ideal future dictionary if it attempts to make distinctions within Late Egyptian vocabulary based on our perceptions of what comprised colloquial and administrative usages.

76. For a summation of the similarities between the language of the treaty and that of "documentary" Late Egyptian, see Goelet and Levine (1998) 257–62.

77. F. Junge (1996) 18, e.g., classifies the treaty as a "Dekorumstext."

78. The treaty is dated to Ramesses' twenty-first regnal year. When the inscription of Mose was executed is not quite clear. There is mention of a "year 18" in the tomb, providing that as a *post quem* date. However, the form of the king's prenomen, R^c-*ms-sw,* may indicate a date slightly later than that. See Kitchen (1977); Spalinger (1980) esp. 95–99.

79. See *RITANC* II:282–83; Kitchen (1999c) 197–204; Davies (1997) 141–49. The reiterative use of negative statements in the poetical sections of the stela is a rhetorical device particularly popular during the Ramesside period; see *Didactic Literature* below.

80. Fischer-Elfert (1986a) 261–76 presents convincing evidence that *The Satirical Letter* must have been composed during the reign of Ramesses II, even though the best-known manuscript, Papyrus Anastasi I, appears to have been written at Memphis no earlier than the reign of Merenptah (see ibid., 249–60). The composition is also attested on ostraca from Deir el-Medina with no substantial differences in textual content. For the text of this key work, see Fischer-Elfert (1983b). On this piece and its place in the curriculum, see *Didactic Literature* below; for a convenient translation in English with extensive notes showing the great number of Semitic words in this text, see Allen (2002) 9–14.

81. Generally speaking, most of the Late Egyptian texts mentioned in the present study are infrequently copied or even cited in the Late Period (see Jasnow [1999] 193–94), but didactic texts such as *The Instruction of Ani* and *The Instruction of Amenemope* represent an exception (see ibid., 195; Baines [1996a] 158–59).

82. For a brief discussion of the approximate scale of time and expense implicit in various forms of writing as well as how these and other factors might influence the script chosen for a certain task, see Parkinson and Quirke (1995) 24–28.

83. O. Turin 57300; see López (1978) pl. 95a.

84. The stages of scribal training were described by Clement of Alexandria in *Stromata* V.4.20, as quoted in Parkinson and Quirke (1995) 29: "the men of learning among the Egyptians learnt first of all that method of writing called the epistolographic, and second the hieratic, which the sacred scribes use, and then, last of all, the hieroglyphic."

85. For discussion of the cursive hieroglyphs and how they were used, see Parkinson and Quirke (1995) 24–28; Fischer (1976b) 39–45; Ali (2001); Goelet (2010). The association of the cursive hieroglyphs with the recondite can be seen as early as the Middle Kingdom. E.g., several among the Ramesseum papyri were written in cursives in columnar format, with the script moving in a retrograde direction. See Gardiner (1955) P. Ram. V (medical; pls. XV–XVII); P. Ram. VII (Sobek hymns; pls. XVIII–XXI); P. Ram. VII (medical and magical; pls. XXII–XXVI). Perhaps the most famous example of such Middle Kingdom arcania is the Berlin Dramatic Papyrus; see Sethe (1928b). The later *Book of the Dead* as well as other New Kingdom religious texts were to employ the combination of script form, columnar format, and direction of writing.

86. See Hornung (1971) pl. 37b, where one can see the preliminary text in cursives underlying the more finished and correct final hieroglyphic text in preparation for the final carving. In a private Dynasty Eighteen tomb, one can see several lines of the red-ochre cursives in columns of text that were never finished; see Brack and Brack (1980) pls. 3, 5. Ostraca in cursive hieroglyphs found in the Theban tomb of a Dynasty Eighteen official named Nankht-Min (TT 87) may have been used as a preparatory stage in the production of a lengthy inscription in that script form; see Guksch (1995) 74–75.

87. This is disputed by Brunner ([1957] 86–89), who believed that the curriculum more probably began with training in the Middle Egyptian classics. However, his opinion was based at least partially on a misevaluation of the level of skill in the script on the "school" ostraca.

88. This old conception of a geographical division in the curriculum is strongly contradicted by McDowell ([2000] 221–33), who has presented a useful compendium on the numerous citations of passages from the *Miscellanies* that have appeared on ostraca found in the Theban region. Furthermore, one of the *Miscellanies* papyri, Papyrus Lansing, can be shown from internal evidence to have been produced in Thebes late in Dynasty Twenty. Several passages from earlier papyri from Memphis are reproduced on this document.

89. Quirke (1996a) 382–83. Quirke's observations can be strengthened and supplemented by similar evidence from the Deir el-Medina ostraca mentioned in the previous note.

90. The *Kemyt* ostraca are a major exception to this rule, as they employed a distinctly archaic form of hieratic. See *Didactic Literature* below. For an introduction to

the didactic methods and texts of the Ramesside Period, see Erman (1925) and Brunner (1957) 89–90. However, some of the theories of these two authors have recently been disputed; see Hagen (2006) and idem (2007).

91. Gasse (1992) 52–53. There is an even more pronounced objective criterion for distinguishing between literary and nonliterary papyri based on fiber arrangement; see "Didactic Literature" below.

92. Gasse (1992) 53.

93. Fischer-Elfert (1999) 381–99.

94. Fischer-Elfert (2003) 120–28.

95. BM EA 5629, conveniently illustrated in Parkinson (1999a) pl. 28. On this object, see also n. 249 below.

96. Ramesside literary ostraca, however, are not necessarily always fraught with errors. Foster (1982) 81–85 notes that the Ashmoleon Ostracon of Sinuhe frequently seems to be more accurate and reliable in places than some Middle Kingdom manuscripts. There is evidence that this huge ostracon, which Parkinson has significantly described as a classroom blackboard, was used as a model text for student copyists. See Parkinson (2004) 61; Kahl (1998) 392–93. I would like to thank Dr. Richard Parkinson for these references.

97. Janssen (1992).

98. Janssen (1987), answering Caminos (1986) 47. McDowell (2000) 233 notes that some of the *Miscellanies* appear to have been written on reused documentary papyri.

99. This holds true for the scripts on most of the *Miscellanies* as well for other Ramesside papyri that contain didactic material based on Middle Kingdom texts; see McDowell (2000) 220 ("beautifully written"). One example among very many might be a frame from Papyrus Sallier II (BM EA 10182.1), a Ramesside copy of *The Instruction of King Amenemhat*, conveniently reproduced in Parkinson (1999a) pl. 8. The script of one of the scribes who also wrote out *Miscellanies* papyri, Innene, is so exemplary that it was chosen as one of the characteristic handwritings of late Dynasty Nineteen in Möller (1927) 10.

100. McDowell (2000) 270. This disproves the oft-cited opinion of Brunner (1957) 87.

101. For an estimate of the skill of those who wrote the "school" ostraca, see Janssen (1992) 86. See also the remarks on the student papyri in n. 99 above.

102. For an evaluation of the ability of Ramesside students to copy texts in the Middle Egyptian dialect, see especially G. Burkard (1977) 316–22. However, Burkard's views on the causes of student errors, particularly those concerning the notorious "Hörfehler," should be tempered; see Schenkel (1978). We have no way of knowing the accuracy of the material on which the students were basing their exercises. Indeed, many student "errors" may have actually been the fault of their instructors' defective models.

103. Goelet (2008) 102–10.

104. Caminos (1986) 46 remarks that there are many possible reasons for the reuse of papyri and that attempts to assign one cause or another are often "*idle* speculation."

105. Quirke (1997) 245–47.

106. Fischer-Elfert (1999) 382 has raised the possibility that the discovery of excerpts from both *The Instruction of a Man for His Son* and *The Loyalist Instruction* on

the same ostracon (O. Gardiner 347) provides some evidence that these works were part of an established sequence (i.e., a curriculum) of didactic texts during the Ramesside period.

107. Much of the discussion of this portion of the present chapter can also be found in two studies of mine: Goelet (2008) 102–10; Goelet (2010).

108. The pioneering compilation of this text, mainly from ostraca from Deir el-Medina, was made in Posener (1951a). For a convenient translation, see Wente (1990) 15–16. For the most recent studies of this text, see Barta (1978); Chappaz (1989); Parkinson (2002) 322–25; Mathieu and Ritter (2008). The basic epistolary formulae employed in this text are attested as early as the Old Kingdom; see Posener-Kriéger (1976) 454–55 and, slightly later, Simpson (1981).

109. Chappaz (1989) 34.

110. Simpson (1981) 173–79.

111. The earliest known examples with an extensive portion of the text are an unpublished papyrus fragment in the University College London collection (P. UCL 32271B recto) and two writing boards (see Quirke [1996a] 381). Parkinson ([2002] 322–23) believes that the text may have been composed early in Dynasty Twelve.

112. For its position in the school curriculum, see "Literature and the Literary Environment" below.

113. This, not incidentally, is the manner in which both wall inscriptions in tombs and *Book of the Dead* manuscripts are composed, as shown by numerous instances in unfinished portions of tombs where the scenes are accompanied by unfilled text columns, such as those in the tomb of Userhat (TT 56; see Beinlich-Seeber and Shedid [1987] pl. 12), and blank sections of papyri. In both tombs and papyri, decoration seems to have proceeded with first the illustrative material, then the text; see James (2001) 142, 144 n. 5.

114. O. Turin 57546; see López (1984) pl. 150. On the same plate, there is also a fragment of a hieratic grain account (O. Turin 57545) that has been similarly overtraced.

115. This is even true of the rare Dynasty Eighteen exemplars of the *Kemyt*; see, e.g., Hayes (1948) pls. I–III. It may be significant that these ostraca were found near the tomb of Senenmut, since this may indicate a connection with scribal training for the purposes of producing tomb inscriptions, on which possibility see the discussions below.

116. Brunner (1980) 383–84: "Der Text wird auch im NR ausschliesslich altertümlich in mittelheiratischer Schrift in senkrechten Zeilen mit MR-Interpunktion geschrieben—wohl als Schultext für Anfänger." See, similarly, Brunner (1957) 83. Chappaz and Parkinson have recently expressed similar views; see n. 108 above. I would, however, doubt whether a text with so many peculiar features and requiring the use of many archaisms in both script and diction would have been used to instruct beginners. Nevertheless, Brunner's observation concerning the hieratic hands is important. The script on most *Kemyt* ostraca may be awkward, but it compares favorably with the writing of an actual student's writing board of the Middle Kingdom (New York MMA 29.9.4); see James (1962) pl. 20.

117. Chappaz (1989) 33–34, remarks that the lack of ligatures would force students to focus more on individual signs. Although copying is most obvious in connection with the *Kemyt* ostraca, we should bear in mind that the primary learning method

underlying didactic materials was probably simply copying texts from a model. Mc-Dowell ([2000] passim) is certainly justified in her frequent use of the word "copyist" in her discussions of the scribes who wrote out Ramesside didactic materials.

118. Some rare exceptions to this rule are offered by exemplars of *The Instruction of King Amenemhat* written in cursive hieroglyphs in lined columns. See Goedicke and Wente (1963) pls. I–II; Parkinson (2002) 73 n. 12. The delineation of the columns is reminiscent more of tomb inscriptions than literary manuscripts. Significantly, one of these ostraca has a copy of the *Kemyt* on its other side. An example of the *Kemyt* in fully formed hieroglyphs is O. IFAO 1175; see Posener (1972) pl. 26.

119. Brunner (1957) 86–87.

120. One needs only to peruse the plates of Posener's publication of the IFAO *Kemyt* ostraca (see Posener [1951b]) to notice the large number of rubricized passages among this material.

121. For a study of some paleographic aspects of the cursive hieroglyphs, see Ali (2001). This script form underwent very little change during the New Kingdom because it was a "book hand" with a very limited usage, mostly in funerary contexts. With the advent of the Third Intermediate Period, the cursive hieroglyphs were used less for such purposes, and hieratic then became a largely fossilized "book hand" for such purposes; see Verhoeven (2001) 8–21. Interestingly enough, one of the earliest known examples of the *Book of the Dead* texts is written on wood in hieratic; see Parkinson and Quirke (1992) 37–51.

122. See Guksch (1995) pl. 14, and note the remarks on the New Kingdom tradition of the Coffin Texts on pp. 74–75. It is important to remember that spells from the Coffin Texts were still being adapted in the course of the Ramesside period for use in the *Book of the Dead* and other religious texts.

123. This important point was first stressed in Brunner (1957) 86–87. The frequency of rubrics, however, may be an indication that training for the *Book of the Dead* was the primary objective behind training in the *Kemyt*.

124. The *Book of the Dead* spells are primarily composed in Middle Egyptian with occasional Late Egyptian intrusions. See Munro (1988) 175–84. Munro's overall characterization of the appearance of Late Egyptian in this corpus is that it is "sporadisch" (184).

125. This usage is not consistent. Perhaps the cursive hieroglyphs were used chiefly in the early part of Dynasty Eighteen, then fell out of use in the Ramesside tombs, which tend to employ fully formed hieroglyphic texts instead. For examples in columnar, cursive hieroglyphs, see Hornung (1982b) pls. 95–96 (*Amduat*; tombs of Thutmosis III and Amenophis II). Contrast the finished forms appearing in similar material of the Ramesside period, in ibid., pls. 102–3 (*Book of Gates* and *Amduat*; tombs of Sety I and Ramesses I).

126. See, e.g., O. Turin 57567; López (1984) pl. 182.

127. BMFA O. 11.1498; Černý (1944) pl. X. Černý (op. cit., 25) suggested that the handwriting on this object bears "a striking similarity" to that of one of the draftsmen who painted in the hieroglyphs in a number of Deir el-Medina tombs at the end of Dynasty Nineteen. The object itself might have been intended as an inexpensive replacement for a funerary stela rather than just a draft text. O. IFAO 1208 (Posener

[1972] pl. 45) seems to be a fragment of a doorway text, with text written on the back. It is striking to note that several of the ostraca that Goedicke and Wente ([1962] 25) identify as "Entwürfe für Grabinschriften" are not in hieratic but in cursive hiero-glyphs (e.g., nos. XXXVI–XXXVII).

128. E.g., O. IFAO 1227 (cursive columnar religious text, facing in the noncanoni-cal direction); see Posener (1972) pl. 56. Significantly, Ramesside magical texts on pa-pyri also prefer the Middle Egyptian dialect and cursive hieroglyphs. It is unclear, however, whether these features might be due to the fact that the texts were copies of older originals.

129. Occasionally, the text will face left, in the noncanonical direction of many in-scriptional religious texts as well as those on papyri. See, e.g., O. Strassbourg H.150; O. Strassbourg H.173 (Koenig [1997] pls. 82, 85; text faces left in noncanonical direction; some text written with top in opposite direction); O. Turin 57440 (López [1978] pl. 146; practice[?] text in columnar cursive on recto; hieratic on verso); O. IFAO 1227 (Posener [1972] pl. 56; a long excerpt of a religious text). In addition, R. J. Demarée ([2002] 13) has identified some cursive hieroglyphic ostraca texts (BM 29509 and 29510) as being "in the style of royal Underworld Books."

130. Černý (1973) 27; McDowell (2000) esp. 231–32 (I would like to thank Dr. Deb-orah Sweeney for this reference).

131. See Posener (1976) for a compilation and study of the stela as well as the other versions of the composition. The text of the Sehetep-ib-Re stela, in turn, owes many aspects of its phraseology to the stela of the vizier Menthuhotep, dated to the reign of Sesostris I. For a brief discussion of the relationship between these two stelae, both of which are significantly didactic in nature as well as double-sided and therefore in-tended for public viewing, see Simpson (1991) 332, 337, noting a suggestion by Berlev that Menthuhotep may have been the author of *The Loyalist Instruction*. Leprohon (2009) has published a new study of the stela text.

132. See "Literature and the Literary Environment" above.

133. Schipper (1998) 161–79. For some arguments for an earlier date in the Middle Kingdom, see Fischer-Elfert (1999) 417–21. Loprieno (1996a) 412 also makes a distinc-tion between the more "jenseitsorientiert" text of the Dynasty Twelve stela and later, more "diesseitsorientiert" hieratic editions. See also Verhoeven (2009).

134. *Ptahhotep* seems to have been part of the curriculum at Deir el-Medina, as shown by a number of ostraca with portions of the text found there. See Fischer-Elfert (1997) 17–34.

135. This is demonstrated not only by Gardiner's discussion of the Middle Egyp-tian dialect (Gardiner [1957] 1–2) but also by the frequent number of citations to *Urk IV* among his references. For another assessment of the somewhat archaic quality of Dynasty Eighteen Egyptian, see Vernus (1996) 557. In this light, it is important to note that Schipper (1998) 179 ascribes the development of the two separate lines of the original Sehetep-ib-Re text to early Dynasty Eighteen. See also Verhoeven (2009).

136. Baines and other authors are unquestionably right to note the existence of both Middle Egyptian and Late Egyptian compositions during the New Kingdom; see Baines (1996a) 157–74. However, the question remains whether this distinction meant as much to the Egyptians who worked with these texts as it does for our classification

schemes. If substantial portions of the "classics" should eventually prove to be more recent creations, then the significance of the two categories should be completely reevaluated.

137. See "Royal Inscriptions" above.

138. Helck (1986) 905–6; Wildung (1980) 663; Björkman (1971) 20–21, 121–22.

139. See "Didactic Literature" above.

140. Gardiner (1916).

141. Ibid.

142. On the problem of the historicity of Ramesses III's texts in the light of texts and the relief scenes from the reign of Merenptah, see Lesko (1980) 83–86.

143. For more extensive expositions on the literary character of royal inscriptions, see Eyre (1996b); Loprieno (1996b); Simpson (1996).

144. Kitchen (1999c).

145. For a comprehensive survey of the wide range of rhetorical and literary devices the Egyptians used in both prose and poetry, see Guglielmi (1996a). Truly, the Egyptians made as skillful use of their language as the Greeks and Romans did.

146. "Flowery," in fact, is precisely the description employed by Schulman ([1987] 30–31) for the lengthy Libyan War inscription of Merenptah. For a recent study of this text see Manassa (2003).

147. See n. 10 above. An interesting feature of several rhetorical stelae dating to the reign of Ramesses II is that they are double-sided, an indication that they were displayed in the open so that they could instruct the literate public about the special qualities of the king. This is also true of the Sehetep-ib-Re stela and the Menthuhotep stela on which it was partially based (see n. 131).

148. For an example found in a chapel at Deir el-Medina, see KRI V.90–91, translated in Peden (1994b) 63–67. There are also two large rhetorical texts on the outside face of the first pylon of Medinet Habu (see n. 157 below). One should probably also include in this category the king's Great Double Stela in Karnak. See KRI V.237–47; Peden (1994b) 115–32.

149. In addition to the current section, see "Indicators of Late Egyptian Dialect" above.

150. Spalinger (2006) 415–28, esp. 415–16.

151. For some fundamental studies of the problem of propaganda in the Egyptian political environment, see Bleiberg (1985/86); Williams (1964); Simpson (1996) with extensive bibliography. However, to me, any attempt to separate texts with a palpable political or religious agenda from those with a "purely" literary intent appears ultimately to impose modern criteria of taste on the ancient material, especially when one considers the probable "state" origin of the preponderance of didactic literature.

152. Gnirs (1996b); Frood (2007) 26.

153. For the most complete study of the "historical section" that occurs at the end of Papyrus Harris I, see Grandet (1994) 1:335–40. Another recent translation appears in Peden (1994b) 211–23.

154. Loprieno (1996b) 277. The Königsnovelle is by no means a topos of royal inscriptions alone but appears in didactic literature and narrative tales as well (see ibid., 281–82). A good overview of this entire complex subject has been given in Osing

(1980) 556–57. The role of the *Königsnovelle* as a means for presenting divine revelations and oracles on behalf of the king is studied at length in Shirun-Grumach (1993).

155. See the general discussion of the composite nature of royal inscriptions in "Verse Points" above.

156. For an analysis of the vocabulary of Ramesses III's "military" inscriptions at Medinet Habu, see Cifola (1991) esp. 10.

157. *KRI* V:20–27; Edgerton and Wilson (1936) 20–34.

158. Piccone (1980).

159. *KRI* V:72. The full text is presented in parallel with the Ramesses II originals in *RITANC* II:258–81. For translations and commentary, see especially Edgerton-Wilson (1936) 119–29; *RITA* II.99–110; *RITANC* II.159–63; Goelet (1991).

160. *KRI* V.72–77; Edgerton-Wilson (1936) 107–36.

161. Goelet (1991) 36.

162. See especially Brunner (1979b).

163. This is not to say, however, that private biographical material was devoid of all literary qualities. There have been a number of recent studies on the problems associated with (auto)biographical texts and the influence of the funerary context on such inscriptions. See Assmann (1983b) and, more recently, Assmann (1996a) and Gnirs (1996b). Of particular interest in this respect is a recent study devoted specifically to the private biographical texts of the Ramesside period, Frood (2007), the introduction of which touches on many of the problems connected to this genre as literary works.

164. Quirke ([1996a] 385–96) has recognized this innovation of Ramesside literature in his two descriptive categories "letter in form, discourse in content" and "letter in form, tale in content." On the literary letter as a Ramesside literary form, see also Goldwasser (1991c).

165. On this issue, see *Verse Points* below.

166. The characteristics of literary papyri are summarized below in *Didactic Literature*.

167. This is very much the point of Janssen's 1992 study. However, there was also a purposeful aspect to the use of Middle Egyptian texts as well.

168. On the question of verse points, see also *Verse Points* below.

169. For an excellent overview of the didactic genre throughout Egyptian history, see Lichtheim (1996).

170. This is a term the Egyptians themselves actually employed. The title rubric of *The Instruction of Amenemope* consists of the phrase *ḥȝty-ꜥ m sbȝyt m ꜥnḫ*, literally "The beginning of the scroll in the teaching in life . . ." See Schott (1990) 308 (no. 1393).

171. Gardiner (1937); Caminos (1956).

172. Helck (1970); the sources for this text have been gathered in Parkinson (1991) 91–122.

173. This attitude is stated in a remarkable passage from Papyrus Anastasi II (6.7–7.5) asserting that one of the advantages of being a scribe is that "you are not under many lords (7.3) and numerous masters. Man comes forth from his mother's womb and runs to his master: the child is in the service of (7.4) a soldier, the stripling is a skirmisher. The old man is put to be a cultivator" (Caminos [1954] 51).

174. The disparity between the authors praised in the *Encomium* and the authors actually represented among student ostraca preserved at Deir el-Medina is discussed in Fischer-Elfert (2003) 123–31.

175. This assumption was based largely on false premises. See *Implications of Literary and Scribal Training* below.

176. On this point, see n. 88 above.

177. Guglielmi ([1994] esp. 68–72) and Hagen (2006) have presented forceful arguments in favor of the humorous and satirical intent of this and other Egyptian didactic texts. Those who believe that "true" satire did not appear in Egypt until well after the Middle and New Kingdoms underestimate both the Egyptians' humanity and the great value of humor as an educational tool for making even the most difficult material more readily accessible. A likely example of humor as an educational technique is the topos of the admonition to the idle scribe that employs an exaggerated description of the scribe's debauchery. Of course, some of these exercises may have had an actual admonitory purpose at the same time.

178. See Guglielmi (1994) 44 nn. 1–3 for a bibliography of this topos. For a study of the image of the soldier in didactic literature and other sources, see Fischer-Elfert (1983a).

179. Even if the text of *The Satirical Letter* may avoid the amusing exaggerations of the *Satire* and the *Miscellanies* (and perhaps *Wenamun*), the cumulative effect of the text was similar: it constantly drummed in the message that any form of military life abroad was fraught with an endless array of difficulties.

180. For a summary of the evidence and reasoning that led Erman to conclude that these were "Schülerhandschriften," see Hagen (2006) 85.

181. Hagen (2006) 93–97. The role of the letter as a framing device is implicitly acknowledged in the rubric name "Brieflehren" that Jäger ([2004] 193–94) chose in his discussion of the satires on professions that appear in the *Miscellanies*. Jäger largely concurs with Hagen's critique of Erman's arguments, but unlike Hagen, he believes that these were ultimately student manuscripts that formed a library or an archive. Each manuscript and each selection within a manuscript, however, should be evaluated on its own merits.

182. On the implications of the orthography, see Goelet (2008) 108–9.

183. See Lichtheim (1980b). Although this genre is usually associated with the Ramesside period, it may have been already in place in Dynasty Eighteen; see Guksch (1994). As noted above (*Royal Inscriptions*), elements of this theme certainly appear in royal inscriptions as well.

184. For the provenance and dating, see the remarks in Gardiner (1937) xviii–xix.

185. On this point, see Groll (1982); Winand (1995).

186. Posener (1976); see n. 133 above.

187. Helck (1969); Goedicke (1988). Fragments of this text have been found at Amarna; see Parkinson (1999b). All known exemplars, including the profuse documentation from Deir el-Medina ostraca, have been gathered in Adrom (2006).

188. Fischer-Elfert ([1999] 334–422) presents a lengthy argument for an intimate relationship between the *Satire on the Trades* and the two loyalist texts *The Instruction of a Man for His Son* and *The Loyalist Instruction*. He sees these as forming a trio

within an instructional curriculum. For some doubts about this suggestion, see Junge (2003) 157 with n. 316.

189. For a summary of past attempts at dating the main sources, all later than Dynasty Twenty, see Laisney (2007) 6–8. On the compositional date of the work, Laisney concludes: "Le contenu ne fournit pas d'indices pour la date de redaction. Il me semble donc que l'on peut dater le texte de la fin de la 20e ou du début de la 21e dyn. Avec comme dates limites, la fin de la 19e dyn. et le début de la 21e dyn" (7). "The contents furnish no indication as to the date of its editing or composition. It therefore seems to me that one might date the text from the end of Dynasty Twenty or the beginning of Dynasty Twenty-one, with upper and lower limits placed at the end of Dynasty Nineteen and the beginning of Dynasty Twenty-one" (author's translation).

190. Posener (1955); Bickel and Mathieu (1993). For a convenient translation of the work and a brief sketch of this personality, see McDowell (1999) 139. Amennakhte seems to have possessed a small library and was also a teacher in the community. He may have composed one additional brief instructional work in the form of a letter; see ibid., 144.

191. Bickel and Mathieu (1993) 49–51. A convenient translation can also be found in McDowell (1999) 140–42.

192. Guglielmi (1983); Foster (1984); Morenz (1998); Vernus (1978); McDowell (1999) 144–47; Fischer-Elfert (2006) 87–92. Like Amennakhte, Menna and Mery-Sekhmet were real figures in the Deir el-Medina community and not pseudepigraphic characters. The *Kemyt* may have been framed by a similar theme involving a wayward son; see Parkinson (2002) 323–24.

193. For the relationship between the three pieces, see n. 188 above.

194. On this point, see Loprieno (1996d) 406–7; Blumenthal (1974).

195. This embourgoisement was by no means an uninterrupted trend in the history of Egyptian literature between the Middle Kingdom and the end of the Ramesside period; see Loprieno (1996d) 405–13. For additional discussion of the intended audience of Ramesside instructions, see Quack (1994) 79–81.

196. Oddly enough, this great classic of Middle Kingdom didactic literature does not seem to have been much used for instructional purposes during the Ramesside period, unless some of the papyrus exemplars of the text from Dynasties Nineteen and Twenty represent student exercises. There are only a few ostraca from Deir el-Medina; see Fischer-Elfert (1997) 18–23. The values that this text preached, however, were certainly in keeping with those of the Ramesside era; see Junge (2003) 154–59. Junge observes that due to its difficulty even for Egyptians, this would have been a problematic text for use as a didactic text in the usual sense of just a copying exercise.

197. The house metaphor underlying this terminology appears also in our poetical term *stanza,* which is derived from the Italian word for "room." On this use of the word *ḥwt,* see Blackman (1937); Guglielmi (1996) 473.

198. Baines (1994); Miosi (1982).

199. On the relationships between Proverbs and *Amenemope* and between Egyptian and Hebrew Wisdom generally, see Williams (1971); Shupak (1993) 342–54. For a more specific analysis of the possible relationship between *Amenemope* and the

biblical Proverbs, including an evaluation of the "monotheistic" features of the Egyptian text, see Laisney (2007) 239–49.

200. Lichtheim (1996) 258–61 provides a good summary of the qualities of the *grw.*

201. This characterization of German pietism is drawn from Berlin (1999) 36–37.

202. The most recent and thorough study of this work to date is Quack (1994).

203. Quack (1994) 82–147 offers separate translations for the three main papyrus exemplars: Papyrus Boulaq 8 (now Cairo CG 58042; really a group of unrelated papyri; see ibid., 5–9), Papyrus Deir el-Medina I, and Papyrus Louvre E 30144.

204. A detailed study and evaluation of parallels within both the Egyptian and Mesopotamian context is available in Quack (1994) 194–220.

205. Quack (1999); Caminos (1968).

206. Now BM EA 10684; since the beginning section of this work is missing and therefore cannot be ascribed to any ancient author, this collection has never received a descriptive name in the literature and is simply called after the name of the original purchaser of the papyrus collection from which it derived.

207. See, e.g., the passage excerpted in McDowell (1999) 138–39, which debates the question of whether wisdom can be taught.

208. This is one of the most anthologized pieces of all Ramesside literature. It appears in Lichtheim (1976) 176–77 as "The Immortality of Writers"; for another convenient translation, see McDowell (1999) 137–38. For additional interesting analyses of the passage, see Williams (1981); Brunner (1966); te Velde (1981) 143–44; Fischer-Elfert (2003).

209. For more on the subject of this and other of the Harpers' Songs, see *Harpers' Songs* below.

210. Sirach 44. The debate concerning whether this wisdom text may or may not have been influenced by demotic wisdom texts, especially the *Wisdom of 'Onkhesh-eshonqi,* is far too long and complex to delineate here. On this question, see, recently, Thissen (1986); Jasnow (1999) 20 n. 38. The opening lines of Sirach in the Septuagint version explicitly state that it was composed in Alexandria during the Ptolemaic era and represents a collection of wisdom from Hebrew as well as other sources. Nevertheless, the passage praising a list of great figures of the Jewish past has no parallel in either Hellenistic Greek or Hebrew sources, but there are undoubtedly some parallels in the Egyptian *Encomium,* albeit directed at great writers, rather than the religious or political figures who are the subject of the biblical parallel (Sirach 44–50). Equally intriguing is the possibility that Egyptian love lyric may have been mediated through Ptolemaic Alexandria and had a subsequent influence on Hellenistic Greek and Arabic love lyric as well; see Guglielmi (1996b) 347 n. 81 with references. Finally, I would note here Roccati's recent remark ([2003] 44) that "for the Hellenistic Period one may perhaps speak of an Egyptian literature in the Greek language."

211. P. Lansing 2.2–2.3; Caminos (1954) 374: "As for writing, to him that knows it, more profitable is it than any office; it is pleasanter (2.3) than bread and beer, than clothing and than ointment. It is more precious than an heritage in Egypt, than a tomb in the West." Bread, beer, clothing, and ointment, significantly enough, represent a standard sequence of gifts in contemporary funerary offering formulae.

212. The most up-to-date treatment of this composition is the two-part work by Fischer-Elfert (1983b and 1986a).

213. For the date of the composition of this work, see Fischer-Elfert (1986a) 261–67.

214. Numerous suggestions as to the meaning of this term and its origin have been put forth. For a detailed summary of the various arguments with bibliography, see Fischer-Elfert (1986a) 244–46; Hoch (1994) 147–49 (no. 190).

215. This work has been recently reexamined; see Dorn (2004) 38–55.

216. Amennakhte was also the scribe who wrote out the Naunakhte documents and may have possessed a small library; see n. 190 above. Bickel and Mathieu ([1993] 37–38) suggest that it was he, not Qenherkhepeshef, who was the owner of the library that we know today as the Chester Beatty Papyri. For the opposite view, see Pestman (1982).

217. O. Gardiner 2; Fischer-Elfert (1986b) 1–4; Bickel and Mathieu (1993) 49–51; also conveniently translated in McDowell (1999) 140–42.

218. O. Petrie 11, conveniently translated in McDowell (1999) 142–43. For a recent comprehensive treatment of the four Deir el-Medina ostraca on which this text appears, see Hagen (2005) 125–29.

219. See *Indicators of Late Egyptian Dialect* above.

220. On this point, see *The Kemyt and the Ramesside School Curriculum* above.

221. For a discussion of the use of narrative in its literary and nonliterary forms, see Quirke (1996b) 263–76, esp. 272–74. By "nonliterary narrative," I mean works such as royal historical inscriptions and private biographical texts, two genres that can be highly polished and that share many features with their literary counterparts, including didactic material. On these topics, see also Gnirs (1996b); Mathieu (2003) 297–306, containing a bibliographic essay on the topic in the notes (301–6).

222. Lichtheim (1976) 197.

223. Of all the narrative tales of the Middle Kingdom, only *The Tale of Sinuhe* is attested during Ramesside times; see Quirke (1996a) 388–89 and n. 249 below. Two possible exceptions are *The Destruction of Mankind*, which was probably written during the Middle Kingdom but of which only New Kingdom exemplars exist (see n. 243 below) and *The Tale of Neferkare and General Sisene*, whose compositional date remains uncertain.

224. Exceptions are *The Tale of the Two Brothers*, whose colophon informs us that it was copied by the well-known apprentice scribe Innene (see n. 36 above), and *Khonsuemhab and the Spirit*, discussed shortly below. *Apophis and Seqenenre*, which has a similar colophon, is part of a student's miscellany.

225. Papyrus Sallier I (now BM EA 10185) contains a copy of *The Instruction of Amenemhat I* and the only extant copy of *Apophis and Seqenenre*.

226. Papyrus Harris 500 (now BM EA 10062) has two lengthy selections of entertainment literature—four groups of love poetry and the *Antef Song* (one of the Harpers' Songs)—in addition to *The Prince Who Knew His Fate* and *Thutmosis III and the Taking of Joppa*; P. Chester Beatty I also contains both entertainment literature (love poetry) and *The Contendings of Horus and Seth*.

227. The colophon of Papyrus D'Orbiney (now BM EA 10183) identifies its copyist as the well-known scribe Innene, who was active in the reign of Merenptah. Innene was also the scribe of several of the *Miscellanies*, but this does not necessarily mean that *The Tale of the Two Brothers* was also copied as a student exercise.

228. Gardiner (1932) vii–xi. Note the observations about colophons and titles in Hagen (2006) 88–92.

229. According to Gasse, literary ostraca similarly have a number of features that allow one to make an a priori selection of literary and documentary materials. See *Implications of Literacy and Scribal Training* above with n. 91.

230. There seems to be no practical reason for this practice. Convenient illustrations of the relationship between the direction of writing and the fiber arrangement on literary and documentary papyri can be found in Junge (1996) 23–24. *The Report of Wenamun* is an exception to this rule, but this could well be an indication that it is not a literary work at all. On this question, see in the current section of this essay. In the case of Middle Kingdom papyri, frequent use of the columnar format meant that this rule did not apply. Nor did it necessarily apply in instances of reuse or when a particularly long text continued on the verso of the papyrus.

231. For Gasse's observations on hieratic style on ostraca, see *Implications of Literacy and Scribal Training* above. There was a slight, similar distinction between literary and documentary hieratic hands in the Middle Kingdom; see Parkinson (2002) 73–74.

232. Parkinson's admirable translations of Middle Kingdom tales (1997) explicitly treats those works as poems.

233. See *Implications of Literacy and Scribal Training* above.

234. On the distinction between literary and documentary Late Egyptian, see *Indicators of Late Egyptian Dialect* above with nn. 75–81. One of the key documents employed in some authors' definition of Late Egyptian is the problematic *The Report of Wenamun,* which many scholars would class as a work of fiction rather than a copy of an actual document. On this controversy, see *Narrative Tales* and n. 257 below.

235. For a discussion (and extensive bibliography) of the relationship between myth and literature in ancient Egypt, see Baines (1996b) 361–77.

236. On this work, see also *Indicators of Late Egyptian Dialect* above.

237. On the verso of the student's miscellany Papyrus Sallier I (now BM EA 10185). This papyrus also contains the sole copy of *The Prince Who Knew His Fate.* The standard edition of the text is Gardiner (1932) 77–80. A convenient translation appears in Simpson, Wente, and Faulkner (1973) 85–91. There are some additional fragments from Deir el-Medina containing parts of a narrative centered on this famous king in the Turin Museum (Turin 1940 + 1941). See Quirke (1996a) 389; McDowell (1992) 103 n. 62.

238. Fragments preserved only on the verso of Papyrus Harris 500 (now BM EA 10060), which is primarily a collection of love poetry on the recto. The standard text edition is Gardiner (1932) 82–85. A colophon at the end indicates that the tale was copied by a military scribe whose name is lost.

239. The late Middle Kingdom Westcar Papyrus contains a cycle of magical tales set in the court of King Sneferu of Dynasty Four. For a discussion of such historical romances and what they reveal about knowledge of history among the workers of Deir el-Medina, see McDowell (1992) esp. 103–4.

240. See McDowell (1992) 103–4; Quirke (1996b) 271. For the text, see Posener (1957) 119–37. A convenient translation appears in Parkinson (1991) 54–56, 156. The later development of the text, which dates to Dynasty Twenty-five, has been treated in Jasnow (1999) 195.

241. Now BM EA 10681; originally part of the Deir el-Medina library that belonged either to Qenherkhepehef or Amennakhte, on which see n. 216 above. The papyrus is now located at the Chester Beatty Gallery and Library, Dublin. For the standard text editions and translations, see Gardiner (1932) 37–60; Gardiner (1931); Lichtheim (1976) 214–23. A more thorough study of the tale, especially from the perspective of myth, is Broze (1997).

242. On this point, see Baines (1996b) 373.

243. The standard edition is now Hornung (1991). A convenient English translation appears in Lichtheim (1976) 197–99. The narrative shares some features with the so-called "Königsnovelle"; see Loprieno (1996b) 291.

244. Both sections of the myth are treated in Maystre (1941).

245. Now BM EA 10183, a good facsimile of which appears in Möller (1909–10) II: pls. 1–20. The standard text edition is Gardiner (1932) 9–30. For studies of the folkloric and religious aspects of the tale, see Hollis (1990); Blumenthal (1972).

246. The bibliography connected with this incident is truly enormous. Particularly interesting treatments from the Egyptological point of view have been produced by Vergote (1959 and 1985) and Redford (1970). For a discussion of the erotic significance of the wife's hair plaiting in this incident, see Derchain (1975b) 56–74.

247. The tale appears on the verso of Papyrus Harris 500 (now BM EA 10060), most of which appears to be a collection of love stories and other entertainment literature. Because it was thus in an ancient anthology, it is one of the rare examples of Ramesside literary material not written on the horizontal fibers of the papyrus. In addition to this tale, the document also contained the story of *Thutmose III and the Taking of Joppa*. The standard text edition of *The Prince Who Knew His Fate* is Gardiner (1932) 1–9. A convenient translation is available in Lichtheim (1976) 200–203.

248. This is the name assigned to the tale by Lichtheim ([1976] 200), but she comments that "The Prince Who Was Threatened by Three Fates" would be more fitting.

249. Several ostracon exemplars of *Sinuhe* are known. For two particularly fine examples, see Barns (1952) and O. BM EA 5629, illustrated in Parkinson (1999a) pl. 29, with a discussion on p. 167 (cat. no. 79). Although their exact provenances are not known, both objects are highly likely to have come from Deir el-Medina. Not only is the Ashmolean Ostracon written in a fine Ramesside hand (inasmuch as the surface permitted), but the text is also among the most accurate; see Foster (1982) 81–85. Ostraca exemplars definitely from the workmen's village are Deir el-Medina 1011, 1045, 1174, 1437, 1438, 1439 (recto), 1440, and 1609, all published by Posener (1951a; 1972; 1978). For a complete listing of the New Kingdom ostraca and papyri sources of *Sinuhe*, see Koch (1990) vi.

250. The standard text edition is Gardiner (1932) 89–94; convenient English translations appear in McDowell (1999) 149–52 and Simpson, Wente, and Faulkner (1973) 137–41. A detailed study is Beckerath (1992) 90–107.

251. Posener (1975) 105–112.

252. On this topic, see Posener (1981) 393–401, which discusses an obscure passage in *The Instruction of Ani*.

253. P. Moscow 120; Gardiner (1932) 61–76. Photographs of the papyrus are available in Korostovtsev (1960).

254. P. Moscow 127; Caminos (1977). This text is also known as the Moscow Literary Letter.

255. For the circumstances of the find, see Caminos (1977) 1.

256. The grammar of *Wenamun* is quite distinct from the other works collected by Gardiner in his *Late-Egyptian Stories*. Černý was so convinced of the document's authenticity that he chose it as an exemplary text in his *Late Egyptian Grammar*, Černý and Groll (1993).

257. The nature of *Wenamun*—whether it is fiction or nonfiction—has been the subject of a long-standing debate. For some recent studies of the question and a review of some of the more recent arguments, pro and con, see Goedicke (1975) 1–11; Moers (1999a) and Moers (1999b); Baines (1999); Eyre (1999b); Scheepers (1992); Spens (1998).

258. See Ignatov (1999), which deals rather briefly with the contrast in the religious perspectives between the inscriptional and papyrus versions of the "Kadesh Poem." Two more substantial comparisons focus on the textual tradition underlying the inscriptional and the two papyrus versions of the story of the battle of Kadesh (P. Sallier III, P. Raifé, and P. Chester Beatty III). See von der Way (1984); Spalinger (2002). However, whether even the papyrus version, called the "Poem of Pentawer," should be considered a poem in the Egyptian context is a difficult question with a largely subjective answer. Nonetheless, I would agree with Gardiner ([1960] 2–3) and Spalinger (op. cit., ix) that this is not a poem in the sense that we think of verse today.

259. See "Ramesside Poetry" and "Verse Points" below. Foster (1995) 11 is quite definite on this point: "But what translator and reader alike need to remember is that, in the mind of the ancient Egyptian author, these hymns, prayers, and songs were meant to be poems."

260. The musical nature of these two (and some other) terms is confirmed by the fact that they are often followed by the prepositions *m* and *m-s₃*, in the sense of "by, along with," governing the name of some musical instrument. See Mathieu (1996) 134 with n. 456.

261. See Goelet (2002); Guglielmi (1996a) 470–72.

262. See Goelet (2002) 75–89, esp. 79–84.

263. Verse points have been identified as one of the first known forms of punctuation in early writing systems. See Winand (1998) 163–77. Given the difficulties of applying any sort of consistent system, let alone a metrical scheme, to these marks, it is probably better to call them by the more neutral term *division markers* (*Gliederungsmittel*), as the terminology implied in the very title of Tacke (2001) implies.

264. The discussion here follows essentially Brunner (1986).

265. For a through synoptic presentation of the various theories concerning metric and its associated literature, see Burkard (1996) 447–63. The term *Gliederungspunkte* was adapted by Morenz (1997) 65.

266. The basic works are Fecht (1963), Fecht (1964), Fecht (1965a), and Fecht (1965b). Fecht has even extended his principles to other early traditions, such as Hebrew and Phoenician; see Fecht (1990). In a more recent article, Fecht (1993) 69–94, he has modified his previous positions slightly. The introduction into the discussion of the term *elevated language,* to take the place of *verse* or *poetry,* is significant and quite helpful.

267. As Fecht (1993) 69 states, "All Egyptian texts with any claim to structure, ranging from the domain of 'literature,' which cannot be defined objectively, to carefully written letters, are metrical in form."

268. Schenkel (1975).

269. Lichtheim (1971–72) 103–10.

270. E.g., see the remarks of Parkinson (2002) 115–17.

271. Foster (1977); Foster (1993); Foster (1988).

272. Foster himself admits that his theory can be expanded to accommodate occasional triplets and quatrains. See Foster (2000) 313.

273. Burkard (1996) 456–63, in the section entitled "Das literarische Gesamtkunstwerk: Versuch einer Synthese."

274. Kitchen (1999c).

275. Tacke (2001) 137, 145.

276. Posener ([1951c] 77) proposed that the practice of providing itemized lists with check marks may have been the inspiration for the development of verse points.

277. On this see, Goelet (1996) pls. IX–X with 112 n. a and 119.

278. Brunner's observation can be applied to another Middle Kingdom literary classic—*The Tale of Sinuhe.* I would like to point out that the two Middle Kingdom papyri preserving the story—"B" and "R"—both have no verse points, but most of the later versions, either on papyrus or ostraca, have verse points present; see Koch (1990) passim. Similar statements can be made about nearly all literary papyri dating to the Middle Kingdom: *The Tale of the Eloquent Peasant,* the Westcar Papyrus, *The Shipwrecked Sailor, The Dispute of a Man with His Ba*—as with *Sinuhe* manuscripts, none of these have verse points.

279. In the case of the *Kemyt,* sometimes a red line would be employed instead of the normal red points. See Parkinson and Quirke (1995) 46.

280. Note Eyre's remark ([1996b] 425) on the presence of verse points in Papyrus Turin 1882, which "mark it either as literature or a scribal exercise."

281. Robertson (1994); Izre'el (1997). On one tablet (Amarna Tablet EA 356, *Adapa and the South Wind*), the points have been heavily used to mark off the individual words and short phrases in the Akkadian text. Recognizing the separate words on a tablet with a continuous cuneiform text would be one of the most important first steps for a beginning student in Akkadian, ancient or modern. For an instance where a red dot (i.e., verse point or division marker) has been added into an Akkadian text to mark a point in dictation rather than a point in meter, see Izre'el (1997) 60–61 n. 88.

282. P. Ramesseum II (now BM EA 10755) came from the so-called Ramesseum library of manuscripts securely dated to the late Middle Kingdom. For a brief discussion and bibliography on this work, see Parkinson (2003) 310–11; Morenz (1997). Parkinson does not believe that the adages derived from a unitary source. There are two other, much more poorly preserved manuscripts from this era that likewise use verse points irregularly; see Parkinson (2003) 300–301. The evidence is too fragmentary to be of much use to our discussion here.

283. For a discussion of the monostichic form in Egyptian didactic literature of the Late Period and a comparison with earlier forms, see Lichtheim (1983) 1–12. For a convenient translation of *The Maxims of Onchsheshonqi,* see Lichtheim (1980a) 159–84. The arrangement in this work may be monostichic, but it is by no means athematic.

284. Morenz (1997) 65. Tacke (2001) employs the similar term *Gliederungsmittel* in the title of his work.

285. For the use of anaphoric elements, see n. 261 above. However, the texts formatted in this fashion were not all literary texts or historical inscriptions; see Grapow (1936).

286. For a photo and a description of the "crossword" format and compositional technique of the famous hymn to Mut, see Parkinson (1999a) 84–85. For a recent translation, see Troy (1997).

287. This arrangement first appears in two Middle Kingdom works: the *Hymns to Senwosret III* (see the facsimiles in Möller [1909–10] I: pls. 4–5 and the remarks of Grapow (1936) 40 and 64 n. 61) and a student's copy of lines from the didactic work *The Maxims of P. Ramesseum II* (see n. 282 above). A Late Egyptian example of this rare form is the laudatory poem addressed to the student's teacher that occurs near the end of the Lansing Papyrus dating near the end of Dynasty Twenty; see Lichtheim (1976) 173–75 and Gardiner (1937) 112–15. Lichtheim (1976) 175 n. 10 describes its structure as follows: "The encomium is metrically structured. Each period begins with *mntk*, 'you are,' and consists of two, three, or four sentences or clauses." The lines vary considerably in length, and verse points are employed erratically. This form of verse arrangement became more common in the Late Period and beyond; see the remarks of Quack (1999) 153–54 with n. 7. This structure also appears in a fragment of *The Instruction of Amenemope* illustrated in Parkinson and Quirke (1995) 44 (fig. 30).

288. Many examples have been collected in Fischer-Elfert (1986b) 13–86.

289. There are a number of love poems on ostraca and a jar. See *The Study of Love Lyrics* below.

290. Lichtheim (1976) 181–93.

291. Foster (1995) 162–71; Foster (1974); Foster (1992). See also, briefly, Foster (2001) 316.

292. Fox (1982); Fox (1985).

293. Meeks (1980).

294. Kitchen (1999c) 330–430.

295. Mathieu (1996).

296. Vernus (1992).

297. Sweeney (2002).

298. In his anthology, Vernus ([1992] 96–126) includes several encomia addressed to deities as *comparativa*. These selections are chiefly addressed to Hathor.

299. As other scholars have done, Mathieu ([1996] 218–20, 223–26) has gathered a number of parallels with didactic literature. These parallels, of course, may be just another indication of the pervasive influence of scribal training on all aspects of Egyptian literature.

300. Guglielmi (1996b) 338. For concurring opinions, see Kitchen (1999c) 315; Mathieu (1996) 22–23, 200–201.

301. Eyre (1996b) 424.

302. Fox (1982) 268–316.

303. Kitchen (1999c) 315, notes a Western Theban or Deir el-Medina origin for all manuscripts, with the possible exception of Papyrus Harris 500.

304. Meeks (1980). However, occasionally the protagonist is of rather lowly status; see Sweeney (2002) 10–11.

305. For a discussion of floral motifs in love poetry and other genres of Egyptian literature, see Derchain (1975a) 65–86.

306. Guglielmi (1996b) 225–337.

307. In this respect, Fox (1985) 234–43 notes a number of parallels in technique especially between love lyric, religious poetry, and royal encomia in both the Egyptian and Hebrew context.

308. P. Harris 500; see Lichtheim (1976) 189. Thus, this Ramesside poem anticipates by many centuries such amatory epigrams as that of Eratosthenes Scholasticus that says, "May I push back the bolts of your door, loosening the bolt-pin, and fixing the middle of the tip of the key pierce the damp base of the folding door" (Paton [1993] 251 [no. 242]). For a list of some possible sexual euphemisms in Egyptian, see Guglielmi (1996a) 491; Schreiber (1991).

309. Less common terms of endearment are "wolf" (*wnš*), "friend," and "my God, my lotus." See Guglielmi (1996b) 343 with nn. 52–55.

310. For detailed studies of the most common topoi in love lyric, see particularly Fox (1985) 267–331; Mathieu (1996) 151–88.

311. Vernus (1992) 38–40 ("La modernite") provides a valuable overview of some thematic similarities between Egyptian and other love poetry through the ages.

312. The term *travestie* is used for this theme, since the lovers in such cases wish that they might be transformed into someone (or something) else, which would allow them to be next to the object of their desire without facing any obstacles or raising any suspicions. The term apparently was first suggested for this context by Görg (1991); see also Guglielmi (1996b) 334.

313. Fox (1985), esp. 267–331 (detailed comparative study of the themes).

314. The universality of the emotion, however, certainly does not lead to common courtship behavior or societal practices. See Sweeney (2002) 27–28.

315. Actually, Nakht-sobek credits himself only with having found a cycle of poems "in a box of scrolls" (P. Chester Beatty I), but most commentators note that he has merely inserted his name in place of another, erased name. See Fox (1985) 68–69, 95. Vernus ([1992] 177 n. 37) sees Nakht-sobek as the copyist for the entire scroll.

316. Recently, Sweeney ([2002] 30) has offered a slightly expanded list. She includes an incomplete poem in the *Miscellanies* (P. Anastasi II, verso 5). See Morenz (1999) and the very poorly preserved Papyrus Deir el-Medina 43, whose exact nature is hard to define. On the latter, see Koenig (1985).

317. For a comprehensive bibliography of the love lyric in this papyrus collection, see Mathieu (1996) 55; Kitchen (1999c) 353.

318. A much-debated alternative interpretation of the word *shmh-jb* is that it is a nominal construction meaning "entertainer." This suggestion finds some support in the parallel titles in Papyrus Chester Beatty I that have, instead, the word *shmht-jb,* a feminine form otherwise unattested. On this point, see Mathieu (1996) 36 n. 29.

319. Kitchen (1999c) 376.

320. Kitchen (1999c) 360–61. The popular name for the poem derives from Foster (1974) 71.

321. For bibliography of the love lyric on Papyrus Chester Beatty I, see Mathieu (1996) 25.

322. The term *stanza* itself, as the Italian word for "room," works from the same metaphorical basis as *ḥwt*, "house." See Blackman (1937). This use of the *grḥ*-sign may, in fact, derive from a practice, found in the Pyramid Texts, of transforming text columns into large *ḥwt*-signs.

323. The alternating boy-girl pattern poses an interesting problem in connection with the third lyric in the poem. If the pattern holds true, this poem would have a young man declaring his love for another young man whom he sees riding by in a chariot. Thus, this verse might well be a homoerotic poem, a conclusion that has often been resisted in the literature. On this point, see Gilliam (2000) 213; Sweeney (2002) 37–38. For an examination of the problematic and much-discussed figure of Mehy in this poem, see Mathieu (1996) 155–57, esp. nn. 520–23.

324. Lichtheim (1976) 182–86; Mathieu (1996) 26–32 with notes on 36–54. In instances such as this, it is sometimes difficult to know whether the Egyptian author was aiming for a play on simple assonance, paronomasia, or wordplay per se; see Guglielmi (1996a) 476–81. Poems based on numbers also occur in religious literature, such as Papyrus Leiden I 350, but this hymn is not especially based on numerical allusions or puns; see Zandee (1947). For a short example on an ostracon, see Fischer-Elfert (1986b) 63–67.

325. This verse collection clearly derives from Deir el-Medina. For comprehensive bibliographies, see Mathieu (1996) 95; Kitchen (1999c) 377.

326. For comprehensive bibliographies on this collection, see Mathieu (1996) 81; Kitchen (1999c) 343.

327. As its very name suggests, the category "miscellanea" refers to a wide range of sources that various authors have considered to be love poetry; there is no set corpus in Egyptological literature. The preponderance of this verse occurs on ostraca, but a few short poems on papyrus should be included as well. Several major collections of these texts have been made: see Mathieu (1996) 113–25; Vernus (1992) 93–94; Kitchen (1999c) 393–419.

328. Rare examples would be a two-line poem ("verso 5") in the student miscellany in Papyrus Anastasi II and the poorly preserved love poem with pastoral motifs on Papyrus Deir el-Medina 43. See Kitchen (1999c) 413–20 for a number of small fragmentary poems that may belong to this genre.

329. On this point, see Simpson (2003) 46.

330. For two examples from Middle Kingdom funerary stelae, see Lichtheim (1972) 193–94.

331. There is a vast bibliography on the subject of the Harpers' Songs, so I here list only a selection of the principle modern studies: Lichtheim (1945); Assmann (1977a); Assmann (1977b) 972–82; Fox (1982); Fox (1977); Osing (1992b). Osing's article adds one more song to the repertory. This is from the tomb of a certain Nefersekheru, located at Zawyet Sultan near Kom el-Ahmar, on which see also Osing et al. (1992b). For recent English translations of the Antef poem, see Kitchen (1999c) 137–42; Foster (1995) 154–56.

332. This point was raised by Goedicke (1977). Osing (1992a) 13–14 notes that this does not eliminate the possibility that the work may have been written during the Middle Kingdom or shortly after, but the numerous Late Egyptianisms in the text in-

dicate that this version of the poem was at least extensively rewritten at a later date. Perhaps it would be best to adopt Kitchen's assessment ([1999c] 137) that the composition date remains uncertain.

333. In addition to their connection with the Beautiful Feast of the Valley, the erotic implications of Egyptian banquet scenes have long been discussed. See, more recently, Haikal (1997).

334. For some skeptical views on the significance of the harp (*bnbnt*) and the sex act (*bnbn*), see Baines (1970); Buchberger (1983).

335. The many common phrases of the Harpers' Songs were noted in the pioneering studies Lichtheim (1945), Wente (1962), and Lorton (1975). These three articles have framed much of the subsequent debate on the significance of this genre, on which see n. 331 above.

336. On the "debate" aspect of the genre, see Osing (1992a) 12–17. In this respect, the three examples of the Harpers' Songs preserved in the Ramesside tomb of Neferhotep are particularly instructive, since they offer contradictory points of view on the efficacy of the tomb, one of them explicitly criticizing the attitude of the *Antef Song*. However, Neferhotep's tomb as a whole is itself an explicit endorsement of the standard views—hardly surprising, since he was a priest of Amun and certainly a member of the establishment.

337. E.g., in one of the poems from Neferhotep's tomb that extols the traditional views of the afterlife, there is the phrase "All of them come to it [i.e., the land of eternity]; / No one may linger in the land of Egypt." See Lichtheim (1976) 116. The same sentiment is also found in the *Antef Song*.

338. Jasnow (1999) 193; Thissen (1992). Thissen believes that the demotic tradition of the Harpers' Songs shows considerable Hellenistic influence.

339. The debate on whether these songs are concerned primarily with pessimism over the afterlife or are simply exhorting their audience to enjoy the here and now has been ably summarized and discussed in Assmann (1977a), cited above in n. 331.

340. For a study of the religious qualities of the descriptions of banquets and of offerings, see Finnestad (1999).

341. On this text, see n. 208 above.

342. On the *Encomium* and the theme of commemoration, see te Velde (1982).

343. A nearly duplicate version of the *Antef Song* seems to be preserved on Leiden K6 from the Saqqara tomb of a certain Pa-Aten-em-Heb. See, most recently, Gessler-Löhr (1989). This tomb has been dated variously to the Amarna period or shortly after, in the reign of Horemheb.

344. See *Royal Inscriptions* above.

345. Zandee (1992).

346. Condon (1978).

347. This assertion, of course, does not take into consideration those chapters that were reeditions of portions of either the Pyramid Texts or the Coffin Texts. For a brief sketch of the complex relationship of the *Book of the Dead* with other religious corpora, see Hornung (1999) 13–14.

348. The thirty lines, of course, would be an allusion to the Sed Festival that would normally be held in the thirtieth year of a king's reign. See Fischer-Elfert (1997) 65–72.

349. Assmann (1996b).

Chapter 9

The Legacy of Ramesses III and the Libyan Ascendancy

STEVEN R. SNAPE

How does one properly assess the legacy of Ramesses III? There are a number of different ways in which this question might be approached. It is clear that Ramesses himself would wish to be regarded as a king from the same mold as his illustrious namesake and predecessor Ramesses II, and his agenda of self-presentation was based on a number of connections between them. The most obvious of these connections begins with the similarity of the royal name itself and includes the stress on building achievements and military accomplishments of a king who is worthy of deification in his own lifetime.[1]

There is a residue of monumental works, most notably Medinet Habu, which, unequaled by his successors (at least until Dynasty Twenty-six), might be thought of as the last in the line of great building achievements of kings of the New Kingdom. Against this, it could be argued that Medinet Habu is Ramesses III's only major building project to survive and therefore that he falls well short of the mark set not only by Ramesses II but also by many kings of the Eighteenth and Nineteenth Dynasties, although one could reply that our view of Ramesses II as a builder might be significantly different had he not included Nubia among the regions that benefited from architectural embellishment during his reign.

As far as military matters are concerned, one might argue that Ramesses III's achievements were, in fact, greater than those of Ramesses II, in that he ensured the very survival of Egypt itself through the crisis of the collapse of the Late Bronze Age world system, which resulted in the effective destruction of other Eastern Mediterranean and Near Eastern powers, most notably the Hittite Empire and Mycenaean hegemony in the Aegean. This was clearly the most important historical aspect of his reign, with Ramesses III supposedly dealing effectively with the major nomadic incursions of the Sea Peoples and the Libyans.

That Ramesses III was provided with the opportunity to emulate his kingly role model through military victories against a significant foreign threat might, perversely, be regarded as a fortuitous circumstance for him. The extent to which this legacy can be regarded as the personal achievement of Ramesses III himself or of Egypt as an effectively marshaled state is debatable, but it is certainly the case that the building works and the evidence for military success come together best in a single source, the king's "Mansion of Millions of Years" at Medinet Habu. This structure is one of the best preserved of all New Kingdom temples and, arguably, the single most useful historical document for the end of the Bronze Age.

As is well known,[2] Ramesses III's memorial temple at Medinet Habu was modeled closely on the Ramesseum both in form and decorative content. Although the temple, especially the scenes that covered its walls, was tailored to the individual requirements of its owner, it was based on the prototype of a temple built to represent the relationship between a king and the gods of Egypt, with that relationship expressed through both generalities and the historical specificity of what a particular king does for a particular god. This is well represented in the memorial temples of the first Ramesside kings and, early in the New Kingdom, by Hatshepsut's temple at Deir el-Bahari, where the building and its figured decoration and textual content make a unified whole of the generality of the nature and operation of the royal relationship with the gods at Thebes and personal achievement. Whether that achievement is in erecting obelisks, obtaining incense from Punt, building sacred barks, or smiting foreigners, it is the fact that it is done for the god that is overwhelmingly important. However, despite this shared background of royal performance in the face of divine expectation, the deliberate modeling of Medinet Habu on the Ramesseum must not be underestimated and is a factor that has been used to cast doubt on the historicity of a significant proportion of the war reliefs at Medinet Habu.[3]

Another document that directly addresses the idea of the legacy of Ramesses III, in the period immediately after his death, is Papyrus Harris I, often referred to as the Great Harris Papyrus, not least from its length at an unrolled forty-two meters.[4] Acquired by the collector A. C. Harris in the winter of

1854–55, it was sold after his death to the British Museum in 1872. It appeared as part of a group of papyri illicitly excavated on the West Bank at Thebes at the same time as other notable papyri, including Papyrus Mayer A and B and the Abbott Papyrus. The possibility that these papyri shared a common findspot suggests a deliberate cache of Late New Kingdom administrative documents particularly concerned with serious administrative problems (e.g., royal tomb robbery) on the West Bank.

The age of Papyrus Harris I—older than other documents in the group—might suggest its long-term residency in a temple archive, perhaps at Medinet Habu itself. Its importance as a deliberate summation of the main achievements of the reign is clear from the extent to which it is one of the major sources for different aspects of Ramesses III's activities as described in this volume, but the specific purpose for which it was written is less obvious. Vernus notes that the majority of this *res gestae* is in hieratic, but with hieroglyphic sections that give it the appearance of being a "sacralised document."[5]

Goedicke goes further, suggesting in relation to a collection of documents that includes Papyrus Harris I and at least some of the judicial/conspiracy papyri, "The idea, as expressed by de Buck, that they were meant as a record of the activity of Ramesses III as king to be presented in that final judgment in the netherworld seems the only plausible explanation. Thus the group of papyri are to be understood as notes for the king in his confession before Osiris."[6] Support for this, perhaps surprising, notion might be found in the suggestion that the original findspot of Papyrus Harris I was a funerary context, possibly originally having been deposited in the tomb of Ramesses III himself and later recovered as part of the Deir el-Bahari cache that was being robbed by the Abd er-Rassoul family in 1855.[7] In this context, a concern with a well-documented personal legacy, of which one could give a full account, might make sense.

However, the legacy of Ramesses III has another aspect in the children, particularly male children, he fathered. The identities and relationships of these royal sons are a major factor in constructing an understanding of the events at the end of the reign of Ramesses III and for most of the remainder of the Twentieth Dynasty. Our starting point for this particular view of the Late New Kingdom is the procession of royal sons at Medinet Habu, and our end point will be a similar procession from the Khonsu temple at Karnak. These lists of royal sons in temples built or decorated by their fathers do not simply provide neat bookends to the period but also exemplify processes and depict individuals who are explicitly linked to the major developments of the period, and they will be examined in that light.

ROYAL SONS AT MEDINET HABU

The main evidence for the succession to the throne of several kings who follow Ramesses III comes from a procession scene of royal sons and daughters at Medinet Habu. At the rear of the second court of the temple is a colonnade forming a portico, the rear wall of which depicts a series of royal children, as though they are walking in procession toward the entrance to the rear rooms.[8] These children appear in mirror image on each side of the doorway and consist of a series of unnamed daughters and named sons. Thirteen sons are shown on the north side of the rear wall of the portico,[9] and thirteen sons are shown on the south.[10] In addition, five further sons are shown on the northern end wall of the portico,[11] but since they are unnamed, they are not discussed here. Since the two processions are essentially identical (relevant differences are noted below), the better-preserved, northern group will be described here and is reproduced as figure 9.1.[12]

Each royal son has before him a deeply incised cartouche of Ramesses III, and each raises his right hand in adoration of the cartouche while holding an ostrich-feather fan in his left (for detail, see plate 9.1). As with much of the decorative scheme at Medinet Habu, identification of Ramesses III with Ramesses II seems to have been an important concern, and the theme of a procession of royal children is a borrowing from a well-known motif of Ramesses II. It might also be noted here that, although not identical, some illustrative elements from the Ramesses II processions are evident at Medinet Habu, as, indeed, is Ramesses III's individual naming of his sons and even giving them titles closely modeled on the sons of Ramesses II (e.g., both kings have sons named Khaemwese who hold the title of *sm*-priest of Ptah at Memphis).

The three sons at the front of the procession are distinguished from the rest of the group by wearing a lappet headdress and a long, transparent overgarment, while the others wear the more abbreviated style of attached hairpiece appropriate to Ramesside royal sons and shorter kilts with long sashes. In this they seem to reflect the practice followed by Ramesses II at, for example, the Luxor Temple,[13] where the first three sons (Amenhirkhopeshef, Ramesses, and Prehirwenemef) are distinguished by carrying ostrich-feather fans and wearing long, transparent overgarments, while the remainder bear bouquets and have shorter kilts. However, the fourth son at Medinet Habu has had the long overgarment added to his figure at a later date.

The first ten princes at Medinet Habu are identified by a vertical text band that runs between them and the Ramesses III cartouche, giving their names and titles. The first three sons have names in cartouches within the vertical

Fig. 9.1. Royal sons at Medinet Habu. (After *MH* V, pl. 301. Courtesy of the
Oriental Institute of the University of Chicago.)

Plate 9.1. First two sons of Ramesses III at Medinet Habu. (Photo by S. Snape.)

text band, namely, son 1 (Ramesses), son 2 (*nb-M3ˁt-Rˁ mry-Imn*), and son 3 (Ramesses *Imn-ḥr-ḫpš.f nṯr-ḥḳ3-Iwnw*).[14] The first four sons have all been given a uraeus. The fourth son, named Ramesses-Sethhirkhopeshef in the framed column, has an additional unframed column of text cut in the space between his body and the framed column enclosing his prenomen, *Wsr-M3ˁt-Rˁ 3ḫ-n-Imn,* on the northern procession and his nomen, Ramesses *Mry-Imn stḫ-ḥr-ḫpš.f* on the southern group.

All of the above is uncontroversial, but the interpretation of this line of princes has given rise to a virtual industry of scholarly debate. It cannot be doubted that, at the time of their carving, these figures were indeed meant to represent sons of Ramesses III; whether their accompanying texts identify them as such is another question. It is equally undebatable that the framed columns containing their names and titles were added after the death of Ramesses III—the names in cartouches that identify them as kings makes that clear. The first four figures are given names in cartouches that identify them as kings, but all the figures in the procession are described in relation to a king who is not them ("king's son of his body"). The specific detail of when these identifying texts were added and who the figures represented were then thought to be is at the heart of the debate surrounding the succession to the throne in the later Twentieth Dynasty.

ROYAL SONS AT MEDINET HABU—RAMESSES IV

There are two major theories that identify the first prince in the Medinet Habu procession (plate 9.1), the most commonly held being that it is Ramesses IV—the name *Ramesses,* when taken together with the Ramesses IV bandeau text that underlies the processional scene, would seem to make that identification almost certain. The succession from Ramesses III to Ramesses IV is one of the best recorded from the New Kingdom.[15] The date of the death of Ramesses III in the third month of Shemu in year 32 of his reign and the accession of Ramesses IV is well documented by two separate sources from Deir el-Medina that refer not just to the death of Ramesses III but also to how the news was conveyed to the workmen involved in constructing the royal tomb.

The first, a necropolis journal, notes that "the Chief of Medjay, Montu-mose, [cam]e [to tell the wor]kmen of the Tomb: 'The falcon has flown [up to heaven, namely the Majesty] (of) King User-Maat-Re Mery-Amen, son of Re, Ramesses Heka-Iunu, l.p.h. [and King] User-Maat-Re Setep-en-Amen, son of Re, Ramesses Mery-[Amen], l.p.h., [the Sover]eign, sits upon the throne of Re in his place.'"[16] A contemporary ostracon notes, "One said, 'The falcon has flown up to heaven.'"[17] Despite a degree of scholarly controversy,[18] it is likely that Ramesses III had died the day before, day 15. The speed with which the Deir el-Medina workmen were told of the king's recent demise strongly suggests that the king had died at Thebes itself, and it was obviously important that the Deir el-Medina team were told, so that the king's tomb could be made ready for the funeral. These preparations are also documented in the Deir el-Medina ostraca. On day 4 of the first month of *akhet,* items of funerary furniture were brought to the tomb,[19] in preparation for the funeral that took place on day 24.[20]

The dual announcement of the death of Ramesses III and the accession of Ramesses IV on the day following the former's death seems to demonstrate an orderly and, indeed, not unexpected succession. The royal titulary adopted at the beginning of his reign indicates that, like Ramesses III before him, Ramesses IV was intent on modeling himself on Ramesses II,[21] although the emendation of his nomen to *Maaty,* "the True/Legitimate One," during his second year[22] might be seen as an attempt to affirm a challenged legitimacy. One might, on admittedly flimsy grounds, attribute this slight evidence for a defensive attitude toward his own legitimacy on the part of Ramesses IV to the circumstances surrounding the death of Ramesses III. These circumstances need now to be considered, if only briefly, particularly in relation to the Medinet Habu procession scene.

ROYAL SONS AT MEDINET HABU—PENTAWERET?

The best-known, most extensive, and most sensational set of legal documents from dynastic Egypt concern the legal proceedings that seem to deal with the aftermath of a possibly successful (and several unsuccessful) attempts to kill Ramesses III. These much-discussed[23] documents are remarkable in a number of different ways. Perhaps the most obvious is the survival of a substantial documentary source whose subject matter is of extreme delicacy—the murder of a divine king by members of his own court/family and the subsequent trial and execution of the guilty individuals.

Opposition to the prevailing political order was unthinkable—possibly quite literally so. The only possible reason for regime change was not a change in the fundamental nature of the regime itself but merely the individual identities of those who operated the most powerful levers of political authority. The office of king was unchallengeable, but the identity of that king was not. Despite the efforts of Ramesses II to develop the idea of a personal divine kingship in a ruler's lifetime and despite some evidence for a continuation of this notion by Ramesses III,[24] the separation between office and office holder was one that was readily apparent, if not to the populace at large, certainly to those individuals closest to the king himself, his family.

The institution of the harem, while seeking to guarantee the existence of a male successor to the throne, also had the effect of creating multiple, potentially competing successors. Ramesses III did not merely manage to generate a series of potential male heirs to the throne, in the same way as Ramesses II, and to list these children on the walls of Medinet Habu, as Ramesses II had done on his temples; he also generated a similarly complex succession crisis—in fact, succession crises. In the case of Ramesses III, not only might this crisis be assumed through the competing claims of the children of favored wives (e.g., Nefertari and Iset-Nofret in the case of Ramesses II), but it can be seen through active plotting that involved not simply maneuvering on the parts of court factions but also the removal of the most obvious impediment to accession to the throne, Ramesses III himself.

As with Papyrus Harris I, the specific purpose of the Harem Conspiracy documentation—the Turin Judicial Papyrus, the Rollin Papyrus,[25] the Lee and Rifaud papyri, Papyrus Rifaud II,[26] and the Varzy Papyrus[27]—is not agreed.[28] It is likely that at least some of these now-separate papyri were once part of an extensive papyrus roll about fifty centimeters in height and up to five meters in length. Groll's view is that the Lee, Rollin, and Varzy papyri are fragments of the same original document,[29] a report on a trial that had just taken place, whereas the Turin Judicial Papyrus represents an attempt to summarize the trial with an emphasis on the types of crime committed and the punishments they attracted, rather than a concern for individual cases, and is, in Goedicke's phrase, "more like an excerpt from this more detailed account."[30] Grandet's view is that the Turin Judicial Papyrus, understandable by all literate Egyptians, was suitable for public broadcast, perhaps in the form of a bulletin set up on a billboard in front of Medinet Habu.[31]

Although much of the specific detail and order of events is lost, the general outline of the Harem Conspiracy is clear. A plot to kill Ramesses III was hatched in the harem and involved both court officials and female members of the royal family itself. It seems to have attempted to use magic and then more direct, practical methods. The outcome of these attempts is not known—perhaps they were successful. However, the plotters did not succeed in their main aim, which was not just to kill Ramesses III but, rather, to kill him and ensure the succession of a prince who is given the pseudonym *Pentaweret*, "He of the Great One." A royal mother, Queen Tiyi, seems to have been plotting here with her son, presumably not a son who was in the immediate line of succession at the end of a reign that was, one could reasonably expect, coming to an end after twenty-nine years anyway. The trial of those responsible for the plot seems to have been complicated by an attempt to pervert the course of justice, which itself resulted in the prosecution of judges set to try the case. A series of executions followed, and presumably because the public execution of high-ranking members of court might be considered bad for morale, there were a number of forced suicides, including those of Queen Tiyi and Pentaweret. The identity of Pentaweret is thus disguised in the court documents, but presumably everyone involved knew who he was—it was simply bad form to use the theophorous royal name of a royal prince in a document of this kind. Although clearly not the heir apparent, it seems unlikely that he would have been very far from the succession. So, if the procession of princes at Medinet Habu does indeed represent sons of Ramesses III, can he be identified?

At first sight, this might seem improbable. Since the names on the list of princes were added after the death of Ramesses III, it would seem unlikely that any descendants of Ramesses III would add the name of an attempted regicide to the monument of his victim/intended victim. However, Leblanc's ingenious, if extremely contentious, theory is to relocate Queen Titi, possible wife of Ramesses X and owner of tomb QV 52 in the Valley of the Queens, to be a queen of Ramesses III and, in fact, the Tiyi of the Harem Conspiracy. Furthermore, Leblanc suggests that the figure of son 4 at Medinet Habu was originally inscribed for Sethhirkhopeshef I but later recut for his son, Sethhirkhopeshef II (i.e., Ramesses VIII), and that Sethhirkhopeshef I was none other than the disgraced Pentaweret.[32] This theory is far from being generally accepted.[33]

ROYAL SONS AT MEDINET HABU—RAMESSES VI

Ramesses IV died after a reign of six years and was succeeded by his son Ramesses V, who himself reigned only four years. Since Ramesses V had died without issue, the succession reverted to the brothers of Ramesses IV—that is, the surviving princes listed in the processional scene at Medinet Habu. As has already been noted, sons 2 and 3 are labeled as *nb-M3ʿt-Rʿ mry-Imn* and Ramesses *Imn-ḥr-ḫpš.f nṯr-ḥḳ3-Iwnw,* and so it would appear that both these figures (i.e., the only two apart from the first figure to have the lappet headdress) should be regarded as representations of Ramesses VI.

The similarity of the cutting of the framed columns of text naming this king and the other royal sons (apart from son 1) makes it very likely indeed that all of these columns were cut during the reign of Ramesses VI. Indeed, another hypothesis regarding this group would regard the entire procession of royal sons at Medinet Habu as being fundamentally the family of Ramesses VI rather than Ramesses III. In this scenario, the first prince "Ramesses" would be the nonreigning father of Ramesses VI (i.e., a predeceasing son of Ramesses III),[34] and all the named sons who follow Ramesses VI would be his own children, not those of Ramesses III.[35]

ROYAL SONS AT MEDINET HABU—RAMESSES VIII

Ramesses VI reigned seven to eight years,[36] as did his successor Ramesses VII,[37] who was probably his son.[38] On the death of Ramesses VII without surviving issue, the succession reverted once more to the son of Ramesses III by another (unknown?) queen, Ramesses VIII (probably son 4 at Medinet Habu—Ramesses-Sethhirkhopeshef). It is clear that the vertical bands of identifying text on the Medinet Habu processional scene were already in place when son 4 became King Ramesses VIII, since he needed additional space to add his newly adopted royal name.

It is also possible that, at the same time this additional text was cut, the figure of son 4 was recut to give him an overgarment similar to those of Ramesses IV and Ramesses VI, as a means of making his royal image match his royal title.[39] He reigned one to three years. The origins of Ramesses IX (who reigned eighteen years) are not clear. He may have been the son of the predeceased Montuhirkhopshef (son 6 in the Medinet Habu procession). The parentage of Ramesses X[40] (who reigned three or more than eight[41] years) and Ramesses XI is unknown. It would be convenient to regard them as son and grandson of Ramesses IX.

INTERNAL AND EXTERNAL AFFAIRS IN THE
LATER TWENTIETH DYNASTY

The net result of this series of generally short reigns is that the gap between the death of Ramesses III and the accession of Ramesses XI could be as little as forty-six years, with a maximum of no more than fifty-seven years. A particularly telling illustration of the brevity of this period is the tenure of the high priesthood of Amun at Karnak by Ramesses-nakht I, which—from his appointment by year 1 of Ramesses IV until his death at some point during the reign of Ramesses IX—spans almost all of this era.[42]

The shortness of these reigns is itself often taken as indicative of the inherent political instability of this period, which is usually dismissed by most general histories of Ancient Egypt as one of generalized decline in royal authority and, with it, the stability and standard of living of the population at large. Most of the evidence for this period is Theban and reflects the particular concerns of two of the constituencies who are best represented in the documentary record of New Kingdom Egypt: kings attempting (and, now, failing dismally) to emulate the building achievements of the past and Deir el-Medina workmen seeking (and similarly struggling) to maintain a semblance of a stable lifestyle. For the former, monumental activity at Thebes shows a consistent decline, especially in the inability of Kings Ramesses IV–X to create significant monuments at Karnak and on the West Bank.

The enormous funerary temple planned by Ramesses IV was far from complete at his death, and work was continued by Ramesses V and Ramesses VI. Nonetheless, little remains today of this structure, whose very form is obscure. No other Ramessides seem even to have attempted to build a "Mansion of Millions of Years" on the West Bank; perhaps the length of their reigns precluded this. The Deir el-Medina gang was doubled by Ramesses IV—largely, one suspects, in an attempt to hasten the completion of a tomb for its assumed imminent use. The desire to maintain a royal tomb at Western Thebes, which would act as a suitable portal to eternity for the king, largely continued for the rest of the Twentieth Dynasty. The halving of the gang by Ramesses VI proved no obstacle to having a major tomb; he simply usurped that of his nephew Ramesses V. Other indicators of a collapse of the interdigitated factors of royal authority and economic stability are well represented in the Theban area by the twin benchmarks of inflation in grain prices (most noticeable during the reign of Ramesses VI)[43] and tomb robbery, which is represented by the well-known series of legal documents from the reign of Ramesses IX.[44]

As far as foreign affairs in the period from the reign of Ramesses IV to that of Ramesses XI are concerned, the fragmentary evidence that exists suggests a gradual retreat from what was left of Egypt's imperial possessions. This is particularly the case in the Levant. The existence of monuments referring to later Ramesside kings is clear enough; what these monuments represent is less so—a statue base of Ramesses VI from Megiddo,[45] for instance, might represent genuine Egyptian control of the area but equally might be "a present or a stray."[46] One interpretation of the available evidence[47] would see an Egyptian presence in the Levant shrinking after the reign of Ramesses III,[48] with the reign of Ramesses VI seeing a catastrophic collapse with the loss of even the southern control point at Deir el-Balah. However loss of empire does not mean loss of influence or contact, and "although the Philistines (and other members of the Sea People confederation) had occupied land once dominated by Egyptian military and bureaucratic personnel, had severed Egypt's lifeline to western Asia, and had destroyed whatever was left of the New Kingdom empire, Philistia evidently became both a market for Egyptian trade goods and an intermediary through which Egypt maintained trade relations with other areas of Palestine."[49]

THE LIBYAN ASCENDANCY

Since the Egyptian sources describe a record of spectacular victories by Egyptian armies against Libyan incursions in the Nineteenth and Twentieth Dynasties,[50] the emergence of a politically powerful and possibly numerous Libyan component to the population of Egypt as the dominant force at the beginning of the Third Intermediate Period needs to be explained. For some scholars, the Third Intermediate Period *is* the Libyan period, and the ascendancy to the highest offices of state and effective control of Egypt by groups and individuals who are, to a greater or lesser extent, "Libyan" is the epoch's single most important defining factor, particularly eclipsing its "Intermediate" character.[51] It is therefore justifiable to question the mechanisms by which these people came to be in Egypt and, perhaps more interestingly, exactly when they arrived. The intention here is not to reprise the evidence of Egypto-Libyan contact in the reign of Ramesses III and before[52] but, rather, to establish a pattern of Libyan presence and settlement in Egypt that began before Ramesses III, gained pace after his reign, and was, in effect, the single most important contributory factor to the eventual end of the New Kingdom and the beginning of the eponymous "Libyan period." The possibilities that will be explored, which might explain the presence and influence of Libyan groups in Egypt at the end of the New Kingdom, are the deliberate settlement of Libyans within Egypt by the Egyptian state for the benefit of the Egyptian state; the successful penetration of the Delta/Nile Valley by Libyans despite the opposition of the Egyptian state; and the presence of Libyans who, increasingly after the reign of Ramesses VI, acted as a sporadically destabilizing influence in the Theban area.

LIBYANS IN EGYPT: PRISONERS OF WAR BEFORE RAMESSES III

Predating the reign of Ramesses III is the evidence for the use of Libyan mercenaries (probably in the strict sense of that word) by the Egyptian state as early as the Amarna period.[53] Much more significant is the process of establishing Libyan "colonies" within Egypt, which began during the reign of Ramesses II and was an important feature of Ramesses III's means of dealing with prisoners of war captured during his Libyan wars. Among the various Egyptian terms that might be translated as "fortress" is one of particular interest to the topic under discussion—*nḫt*. The word is derived from *nḫt/nḫtw*, "strong/strength," which lends itself to the conventional English translation "stronghold." However, it is possible to go beyond this bland description to detail a more nuanced functional meaning for the term as it applies to Egyptian military installations, which is of importance to our understanding of at least some aspects of the emergence of the Libyans at the end of the New Kingdom.[54] The earliest substantive use of the term is in the annals of Thutmose III, where the "children of the ruler were brought to be in *nḫtw* in Egypt. Whoever died among these rulers his Majesty will cause his son to stand upon his place."[55] Thus the *nḫt* is described in terms of a facility used to house vassal hostages against the good behavior of their royal fathers and to provide a ruling heir on the death of those rulers. Although it is not specifically stated, the role of the *nḫt* as a place to facilitate the Egyptianification of the children of vassals to prepare them to rule an Egyptian imperial possession, having absorbed a suitably Egyptian worldview, is implied.

The next use of *nḫtw* as instruments of Egyptian imperialism is attested under Ramesses II, where they are used to house not indigenous elites to prepare them for rule but rank-and-file Libyan soldiers. At Abu Simbel, Ramesses claims that "he has settled the Libyans (Tjehenu) on the ridges (*tstw*). Filled are the *nḫtw* he has built."[56] The context of this text is one of settling easterners in the west, westerners in the east, and so on. Therefore an "eastern" location for the Libyan settlement should probably be understood; the "ridges" mentioned would therefore be identified with either the hills of Canaan or, perhaps more likely, the sandy "geziras"/"turtlebacks" of the Eastern Delta.[57]

Other references to the establishment of specific locations where Libyans can be processed into effective members of the Egyptian armed forces include a block found at Suez that refers to "[resettling the] Libyans in settlements (*dmiw*) bearing his name"[58] and Stela Tanis II, which states, "He has captured the country of the West, transformed into soldiery, to serve him."[59] Although the specific locations of the *dmiw* and where the transforming into soldiery took place are not stated in either text, the East Delta provenance of each source is striking.

LIBYANS IN EGYPT: PRISONERS OF WAR FROM THE
REIGN OF RAMESSES III

This process of creating military settlements of captured Libyans is very evident in the reign of Ramesses III. The most explicit text is the Rhetorical Stela from chapel C at Deir el-Medina, which says of the king:

> He has captured the land of the (Tjemehu), Libu and Meshwesh. He made them cross the Nile streams, brought to Egypt and made (to settle) into *nḫtw* by the victorious king so that they might hear the speech of the (Egyptian) people before following their king. He made their speech disappear, changing their tongues; and they went upon the road which (they) had not descended . . . When they reached the district of the king they were made into shield-bearers, followers and fan-bearers following the king.[60]

The Medinet Habu text of the war of year 5 similarly notes, "Their leaders were rounded up and made into groups (*mhwt*), in fortresses[61] (*nḫtw*) and branded with the great name of His Majesty."[62]

The process of settlement and (partial) integration is also referred to at some length in Papyrus Harris I, which describes Ramesses III taking tens of thousands of foreign captives (including Libyan groups headed by the Meshwesh and Libu) and having "settled their leaders (*ḥꜣwtyw*—or "best soldiers"?)[63] in forts (*nḫtw*) bearing my name. I appointed troop-commanders (*ḥryw-pḏt*) for them and tribal chiefs (*ꜥꜣ n mhwt*),[64] branded and reduced to slaves, . . . their wives and children being similarly treated."[65] *Mhwt* implies tribal groups, which seems to suggest that existing tribal/clan groupings were maintained rather than broken up. The involvement of both "troop-commanders" and "tribal leaders" strongly suggests a mode of administration that involved Egyptian military officers acting through the (now bilingual?) Libyan tribal leaders.[66] This might imply that the Egyptians themselves chose the tribal leaders. However, a potential future problem for the Egyptian state was that if, as is suggested, whole communities of Libyans were being settled in "strongholds," this may well have left intact aspects of their traditional social and political structures that would make possible a continued sense of group identity, able to assert itself when the opportunity arose.

It is very likely that these *nḫtw* were also carefully situated so they could act as effective military bases and/or that the foreigners "trained" in the *nḫtw* were disseminated into the locality. This is suggested by an East Delta location for *nḥtw* that contain Libyans. Sherden are also attested in association with *nḥtw*, including in late Twentieth Dynasty references to commanders of either the "great *nḥt* of the Sherden" or the "five *nḥtw* of the Sherden."[67] It is uncertain whether any of these are the known *nḥtw* named on the so-called Endowment Stela of the reign of Ramesses III from the region of Herakleopolis; the *nḥt,* called "Ramesses, Ruler of Heliopolis, Beloved of His Army," seems to have been a self-supporting institution, having been endowed with the economic resources to make it self-sufficient, and was also associated with Libyan soldiery as late as the reign of Shoshenq I.[68] While Grandet is of the opinion that the Sherden were settled here as a mercenary colony to protect the vulnerable entry point from the west via the Faiyum region,[69] Morris's view is that they were primarily settled here as an Egyptian heartland where they could also exploit underutilized agricultural land. Certainly the settlement of Sherden in the area of the mouth of the Faiyum is supported by evidence from the Wilbour Papyrus[70] suggesting that Sherden veterans/reservists were common in this region by the reign of Ramesses V. It seems most likely that Sherden who were "processed" in this *nḥt* of Ramesses III, "beloved of his army," were then dispersed in the region around the place where they had been acculturated, which might conceivably act as a rallying point for the collection of what were now effectively reservists. Unfortunately, the specific location of this *nḥt* is not known.

It is possible to envisage a similar, more substantial (though less well-documented) effect with the Libyans, especially in the Eastern Delta. "Processed" in the *nḥtw* of the Eastern Delta, their dissemination as reservists around the Eastern Delta would potentially make them a dominant group at the collapse of the New Kingdom. The only problematic aspect here is the mechanism by which substantial numbers of immigrants were settled in what one imagines (on the basis of little definite evidence, although important later Libyan centers, such as Bubastis and Mendes, at least were well settled from the Old Kingdom onward) was a fairly well-populated region.

LIBYANS IN EGYPT: CONTINUED ATTEMPTS AT PENETRATION

In addition to the invitation to mercenaries (presumably no longer valid by the reign of Ramesses III) and the deliberate settlement of prisoners of war, there was a third way in which a Libyan presence in Egypt might be established—continued attempts at penetration into the Nile Valley and Delta. One mechanism for this might be the survivors of the major attempted Libyan incursion under Merenptah and Ramesses III making their way south to try to enter the Nile Valley on a more piecemeal basis, using the oasis routes.[71] The evidence of the presence of Tjemeh Libyans seized near Wadi es-Sebua by Setjau in year 44 of Ramesses II might suggest that southern penetration, while not as ideal as the penetration into the Western Delta, was simply an alternative option taken up by other Libyan groups not necessarily associated with the military defeats further north.

It is also possible, of course, that the Egyptian accounts of Ramesses III's Libyan wars may simply have overstated their success. Leahy, for example, makes a distinction between the attempted invasions of Egypt during the reign of Ramesses III by the Sea Peoples and the Libyans; that of the former was "largely transient and repulsed," while the latter was "sustained and successful."[72] Indeed, despite the series of loudly trumpeted Egyptian victories over Libyans from early in the Nineteenth Dynasty onward, Leahy regards the period from Seti I to Ramesses III as a "series of conflicts in which the Libyans slowly gained ascendancy."[73] More radically, it has even been suggested that the year 5 victory over the Libyans claimed by Ramesses III was a fiction, simply copied from the nearby, now badly destroyed memorial temple of Merenptah, from now-lost reliefs describing his (genuine) year 5 Libyan war.[74]

In this rather unlikely eventuality, it might be argued that the copied reliefs represented a form of "execration text"—an attempt to apotropaically destroy an enemy that was beyond practical reach, not because it was a located in a faraway land, but because the Libyans had proved themselves to be a problem incapable of a simple military solution, one that (in a curious parallel to the situation described in the Harem Conspiracy papyri) required the application of both practical and magical measures for its resolution. If this were the case, then, in this instance at least, the memorial temple of Merenptah with its (we assume) now-lost scenes of a year 5 victory against the Libyans would provide a more suitable model for copying than the usual source, the Ramesseum.

However, on balance of probabilities, the coincidence of both Merenptah and Ramesses III having a year 5 war against a Libyan enemy is not good enough grounds for dismissing the latter as a historical fiction, even if the actual results of that war seem less clear-cut than described. In addition, even if a year 5 Libyan war of Ramesses III can be dismissed as an aspirational fiction, one would also have to explain the nature and results of Ramesses III's year 11 Libyan war. However, it has already been noted that, while we might accept the battlefield victories of years 5 and 11, these wars did not decisively end the threat posed by continued attempts at immigration by significant numbers of

Libyans, let alone the low-level and occasional infiltration by smaller groups, even during the reign of Ramesses III itself. This is attested in two ways; by measures taken against Libyan immigration by Ramesses III in addition to the direct military conflicts of years 5 and 11 and by references to the extent to which, in the later part of the reign, all of these efforts can be demonstrated to have fallen short in any aspiration to make Egypt Libyan-proof.

In Papyrus Harris I, it is claimed that Ramesses III built a series of mud-brick walls thirty cubits (over fifteen meters) in height around the temple enclosures of a series of temples in Middle/Upper Egypt. This he did for the temples of Thoth at Hermopolis Magna, Wepwawet at Asyut, and Onuris-Shu at This; at nearby Abydos, the temple of Osiris was fortified so that it was like "a mountain of iron."[75] The impression given is that these are defenses against a Libyan force that was large enough to wreak havoc by descending on large cities but not large (and slow-moving?) enough to be tracked and neutralized by the Egyptian army, assuming the continued battle-readiness of that army.

It is particularly notable that these defended sites are at or near the Nile Valley termini of routes from the oases. This process of providing substantial fortifications for existing population centers is heavily reminiscent of a similar program by Ramesses II on the western edge of the Delta.[76] The Upper Egyptian locales of these fortified locations is also noteworthy. Although Papyrus Harris I concerns itself with the whole of Egypt, rather than just the south, the cities that have been given special protection are southern. It may well be that the Meshwesh/Libu Libyans were following the pattern set by Tjehenu/Tjemeh Libyans in ranging far to the south of the Mediterranean coast, at least in the oases and close to the Nile Valley in the period following year 11.

Unfortunately, the chronological relationship between the defensive measures taken at these temple sites and the Libyan wars themselves is not known, so it cannot be said whether they were built in response to the emerging Libyan threat early in the reign or the continued threat after the year 5/11 wars. One might argue that part of the reason for this defensive strategy may well have been the perception/actuality that Middle and Upper Egypt were less well defended against incursions from the west in comparison to the Western Delta. Conversely, it may be that the need to defend Middle/Upper Egypt from Libyan incursions was an achievable priority at a time when Libyan penetration of the Western Delta was a reality that could not be easily rolled back. It is notable that similar defensive works are not mentioned in relation to cities in the Western Delta—surely a priority if the fortified cities of Ramesses II had been overrun early in the reign of Ramesses III, as seems likely given the extent of Libyan penetration in the Western Delta described in Papyrus Harris I.

Although fortresses and fortress towns from the Western Delta/Mediterranean coast are depicted at Medinet Habu, there is, to date, no specific evidence, either archaeological or textual, to indicate that they were still being maintained by the end of the reign. Indeed, it is striking that even a cursory overview of archaeological material that provides evidence for monumental activity by Ramesses III in the Delta demonstrates a pattern of it being specifically concentrated in the Eastern Delta,[77] especially on sites that are particularly associated with Third Intermediate Period activity.[78] One site that does seem to have had its defenses enhanced with a substantial mud-brick enclosure wall by Ramesses III is Tell el-Yehudieh,[79] although we do not know whether this occurred because of the threat from the east, to house Libyans in a *nḥt,* or both.

LIBYAN ACTIVITY BETWEEN THE REIGNS OF RAMESSES III AND RAMESSES VI

After Ramesses III, there is no record of attempted mass migration into Egypt from Libya; or, rather, there is no evidence of attempted mass migration that was opposed by military force on the part of the Egyptians and that resulted in a superficially decisive victory, which could be appropriately represented in a monumental form. On the contrary, our evidence for Libyan/Egyptian interaction in the post–Ramesses III Twentieth Dynasty is of Libyan activity in the Theban area during the period and the presence of significant numbers of Libyans in the Delta at the end of the period, while large-scale Libyan migration into the Delta in the latter part of the Twentieth Dynasty seems more likely than not. An ostracon from year 28 of Ramesses III refers to the descent of the "enemy" that disrupted work on the royal tomb.[80]

If the references to the "enemy" in texts that describe external forces causing problems for the Deir el-Medina workforce refer to Libyans, then clearly these raids had already begun before the end of the reign of Ramesses III himself. Papyrus Turin 2044, dating to year 1 of (probably) Ramesses VI,[81] notes that the "enemy" had reached and destroyed the town of Per-Nebyt, from where they seemed to pose a potential threat to Western Thebes. While it is possible that the "enemy" are Egyptian and therefore that this document might be used to support the notion of a civil war between Ramesses V and Ramesses VI, the lack of civil disruption at Thebes might make it more likely that the "enemy" referred to are a group of Libyans whose specific identity was not known by the scribe at the time of writing.

Evidence that the burial of Ramesses V was postponed until in year 2 of Ramesses VI[82] might also be seen as a temporary worsening of the security situation on the West Bank at Thebes early in the reign. It is tempting to use this fragmentary evidence to suggest a significant Libyan conflict early in the reign of Ramesses VI.[83] A scene on the upper portion of the south face of the vestibule of the second pylon at Karnak depicts Ramesses VI in the act of smiting a group of defeated enemies. The restored text of this scene seems to lend itself to an interpretation of a successfully thwarted invasion—"I have brought for thee all foreign hill-countries (*ḫ3swt*) which fall to attacking thy boundaries"—but the presence of an adjacent and very similar scene/accompanying text of Ramesses II might suggest an emulation of the royal predecessor. A copying of the Ramesses II scene might be explained as a mimicking of the mode of presentation that nevertheless reflected a genuinely historical event, but the figures of foreign captives on the Ramesses VI scene are so poorly preserved that it is not possible to assign to them a specific identity that might support a contemporary reality. Even more suggestive is the well-known statue of Ramesses VI, again from Karnak, showing a striding king accompanied by a lion and grasping the hair of a cowering Libyan captive.[84] There is no indication that this statue is connected with a specific event, but it suggests that the feeling that the king should be and was smiting Libyans, if only in a very general sense, was a contemporary concern.

LIBYAN ACTIVITY DURING THE REIGNS OF RAMESSES IX—RAMESSES XI

From the later part of the Twentieth Dynasty, there are a number of texts in the copious documentation associated with Deir el-Medina that refer, usually in passing, to the presence or arrival of Libyans.[85] It would appear that, by this time, the arrival of Libyans was not always an unexpected event. Papyrus Turin 2074[86] (from year 8 of Ramesses IX) describes the workmen at Deir el-Medina being warned by the vizier that "the Meshwesh are coming to Thebes," which, the same document reports, indeed happened eleven days later.

The notion that these Meshwesh were moving southward through Middle Egypt toward Thebes rather than descending from the Western Desert seems a more likely scenario, one that would suggest a serious, largely unchecked Libyan presence in Middle/Lower Egypt. However, as Haring notes, the same text refers to a trading arrangement between two individuals at Deir

el-Medina involving "that which he obtained from the Libu"[87]—a different
Libyan group to the Meshwesh is being described here, one (of uncertain
size) that seems to be active in trade in the Theban area. However, raids from
the desert are clearly noted in the journal text of Papyrus Turin 2071[88] (from
years 10–11 of Ramesses IX), which refers to the descent (*h3y*) of the desert
people (*h3styw*) from the town (*dmi*) of *Smn*.

In the days that follow, the journal records inactivity (*wsf*) because of the
desert people. More specific is the record of "inactivity of the crew because of
the Meshwesh," who are presumably to be identified as the desert people of
the earlier entries. The most likely candidate for *Smn* is in the vicinity of the
village of Al-Mahamid Qibly, 14.5 kilometers south of Armant, which has
produced a cache of monuments naming "Sobek of *Smn*," the latest of which
was donated by Ramesses II.[89] This area is close to a natural entry point to
the Nile Valley for a route from the Kharga Oasis, an indicator that Thebes
might have been menaced by Libyan groups coming from the immediate
south, as well as the west and north. Routes from the oases provided a natural means for Libyans based in Dakhleh/Kharga to descend on western
Thebes. It is particularly noticeable that the securing of the desert routes immediately to the west of Thebes, on the Farshut Road, the "Road of Horses,"
was one of the most notable acts of the High Priest Menkheperre in the
Twenty-first Dynasty.[90]

The regularity with which the "desert people" descend on the area of Deir
el-Medina between years 10 and 15 of Ramesses IX is striking, although
whether these are attacks on the village or the activities of a nomadic population coming down to the Nile Valley to trade is unclear.[91] Inactivity by the
Deir el-Medina gang because of the "desert people" is also attested from year
3 of Ramesses X.[92] Probably by year 17 of Ramesses XI, if not earlier, the situation had become so severe that the villagers of Deir el-Medina decamped
permanently to Medinet Habu,[93] not merely because it was the administrative center of Western Thebes, but because of the practical protection its
walls afforded.

A particularly informative document probably from year 12 of Ramesses
XI[94] casts significant light on the situation on the West Bank at Thebes. The text
describes itself as "Town-register of the West of Thebes (literally "the city"),
from the temple of Menmaatre (i.e., the Qurna temple of Seti I) to the settlement of Maiunehes." The register is a list of 182 houses and three temples—the
Seti temple at Gurna, the Ramesseum, and Medinet Habu. Of the 182 houses
listed, only ten are located in the area between the Seti temple and the Ramesseum, and of these, seven are occupied by priests, two by Medjay, and one by a

stable master. Between the Ramesseum and Medinet Habu, fourteen houses are listed, ten of which are occupied by priests. In startling contrast to what appears to be a skeleton staff of priests operating the memorial temples of Seti I and Ramesses II, 155 houses are listed as being situated south of Medinet Habu, perhaps clustering around the temple itself, and these householders represent a wide spectrum of trades as well as the administrative officials for the area, including the mayor of Western Thebes himself.

Kemp regards these houses not as being located to the south of Medinet Habu but as the "second-stage" town that developed within the enclosure wall of the temple complex itself.[95] This significant concentration of occupation around a comfortingly strongly fortified keep in the form of the Medinet Habu temple might well have developed as a result of the desire for security at a time when Libyans were raiding almost unchecked around the West Bank. This drawing in on the West Bank might also explain why the Ramesseum itself was abandoned to be robbed by members of the temple staff of Medinet Habu itself before year 9 of Ramesses XI,[96] and it might be a contributory reason for Ramesses XI ultimately abandoning the Valley of the Kings as a place for his own burial.

One of the most remarkable documents for Libyans in Egypt during the later part of the Ramesside period refers to their presence in the district of Per-Hebyt in the reign of Ramesses XI.[97] This is particularly important since Per-Hebyt—modern Behbeit el-Hagar—is precisely the sort of Delta location where we would expect Libyans to be present but, equally, is the sort of place for which we have minimal documentation. The context in which the document was written is uncertain, but it seems to refer to a vizieral order to an unnamed official to take part in a police operation to ascertain the intentions of a group of Meshwesh of unstated size. Whatever the intentions involved here, this operation is one of monitoring rather than action. This document serves to remind us that Libyan activity in Egypt toward the end of the Twentieth Dynasty—which is reasonably well documented in Thebes—is likely to have been considerably more significant in northern Egypt.

RAMESSES XI AND THE END OF THE NEW KINGDOM

It must be admitted from the outset that the nature and chronology of events and individuals at the transition from the New Kingdom to the Third Intermediate Period is far from being a matter of scholarly consensus. Apart from the problems concerning the quasi-royal individuals who emerge at this time, the nature of the reigns of even "real" kings is a matter of dispute—the lineal succession of Ramesses IX, X, and XI has recently been challenged by those who would reclassify these three kings as rulers of territorially limited authority whose "reigns" are not sequential but overlapping.[98] If true, this might signal the beginning of the Third Intermediate Period at a date even earlier than other convenient events, especially the death of Ramesses XI or the beginning of the *wḥm mswt*. Indeed, what constitutes an effective marker of the end of the New Kingdom is itself a problem. This might be best thought of as the point where the struggle for power between nonroyal individuals becomes the central issue in determining who holds real control in Egypt, superseding attempts by the crown to suppress challenges to royal authority.

It is probably true to say that while the death of Ramesses XI might represent one convenient "official" end of the line of New Kingdom kings, it in reality simply ushered in a period where the fragmented nature of power within the state, which had developed during that king's reign, had fewer checks on its overt display. It is also clear that individuals of Libyan origin or with Libyan connections were among the dominant political figures at this time. The most obvious way this might be imagined as operating is in the emergence of a Libyan military elite as holders of the highest military offices within the state system, well positioned to act as power brokers between competing factions or as warlords with their own royal ambitions. This Libyan presence in the upper levels of state administration need not have been limited to the army; although a military career was an obvious route to success for captured warriors and their descendants, a wider penetration of offices of influence at court even as early as the reign of Ramesses III is indicated by, for example, the identity of one of the plotters in the Harem Conspiracy, "the Libu, Yanini, who had been a butler."[99]

While the detail is contentious, the fact that holders of major state offices were in open competition with each other during the reign of Ramesses XI and, in being so, were undermining royal authority is obvious. Once again we tend to see national events through the lens of Theban evidence at this time, but even this partial picture is enough to give a general sense of the disintegration of central control. Challenges to the status quo include the "suppression" of Amenhotep, high priest of Amun, by an unnamed party and the reinstatement of Amenhotep by the Viceroy of Kush, Panehesy, probably as an attempt by Ramesses XI, now effectively a northern king, to assert control in southern Egypt.

Panehesy seems to have brought Upper Egypt under his control by martial law, possibly as early as year 9 and certainly by year 12 of Ramesses XI. An early, though not atypical, example of the ways in which army leaders, supposedly acting under royal instruction, regarded themselves as independent agents is illustrated by the probable ejection of Amenhotep from the High Priesthood of Amun by Panehesy in year 17. The objectives being followed by Panehesy when he took his army north into Middle Egypt, before eventually being forced back into Nubia, are unclear. What is clear is that this might be regarded as the point at which any control over Nubia was lost by the Egyptian state and that southern Egypt was, however briefly, in a state of civil war: this time was remembered in later memory as the "year of the hyenas when one was hungry."[100]

THE LIBYAN ASCENDANCY AND THE *WḤM MSWT*

Year 19 of Ramesses XI marked the beginning of a period referred to as the *wḥm mswt* (literally "repeating of births"), often referred to as the "Renaissance period." What was intended by this is uncertain—a new start certainly, but one in which the new start itself was the defining moment of what followed. The practice of dating the rest of the reign of Ramesses XI by reference to the years of the *wḥm mswt* is a striking example of the ways in which both the reality and the appearance of royal authority was being undermined.

In the conventional view of this period, the most obvious political result of the *wḥm mswt* at Thebes was that General Herihor replaced the truculent Panehesy as the effective power in Upper Egypt and theoretical power in Nubia, while an individual whom Manetho names as Smendes, who may or may not have a family connection to Herihor, was the real power in the land in the Delta, based at Tanis. The early career of Herihor, before his arrival at Thebes, probably at the beginning of the *wḥm mswt,* is unclear. It is likely that he had a military background and that his assumption of priestly titles at Thebes was part of his taking the reins of power for Ramesses XI, whereas his later self-promotion to king at Thebes was clearly not. It has been noted[101] that one of the scenes depicting Herihor as king at the Khonsu temple has him offering to "Horus of 'The Camp'" which may be a reference to El-Hibeh, one of the fortified settlements in Middle Egypt that may have been one of the fortresses (*nḫtw*) of militarized Libyan settlement from earlier in the Ramesside period.[102]

Ramesses XI seems to have spent the last decade of his reign as a ceremonial figurehead in Memphis. Thus, assuming the Libyan connections of Herihor and Smendes, the *wḥm mswt* saw Libyans taking the reins of power in the key areas—military leadership, the High Priesthood of Amun at Thebes, and control of the Delta and access to the east through Tanis. It is notable that the reign of Ramesses XI saw the abandonment of the Valley of the Kings as the royal burial place; the location of the burials of kings of the Twenty-first Dynasty at Tanis is one of the obvious features of a Theban/Tanite split that typified the early part of the Third Intermediate Period. The burial place of Ramesses XI is not known, but it is unlikely to have been anywhere south of Memphis.

Herihor seems to have been the agent who brought about any renaissance-like activity in the south. At Thebes, he brought tomb robbers to trial,[103] ordered the reburial of plundered kings, and carried out building repairs at Karnak. Perhaps most significantly, he carried out a major decorative project at the Khonsu temple at Thebes, which will be discussed below. After year 7 of the *whm mswt*, Herihor was succeeded in Upper Egypt by a man who similarly combined the office of High Priest of Amun and military functions, Piankh. This individual, who may have been related to Herihor by marriage, may have continued the civil war in the south against Panehesy, but he may have only ruled for four years of the *whm mswt* before passing his offices on to his son Pinudjem. On the death of Ramesses XI, he was succeeded by Smendes/Nesubanebdjed,[104] who reigned for twenty-five or twenty-six years.[105] For the first fifteen years of this reign, the effective instrument of governance in Upper Egypt was Pinudjem, who was calling himself king by year 16 of Smendes; by that year, the High Priest of Amun was Pinudjem's son, Masaharta.

Much of this account of the period is disputed, in particular by those scholars who have put forward a revisionist view that would read the evidence for this period as supporting a reversal of the succession from Herihor-Piankh to Piankh-Herihor.[106] The most extreme view would have Pinudjem succeeding Ramesses XI, so that Wenamun would have embarked on his expedition in year 5 of Pinudjem rather than that of the *whm mswt*, while Pinudjem himself would be a son of Piankh and brother of the Nodjmet who married Herihor.[107]

THE NATURE OF THE LIBYAN SETTLED PRESENCE IN EGYPT

Libyan penetration of Egypt can be seen at this time not only through the actions of high-ranking individuals of Libyan origin but also by more routine references to lower-status Libyans in the Theban area. Evidence for this comes from a letter from Piankh to the Scribe of the Tomb Djehutymose requesting that the latter deal with some issue that had arisen regarding the "rations for the Meshwesh"; it is possible that this particular group of Meshwesh-Libyans were involved in Piankh's Nubian campaign of year 10 of the *whm mswt*.[108] Perhaps they were the same as the sizable contingent of Meshwesh in the army of Piankh who are referred to in another letter of the same period.[109] Another document from the *whm mswt* (year 2), Papyrus Mayer A, describes the interrogation of the brewer Nepare in relation to a quantity of silver found in his possession; his alibi is that he obtained it not from the robbing of a royal tomb but from the Meshwesh.[110] Whether this means that the presence of Meshwesh-Libyans in the Theban area during the *whm mswt* had been normalized—that is, whether or not they should be regarded as an unstable marginal element—is not obvious.

Significant foreign immigration was not new to Egypt, nor was immigration that produced individuals of foreign origin who rose to positions of prominence within the state. What was different in the case of the Libyans was the extent to which Libyans (to simplify) retained their own cultural traditions.[111] This may, in part, have been due to the "speed and scale of their intrusion and the density of their settlement in Egypt, which enabled them to maintain a greater degree of ethnic integrity."[112] In general, the Libyans seem to have embraced the multicultural nature of Late New Kingdom Egypt more happily than its integrative aspects. However, detecting specifically "Libyan" cultural artifacts is not easy, particularly if one remembers that the supposed intrusive Libyan element is as strikingly indistinct as a cultural horizon in "Libya" itself throughout the Bronze Age, apart from the evidence provided by a very limited amount of work done on those few sites that can really be regarded as "Libyan"[113] and the sometimes problematic interpretation of Egyptian illustrations of Libyan material culture at, for instance, Medinet Habu.[114]

Another approach is to seek changes to Egyptian norms of cultural behavior that may have been influenced by the presence of an increasingly important Libyan contingent among elites in Egypt, which might have brought about the adaptation of those norms to suit the requirements of conservative Libyans and aspirant elite Egyptians. But claims that, for instance, changes in burial practices at both the royal and private level in the Third Intermediate Period are due to the absorption of Libyan practices are impossible to prove given the lack of evidence from Libya itself.

One example of a Libyan practice that seems to have been adapted to Egyptian usage is an interest in genealogy as an aspect of self-presented identity.[115] The best example here is the concentration on long genealogies on private monuments in Egypt (e.g., block statues), which is often thought to have developed from the long verbal genealogies held by nomadic, nonliterate Libyans. There are several potential reasons why an immigrant community would have a particular interest in the subject of genealogy, particularly written genealogy. Most obviously, there is the possibility that existing genealogies are nurtured to preserve a sense of identity and connection to the "homeland," a point of bonding for community groups who might well share that genealogy. The safeguarding of this information is the preservation of an essential element of communal identity. However, if this information is lost or never existed in the first place, this may give rise to the process of discovered identity. In this case, a community or, more usually, an individual might seek their "roots" in an ancestry and homeland from which the individual's ancestors had been dislocated.

An important issue in both these cases is that of illiteracy. A community may not have written records of its ancestors because the community itself is effectively illiterate. That illiteracy may be as a result of a disruptive translation of the community itself, removing individuals from organized social structures and transporting them to new situations in an ad hoc manner. The extent to which communal memories of homeland and ancestry are retained will depend on the extent to which original groups are kept together and the extent that individual and group memory is passed down from generation to generation, through the mechanism of oral history, until it reaches an individual who is in a position to commit this family history to written record. The other possibility is a community that is itself intrinsically illiterate, where oral history is the only means of retaining any sense of group and individual history. This seems to be the case with the Libyans. Although the extent to which the "new" Libyan groups (Meshwesh, Libu) can be regarded as "nomadic" and therefore candidates for classic owners of a nonliterate oral tradition is uncertain, there is no evidence for any textual material connected to any of these groups.

It is clear that the Libyans who are visible in Egypt at the end of the Twentieth Dynasty are a collection of groups who may have had, broadly speaking, a common ethnic/geographical origin but who arrived in Egypt at different times, with different experiences of arrival and varying levels of acculturation. It would appear that the retention and projection of the Libyan identity was of significant importance for many of them and, as we have seen, that the extent to which they acculturated was limited. The retention of ethnic identity by the Libyans in Egypt indicates that they saw little need to present themselves in the way other immigrant groups did, as "Egyptian," and that their level of acculturation was one of choice. Moreover, it appears to be that the assertion of their own status within their Libyan peer groups by displaying elite ancestry was more important to them than how they appeared to Egyptians. It might well have been a cause for surprise among the officials of the Egyptian state to realize that the scruffy desert nomads with whom they were forced to deal regarded themselves as more aristocratic than the officials.

Individuals in the Third Intermediate Period who could claim ancestry back to identifiable immigrant groups who came of their own volition were quite capable and more than willing to display their aristocratic Libyan heritage. A good example is the Memphite priest Pasenhor "B," whose Serapeum stela is conventionally dated to year 37 of Shoshenq V.[116] This is a typical "Libyan" autobiography in that the main aim is the construction of an astonishingly long genealogy, which, in this case, stretches back to and beyond Shoshenq I. Of particular interest is that Pasenhor gives his earliest known ancestor—Buyuwawa the Tjehenu—whose own immediate descendants were four generations of "Great Chiefs of the Ma" (Mawasun, Neb-neshi, Paihuty, and Shoshenq "A") and then Shoshenq I's own father, Great Chief of the Ma and God's Father Nimlot "A." Thus the Twenty-second Dynasty had its origins in a long-established Libyan family. Precisely when the family settled in Egypt is not clear, although it is tempting to think of Buyuwawa as a first-generation immigrant. If this is the case, then placing him six generations (ca. 150 years?) before Shoshenq I (ca. 945 BC) would put him at about 1095 BC, in the *whm mswt*.

On a wider level, the Pasenhor stela does more for our awareness of the nature of the Libyan ascendancy in Egypt than simply establish a good Libyan ancestry for Shoshenq I and his descendants. It also gives a sense of the mixture of retention of Libyan identity and acculturation by this family that had been perfectly capable of retaining long ancestor strings, necessary not only for retaining their original *identity* as part of an immigrant community but also (and originally primarily) for *status* within that community. Pasenhor himself is Libyan aristocracy, because he can trace his ancestry back not merely to King Shoshenq I but far beyond that, to the Great Chiefs of the Ma. Indeed, it is noticeable that this Title—"Great Chief of the Ma"—is the title that carries real power in the Third Intermediate Period, with Egyptian royal titles as largely mere titulary trappings. The immediate forebears of Pasenhor have titles that depict them as conventional Egyptian officeholders, combining the titles of General, Overseer of Upper Egypt, and Overseer of Priests at (interestingly enough) Herakleopolis.

One specific aspect of detectable Libyanness that is often cited as a marker for their presence is the appearance of Libyan personal names in the Egyptian epigraphic record. These names are distinctly un-Egyptian and, occurring in several generations in the Third Intermediate Period, are well attested and recognizable, such as the several royal individuals named Shoshenq, Osorkon, and Takelot. The use of Libyan names by individuals indicates that their bearers have no desire to conceal their ethnic identity or to acculturate by assuming an Egyptian name, although this did occur. It is unlikely that Egyptians would take on Libyan names, although the situation might conceivably have changed later in the Twenty-first and Twenty-second Dynasties, when the cachet attached to Libyan royal names might have given them a more widespread currency.[117] Perhaps most striking of all is the cultural confidence of ethnic Libyans with Egyptianizing names who chose to give their children Libyan names. This seems to have been precisely the case with Herihor himself.

HERIHOR AT THE KHONSU TEMPLE: KINSHIP AND KINGSHIP

The Khonsu Temple within the Amen enclosure at Karnak is one of the most intriguing monuments of this period. It was begun by Ramesses III, but the bulk of the temple—pylon, courtyard, and first hypostyle hall—was the work of Ramesses XI and Herihor.[118]

The connection with Ramesses III may not have been coincidental but might be seen as an attempt to establish legitimacy by referring to a monument that the last significant king of Egypt started and with decoration using forms that derive from New Kingdom "Mansions of Millions of Years," not least Medinet Habu itself. The interplay in the decoration between the two principal protagonists—Herihor as High Priest of Amun cutting scenes for Ramesses XI—is an interesting one; there is an ambiguity in the texts themselves as to who commissioned the work, some naming Ramesses XI, others Herihor.[119] The distribution of texts at the Khonsu temple mirror this ambiguity—the hypostyle hall primarily contains texts that refer to Herihor by his "preroyal" titles as High Priest of Amun, while the (later?) texts in the courtyard give Herihor royal titulary.[120]

Since the Ramesses XI/Herihor texts and reliefs in the Khonsu temple are largely undated, it is impossible to give a firm chronological sequence to the emergence of Herihor as a royal figure in his own right. Herihor's specific royal titulary is derived from Ramesside prototypes and stresses his role as builder at Thebes[121]—very appropriate given that this seems to be the only place where he is called king. The scenes in the forecourt show most clearly the personal agenda of Herihor in the projection of his nascent kingship, drawing on themes and motifs borrowed from his Ramesside predecessors— his is the first surviving temple at Thebes to do this since Ramesses III at Medinet Habu. These motifs include the definition of a personal relationship between Herihor and Amun, evidenced by the things the king did for the god. In the absence of specific wars to boast of, this is achieved by the long-established mechanism of refurbishing the bark of Amun and organizing its use during the Opet Festival. The Khonsu temple, situated in the southwest corner of the Amun enclosure at Karnak and orientated to face south toward the Luxor Temple, would serve as a suitable starting point for this most important of Theban festivals. Herihor also claims to have constructed the processional bark for Amun from Lebanese cedar.[122] This has been seized on by those who wish to see *The Report of Wenamun* as reflecting a genuine mission rather than a tale of the "state of the nation."

ROYAL SONS AT THE KHONSU TEMPLE

The most famous scene on the walls of the Khonsu Temple shows the procession of the sons of Herihor, located immediately below the scene of the towing of the barks of the Theban triad at the Opet Festival. Historically, the main point at issue is the extent to which this scene supports the notion that Piankh was the son of Herihor. Based on a misinterpretation by Lepsius, it was taken as evidence of such relationship, but the careful publication of the monument by the University of Chicago has shown this not to be the case.[123]

The processional scene from the Khonsu temple consists of a row of royal sons above a row of royal daughters. The procession of royal sons (fig. 9.2) is not directly similar to those of Ramesses II or III, discussed above, particularly inasmuch as the procession is led by a queen, the great royal wife Nodjmet, and because all nineteen royal sons are named. However, one similarity that this scene does share with its Ramesses II and III predecessors is that the first three princes are given specific distinction, by bearing ostrich-feather fans and wearing overgarments while the remaining sons carry bouquets and have short kilts and sashes—in fact, this seems to be copied from the Ramesses II tradition rather than that of Ramesses III, as at the Luxor Temple (plate 9.2).

There is a regularity in the way the sons are identified; the sixteen bouquet carriers have outstretched left arms, above which is the label "King's son of his body," while below each arm is the son's name—none is given a title. In contrast, the first three sons have priestly and administrative titles in addition to their filiations. The main point of interest in the procession of the sons (apart from their remarkable number apparently born to a single mother) is the mixture of Egyptian and Libyan names they bear. While most, like Herihor himself, bear identifiable Egyptian appellations, sons 7 (Masaharta), 8

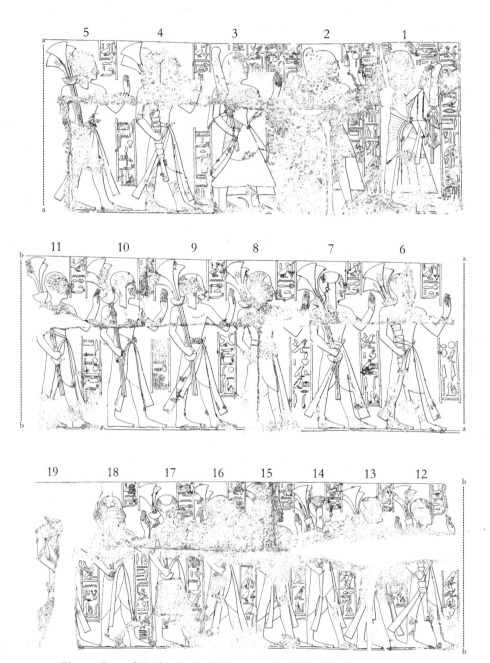

Fig. 9.2. Sons of Herihor in the Khonsu temple. (After *Khonsu* I, pls. x–xi.
Courtesy of the Oriental Institute of the University of Chicago.)

Plate 9.2. First four sons of Ramesses II at Luxor. (Photo by S. Snape.)

(Masaqaharta), 16 (Nawasun), 17 (Osorkon), and 19 (Madenen) have names that identify them as Libyans. The odd man out in the list is son 18, the "God's Father of Amun, Espaneferhor, son of Pinudjem" whose name and title is a recutting over an erasure.[124] The implications of these Libyan names being given to children of such an obviously high-ranking figure have been much debated.

We know nothing of Herihor's ancestors, which is a little strange given the later emphasis on genealogies as part of the assertion of Libyan identity, but Herihor may well be trying to formulate an appropriately royal identity for himself within what he perceives to be appropriate Egyptian models of self-presentation. He has an Egyptian name, as does his wife, Nodjmet, which reveals little about the reality of the ethnic identity of this couple. It is easier to imagine Herihor as a Libyan with an Egyptian name giving traditional Libyan names to some of his children than as an Egyptian giving his Egyptian children Libyan names when they had no precedent of associated authority (e.g., the later King Osorkon).

However, the presence of this row of "royal" sons at Karnak may be used to draw some wider conclusions about the nature of the Libyan ascendancy at the end of the New Kingdom. The first and rather obvious point is that these Libyans, though possessed of their own specific Libyan identity, were nonetheless willing and able to use Egyptian prototypes for appropriate self-presentation as Egyptian rulers. It is by no means unlikely that Herihor had the degree of iconographic sophistication necessary to present himself at the Khonsu temple not just as a king doing kingly things but as one who could make specific reference to other monuments, namely, those of Ramesses II and Ramesses III.

It is also possible that this particular means of self-presentation fitted perfectly well within Libyan notions of the importance of kinship structures at the level of paramount leader. The role of the "tribal leader" among Libyan groups in Egypt had shifted from that of "cultural broker,"[125] at the time of their attempted acculturation by the Egyptian state, to one where they are now the leaders of that state, whose cultural identity is likely to have been sustained through safeguarding traditional kinship structures. It may be that O'Connor's hypothesis[126] concerning the "nomadic state" as a model for Libyan political organization might be given a speculative revision in that the notion of a "nomadic state" and its establishment in Egypt does not necessarily require the acquisition of territory and the sedentarization of the nomadic group on that territory, thus forming a foothold for later expansion.

What may have been happening, particularly in the Delta, during the

Twentieth Dynasty was not necessarily the evolution of a political structure and social differentiation and social stratification of a type recognizable to the Egyptians among the West Delta Libyans in territory they controlled. Instead, it may have been that a more important factor, particularly among the East Delta Libyans, was the cohesive and leadership role, at least at the "clan" level, provided by bonds of kinship. Kinship among nomadic groups is a well-studied area, although there is little consensus about a universally applicable level of importance for this feature among various nomadic groups. In economic terms, Khazanov stresses the importance of "neighbourliness" rather than kinship as the most important social institution for the operation of economic aspects of a nomadic lifestyle.[127]

However, with the dislocation of communities and the economic basis of a pastoralist lifestyle, kinship would become the dominant aspect of interaction, given that social function would become more important with the radical change in economic activity. One might therefore speculate that the kinship structure that was the bedrock of the immigrant Libyan community in Egypt gave them a particular advantage at a time of political and economic disintegration, because of the flexibility and continued effectiveness of that structure. Herihor, at the Khonsu temple, may be displaying for our admiring view not merely the Egyptian "King's sons of his body" but also a unit of his Libyan segmentary lineage system,[128] his *mhwt,* his "tribe."

Notes

1. For a royal statue cult of Ramesses III at Memphis, see Schulman (1963). These statue cults were an important aspect of Ramesses II's projection of aspects of his own divinity during his lifetime; see Habachi (1969).

2. See chapter 6 in this volume.

3. See chapter 6 above.

4. For a summary of the history of the papyrus, and its study, see Grandet (1994) 3–18.

5. Vernus (1990) 46.

6. Goedicke (1963) 92.

7. Grandet (1994) 15 n. 43.

8. PM II.502–3.

9. *MH* V, pl. 301.

10. *MH* V, pl. 299.

11. *MH* V, pl. 302.

12. Adapted from *MH* V, pl. 301, apart from the final three unnamed sons from this group.

13. PM II.308, reproduced here as plate 9.2.

14. Probably this rather than *Ìmn-nṯr-ḥḳȝ-Ìwnw*?

15. Conveniently summarized in Peden (1994a).

16. P. Turin Cat. 1949+1946 verso; *KRI* V.557–58.

17. O. Deir el-Medina 0039 recto 16: *KRI* V.553.5.

18. The theory, first promoted by Cerny (1936), was questioned by Helck (1959) but supported by Goedicke (1963).

19. O. Deir el-Medina 0040 rt. 2: *KRI* VI.106.4.

20. O. Deir el-Medina 0040 rt. 14–15: *KRI* VI.107.1–2.

21. Peden (1994a) 15; Kitchen (1987) 137.

22. The problem of exactly when in year 2 this change took place is discussed in Peden (1994a) 15 n. 2.

23. E.g., Ritner (1997); Leblanc (2001). A readable overview of the Harem Conspiracy papyri and their contents can be found in Redford (2002).

24. See n. 1 above.

25. Worthington (2001).

26. Koenig (1989).

27. Loffet and Matoian (1996) 29.

28. Koenig (2001).

29. Groll (1980) 67.

30. Goedicke (1963) 92.

31. Grandet (1993) 341.

32. Leblanc (2001) 163.

33. For a probable family tree for the Twentieth Dynasty and discussion of the evidence, see Dodson and Hilton (2004) 186–87.

34. For a summary, see Kitchen (1982) esp. 116 n. 1.

35. Altenmüller (1994b) and references cited.

36. For a summary of the activities of this more energetic late Ramesside ruler, see Amer (1985).

37. Eyre (1980). For the accession dates of the kings of the Twentieth Dynasty, see Demarée (1993) 52; Beckerath (2002).

38. On a fragmentary doorjamb from Deir el-Medina, Ramesses VII honors Ramesses VI as "his father." See Kitchen (1972) 182.

39. Leblanc (2001) 158–59.

40. For a discussion of his monuments, including his tomb, KV 18, see Jenni (2000).

41. Bierbrier (1975b).

42. Kitchen (1995) 246.

43. Illustrated most graphically by the table in Trigger et al. (1983) 228, fig. 3.10.

44. Especially the Abbott and Leopold-Amherst papyri and Papyrus Mayer B: see Peden (1994b) 225–64.

45. PM VII.381.

46. Kitchen (1984c) 124.

47. Finkelstein (2000) 161–62.

48. On the basis of the evidence of scarabs bearing royal names, however, there seems to be continuity of Egyptian control from Ramesses III to Ramesses IV at Megiddo, Beth Shan, Gezer, Ashdod, and Tell Far'ah South at least. See Brandl (2004) 61.

49. Weinstein (1998) 191.

50. It must be noted, however, that in the case of both Merenptah and Ramesses III, these campaigns were launched against Libyan groups who had already penetrated and were established in northern Egypt.

51. Leahy (1985) 53.

52. For this, see the discussion of Ramesses III's Libyan Wars in this volume.

53. Trigger et al. (1983) 272.

54. The term is discussed in Morris (2005) 820–21 and passim.

55. Morris (2005) 96 n. 252; *Urk* IV.690.

56. *KRI* II.206.15–16; *RITA* II.67.

57. *RITANC* II.118.

58. *KRI* II.406.4; *RITA* II.232.

59. *KRI* 289.16; *RITA* II.119.

60. *KRI* V.91. These attempts may well have been viewed in a somewhat sardonic light by Deir el-Medina villagers, who were not long spared from the attentions of Libyans who were less well acculturated.

61. The word has no hieroglyphic determinative for a building, but "fortresses" is probably correct here; see Peden (1994b) 15.

62. *KRI* 24.2–3.

63. Grandet (1994) 337.

64. O'Connor (1990) makes the important point that in the New Kingdom, the term *mhwt*, although originating in general terms for "family," is only applied to nomadic, non-Egyptian groups, specifically the Libyans and the Shasu (Giveon [1971] 240–41), where, by context, it must refer to a large familial grouping, perhaps a "clan" or "tribe." In addition, there seem to be distinctions among the words used for leaders among the Libyans, with *wr* referring to something like a paramount leader, while ꜥꜣ referred to an "elder" or "clan chief." In this context, it is appropriate that the charge over the settled Libyans goes not to the dispossessed *wr* (presumably pharaoh is now the *wr*) but to ancestral chiefs.

65. Peden (1994b) 217.

66. O'Connor (1990) 79–80.

67. Morris (2005) 734.

68. *KRI* V.270; Kessler (1975).

69. Grandet (1994) 203–4.

70. Gardiner (1941–48). Note also that the same document refers to settled Tjuku Libyans in the vicinity of Herakleopolis.

71. Kitchen (1990) 21.

72. Leahy (1985) 53.

73. Leahy (1999b) 446.

74. Haring (1997) 69–70.

75. Grandet (1994) 304–6.

76. At Tell Abqa'in, Kom Firin, and Kom el-Hisn—see Snape (2003).

77. E.g., Nebesheh (PM IV.8), Qantir (PM IV.10; *KRI* V.258), Tell Umm Harb (PM IV.44), Tell Rataba (PM IV.55).

78. E.g. Bubastis (PM IV.29; *KRI* V.259), Mendes (PM IV.35), Leontopolis (PM IV.38; *KRI* V.259), Tanis (PM IV.17, 25; *KRI* V.248–49, 258–59).

79. Du Mesnil du Buisson (1929) 164.

80. O. Deir el-Medina 35; *KRI* V.520–21.

81. *KRI* VI.342–43.

82. O. Cairo 25.254; *KRI* VI.343.

83. Amer (1985).

84. PM II.141.

85. The most useful summary of this material is in Haring (1992).

86. *KRI* VI.608–9; Haring (1992) 73.

87. Haring (1992) 73.

88. *KRI* VI.637–39.

89. Bakry (1971) 143.

90. Darnell (2002) 151:

91. For the former view, see Gutgesell (1983) 143.

92. Haring (1992) 76.

93. Haring (1997) 279.

94. BM 10068; Peet (1930) 79ff. The text discussed here is dated to year 12 of an unnamed king, but since it is on the verso of a text dated to year 17 of Ramesses IX, Ramesses XI is one of only two serious contenders, the other being the *wḥm mswt* itself.

95. Kemp (1972) 665–66.

96. BM 10053; Peden (1994b) 265–70.

97. P. Louvre 3169; Kitchen (1994) 22–23.

98. Thijs (2005) 77 n. 33.

99. P. Jud. Turin 4, 15: Peden (1994b) 203.

100. Peet (1930) 153.

101. Epigraphic Survey (1979) 4 and pl. 14.

102. Epigraphic Survey (1979) xiii–xiv. That El-Hibeh was the findspot for the *We-namun* papyrus may not be coincidental.

103. For a convenient translation, see Peden (1994b) 271–76.

104. The Egyptian form of his name, like the Manethonian Greek, implies an association with the Delta city of Mendes.

105. The earlier date is from the so-called Banishment Stela; the later is from Manetho.

106. Jansen-Winkeln (1992); Thijs (2005).

107. Thijs (1998b) 106. For a variant view, see Broekman (2002).

108. P. Bibliothèque Nationale 197, I; Haring (1992) 77–78.

109. BM EA 75019+10302; Demarée (2006) 15–18. This letter refers to the "great ones" (ꜥꜣw) of the Meshwesh who were with Piankh (or, possibly, Panehesy?) and specifically to the *wr* Imtuy and one hundred chariots. The fragmentary end of the letter makes some reference to a *nḫt*-fortress.

110. Peet (1930).

111. Leahy (1985) 51.

112. Leahy (1985) 54.

113. Simpson (2002).

114. Richardson (1999).

115. An awareness of ancestry and displayed genealogy was not unknown to New Kingdom Egyptians themselves. See chapter 4 in this volume.

116. Kitchen (1986) 105 and references cited.

117. Leahy (1985) 54.

118. PM II.224–44. See especially Epigraphic Survey 2 (1981) xvii ff.

119. Epigraphic Survey (1981) xviii n. 9.

120. Epigraphic Survey (1981) xviii.

121. Bonhême (1987) 26–34.

122. Epigraphic Survey (1981) 30, pl. 143C.

123. Epigraphic Survey (1979) x–xi.

124. Epigraphic Survey (1979) 13 n. j.

125. Obermeyer (1973).

126. O'Connor (1990) 107–8.

127. Khazanov (1994) 135.

128. Bastug (1998).

Contributors

ERIC H. CLINE

Eric H. Cline is associate professor of classics, history, and anthropology and chair of the Department of Classical and Near Eastern Languages and Civilizations at the George Washington University, in Washington, DC. He received his Ph.D. in ancient history from the University of Pennsylvania. His specialty is interconnections in the ancient world during the Late Bronze Age. He has published extensively, including *The Battles of Armageddon: Megiddo and the Jezreel Valley from the Bronze Age to the Nuclear Age* (Ann Arbor: University of Michigan Press, 2000) and *Sailing the Wine-Dark Sea: International Trade and the Late Bronze Age Aegean* (Oxford: Tempus Reparatum, 1994). He was coeditor of *Amenhotep III: Perspectives on His Reign* (Ann Arbor: University of Michigan Press, 1998).

CHRISTOPHER J. EYRE

Christopher J. Eyre is professor of Egyptology at the University of Liverpool. He received his M.A. and D.Phil. from Oxford University. His primary research interests and principal areas of publication lie in the realm of social and economic history. He wrote *The Cannibal Hymn: A Cultural and Literary Study* (Liverpool: Liverpool University Press, 2002), edited the *Proceedings of the Seventh International Congress of Egyptologists, Cambridge, 3–9 September 1995* (Leuven: Peeters, 1998), and has published extensively elsewhere, including contributions to *A Late Egyptian Grammar* (Rome: Editrice Pontificio Istituto Biblico, 1993) and *The Memphite Tomb of Horemheb, Commander-in-Chief of Tut'ankhamun* (London: Egypt Exploration Society, 1989).

OGDEN GOELET, JR.

Ogden Goelet, Jr., is a research professor in Egyptian language and culture in the Department of Middle Eastern and Islamic Studies at New York University. He holds a B.A. from Harvard University and a Ph.D. from Columbia University. He has published extensively on Egyptian literature, the *Book of the Dead,* and the Ramesside period. He codirects an epigraphical expedition at the Ramesses II temple at Abydos.

PETER W. HAIDER

Peter W. Haider is associate professor of ancient history and comparative historical science (emeritus) at the Institute of Ancient History and the Ancient Near East at the University of Innsbruck, Austria. He studied ancient history, classical archaeology, ancient Near Eastern studies, and Egyptology. He received his Ph.D. and his Ph.Habil. in ancient history and comparative historical science from the University of Innsbruck. His specialities are ancient religions, interconnections and intercultural contacts, and transfer of cultural assets in the ancient world from the Bronze Age to the Roman Empire. Apart from seventy-five papers, he has published several books, including *Griechenland–Nordafrika* (Darmstadt: Wissenschaftliche Buchgesellschaft, 1988), *Religionsgeschichte Syriens: Von den Anfängen bis zur Gegenwart* (Stuttgart: Kohlhammer, 1996), and *Einblicke in die Religion Altägyptens* (Innsbruck: Studien Verlag, 2002).

CAROLYN R. HIGGINBOTHAM

Carolyn R. Higginbotham is professor of Hebrew Bible at Christian Theological Seminary in Indianapolis, Indiana. She received her Ph.D. in Near Eastern studies (Hebrew Bible) from the Johns Hopkins University. She has published several articles on the Ramesside period as well as *Egyptianization and Elite Emulation in Ramesside Palestine: Governance and Accommodation on the Imperial Periphery* (Leiden: Brill, 2000).

KENNETH A. KITCHEN

Kenneth A. Kitchen is emeritus professor of Egyptology at the University of Liverpool. He is a leading expert on the Nineteenth Dynasty and on the international connections of Egypt during the New Kingdom period. He is the author of numerous books and articles, including *Pharaoh Triumphant: Life and Times of Ramesses II, King of Egypt* (Warminster: Aris and Phillips, 1982), *The Third Intermediate Period in Egypt, 1100–650 B.C.* (Warminster: Aris and Phillips, 1986), and a series of volumes on Ramesside inscriptions.

BOJANA MOJSOV

Bojana Mojsov holds a Ph.D. from the Institute of Fine Arts at New York University. She has published several papers on the Ramesside period and two books entitled *Osiris: Death and Afterlife of a God* (Oxford: Blackwell, 2005) and *Alexandria Lost* (London: Duckworth, 2010). Dr. Mojsov has been a member of the Egyptological team working to update the documentation of the tomb of Seti I in the Valley of the Kings, Luxor.

DAVID O'CONNOR

David O'Connor is the Lila Acheson Wallace Professor of Ancient Egyptian Art at the Institute of Fine Arts at New York University. Formerly professor of Egyptology at the University of Pennsylvania for many years, he received his Ph.D. in Egyptology from Cambridge University. He has published extensively, including *Ancient Nubia: Egypt's Rival in Africa* (Philadelphia: University Museum Press, 1993), and coauthored *Ancient Egypt: A Social History* (Cambridge: Cambridge University Press, 1983). His latest book is *Abydos: Egypt's First Pharaohs and the Cult of Osiris* (Thames and Hudson, 2009). He was coeditor of *Amenhotep III: Perspectives on His Reign* (Ann Arbor: University of Michigan Press, 1998).

STEVEN R. SNAPE

Steven R. Snape is senior lecturer in Egyptian archaeology at the University of Liverpool, from where he also received his B.A. and Ph.D. He is also keeper of the Garstang Museum of Archaeology at Liverpool. His primary research interest concerns Egyptian imperial activity in the Ramesside period, especially in contact with Libyan groups. He has excavated extensively in Egypt, most notably at the Ramesside fortress town of Zawiyet Umm el-Rakham, a site on which he has published widely, including (with P. Wilson) *Zawiyet Umm el-Rakham I: The Temple and Chapels* (Bolton: Rutherford, 2007).

EMILY TEETER

Emily Teeter is a research associate and coordinator of special exhibits at the Oriental Institute of the University of Chicago. She received her Ph.D. from that institution's Department of Near Eastern Languages and Civilizations. Dr. Teeter is the author of a wide range of scholarly and popular books and articles. For the past decade, she has been working on the publication of the small finds from the Oriental Institute's excavation at Medinet Habu from 1926 to 1933.

JAMES M. WEINSTEIN

James M. Weinstein is editor of the *Bulletin of the American Schools of Oriental Research* and an adjunct professor of classics in the Department of Classics at Cornell University. He received his Ph.D. in Egyptology from the University of Pennsylvania and is the author of numerous articles.

Bibliography

Abitz, F.

1984   *König und Gott: Die Götterszenen in den ägyptischen Königsgräbern von Thutmosis IV. bis Ramses III.* Wiesbaden: Otto Harrassowitz.

1986   *Ramesses III in den Graebern seiner Sohne.* Orbis Biblicus et Orientalis 72. Freiburg and Gottingen: Schweiz Universitätsverlag

Adrom, F.

2006   *Die Lehre des Amenemhet.* Bibliotheca Aegyptiaca 19. Turnhout: Brepols.

Aldred, C.

1961   *The Egyptians.* New York: Frederick A. Praeger.

1979a   Statuaire. In *Le Monde Egyptien*, vol. II, *L'Empire des Conquérants*, ed. J. Leclant, 139–203. Paris: Gallimard.

1979b   More Light on the Ramesside Tomb Robberies. In *Glimpses of Ancient Egypt: Studies in Honour of H. W. Fairman*, ed. John Ruffle, G. A. Gaballa, and Kenneth A. Kitchen, 92–99. Warminster: Aris and Phillips.

Ali, M. S.

2001   Die Kursivhieroglyphen: Eine paläographische Betrachtung. *GM* 180:9–21.

Allam, S.

1973   *Hieratische Ostraka und Papyri aus der Ramessidenzeit.* Tübingen: Im Selbstverlag des Herausgebers.

1997   La vie municipale à Deir el-Médineh: Les supérieurs (*Hwtjw/Hntjw*) du village. *BIFAO* 97:1–17.

Allam, S., ed.

1994   *Grund und Boden in Altägypten.* Tübingen: Im Selbstverlag des Herausgebers.

Allen, J. P.

1989   The Cosmology of the Pyramid Texts. *Yale Egyptological Studies* 3:89–101.

1994   Colloquial Middle Egyptian: Some Observations on the Language of Heqa-Nakht. *LingAeg* 4:1–12.

2002   The Craft of the Scribe (Papyrus Anastasi I). In *The Context of Scripture,* vol. III, *Archival Documents from the Biblical World,* ed. William W. Hallo and K. L. Younger, Jr., 9–14. Leiden: E. J. Brill.

2003   Response to J. Baines. In *Egyptology at the Dawn of the Twenty-first Century,* ed. Z. Hawass and L. P. Brock, 3:27–28. Cairo: American University in Cairo Press.

2009   Old and New in the Middle Kingdom. In *Archaism and Innovation. Studies in the Culture of Middle Egyptian Egypt,* ed. David P. Silverman et al., 263–75. New Haven and Philadelphia: Yale University and the University of Pennsylvania Museum.

Altenmüller, H.

1982   Tausret und Sethnacht. *JEA* 68:107–15.

1992   Bemerkungen zu den neugefundenen Daten im Grab der Königin Twosre (KV 14) im Tal der Könige von Theben. In *After Tutankhamun,* ed. C. N. Reeves, 141–64. London: Kegan Paul International.

1994a   Das Graffito 551 aus der thebanischen Nekropole. *SAK* 21:19–28.

1994b   Prinz Mentu-her-chopeschef aus der 20. Dynastie. *MDAIK* 50:1–12.

1996   Das präsumtive Begräbnis des Siptah. *SAK* 23:1–9.

Amer, A. M. A.

1985   Reflections on the Reign of Ramesses VI. *JEA* 71:66–70.

Andrzejewski, T.

1962   Le Livre des Portes dans la salle du sarcophage du tombeau de Ramses III. *ASAE* 57:1–6.

Anthes, R.

1930   Die Vorfuehrung der Gefangenen Feinde vor dem Koenig. *ZÄS* 65:26–35.

Arnold, D.

1992   *Die Tempel Ägyptens: Götterwohnungen, Kultstätten, Baudenkmäler.* Düsseldorf: Artemis and Winkler.

2005   The Temple of Hatshepsut at Deir el-Bahri. In *Hatshepsut: From Queen to Pharaoh,* ed. C. Roehrig, 135–40. Metropolitan Museum of Art Series. New Haven: Yale University Press.

Artzy, M.

1997   Nomads of the Sea. In *Res Maritimae: Cyprus and the Eastern Mediterranean from Prehistory to Late Antiquity,* ed. S. Swiny, R. L. Hohlfelder, and H. W. Swiny, 1–16. Cyprus American Archaeological Research Institute Monograph Series, vol. 1; American Schools of Oriental Research Archaeological Reports, no. 4. Atlanta: Scholars Press.

2006   The Carmel Coast during the Second Part of the Late Bronze Age: A Center for Eastern Mediterranean Transshipping. *BASOR* 343:45–64.

Assmann, J.

1975   *Ägyptische Hymnen und Gebete.* Zurich: Artemis.

1977a   Fest des Augenblicks—Verheißung der Dauer: Die Kontroverse der ägyptischen Harfnerlieder. In *Fragen an die altägyptischen Literatur,* ed. J. Assmann et al., 55–84. Wiesbaden: Reichert.

1977b   Harfnerlieder. *LÄ* II.972–82.

1979   Weisheit, Loyalismus und Frömmigkeit. In *Studien zu altägyptischen Lebenslehre,* ed. E. Hornung and O. Keel, 11–17. Orbis Biblicus et Orientalis 28. Göttingen: Vandenhoeck und Ruprecht.

1980   Die "Loyalistische Lehre" Echnatons. *SAK* 8:1–32.

1983a   Die Rubren in der Überlieferung der Sinuhe-Erzählung. In *Fontes atque Pontes: Eine Festgabe für Hellmut Brunner,* ed. M. Görg, 18–43. Ägypten und Altes Testament 5. Wiesbaden: Otto Harrassowitz.

1983b   Schrift, Tod und Identität: Das Grab als Vorschule der Literatur im alten Ägypten. In *Schrift und Gedächtnis: Archäologie der literarischen Kommunkation,* vol. I, ed. A. Assmann, J. Assmann, and Chr. Hardmeier, 64–93. Munich: W. Fink.

1983/84   Krieg und Frieden im alten Ägypten: Ramses II. und die Schlacht bei Kadesch. *Mannheimer Forum* 83–84:173–231.

1984   Vergeltung und Erinnerung. In *Studien zu Sprache und Religion Ägyptens,* vol. 2, *Religion: Zu Ehren von Wolfhart Westendorf überreicht von seinen Freunden und Schülern,* ed. F. Junge, 687–701. Göttingen: Göttingen University.

1985   Gibt es eine "Klassik" in der ägyptischen Literaturgeschichte? Ein Beitrag zur Geistesgeschichte der Ramessidenzeit. In *XXII. Deutscher Orientalistentag: Vom 21. bis 25. März 1983 in Tübingen,* ed. W. Röllig, 35–52. ZDMG Supplement 6 Stuttgart: Franz Steiner.

1989   State and Religion in the New Kingdom. In *Religion and Philosophy in Ancient Egypt,* ed. J. P. Allen, J. Assmann, A. B. Lloyd, R. K. Ritner, and D. P. Silverman, 55–88. Yale Egyptological Studies 3. New Haven: Yale University Press.

1990   *Ma'at: Gerechtigkeit und Unsterblichkeit im Alten Ägypten.* Munich: C. H. Beck.

1995   *Egyptian Solar Religion in the New Kingdom: Re, Amun, and the Crisis of Polytheism.* Trans. A. Alcock. London: Kegan Paul International.

1996a   Der literarische Aspekt des ägyptischen Grabes und seine Funktion im Rahmen des "Monumentalen Diskurses." In *Ancient Egyptian Literature: History and Forms,* ed. A. Loprieno, 97–104. Probleme der Ägyptologie 10. Leiden: E. J. Brill.

1996b   Verkünden und Verklären: Grundformen Hymnischer Rede im Alten Ägypten. In *Ancient Egyptian Literature: History and Forms,* ed. A. Loprieno, 313–34. Probleme der Ägyptologie 10. Leiden: E. J. Brill.

2001   *The Search for God in Ancient Egypt.* Ithaca: Cornell University Press.

Assmann, J., and Blumenthal, E., eds.

1999   *Literatur und Politik im pharaonischen und ptolemäischen Ägypten.* Bibliothèque d'Étude 127. Cairo: Institut français d'archéologie orientale.

Athanasi, G. di

1836   *A Brief Account of the Researches and Discoveries in Upper Egypt, Made under the Direction of Henry Salt, esq.* London: J. Hearne.

Aufrère, S., Golvin, J.-Cl., and Goyon, J.-Cl.

1997   *L'égypte restituée.* Vol. I, *Sites, et temples de Haute Égypte.* Paris: Editions Errance.

Avner, U.
    1972   Naḥal Roded. *IEJ* 22:158.
Badawy, A.
    1968   *A History of Egyptian Architecture: The Empire.* Berkeley and Los Angeles: University of California Press.
Baer, K.
    1962   The low price of land in Ancient Egypt. *JARCE* 1:25–45.
Baines, J.
    1970   *Bnbn:* Mythological and Linguistic Notes. *Or* 39:389–404.
    1985   *Fecundity Figures.* Warminster: Aris and Phillips.
    1987   Practical Religion and Piety. *JEA* 73:79–98.
    1991   Society, Morality, and Social Practice. In *Religion in Ancient Egypt: Gods, Myths, and Personal Practice,* ed. Byron Schafer, 123–200. Ithaca: Cornell University Press.
    1994   Contexts of Fate: Literature and Practical Religion. In *The Unbroken Reed: Studies in the Culture and Heritage of Ancient Egypt in Honour of A. F. Shore,* ed. C. Eyre et al., 35–52. London: Egypt Exploration Society.
    1995   Kingship, Definition of Culture, and Legitimation. In *Ancient Egyptian Kingship,* ed. D. O'Connor and D. Silverman, 3–47. Probleme der Ägyptologie 9. Leiden: E. J. Brill.
    1996a   Classicism and Modernism in the Literature of the New Kingdom. In *Ancient Egyptian Literature: History and Forms,* ed. A. Loprieno, 157–74. Probleme der Ägyptologie 10. Leiden: E. J. Brill.
    1996b   Myth and Literature. In *Ancient Egyptian Literature: History and Forms,* ed. A. Loprieno, 361–77. Probleme der Ägyptologie 10. Leiden: E. J. Brill.
    1999   On *Wenamun* as a Literary Text. In *Literatur und Politik im pharaonischen und ptolemäischen Ägypten,* ed. J. Assmann and E. Blumenthal, 209–33. Bibliothèque d'Étude 127. Cairo: Institut français d'archéologie orientale.
    2003   Research on Egyptian Literature: Background, Definitions, Prospects. In *Egyptology at the Dawn of the Twenty-first Century,* ed. Z. Hawass and L. P. Brock, 3:1–26. Cairo: American University in Cairo Press.
Baines, J., and Parkinson, R. B.
    1997   An Old Kingdom Record of an Oracle? Sinai Inscription 13. In *Essays on Ancient Egypt in Honour of Herman te Velde,* ed. J. van Dijk, 9–27. Egyptological Memoirs. Gröningen: Styx.
Bakry, H.
    1971   The Discovery of a Temple of Sobk in Upper Egypt. *MDAIK* 27:131–46.
    1973   The Discovery of a Temple of Merenptah at On. *Aegyptus* 53:3–21.
Baldwin Smith, E.
    1938   *Egyptian Architecture as Cultural Expression.* New York: D. Appleton-Century.
Barako, T. J.
    2000   The Philistine Settlement as Mercantile Phenomenon? *AJA* 104:513–30.
    2007   *Tel Mor: The Moshe Dothan Excavations, 1959–1960.* IAA Reports, no. 32. Jerusalem: Israel Antiquities Authority.

Barguet, P.

    1962   *Le Temple d'Amon-Re a Karnak: Essaie d'exegese.* RAPH 21. Cairo: Institut français d'archéologie orientale.

Barns, J. W. B.

    1952   *The Ashmolean Ostracon of Sinuhe.* Oxford: Oxford University Press.

Barta, W.

    1978   Das Schulbuch Kemit. *ZÄS* 105:6–14.

Bass, G.

    1967   *Cape Gelidonya: A Bronze Age Shipwreck.* Transactions of the American Philosophical Society, n.s., 57, pt. 8. Philadelphia: American Philosophical Society.

    1997   Sailing between the Aegean and the Second Millenium BC. In *The Aegean and the Orient in the Second Millenium: Proceedings of the 50th Anniversary Symposium, Cincinnati, 18–20 April,* ed. E. Cline and D. Harris-Cline, 183–89. Liège: Universié de Liège; Austin: University of Texas.

Bastug, S.

    1998   The Segmentary Lineage System: A Reappraisal. In *Changing Nomads in a Changing World,* ed. J. Ginat and A. M. Khazanov, 94–123. Sussex: Sussex Academic Press.

Beckerath, J. von

    1984   *Handbuch der ägyptischen Königsnamen.* Münchner Ägyptologische Studien 20. Munich: Deutscher Kunstverlag.

    1992   Zur Geschichte von Chonsuemhab und dem Geist. *ZÄS* 119:90–107.

    1997a   *Chronologie des pharaonischen Ägypten.* Münchner Ägyptologische Studien 46. Mainz: P. von Zabern.

    1997b   Nochmals zu den Thronbesteigungsdaten Ramses' V. und VII. *GM* 157: 7–10.

    2001   Bemerkungen zur Chronologie der Grabräuberpapyri. *ZÄS* 127:111–16.

    2002   Zur Geschichte der mittleren XX. Dynastie. *GM* 188:15–19.

Beckman, G.

    1996   Texts: Akkadian/Ugarit. In *Sources for the History of Cyprus.* Vol. II, *Near Eastern and Aegean Texts from the Third to the First Millennia BC,* ed. A. B. Knapp, 26–28. Altamont, NY: Greece and Cyprus Research Center.

Beinlich-Seeber, C., and Shedid, A. G.

    1987   *Das Grab des Userhat (TT 56).* AV 50. Mainz: P. von Zabern.

Bell, L.

    1980   Only One High Priest Ramessenakht and the Second Prophet Nesamun His Younger Son. *Serapis* 6:7–27.

    1997   The New Kingdom "Divine Temple": The Example of Luxor. In *Temples of Ancient Egypt,* ed. B. Shafer, 127–84. Ithaca: Cornell University Press.

Belzoni, G.

    1820   *Narrative of the Operations and Recent Discoveries within the Pyramids, Temples, Tombs, and Excavations in Egypt and Nubia.* London: J. Murray. Reprint, Westmead: Gregg, 1971.

Benson, M., and Gourlay, J.

    1899   *The Temple of Mut in Asher.* London: J. Murray.

Berlin, I.

1999   *The Roots of Romanticism.* Princeton: Princeton University Press.

Betancourt, P. P.

2000   The Aegean and the Origin of the Sea Peoples. In *The Sea Peoples and Their World: A Reassessment,* ed. E. D. Oren, 297–303. University Museum Monograph 108. Philadelphia: University Museum, University of Pennsylvania.

Bianchi, R.

1988   *Cleopatra's Egypt: Age of the Ptolemies.* Catalog of an exhibition at the Brooklyn Museum, October 7, 1988– January 2, 1989. New York: Brooklyn Museum.

Bickel, S., and Mathieu, B.

1993   L'écrivain Amennakht et son *Enseignment. BIFAO* 93:31–59.

Bierbrier, M. L.

1972   A Second High Priest Ramessesnakht. *JEA* 58:195–99.

1975a   *The Late New Kingdom in Egypt (c. 1300–664 B.C.): A Genealogical and Chronological Investigation.* Warminster: Aris and Phillips.

1975b   The Length of the Reign of Ramesses X. *JEA* 61:251.

1977   Hoherpriester des Amun [in English]. *LÄ* II.1241–49.

Bietak, M.

1975   *Tell el-Daba.* Vol. II. Vienna: Österreichischen Akademie der Wissenschaften.

1991   Zur Landnahme Palästinas durch die Seevölker und zum Ende der ägyptischen Provinz Kana'an. *MDAIK* 47:35–50.

1993   The Sea Peoples and the End of the Egyptian Administration in Canaan. In *Biblical Archaeology Today, 1990: Proceedings of the Second International Congress on Biblical Archaeology, Jerusalem, June–July 1990,* ed. A. Biran and J. Amiran, 292–306. Jerusalem: Israel Exploration Society.

Birch, S.

1876   *Remarks upon the Cover of the Granite Sarcophagus of Ramesses III.* Cambridge: Cambridge Antiquarian Society.

Bissing, F. W. von

1914   *Denkmaeler aegyptischer Skulptur.* Munich: F. Bruckmann.

Bittel, K.

1983   Die archäologische Situation in Kleinasien um 1200 v.Chr. und während der nachfolgenden vier Jahrhunderte. In *Griechenland, die Ägäis und die Levante während der "Dark Ages" vom 12. Bis zum 9. Jh. v.Chr.,* ed. S. Deger-Jalkotzy, 25–47. Österreichische Akademie der Wissenschaften, philosophisch-historische Klasse, Sitzungsberichte, vol. 418. Vienna: Verlag der Österreichischen Akademie der Wissenschaften.

Björkman, G.

1971   *Kings at Karnak. A Study of the Treatment of the Monuments of Royal Predecessors in the Early New Kingdom.* Boreas 2. Uppsala: Almqvist und Wiksell.

Blackman, A. M.

1925   Oracles in Ancient Egypt. *JEA* 11:249–55.

1937   The Use of the Egyptian Word *Ht* "House" in the Sense of "Stanza." *Or* 7:64–66.

Bleiberg, E.

1985/86   Historical Texts as Political Propaganda. *BES* 7:5–13.

Blumenthal, E.

1972   Die Erzählung des Papyrus d'Orbiney als Literaturwerk. *ZÄS* 99:1–17.

1974   Eine neue Handschrift der "Lehre eines Mannes für seinen Sohn." In *Festschrift zum 150 jährigen Bestehen des Berliner Ägyptischen Museums,* ed. W. Müller, 55–66. Mitteilungen aus den Ägyptischen Sammlung 8. Berlin: Akademie Verlag.

Blyth, E.

2006   *Karnak: Evolution of a Temple.* London and New York: Routledge.

Bonhême, M.-A.

1987   *Les noms royaux dans L'Egypte de la troisième période intermédiaire.* Cairo: Institut français d'archéologie orientale.

Boorn, G. P. F. van den

1988   *The Duties of the Vizier: Civil Administration in the Early New Kingdom.* New York: Kegan Paul.

Boraik, M.

2007   Stela of Bakenkhonsu, High Priest of Amun-Re. *Memnonia* 18:119–26.

Borchardt, L.

1926   Jubilaeumsbilder. *ZÄS* 61:37–51.

1936   *Statuen und Statuetten von Koenige und Privatleuten im Museum von Kairo, Nos. 1542–1808.* Vol. II (Berlin, 1925). Catalogue general des antiquites egyptiennes du Musee du Caire. Berlin: Reichsdruckerei.

Borchhardt, H.

1972   *Homerische Helme.* Mainz: P. von Zabern.

Bosticco, S.

1965   *Le Stele Egiziane.* Pt. 2. Rome: Instituto Poligrafico.

Botti, G., and Peet, T. E.

1928   *Il giornale della necropoli di Tebe.* Turin: Fratelli Bocca.

Bowman, A. K., and Rogan, E., eds.

1999   *Agriculture in Egypt: From Pharaonic to Modern Times.* Proceedings of the British Academy 96. Oxford: Oxford University Press.

Brack, A., and Brack, A.

1980   *Das Grab des Haremheb: Theben Nr. 78.* AV 35. Mainz: P. von Zabern.

Brand, P. J.

2000   *The Monuments of Seti I: Epigraphic, Historical, and Art Historical Analysis.* Probleme der Ägyptologie 16. Leiden: E. J. Brill.

Brandl, B.

2004   Scarabs and Plaques Bearing Royal Names of the Early 20th Egyptian Dynasty Excavated in Canaan—from Sethnakht to Ramesses IV. In *Scarabs of the Second Millennium BC from Egypt, Nubia, Crete, and the Levant:*

Chronological and Historical Implications: Papers of a Symposium, Vienna, 10th–13th of January 2002, ed. M. Bietak and E. Czerny, 57–71. Denkschriften der Gesamtakademie, vol. 35. Vienna: Verlag der Österreichischen Akademie der Wissenschaften.

Breasted, J. H.

1912   *The Development of Religion and Thought in Ancient Egypt*. New York: Charles Scribner's Sons.

2001   *Ancient Records of Egypt*. Vols. 3– 4. Urbana: University of Illinois Press.

Broekman, G. P. F.

2002   The Founders of the Twenty-first Dynasty and Their Family Relationships. *GM* 191:11–18.

Brovarski, E.

1984   Sokar. *LÄ* III.1055–74.

Broze, M.

1997   *Les aventures d'Horus et Seth dans le Papyrus Chester Beatty I: Mythe et roman en Egypte ancienne*. Orientalia Lovaniensia Analecta 78. Louvain: Peeters.

Brug, J.

1985   *A Literary and Archaeological Study of the Philistines*. Oxford: British Archaeological Reports.

Brunner, H.

1957   *Altägyptische Erziehung*. Wiesbaden.

1958   Eine Dankstele an Upuaut. *MDAIK* 16:5–19.

1979a   Sokar im Totentempel Amenophis III. In *Festschrift für Elmar Edel*, ed. Manfred Görg and Edgar Pusch, 60–65. Ägypten und Altes Testament 1. Bamberg: M. Görg.

1979b   Zitate aus Lebenslehren. In *Studien zu altägyptische Lebenslehren*, ed. E. Hornung and O. Keel, 105–71. Orbis Biblicus et Orientalis 28. Göttingen: Vandenhoeck und Ruprecht.

1980   Kemit. *LÄ* III.383–84.

1986   Verspunkte. *LÄ* VI.1017–18.

Bruyère, B.

1930   *Meret Seger à Deir el Médineh*. MIFAO 58. Cairo: Institut français d'archéologie orientale.

Bryce, T. R.

1979   The Role of the Lukki People in Late Bronze Age Anatolia. *Antichthon* 13:1–11.

1986   *The Lycians: A Study of Lycian History and Civilisation to the Conquest of Alexander the Great*. Vol. 1, *The Lycians in Literary and Epigraphic Sources*. Copenhagen: Museum Tusculanum Press.

1992   Lukki Revisited. *JNES* 51:121–30.

Buchberger, H.

1983   Sexualität und Harfenspiel: Notizen zur "sexuellen" Konnotation der altägyptischen Ikonographie. *GM* 66:11–43.

1991   *Ḥtp ʿn ʾIpw-rs.ti:* Der Brief auf dem Gefäß München ÄS 4313. *SAK* 18: 49–87.

Buchholz, H.-G.

1959   Keftiubarren und Ertzhandel im zweiten vorchristlichen Jahrtausend. *Prähistorische Zeitschrift* 37:1–40.

1974   Ägäische Funde und Kultureinflüsse in den Randgebieten des Mittelmeers: Forschungsbericht über Ausgrabungen und Neufunde, 1960–1970. *Archäologischer Anzeiger des Deutschen Archäologischen Instituts* 89:325–462.

1988   Der Metallhandel des zweiten Jahrtausends im Mittelmeerraum. In *Society and Economy in the Eastern Mediterranean (c. 1500–1000 B.C.): Proceedings of the International Symposium Held at the University of Haifa from the 28th of April to the 2nd of May 1985*, ed. M. Heltzer and E. Lipinski, 187–228. Orientalia Lovanensia Analecta 23, Louvain: Peeters.

Budge, W.

1893   *A Catalogue of the Egyptian Collection in the Fitzwilliam Museum.* Cambridge: Cambridge University Press.

Buecher, P., and Leclant, J.

1956   La collection de L'Institut D'Égyptologie de l'Université de Strasbourg. *Bulletin de la Societe Academique du Bas-Rhin* 75–78 (n.s., 57–60): 100–109.

Bunimovitz, S.

1988–89   An Egyptian "Governor's Residency" at Gezer?—Another Suggestion. *Tel Aviv* 15–16:68–76.

Bunimovitz, S., and Faust, A.

2001   Chronological Separation, Geographical Segregation, or Ethnic Demarcation? Ethnography and the Iron Age Low Chronology. *BASOR* 322: 1–10.

Burkard, G.

1977   *Textkritische Untersuchungen zu ägyptischen Weisheitslehren des Alten und Mittleren Reiches.* Ägyptologische Abhandlungen 34. Wiesbaden: Otto Harrassowitz.

1996   Metrik, Prosodie und formaler Aufbau ägyptischer literarischer Texte. In *Ancient Egyptian Literature: History and Forms*, ed. A. Loprieno, 447–63. Probleme der Ägyptologie 10. Leiden: E. J. Brill.

Butzer, K. W.

1976   *Early Hydraulic Civilization in Egypt: A Study in Cultural Ecology.* Chicago: University of Chicago Press.

Calverly, A. M., and Broome, M. F.

1938   *The Temple of King Sethos I at Abydos.* Vol. 3, *The Osiris Complex.* London: Egypt Exploration Society; Chicago: University of Chicago Press.

Caminos, R. A.

1954   *Late-Egyptian Miscellanies.* Brown Egyptological Studies 1. London: Oxford University Press.

1968   A Fragmentary Hieratic School-Book in the British Museum. *JEA* 54:114–22.

1972   Another Hieratic Manuscript from the Library of Pwerem Son of Ḳiḳi." *JEA* 58:205–24.

1977   *A Tale of Woe.* Oxford: Griffith Institute.

1986   Some Comments on the Reuse of Papyrus. In *Papyrus: Structure and Usage,* ed. M. L. Bierbrier, 43–61. London: British Museum.

Capart, J., Gardiner, A. H., and van de Walle, B.

1936   New Light on the Ramesside Tomb-Robberies. *JEA* 22:169–93.

Cardon, P.

1980   Amenmesse: An Egyptian Royal Head of the Nineteenth Dynasty in the Metropolitan Museum. *MMJ* 14:5–14.

Cavillier, G.

2008   *Migdol: Richerche su modelli di architettura militare di età ramesside (Medinet Habu).* BAR International Series 1755. Oxford: Archaeopress.

Černý, J.

1934   Fluctuations in Grain Prices during the Twentieth Dynasty. *Archive Orientalni* 6:173–78.

1939   *Late Ramesside Letters.* Bibliotheca Aegyptiaca IX. Brussels: Édition de la Fondation égyptologique Reine Élisabeth.

1936   Das Datum des Todes Ramses III. und der Thronbesteigung Ramses IV. *ZÄS* 72:109–18.

1954   Prices and Wages in Egypt in the Ramesside Period. *Cahiers d'Histoire Mondiale* 1:903–21.

1958a   A Hieroglyphic Ostracon in the Museum of Fine Arts Boston. *JEA* 44:23–25.

1958b   Queen Ese of the Twentieth Dynasty and Her Mother. *JEA* 44:31–37.

1962   Egyptian Oracles. In *A Saite Oracle Papyrus from Thebes in the Brooklyn Museum (Papyrus Brooklyn 47.218.3),* ed. Richard A. Parker, 35–48. Providence: Brown University Press.

1973   *A Community of Workmen at Thebes in the Ramesside Period.* Bibliothèque d'Étude 50. Cairo: Institut français d'archéologie orientale.

Černý, J., and Groll, S. I.

1993   *A Late Egyptian Grammar.* 4th ed. Studia Pohl: Series Maior 4. Rome: Biblical Institute Press.

Chadefaud, C.

1982   *Les Statues porte-enseignes de l'Egypte ancienne (1580–1085 avant J.C.).* Paris: C. Chadefaud.

Chappaz, J.-L.

1989   Remarques sur un exercise scolaire. *Bulletin de la Société d'égyptologie de Genève* 13:33–43.

Chevrier, H.

1933   *Le Temple reposoir de Ramsès III: à Karnak.* Cairo: Institut français d'archéologie orientale.

Christophe, L. A.

1949   La stèle de l'an III de Ramsès IV au Ouâdi Hammâmât (no. 12). *BIFAO* 48:1–38.

Cifola, B.

1988   Ramses III and the Sea Peoples: A Structural Analysis of the Medinet Habu Inscriptions. *Or,* n.s., 57:275–306.

1991   The Terminology of Ramses III's Historical Records with a Formal Analysis of the War Scenes. *Or,* n.s., 60: 9–57.

Clayton, P.

1972   Royal Bronze Shabti Figurines. *JEA* 58:167–75.

Cline, E. H.

1991   Orientalia in the Late Bronze Age Aegean: A Catalogue and Analysis of Trade and Contacts between the Aegean and Egypt, Anatolia and the Near East. Ph.D. diss., University of Philadelphia.

1994   *Sailing the Wine-Dark Sea: International Trade and the Late Bronze Age Aegean.* BAR International Series 591. Oxford: Tempus Reparatum.

1995   Egyptian and Near Eastern Imports at Late Bronze Age Mycenae. In *Egypt, the Aegean, and the Levant: Interconnections in the Second Millenium BC,* ed. W. V. Davies and L. Schofield, 91–115. London: British Museum Press.

Cline, E. H., and O'Connor, D.

2003   The Mystery of the "Sea Peoples." In *Mysterious Lands,* ed. D. O'Connor and S. Quirke, 107–38. London: UCL Press.

Cline, E. H., and Yasur-Landau, A.

2009   Domination and (In)visibility: Reading Power Relations at Tel Mor. http://www.ajaonline.org/pdfs/book_reviews/113.1/00_Cline.pdf.

Cohen-Weinberger, A.

1998   Petrographic Analysis of the Egyptian Forms from Stratum VI at Tel Beth-Shean. In *Mediterranean Peoples in Transition, Thirteenth to Early Tenth Centuries BCE: In Honor of Professor Trude Dothan,* ed. S. Gitin, A. Mazar, and E. Stern, 406–12. Jerusalem: Israel Exploration Society.

Collombert, Ph., and Coulon, L.

2000   Les dieux contre la mer: Le début du "papyrus d'Astarté" (pBN 202). *BIFAO* 100:193–242.

Condon, V.

1978   *Seven Royal Hymns of the Ramesside Period: Papyrus Turin CG 54031.* Münchner Ägyptologische Studien 37. Munich: Deutscher Kunstverlag.

Cooney, K.

2000   The Edifice of Taharqa by the Sacred Lake: Ritual Function and the Role of the King. *JARCE* 37:15–50.

Coulon, L., Leclère, F., and Marchand, S.

1995   Catacombes osiriennes de Ptolémée IV à Karnak. *Cahiers de Karnak* X:205–52. Paris: Centre National de la Recherche Scientifique.

Cruz-Uribe, E.

1994   A Model for the Political Structure of Ancient Egypt. In *For His Ka: Essays Offered in Memory of Klaus Baer,* ed. D. P. Silverman, 45–53. Studies in Ancient Oriental Civilization 55. Chicago: Oriental Institute.

Daressy, G.

1897   *Notice explicative des ruines de Médinet Habou.* Cairo: Service des Antiquités de l'Égypte.

1902   *Fouilles de la Vallée des Rois (1898–1899).* Catalogue general des antiquites egyptiennes du Musee du Caire. Cairo: Institut français d'archéologie orientale.

1905   *Statues des divinites.* Vols. I–II. Catalogue general des antiquites egyptiennes du Musee du Caire. Cairo: Institut français d'archéologie orientale.

1917   Une inscription d'Achmoun et la géographie du nome Libique. *ASAE* 16:221–46.

Darnell, J. C.

2002   Opening the Narrow Doors of the Desert: Discoveries of the Theban Desert Road Survey. In *Egypt and Nubia: Gifts of the Desert,* ed. R. Friedman, 132–55. London: British Museum Press.

David, A. R.

1973   *Religious Ritual at Abydos (c. 1300BC).* Warminster: Aris and Phillips.

Davies, B. G.

1977   *Egyptian Historical Inscriptions of the Ninetheenth Dynasty, Documenta Mundi. Aegyptiaca* 2. Jonsered: Paul Åströms förlag.

Davies, N.

1926   *The Tomb of Huy.* London: Egypt Exploration Society.

Dawson, W. R.

1925   An Oracle Papyrus: B.M. 10335. *JEA* 11:247–48.

Deger-Jalkotzy, S.

1998   The Last Mycenaeans and Their Successors Updated. In *Mediterranean Peoples in Transition, Thirteenth to Early Tenth Centuries BCE: In Honor of Professor Trude Dothan,* ed. S. Gitin, A. Mazar, and E. Stern, 114–28. Jerusalem: Israel Exploration Society.

Del Monte, G. F., and Tischler, J.

1978   *Die Orts- und Gewässernamen der hethitischen Texte.* Répertoire Géographique des Textes Cunéiformes 6. Beihefte zum Tübinger Atlas des Vorderen Orients, Series B, no. 7/6. Wiesbaden: Reichert.

1992   *Die Orts- und Gewässernamen der hethitischen Texte.* Répertoire Géographique des Textes Cunéiformes 6/2. Beihefte zum Tübinger Atlas des Vorderen Orients, Reihe B, no. 7/6. Reprint. Wiesbaden: Reichert.

Demarée, R. J.

1993   The King Is Dead—Long Live the King. *GM* 137:49–52.

2002   *Ramesside Ostraca.* London: British Museum Press.

2006   *The Bankes Late Ramesside Papyri,* London: British Museum Press.

Demarée, R. J., and Egberts, A., eds.

2000   *Deir el-Medina in the Third Millennium AD: A Tribute to Jac. J. Janssen.* Egyptologische Uitgaven XIV. Leiden: Nederlands Institutet voor het Nabije Oosten.

Demarée, R. J., and Janssen, J. J., eds.

1982   *Gleanings from Deir el-Medîna.* Egyptologische Uitgaven I. Leiden: Nederlands Institutet voor het Nabije Oosten.

Derchain, Ph.

1975a   Le lotus, la mandragore et le perséa. *Chronique d'Égypt* 50:65–86.

1975b   La perruque et le crystal. *SAK* 2:56–74.

Der Manuelian, P.

    1975   Semi-literacy in Egypt: Some Erasures from the Amarna Period. In *Gold of Praise: Studies in Honor of Edward F. Wente,* ed. E. Teeter and J. A. Larson, 285–98. Studies in Ancient Oriental Civilization 58. Chicago: Oriental Institute.

Dever, W. G.

    1993   Gezer. In *The New Encyclopedia of Archaeological Excavations in the Holy Land,* ed. E. Stern, 2:496–506. New York: Simon and Schuster.

Dijk, J. van

    1994   The Nocturnal Wanderings of King Neferkare. In *Hommages à Jean Leclant,* ed. C. Berger et al., 4:387–93. Bibliothèque d'Étude 106, no. 4. Cairo: Institut français d'archéologie orientale.

Dodson, A.

    1986   Was the Sarcophagus of Ramesses III Begun for Sethos II? *JEA* 72:196–98.

Dodson, A., and Hilton, D.

    2004   *The Complete Royal Families of Ancient Egypt.* London: Thames and Hudson.

Donker van Heel, K., and Haring, B. J. J.

    2003   *Writing in a Workmen's Village: Scribal Practice in Ramesside Deir el-Medina.* Egyptologische Uitgaven XVI. Leiden: Nederlands Instituut voor het Nabije Oosten.

Doresse, M.

    1979   Le Dieu Voilé dans sa châsse et la Fête du Début de la Decade, IV: La Fête da la Décade. *RdÉ* 31:36–65.

Dorn, A.

    2004   Die Lehre Amunnachts. *ZÄS* 131:38–55.

    2006   *M33-nḫt.w=f,* ein(?)einfacher Arbeiter, Schreibt Briefe. In *Living and Writing in Deir el-Medine. Socio-historical Embodiment of Deir el-Medine Texts,* ed. A. Dorn and T. Hofmann, 67–85. *Aegyptiaca Helvetica* 19. Basel: Schwabe.

Dothan, M.

    1993   Mor, Tel. In *The New Encyclopedia of Archaeological Excavations in the Holy Land,* ed. E. Stern, 3:1073–74. New York: Simon and Schuster.

Dothan, M., and Porath, Y.

    1993   *Ashdod.* Vol. 5, *Excavation of Area G: The Fourth–Sixth Seasons of Excavations, 1968–1970.* 'Atiqot 23. Jerusalem: Israel Antiquities Authority.

Dothan, T.

    1982   *The Philistines and Their Material Culture.* New Haven: Yale University Press.

    1993   Deir el-Balaḥ. In *The New Encyclopedia of Archaeological Excavations in the Holy Land,* ed. E. Stern, 1:343–47. New York: Simon and Schuster.

    1995   The "Sea Peoples" and the Philistines of Ancient Palestine. In *Civilizations of the Ancient Near East,* ed. J. M. Sasson et al., 1267–79. Peabody, MA: Hendrickson.

1998   Initial Philistine Settlement: From Migration to Coexistence. In *Mediterranean Peoples in Transition, Thirteenth to Early Tenth Centuries BCE: In Honor of Professor Trude Dothan,* ed. S. Gitin, A. Mazar, and E. Stern, 148–61. Jerusalem: Israel Exploration Society.

2000   Reflections on the Initial Phase of Philistine Settlement. In *The Sea Peoples and Their World: A Reassessment,* ed. E. D. Oren, 145–58. University Museum Monograph 108. Philadelphia: University Museum, University of Pennsylvania.

Dothan, T., and Dothan, M.

1992   *People of the Sea: The Search for the Philistines.* New York: Macmillan.

Drenkhahn, R.

1980   *Die Elephantine-Stele des Sethnacht und ihr historischer Hintergrund.* Ägyptologische Abhandlungen 36. Wiesbaden: Otto Harrassowitz.

Drews, R.

1992   Herodotus 1.94, the Drought ca. 1200 BC, and the Origin of the Etruscans. *Historia* 41:14–39.

1993   *The End of the Bronze Age.* Princeton: Princeton University Press.

1998   Canaanites and Philistines. *JSOT* 81:39–61.

2000   Medinet Habu: Oxcarts, Ships, and Migration Theories. *JNES* 59 3: 161–90.

Drioton, E.

1939   Une statue prophylactique de Ramses III. *ASAE* 39:57–89.

du Mesnil du Buisson, R.

1929   Compte rendu sommaire d'une Mission à Tell el-Yahoudiyé. *BIFAO* 29:155–78.

Edel, E.

1961   Ein kairener fragment mit einem Bericht über den libyerkrieg Merneptahs. *ZÄS* 86:101–3.

1966   *Die Ortsnamenlisten Amenophis' III.* Bonner Biblische Beiträge 25. Bonn: Peter Hanstein Verlag.

1975   Neue Identifikationen topographischer Namen in den konventionellen Namenszusammenstellungen des Neuen Reiches. *SAK* 3:49–73.

1984   Die Sikeloi in den ägyptischen Seevölkertexten. *BN* 23:7–8.

1985   Der Seevölkerbericht aus dem 8. Jahr Ramses' III (*MH* II, pl. 46, 15–18): Übersetzung und Struktur. In *Mélanges Gamal Eddin Mokhtar,* I:223–37. Caire: Institut française d'archéologie orièntale.

Edgerton, W. F., and Wilson, J. A.

1936   *Historical Records of Ramses III: The Texts in "Medinet Habu" Volumes I and II Translated with Explanatory Notes.* Studies in Ancient Oriental Civilization 12. Chicago: University of Chicago Press.

Eichler, S. S.

2000   *Die Verwaltung des "Hauses des Amun" in der 18. Dynastie.* BSAK 7. Hamburg: Helmut Buske.

Eigner, D.

1984   *Die Monumenltalen Grabbauten der Spätzeit in der Thebanischen Nekropole.* Untersuchungen der Zweigstelle Kairo des Österreichischen

Archäologischen Instituts VI. Vienna: Österreichischen Akademie der Wissenschaften.

el-Sabban, S.

2000   *Temple Festival Calendars of Ancient Egypt.* Trowbridge: Liverpool University Press.

Endesfelder, E., et al.

1977   *Ägypten und Kusch.* Schriften zur Geschichte und Kultur des Alten Orients 13. Berlin: Akademie Verlag.

Epigraphic Survey

1930–70   *Medinet Habu.* Vols. I–VIII. Oriental Institute Publications. Chicago: University of Chicago Press.

1979   *The Temple of Khonsu.* Vol. I, *Scenes of King Herihor in the Court.* Oriental Institute Publications 100. Chicago: Oriental Institute.

1981   *The Temple of Khonsu.* Vol. II, *Scenes and Inscriptions in the Court and the First Hypostyle Hall.* Oriental Institute Publications 103. Chicago: Oriental Institute.

Erichsen, W.

1933   *Papyrus Harris I, Hieroglyphische Transkription.* Bibliotheca Aegyptiaca V. Brussels: Fondation Égyptologique Reine Élisabeth.

Erman, A.

1911   Denksteine aus der thebanischen Gräberstadt. *Sitzungsberichte der Preussischer Akademie der Wissenschaften, Berlin,* 1086–1110.

1925   *Die ägyptischen Schülerhandschriften.* APAW 1925, 2. Berlin: W. DeGruyter.

Eyre, C. J.

1979   A 'Strike' Text from the Theban Necropolis. In *Glimpses of Ancient Egypt: Studies in honour of H. W. Fairman,* ed. John Ruffle, G. A. Gaballa, and Kenneth A. Kitchen, 80– 91. Warminster: Aris and Phillips.

1980   The Reign-Length of Ramesses VII. *JEA* 66:168–70.

1984a   A Draughtsman's Letter from Thebes. *SAK* 11:195–207.

1984b   Crime and Adultery in Ancient Egypt. *JEA* 70:92–105.

1987a   Work and the Organization of Work in the New Kingdom. In *Labor in the Ancient Near East,* ed. Marvin A. Powell, 167–221. New Haven: American Oriental Society.

1987b   Papyrus Deir el-Medîna XXIV: An Appeal for Wages? *GM* 98:11–21.

1990   The Semna Stelae: Quotation, Genre, and Functions of Literature. In *Studies in Egyptology Presented to Miriam Lichtheim,* ed. S. I. Groll, I:134–65. Jerusalem: Magnes Press.

1992   The Adoption Papyrus in Social Context. *JEA* 78:207–21.

1994a   Feudal Tenure and Absentee Landlords. In *Grund und Boden in Altägypten,* ed. Schafik Allam, 107–33. Tübingen: Im Selbstverlag des Herausgebers.

1994b   The Water Regime for Orchards and Plantations in Pharaonic Egypt. *JEA* 80:57–80.

1996a   Ordre et désordre dans la campagne égyptienne. In *Égypte pharaonique: Pouvoir, société,* ed. B. Menu, 179–93. Méditerranées 6/7. Paris: L'Harmattan.

1996b   Is Egyptian Historical Literature "Historical" or "Literary"? In *Ancient*

Egyptian Literature: History and Forms, ed. A. Loprieno, 415–33. Probleme der Ägyptologie 10. Leiden: E. J. Brill.

1997   Peasants and "Modern" Leasing Strategies in Ancient Egypt. *Journal of the Economic and Social History of the Orient* 40, no. 4:367–90.

1999a   The Village Economy in Pharaonic Egypt. In *Agriculture in Egypt: From Pharaonic to Modern Times,* ed. A. K. Bowman and E. Rogan, 33–60. Proceedings of the British Academy 96. Oxford: Oxford University Press.

1999b   Irony in the Story of Wenamun: The Politics of Religion in the 21st Dynasty. In *Literatur und Politik im pharaonischen und ptolemäischen Ägypten,* ed. J. Assmann and E. Blumenthal, 235–52. Bibliothèque d'Étude 127. Cairo: Institut français d'archéologie orientale.

2000   Pouvoir central et pouvoirs locaux: Problèmes historiographiques et méthodologiques. In *Égypte pharaonique: Déconcentation, cosmopolitisme,* ed. B. Menu, 15–39. Méditerranées 24. Paris: L'Harmattan.

2004   How Relevant Was Personal Status to the Functioning of the Rural Economy in Pharaonic Egypt? In *La dépendence rurale en Égypte ancienne et dans l'Antiquité proche orientale,* ed. B. Menu. Cairo: Institut français d'archéologie orientale.

Fairman, H.

1938   Preliminary Report on the Excavation at Sudla, Sesebi, and Amara West, Anglo-Egyptian Sudan, 1937–1938. *JEA* 24:151–56.

1939   Preliminary Report on the Excavation at Amara West, Anglo-Egyptian Sudan, 1938–1939. *JEA* 25:139–44.

Faulkner, R. O.

1975   Egypt from the Inception of the Nineteenth Dynasty to the Death of Rameses III. In *The Cambridge Ancient History,* vol. 2, pt. 2, 217–51. Cambridge: Cambridge University Press.

1999   *A Concise Dictionary of Middle Egyptian.* Oxford: Oxford University Press.

Faust, M.

1969   Der ägäische Ortsname Mino(i)a. *Zeitschrift für vergleichende Sprachforschung* 83:88–107.

Fecht, G.

1963   Die Wiedergewinnung der altägyptischen Verskunst. *MDAIK* 19:54–96.

1964   Die Form der altägyptischen Literatur: Metrische und stilistische Analyse. *ZÄS* 91:11–63.

1965a   Die Form der altägyptischen Literatur: Metrische und stilistische Analyse Schluss. *ZÄS* 92:10–32.

1965b   *Literarische Zeugnisse zur "personliche Frömmigkeit" in Ägypten: Analyse der Beispiele in den ramessidischen Schulpapyri.* Heidelberg: Carl Winter Universitätsverlag.

1993   The Structural Principle of Ancient Egyptian Elevated Language. In *Verse in Ancient Near Eastern Prose,* ed. J. C. de Moor and W. G. E. Watson, 69–94. Neukirchen-Vluyn: Neukirchener Verlag.

Feldman, M.

2009   Hoarded Treasures: The Megiddo Ivories and the End of the Late Bronze Age. *Levant* 41:175–94.

Fimmen, D.
   1924   *Die kretisch-mykenische Kultur.* Leipzig and Berlin: B. G. Teubner.
Finkelstein, I.
   1995   The Date of the Settlement of the Philistines in Canaan. *Tel Aviv* 22: 213–39.
   1996   The Stratigraphy and Chronology of Megiddo and Beth-Shan in the 12th–11th Centuries B.C.E. *Tel Aviv* 23:170–84.
   1998a   Bible Archaeology or Archaeology of Palestine in the Iron Age? A Rejoinder. *Levant* 30:167–74.
   1998b   Philistine Chronology: High, Middle, or Low? In *Mediterranean Peoples in Transition, Thirteenth to Early Tenth Centuries BCE: In Honor of Professor Trude Dothan,* ed. S. Gitin, A. Mazar, and E. Stern, 140–47. Jerusalem: Israel Exploration Society.
   2000   The Philistine Settlements: When, Where, and How Many? In *The Sea Peoples and Their World: A Reassessment,* ed. E. D. Oren, 159–80. University Museum Monograph 108. Philadelphia: University Museum, University of Pennsylvania.
   2009   Destructions: Megiddo as a Case Study. In *Exploring the* Longue Durée: *Essays in Honor of Lawrence E. Stager,* ed. J. D. Schloen, 113–26. Winona Lake, IN: Eisenbrauns.
Finley, M.
   1963   *The Ancient Greeks.* New York: Viking.
Finnestad, R. B.
   1997   Temples of the Ptolemaic and Roman Periods: Ancient Traditions in New Contexts. In *Temples of Ancient Egypt,* ed. B. Shafer, 185–237. Ithaca: Cornell University Press.
   1999   Enjoying the Pleasures of Sensation: Reflections on a Significant Feature of Egyptian Religion. In *Gold of Praise: Studies on Ancient Egypt in Honor of Edward F. Wente,* ed. E. Teeter and J. A. Larson, 111–19. Studies in Ancient Oriental Civilization 58. Chicago: Oriental Institute.
Fischer, E.
   2007   *Ägyptische und ägyptisierende Elfenbeine aus Megiddo und Lachish: Inschriftenfunde, Flaschen, Löffel.* Alter Orient und Altes Testament, vol. 47. Münster: Ugarit-Verlag.
Fischer, H. G.
   1976a   *Egyptian Studies.* Vol. I, *Varia.* New York: Metropolitan Museum of Art.
   1976b   Archaeological Aspects of Epigraphy and Palaeography. In *Ancient Egyptian Epigraphy and Palaeography,* ed. H. G. Fischer and R. Caminos, 29–50. New York: Metropolitan Museum of Art.
   1977   *The Orientation of Hieroglyphs.* Pt. 1, *Reversals.* Egyptian Studies II. New York: Metropolitan Museum of Art.
Fischer-Elfert, H.-W.
   1983a   Morphologie, Rhetorik und Genese der Soldatencharakteristik. *GM* 66:45–65.
   1983b   *Die Satirische Streitschrift des Papyrus Anastasi I: Textzusammenstellung.* KÄT. Wiesbaden: Otto Harrassowitz.

1986a   *Die Satirische Streitschrift des Papyrus Anastasi I: Übersetzung und Kommentar.* Ägyptologische Abhandlungen 44. Wiesbaden: Otto Harrassowitz.

1986b   *Literarische Ostraka der Ramessidenzeit in Übersetzung.* KÄT. Wiesbaden: Otto Harrassowitz.

1991   Bemerkungen zum Feldinventar des Papyrus Louvre AF 6345 und der Griffith Fragments. *Enchoria* 18:27–36.

1993   Vermischtes II. *GM* 135:31–37.

1997   *Lesefunde im literarischen Steinbruch von Deir el-Medineh.* KÄT 12. Wiesbaden: Otto Harrassowitz.

1999   *Die Lehre eines Mannes für seinen Sohn: Eine Etappe auf dem "Gottesweg" des loyalen und solidarischen Beamten des Mittleren Reiches.* Ägyptologische Abhandlungen 60. Wiesbaden: Otto Harrassowitz.

2003   Representations of the Past in New Kingdom Literature. In *"Never Had the Like Occurred": Egypt's View of Its Past,* ed. W. J. Tait, 119–37. London: UCL Press.

2006   Literature as a Mirror of Private Affairs: The Case of *Mnn3* (i) and his son *Mrj-shm.t* (iii). In *Living and Writing in Deir el-Medine: Socio-historical Embodiment of Deir el-Medine Texts,* ed. A. Dorn and T. Hofmann, 87–92. Aegyptiaca Helvetica 19. Basel: Schwabe.

Foster, J. L.

1974   *Love Songs of the New Kingdom.* Austin: University of Texas Press.

1977   *Thought Couplets and Clause Sequences in a Literary Text: The Maxims of Ptahhotep.* Toronto: Society for the Study of Egyptian Antiquities.

1982   Cleaning up Sinuhe. *JSSEA* 12:81–85.

1984   Oriental Institute Ostracon 12074: "Menna's Lament" or "Letter to a Wayward Son." *JSSEA* 14:88–99.

1988   "The Shipwrecked Sailor": Prose or Verse? *SAK* 15:69–109.

1992   *Echoes of Egyptian Voices. An Anthology of Ancient Egyptian Poetry.* Oklahoma Series in Classical Culture 12. Norman: University of Oklahoma Press.

1993   *Thought Couplets in the "Tale of Sinuhe."* Münchner Ägyptologische Untersuchungen 3. Frankfurt.

1995   *Hymns, Prayers, and Songs: An Anthology of Ancient Egyptian Lyric Poetry.* Atlanta: Scholars Press.

2001   Lyric. In *Oxford Encyclopedia of Ancient Egypt,* ed. D. B. Redford, 2:312–17. Oxford: Oxford University Press.

Fox, M. V.

1977   A Study of Antef. *Or* 46:393–423.

1982   The Entertainment Song Genre in Egyptian Literature. In *Egyptological Studies,* ed. S. Groll, 268–316. Scripta Hierosolymita 28. Jerusalem: Magnes Press.

1985   *The Song of Songs and the Ancient Egyptian Love Songs.* Madison: University of Wisconsin Press.

Frandsen, P. J.

1990   Editing Reality: The Turin Strike Papyrus. In *Studies in Egyptology Pre-*

sented to Miriam Lichtheim, ed. S. I. Groll, I:166–99. Jerusalem: Magnes Press.

Frankfort, H.

1946   Myth and Reality. In *The Intellectual Adventure of Ancient Man,* ed. Henri Frankfort, John Wilson, Thorkild Jacobsen, and William Irwin, 2–27. Chicago: University of Chicago Press.

Frantz-Murphy, G.

1986   *The Agrarian Administration of Egypt from the Arabs to the Ottomans.* Cairo: Institut français d'archéologie orientale.

Frood, E.

2007   *Biographical Texts from Ramessid Egypt.* Society of Biblical Literature Writings from the Ancient World 26. Atlanta: Scholars Press.

Gaballa, G. A., and Kitchen, K. A.

1969   The Festival of Sokar. *Or* 38:1–76.

Gadot, Y.

2006   Aphek in the Sharon and the Philistine Northern Frontier. *BASOR* 341:21–36.

Gardiner, A. H.

1916   The Defeat of the Hyksos by Kamose: The Carnavon Tablet, no. 1. *JEA* 3:95–110.

1918   The Delta Residence of the Ramessides. *JEA* 5:127–38, 179–200, 242–71.

1931   *The Library of Chester Beatty: The Chester Beatty Papyri, No. I.* London: Oxford University Press.

1932   *Late-Egyptian Stories.* Bibliotheca Aegyptiaca I. Brussels: Édition de la Fondation égyptologique Reine Élisabeth.

1937   *Late-Egyptian Miscellanies.* Bibliotheca Aegyptiaca VII. Brussels: Édition de la Fondation égyptologique Reine Élisabeth.

1941a   Adoption Extraordinary. *JEA* 26:23–29.

1941b   Ramesside Texts Relating to the Taxation and Transport of Corn. *JEA* 27:19–73.

1941–48   *The Wilbour Papyrus.* 3 vols. Oxford: Oxford University Press.

1947   *Ancient Egyptian Onomastica.* Vols. I–II. London: Oxford University Press.

1955   *The Ramesseum Papyri: Plates.* Oxford: Oxford University Press.

1957   *An Egyptian Grammar.* 3rd ed. Oxford: Oxford University Press.

1960   *The Kadesh Inscriptions of Ramesses II.* Oxford: Griffith Institute.

1961   *Egypt of the Pharaohs.* Oxford: Oxford University Press.

Gardiner, A., Peet, T. E., and Černý, J.

1952   *The Inscriptions of Sinai.* Vol. I. Memoirs of the Egypt Exploration Society, vol. 36. London: Egypt Exploration Society.

1955   *The Inscriptions of Sinai.* Vol. II. Memoirs of the Egypt Exploration Society, vol. 45. London: Egypt Exploration Society.

Gasse, A.

1988   *Données nouvelles administratives et sacerdotales sur l'organisation du domaine d'amon XXe–XXIe dynasties à la lumière des papyrus Prachov, Reinhardt et Grundbuch (avec édition princeps des papyrus Louvre AF 6345 et 6346–7).* Cairo: Institut français d'archéologie orientale.

1992 Les ostraca hiératiques littéraires de Deir el-Medina: Nouvelles orienta-
tions de la publication. In *Village Voices: Proceedings of the Symposium
"Texts from Deir el-Medina and Their Interpretation," Leiden, May 31–
June 1, 1991*, ed. R. J. Demarée and A. Egberts, 51–70. Leiden: Nederlands
Institutet voor het Nabije Oosten.

Gessler-Löhr, B.

1989 Bemerkungen zu einigen *wbȝw njswt* der Nach-Amarnazeit. *GM* 112:27–34.

Gibson, M.

1987 Introduction to *The Organization of Power: Aspects of Bureaucracy in the
Ancient Near East*, ed. McGuire Gibson and Robert D. Biggs. Studies in
Ancient Oriental Civilization 46. Chicago: Oriental Institute.

Gilboa, A.

2005 Sea Peoples and Phoenicians along the Southern Phoenician Coast: A
Reconciliation; An Interpretation of Šikila (SKL) Material Culture.
BASOR 337:47–78.

Gillam, R. A.

2000 The Mehy Papers: Text and Lifestyle in Translation. *Chronique d'Égypte*
75:207–16.

Gilula, M.

1976 An Inscription in Egyptian Hieratic from Lachish. *Tel Aviv* 3:107–8.

Gitin, S., Mazar, A., and Stern, E., eds.

1998 *Mediterranean Peoples in Transition, Thirteenth to Early Tenth Centuries
BCE: In Honor of Professor Trude Dothan*. Jerusalem: Israel Exploration
Society.

Giveon, R.

1971 *Les bédouins Shosou des documents Égyptiens*. Documenta et Monumenta Orientis Antiqui, vol. 18. Leiden: E. J. Brill.

1983 An Inscription of Ramesses III from Lachish. *Tel Aviv* 10:176–77.

1985 Dating the Cape Gelidonya Shipwreck. *Anatolian Studies* 55:99–101.

Giveon, R., Sweeney, D., and Lalkin, N.

2004 The Inscription of Ramesses III. In *The Renewed Archaeological Excavations at Lachish (1973–1994)*, ed. D. Ussishkin, 3:1626–28. Monograph Series, no. 22. Tel Aviv: Emery and Claire Yass Publications in Archaeology,
Institute of Archaeology, Tel Aviv University.

Gnirs, A. M.

1989 Haremhab—ein Staatsreformator? Neue Betrachtungen zum Haremhab-
Dekret. *SAK* 16:83–110.

1996a *Militär und Gesellschaft: Ein Beitrag zur Sozialgeschichte des Neuen Reiches*. Studien zur Archäologie und Geschichte Altägyptens 17. Heidelberg: Heidelberger Orientverlag.

1996b Die ägyptische Biographie. In *Ancient Egyptian Literature: History and
Forms*, ed. A. Loprieno, 191–241. Probleme der Ägyptologie 10. Leiden: E.
J. Brill.

Goedicke, H.

1963 Was Magic Used in the Harem Conspiracy against Ramesses III? *JEA*
49:71–92.

1975   *The Report of Wenamun.* Baltimore: Johns Hopkins University Press.

1977   The Date of the "Antef-Song." In *Fragen an die altägyptischen Literatur,* ed. J. Assmann et al., 185–96. Wiesbaden: Reichert.

1986   Vergöttlichung. *LÄ* VI.989–92.

1988   *Studies in the Instruction of King Amenemhet for His Son.* Varia Aegyptiaca Supplement 2. San Antonio: Van Siclen Books.

Goedicke, H., and Wente, E. F.

1963   *Ostraka Michaelides.* Wiesbaden: Otto Harrassowitz.

Goelet, O.

1991   The Blessing of Ptah. In *Fragments of a Shattered Visage: Proceedings of the International Symposium on Ramesses the Great,* ed. E. Bleiberg and R. Freed, 28–37. Monographs of the Institute of Egyptian Art and Archaeology 1. Memphis, TN: Memphis State University.

1996   A New "Robbery" Papyrus: Rochester MAG 51.346.1. *JEA* 82:107–27.

2002   The Anaphoric Style in Egyptian Hymnody. *JSSEA* 28:75–89.

2003   Ancient Egyptian Scripts—Literary, Sacred, and Profane. In *Semitic Papyrology in Context: A Climate of Creativity; Papers from a New York University Conference Marking the Retirement of Baruch A. Levine,* ed. L. H. Schiffman, 1–21. Culture and History of the Ancient Near East. Vol. 14. Leiden: E. J. Brill.

2008   Writing Ramesside Hieratic: What the *Late-Egyptian Miscellanies* Tell Us about Scribal Education. In *Servant of Mut: Studies in Honor of Richard A. Fazzini,* ed. S. H. D'Auria, 102–10. Probleme der Ägyptologie 28. Leiden: E. J. Brill.

2010   Observations on Copying and the Hieroglyphic Tradition in the Production of the *Book of the Dead.* In *Offerings to the Discerning Eye: An Egyptological Medley in Honor of Jack A. Josephson,* ed. Sue H. D'Auria, 121–32. Leiden: Brill.

Goelet, O., and Levine, B.

1998   Making Peace in Heaven and on Earth: Religious and Legal Aspects of the Treaty between Ramesses II and Hattušili III. In *Boundaries of the Ancient Near Eastern World: A Tribute to Cyrus H. Gordon,* ed. M. Lubetsky et al., 252–99. Sheffield: Sheffield University Press.

Goldwasser, O.

1984   Hieratic Inscriptions from Tel Sera' in Southern Canaan. *Tel Aviv* 11:77–93.

1991a   An Egyptian Scribe from Lachish and the Hieratic Tradition of the Hebrew Kingdoms. *Tel Aviv* 18:248–53.

1991b   A Fragment of an Hieratic Ostracon from Tel Haror [in Hebrew]. *Qadmoniot* 24: 19.

1991c   On Dynamic Canonicity in Late-Egyptian: The Literary Letter and the Personal Prayer. *LingAeg* 1:129–41.

1999   "Low" and "High" Dialects in Ramesside Egyptian. In *Textcorpus und Wörterbuch: Aspekte zur ägyptischen Lexikographie,* ed. S. Grunert and I. Hafemann, 311–28. Probleme der Ägyptologie 14. Leiden: E. J. Brill.

2001   Poetic License in Nineteenth Dynasty Non-Literary Late Egyptian. *LingAeg* 9:123–38.

Goldwasser, O., and Wimmer, S.

1999 Hieratic Fragments from Tell el-Far'ah (South). *BASOR* 313:39–42.

Görg, M.

1991 "Travestie" im Hohen Lied. In *Aegyptiaca—Biblica,* 319–33. Ägypten und Altes Testament 11. Wiesbaden: Otto Harrassowitz.

Goyon, J.-C.

1971 Un parallele tardif d'une formule des inscriptions de la statue prophylactique de Ramses III au Musee du Caire (Papyrus Brooklyn 47.218.138, col.x+13, 9 a 15). *JEA* 57:154–59.

Graefe, E.

1979 König und Gott als Garanten der Zukunft. In *Aspekt der Spatägyptischen Religion,* ed. W. Westendorf, 47–78. Göttinger Orientforschungen series 4, vol. 9. Wiesbaden: Otto Harrassowitz.

Graindorge, C.

2000 Sokar. In *The Oxford Encyclopedia of Ancient Egypt,* ed. D. B. Redford, 3:305–7. Oxford: Oxford University Press.

Grandet, P.

1990 Un texte historique de Ramsès III à El-Kâb (et autres textes ramessides). *RdÉ* 41:95–99, pls. 5–6.

1993 *Ramsès III, histoire d'un règne.* Paris: Pygmalion Gérard Watelet.

1994 *Le Papyrus Harris I.* Vols. I–II. Bibliothèque d'Étude 109, nos. 1–2. Cairo: Institut français d'archéologie orientale.

1999 *Le Papyrus Harris I (BM 9999).* Vol. III. Bibliothèque d'Étude 129. Cairo: Institut français d'archéologie orientale.

2000 L'execution du chancelier Bay O.IFAO 1864. *BIFAO* 100:339–45.

2003 *Catalogue des ostraca non littéraires de Deir el-Medina.* Vol. IX. Cairo: Institut français d'archéologie orientale.

Grapow, H.

1936 *Sprachliche und schriftliche Formung ägyptischer Texte.* Leipziger Äegyptologische Studien 7. Glückstadt: J. J. Augustin.

Grdseloff, B.

1949 A New Middle Kingdom Letter from El-Lahun. *JEA* 35:59–62.

Groenewegen-Frankfort, H.

1951 *Arrest and Movement.* Reprint, Cambridge, MA: Belknap Press, 1987.

Groll, S. I.

1973a Late Egyptian of Non-literary Texts of the 19th Dynasty. In *Orient and Occident,* ed. H. A. Hoffner, 67–70. *Alter Orient und Altes Testament* 22. Kevalaer: Butzon und Bercker.

1973b A Note on the Hieratic Texts from Tel Sera' [in Hebrew]. *Qadmoniot* 6:56–57.

1980 The Stenographic Style of Papyrus Lee, Papyrus Rollin, Papyrus Varzy, and the Judicial Papyrus of Turin. In *The Bible World: Essays in Honor of Cyrus H. Gordon,* ed. G. Rendsburg, 67–77. New York: Ktav.

1982 Diachronic Grammar as a Means of Dating Undated Texts. In *Egyptological Studies,* ed. S. I. Groll, 11–104. Scripta Hierosolymitana 28. Jerusalem: Magnes Press.

1986   The *sḏm.n.f* Formations in the Non-literary Documents of the 19th Dynasty. In *Crossroad: Chaos or the Beginning of a New Paradigm,* ed. G. Englund and P. J. Frandsen, 167–79. CNI Publications 1. Copenhagen: Carsten Niebuhr Institute of Ancient Near East Studies.

Guglielmi, W.

1983   Eine "Lehre" für einen reiselustigen Sohn: Ostracon Oriental Institute 12704. *Die Welt des orient* 14:147–66.

1994   Berufssatiren in der Tradition des Cheti. In *Zwischen den beiden Ewigkeiten: Festschrift Gertrud Thausing,* ed. M. Bietak et al., 44–72. Vienna: Im Eigenverlag des Institutes für Ägyptologie der Universität Wien.

1996a   Der Gebrauch rhetorischer Stillmittel in der ägyptischen Literatur. In *Ancient Egyptian Literature: History and Forms,* ed. A. Loprieno, 465–97. Probleme der Ägyptologie 10. Leiden: E. J. Brill.

1996b   Die altägyptische Liebespoesie. In *Ancient Egyptian Literature: History and Forms,* ed. A. Loprieno, 335–47. Probleme der Ägyptologie 10. Leiden: E. J. Brill.

Guksch, H.

1994   "Sehnsucht nach der Heimatstadt": Ein ramessidisches Thema? *MDAIK* 50:101–6.

1995   *Die Gräber des Nacht-Min und des Men-cheper-Ra-seneb: Theben Nr. 87 und 79.* AV 34. Mainz: P. von Zabern.

Gutgesell, M.

1983   *Die Datierung der Ostraka und Papyri aus Deir el-Medina und ihre ökonomische Interpretation.* Hildesheim: Gerstenberg.

Habachi, L.

1969   *Features of the Deification of Ramesses II.* Abhandlungen des Deutschen Archäologischen Instituts, Abteilungen Kairo 5. Glückstadt: J. J. Augustin.

1972   *The Second Stela of Kamose and His Struggle against the Hyksos Ruler and His Capital.* AV 8. Glückstadt: J. J. Augustin.

1974   Three Large Rock-Stelae Carved by Ramesses III near the Quarries. *JARCE* 11:69–75.

Haeny, G.

1967   Zum Hohen Tor von Medinet Habu. *ZÄS* 94:71–78.

1981   (ed.) *Untersuchungen im Totentempel Amenophis III.* Beiträge zur Ägyptische Bauforschung und Altertumskunde 11. Wiesbaden: Franz Steiner.

1997   New Kingdom "Mortuary Temples" and "Mansions of Millions of Years." In *Temples of Ancient Egypt,* ed. B. Shafer, 86–90, 123–26. Ithaca: Cornell University Press.

Hagen, F.

2005   The Prohibitions: A New Kingdom Didactic Text. *JEA* 91:125–29.

2006   Literature, Transmission, and the Late Egyptian Miscellanies. In *Current Research in Egyptology 2004: Proceedings of the Fifth Annual Symposium, University of Durham 2004,* ed. R. J. Dann, 84–99. Oxford: Oxbow Books.

2007   Ostraca, Literature and Teaching at Deir el-Medina. In *Current Research in Egyptology 2005: Proceedings of the Sixth Annual Symposium Which*

Took Place at the University of Cambridge, 6–8 January 2005, ed. R. Mairs and A. Stevenson, 38–51. Oxford: Oxbow Books.

Haider, P. W.

1988   *Griechenland–Nordafrika*. Impulse der Forschung 53. Darmstadt: Wissenschaftliche Buchgesellschaft.

1999a   Zur historischen Geographie Westkleinasiens im 13. Jh. v.Chr. In *100 Jahre Österreichische Forschungen in Ephesos: Akten des Symposions Wien 1995*, ed. H. Friesinger and F. Krinzinger, 665–75. Vienna: Verlag der Österreichischen Akademie der Wissenschaften.

1999b   Vom Nil zum Mäander: Die Beziehungen zwischen dem Pharaonenhof und dem Königreich Arzawa in Westkleinasien. In *Steine und Wege: Festschrift für Dieter Knibbe zum 65. Geburtstag*, ed. P. Scharrer, H. Täuber, and H. Thür, 205–19. Vienna: Österreichisches Archäologisches Institut.

Haikal, F.

1997   Thoughts and Reflections on the Love Songs in Ancient Egypt. In *L'Imperio Ramesside: Convengo Internazionale in onore di Sergio Donandoni, Vicino Oriente*, ed. I. Brancoli et al., 77–85. Rome: Dipartimento di Scienze Storiche Archeologiche e Antropologiche nell'Antichità.

2003   Response to J. Baines. In *Egyptology at the Dawn of the Twenty-first Century*, ed. Z. Hawass and L. P. Brock, 3:29–32. Cairo: American University in Cairo Press.

Halpern, B.

2000   Centre and Sentry: Megiddo's Role in Transit, Administration, and Trade. In *Megiddo III: The 1992–1996 Seasons*, ed. I. Finkelstein, D. Ussishkin, and B. Halpern, 2:535–75. Monograph Series, no. 18. Tel Aviv: Emory and Claire Yass Publications in Archaeology, Institute of Archaeology, Tel Aviv University.

Haring, B. J. J.

1992   Libyans in the Late Twentieth Dynasty. In *Village Voices: Proceedings of the Symposium "Texts from Deir el-Medîna and Their Interpretation," Leiden, May 31–June 1, 1991*, ed. R. J. Demarée and A. Egberts, 71–80. Leiden: Nederlands Institutet voor het Nabije Oosten.

1997   *Divine Households: Administrative and Economic Aspects of the New Kingdom Royal Memorial Temples in Western Thebes*. Leiden: Nederlands Instituut voor het Nabije Oosten.

Harrison, T. P.

2004   *Megiddo 3: Final Report of the Stratum VI Excavations*. Oriental Institute Publications 127. Chicago: Oriental Institute.

Hartwig, M.

2003   Style and Visual Rhetoric in Theban Tomb Painting. In *Egyptology at the Dawn of the Twenty-first Century*, ed. Z. Hawass and L. P. Brock, 2:298–307. Cairo: American University in Cairo Press.

2004   *Tomb Painting and Identity in Ancient Thebes, 1419–1372 BCE*. Monumenta Aegyptiaca X. Brussels: Fondation Egyptologique Reine Elisabeth; Turnhout: Brepols.

Hayes, W. C.
1948   A Much-Copied Letter of the Early Middle Kingdom. *JNES* 7:1–10.
1959   *The Scepter of Egypt.* Vol. II. Cambridge, MA: Harvard University Press.

Heinhold-Krahmer, S.
1977   *Arzawa: Untersuchungen zu seiner Geschichte nach den hethitischen Quellen.* Carl Winter Universitätsverlag.

Helck, W.
1956   Die Inschrift über die Belohnung des Hohenpriesters *Imn-htp. MIO* 4:161–78.
1958   *Zur Verwaltung des Mittleren und Neuen Reichs.* Leiden: E. J. Brill.
1959   *Bemerkungen zu den Tronbesteigungsdaten im Neuen Reich.* Studia Biblica et Orientalia III:124–25.
1961–70 *Materialien zur Wirtschaftsgeschichte des Neuen Reiches.* Abhandlungen des Geistes- und Socialwissenschaftlichen Klasse, Akademie der Wissenschaften und Literatur in Mainz 1960 Nr. 10 und 11(=Teil I, II); 1963 Nr. 2 und 3(=Teil III, IV); 1964, Nr. 4(=Teil V); 1969 Nr. 4(=Teil VI); Indices, by I. Hoffman, 1969 Nr. 13. Wiesbaden: Franz Steiner.
1963   Der Papyrus Berlin P 3047. *JARCE* 2:65–73.
1964   *Materialien zur Wirtschaftsgeschichte des Neuen Reiches.* Pt. V. Akademie der Wissenschaften und Literatur Mainz, Abhandlungen der geistes- und sozialwissenschaftlichen Klasse 1960: 10–11. Wiesbaden: Franz Steiner.
1966   Zum Kult an Koenigsstatuen. *JNES* 25:32–41.
1967   Eine Briefsammlung aus der Verwaltung des Amuntempels. *JARCE* 6:135–51.
1968   *Die Ritualszenen auf der Umfassungsmauer Ramses' II. in Karnak.* Ägyptologische Abhandlungen 18. Wiesbaden: Otto Harrassowitz.
1969   *Der Text der "Lehre Amenemhets I. für seinen Sohn."* Wiesbaden: Otto Harrassowitz.
1972   *Die Ritualdarstellungen des Ramesseums.* Ägyptologische Abhandlungen 25. Wiesbaden: Otto Harrassowitz.
1975   *Wirtschaftsgeschichte des Alten Ägypten im 3. und 2. Jahrtausend vor Chr.* Leiden: E. J. Brill.
1980   Ein "Feldzug" unter Amenophis IV. gegen Nubien. *SAK* 8:117–22.
1983a   Asja. *ZÄS* 11:29–36.
1983b   *Historisch-Biographische Texte der 2. Zwischenzeit und neue Texte der 18. Dynastie.* 2nd ed. KÄT. Wiesbaden: Otto Harrassowitz.
1986   Usurpierung. *LÄ* VI.905–6.
1987   Nochmals zu Ramses' III. Seevölkerbericht. *SAK* 14:129–45.
1995   *Die Beziehungen Ägyptens und Vorderasiens zur Ägäis bis ins 7. Jahrhundert v.Chr.* Darmstadt: Wissenschaftliche Buchgesellschaft.

Higginbotham, C. R.
1999   The Statue of Ramses III from Beth Shean. *Tel Aviv* 26:225–32.
2000   *Egyptianization and Elite Emulation in Ramesside Palestine: Governance and Accommodation on the Imperial Periphery.* Culture and History of the Ancient Near East, vol. 2. Leiden: E. J. Brill.

Hoch, J. E.

1994   *Semitic Words in Egyptian Texts of the New Kingdom and Third Interme-diate Period.* Princeton: Princeton University Press.

Hoffmeier, J. K., and Moshier, S. O.

2006   New Paleo-Environmental Evidence from North Sinai to Complement Manfred Bietak's Map of the Eastern Delta and Some Historical Impli-cations. In *Timelines: Studies in Honour of Manfred Bietak,* ed. E. Czerny, I. Hein, H. Hunger, D. Melman, and A. Schwab, 2:167–76. Orientalia Lo-vaniensia Analecta 149. Louvain: Peeters.

Hoffner, H. A.

1989   The Last Days of Khattusha. In *The Crisis Years: The 12th Century B.C.; From beyond the Danube to the Tigris,* ed. W. A. Ward and M. Sharp Joukowsky, 46–55. Dubuque, IA: Kendall/Hunt.

Hölbl, G.

1983   Die historischen Aussagen der ägyptischen Seevölkerinschriften. In *Griechenland, die Ägäis und die Levante während der "Dark Ages" vom 12. Bis zum 9. Jh. v.Chr.,* ed. S. Deger-Jalkotzy, 121–38. Österreichische Akademie der Wissenschaften, philosophisch-historische Klasse, Sitz-ungsberichte, vol. 418. Vienna: Verlag der Österreichischen Akademie der Wissenschaften.

Hollis, S. T.

1990   *The Ancient Egyptian "Tale of Two Brothers": The Oldest Fairy Tale in the World.* Oklahoma Series in Classical Culture 7. Norman: University of Oklahoma Press.

Hölscher, U.

1934–54   *The Excavation of Medinet Habu.* Vols. I–V. Chicago: University of Chicago Press.

Hornemann, B.

1951   *Types of Ancient Egyptian Statuary.* Vol. I. Copenhagen: Munksgaard.

1957   *Types of Ancient Egyptian Statuary.* Vol. II. Copenhagen: Munksgaard.

1966   *Types of Ancient Egyptian Statuary.* Vol. V. Copenhagen: Munksgaard.

Hornung, E.

1964   *Untersuchungen zur Chronologie und Geschichte des Neuen Reiches.* Weis-baden: Otto Harrassowitz.

1971   *Das Grab des Haremhab im Tal der Könige.* Bern: Francke.

1982a   *Conceptions of God in Ancient Egypt.* Ithaca: Cornell University Press.

1982b   *Das Tal der Könige: Die Ruhestätte der Pharaonen.* Zurich: Artemis.

1991   *Der ägyptische Mythos von der Himmelskuh: Eine Ätiologie des Unvol-lkommenen.* 2nd ed. Orbis Biblicus et Orientalis 46. Göttingen: Vanden-hoeck und Ruprecht.

1999   *The Ancient Egyptian Books of the Afterlife.* Ithaca: Cornell University Press.

Ignatov, S.

1999   Literature and Politics in the Time of Ramesses II: The Kadesh Inscrip-tions. In *Literatur und Politik im pharaonischen und ptolemäischen*

Ägypten, ed. J. Assmann and E. Blumenthal, 7–9. Bibliothèque d'Étude 127. Cairo: Institut français d'archéologie orientale.

Iskander, S.
2002 The Reign of Merenptah. Ph.D. diss., New York University.

Izre'el, S.
1997 *The Amarna Scholarly Tablets.* Cuneiform Monographs 9. Gronigen: Styx.

Jäger, S.
2004 *Altägyptische Berufstypologien.* Lingua Aegyptia Studia Monographica 4. Göttingen: Seminar für Ägyptologie und Koptologie.

James, F. W.
1966 *The Iron Age at Beth Shan: A Study of Levels VI–IV.* Philadelphia: University Museum, University of Pennsylvania.

James, T. G. H.
1962 *The Hekanakhte Papers and Other Early Middle Kingdom Documents.* Metropolitan Museum of Art Egyptian Expedition Publications 14. New York: Metropolitan Museum of Art.

2001 Vignettes in the Papyrus of Ani. In *Colour and Painting in Ancient Egypt,* ed. W. V. Davies, 141–44. London: British Museum Press.

Jankhun, D.
1973 Maat die Herrin des Westens. *GM* 8:19–22.

Jansen-Winkeln, K.
1984 *Ägyptische Biographien der 22. und 23. Dynastie.* Ägypten und Altes Testament 8. Wiesbaden: Otto Harrassowitz.

1991 Ein Siegelabdruck mit Motto. *Varia Aegyptiaca* 7:29–30.

1992 Das ende des Neuen Reiches. *ZÄS* 119:22–37.

1994 Der Beginn der libyschen Herrschaft in Ägypten. *BN* 71:78–97.

1995a Die Plünderung der Königsgräber des Neuen Reiches. *ZÄS* 122:62–78.

1995b Diglossie und Zweisprächigkeit im alten Ägypten. *Wiener Zeitschrift für die Kunde des Morgenländes* (Vienna) 85:85–115.

2007 *Inschriften der Spätzeit.* Pt. II, *Die 22.–24. Dynastie.* Wiesbaden: Otto Harrassowitz.

Janssen, J. J.
1975a *Commodity Prices from the Ramesside Period: An Economic Study of the Village of Necropolis Workmen at Thebes.* Leiden: E. J. Brill.

1975b Prolegomena to the Study of Egypt's Economic History during the New Kingdom. *SAK* 3:127–85.

1979a The Role of the Temple in the Egyptian Economy during the New Kingdom. In *State and Temple Economy in the Ancient Near East,* ed. E. Lipinski, II:505–15. Orientalia Lovaniensia Analecta 6. Louvain: Department Oriëntalistiek.

1979b Background Information on the Strikes of Year 29 of Ramesses III. *OA* 18:301–8.

1982 The Mission of the Scribe Pesiur. In *Gleanings from Deir el-Medîna,* ed. R. J. Demarée and J. J. Janssen, 133–47. Egyptologische Uitgaven I. Leiden: Nederlands Institutet voor het Nabije Oosten.

1987   The Price of Papyrus. *DE* 9:33–35.

1991   *Late Ramesside Letters and Communications.* Hieratic Papyri in the British Museum VI. London: British Museum.

1992   Literacy and Letters at Deir el-Medîna. In *Village Voices: Proceedings of the Symposium "Texts from Deir el-Medîna and Their Interpretation," Leiden, May 31–June 1, 1991,* ed. R. J. Demarée and A. Egberts, 81–94. Leiden: Nederlands Institutet voor het Nabije Oosten.

1995   Papyrus Baldwin Rediscovered. *GM* 147:53–60.

1997   *Village Varia: Ten Studies on the History and Administration of Deir el-Medina.* Egyptologische Uitgaven XI. Leiden: Nederlands Instituut voor het Nabije Oosten.

Jasnow, R.

1999   Remarks on Continuity in Egyptian Literary Tradition. In *Gold of Praise: Studies in Honor of Edward F. Wente,* ed. E. Teeter and J. A. Larson, 193–205. Studies in Ancient Oriental Civilization 58. Chicago: University of Chicago Press.

2003   Response to J. Baines. In *Egyptology at the Dawn of the Twenty-first Century,* ed. Z. Hawass and L. P. Brock, 3:33–37. Cairo: American University in Cairo Press.

Jenni, H., ed.

2000   *Das Grab Ramses' X. (KV 18).* Aegyptiaca Helvetica 16. Basel: Schwabe.

Jéquier, G.

1933   Deux statuettes égyptiennes d'époque ramesside. *Bulletin de la Société neuchâteloise de Géographie* 42:19–24.

Johnson, W. R.

1998   Monuments and Monumental Art under Amenhotep III. In *Amenhotep III: Perspectives on His Reign,* ed. D. O'Connor and E. H. Cline, 63–94. Ann Arbor: University of Michigan Press.

1999   The Small Temple of Amun at Medinet Habu. *Bulletin of the American Research Center in Egypt* 180:12–13.

Junge, F.

1973   Zur Fehldatierung des sog: Denkmals memphitischer Theologie oder Der Beitrag der ägyptischen Theologie zur Geistesgeschichte der Spätzeit. *MDAIK* 29:195–204.

1985   Sprachstufen und Sprachgeschichte. In *XXII. Deutscher Orientalistentag: Vom 21. bis 25. März 1983 in Tübingen,* ed. W. Röllig, 17–34. ZDMG Supplement 6. Stuttgart: Franz Steiner.

1996   *Neuägyptisch: Einführung in die Grammatik.* Wiesbaden: Otto Harrassowitz.

2003   *Die Lehre Ptahhoteps und die Tugenden der ägyptischen Welt.* Orbis Biblicus et Orientalis 193. Fribourg and Göttingen: Academic Press.

2005   *Late Egyptian Grammar: An Introduction.* 2nd English ed. Trans. D. Warburton. Oxford: Oxford University Press.

Junker, H.

1940   *Giza.* Vol. IV. Vienna: Leipzig Hölder-Pichler-Tempsky A.G.

Kahl, J.

1998   "Es ist vom Anfang bis zum Ende so gekommen, wie es in der Schrift gefunden worden war": Zur Überlieferung der Erzählung des Sinuhe. In *"Und Mose schrieb dieses Lied auf": Studien zum Alten Testament und zum Alten Orient, Festschrift Oswald Loretz,* ed. M. Dietrich and I. Kottsieper, 383–400. Alter Orient und Altes Testament 250. Münster: Ugarit-Verlag.

Kanta, A.

1980   *The Late Minoan III Period in Crete.* Studies in Mediterranean Archaeology 58. Göteborg: Paul Åströms Förlag.

Kaplony, P.

1977   Die Definition der schönen Literatur im Alten Ägypten. In *Fragen an die altägyptischen Literatur,* ed. J. Assmann et al., 289–314. Wiesbaden: Reichert.

Karageorghis, V.

1989   The Crisis Years: Cyprus. In *The Crisis Years: The 12th Century B.C.; From beyond the Danube to the Tigris,* ed. W. A. Ward and M. Sharp Joukowsky, 79–86. Dubuque, IA: Kendall/Hunt.

Katary, S. L. D.

1989   *Land Tenure in the Ramesside Period.* London: Kegan Paul International.

1999   Land-Tenure in the New Kingdom: The Role of Women Smallholders and the Military. In *Agriculture in Egypt: From Pharaonic to Modern Times,* ed. A. K. Bowman and E. Rogan, 61–82. Proceedings of the British Academy 96. Oxford: Oxford University Press.

Keel, O., and Münger, S.

2005   The Stamp Seal Amulets. In *Ashdod,* vol. 6, *The Excavations of Areas H and K (1968–1969),* ed. M. Dothan and D. Ben-Shlomo, 273–79. IAA Reports, no. 24. Jerusalem: Israel Antiquities Authority.

Kees, H.

1983   *Der Götterglaube im alten Ägypten.* Berlin: Akademie Verlag.

Keller, C. A.

1994   Speculations Concerning Interconnections between the Royal Policy and Reputation of Ramesses IV. In *For His Ka: Essays Offered in Memory of Klaus Baer,* ed. D. P. Silverman, 145–57. Studies in Ancient Oriental Civilization 55. Chicago: Oriental Institute.

Kemp, B. J.

1972   Temple and Town in Ancient Egypt. In *Man, Settlement, and Urbanism,* ed. P. J. Ucko, R. Tringham, and G. W. Dimbleby, 657–80. London: Duckworth.

2006   *Ancient Egypt: Anatomy of a Civilization.* London and New York: Routledge.

Kessler, D.

1975   Eine Landeschenkung Ramses' III. zugunsten eines "Grossen der *thrw*" aus *mr-mšꜥ.f. SAK* 2:103–34.

Khazanov, A. M.

1994   *Nomads and the Outside World.* 2nd ed. Wisconsin: University of Wisconsin Press.

Killebrew, A. E.

1998   Mycenaean and Aegean-Style Pottery in Canaan during the 14th–12th Centuries BC. In *The Aegean and the Orient in the Second Millennium: Proceedings of the 50th Anniversary Symposium, Cincinnati, 18–20 April 1997*, ed. E. H. Cline and D. Harris-Cline, 159–69. Liège: Université de Liège; Austin: University of Texas.

2000   Aegean-Style Early Philistine Pottery in Canaan during the Iron I Age: A Stylistic Analysis of Mycenaean IIIC:1b Pottery and Its Associated Wares. In *The Sea Peoples and Their World: A Reassessment*, ed. E. D. Oren, 233–53. University Museum Monograph 108. Philadelphia: University Museum, University of Pennsylvania.

2005   *Biblical Peoples and Ethnicity: An Archaeological Study of Egyptians, Canaanites, Philistines, and Early Israel (ca. 1300–1100 B.C.E.).* SBL Archaeology and Biblical Studies, no. 9. Atlanta: Society of Biblical Literature.

2008   Aegean-Style Pottery and Associated Assemblages in the Southern Levant: Chronological Implications regarding the Transition from the Late Bronze II to the Iron I and the Appearance of the Philistines. In *Israel in Transition: From Late Bronze II to Iron IIa (c. 1250–850 B.C.E.)*, vol. 1, *The Archaeology*, ed. L. L. Grabbe, 54–71. Library of Hebrew Bible/Old Testament Studies 491; European Seminar in Historical Methodology 7. London: T&T Clark.

Killebrew, A. E., Goldberg, P., and Rosen, A. M.

2006   Deir el-Balah: A Geological, Archaeological, and Historical Reassessment of an Egyptianizing 13th and 12th Century B.C.E. Center. *BASOR* 343:97–119.

Kitchen, K. A.

1969–90   *Ramesside Inscriptions: Historical and Biographical.* Vols. I–VIII. Oxford: Blackwell.

1972   Ramesses VII and the Twentieth Dynasty. *JEA* 58:182–94.

1973   The Philistines. In *Peoples of Old Testament Times*, ed. D. J. Wiseman, 53–78. Oxford: Clarendon.

1977   Historical Observations on Ramesside Nubia. In *Ägypten und Kusch*, ed. E. Endesfelder et al., 211–25. Schriften zur Geschichte und Kultur des Alten Orients 13. Berlin: Akademie Verlag.

1982a   *Pharaoh Triumphant: The Life and Times of Ramesses II, King of Egypt.* Warminster: Aris and Phillips.

1982b   The Twentieth Dynasty Revisited. *JEA* 68:116–25.

1984a   A Note on Bandeau Texts in New Kingdom Temples. In *Studien zu Sprache und Religion Ägyptens: Zu Ehren von Wolfhart Westendorf überreicht von seinen Freunden und Schülern*, ed. F. Junge, 547–53. Göttingen: Göttingen University.

1984b   Family Relationships of Ramesses IX and the Late Twentieth Dynasty. *SAK* 11:127–34.

1984c   Ramses V–XI. *LÄ* V:124–28.

1985   Les suites des guerres libyennes de Ramsès III. *RdÉ* 36:177–79.

1986   *The Third Intermediate Period in Egypt, 1100–650 B.C.* 2nd ed. Warminster: Aris and Phillips.

1987   The Titularies of the Ramesside Kings as Expression of Their Ideal Kingship. *ASAE* 71:131–41.

1990   The Arrival of the Libyans in Late New Kingdom Egypt. In *Libya and Egypt, c. 1300–750 BC*, ed. Anthony Leahy, 15–27. London: Centre of Near and Middle Eastern Studies, School of Oriental and African Studies, and Society for Libyan Studies.

1995   *The Third Intermediate Period in Egypt.* 2nd ed. Warminster: Aris and Phillips.

1999a   Notes on a Stela of Ramesses II from Near Damascus. *GM* 173:133–38.

1999b   The Wealth of Amun of Thebes under Ramesses II. In *Gold of Praise: Studies on Ancient Egypt in Honor of Edward F. Wente*, ed. E. Teeter and J. A. Larson, 235–38. Studies in Ancient Oriental Civilization 58. Chicago: Oriental Institute.

1999c   *Poetry of Ancient Egypt.* Documenta Mundi Aegyptiaca 1. Jonsered: Paul Åströms Förlag.

2004   *The Third Intermediate Period in Egypt, 1100–650 B.C.* London: Aris and Phillips.

2009   Egyptian New-Kingdom Topographical Lists: An Historical Resource with "Literary" Histories. In *Causing His Name to Live: Studies in Egyptian Epigraphy and History in Memory of William J. Murnane*, ed. P. J. Brand and L. Cooper, 129–35. Culture and History of the Ancient Near East, vol. 37. Leiden: E. J. Brill.

Kitchen, K. A., and Gaballa, G. A.

1969   Ramesside Varia II. *ZÄS* 96:14–28.

Kitchen, K. A., and Ockinga, B. G.

1992   A Memphite Monument of the Vizier *T3* in Sydney. *MDAIK* 48:99–103, pls. 20–21.

Klengel, H.

1992   *Syria, 3000 to 300 B.C.: A Handbook of Political History.* Berlin: Akademie Verlag.

1999   *Geschichte des Hethitischen Reiches.* Leiden: E. J. Brill.

Kling, B. B.

2000   Mycenaean IIIC:1b and Related Pottery in Cyprus: Comments on the Current State of Research. In *The Sea Peoples and Their World: A Reassessment*, ed. E. D. Oren, 281–95. University Museum Monograph 108. Philadelphia: University Museum, University of Pennsylvania.

Knapp, A. B.

1992   Bronze Age Mediterranean Island Cultures and the Ancient Near East. Pt. 2. *Biblical Archaeologist* 55, no. 3:112–28.

Koch, R.

1990   *Die Erzählung des Sinuhe.* Bibliotheca Aegyptiaca 17. Brussels: Fondation Égyptologique Reine Elisabeth.

Koenig, Y.

1985   Notes sur un papyrus littéraire fragmentaire, P. Deir el-Médineh, no. 43. *CRIPEL* 7:71–73.

1989   Nouveaux textes Rifaud II (document E). *CRIPEL* 11:53–58.

1997   *Les ostraca hiératiques inédits de la Bibliothèque Nationale et Université de Strasbourg.* DFIFAO 33. Cairo: Institut français d'archéologie orientale.

2001   À propos de la conspiration du harem. *BIFAO* 101:293–314.

Korostovtsev, M.

1960   *Puteshestviye Un-Amuna v Bibl. Egiptskiy iyeraticheskiy papyrus n° 120 Gosudarstvennogo muzeya izobrazitel'nykh iskusstv im. A. S. Pushkina v Moskve.* Moscow: Akademija nauk SSR. Institut vostokevedenija.

Kozloff, A., Bryan, B., and Berman, L.

1992   *Egypt's Dazzling Sun: Amenhotep III and His World.* Catalog of an exhibition at the Cleveland Museum of Art. Bloomington: Indiana University Press.

Krauss, R.

1994   Ein wahrscheinlicher Terminus post quem für das Ende von Lachish VI. *MDOG* 126:123–30.

Kroeber, B.

1970   Die Neuägyptizismen vor der Amarnazeit: Studien zur Entwicklung der ägyptischen Sprache vom Mittleren zum Neuen Reich. Ph.D. diss., University of Tübingen.

Kruchten, J.-M.

1981   *Le Décret d'Horemheb: Traduction, commentaire épigraphique, philologique et institutionnel.* Brussels: Éditions de l'Université.

1989   *Les annales des prêtres de Karnak (XXI–XXIIImes dynasties) et autres textes contemporains relatifs à l'initiation des prêtres d'Amon.* Orientalia Lovaniensia Analecta 32. Louvain: Departement Oriëntalistik.

1999   From Middle Egyptian to Late Egyptian. *LingAeg* 6:1–97.

2001   Oracles. In *The Oxford Encyclopedia of Ancient Egypt,* ed. D. B. Redford, 2:609–12. Oxford: Oxford University Press.

Lackenbacher, S.

1995   Une correspondance entre l'administration du pharaon Merneptah et le roi d'Ugarit. In *Le pays d'Ougarit autour de 1200 av. J.-C.: Actes du Colloque International Paris, 28 juin–1er juillet 1993,* ed. M. Yon, M. Szneyzer, and P. Bordreuil, 77–83. Ras Shamra-Ougarit XI. Paris: Èdition Recherche sur les Civilisations.

Lacovara, P.

1997   *The New Kingdom Royal City.* London: Kegan Paul International.

Laisney, V. M.-P.

2007   *L'Enseignement d'Aménémopé.* Studia Pohl: Series Maior 19. Rome: Pontifical Biblical Institute.

Leahy, A.

1985   The Libyan Period in Egypt: An Essay in Interpretation. *Libyan Studies* 16:51–65.

1999a   In the House of the Phoenix at Thebes (Cairo JE 36938). In *Studies on*

Ancient Egypt in Honour of H. S. Smith, ed. A. Leahy and J. Tait, 185–92. Occasional Publications 13. London: Egypt Exploration Society.

1999b   Libyans. In *Encyclopedia of the Archaeology of Ancient Egypt*, ed. K. A. Bard, 445–47. London and New York: Routledge.

2001   Sea Peoples. In *The Oxford Encyclopedia of Ancient Egypt*, ed. D. Redford, 3:257–60. New York: Oxford University Press.

Leahy, A., ed.

1990   *Libya and Egypt, c. 1300–750 BC*. London: Centre of Near and Middle Eastern Studies, School of Oriental and African Studies, and Society for Libyan Studies.

Leblanc, C.

1997   Quelques reflexions sur le programme iconographique et le fonction des temples de millions d'années. In *The Temple in Ancient Egypt*, ed. S. Quirke, 49–56. London: British Museum.

2001   La véritable identité de Pentaouret, le prince "maudit." *RdÉ* 52:151–81.

Leclant, J.

1961   Découverte de monuments égyptiens ou égyptisants hors de vallée du Nil, 1955–1960. *Or* 30:391–406.

1965   *Recherches sur Les Monumentes Thébains de la XXVe Dynastie dite Éthiopienne*. Bibliotheque d'Étude 36. Cairo: Institut français d'archéologie orientale.

1996   L'Ègypte et l'Ègéen au second millenaire. In *Atti memorie del secondo congresso internazionale di micenologia*, 613–25. Rome: Editioni dell'Ateno.

1982   Fouilles et travaux en Égypte et au Soudan, 1980–1981. *Or* 51:411–92.

Leclere, F.

1996   A Cemetery of Osirid Figures at Karnak. *Egyptian Archaeology* 9:9–12.

Lecuyot, G.

2000   Ta Set Neferu, the Valley of the Queens: A Brief History of Its Excavation. *KMT* 11, no. 2 (Summer): 42–55.

Legrain, G.

1906   *Statues et statuettes de rois et de particuliers*. Vol. II. Catalogue general des antiquites egyptiennes du Musee du Caire. Cairo: Institut français d'archéologie orientale.

1929   *Les temples de Karnak*. Brussels: Vromant and Company.

Lehmann, G. A.

1979   Die Sikalaju: Ein neues Zeugnis zu den "Seevölker"-Heerfahrten im späten 13. Jh. v.Chr. (RS 34.129). *Ugarit-Forschungen* 11:481–94.

1983   Zum Auftreten von "Seevölker"-Gruppen im östlichen Mittelmeerraum: Eine Zwischenbilanz. In *Griechenland, die Ägäis und die Levante während der "Dark Ages" vom 12. Bis zum 9. Jh. v.Chr.*, ed. S. Deger-Jalkotzy, 79–92. Österreichischen Akademie der Wissenschaften, philologisch-historische Klasse, Sitzungsberichte, vol. 418. Vienna: Verlag der Österreichischen Akademie der Wissenschaften.

Leibovitch, J.

1938   *Ancient Egypt: An Easy Introduction to Its Archaeology, Including a Short*

Account of the Egyptian Museum, Cairo, with a Description of Giza and Saqqara. Cairo: L. Baroukh.

Leprohon, R. J.

2009   The Stela of Sehetepibre (CG 20538). In *Archaism and Innovation. Studies in the Culture of Middle Egyptian Egypt,* ed. David P. Silverman et al., 277–92. New Haven and Philadelphia: Yale University and the University of Pennsylvania Museum.

Lesko, L. H.

1980   The Wars of Ramses III. *Serapis* 6:83–86.

1986   Three Late Egyptian Stories Reconsidered. In *Egyptological Studies in Honor of Richard A. Parker: Presented on the Occasion of His 78th Birthday, December 10, 1983,* ed. L. H. Lesko, 98–103. Hanover, NH: University Press of New England.

1989   Egypt in the 12th century B.C. In *The Crisis Years: The 12th Century B.C.; From beyond the Danube to the Tigris,* ed. W. Ward and M. Sharp Joukowsky, 151–56. Dubuque, IA: Kendall/Hunt.

Lesko, L. H., and B. S. Lesko, eds.

1982   *A Dictionary of Late Egyptian.* Vol. I. Berkeley and Los Angeles: University of California Press.

Levy, T. E., and Higham, T., eds.

2005   *The Bible and Radiocarbon Dating: Archaeology, Text, and Science.* London: Equinox.

Lichtheim, M.

1945   The Songs of the Harpers. *JNES* 4:172–212.

1971–72   Have the Principles of Ancient Egyptian Metrics Been Discovered? *JARCE* 9:103–10.

1973   *Ancient Egyptian Literature.* Vol. I, *The Old and Middle Kingdom.* Berkeley and Los Angeles: University of California Press.

1976   *Ancient Egyptian Literature.* Vol. II, *The New Kingdom.* Berkeley and Los Angeles: University of California Press.

1980a   *Ancient Egyptian Literature.* Vol. 3, *The Late Period.* Berkeley and Los Angeles: University of California Press.

1980b   The Praise of Cities in the Literature of the Egyptian New Kingdom. In *Panhellenica: Essays in Ancient History and Historiography in Honor of Truesdell S. Brown,* ed. S. M. Burstein and L. A. Okin, 15–23. Lawrence, KA: Coronado.

1983   *Late Egyptian Wisdom Literature in the International Context: A Study of Demotic Instructions.* Orbis Biblicus et Orientalis 52. Göttingen: Vandenhoeck und Ruprecht.

1992   *Maat in Egyptian Autobiographies and Related Studies.* Orbis Biblicus et Orientalis 120. Göttingen: Vandenhoeck und Ruprecht.

1996   Didactic Literature. In *Ancient Egyptian Literature: History and Forms,* ed. A. Loprieno, 243–62. Probleme der Ägyptologie 10. Leiden: E. J. Brill.

1997   *Moral Values in Ancient Egypt.* Orbis Biblicus et Orientalis 155. Göttingen: Vandenhoeck und Ruprecht.

Lilyquist, C.

2008   Ramesside Vessels from Sinai. In *Servant of Mut: Studies in Honor of Richard A. Fazzini*, ed. S. H. D'Auria, 155–65. Probleme der Ägyptologie 28. Leiden: E. J. Brill.

Loffet, H., and Matoian, V.

1996   Le papyrus de Varzy. *RdÉ* 47:29–36.

Logan, T.

2000   The *Jmyt-pr* Document: Form, Function, and Significance. *JARCE* 37: 49–74.

López, J.

1976   *Ostraca Ieratici N. 57093–57319.* Catalogo generale del Museo Egizio di Torino, vol. 3, 2. Milan: Cisalpino-La Goliardica.

1984   *Ostraca Ieratici N. 57450–57568 Tabelle Lignee N. 58001–58007.* Catalogo generale del Museo Egizio di Torino, vol. 3, 4. Milan: Cisalpino–La Goliardica.

Loprieno, A.

1996a   Loyalist Instructions. In *Ancient Egyptian Literature: History and Forms*, ed. A. Loprieno, 403–14. Probleme der Ägyptologie 10. Leiden: E. J. Brill.

1996b   The "King's Novel." In *Ancient Egyptian Literature: History and Forms*, ed. A. Loprieno, 275–95. Probleme der Ägyptologie 10. Leiden: E. J. Brill.

1996c   Defining Egyptian Literature: Ancient Texts and Modern Literary Theory. In *The Study of the Ancient Near East in the Twenty-first Century: The William Foxwell Albright Centennial Conference*, ed. J. S. Cooper and G. M. Schwartz, 209–32. Winona Lake, IN: Eisenbrauns.

1996d   Loyalty to the King, to God, to Oneself. In *Studies in Honor of William Kelly Simpson*, ed. P. Der Manuelian, II:533–52. Boston: Department of Ancient Egyptian, Nubian, and Near Eastern Art, Museum of Fine Arts.

1996e   Linguistic Variety and Egyptian Literature. In *Ancient Egyptian Literature: History and Forms*, ed. A. Loprieno, 515–29. Probleme der Ägyptologie 10. Leiden: E. J. Brill.

1998   Le pharaon reconstruit: La figure du roi dans la littérature égyptienne au 1er millénaire avant J.C. *BSFÉ* 142:4–24.

Loretz, O.

1995   Les *Serdanu* et la fin d'Ougarit: À propos des documents d'Ègypte, de Byblos et d'Ougarit relatifs aux Shardana. In *Le pays d'Ougarit autour de 1200 av. J.-C.: Actes du Colloque International Paris, 28 juin–1er juillet 1993*, ed. M. Yon, M. Szneycer, and P. Bordreuil, 125–40. Ras Shamra-Ougarit XI. Paris: Èdition Recherche sur les Civilisations.

Lorton, D.

1975   The Expression *iri hrw nfr. JARCE* 12:23–31.

1995   Legal and Social Institutions of Pharaonic Egypt. In *Civilizations of the Ancient Near East*, ed. J. M. Sasson, 345–62. Peabody, MA: Hendrickson.

Loud, G.

1939   *The Megiddo Ivories.* Oriental Institute Publications 52. Chicago: University of Chicago Press.

1948 *Megiddo II: Seasons of 1935–39.* 2 vols. Oriental Institute Publications 62. Chicago: University of Chicago Press.

Luft, U. H.

1976 Seit der Zeit Gottes. *Studia Aegyptiaca* 2:47–78.

2001 Religion. In *The Oxford Encyclopedia of Ancient Egypt,* ed. D. B. Redford, 3:139–45. Oxford: Oxford University Press.

Macalister, R. A. S.

1912 *The Excavation of Gezer, 1902–1905 and 1907–1909.* 3 vols. London: J. Murray.

Macdonald, E., Starkey, J. L., and Harding, G. L.

1932 *Beth-Pelet. II.* Publications of the Egyptian Research Account 52. London: British School of Archaeology in Egypt.

Machinist, P.

2000 Biblical Tradition: The Philistines and Israelite History. In *The Sea Peoples and Their World: A Reassessment,* ed. E. D. Oren, 53–83. University Museum Monograph 108. Philadelphia: University Museum, University of Pennsylvania.

Maeir, A. M.

1988–89 Remarks on a Supposed "Egyptian Residency" at Gezer. *Tel Aviv* 15–16:65–67.

Maeir, A. M., Martin, M., and Wimmer, S. J.

2004 An Incised Hieratic Inscription from Tell eṣ-Ṣâfī, Israel. *Ägypten und Levante* 14:125–34.

Manassa, C.

2003 *The Great Karnak Inscription of Merneptah: Grand Strategy in the 13th Century BC.* Yale Egyptological Seminar. New Haven and Oxford: Yale University Press and Oxford University Press.

Manning, J. G.

2003 *Land and Power in Ptolemaic Egypt.* Cambridge: Cambridge University Press.

Maravelia, A.-A.

2003 Some Aspects of Ancient Egyptian Social Life from the Study of the Principal Love Poem's Ostraca from Deir el-Medina. In *Egyptology at the Dawn of the Twenty-first Century,* ed. Z. Hawass and L. P. Brock, 3:281–88. Cairo: American University in Cairo Press.

Marciniak, M.

1982 Deux campagnes épigraphiques au tombeau du Ramsès III dans la Valée des Rois. *Africana Bulletin* 31:37–74.

Margalith, O.

1994 *The Sea Peoples in the Bible.* Wiesbaden: Otto Harrassowitz.

Martin, G. T.

2000 Memphis: The Status of a Residence City in the Eighteenth Dynasty. In *Abusir and Saqqara in the Year 2000,* ed. M. Bárta and J. Krejcí, 99–120. Archiv Orientalní Supplementa IX. Prague: Academy of Sciences of the Czech Republic.

Martin, M. A. S.

2004   Egyptian and Egyptianized Pottery in Late Bronze Age Canaan. *Ägypten und Levante* 14:265–84.

2006   The Egyptianized Pottery Assemblage from Area Q. In *Excavations at Tel Beth-Shean, 1989–1996*. Vol. 1, *From the Late Bronze Age IIB to the Medieval Period*, ed. A. Mazar, 140–57. Jerusalem: Israel Exploration Society.

2009   Egyptian Fingerprints at Late Bronze Age Ashkelon: Egyptian-Style Beer Jars. In *Exploring the* Longue Durée: *Essays in Honor of Lawrence E. Stager*, ed. J. D. Schloen, 297–304. Winona Lake, IN: Eisenbrauns.

2011   Egyptian-Type Pottery at Late Bronze Megiddo. In *The Fire Signals of Lachish: Studies in the Archaeology and History of Israel in the Late Bronze Age, Iron Age, and Persian Period in Honor of David Ussishkin*, ed. I. Finkelstein and N. Na'aman, 159–78. Winona Lake, IN: Eisenbrauns.

Martin, M. A. S., and Ben-Dov, R.

2007   Egyptian and Egyptian-Style Pottery at Tel Dan. *Ägypten und Levante* 17:191–203.

Maspéro, G.

1896   *The Struggle of the Nations*. Ed. A. H. Sayce. Trans. M. L. McClure. New York: D. Appleton and Company.

1915   *Guide au visiteur au Musee de Caire*. Cairo: Institut français d'archéologie orientale.

Master, D.

2009   The Renewal of Trade at Iron Age I Ashkelon. In *Eretz-Israel*, vol. 29 (Ephraim Stern volume), 111*–122*. Jerusalem: Israel Exploration Society.

Mathieu, B.

1996   *La poésie amoureuse de l'Égypte ancienne: Recherches sur un genre littéraire au Nouvel Empire*. Bibliothèque d'Étude 115. Cairo: Institut français d'archéologie orientale.

2003   La litérature narrative de l'Égypte ancienne: Un bilan. In *Egyptology at the Dawn of the Twenty-first Century*, ed. Z. Hawass and L. P. Brock, 3:296–306. Cairo: American University in Cairo Press.

Mattieu, B., and Ritter, V.

2008   Les section finales du manuel scolaire Kémyt (CXV–XVII). In *Mélanges offerts à François Neveu par ses amis, élèves et collégues à l'occasion de son soixante-quinzième anniversaire*, ed. C. Gallois, P. Grandet, and L. Pantalacci, 193–238. Bibliothèque d'Étude 145. Cairo: Institut français d'archéologie oriental.

Maystre, C.

1941   Le livre de la vache du ciel. *BIFAO* 40:53–115.

Mazar, A.

1988   Some Aspects of the "Sea Peoples" Settlement. In *Society and Economy in the Mediterranean (c. 1500–1000 B.C.): Proceedings of the International Symposium Held at the University of Haifa from the 28th of April to the 2nd of May 1985*, ed. M. Heltzer and E. Lipinski, 251–60. Orientalia Lovanensia Analecta 23. Louvain: Peeters.

1997   Iron Age Chronology: A Reply to I. Finkelstein. *Levant* 29:157–67.

2000   The Temples and Cult of the Philistines. In *The Sea Peoples and Their World: A Reassessment,* ed. E. D. Oren, 213–32. University Museum Monograph 108. Philadelphia: University Museum, University of Pennsylvania.

2002   Megiddo in the Thirteenth–Eleventh Centuries BCE: A Review of Some Recent Studies. In *Aharon Kempinski Memorial Volume: Studies in Archaeology and Related Disciplines,* ed. S. Aḥituv and E. D. Oren, 264–82. Beer-Sheva, vol. 15. Beer-Sheva: Ben-Gurion University of the Negev Press.

2003   Beth Shean in the Second Millennium B.C.E.: From Canaanite Town to Egyptian Stronghold. In *The Synchronisation of Civilisations in the Eastern Mediterranean in the Second Millennium B.C. II, Proceedings of the SCIEM 2000-EuroConference, Haindorf, 2nd of May–7th of May 2001,* ed. M. Bietak, 323–39. Denkschriften der Gesamtakademie, vol. 29. Vienna: Verlag der Österreichischen Akademie der Wissenschaften.

2006   *Excavations at Tel Beth-Shean, 1989–1996.* Vol. 1, *From the Late Bronze Age IIB to the Medieval Period.* Jerusalem: Israel Exploration Society.

2008a   From 1200 to 850 B.C.E.: Remarks on Some Selected Archaeological Sites. In *Israel in Transition: From Late Bronze II to Iron IIa (c. 1250–850 B.C.E.),* vol. 1, *The Archaeology,* ed. L. L. Grabbe, 86–120. Library of Hebrew Bible/Old Testament Studies 491; European Seminar in Historical Methodology 7. London: T&T Clark.

2008b   Tel Beth-Shean. In *The New Encyclopedia of Archaeological Excavations in the Holy Land,* ed. E. Stern, vol. 5 (supplementary volume), 1619–22. Jerusalem: Israel Exploration Society.

Mazar, A., and Ben-Shlomo, D.

2005   Stratigraphy and Building Remains. In *Ashdod,* vol. 6, *The Excavations of Areas H and K (1968–1969),* by M. Dothan and D. Ben-Shlomo, 11–61. IAA Reports, no. 24. Jerusalem: Israel Antiquities Authority.

Mazar, A., and Mullins, R. A.

2007   Introduction and Overview. In *Excavations at Tel Beth-Shean, 1989–1996,* vol. 2, *The Middle and Late Bronze Age Strata in Area R,* ed. A. Mazar and R. A. Mullins, 1–22. Jerusalem: Israel Exploration Society.

McDowell, A. G.

1990   *Jurisdiction in the Workmen's Community of Deir el-Medîna.* Leiden: Nederlands Instituut voor het Nabije Oosten.

1992   Awareness of the Past in Deir el-Medîna. In *Village Voices: Proceedings of the Symposium "Texts from Deir el-Medîna and Their Interpretation," Leiden, May 31–June 1, 1991,* ed. R. J. Demarée and A. Egberts, 95–109. Leiden: Nederlands Institutet voor het Nabije Oosten.

1996   Student Exercises from Deir el-Medina: The Dates. In *Studies in Honor of William Kelly Simpson,* ed. P. Der Manuelian, II:601–8. Boston: Department of Ancient Egyptian, Nubian, and Near Eastern Art, Museum of Fine Arts.

1999   *Village Life in Ancient Egypt.* Oxford: Oxford University Press.

2000   Teachers and Students at Deir el-Medina. In *Deir el-Medîna in the Third*

Millennium AD: A Tribute to Jac. J. Janssen, ed. R. J. Demarée and E. Egberts, 217–33. Egyptologische Uitgaven XIV. Leiden: Nederlands Institutet voor het Nabije Oosten.

Meeks, D.

    1979   Les donations aux temples dans l'Égypte du 1er millénaire avant J.-C. In *State and Temple Economy in the Ancient Near East,* ed. E. Lipinski, II:605–87. Orientalia Lovaniensia Analecta 6. Louvain: Department Oriëntalistiek.

    1980   Liebeslieder. *LÄ* III.1048–52.

    1997   Les emprunts Égyptiens aux langues sémitiques durant le Nouvel Empire et la Troisième Période Intermédiare: Les aléas du comparatisme. *Bibliotheca Orientalis* 54:32–61.

Megally, M.

    1975   À propos de la dualité dans l'administration au nouvel empire. In *Actes du XXIXe Congrès internationale des Orientalistes, Égyptologie,* 2:76–81. Paris: L'Asiathèque.

    1977   *Recherches sur l'économie l'administration et la comptabilité égyptiennes à la XVIIIe dynastie d'après le papyrus E. 3226 du Louvre.* Cairo: Institut français d'archéologie orientale.

Menu, B.

    1998   *Recherches sur l'histoire juridique, économique et sociale de l'ancienne Égypte.* Vol. II. Cairo: Institut français d'archéologie orientale.

Merrillees, R. S.

    1989   The Crisis Years: Cyprus, a Rejoinder. In *The Crisis Years: The 12th Century B.C.; From beyond the Danube to the Tigris,* ed. W. A. Ward and M. Sharp Joukowsky, 87–92. Dubuque, IA: Kendall/Hunt.

Meskell, L.

    1999   *Archaeologies of Social Life: Age, Sex, Class, et cetera in Ancient Egypt.* Oxford: Blackwell.

    2002   *Private Life in New Kingdom Egypt.* Princeton: Princeton University Press.

Meyer, E.

    1928   *Geschichte des Altertums.* Vol. II, pt. 1. Stuttgart: J. G. Cotta.

Miosi, F. T.

    1982   God, Fate, and Free Will in Egyptian Wisdom Literature. In *Studies in Philology in Honour of Ronald James Williams,* ed. G. A. Kadish and G. E. Freeman, 69–111. Toronto: Society for the Study of Egyptian Antiquities.

Moers, G.

    1999a   Fiktionalität und Intertextualität als Parameter ägyptologischer Literaturwissenschaft: Perspektiven und Grenzen der Anwendung zeitgenößischer Literaturtheorie. In *Literatur und Politik im pharaonischen und ptolemäischen Ägypten,* ed. J. Assmann and E. Blumenthal, 37–52. Bibliothèque d'Étude 127. Cairo: Institut français d'archéologie orientale.

Moers, G., ed.

    1999b   *Definitely Egyptian Literature: Proceedings of the Symposium "Ancient Egyptian Literature: History and Forms," Los Angeles, March 24–26, 1995.* Göttingen: Lingua Aegyptia.

Moftah, R.

1985   Studien zum Ägyptischen Königsdogma im Neuen Reich. Deutsches Archäologisches Instituts, Abteilung Kairo, Sonderschriften 20. Mainz: P. von Zabern.

Möller, G.

1909–10   Hieratische Lesestücke für den akademischen Gebrauch. 3 vols. Leipzig: J. C. Hinrichs.

1927   Hieratische Paläographie. Vol. II. 2nd ed. Leipzig: J. C. Hinrichs.

Monnet, J.

1965   Remarques sur la famille et les successeurs de Ramsès III. BIFAO 63: 209–36.

Morales, A. J.

2001   The Suppression of the High Priest Amenhotep: A Suggestion to the Role of Panehsi. GM 181:59–75.

Moran, W. L.

1992   The Amarna Letters. Baltimore: Johns Hopkins University Press.

Morenz, L. D.

1997   Eine Maxime aus der Sammlung weisheitlicher Sprüche des Papyrus Ramesseum II. DE 39:65–70.

1998   Sa-mut/kyky und Menna, zwei reale Leser/Hörer des Oasenmannes aus dem Neuen Reich? GM 165:73–81.

1999   Einem Dichter über die Schulter geschaut—ein en passant skizzerties Epigram. DE 43:19–26.

Morenz, S.

1973   Egyptian Religion. Ithaca: Cornell University Press.

1984   Die Heraufkunft des transzendenten Gottes in Ägypten. Berlin: Akademie Verlag.

Morris, E. F.

2005   The Architecture of Imperialism: Military Bases and the Evolution of Foreign Policy in Egypt's New Kingdom. Probleme der Ägyptologie 22. Leiden: E. J. Brill.

Mountjoy, P. A.

1988   LH III C Late versus Submycenaean. Jahrbuch des Deutschen Archäologischen Instituts 103:1–33.

Muhly, J. D.

1977   The Copper Ox-Hide Ingots and the Bronze Age Metals Trade. Iraq 39:73–82.

1989   The Organisation of the Copper Industry in Late Bronze Age Cyprus. In Early Society in Cyprus, ed. E. Peltenburg, 298–314. Edinburgh: Edinburgh University Press.

Muhly, J. D., Wheeler, T. S., and Maddin, R.

1977   The Cape Gelidonya Shipwreck and the Bronze Age Metals Trade in the Eastern Mediterranean. Journal of Field Archaeology 4:353–62.

Müller, H.

1961   5000 Jahre aegyptische Kunst: [Ausstellung] 15. Mai bis 27. August 1961 in Villa Hügel, Hessen. Essen: Der Verein.

Munro, I.
1988   *Untersuchungen zu den Totenbuch-Papyri der 18. Dynastie*. London: Kegan Paul International.

Munro, P.
1973   *Die spatägyptischen Totenstelen*. Ägyptologische Forschungen 25. Glückstadt: J. J. Augustin.

Murnane, W. J.
1978   *United with Eternity: A Concise Guide to Medinet Habu*. Chicago: University of Chicago Press; Cairo: American University in Cairo Press.

1995   *Texts from the Amarna Period in Egypt*. Atlanta: Scholars Press.

2001   Medinet Habu. In *The Oxford Encyclopedia of Ancient Egypt*, ed. D. B. Redford, 2:356–58. Oxford: Oxford University Press.

Murnane, W. J., and Van Siclen III, C. C.
1993   *The Boundary Stelae of Akhenaten*. London: Kegan Paul International.

Murray, E.
1930   *Egyptian Sculpture*. London: Duckworth.

Mysliwiec, K.
1976   *Le portrait royal dans le bas-relief du Nouvel Empire*. Warsaw: Editions scientifiques de Pologne.

Negbi, O.
1991   Were There Sea Peoples in the Central Jordan Valley at the Transition from the Bronze Age to the Iron Age? *Tel Aviv* 18:205–43.

Nelson, H. H.
1942   The Identity of Amon-Re of United-with-Eternity. *JNES* 1:127–55.

1943   The Naval Battle Pictured at Medinet Habu. *JNES* 2:40–45.

1981   *The Great Hypostyle Hall at Karnak*. Vol. I, pt. 1, *The Wall Reliefs*. Oriental Institute Publications 106. Chicago: Oriental Institute.

Nelson, H. H., and Hölscher, U.
1934   *Work in Western Thebes, 1931–33*. Oriental Institute Communications 18. Chicago: University of Chicago Press.

Nelson, H. H., et al.
1936   *Reliefs and Inscriptions at Karnak*. Vols. I–II. Oriental Institute Publications 35. Chicago: University of Chicago Press.

Nibbi, A.
1975   *The Sea Peoples and Egypt*. Park Ridge, NJ: Noyes.

Niemeier, W.-D.
1998   The Mycenaeans in Western Anatolia and the Problem of the Origins of the Sea Peoples. In *Mediterranean Peoples in Transition, Thirteenth to Early Tenth Centuries BCE: In Honor of Professor Trude Dothan*, ed. S. Gitin, A. Mazar, and E. Stern, 17–65. Jerusalem: Israel Exploration Society.

Nims, C.
1954   Popular Religion in Ancient Egyptian Temples. In *Proceedings of the 23rd International Congress of Orientalists*, ed. D. Sinor, 79–80. London: Royal Asiatic Society.

1955   Places about Thebes. *JNES* 14:110–23.

1964   *Thebes of the Pharaohs*. London: Elek Books.

1971   The Eastern Temple at Karnak. *Beiträge zur Ägyptischen Bauforschung und Altertumskunde* 12:107–11.

1973   Review of G. Bjorkman, *Kings at Karnak. JNES* 34:76.

1976   Ramesseum Sources of Medinet Habu Reliefs. In *Studies in Honor of George R. Hughes*, ed. J. H. Johnson and E. F. Wente, 169–75. Studies in Ancient Oriental Civilization 39. Chicago: Oriental Institute.

Niwinski, A.

1987–88   The Solar-Osirian Unity as a Principle of the Theology of the "State of Amun" in Thebes in the 21st Dynasty. *Jaarbericht van het Vooraziatische-Egyptische Genootschap "Ex Orient Ex"* 30:89–106.

1995   Le passage de la XXe à la XXIIe dynastie: Chronologie et histoire politique. *BIFAO* 95:329–60.

Nur, A., and Cline, E. H.

2000   Poseidon's Horses: Plate Tectonics and Earthquake Storms in the Late Bronze Age Aegean and Eastern Mediterranean. *Journal of Archaeological Science* 27:43–63.

Obermeyer, G. J.

1973   Leadership and Transition in Bedouin Society: A Case Study. In *The Desert and the Sown: Nomads in the Wider Society*, ed. C. Nelson, 159–73. Berkeley: Institute of International Studies.

Ockinga, B.

2000   Piety. In *The Oxford Encyclopedia of Ancient Egypt*, ed. D. B. Redford, 3:44–47. Oxford: Oxford University Press.

O'Connor, D.

1972   The Geography of Settlement in Ancient Egypt. In *Man, Settlement, and Urbanism*, ed. P. J. Ucko, R. Tringham, and G. W. Dimbleby, 681–98. London: Duckworth.

1983   New Kingdom and Third Intermediate Period. In *Ancient Egypt: A Social History*, by B. G. Trigger, B. J. Kemp, D. O'Connor, and A. B. Lloyd, 183–78. Cambridge: Cambridge University Press.

1990   The Nature of Tjemhu (Libyan) Society in the Later New Kingdom. In *Libya and Egypt, c. 1300–750 BC*, ed. A. Leahy, 29–113. London: Centre of Near and Middle Eastern Studies, School of Oriental and African Studies, and Society for Libyan Studies.

1991   Mirror of the Cosmos: The Palace of Merenptah. In *Fragments of a Shattered Visage: Proceedings of the International Symposium on Ramesses the Great*, ed. E. Bleiberg and R. Freed, 167–98. Monographs of the Institute of Egyptian Art and Archaeology 1. Memphis, TN: Memphis State University.

1995   Beloved of Maat, the Horizon of Re: The Royal Palace in New Kingdom Egypt. In *Ancient Egyptian Kingship*, ed. D. O'Connor and D. Silverman, 263–300. Probleme der Ägyptologie 9. Leiden: E. J. Brill.

2000   The Sea Peoples and the Egyptian Sources. In *The Sea Peoples and Their World: A Reassessment*, ed. E. D. Oren, 85–102. University Museum Monograph 108. Philadelphia: University Museum, University of Pennsylvania.

2005   The Eastern High Gate: Sexualized Architecture at Medinet Habu? In

Structure and Significance: Thoughts on Ancient Egyptian Architecture, ed. P. Janosi, 439–54. Vienna: Verlag der Österreichischen Akademie der Wissenschaften.

Oren, E. D.

1973   *The Northern Cemetery of Beth Shan*. Leiden: E. J. Brill.

1993a   Haror, Tel. In *The New Encyclopedia of Archaeological Excavations in the Holy Land*, ed. E. Stern, 2:580–84. New York: Simon and Schuster.

1993b   Sera', Tel. In *The New Encyclopedia of Archaeological Excavations in the Holy Land*, ed. E. Stern, 4:1329–35. New York: Simon and Schuster.

Oren, E. D., ed.

2000   *The Sea Peoples and Their World: A Reassessment*. University Museum Monograph 108. Philadelphia: University Museum, University of Pennsylvania.

Osing, J.

1975   *Der Tempel Sethos' I. in Gurna*. Deutsches Archäologisches Instituts, Abteilung Kairo, Archäologische Veröffentlichungen 20. Mainz: P. von Zabern.

1980   Königsnovelle. *LÄ* III: 556–57.

1992a   Les chants du harpiste au Nouvel Empire. In *Aspects de la culture pharaonique: Quatre leçons au Collège de France*, ed. J. Osing, 11–24. Memoires de l'academie des inscriptions et belles lettres, n.s., 12. Paris: Diffusion de Boccard.

Osing, J. et al., eds.

1992b   *Das Grab des Nerfersecheru in Zawyet Sultan*. AV 88. Mainz : P. von Zabern.

Otten, H.

1983   Die letzte Phase des hethitischen Großreiches nach den Texten. In *Griechenland, die Ägäis und die Levante während der "Dark Ages" vom 12. bis zum 9. Jh. v.Chr.*, ed. S. Deger-Jalkotzy, 13–21. Österreichische Akademie der Wissenschaften, philosophisch-historische Klasse, Sitzungsberichte, vol. 418. Vienna: Verkag der Österreichischen Akademie der Wissenschaften.

Panitz-Cohen, N., and Mazar, A., eds.

2009   *Excavations at Tel Beth-shean 1989–1996*. Vol. 3, *The 13th–11th Century BCE Strata in Areas N and S*. Jerusalem: Israel Exploration Society.

Parker, R.

1950   *The Calendars of Ancient Egypt*. Studies in Ancient Oriental Civilization 26. Chicago: University of Chicago Press.

Parker, R., Leclant, J., and Goyon, J.-C.

1979   *The Edifice of Taharqa by the Sacred Lake of Karnak*. Providence: Brown University Press; London: Lund Humphries.

Parkinson, R. B.

1991a   Teachings, Discourses, and Tales from the Middle Kingdom. In *Middle Kingdom Studies*, ed. S. G. Quirke, 91–122. New Malden, Surrey: SIA Publishing.

1991b   *Voices from Ancient Egypt: An Anthology of Middle Kingdom Writings*. Norman: University of Oklahoma Press.

1997   *The Tale of Sinuhe and Other Ancient Egyptian Poems, 1940–1640 BC*. Oxford: Oxford University Press.

1999a   *Cracking Codes: The Rosetta Stone and Decipherment*. Berkeley and Los Angeles: University of California Press.

1999b   *The Teaching of King Amenemhat I* at El-Amarna: British Museum EA 57458 and 57479. In *Studies on Ancient Egypt in Honour of H. S. Smith*, ed. A. Leahy and J. Tait, 221–26. Occasional Publications 13. London: Egypt Exploration Society.

2002   *Poetry and Culture in Middle Kingdom Egypt: A Dark Side to Perfection*. Athlone Publications in Egyptology and Ancient Near Eastern Studies. London and New York: Athlone.

2004   The History of a Poem: Middle Kingdom Literary Manuscripts and Their Reception. In *Kon-Texte: Akten des Symposions "Spurensuche—Altägypten im Spiegel seiner Texte," München 2. bis 4. Mai*, ed. G. Burkard et al., 51–63. Wiesbaden: Harrassowitz Verlag.

Parkinson, R. B., and Quirke, S. G.

1992   The Coffin of Prince Herunefer and the Early History of the *Book of the Dead*. In *Studies in Pharaonic Religion and Society in Honor of J. Gynn Griffiths*, ed. A. B. Lloyd, 37–51. London: Egypt Exploration Society.

1995   *Papyri*. London: Egyptian Bookshelf.

Paton, W. R., trans.

1993   *The Greek Anthology*. Vol. I, *Books I–VI*. Loeb Classical Library 67. London: W. Heinemann.

Peden, A. J.

1994a   *The Reign of Ramesses IV*. Warminster: Aris and Phillips.

1994b   *Egyptian Historical Inscriptions of the Twentieth Dynasty*. Documentat Mundi Aegyptiaca 3. Jonsered: Paul Åströms Förlag.

2001   *The Graffiti of Pharaonic Egypt: Scope and Roles of Informal Writings (c. 3100 –332 BC)*. Leiden: E. J. Brill.

Peet, T. E.

1930   *The Great Tomb-Robberies of the Twentieth Egyptian Dynasty*. London: London University Press.

Perdriaud, H.

2002   Le cas des neuf cents "disparus" de la stèle de l'An 3 de Ramsès IV au Ouâdi Hammâmât. *GM* 186:89–97.

Pestman, P. W.

1982   Who Were the Owners in the "Community of Workmen" of the Chester Beatty Papyri. In *Gleanings from Deir el-Medîna*, ed. R. J. Demarée and J. J. Janssen, 155–72. Egyptologische Uitgaven I. Leiden: Nederlands Institutet voor het Nabije Oosten.

Peterson, B. E. J.

1973   *Zeichnungen aus einer Totenstadt*. Medelhavsmuseet Bulletin 7–8. Stockholm: Medelhavsmuseet.

Petrie, W. M. F.

1896   *Koptos*. London: B. Quaritch.

1906   *Hyksos and Israelite Cities*. London: Office of the School of Archaeology.

1909   *The Arts and Crafts of Ancient Egypt.* London: T. N. Foulis.

1925   *A History of Egypt.* Vol. III. London: Methuen and Company.

1930   *Beth-Pelet. I.* Publications of the Egyptian Research Account 48. London: British School of Archaeology in Egypt.

Phillips, J.

1991   The Impact and Implications of the Egyptian and Egyptianizing Objects found in Bronze Age Crete ca. 3000–ca. 1100 B.C. Ph.D. diss, University of Toronto.

Piankoff, A.

1964   *The Litany of Re.* Princeton: Princeton University Press.

Piccone, P. A.

1980   On the Use of the *sḏm.n.f* in the Historical Texts of Ramesses III at Medinet Habu. *Serapis* 6:103–16.

Pillet, M.

1922   Le Temple de Ramses III du Sud (enceinte de Mut). *ASAE* 22:257–59.

Polz, D.

1998   The Ramsesnakht Dynasty and the Fall of the New Kingdom: A New Monument in Thebes. *SAK* 25:257–93.

Porter, B., and Moss, R. L. B.

1934   *Topographical Bibliography of Ancient Egyptian Hieroglyphic Texts, Reliefs, and Paintings.* Vol. IV, *Lower and Middle Egypt (Delta and Cairo to Asyut).* Oxford: Oxford University Press.

1937   *Topographical Bibliography of Ancient Egyptian Hieroglyphic Texts, Reliefs, and Paintings.* Vol. V, *Upper Egyptian Sites.* Oxford: Oxford University Press.

1939   *Topographical Bibliography of Ancient Egyptian Hieroglyphic Texts, Reliefs, and Paintings.* Vol. VI, *Upper Egypt: Chief Temples (Excluding Thebes); Abydos, Dendera, Esna, Edfu, Kom Ombo, and Philae.* Oxford: Oxford University Press.

1951   *Topographical Bibliography of Ancient Egyptian Hieroglyphic Texts, Reliefs, and Paintings.* Vol. VII, *Nubia, the Deserts, and Outside Egypt.* Oxford: Oxford University Press.

1960   *Topographical Bibliography of Ancient Egyptian Hieroglyphic Texts, Reliefs, and Paintings.* Vol. I, *The Theban Necropolis.* Pt. 1, *Private Tombs.* 2nd ed. Oxford: Clarendon.

1964   *Topographical Bibliography of Ancient Egyptian Hieroglyphic Texts, Reliefs, and Paintings.* Vol. I, *The Theban Necropolis.* Pt. 2, *Royal Tombs and Smaller Cemeteries.* 2nd ed. Oxford: Clarendon.

1972   *Topographical Bibliography of Ancient Egyptian Hieroglyphic Texts, Reliefs, and Paintings.* Vol. II, *Theban Temples.* 2nd ed. Oxford: Clarendon.

1974   *Topographical Bibliography of Ancient Egyptian Hieroglyphic Texts, Reliefs, and Paintings.* Vol. III, *Memphis.* Pt. 1, *Abu Rawash to Abusir.* 2nd ed. Oxford: Clarendon.

1981   *Topographical Bibliography of Ancient Egyptian Hieroglyphic Texts, Reliefs, and Paintings.* Vol. III, *Memphis.* Pt. 2, *Saqqara to Dahshur.* 2nd ed. Oxford: Clarendon.

Porter, R. M.

1998 An Egyptian Temple at Beth Shean and Ramesses IV. In *Proceedings of the Seventh International Congress of Egyptologists, Cambridge, 3–9 September 1995*, ed. C. J. Eyre, 903–10. Orientalia Lovaniensia Analecta 82. Louvain: Peeters.

2008 A Note on Ramesses IV and "Merneptah" at Beth Shean. *Tel Aviv* 35: 244–48.

Posener, G.

1951a *Catalogue des ostraca hiératiques littéraires de Deir el Médineh. Nos. 1001 à 1108.* Cairo: Institut français d'archéologie orientale.

1951b *Catalogue des ostraca hiératiques littéraires de Deir el Médineh. Nos. 1109 à 1167.* Cairo: Institut français d'archéologie orientale.

1951c Sur l'emploi de l'encre rouge dans les manuscripts égyptiens. *JEA* 37: 75–80.

1955 L'exorde de l'instruction éducative d'Amennakhte (Recherches littéraires V). *RdÉ* 10:61–74.

1956 *Littérature et Politique dans l'Égypt de la XIIe Dynastie.* Paris: Librairie ancienne Honoré Champion.

1957 Le conte de Néferkarê et de général Seséné (Recherches littéraires VI). *RdÉ* 11:119–37.

1972 *Catalogue des ostraca hiératiques littéraires de Deir el Médineh. Nos. 1109 à 1266.* Cairo: Institut français d'archéologie orientale.

1975 Les ostraca numérotés et le Conte du Revenant. In *Drevnii Vostok: K semidesiatipiatiletiiu akademika M. A. Korostovtseva,* ed. I. S. Katsnelson, 1:105–12. Moscow: Nauka.

1976 *L'enseignement loyaliste: Sagesse égyptienne du Moyen Empire.* Centre de recherches d'histoire et de philologie 2; Hautes études orientales 5. Geneva: Droz.

1978 *Catalogue des ostraca hiératiques littéraires de Deir el Médineh. Nos. 1267 à 1606.* Cairo: Institut français d'archéologie orientale.

1981 Les ʿafarit dans l'ancienne Égypt. *MDAIK* 37:393–401.

Posener-Kriéger, P.

1976 *Les archives du temple funeraire du Néferirkarê-Kakaï: Les papyrus d'Abousir.* Vol. II. Bibliothèque d'Étude 65, no. 2. Cairo: Institut français d'archéologie orientale.

1981 Construire une tombe à l'ouest de *Mn-nfr* (P. Caire 52002). *RdÉ* 33:47–58.

1996 Au plaisir des paléographes: Papyrus Caire JE 52003. In *Studies in Honor of William Kelly Simpson,* ed. P. Der Manuelian, II:655–64. Boston: Museum of Fine Arts.

Pritchard, J. B.

1969 *Ancient Near Eastern Texts Relating to the Old Testament.* 3rd ed. Princeton: Princeton University Press.

1980 *The Cemetery at Tell es-Saʿidiyeh, Jordan.* University Museum Monograph 41. Philadelphia: University Museum, University of Pennsylvania.

Quack, J. F.

1994 *Die Lehren des Ani: Ein neuägyptischer Weisheitstext in seinem kulturellen*

Umfeld. Orbis Biblicus et Orientalis 141. Göttingen: Vandenhoeck und Ruprecht.

1996   *k3t3w* und *i3sy*. *Ägypten und Levante* 6:75–81.

1999   A New Bilingual Fragment from the British Museum: Papyrus BM EA 69574. *JEA* 85:154–64.

2000   Eine Revision im Tempel von Karnak (Neuanalyse von Papyrus Rochester MAG 51.346.1). *SAK* 28:219–32.

Quaegebeur, J.

1977   Les saints égyptiens préchrétiens. *Orientalia Lovaniensia Periodica* 8: 129–43.

Quirke, S. G.

1996a   Archive. In *Ancient Egyptian Literature: History and Forms,* ed. A. Loprieno, 379–401. Probleme der Ägyptologie 10. Leiden: E. J. Brill.

1996b   Narrative Literature. In *Ancient Egyptian Literature: History and Forms,* ed. A. Loprieno, 263–76. Probleme der Ägyptologie 10. Leiden: E. J. Brill.

1997   Review of J. Zandee, *Der Amunhymnus des Papyrus Leiden I 344, Verso*. *JEA* 83:245–47.

Raban, A.

1988   The Constructive Maritime Role of the Sea Peoples in the Levant. In *Society and Economy in the Eastern Mediterranean (c. 1500–1000 B.C.): Proceedings of the International Symposium Held at the University of Haifa from the 28th of April to the 2nd of May 1985,* ed. M. Heltzer and E. Lipinski, 261–94. Orientalia Lovanensia Analecta 23. Louvain: Peeters.

Raban, A., and Stieglitz, R. R.

1991   The Sea Peoples and Their Contributions to Civilization. *BAR* 17, no. 6:34–42, 92–93.

Ranke, H.

1950   The Egyptian Collections of the University Museum. *University of Pennsylvania University Museum Bulletin* 15, nos. 2–3:5–109.

Raven, M. J.

2000   Twenty-five Years of Work in the New Kingdom Necropolis of Saqqara: Looking for Structure. In *Abusir and Saqqara in the Year 2000,* ed. M. Bárta and J. Krejcí, 133–44. Archiv Orientalní Supplementa IX. Prague: Academy of Sciences of the Czech Republic.

Redford, D. B.

1984   New Light on Temple J at Karnak. *Or* 55:1–15.

1986   *Pharaonic King-Lists, Annals, and Day-Books: A Contribution to the Study of the Egyptian Sense of History*. Society for the Study of Egyptian Antiquities Publication IV. Mississauga: Benben.

1990   The Sea and the Goddess. In *Studies in Egyptology Presented to Miriam Lichtheim,* ed. S. I. Groll, II:824–35. Jerusalem: Magnes Press.

1992   *Egypt, Canaan, and Israel in Ancient Times*. Princeton: Princeton University Press.

1995   The Concept of Kingship during the Eighteenth Dynasty. In *Ancient Egyptian Kingship,* ed. D. O'Connor and D. Silverman, 157–84. Probleme der Ägyptologie 9. Leiden: E. J. Brill.

2000   Egypt and Western Asia in the Late New Kingdom: An Overview. In *The Sea Peoples and Their World: A Reassessment,* ed. E. D. Oren, 1–20. University Museum Monograph 108. Philadelphia: University Museum, University of Pennsylvania.

Redford, D. B., ed.

1970   *A Study of the Biblical Story of Joseph: Genesis 37–50.* Supplements to Vetus Testamentum 20. Leiden: E. J. Brill.

Redford, S.

2002   *The Harem Conspiracy: The Murder of Ramesses III.* DeKalb, IL: Northern Illinois University.

Richardson, S.

1999   Libya Domestica: Libyan Trade and Society on the Eve of the Invasions of Egypt. *JARCE* 36:149–64.

Ricke, H.

1981   Ein Sokartempel? In *Untersuchungen im Totentempel Amenophis' III,* ed. G. Haeny, 31–37. Beiträge zur Ägyptischen Bauforschung und Altertumskunde 11. Wiesbaden: Franz Steiner.

Ricke, H., Hughes, G. R., and Wente, E. F.

1967   *The Beit el-Wali Temple of Ramesses II.* Oriental Institute Nubian Expedition I. Chicago: University of Chicago Press.

Ritner, R. K.

1997   *The Mechanics of Ancient Egyptian Magical Practice.* Chicago: Oriental Institute.

Robertson, A. F.

1994   Word Dividers, Spot Markers, and Clause Markers in Old Assyrian, Ugaritic, and Egyptian Texts: Sources for Understanding the Use of the Red Ink Points in the Two Amarna Literary Texts, Adapa and Ereshkigal, found in Egypt. Ph.D. Diss., New York University.

Roccati, A.

2003   Response to J. Baines. In *Egyptology at the Dawn of the Twenty-first Century,* ed. Z. Hawass and L. P. Brock, 3:38–44. Cairo: American University in Cairo Press.

Roeder, G.

1960   *Mythen und Legenden um Aegyptischen Gottheiten und Pharaonen.* Zurich: Artemis.

Romer, J.

1981   *Valley of the Kings.* London: Michael Joseph and Rainbird.

Römer, M.

1994   *Gottes- und Priesterherrschaft in Ägypten am Ende des Neuen Reiches: Ein religionsgeschichtliches Phänomen und seine sozialen Grundlagen.* Ägypten und Altes Testament 21. Wiesbaden: Otto Harrassowitz.

1998   Gold/Silber/Kupfer—Geld oder nicht? Die Bedeutung der drei Metalle als allgemeine Äquivalente im Neuen Reich mit einem Anhang zu den Geldtheorien der Volkswirtschaftslehre. *SAK* 26:119–42.

Rossellini, I.

1977   *Monumenti del'Egitto e della Nubia.* Vol. III, *Monumenti del Culto.* Reprint. Geneva: Editions de Belles-lettres.

Rothenberg, B.

    1988   *The Egyptian Mining Temple at Timna.* Researches in the Arabah, 1959–1984, vol. 1. London: Institute for Archaeo-Metallurgical Studies.

Rowe, A.

    1930   *The Topography and History of Beth-Shan.* Publications of the Palestine Section of the Museum of the University of Pennsylvania 1. Philadelphia: University of Pennsylvania Press.

    1940   *The Four Canaanite Temples of Beth Shan.* Philadelphia: University of Pennsylvania Press for the University Museum.

Sadek, A.

    1988   *Popular Religion in Egypt during the New Kingdom.* Hildesheimer Ägyptologische Beiträge 27. Hildesheim: Gerstenberg.

Saleh, M., and Sourouzian, H.

    1987   *Official Catalog: The Egyptian Museum Cairo.* Mainz: P. von Zabern.

Sandars, N. K.

    1978   *The Sea Peoples.* London: Thames and Hudson.

    1985   *The Sea Peoples.* 2nd ed. London: Thames and Hudson.

Sandman, M.

    1938   *Texts from the Time of Akhenaten.* Bibliotheca Aegyptiaca 8. Brussels: Fondation Égyptologique Reine Élisabeth.

Säve-Söderbergh, T., and Troy, L.

    1991   *New Kingdom Pharaonic Sites: The Finds and the Sites.* Scandinavian Joint Expedition to Sudanese Nubia, vol. 5:2. Uppsala: Scandinavian Joint Expedition to Sudanese Nubia.

Scamuzzi, E.

    1965   *Egyptian Art in the Egyptian Museum in Turin.* New York: Harry N. Abrams.

Schachermeyr, F.

    1979   *Die Ägäische Frühzeit.* Vol. III, *Kreta zur Zeitalter der Wanderungen vom Ausgang der minoischen Ära bis zur Dorisierung der Insel.* Österreichische Akademie der Wissenschaften, philosophisch-historische Klasse, Sitzungsberichte, vol. 355. Vienna: Verlag der Österreichischen Akademie der Wissenschaften.

    1980   *Die Ägäische Frühzeit.* Vol. IV, *Griechenland im Zeitalter der Wanderungen.* Österreichische Akademie der Wissenschaften, philosophisch-historische Klasse, Sitzungsberichte, vol. 372. Vienna: Verlag der Österreichischen Akademie der Wissenschaften.

    1982   *Die Ägäische Frühzeit.* Vol. V, *Die Levante im Zeitalter der Wanderungen vom 13. Bis zum 11. Jahrhundert v.Chr.* Österreichische Akademie der Wissenschaften, philosophische-historische Klasse, Sitzungsberichte, vol. 387. Vienna: Verlag der Österreichischen Akademie der Wissenschaften.

Schaedel, H. D.

    1936   *Die Listen des Grossen Payprus Harris.* Leipziger Ägyptologische Studien 6. Glückstadt: J. J. Augustin.

Schaeffer, C. F. A.

    1968   *Ugaritica.* Vol. 5. Mission de Ras Shamra 16. Paris: Geuthner.

Scheepers, A.

1992   Le récit d'Ounamon: Un texte "littéraire" ou "non-littéraire." In *Amosi-adès: Mélanges offerts au professeur Claude Vandersleyen par ses anciens étudiants,* ed. C. Obsomer and A. L. Oosthoeck, 355–65. Louvain-la-Neuve: Université Catholique de Louvain.

Schenkel, W.

1975   Zur Relevanz der altägyptischen "Metrik." *MDAIK* 28:103–7.

1978   Kritisches zur Textkritik: Die sogenannten Hörfehler. *GM* 29:119–26.

Schiaparelli, E.

1924   *Relazione sui lavori della Missione Archeologica Italiana in Egitto (anni 1903–1920).* Vol. I, *Esplorazione della Valle delle Regine.* Turin: Giovanni Chiantore.

Schipper, B. U.

1998   Von der "Lehre des Sehetep-jb-Re'" zur "Loyalistischen Lehre." *ZÄS* 125:161–79.

Schott, S.

1934   The Feasts of Thebes. In *Work in Western Thebes, 1931–33,* ed. H. H. Nelson and U. Hölscher, 63–90. Oriental Institute Communications 18. Chicago: University of Chicago Press.

1990   *Bücher und Bibliotheken im Alten Ägypten: Verzeichnis der Buch- und Spruchtitel und der Termini technici.* Wiesbaden: Otto Harrassowitz.

Schreiber, S.

1991   "Keusch wie kaum ein anderes Volk"? Einige Anmerkungen zum Sexual-Vokabular der alten Ägypter. In *Ägypten im Afro-Orientalischen Kontext: Gedenkschrift Peter Behrens,* ed. D. Mendel and U. Claudi, 315–35. Köln: Institut für Afrikanistik.

Schulman, A. R.

1963   A Cult of Ramesses III at Memphis. *JNES* 22:177–84.

1964   *Military Rank, Title, and Organization in the Egyptian New Kingdom.* Münchner Ägyptologische Studien 6. Berlin: Verlag Bruno Hessling.

1976   The Royal Butler Ramessesemperrē. *JARCE* 13:117–30.

1987   The Great Historical Inscription of Merenptah at Karnak: A Partial Reappraisal. *JARCE* 24:21–34.

Seeber, C.

1976   *Untersuchungen zur Darstellung des Totengerichts im alten Ägypten.* Münchner Ägyptologische Studien 35. Munich: Deutscher Kunstverlag.

Seele, K. C.

1935   A Hymn to Amon-Re on a Tablet from the Temple of Karnak. In *From Pyramids to Paul: Studies Presented in Honor of George Livingston Robinson,* ed. L. G. Leary, 224–41. New York: Thomas Nelson and Sons.

1959   *The Tomb of Tjanefer at Thebes.* Chicago: University of Chicago Press.

Seguin, J.

2007   *Le Migdol du Proche-Orient à l'Égypte.* Paris: Presses de l'Université Paris-Sorbonne.

Seidlmayer, S. J.

1998   Epigraphische Bemerkungen zur Stele des Sethnachte aus Elephantine.

In *Stationen: Beiträge zur Kulturgeschichte Ägyptens Reiner Stadelmann Gewidmet,* ed. H. Guksch and D. Polz, 363–86. Mainz: P. von Zabern.

2001   *Historische und Moderne Nilstände.* Berlin: Achet Verlag.

Sethe, K.

1928a   *Ägyptische Lesestücke zum Gebrauch und akademischen Unterricht: Texte des Mittleren Reiches.* 4th ed. Hildesheim: G. Olms.

1928b   *Dramatische Texte zu altägyptischen Mysterienspielen.* Untersuchungen zur Geschichte und Altertumskunde Ägyptens 10. Leipzig: J. C. Hinrichs.

Sherratt, S.

1998   "Sea Peoples" and the Economic Structure of the Late Second Millennium in the Eastern Mediterranean. In *Mediterranean Peoples in Transition, Thirteenth to Early Tenth Centuries: In Honor of Professor Trude Dothan,* ed. S. Gitin, A. Mazar, and E. Stern, 292–313. Jerusalem: Israel Exploration Society.

Shirun-Grumach, I.

1993   *Offenbarung, Orakel und Königsnovelle.* Ägypten und Altes Testament 24. Wiesbaden: Otto Harrassowitz.

Shupak, N.

1993   *Where Can Wisdom Be Found? The Sage's Language in the Bible and in Ancient Egyptian Literature.* Orbis Biblicus et Orientalis 130. Göttingen: Vandenhoeck und Ruprecht.

Siclen, C. C. van, III

1973   The Accession Date of Amenhotep III and the Jubilee. *JNES* 32:290–300.

Silverman, D. P.

1991   Texts from the Amarna Period and Their Position in the Development of Ancient Egyptian. *LingAeg* 1:301–14.

Silverman, D. P., ed.

1994   *For His Ka: Essays Offered in Memory of Klaus Baer.* Studies in Ancient Oriental Civilization 55. Chicago: Oriental Institute.

Simons, J.

1937   *Handbook for the Study of Egyptian Topographical Lists Relating to Western Asia.* Leiden: E. J. Brill.

Simpson, F. S.

2002   Evidence for a Late Bronze Age Libyan Presence in the Egyptian Fortress at Zawiyet Umm el-Rakham. Ph.D. diss., University of Liverpool.

Simpson, W. K.

1981   The Memphite Epistolary Formula on a Jar Stand of the First Intermediate Period from Naga ed-Deir. In *Studies in Ancient Egypt, the Aegean, and the Sudan: Essays in Honor of Dows Dunham on the Occasion of His 90th Birthday, June 1, 1980,* ed. W. K. Simpson and W. M. Davies, 173–79. Boston: Museum of Fine Arts.

1991   Menthuhotep, Vizier of Sesostris I, Patron of Art and Architecture. *MDAIK* 47:331–40.

1995   *Inscribed Material from the Pennsylvania-Yale Expedition to Abydos.* New Haven and Philadelphia: Peabody Museum of Natural History at Yale and University of Pennsylvania Museum of Archaeology and Anthropology.

1996   *Belles lettres* and propaganda. In *Ancient Egyptian Literature: History and Forms,* ed. A. Loprieno, 435–43. Probleme der Ägyptologie 10. Leiden: E. J. Brill.

2003   Response to J. Baines. In *Egyptology at the Dawn of the Twenty-first Century,* ed. Z. Hawass and L. P. Brock, 3:45–47. Cairo: American University in Cairo Press.

Simpson, W. K., Wente, E., and Faulkner, R. O., trans.

1973   *Ancient Egyptian Literature.* 2nd ed. New Haven: Yale University Press.

Singer, I.

1986–87   An Egyptian "Governor's Residency" at Gezer? *Tel Aviv* 13–14:26–31.

1988a   The Origin of the Sea Peoples and Their Settlement on the Coast of Canaan. In *Society and Economy in the Eastern Mediterranean (c. 1500–1000 B.C.): Proceedings of the International Symposium Held at the University of Haifa from the 28th of April to the 2nd of May 1985,* ed. M. Heltzer and E. Lipinski, 239–50. Orientalia Lovanensia Analecta 23. Louvain: Peeters.

1988b   Merneptah's Campaign to Canaan and the Egyptian Occupation of the Southern Coastal Plain of Palestine in the Ramesside Period. *BASOR* 269:1–10.

1988–89   The Political Status of Megiddo VIIA. *Tel Aviv* 15–16:101–12.

1994   Egyptians, Canaanites, and Philistines in the Period of the Emergence of Israel. In *From Nomadism to Monarchy: Archaeological and Historical Aspects of Early Israel,* ed. I. Finkelstein and N. Na'aman, 282–338. Washington, DC: Biblical Archaeology Society.

2000   New Evidence on the End of the Hittite Empire. In *The Sea Peoples and Their World: A Reassessment,* ed. E. D. Oren, 21–33. University Museum Monograph 108. Philadelphia: University Museum, University of Pennsylvania.

Smith, H. S.

1976   *Excavations at Buhen.* Vol. II, *The Fortress of Buhen: The Inscriptions.* Excavation Memoirs 48. London: Egypt Exploration Society.

Smith, S. T.

1995   *Askut in Nubia: The Economics and Ideology of Egyptian Imperialism in the Second Millennium B.C.* New York: Kegan Paul.

Snape, S.

1998   Walls, Wells, and Wandering Merchants: Egyptian Control of Marmarica in the Late Bronze Age. In *Proceedings of the Seventh International Congress of Egyptologists, Cambridge, 3–9 September 1995,* ed. C. J. Eyre, 1081–84. Orientalia Lovaniensia Analecta 82. Louvain: Peeters.

2003   The Emergence of Libya on the Horizon of Egypt. In *Mysterious Lands,* ed. D. O'Connor and S. Quirke, 93–106. London: UCL Press.

Spalinger, A. J.

1980   Historical Observations on the Military Reliefs of Abu Simbel and Other Ramesside Temples in Nubia. *JEA* 66:83–99.

1986   Two Ramesside Rhetorical Poems. In *Egyptological Studies in Honor of Richard A. Parker,* ed. Leonard H. Lasko, 136–64. Providence: Brown University.

2002   *The Transformation of an Ancient Egyptian Narrative: P. Sallier III and the Battle of Kadesh.* Göttinger Orientforschungen, Series 4, vol. 40. Wiesbaden: Otto Harrassowitz.

2006   New Kingdom Eulogies of Power: A Preliminary Analysis. In *Es werde niedergelegt als Schriftstück: Festschrift für Hartwig Altenmüller zum 65. Geburtstag,* ed. N. Kloth et al., 415–28. BSAK 9. Hamburg: Helmut Buske.

Spence, K.

1997   Orientation in Ancient Egyptian Royal Architecture. Ph.D. diss., University of Cambridge.

Spens, R. de

1998   Droit internationale et commerce au début de la XXIe dynastie: Analyse juridique du rapport d'Ounamon. In *Le commerce en Égypte ancienne,* ed. N. Grimal and B. Menu, 105–26. Bibliothèque d'Étude 121. Cairo: Institut français d'archéologie orientale.

2000   La XXIe dynastie: Un état décentralisé. In *Égypte pharaonique: Déconcentation, cosmopolitisme,* ed. B. Menu, 81–97. Paris: L'Harmattan.

Spiegelberg, W.

1909   *Ausgewählte Kunst-Denkmäler der aegyptischen Sammlung der Kaiser Wilhelms-Universität Strassburg.* Strassburg: Schlesier und Schweikhardt.

Spieser, C.

2000   *Les noms du Pharaon comme êtres autonomes au Nouvel Empire.* Orbis Biblicus et Orientalis 174. Göttingen: Vandenhoeck und Ruprecht.

Stadelmann, R.

1973   Tempelpalast und Erscheinungsfenster in den Thebanischen Totentempeln. *MDAIK* 29:221–42.

1980   Medinet Habu. *LÄ* III.1255–71.

1984   Seevolker. *LÄ* V.814–22.

1994   Royal Palaces of the Late New Kingdom in Egypt. In *Essays in Egyptology in Honor of Hans Goedicke,* ed. B. Bryan and D. Lorton, 309–15. San Antonio: Van Siclen Books.

1996   Temple Palace and Residential Palace. In *House and Palace in Ancient Egypt,* ed. M. Bietak, 225–30. Vienna: Verlag der Österreichischen Akademie der Wissenschaften.

Stager, L. E.

1995   The Impact of the Sea Peoples in Canaan (1185–1150 BCE). In *The Archaeology of Society in the Holy Land,* ed. T. E. Levy, 332–48. New York: Facts on File.

2008   Tel Ashkelon. In *The New Encyclopedia of Archaeological Excavations in the Holy Land,* ed. E. Stern, vol. 5 (supplementary volume), 1578–86. Jerusalem: Israel Exploration Society.

2009   A Pictorial Potsherd from Ashkelon Depicting a Philistine Ship. In *Eretz-Israel,* vol. 29 (Ephraim Stern volume), 209*–215*.

Stager, L. E., Schloen, J. D., Master, D. M., Press, M. D., and Aja, A.

2008   Stratigraphic Overview. In *Ashkelon 1: Introduction and Overview (1985–2006),* ed. L. E. Stager, J. D. Schloen, and D. M. Master, 215–323. Winona Lake, IN: Eisenbrauns.

Steindorf, W.

1917   Die blaue Koenigskrone. *ZÄS* 53:71–85.

Steinmann, F.

1984   Untersuchungen zu den in der handwerklich-künstlicherischen Produktion beschäftigen Personen und Berufsgruppen des Neuen Reichs. Pt. IV, Bermerkungen zur Arbeitsorganisation. *ZÄS* 111:30–40.

Stern, E.

1994   *Dor, Ruler of the Seas: Twelve Years of Excavations at the Israelite-Phoenician Harbor Town on the Carmel Coast.* Jerusalem: Israel Exploration Society.

1998   The Relations between the Sea Peoples and the Phoenicians in the Twelfth and Eleventh Centuries BCE. In *Mediterranean Peoples in Transition, Thirteenth to Early Tenth Centuries BCE: In Honor of Professor Trude Dothan,* ed. S. Gitin, A. Mazar, and E. Stern, 345–52. Jerusalem: Israel Exploration Society.

2000   The Settlement of Sea Peoples in Northern Israel. In *The Sea Peoples and Their World: A Reassessment,* ed. E. D. Oren, 197–212. University Museum Monograph 108. Philadelphia: University Museum, University of Pennsylvania.

Stevenson Smith, W.

1958   *The Art and Architecture of Ancient Egypt.* New Haven: Yale University Press. Reprint, 1998.

Stiebing, W. H., Jr.

2001   When Civilization Collapsed: Death of the Bronze Age. *Archaeology Odyssey* 4/5:16–26, 62.

Strobel, A.

1976   *Der bronzezeitliche Seevölkersturm.* Zeitschrift für die alttestamentliche Wissenschaft, volume 145. Berlin and New York: Walter de Gruyter.

Sweeney, D.

1998   The Man on the Folding Chair: An Egyptian Relief from Beth Shean. *IEJ* 48:38–53.

2002   Gender and Language in the Ramesside Love Songs. *BES* 16:27–50.

2004   The Hieratic Inscriptions. In *The Renewed Archaeological Excavations at Lachish (1973–1994),* ed. D. Ussishkin, 3:1601–17. Monograph Series, no. 22. Tel Aviv: Emery and Claire Yass Publications in Archaeology, Institute of Archaeology, Tel Aviv University.

Tacke, N.

2001   *Verspunkte als Gliederungsmittel in ramessidischen Schülerhandschriften.* Studien zur Archäologie und Geschichte Altägyptens 22. Heidelberg: Heidelberger Orientverlag.

Tallet, P.

1999   Deux prêtres-*sem* thébains de la XXe dynastie. *BIFAO* 99:411–22.

2000   Des étrangers dans les campagnes d'Égypte au Nouvel Empire. In *Égypte pharaonique: Déconcentation, cosmopolitisme,* ed. B. Menu, 135–44. Paris: L'Harmattan.

Taraqji, A. F., and Yoyotte, J.

1999a   Témoignages égyptiens de la région de Damas. *BSFÉ* 144:40–43.

1999b   La Stèle de Ramsès II à Keswé et sa signification historique. *BSFÉ* 144: 44–58.

Teeter, E.

1997   *The Presentation of Maat: Ritual and Legitimacy in Ancient Egypt.* Studies in Ancient Oriental Civilization 57. Chicago: Oriental Institute.

Teeter, E., and Larson, J. A., eds.

1999   *Gold of Praise: Studies on Ancient Egypt in Honor of Edward F. Wente.* Studies in Ancient Oriental Civilization 58. Chicago: Oriental Institute.

te Velde, H.

1982   Commemoration in Ancient Egypt. *Visible Religion* 1:135–53.

Thijs, A.

1998a   Piankh's Second Nubian campaign. *GM* 165:99–103.

1998b   Two Books for One Lady. *GM* 163:101–10.

2000   "Please tell Amon to bring me back from Yar": Dhutmose's Visits to Nubia. *GM* 177:63–70.

2003   The Troubled Careers of Amenhotep and Panehsy: The High Priest of Amun and the Viceroy of Kush under the Last Ramessides. *SAK* 31: 289–306.

2005   In Search of King Herihor and the Penultimate Ruler of the 20th Dynasty. *ZÄS* 132:73–91.

Thissen, H.-J.

1986   Review of J. T. Sanders, *Ben Sira and Demotic Wisdom. Enchoria* 14: 199–201.

1992   *Der verkommene Harfenspieler: Eine altägyptische Invektive (P. Wien KM 3877).* Demotische Studien 11. Sommerhausen: Gisela Zauzich Verlag.

Thomas, E.

1966   *The Royal Necropoleis of Thebes.* Princeton: Princeton University Press.

Trigger, B. G., Kemp, B. J., O'Connor, D., and Lloyd, A. B.

1983   *Ancient Egypt: A Social History.* Cambridge: Cambridge University Press.

Troy, L.

1997   Mut Enthroned. In *Essays on Ancient Egypt in Honour of Herman te Velde,* ed. J. van Dijk, 301–15. Egyptological Memoirs. Gröningen: Styx.

Tubb, J. N.

1995   An Aegean Presence in Egypto-Canaan. In *Egypt, the Aegean, and the Levant: Interconnections in the Second Millennium B.C.,* ed. W. V. Davies and L. Schofield, 136–45. London: British Museum Press.

2000   Sea Peoples in the Jordan Valley. In *The Sea Peoples and Their World: A Reassessment,* ed. E. D. Oren, 181–96. University Museum Monograph 108. Philadelphia: University Museum, University of Pennsylvania.

Tufnell, O.

1958   *Lachish IV (Tell ed-Duweir): The Bronze Age.* 2 vols. London: Oxford University Press.

Uehlinger, C.

1988   Der Amun-Tempel Ramses' III. in *p3-Knᶜn,* seine südpalästinischen Tempelgüter und der Übergang von der Ägypter-zur Philisterherrschaft: Ein Hinweis auf einige wenig beachtete Skarabäen. *ZDPV* 104:6–25.

Uphill, E.

1972   The Concept of the Egyptian Palace as a "Ruling Machine." In *Man, Settlement, and Urbanism,* ed. P. J. Ucko, R. Tringham, and G. W. Dimbleby, 721–34. London: Duckworth.

Ussishkin, D.

1983   Excavations at Tel Lachish, 1978–1983: Second Preliminary Report. *Tel Aviv* 10:97–175.

1995   The Destruction of Megiddo at the End of the Late Bronze Age and Its Historical Significance. *Tel Aviv* 22:240–67.

1998   The Destruction of Megiddo at the End of the Late Bronze Age and Its Historical Significance. In *Mediterranean Peoples in Transition, Thirteenth to Early Tenth Centuries BCE: In Honor of Professor Trude Dothan,* ed. S. Gitin, A. Mazar, and E. Stern, 197–219. Jerusalem: Israel Exploration Society.

2008   The Date of the Philistine Settlement in the Coastal Plain: The View from Megiddo and Lachish. In *Israel in Transition: From Late Bronze II to Iron IIa (c. 1250–850 B.C.E.),* vol. 1, *The Archaeology,* ed. L. L. Grabbe, 203–16. Library of Hebrew Bible/Old Testament Studies 491; European Seminar in Historical Methodology 7. London: T&T Clark.

Vagnetti, L.

2000   Western Mediterranean Overview: Peninsular Italy, Sicily, and Sardinia at the Time of the Sea Peoples. In *The Sea Peoples and Their World: A Reassessment,* ed. E. D. Oren, 305–26. University Museum Monograph 108. Philadelphia: University Museum, University of Pennsylvania.

Valbelle, D.

1985   *"Les Ouvriers de la Tombe": Deir el-Médineh à l'époque ramesside.* Cairo: Institut français d'archéologie orientale.

Vallogia, M.

1976   *Recherche sur les messagers* (wpwtyw) *dans les sources égyptiennes profanes.* Paris: Droz.

van Dam, K.

1988   De Geschiedenis de Strijd van Horus en Seth. *De Ibis* 13:34–48.

Vandier, J.

1958   *Manuel d'archèologie egyptienne.* Vol. III, *Les grandes èpoques: La Statuaire.* Paris: Éditions A. et J. Picard.

1963   Une buste de Mineptah. *La Revue du Louvre et des Musees de France* 13:153–58.

Van Dijk, J.

1998   The Amarna Period and the Late New Kingdom. In *The Oxford History of Ancient Egypt,* ed. I. Shaw, 272–313. Oxford: Oxford University Press.

van Essche, E.

1979   Quelques réflexions sur l'espace et le récit à Médinet Habou. *Annales d'histoire de l'art et d'archaeologie* 11:7–24.

van Essche-Merchez, E.

1992   La syntaxe formelle des reliefs et de la grande inscription de l'an 8 de Ramsès III à Médinet Habou. *Chronique d'Égypte* 67:211–39.

1994 Pour une lecture "stratigraphique" des parois du temple de Ramsès III à Médinet Habou. *RdÉ* 45:87–115.

Vanschoonwinkel, J.

1991 *L'Ègée et la Méditerranée orientale à la fin du Iie millénaire.* Archaeologia Transatlantica IX. Louvain-la-Neuve: Université Catholique de Louvain.

Ventura, R.

1976 An Egyptian Rock Stela in Timna'. *Tel Aviv* 1:60–63.

1985 *Living in a City of the Dead.* Orbis Biblicus et Orientalis 69. Göttingen: Vandenhoeck und Ruprecht.

Vernus, P.

1978 Litterature et autobiographie. Les inscriptions de *S3-Mwt* surnommé *Kyky. RdÉ* 30:115–46.

1990 Les espaces de l'écrit dans l'Egypte pharaonique. *BSFÉ* 119:35–56.

1992 *Chants d'amour de l'Egypte antique.* Paris: La Salamandre.

1996a L'intertextualité dans la culture pharaonique: L'Enseignment de Ptahhotep et le graffito *djmny* (Ovadi Hammâmat n 3042). *GM* 147 (1995) 103–9.

1996b Langue littéraire et diglossie. In *Ancient Egyptian Literature, History and Forms,* ed. A. Loprieno, 555–64. Leiden: E. J. Brill.

2009 Von der "Loyalistischen Lehre" zur "Lehredes kairsu": Eine neue Textquelle in Assiut und deren Auswirkungen. *ZÄS* 136:87–98.

Vercoutter, J.

1956 *L'Ègypte et le monde égéen préhellenique.* Bibliothèque d'Étude, T. XXII. Cairo: Institut français d'archéologie orientale.

Vergote, J.

1959 *Joseph en Égypte.* Louvain: Publications Universitaires.

1985 Joseph en Égypte: 25 ans après. In *Pharaonic Egypt: The Bible and Egypt,* ed. S. I. Groll, 289–306. Jerusalem: Magnes Press.

Verhoeven, U.

2001 *Untersuchungen zur späthieratischen Buchschrift.* Orientalia Lovaniensia Analecta 99. Louvain: Peeters.

Vernus, P.

1975 Un texte oraculaire de Ramsès IV. *BIFAO* 75:102–10.

1978 Littérature et autobiographie: Les inscriptions de *S3-Mwt* surnommé *Kyky. RdÉ* 30:115–46.

1980 Un example de rhétorique politique: Le discours du vizir *TA* (P. Turin 1880, ro 2: 20–3, 4. *RdÉ* 32:121–24.

1982–83 Études de philologie et de linguistique (II). *RdÉ* 34:115–28.

1992 *Chants d'amour de l'Égypte antique.* Paris: La Salamandre.

1993 *Affaires et scandales sous les Ramsès: La crise des valeurs dans l'Égypte du Nouvel Empire.* Paris: Pygmalion/Gérard Watelet.

1995a *Essai sur la conscience de l'histoire dans l'Égypte pharaonique.* Paris: Honoré Champion.

1995b L'intertextualité dans la culture pharaonique: L'Enseignment de Ptahhotep et le graffito djmny (Ouadi Hammâmat n⁰ 3042). *GM* 147:103–9.

1996 Langue littéraire et diglossie. In *Ancient Egyptian Literature: History and*

Forms, ed. A. Loprieno, 555–64. Probleme der Ägyptologie 10. Leiden: E. J. Brill.

Vinson, S.

1995   In Defense of an Ancient Reputation. *GM* 146:93–102.

Vleeming, S. P.

1982   The Days on Which the *Qnbt* Used to Gather. In *Gleanings from Deir el-Medîna,* ed. R. J. Demarée and J. J. Janssen, 183–92. Egyptologische Uitgaven I. Leiden: Nederlands Institutet voor het Nabije Oosten.

1993   *Papyrus Reinhardt: An Egyptian Land List from the Tenth Century B.C.* Berlin: Akademie Verlag.

Vomberg, P.

2004   *Das Erscheinungsfenster innerhalb der amarnazeitlichen Palastarchitektur: Herkunft-Entwicklung-Fortleben.* Wiesbaden: Harrassowitz Verlag.

von der Way, T.

1984   *Die Textüberlieferung Ramses' II. zur Qadeš-Schlacht: Analyse und Struktur.* Hildesheimer Ägyptologische Beiträge 22. Hildesheim: Gerstenberg.

Wachsmann, S.

1981   The Ships of the Sea Peoples. *International Journal of Nautical Archaeology* 10, no. 3:187–220.

1982   The Ships of the Sea Peoples (*IJNA* 10.3: 187–220): Additional Notes. *International Journal of Nautical Archaeology* 11, no. 4:297–304.

1997   Were the Sea Peoples Mycenaeans? The Evidence of Ship Iconography. In *Res Maritimae: Cyprus and the Eastern Mediterranean from Prehistory to Late Antiquity,* ed. S. Swiny, R. L. Hohlfelder, and H. W. Swiny, 339–56. Cyprus American Archaeological Research Institute Monograph Series, vol. 1; American Schools of Oriental Research Archaeological Reports, no. 4. Atlanta: Scholars Press.

1998   *Seagoing Ships and Seamanship in the Bronze Age Levant.* College Station: Texas A&M University Press.

2000   To the Sea of the Philistines. In *The Sea Peoples and Their World: A Reassessment,* ed. E. D. Oren, 103–43. University Museum Monograph 108. Philadelphia: University Museum, University of Pennsylvania.

Ward, W. A.

1994   Foreigners Living in the Village. In *Pharaoh's Workers: The Villagers of Deir el Medina,* ed. L. H. Lesko, 61–85. Ithaca: Cornell University Press.

Ward, W. A., and Joukowsky, M. S., eds.

1992   *The Crisis Years: The 12th Century B.C.; From beyond the Danube to the Tigris.* Dubuque, IA: Kendall/Hunt.

Warren, P. M.

1989   Egyptian Stone Vase from the City of Knossos: Contributions toward Minoan Economic and Social Structure. *Ariadne* 5:1–9.

Weeks, K., ed.

2000   *Atlas of the Valley of the Kings.* Cairo: American University in Cairo Press.

Weinstein, J. M.

1981   The Egyptian Empire in Palestine: A Reassessment. *BASOR* 241:1–28.

1992   The Collapse of the Egyptian Empire in the Southern Levant. In *The Crisis Years: The 12th Century B.C.; From beyond the Danube to the Tigris,* ed. W. A. Ward and M. Sharp Joukowsky, 142–50. Dubuque, IA: Kendall/Hunt.

1993   The Scarabs, Plaques, Seals, and Rings. In *The Late Bronze Egyptian Garrison at Beth Shan: A Study of Levels VII and VIII,* ed. F. W. James and P. E. McGovern, 221–25. University Museum Monograph 85. Philadelphia: University Museum, University of Pennsylvania.

1998   Egyptian Relations with the Eastern Mediterranean World at the End of the Second Millennium BCE. In *Mediterranean Peoples in Transition, Thirteenth to Early Tenth Centuries BCE: In Honor of Professor Trude Dothan,* ed. S. Gitin, A. Mazar, and E. Stern, 188–96. Jerusalem: Israel Exploration Society.

Wente, E. F.
1961   A Letter of Complaint to the Vizier To. *JNES* 20:252–57.
1962   Egyptian "Make Merry" Songs Reconsidered. *JNES* 21:118–28.
1967   *Late Ramesside Letters.* Studies in Ancient Oriental Civilization 33. Chicago: University of Chicago Press.
1990   *Letters from Ancient Egypt.* Society of Biblical Literature Writings from the Ancient World 1. Atlanta: Scholars Press.
2001   Monotheism. In *The Oxford Encyclopedia of Ancient Egypt,* ed. D. B. Redford, 2:432–35. Oxford: Oxford University Press.

Wildung, D.
1977   *Egyptian Saints: Deification in Pharaonic Egypt.* New York: New York University Press.
1980   Reaktivierung der Vergangenheit. *LÄ* III.663.

Wilkinson, J.
1835   *Topography of Thebes and General View of Egypt.* London: J. Murray.

Wilkinson, R.
2000   *The Complete Temples of Ancient Egypt.* London: Thames and Hudson.

Williams, R. J.
1964   Literature as a Medium of Political Propaganda in Ancient Egypt. In *The Seed of Wisdom: Essays in Honour of T. J. Meek,* ed. W. S. McCullough, 14–30. Toronto: University of Toronto Press.
1971   Egypt and Israel. In *The Legacy of Egypt,* ed. J. R. Harris, 257–90. Oxford: Clarendon.

Wilson, J. A.
1956   *The Culture of Ancient Egypt.* Chicago: University of Chicago Press.
1969   The War against the Peoples of the Sea. In *Ancient Near Eastern Texts Relating to the Old Testament,* ed. J. Pritchard, 262–63. 3rd ed. Princeton: Princeton University Press.

Wimmer, S.
1998   (No) More Egyptian Temples in Canaan and Sinai. In *Jerusalem Studies in Egyptology,* ed. I. Shirun-Grumach, 87–123. Ägypten und Altes Testament 40. Wiesbaden: Otto Harrassowitz.
2008   A New Hieratic Ostracon from Ashkelon. *Tel Aviv* 35:65–72.

Wimmer, S. J., and Maeir, A. M.

2007 "The Prince of Safit?": A Late Bronze Age Hieratic Inscription from Tell es-Ṣāfī/Gath. *ZDPV* 123:37–48.

Winand, J.

1995 La grammaire au secours de la datation des textes. *RdÉ* 46:187–201.

1998 La punctuation avant la punctuation: L'organisation du message écrit dans l'Égypte pharaonique. In *À qui appartient la ponctuation? Actes du colloque internationale et interdisciplinaire du Liège (13–15 mars 1997), Champs linguistiques*, ed. J.-M. Defays, 163–77. Brussels: Duculot.

Winnicki, J.

1987 Vier demotische Graffiti in den Koenigsgraber in Theben. *Enchoria* 15:163–68.

Woldering, I.

1955 *Bildkataloge des Kestner-Museums, Hannover: Ausgewaehlte Werke der Aegyptischer Sammlung.* Hannover: Kestner-Museum.

Worthington, M.

2001 Einiges über die Paläographie des Papyrus Rollin. *GM* 183:93–98.

Wreszinski, W.

1923 (1913–36) *Atlas zur altägyptischen Kulturgeschichte.* vols. 1–5. Leipzig: J. C. Hinrich.

Yadin, Y.

1968 And Dan, Why Did He Remain in Ships? *Australian Journal of Biblical Archaeology* 1:9–23.

Yannai, E.

2002 A Stratigraphical and Chronological Reappraisal of the "Governor's Residence" at Tell el-Far'ah (South). In *Aharon Kempinski Memorial Volume: Studies in Archaeology and Related Disciplines*, ed. S. Ahituv and E. D. Oren, 368–76. Beer-Sheva, vol. 15. Beer-Sheva: Ben-Gurion University of the Negev Press.

Yasur-Landau, A.

2010 *The Philistines and Aegean Migration at the End of the Late Bronze Age.* New York: Cambridge University Press.

Yon, M.

1989 The End of the Kingdom of Ugarit. In *The Crisis Years: The 12th Century B.C.; From beyond the Danube to the Tigris*, ed. W. A. Ward and M. Sharp Joukowsky, 111–22. Dubuque, IA: Kendall/Hunt.

Younker, R. W.

2003 The Emergence of Ammon: A View of the Rise of Iron Age Polities from the Other Side of the Jordan. In *The Near East in the Southwest: Essays in Honor of William G. Dever*, ed. B. A. Nakhai, 153–76. Annual of the American Schools of Oriental Research, vol. 58. Boston American Schools of Oriental Research.

Yoyotte, J.

1958 The Tomb of a Prince Ramesses in the Valley of the Queens (No. 53). *JEA* 44:26–30.

Yurco, F.

1997   Merenptah's Wars, the "Sea Peoples," and Israel's Origins. In *Ancient Egypt, the Aegean, and the Near East: Studies in Honor of Martha Rhoads Bell*, vol. 2, ed. J. A. Phillips et al., 497–506. San Antonio: Van Siclen Books.

Žabkar, L.

1965   *A Study of the Ba Concept in Ancient Egyptian Texts*. Studies in Ancient Oriental Civilization 34. Chicago: University of Chicago Press.

Zandee, J.

1947   *De Hymnen aan Amon van Papyrus Leiden I 350*. Oudheidkundig Mededelingen uit het Rijksmuseum van Oudheden te Leiden. 28. Leiden: E. J. Brill.

1992   *Der Amunhymnus des Papyrus Leiden I 344, Verso*. 3 vols. Collections of the National Museum of Antiquities at Leiden 7. Leiden: Rijksmuseum van Oudheden.

Zangger, E.

1994   *Ein neuer Kampf um Troja: Archäologie in der Krise*. Munich: Droemer Knaur.

1995   Who Were the Sea Peoples? *Aramco World* 46, no. 3:21–31.

Zertal, A.

2001   The "Corridor-builders" of Central Israel: Evidence for the Settlement of the "Northern Sea Peoples"? In *Defensive Settlements of the Aegean and the Eastern Mediterranean after c. 1200 B.C.: Proceedings of an International Workshop Held at Trinity College Dublin, 7th–9th May 1999*, ed. V. Karageorghis and C. E. Morris, 215–32. Nicosia: Anastasios G. Leventis Foundation.

Zibelius, K.

1972   *Afrikanische Orts- und Völkernamen in hieroglyphischen und hieratischen Texten*. Beihefte zum Tübinger Atlas des Vorderen Orients, Series B (Geisteswissenschaften), no. 1. Wiesbaden: Reichert.

Title Index

Subject Index